THE BIRTHPLACE OF
ABRAHAM LINCOLN
Nolin Creek, La Rue Co., Ky., U.S.A.

BY JON MEACHAM

And There Was Light: Abraham Lincoln and the American Struggle

His Truth Is Marching On: John Lewis and the Power of Hope

The Hope of Glory: Reflections on the Last Words of Jesus from the Cross

The Soul of America: The Battle for Our Better Angels

Destiny and Power: The American Odyssey of George Herbert Walker Bush

Thomas Jefferson: The Art of Power

American Lion: Andrew Jackson in the White House

American Gospel: God, the Founding Fathers, and the Making of a Nation

Franklin and Winston: An Intimate Portrait of an Epic Friendship

Voices in Our Blood: America's Best on the Civil Rights Movement (EDITOR)

AND THERE
WAS LIGHT

AND THERE WAS LIGHT

ABRAHAM LINCOLN

AND THE

AMERICAN STRUGGLE

Jon Meacham

RANDOM HOUSE
New York

Published in the United States by Random House, an imprint and
division of Penguin Random House LLC, New York.

RANDOM HOUSE and the HOUSE colophon are registered trademarks of
Penguin Random House LLC.

Image permissions located on page 639.

LIBRARY OF CONGRESS CATALOGING-IN-PUBLICATION DATA
Names: Meacham, Jon, author.
Title: And there was light : Abraham Lincoln and the American struggle /
Jon Meacham.
Other titles: Abraham Lincoln and the American struggle
Description: First edition. | New York : Random House, [2022] |
Includes bibliographical references and index.
Identifiers: LCCN 2022023164 (print) | LCCN 2022023165 (ebook) |
ISBN 9780553393965 (hardcover) | ISBN 9780553393972 (ebook)
Subjects: LCSH: Lincoln, Abraham, 1809–1865—Views on slavery. |
Lincoln, Abraham, 1809–1865—Religion. | Presidents—United States—
Biography. | United States—Race relations—History—19th century. |
Slavery—Political aspects—United States—History—19th century. |
Slaves—Emancipation—United States. | United States—Politics
and government—1861–1865. | United States—Politics and
government—1845–1861.
Classification: LCC E457.2 .M479 2022 (print) | LCC E457.2 (ebook) |
DDC 973.7/11—dc23/eng/20220623
LC record available at https://lccn.loc.gov/2022023164
LC ebook record available at https://lccn.loc.gov/2022023165

Printed in the United States of America on acid-free paper

randomhousebooks.com

2 4 6 8 9 7 5 3 1

FIRST EDITION

Book design by Simon M. Sullivan

FRONT ENDPAPER: An artist's 1897 depiction of the Kentucky log cabin
where Abraham Lincoln was born.

FRONTISPIECE: The sixteenth president of the United States, as
photographed by Alexander Gardner in Washington, D.C.,
circa February 1865.

BACK ENDPAPER: The White House as it appeared in 1866, the year after
Lincoln's assassination.

To Gina Centrello

And, as ever, for Keith, Mary, Maggie, and Sam

I do not despair of this country. . . . The fiat of the Almighty, "Let there be Light," has not yet spent its force.

—Frederick Douglass

I do not pretend to understand the moral universe; the arc is a long one, my eye reaches but little ways; I cannot calculate the curve and complete the figure by the experience of sight; I can divine it by conscience. And from what I see I am sure it bends towards justice.

—Theodore Parker

Moral cowardice is something which I think I never had.

—Abraham Lincoln

Contents

PART III: RIGHT MAKES MIGHT
1859-1861

PART IV: MY WHOLE SOUL IS IN IT
1861-1863

PART V: A NEW BIRTH OF FREEDOM
1863-1864

PART VI: HIS ILLIMITABLE WORK
1864 to the End

A Big, Inconsistent, Brave Man

T HE STORM HAD COME FROM THE SOUTH. At dawn on Saturday, March 4, 1865, the day of Abraham Lincoln's second inauguration, gales of wind and sheets of rain roared across the Potomac and struck Washington, destroying trees and soaking the city. Pennsylvania Avenue was a sea of mud, thick and soggy. It had already been raining for two days running; the Army Corps of Engineers considered constructing pontoon bridges to make the city's main thoroughfare passable. A foot could sink as deep as a knee in the ooze.

The wet wartime capital was at once festive and solemn. Willard's Hotel, next door to the Treasury Building, was packed with 1,008 guests, and *The Daily National Republican* reported that twelve hundred inauguration-goers had swarmed the hotel's dining tables. "The other hotels in the city were also full, not being able to accommodate another boarder," the newspaper wrote. "The crowd in the city perfectly awful," the diarist Nathan W. Daniels observed, "every available place taken up—the crowd fairly packed Pennsylvania Avenue from one end to the other, the cortege itself extending over a mile in length." Boswell's Fancy Store at 302 E Street, near Fourteenth Street, advertised "Flags, Flags, For The Inauguration: Silk, Bunting, Delain and Muslin Flags on sticks" as well as "Chinese Lanterns, Fireworks, &c." The retailers Burns & Wilson at 340 Pennsylvania Avenue, between Ninth and Tenth streets, let it be known that "ladies intending to honor the inauguration ball with their presence will want to appear with white slippers and white gaiters," which Burns & Wilson were "now selling at the lowest price."

What the journalist Noah Brooks, an intimate of President Lincoln's, recalled as the "dark and dismal" weather improved slightly as the crowds slogged to the Capitol for the inaugural ceremonies. Completed in the war years, the building's cast-iron dome loomed above Washington. The president had made sure that the project continued even as the struggle unfolded. Workers, many of them enslaved until Lincoln had signed the bill for emancipation in the District of Columbia in 1862, stayed on the job. "It seemed a strange contradiction to see the workmen . . . going on with their labor," *The New York Times* had written, "the click of the chisel, the stroke of the hammer" amid "the tramp of the battalions drilling in the corridors." Lincoln understood the significance of perseverance. "If people see the Capitol going on," he had said, "it is a sign we intend the Union shall go on."

And it had. Now Lincoln stood again where he had stood four years before, on the East Front of the Capitol. Hundreds of thousands of Americans who had been alive on March 4, 1861, were dead, slain by one another's hands. Innumerable others were wounded and maimed in body and in spirit. Everything had hung in the balance since Fort Sumter. "We are now on the brink of destruction," Lincoln had said after a late 1862 Union defeat at Fredericksburg. "It appears to me the Almighty is against us, and I can hardly see a ray of hope." Until victories at Gettysburg and Vicksburg in the summer of 1863, the war had seemed lost. Even afterward the president had expected to lose reelection in 1864. Now, in the late winter of 1865, Union forces were poised for ultimate victory. And at last, slavery was in its final months of life in the United States.

Emancipation had created a different country—and the man at the pinnacle of power, about to address the nation on the occasion of his second inauguration, had put antislavery principle into practice, pursuing justice at perilous moments when a purely political man might have chosen a different course. Successive generations have variously depicted Lincoln as a secular saint, the savior of Union, and the Great Emancipator; as a grasping tyrant; or as a calculating political creature imprisoned by public opinion and white prejudice. The truth is more complicated. Driven by the convictions that the Union was sacred and that slavery was wrong, Lincoln was instrumental in saving one and in destroying the other, expanding freedom and preserving an experiment in popular government that nearly came to an end on his watch. In him we can engage not only the possibilities and the limitations of the presidency, but the possibilities and limitations of America itself.

There were political and practical reasons for Lincoln to do what he did. Yet there were also political and practical reasons for him to do the opposite of what he did. A constant in his calculus—sometimes decisive, sometimes not, but always there—was his moral opposition to human enslavement. This book charts Lincoln's struggle to do right as he defined it within the political universe he and his country inhabited—not to celebrate him for moral perfection, for he was morally imperfect, but to illustrate that progress comes when Americans recognize that all, not just some, possess common rights and are due common respect. Such is a pragmatic vision with a moral component: If the rights of others are sacrosanct, then so are yours. In a democracy, the pursuit of power for power's sake, devoid of devotion to equal justice and fair play, is tempting but destructive.

All anyone knew of the second inaugural speech before its delivery was that it would be pithy. "The address will probably be the briefest one ever delivered," *The New York Herald* reported in a preview. Lincoln, who had written every word of it himself, had had the speech printed in two columns. He would read it, with his spectacles, standing behind a small table fashioned from cast-iron pieces left over from the construction of the Capitol dome. Benjamin Brown French, the marshal for the ceremonies, made sure a glass of water was within the president's reach.

To Frederick Douglass, who braved the mud to hear the president in the open air, Lincoln's ensuing address "sounded more like a sermon than a state paper." In fact, it was both. "The conscience of the nation must be roused," Douglass, the abolitionist, editor, and orator who had escaped slavery in Maryland, had long argued. "Our enterprise is eminently a religious one, dependent for success entirely on the religious sentiment of the people," the abolitionist Wendell Phillips wrote. As president, Lincoln remarked that he had been "brought to a living reflection that nothing in my power whatever would . . . succeed without the direct assistance of the Almighty." He moved toward emancipation amid a deepening sense that his duty lay in attempting to discern and to apply the will of the divine to human affairs.

Lincoln's own faith in the unseen was elusive but real. In 1862, Lincoln closed a message to Congress by speaking of "my great responsibility to my God, and to my country"—a sign that the two were connected in the president's mind and heart. Raised in an antislavery Baptist ethos in Kentucky and in Indiana, Lincoln was not an orthodox Christian. He never sought to declare a traditional faith. There was no in-breaking light, no thunderbolt on the road to Damascus, no conviction that, as the Epistle to the Philippians put it, "every knee should bow" and declare Jesus as Lord. There was, rather, a steadily stronger embrace of the right in a world of ambition and appetite.

To Lincoln, God whispered His will through conscience, calling humankind to live in accord with the laws of love. Lincoln believed in a transcendent moral order that summoned sinful creatures, in the words of Micah, to do justice, to love mercy, and to walk humbly with their God—eloquent injunctions, but staggeringly difficult to follow. "In the material world, nothing is done by leaps, all by gradual advance," the New England abolitionist Theodore Parker observed. Lincoln agreed. "I may advance slowly," the president reputedly said, "but I don't walk backward." His steps were lit by political reality, by devotion to the Union, and by the importuning of conscience.

In the first winter of the war, the Lincolns had lost their eleven-year-old son Willie to typhoid fever. Afterward, Phineas D. Gurley, the pastor of the New York Avenue Presbyterian Church in Washington, had offered the president a religious explanation for tragedy and for pain. "God's ways," Gurley said, "are not our ways." The believer must endure suffering, confident that somehow and someday, as promised in scripture, the Lord will make all things new. "What we need in the hour of trial . . . is confidence in Him who sees the end from the beginning," Gurley said. "Only let us bow in His presence with a humble and teachable spirit, be still and know that He is God; let us hear His voice, and inquire after His will."

Let us hear His voice: Gurley was describing the means by which humankind weighed right and wrong. "I have often wished that I was a more devout man than I am," Lincoln said in his White House years. "Nevertheless, amid the greatest difficulties of my Administration, when I could not see any other resort, I would place my whole reliance on God, knowing that all would go well, and that He would decide for the right."

In this Lincoln was in tune with the times—and with the timeless. "Look at the facts of the world," Theodore Parker said. "You see a continual and progressive triumph of the right. I do not pretend to understand the moral universe; the arc is a long one, my eye reaches but little ways; I cannot calculate the curve and complete the figure by the experience of sight; I can divine it by conscience. And from what I see I am sure it bends towards justice." Whenever history feels inevitable or problems intractable, Lincoln is there, an example of how even the most imperfect of people, leading the most imperfect of peoples, can help bend that arc. Such progress, Frederick Douglass remarked, can come only after storm and strife. "This struggle may be a moral one, or it may be a physical one, and it may be both moral and physical, but it must be a struggle," he said. "Power concedes nothing without a demand. It never did and it never will."

A man of power, Lincoln demanded that the nation follow a moral course through the brute physicality of the Civil War. His "ancient faith," Lincoln once said, "teaches me that 'all men are created equal'; and that there can be no moral right in connection with one man's making a slave of another." In common usage, to say something is moral is to say that it is in harmony with the commandment that one ought to do unto others as we would have them do unto us. This is not just the stuff of sermons. From Plato to Kant, the substance of what is known as the Golden Rule—one common to the world's religious and moral traditions—has occupied philosophers across the ages.

Lincoln's own sensibility—both moral and political—was founded on this injunction. "As I would not be a *slave*, so I would not be a *master*," he once wrote. "This expresses my idea of democracy." For Lincoln, a world in which power was all, in which the assertion of a singular will trumped all, in which brute force dictated all, was not moral but immoral, not democratic but autocratic, not just but unjust. The task of history was to secure advances in a universe that tends to disappoint. Goodness would not always be rewarded. The innocent would suffer. Violence would at times defeat virtue. Such was the way of things, but to Lincoln the duty of the leader and of the citizen was neither to despair nor to seek solace and security with the merely strong, but to discern and to pursue the right.

The president had quietly arrived at the Capitol early on March 4 to sign last-minute legislation. Lincoln had begun the day in his suite on the second floor of the White House. The president slept in a room that faced south, toward the enemy. Lincoln's eyes opened to light that came in through two large windows that faced out onto the Potomac River—and onto seceded Virginia. From this vantage point he could see the unfinished Washington Monument, then standing only 156 feet out of a projected 500 feet, which sat in a cluttered field where cattle grazed on the banks of Tiber Creek. Beyond this lay the river, and the hills of Arlington. Early in the rebellion, now entering its fifth year, Union troops had secured the heights, which Lincoln could see from his bedroom, for fear that Confederate artillery would use them to launch cannonballs into the windows of the White House.

The mansion's second floor was both home and office. Noah Brooks noted "dark mahogany doors, old style mantels and paneled wainscoting" that were "more suggestive of the days of the Madisons and Van Burens than of the present." Mrs. Lincoln's bedroom was between a large oval library and her husband's chamber. Though the plumbing was impressively modern, with pipes for hot water and a flushing toilet in a water closet in the president's small dressing room, the First Lady had thought the suite's furniture a "degradation" when the Lincolns arrived in 1861, and she soon renovated much of the mansion at great expense. The president was furious when he saw the bills for what he denounced as this *"damned old house"*—the basement of which, one White House secretary said, was "perennially overrun with rats, mildew and foul smells."

Lincoln, who kept what his aides called "farm hours," liked to rise early. With the help of his White House usher and valet, William Slade, a leader of the free Black community of Washington, the president would dress, usually in a black suit, white shirt, and what the Victorians called a stock, a permanently tied black bow attached to a longer strip of cloth that hooked around the neck. Tucking his heavy gold watch, which hung from a handsome chain, into his pocket, Lincoln would make sure he had a pair of spectacles for the day ahead. There would be a breakfast of coffee, eggs, and toast, and then some private time before callers began marching over the worn stones of the portico into the White House to mount the staircase that connected the formal rooms to the more prosaic second floor.

It was the life he had chosen. He loved apples, anecdotes, newspapers, political gossip, strong coffee, oysters, fine horses, and his children's pets—the cats as well as the goats, Nanny and Nanko. He neither drank nor smoked nor chewed tobacco, enjoyed—to his wife's chagrin— flirting with women, and indulged his sons, allowing them to clamber over him and run wild, often to the amazement and annoyance of his staff and guests. A self-taught reader of philosophy and political economy, of the King James Bible, of Shakespeare, and of Robert Burns, Lincoln made his living practicing law, but politics was his vocation.

"Every man is said to have his peculiar ambition," he remarked when first offering himself to voters, in Illinois, at the age of twenty-three. "Whether it be true or not, I can say for one that I have no other so great as that of being truly esteemed of my fellow men, by rendering myself worthy of their esteem." Always ready for rejection, Lincoln knew enough of the world to understand that failure was an unavoidable element of life. Should he lose the race, he said, "I have been too familiar with disappointments to be very much chagrined." But he felt defeat and pain deeply—always had, at least since the loss of his mother, who died when he was very young. Intellectually Lincoln grasped the inevitability of tragedy. Emotionally he was entirely human, flesh and blood.

When he failed to win a U.S. Senate seat in 1855, he fell into a depression, yet found relief in action. "That man who thinks Lincoln calmly gathered his robes about him, waiting for the people to call him, has a very erroneous knowledge of Lincoln," his Illinois law partner William Herndon wrote. "He was always calculating and planning ahead. His ambition was a little engine that knew no rest."

But in what direction was that engine heading? Was it simply toward the acquisition of place and power—the holding of office to win, as he put it, the "esteem" of the world? Lincoln had a prodigious memory, both for literature and for politics. "Your district did not give me so strong a vote at the last election as it did in 1860," Lincoln remarked to a visiting banker after his 1864 reelection. "I think, sir, that you must be mistaken," the banker replied. "I have the impression that your majority was considerably increased at the last election."

"No," Lincoln said, "you fell off about six hundred votes." The numbers were checked. Lincoln was right. "It was in the world of politics that he lived," Herndon wrote. "Politics were his life, newspapers his food, and his great ambition his motive power." To see him only as a political creature, however, is to give the means of his life priority over its ends—ends he would lay out in detail in his second inaugural address.

Mrs. Lincoln left the White House about eleven o'clock on the morning of March 4. Her carriage, it was reported, was cheered by a crowd that "thought . . . the President was within the vehicle." People were everywhere. The throngs also included—unusually—many

Black Americans, including Black soldiers in Union blue. "Thousands of colored folk, heretofore excluded from such reunions, were mingled for the first time with the white spectators," an observer said.

They were there to see a man who never quite looked the part he was supposed to play. The president, the writer Nathaniel Hawthorne observed, was "about the homeliest man I ever saw." Hawthorne found Lincoln one day in the White House "dressed in a rusty black frock-coat and pantaloons, unbrushed, and worn so faithfully that the suit had adapted itself to the curves and angularities of his figure, and had grown to be an outer skin of the man. He had shabby slippers on his feet." A photograph taken in the winter of 1865 by Alexander Gardner, a former associate of Mathew Brady's, depicted a weary Lincoln whose worn features and sunken eyes made him seem much older than his fifty-six years.

As Hawthorne had observed, the president often appeared slightly unkempt. Part of the reason was Lincoln's thick and ungovernable black hair, once plentiful, but now thinning above an exhausted and nearly gaunt face. Once, when he was handed a small hairbrush, he said, "Why, I can't do anything with such a thing as that. It wouldn't go through my hair. Now, if you have anything you comb your horse's mane with, that might do."

He put on no airs. "People seemed delighted to find in the ruler of the nation freedom from pomposity and affectation," Noah Brooks wrote of Lincoln. When a friend addressed Lincoln as "Mr. President," he was told, "Now call me Lincoln, and I'll promise not tell of the breach of etiquette—if you won't—and I shall have a resting-spell from 'Mister President.'" Musing about an acquaintance from Illinois who was seeking a federal job, Lincoln said, "Well, now, I never thought M— had any more than average ability when we were young men together; really I did not. . . . But, then, I suppose he thought just the same about me; he had reason to, and—here I am!"

Now here he was on the East Front, in a black Brooks Brothers suit, seated next to the new vice president, Andrew Johnson of Tennessee. Spotting Frederick Douglass, the president pointed him out to Johnson, who, addled from an infusion of preinaugural whiskey, gazed on Douglass with "bitter contempt and aversion" before managing what Douglass thought "the bland and sickly smile of the demagogue." Douglass turned to Mrs. Louise Dorsey of Philadelphia and remarked,

"Whatever Andrew Johnson may be, he certainly is no friend of our race."

Lincoln rose to deliver his address with what observers thought a "clear, resonant" voice. The previous year, in an unsettling military hour around the time of the Wilderness Campaign, Lincoln had wondered aloud: "Why do we suffer reverses after reverses? Could we have avoided this terrible, bloody war? Was it not forced upon us? Is it ever to end?"

Now he would venture some answers to his own anguished questions.

"Fellow countrymen," Lincoln said, "at this second appearing to take the oath of the presidential office, there is less occasion for an extended address than there was at the first. Then a statement, somewhat in detail, of a course to be pursued, seemed fitting and proper." His task today was less about *how* the nation must move forward than it was about *why* he believed the war had been fought, and what it meant. He had begun his presidency with a brief on secession and Union—a brief that had included support for a constitutional amendment that would have banned the federal government from abolishing slavery where it existed at the time. He was opening his second term with a searching statement about human nature, the relationship between the temporal and the divine, and the possibilities of redemption and of renewal.

Lincoln acknowledged that mortal powers were limited. "Both parties deprecated war; but one of them would *make* war rather than let the nation survive; and the other would *accept* war rather than let it perish," he said. "And the war came." The gulf between North and South was so profound, so unbridgeable, that only the clash of arms could decide the contest between freedom and bondage. In a speech that stipulated the ambiguity of the world, Lincoln was unambiguous about why the war had come: slavery. "One eighth of the whole population were colored slaves, not distributed generally over the Union, but localized in the Southern part of it," the president said. "These slaves constituted a peculiar and powerful interest. All knew that this interest was, somehow, the cause of the war." There was no escaping this central truth.

Lincoln turned to the perils of self-righteousness and self-certitude, North and South. "Both read the same Bible, and pray to the same God," he said, "and each invokes His aid against the other." Then the president rendered a moral verdict: "It may seem strange that any men should dare to ask a just God's assistance in wringing their bread from the sweat of other men's faces; but let us judge not that we be not judged." In speaking of the strangeness of profiting from the labor of others—a subtle but unmistakable indictment of slave owners—the president drew on the third chapter of the Book of Genesis: "In the sweat of thy face," the Lord commanded, "shalt thou eat bread." Adam and Eve are being expelled from the Garden of Eden; the whole structure of the world as we know it was being formed in this moment. To work for one's own wealth, rather than taking wealth from others, was the will of God.

In the same breath in which he framed slavery as a violation of God's commandment, Lincoln invoked the words of Jesus: *Judge not.* This injunction is found in the Gospel of Matthew, in a plea for forbearance, forgiveness, and proportion: "Judge not, that ye be not judged." The president believed he was doing the right thing—yet he knew that those who opposed him believed the same. "The prayers of both could not be answered; that of neither has been answered fully," Lincoln said of North and South. "The Almighty has His own purposes."

Lincoln had come to believe that the Civil War might well be a divine punishment—a millstone—for a national sin. The president hoped the strife would soon be over, and the battle won. "Yet," Lincoln said, "if God wills that it continue, until all the wealth piled by the bondman's two hundred and fifty years of unrequited toil shall be sunk, and until every drop of blood drawn with the lash, shall be paid by another drawn with the sword, as was said three thousand years ago, so still it must be said, 'the judgments of the Lord, are true and righteous altogether.'" To Frederick Douglass, "these solemn words . . . struck me at the time, and have seemed to me ever since to contain more vital substance than I have ever seen compressed in a space so narrow."

Lincoln's point was a startling one from an American president: God was exacting blood vengeance for the sin of human enslavement in a specific place and a specific time—in the United States of America in the mid-nineteenth century. This was not routine political rhetoric. In the Second Inaugural Address, Lincoln was affirming a vision of history as understood in the Bible: that there was a beginning, and there will be an end. In the meantime, the only means available to a nation "under God" to prosper was to seek to follow the commandments of that God.

The alternative? Chaos and the reign of appetite without restriction and without peace. Lincoln once said that "the author of our being, whether called God or Nature (it mattered little which), would deal very mercifully with poor erring humanity in the other, and, he hoped, better world." Until then, "poor erring humanity" was charged with making its words and work acceptable in the sight of a God who had enjoined humankind to love one another as they would be loved. That is where Lincoln left the matter in his peroration on Saturday, March 4. "With malice toward none; with charity for all; with firmness in the right, as God gives us to see the right, let us strive on to finish the work we are in; to bind up the nation's wounds, to care for him who shall have borne the battle, and for his widow, and his orphan—to do all which may achieve and cherish a just, and a lasting peace among ourselves, and with all nations."

His speech done, Lincoln turned to Chief Justice Salmon P. Chase for the oath of office. The sun came through the clouds. "It made my heart jump!" the president recalled of the breaking light. Lincoln, Noah Brooks wrote, "was just superstitious enough to consider it a happy omen." A Black man who worked at the Washington Navy Yard, Michael Shiner, recorded the moment in his diary: "The wind ceas[ed] blowing the rain ceased raining and the Sun came out and it was as clear as it could be."

The chief justice noted the passage of the Bible the president kissed—Isaiah 5:27–28, which reads: "None shall be weary nor stumble among them; none shall slumber nor sleep; neither shall the girdle of their loins be loosed, nor the latchet of their shoes be broken: Whose arrows are sharp, and all their bows bent, their horses' hoofs shall be counted like flint, and their wheels like a whirlwind."

There would be no rest. The wheels turned. The work went on.

Later that afternoon, the president would ask Frederick Douglass what he'd thought of the speech.

"Mr. Lincoln," Douglass replied, "that was a sacred effort."

Hated and hailed, excoriated and revered, Abraham Lincoln served as president of the United States in an existential hour. Other presidents have been confronted with momentous decisions—of war and peace, of life and death, of freedom and power. It was Lincoln's lot to adjudicate whether the nation would, in his phrase, remain "half *slave* and half *free*"—and whether the American experiment would survive the treason of a rebellious white South that put its own interests ahead of the Union itself. The issue was not only political and economic. It was also religious and cultural. The slaveholding South believed it had God and history on its side. The fate of the Union, the possibilities of democracy, and the future of slavery, then, were the stakes of a war that Abraham Lincoln chose to wage to total victory—or to defeat.

A president who led a divided country in which an implacable minority gave no quarter in a clash over power, race, identity, money, and faith has much to teach us in a twenty-first-century moment of polarization, passionate disagreement, and differing understandings of reality. For while Lincoln cannot be wrenched from the context of his particular times, his story illuminates the ways and means of politics, the marshaling of power in a democracy, the durability of racism, and the capacity of conscience to help shape events.

For many Americans, to see Lincoln whole is to glimpse ourselves in part—our hours of triumph and of grace, and our centuries of failures and of derelictions. This is why his story is neither too old nor too familiar. For so long as we are buffeted by the demands of democracy, for so long as we struggle to become what we say we already are—the world's last, best hope, in Lincoln's phrase—we will fall short of the ideal more often than we meet the mark. It is a fact of American history that we are not always good, but that goodness is possible. Not universal, not ubiquitous, not inevitable—but possible.

Lincoln governed a nation in which a violent and vociferous element was captive to its own visions and controlled by its own interests. "Domestic slavery is the great distinguishing characteristic of the southern states, and is, in fact, the only important institution which they can claim as peculiarly their own," Abel P. Upshur, a Virginian who served as secretary of state under John Tyler, wrote in 1839. White Southerners dreamed of a slave empire headquartered in the American South but stretching to Cuba, to Mexico, and other parts of Central and South America. Such a white-dominated new nation, a Charleston, South Carolina, newspaper wrote, would ensure slaveholders "a great destiny."

Rebellious white Southerners were unambiguous about their cause. Alexander Stephens, the vice president of the Confederacy, said the "corner-stone" of the new nation was slavery and white supremacy. "That slavery is sanctioned by the Bible seems scarcely to admit of a doubt," the Baptist I. T. Tichenor of Alabama said during the war. In 1863, the Savannah, Georgia, *Daily Morning News* described its understanding of war aims simply and clearly. "As a people," the newspaper said, "we are fighting to maintain the Heaven ordained supremacy of the white man over the inferior or colored race."

Racism—the conviction that one could view and treat people differently based on innate characteristics such as skin color—was, and is, a formative force in American life. As a term, "racism" came into currency in the twentieth century, but it captures the legal, political, and social realities that had constrained the lives of Black Americans since at least Jamestown. John H. Van Evrie of New York published popular titles such as *White Supremacy and Negro Subordination: Or, Negroes a Subordinate Race and (So-Called) Slavery Its Normal Condition.* "All the arguments of abolitionists, based upon appeals to the assertion that the negro is 'a man and a brother,' are gross self-delusions," an Episcopal clergyman, James Warley Miles, wrote in 1861. "The idea of the equality of race is a figment," *The New Orleans Bee* argued on the eve of the Civil War. "Neither politically nor socially, nor legally can it be said to exist. Mentally or physically the weak are ever subjugated by the strong, and the grades of society are as numerous as the [rungs] of a ladder."

Even the era's more progressive voices often expressed racist views. "We do not say that the black man is, or shall be, the equal of the white man; or that he shall vote or hold office, however just such a position may be," the abolitionist Ohio lawmaker Joshua Giddings said; "but we assert that he who murders a black man shall be hanged; that he who robs a black man of his liberty or his property shall be punished like other criminals." "The natural equality of all men I believe in, as far as the rights are concerned," said Henry Wilson, who had helped found the Free Soil Party and became a leading Radical Republican. "So far as mental or physical equality is concerned, I believe the African race inferior to the white race." Senator Lyman Trumbull, a Republican from Lincoln's Illinois, would author a landmark Civil Rights Act in 1866. In 1858, though, he remarked: "I want to have nothing to do either with the free negro or the slave negro. We, the Republican party, are the white man's party. . . . I would be glad to see this country relieved of them."

In this atmosphere of anti-Black racism, Lincoln defended Black Americans as fellow human beings whose fundamental rights were protected in the Declaration of Independence—hardly the most common of arguments in his time. He did not waver from a morally informed insistence that slavery be put on a path to "ultimate extinction"—a view that only a minority of white Americans appeared to share. He maintained his antislavery position to his political detriment throughout the 1850s, winning no office between a single term in the U.S. House and his election to the presidency in 1860. Vitally, he refused to retreat from his antislavery commitment during the crisis over secession in 1860–61. He stood by emancipation after 1862, declining to give in to pressure for a negotiated peace with the Confederacy in order to end a wearying war. He ran for reelection in 1864 on a platform calling for an abolitionist constitutional amendment. The preponderance of his words and actions, moreover, pointed toward a future in which race would be irrelevant to human rights not only in theory but in practice.

"Viewed from the genuine abolition ground," Frederick Douglass said in 1876, "Mr. Lincoln seemed tardy, cold, dull, and indifferent: but measuring him by the sentiment of his country, a sentiment he was bound as a statesman to consult, he was swift, zealous, radical, and determined." Writing in 1922, after Reconstruction had given rise to Jim Crow segregation and to the denial of many basic civil liberties for Black Americans, W.E.B. Du Bois observed, "Abraham Lincoln was a Southern poor white . . . poorly educated and unusually ugly, awkward, ill-dressed . . . —cruel, merciful; peace-loving, a fighter; despising Negroes and letting them fight and vote; protecting slavery and freeing slaves. He was a man—a big, inconsistent, brave man." In the wake of the civil rights movement of the 1950s and '60s, the editor and journalist Lerone Bennett, Jr., argued that Lincoln was a white supremacist. "Lincoln must be seen as the embodiment, not the transcendence, of the American tradition," Bennett wrote, "which is, as we all know, a racist tradition."

It is true that Lincoln was neither an immediate abolitionist nor an explicit advocate of a racially integrated and egalitarian country. For much of his life he was a gradual emancipationist who wanted to compensate slave owners and who supported proposals for the voluntary removal of Black Americans from the national homeland—a project he only "sloughed off," in his assistant secretary John Hay's phrase, late in the war. Until the beginning of his second term as president Lincoln did not press for Black people to be afforded the rights of citizenship enjoyed by white people. He even portrayed his decision on wartime emancipation as a last resort based on military rather than moral considerations. "It had got to be midsummer, 1862," Lincoln recalled in 1864. "Things had gone on from bad to worse, until I felt that we had reached the end of our rope on the plan of operations we had been pursuing; that we had about played our last card, and must change our tactics, or lose the game! I now determined upon the adoption of the emancipation policy." As he said many times, to many people, in public and in private, his primary official duty was not to destroy slavery in the short term (though he did seek to end it in the fullness of time) but to save the Union. For much of his life and of his presidency Lincoln appeared to believe that anti-Black prejudice made a multiracial democracy an impossibility.

Yet to depict Lincoln as only a reluctant warrior against slavery and for an egalitarian future fails to do him justice. To him, slavery was akin to cancer—a deadly disease that one might try to manage but that usually proved fatal. "You may have a wen or a cancer upon your person and not be able to cut it out lest you bleed to death," Lincoln remarked; "but surely it is no way to cure it, to engraft it and spread it over your whole body. That is no proper way of treating what you regard a wrong." As he confronted the question in Illinois and on the national stage, he juggled political reality, cultural custom, and his own moral convictions—convictions that he hoped the nation would come to share. Lincoln was propelled by antislavery principles that led him to emancipation and to suggest suffrage for at least some Black Americans—a prospect he raised in a speech that prompted John Wilkes Booth to pledge to kill him.

Anathema to much of the white South and to its allies in the North because of his antislavery creed, Lincoln also frustrated some abolitionists who were more advanced than he on freedom and egalitarianism. He was attacked for defending a Constitution with proslavery elements and for preserving a politics in which racial prejudice was a predominant factor. The implication of such criticism was that Lincoln made a fetish of the Union at the expense of pursuing true justice. Without Union, however, there could be no freedom for the enslaved. Had Lincoln simply bid the South well and set about creating a separate, free nation, he would have consigned millions of enslaved Black people and their progeny to unrelenting and unrepentant masters. Frederick Douglass called the Constitution a "glorious liberty document" and said he would "prefer the Union even with Slavery than to allow the Slaveholders to go off and set up a Government." An independent Confederate States of America with perhaps the sanction and recognition of the North might well have expanded its reach southward. Many of the enslaved could likely have escaped to free territory, but many more would have been perpetually trapped. Thus, after the Emancipation Proclamation of January 1, 1863, Lincoln's war for Union was simultaneously a war for Union and for freedom in the seceded states. After congressional passage of the Thirteenth Amendment in early 1865, it became a war for Union and for emancipation for all.

The devil, as Shakespeare wrote, can quote scripture to his purpose, and the historical war over Lincoln and race is a long-running conflict in which scholars and observers deploy quotations from the Lincoln canon to support different arguments—a conflict at once rooted in and reflective of the American experience. "I have only to say, let us discard all this quibbling about this man and the other man—this race and that race and the other race being inferior, and therefore they must be placed in an inferior position," Lincoln said in Chicago in 1858. "Let us discard all these things, and unite as one people throughout this land, until we shall once more stand up declaring that all men are created equal." In the same period in which he said this, though, he declined to be portrayed as an egalitarian. "I will say then that I am not, nor ever have been in favor of bringing about in any way the social and political equality of the white and black races," Lincoln remarked in an 1858 debate with Stephen Douglas, "that I am not, nor ever have been in favor of making voters or jurors of negroes, nor of qualifying them to hold office, nor to intermarry with white people; and I will say in addition to this that there is a physical difference between the white and black races which I believe will forever forbid the two races living together on terms of social and political equality. And inasmuch as they cannot so live, while they do remain together there must be the position of superior and inferior, and I as much as any other man am in favor of having the superior position assigned to the white race."

That Lincoln made such points for political reasons while pursuing policies that would enable the principles of the Declaration to prevail is true. But we do neither Lincoln nor ourselves any favors by casting him as a kind of Martin Luther King, Jr., in a stovepipe hat. As a white American man engaged in the accumulation and exercise of power, Lincoln did much good—and left much undone. Taken all in all—which is how we should take him, all in all—he was a human being who sought to do right more often than he did wrong.

In that struggle, Lincoln's view that a Black person had the "right to eat the bread, without leave of anybody else, which his own hand earns" was progressive for the America of the time. His insistence that slavery be contained and not extended into new territories in the period leading up to the Civil War, his Emancipation Proclamation, and his support of the abolitionist Thirteenth Amendment were essential chapters in the story of liberty. A man professing more explicitly egalitarian convictions about race—a William Lloyd Garrison, for instance, or the Massachusetts senator Charles Sumner—could never have won the presidency in a nation suffused with anti-Black prejudice, and would therefore have been unable to do what Lincoln did to make justice possible.

The saga of race in America is a tragic one—and it unfolds still. In Lincoln's hour upon the stage, many hoped he would go farther along the road toward equality than he did; many feared any step at all. But on he walked.

He was an architect of the ideal of a working middle class—the class to which he had won entry as a child of the frontier who became a lawyer—and saw government as a force for good. "I want every man to have a chance—and I believe a black man is entitled to it—in which he *can* better his condition—when he may look forward and hope to be a hired laborer this year and the next, work for himself afterward, and finally to hire men to work for him! That is the true system," Lincoln said in 1860. He understood the power of the vote. "I am opposed to the limitation or lessening of the right of suffrage; if anything, I am in favor of its extension or enlargement," Lincoln once told William Herndon. "I want to lift men up—to broaden rather than contract their privileges." Education mattered, too, so that "every man may . . . be enabled to read the histories of his own and other countries, by which he may duly appreciate the value of our free institutions."

In these pursuits Lincoln was committed to what Theodore Parker defined as the "American Idea," which was a "composite idea . . . of three simple ones: 1. Each man is endowed with certain unalienable rights. 2. In respect of these rights all men are equal. 3. A government is to protect each man in the entire and actual enjoyment of all the unalienable rights. . . . The idea demands . . . a democracy—a government of all, for all, and by all."

The work of a democracy devoted to such an idea is to lead a sufficient number of individuals to share a moral vision about power, liberty, justice, security, and opportunity in the hope that people—and peoples—might be in closer harmony with the good. As a multitude of individuals, a nation possesses a collective conscience—one manifested in how that nation chooses, through the means of politics, to view rights and responsibilities.

Conscience in America has been largely rooted in religious traditions. "I do not know if all Americans have faith in their religion—for who can read to the bottom of hearts?—but I am sure that they believe it necessary to the maintenance of republican institutions," Alexis de Tocqueville wrote during the age of Jackson. "This opinion does not belong only to one class of citizens or to one party, but to the entire nation; one finds it in all ranks." For all the perils of religion—among them the divine sanction a believer might feel for any course of action and the potential for the kinds of sectarian conflicts that had roiled the Old World—the first generation of the Republic's leaders, as well as their successors, acknowledged religious belief and sought to deploy it for the good. "Whatever may be conceded to the influence of refined education on minds of peculiar structure," George Washington wrote, "reason and experience both forbid us to expect that national morality can prevail in exclusion of religious principle." A citizen (or a president) motivated by religiously informed impulses may undertake work that will make the lives of believers and of secularists better, just as a citizen (or a president) motivated by impulses that have nothing to do with religion may undertake work that will make the lives of secularists and of believers better.

To lead, Lincoln forged a faith of his own. His invocations of the Lord summon biblical images, as though Lincoln played the part of a patriarch or a prophet of old. But Lincoln was not a passive actor handing down commandments he received from on high. Though he spoke of tragedy and of fate, sometimes musing that all of history was predestined, he gave his life to a pursuit, politics, which valued individual action, both at the ballot box and in office.

In this he shaped history amid the polarized elements of the age—Southern slaveholders, white racists, unflinching abolitionists, and temporizing politicians. To save the country he loved, Lincoln was sustained by all sorts and conditions of religion and philosophy, drawing from, among other things, the King James Version of the Bible, the Declaration of Independence, and the New England Transcendentalism of Parker and of Ralph Waldo Emerson. His creed was of his own making—and it was always evolving, with enormous consequences for the nation he led and for the nation he left behind.

Emancipation was not foreordained. The closest parallel to the American experience with ending slavery, that of the British Empire in the 1830s, was a story of gradual, compensated emancipation. The compensation was paid not to the enslaved but to the slaveholders, and the timing was not immediate but tiered. It is estimated that the sum, which underwrote the ultimate liberation of about eight hundred thousand enslaved people, was equal to 40 percent of Great Britain's annual expenditure, and the instruments that financed abolition were not fully paid off until 2015—a century and three quarters later. Lincoln's decision to seek total abolition for nearly four million people through a constitutional amendment was, in context, radical and revolutionary—and he risked not only his own reelection but the whole of the cause of Union to pursue it. Under pressure to rescind emancipation, Lincoln stood fast. "They tell me some [want] you [to] take back the Proclamation," Hannah Johnson, the mother of a Black Union soldier, wrote Lincoln. "Don't do it. When you are dead and in Heaven, in a thousand years that action of yours will make the Angels sing your praises."

The Lincoln who left the White House for Ford's Theatre on the evening of Good Friday 1865 had met the exigencies of war with a political sensibility but also with a hardening moral resolve and a deepening philosophical consciousness. "The failure to recognize the attributes of flexibility and the capacity for growth in Lincoln and, instead, to treat him as a static, stunted figure," the historian John Hope Franklin remarked, "is to misuse the legacy that he has left for all of us."

In the estimation of the editor Horace Greeley, "Mr. Lincoln was essentially a growing man." Francis B. Carpenter, an artist who worked in the White House for six months, wrote, "I am not one of those inclined to believe that Mr. Lincoln, in the closing months of his career, reached the full measure of his greatness. Man may not read the future: but it is my firm conviction, that, had he lived through his second term, he would have continued to grow, as he had grown, in the estimation and confidence of his countrymen; rising to a grander moral height with every emergency." Lincoln's election and the secession crisis, according to the journalist Noah Brooks, had "determined him in what he called 'a process of crystallization' then going on in his mind."

While Lincoln did grow and change in the presidential years, the antislavery commitment that found its fullest expression during the Civil War was no newfound thing. The war came, in fact, because slave-owning Southerners believed him an unappeasable foe of what were euphemistically referred to as their "domestic institutions." He knew what was right, and he knew what was wrong. But he also knew that the task of the politician is not the same as the task of the philosopher. Absolute consistency is not a luxury available to the office-seeking and office-holding leaders of a democracy. True greatness in the political arena comes when moral convictions are brought to bear amid conflicting interests. That, in the end, is what Abraham Lincoln did: Amid the myriad forces of politics and of the competing claims of power, he held fast to his view that slavery must end and justice must be pursued. Four miles away from Lincoln's White House, at the Washington Navy Yard, the laborer Michael Shiner understood the president. "The Hon Abraham Lincoln . . . was as brave [a] man that ever live[d] on the face of earth," Shiner wrote, "and all that he done he done it with clear [conscience] before his creator."

Lincoln surely sought to do so. "Moral cowardice is something which I think I never had," he remarked. We study Lincoln not because he was perfect but because he was a man whose inconsistencies resonate even now. So, too, does his bigness. No Olympian, he did not act alone. With courage, Black Americans rose against enslavement; with conscience, Abraham Lincoln held a nation together when a permanent fracture would have given unchecked power to a hegemonic white Southern order with designs on expanding its slavery-based empire.

Offered the opportunity to save the Union and avoid war by making concessions to slavery, Lincoln refused. Urged to abandon emancipation to increase his chances of reelection in 1864, he declined. Both decisions offer tangible evidence of Lincoln's antislavery convictions and of his devotion to democracy in the battle against a race-based autocracy. "I do not despair of this country," Frederick Douglass said. "The fiat of the Almighty, 'Let there be Light,' has not yet spent its force." And it fell to Abraham Lincoln to shed that light in the darkest of hours.

Lincoln was not all he might have been—vanishingly few human beings are—but he was more than many men have been. We could have done worse. And we have. And, as Lincoln himself would readily acknowledge, we can always do better. In that cause, we must try to see Abraham Lincoln—and ourselves—whole.

His story begins not in a White House under siege, nor in the hilltop Capitol of the United States, nor even on the corpse-strewn battlefields of the Civil War, but in the forested interior of a nascent nation in the first years of the nineteenth century—a world of screaming panthers and circuit-riding preachers, of small cabins and big dreams.

AND THERE
WAS LIGHT

PART I

CLOTHED IN BONE & NERVE

Beginnings to 1846

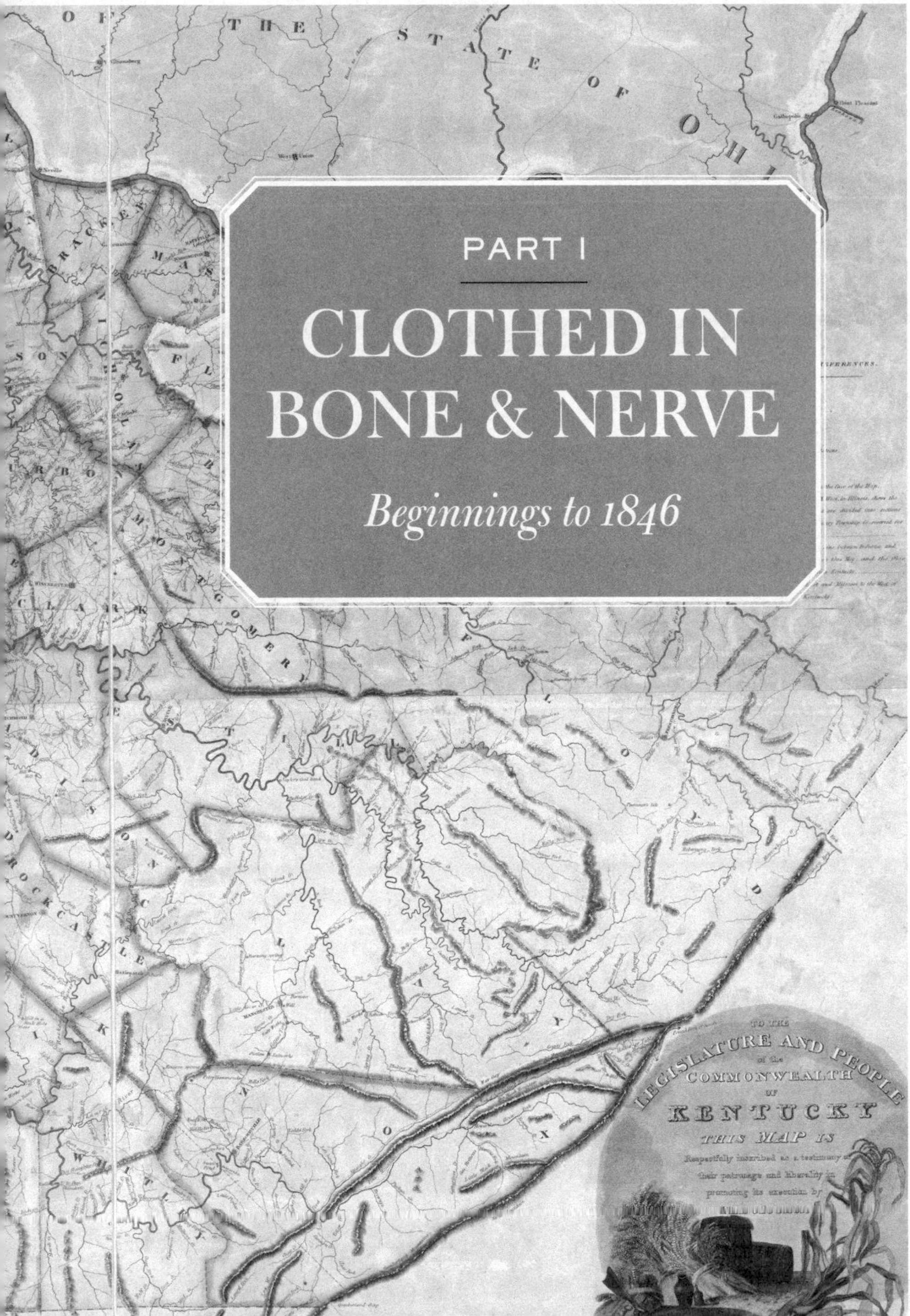

CHAPTER ONE

My Mind and Memory

"The short and simple annals of the poor." That's my life, and
that's all you or anyone else can make out of it.

—ABRAHAM LINCOLN, writing in 1860

Equal rights for all men: Emancipation!

—THE REVEREND ADAM SHOEMAKER, an influential Baptist in
the world of Lincoln's youth

THE ROADS WERE ROUGH, the conversation unusual. In about his
fortieth year, around 1850, Abraham Lincoln folded his long, angular frame into a one-horse buggy in Springfield, Illinois, for the
nineteen-mile trip from the capital city to the courthouse in Petersburg, the seat of neighboring Menard County. He was riding with his
law partner William Herndon, who recalled that the case they were to
try "was one in which we were likely . . . to touch upon the subject of
hereditary traits."

Pondering the subject, Lincoln spoke of his mother, the late Nancy
Hanks Lincoln. It was a striking, introspective, and candid moment.
"He said . . . that she was the illegitimate daughter of Lucey Hanks and
a well-bred Virginia farmer or planter," Herndon recalled, "and he argued that from this last source"—the Virginia grandfather—"came his
power of analysis, his logic, his mental activity, his ambition." Lincoln
had thought much on the subject. "His theory . . . had been that . . . illegitimate children are oftentimes sturdier and brighter than those
born in lawful wedlock," Herndon said, "and in his case, he believed
that his better nature and finer qualities came from this broad minded,
unknown Virginian."

The buggy bumped along. Lincoln was pensive. "The revelation—
painful as it was—called up the recollection of his mother, and . . . he
added ruefully, 'God bless my mother; all that I am or ever hope to be I

owe to her,' and immediately lapsed into silence." Lincoln's quiet was more anguished than peaceful. "Burying himself in thought," his companion recalled, "he drew round him a barrier which I feared to penetrate."

Herndon was struck by the details of the exchange and the depth of feeling evident in Lincoln's tone. Aside from the date and location of his birth—Sunday, February 12, 1809, in Hardin County, Kentucky* —Lincoln "usually had but little to say of himself, the lives of his parents, or the history of the family," Herndon recalled. "There was something about his origin he never cared to dwell upon." To a correspondent who asked for information on his background once he became a national figure, Lincoln said, "There is not much of it, for the reason, I suppose, that there is not much of me."

There was, in fact, much to Lincoln—and the best parts of him, he believed, came not from those forebears whom he knew, but from those he did not: the mysterious Virginia gentleman grandfather and long-dead Lincolns. The roots of his ambition to rise above his frontier birth may lie in his imaginative connection to ancestors, known and unknown, who had left a mark on the world. As a child and a youth, living in poverty, embarrassed by stories of promiscuity in his mother's family, and facing a life of spirit-sapping labor and drudgery, Lincoln likely sought solace in the belief that he was a son of forebears who had transcended their time and place. If they could do so, the young Lincoln believed, then perhaps he could, too.

The family's New World saga had begun with Samuel Lincoln, who had emigrated from Norwich, England, settling in Hingham, Massachusetts, about 1637. Puritan dissenters in England, the Lincolns of Hingham were prominent in their religious community in the Massachusetts Bay Colony, prospering in business and helping to build Hingham's handsome Old Ship Church. Samuel and his wife, Martha Lincoln, had eleven children. One of their grandchildren, Mordecai, became a successful man in central Pennsylvania, marrying Hannah Saltar, a well-connected daughter of a New Jersey family that included lawmakers in the colonial assembly and an acting royal governor.

* Lincoln's birthplace—Sinking Spring Farm—is located in present-day LaRue County, Kentucky.

In 1716, Hannah Lincoln gave birth to John Lincoln, who continued the family's migration south and west when he and his wife, Rebecca Flowers Lincoln, settled on a large farm on Linville Creek in the Shenandoah Valley in 1766. (He was to be known to history as "Virginia John" Lincoln.) Their son Abraham, the grandfather of the sixteenth president, had been born in Pennsylvania in 1744 and became an eager militiaman, earning the rank of captain. In 1774, he fought in Lord Dunmore's War, a conflict between colonial forces under the command of John Murray, Lord Dunmore, the royal governor of Virginia, and a Shawnee-led Indian confederacy. Four years later, Lincoln was part of General Lachlan McIntosh's operation to capture Britain's Fort Detroit, a center of frontier resistance to the American Revolution; the campaign failed for lack of men and supplies.

Following familial pattern, Captain Abraham soon pressed on—in his case, leaving his father's orbit in the Shenandoah for the Kentucky wilderness in 1780. In 1786, an Indian attacked and killed Captain Abraham—"not in battle," as Lincoln would tell the story, "but by stealth, when he was laboring to open a farm in the forest." According to tradition, the Indian warrior was then about to take one of Captain Abraham's young sons captive. Another son, Mordecai, "jumped over the fence—ran to the fort" and shot the Indian at a distance of about 160 paces. He had aimed ("drew his 'beed'") at a silver half-moon medallion the Indian was wearing. The assailant was discovered, dead, the next day. "The story of his death by the Indians, and of Uncle Mordecai, then fourteen years old, killing one of the Indians," Abraham Lincoln would recall of his grandfather, "is the legend more strongly than all others imprinted on my mind and memory." The younger son who was saved that day, Thomas Lincoln, would become the father of Abraham Lincoln.

The slaying of Captain Abraham was the transformative event of Thomas Lincoln's life. His father's death diminished the family's capacities, and, as the youngest son, Thomas found himself in a particular predicament. Mordecai Lincoln, having saved Thomas's life, lost interest in the boy's fortunes. "Owing to my father being left an orphan at the age of six years, in poverty, and in a new country, he became a wholly uneducated man," Abraham Lincoln wrote. A kinswoman of Mary Lincoln's recalled that "the reason why Thomas Lincoln grew up unlettered was that his brother Mordecai, having all the land in his possession . . .

turned Thomas out of the house when the latter was 12 years old; so he went out among his relations . . . and there grew up." Thomas, then, was not part of the more successful and established branch of his family. "These Lincolns," a contemporary recalled, "were excellent men—plain, moderately educated, candid in their manners and intercourse, and looked upon as honorable as any men I have ever heard of."

But not Thomas Lincoln. His son was blunt about his father's plight: "Thomas . . . by the early death of his father and very narrow circumstances of his mother, even in childhood was a wandering laboring boy and grew up literally without education," Abraham Lincoln recalled. "He never did more in the way of writing than to bunglingly write his own name." Described as "an uneducated man, a plain unpretending plodding man [who] attended to his work, peaceable good and good natured," Thomas was hired out for a year with an uncle, Isaac Lincoln, who had settled on the Watauga, a stream of the Holston River in what became upper East Tennessee. Forever struggling, Thomas became a carpenter and a farmer. "He was, we are told," William Herndon wrote, "five feet ten inches high, weighed one hundred and ninety-five pounds, had a well-rounded face, dark hazel eyes, coarse black hair, and was slightly stoop-shouldered." By 1806, Thomas had met and, in a ceremony conducted by the Methodist minister Jesse Head, married Nancy Hanks, a daughter of Lucey Hanks and, as Abraham Lincoln believed, the unknown Virginia gentleman.

The Hanks family was a source of embarrassment to Abraham Lincoln. He described his grandmother Lucey, whom a grand jury once charged with fornication, as "a halfway prostitute." In kinder moments, he cast her as a victim. "My mother's mother was poor and credulous, &c.," he said, "and she was shamefully taken advantage of by the man." Lincoln lived, too, with rumors that he was not the son of Thomas Lincoln.* "That Nancy Hanks was of low character but . . . Thomas Lincoln married her," recalled John B. Helm, a Kentucky neighbor of the Lincolns'. One story in local circles was that Nancy Hanks had been impregnated by a man named Abraham Enlow (also sometimes spelled "Enloe") before her marriage to Thomas Lincoln and that Abraham

---

* As late as 1922, in *The Crisis*, the magazine of the National Association for the Advancement of Colored People, W.E.B. Du Bois would write, almost casually, that Lincoln was "of illegitimate birth."

Lincoln was Enlow's natural son. "She was a woman that did not bear a very virtuous name, and it was hard to tell who was the father of Abe," a Kentucky contemporary of Lincoln's recalled. The story circulated for decades—and Enlow insisted it was true. However, as Herndon was told, "Abe Enlow was as low a fellow as you could find."

The Hankses "were peculiar to the civilization of early Kentucky," Herndon recalled. "Illiterate and superstitious, they corresponded to that nomadic class still to be met with throughout the South, and known as 'poor whites.'" A Lincoln neighbor recalled that Abraham's mother, Nancy, was "Loose," observing "that not only was Nancy Hanks an illegitimate child herself but that Nancy was not what she ought to have been." The "reputation of Mrs. Lincoln," Herndon wrote, "is that she was a bold—reckless—daredevil kind of a woman, stepping to the very verge of propriety." Or past that verge: Herndon was convinced she "fell in Kentucky about 1805—fell when unmarried—fell afterward." John B. Helm recalled the Hankses at camp meeting revivals: "The Hankses were the finest singers and finest shouters in our country—the only drawback on them was that some nine months after these interesting meetings some of them were likely to have babies." Whatever the truth, such talk about Lincoln's grandmother and mother may well account for Lincoln's reluctance to discuss his ancestry and upbringing.

Nancy Hanks "was above the ordinary height in stature, weighed about 130 pounds, was slenderly built," Herndon reported. "Her skin was dark; hair dark brown; eyes gray and small; forehead prominent; face sharp and angular, with a marked expression of melancholy which fixed itself in the memory of everyone who ever saw or knew her." Raised by relatives, Nancy was "rude & rough," her son recalled. "She could not be held to forms & methods of things; & yet she was a fine woman naturally. It is quite possible that a knowledge of her origin made her defiant & desperate; she was very sensitive, sad sometimes—gloomy."

Her husband shared Nancy's tendency toward depression. "He often became depressed and withdrew into himself, sometimes wandering out . . . for hours on end," the Lincoln historian Michael Burlingame wrote of Thomas. "Bouts of depression would hardly be surprising in a man who, as a boy, had witnessed his father's murder and then endured wandering, rootless poverty and hard labor." Thomas Lincoln was known to remark that "everything that I ever touched either died, got killed, or was lost." Thomas's brother Mordecai also suffered from what a kinswoman called "the Lincoln horrors," a pattern of melancholy. Another relative was committed to the Illinois Hospital for the Insane after a finding that her condition was "with *her* hereditary."

The world into which Abraham Lincoln was born on Sunday, February 12, 1809, at the family's tiny (sixteen by eighteen feet) dirt-floored cabin at Sinking Spring Farm on Nolin Creek near Hodgenville, Kentucky, was materially and emotionally impoverished. "Why, Scripps, it is a great piece of folly to attempt to make anything out of me or my early life," Lincoln remarked to the *Chicago Tribune*'s John L. Scripps in 1860. "It can all be condensed into a single sentence, and that sentence you will find in Gray's Elegy, 'The short and simple annals of the poor.' That's my life, and that's all you or anyone else can make out of it."

There was little romance to Lincoln's first years. He remembered the cold of the winters, his toes sticking out of his boots, the tattered clothes. "To all human appearance the early life of Abraham Lincoln was as unpromising for becoming a great man as you could imagine," a Kentucky neighbor, Samuel Haycraft, recalled in 1865, "indeed I would say it was forbidding, and proves to me that nature bestowed upon him an irrepressible will and innate greatness of mind, to enable [him] to break through all those barriers & iron gates and reach the portion he did in life."

The Kentucky of Lincoln's early years was demanding, depleting, and dangerous. Kentucky, Lincoln would later read in a book of American history, was known "by the name of the Dark and Bloody Ground . . . it became a theater of war, and the residence only of wild beasts." Thomas Lincoln moved the family—which included Lincoln's older sister, Sarah—to nearby Knob Creek in 1811. "My earliest recollection," Lincoln later wrote, "is of the Knob Creek place." The family's farm there was near the road between Bardstown, Kentucky, and Nashville. It was a poor place. "The 30 acre farm in Ky was a knotty—[as] knobby as a piece of land could be—with deep hollows—ravines—cedar trees Covering the parts—knobs . . . thick as trees could grow," Lincoln cousin Dennis Hanks recalled. Soldiers returning home from fighting the War of 1812 found the Lincolns welcoming. The family, it was recalled, "fed and cared for them by Companies—by strings of them." A younger brother, named Thomas, was born and lived but briefly. During the Knob Creek period Lincoln received a smattering of education in what he called "A.B.C. schools" conducted by Zachariah Riney and Caleb Hazel. These few but valuable hours of instruction helped Lincoln learn to write, a skill he also studied with Dennis Hanks, who "taught Abe . . . with a buzzard's quillen which I killed with a rifle & having made a pen—put Abe's hand in mine & moving his fingers by my hand to give him the idea of how to write." Lincoln loved the experience. "It was his custom to form letters, to write words and sentences wherever he found suitable material," John L. Scripps reported. "He scrawled them with charcoal, he scored them in the dust, in the sand, in the snow—anywhere and everywhere."

Abraham Lincoln's Kentucky childhood was spent near the Louisville-to-Nashville Cumberland Road, and there is speculation that he encountered slave drivers along the route. "I remember when I was a boy one night a gang of slaves was driven up to my father's house at dusk," a contemporary of Lincoln's told the writer Louis A. Warren. "The slave dealer wanted to put them in the barn for the night but father was afraid of fire and would not allow it. We had a big haystack outdoors and all the slaves, men, women, and children, were chained together and slept on the haystack that night. Some of the women had babies in their arms. I have never forgotten that sight." Warren's conclusion: "One such scene as that would be sufficient to impress it indelibly in any boy's mind. . . . Abraham Lincoln, as a boy, must have observed these people herded much the same as cattle and driven along the public highway." Discussing slavery with a young office boy in the early 1850s, Lincoln remarked, "I saw it all myself when I was only a little older than you are now, and the horrid pictures are in my mind yet."

The Lincolns appear to have been broadly antislavery in a time and place where slavery was a fact of life. African slavery existed in Spanish holdings in the New World as early as 1502; it had come to English North America by 1619. Over the three-hundred-odd-year course of the Atlantic slave trade, some 12.5 million Black people were enslaved and brought across the ocean. The population of enslaved people in the United States increased fivefold, to about four million, between the Treaty of Paris in 1783, which ended the Revolutionary War, and the inauguration of Abraham Lincoln in 1861.

Slavery was an ancient institution. "From the hour of their birth," Aristotle had written, "some are marked out for subjection, others for rule." Often, though, slavery had been based more on conquest than on race. The historian David Brion Davis reported that the Sumerian term for "slave" translates as "male (or female) of a foreign country." For much of recorded history, the enslaved in a society could come from anywhere, and enslavement meant that they were seen as objects to be controlled and exploited, not as human beings with agency.

Christianity had offered the chance for all that to change. For nearly a millennium and a half, much of the Western world had been theoretically governed on the biblical assertion that all human creatures were made in the image of God and all were, in Christian terms, open to redemption. By the sixteenth century, however, the rush to exploit slavery in the Western Hemisphere proved profit and power to be more compelling than respect for the sanctity of the individual. Geopolitics also played a key role. Portuguese traders turned to Africa to supply the demand for enslaved labor partly because Turkish control of the Mediterranean foreclosed access to the Balkans and other parts of Europe—regions that had long been a source for enslavers.

The imperial demands for forced labor in the Atlantic world came at about the same time the European Enlightenment, which did so much to advance liberty and learning, was helping to create a scientific vernacular and a climate of opinion in which Black people could be seen as inherently subordinate to people of other races. In a representative example, in 1735, the Swedish taxonomist Carl Linnaeus wrote that "*H. sapiens afer*"—Africans—were "sluggish, lazy . . . [C]rafty, slow, careless. Covered by grease. Ruled by caprice." Some writers went so far as to assert that Black people were a wholly separate—and lower—order of creation; others that they were human but had lesser capacities than non-Black people. Other works that contributed to scientific racism included Johann Friedrich Blumenbach's 1776 *On the Natural Varieties of Mankind;* Thomas Jefferson wrote of alleged Black inferiority in his *Notes on the State of Virginia.* "The ethnologist," the twentieth-century scholar William Sumner Jenkins observed, "had attempted to prove by deductions from science that the Bible doctrine of the unity of the races was not true, that Negroes belonged to a different species, were not human and, therefore, might be enslaved with perfect consistency with the theory of absolute social equality."

The racial dimension of American slavery fueled anti-Black discrimination and white supremacist ideology, and the mid-nineteenth century would see the spread of pseudoscientific racist theories. Born in Columbia, South Carolina, and educated at the University of Pennsylvania, Josiah Clark Nott long argued for "polygenesis," which asserted that "human races are distinct, . . . with separate origins." Another influential advocate of polygenesis, Samuel George Morton of Philadelphia, published *Crania Americana*, which claimed, based on skull dimensions, that Black people were intellectually inferior. In a typology of racial categories, Morton wrote that the "Ethiopian race" was "characterized by a black complexion . . . the negro is joyous, flexible and indolent." The Swiss-born Harvard University professor Louis Agassiz was also crucial in this movement. Agassiz commissioned daguerreotypes of the enslaved as part of his work and contributed to a volume based on Morton's papers, co-edited by Nott, entitled *Types of Mankind: Or, Ethnological Researches, Based Upon the Ancient Monuments, Paintings, Sculptures, and Crania of Races, and Upon Their Natural, Geographical, Philological and Biblical History.*

The rise of African slavery, racial prejudice, and the ethnological arguments for Black inferiority intersected in the New World with tragic results. "The negro race, from the first, was regarded with disgust, and its union with the whites forbidden under ignominious penalties," the nineteenth-century historian George Bancroft wrote. On a visit to British North America around 1730, the Anglo-Irish bishop and philosopher George Berkeley reported finding "an irrational contempt of the blacks, as creatures of another species, who had no right to be instructed or admitted to the sacraments." Long afterward, in the 1850s, an English observer wrote: "There seems, in short, to be a fixed notion throughout the whole of the States, whether slave or free, *that the colored is by nature a subordinate race*; and that, in no circumstances, can it be considered equal to the white."

In the age of the American Revolution, the hypocrisy at the heart of the national experiment did not go unnoted. "How is it," Samuel Johnson asked, "that we hear the loudest yelps for liberty among the drivers of Negroes?" Calls for the abolition of slavery in what became the United States dated from 1688, when Quakers in Germantown, Pennsylvania, wrote a "Petition Against Slavery." In the eighteenth century, figures such as Anthony Benezet, Ralph Sandiford, and Benjamin Lay published antislavery tracts. "The Colour of a Man avails nothing, in Matters of Right and Equity," the New Jersey Quaker John Woolman argued in *Some Considerations on the Keeping of Negroes*, published in 1754. The African-born Phillis Wheatley—she was sold into enslavement and brought to Massachusetts in 1761—became a noted poet. The patriot-physician Benjamin Rush praised her "singular genius," and Wheatley corresponded with George Washington, whom she praised as a "great chief" in "freedom's cause." The first formal American abolition organization, the Society for the Relief of Free Negroes, Unlawfully Held in Bondage, was founded at the Rising Sun Tavern in Philadelphia on Friday, April 14, 1775, just five days before the Battle of Lexington and Concord. In Massachusetts, Elizabeth Freeman, an enslaved woman, successfully sued for her liberty on the basis of the state's 1780 constitutional claim that "all men are born free and equal, and have certain natural, essential, and unalienable rights." She saw the implications of the American promise more clearly than many, and she acted on that understanding.

Freeman's suit foreshadowed much. Between 1777 and 1817, eight states pursued abolition. Slavery was banned in Vermont by its 1777 constitution; in Massachusetts by judicial rulings in 1781–83; in Pennsylvania, Connecticut, Rhode Island, New York, and New Jersey by gradual emancipation laws from 1780 to 1808; and in New York by an 1817 general emancipation bill that went into effect in 1827. At the federal level, the Confederation Congress approved the Northwest Ordinance in 1787. Upheld two years later by the first Congress that met under the new federal constitution, the document was formally entitled "An Ordinance for the Government of the Territory of the United States North-West of the River Ohio." Under its provisions, there could be "neither slavery nor involuntary servitude" in the territories that would give rise to Ohio, Indiana, Illinois, Michigan, Wisconsin, and part of Minnesota. Border and Southern states, meanwhile, protected and nurtured slavery, ever suspicious that antislavery northerners would try to advance abolition. In 1790, during the First Congress, Representative Thomas Tudor Tucker of South Carolina dismissed talk of a "general emancipation of slaves by law," saying: "This would never be submitted to by the Southern States without a civil war."

The Kentucky into which Abraham Lincoln was born was very much part of the growing slave-based order. In 1792, the convention called to draft a state constitution had rejected the emancipationist pleas of the Presbyterian minister David Rice, who had published a pamphlet, *Slavery Inconsistent with Justice and Good Policy*, on the subject. Instead the Kentucky delegates, under the sway of the proslavery George Nicholas, insisted on Article IX: "The legislature shall have no power to pass laws for the emancipation of slaves without the consent of their owners, or without paying their owners, previous to such emancipation, or a full equivalent in money, for the slaves so emancipated." Slavery was thus ensured in the Commonwealth of Kentucky, the first Land of Lincoln.

The 1800 census for Hardin County, where Thomas and Nancy Lincoln began their married life, reported a population of 3,653, comprised of 3,317 white people, 325 enslaved people, and eleven free Black people—meaning about 9 percent of the county was made up of slaves. By 1811, two years after Abraham Lincoln's birth, tax records show that the enslaved population had risen to 1,007; it is estimated that there were an "average of at least two slaves for each [white] family" in Hardin County.

Though there were slave owners in both the Lincoln and Hanks families in the late eighteenth and early nineteenth centuries, Thomas Lincoln, who chose to join antislavery churches in Kentucky and in Indiana, was not among them. The "daily experience and observation" of struggling white men such as Thomas Lincoln, John L. Scripps wrote in 1860, led to a conviction that "slavery oppresses the poorer classes, making their poverty and social disrepute a permanent condition through the degradation which it affixes to labor."

In the autumn of 1816, when Abraham was seven, Thomas took his family from Kentucky to land on Little Pigeon Creek in Spencer County, Indiana. Looking back, Scripps suggested that Thomas Lincoln had "wisely resolved to remove his young family from [the] presence" of slavery. "It is said . . . that Mr [Thomas] Lincoln left the State of Ky because and only because Slavery was there," Dennis Hanks recalled. "This is untrue. He movd off to better his Condition—to a place where he could buy land for . . . $1.25 per acre—Slavery did not operate on him. I know too well this whole matter." Hanks was not denying that slavery was an issue for Thomas; he just did not believe it to be the sole or controlling one. Land in Indiana, where the Northwest Ordinance had banned slavery, was cheap and plentiful, and white farmers without enslaved labor had more opportunity in the absence of slave-owning competitors. It is reasonable, then, to surmise that slavery did "operate" on Thomas Lincoln to the extent that a free territory was more congenial to him than a slave one. When Abraham Lincoln recalled that his father's move was "chiefly on account of the difficulty in land titles in Ky," the son tellingly noted that the decision was also "partly on account of slavery," and a closer examination of the elder Lincolns' world suggests that Thomas Lincoln's antislavery inclinations had moral as well as economic components.

The religious argument against slavery had been evident in the 1780s Kentucky of Thomas's childhood. "Being conscious to myself that the practice of holding slaves in perpetual slavery is repugnant to the Golden Law of God and the unalienable rights of mankind," one slave owner in Jefferson County wrote in a 1787 legal document, "[I] do . . . emancipate, set free, and discharge all my negroes hereafter mentioned." In 1796, a Baptist church in the region posed the question "Is slavery oppression or not? The query being taken up was answered in the affirmative. It was oppression." It was also asked: "Can we, as a church, have fellowship with those that hold the righteousness of perpetual slavery?" The verdict: No. In the same year, a minister in the Lincolns' neighborhood, the Reverend Josiah Dodge, helped found what was called an "Emancipation church" about thirty miles away, in Bardstown. One of the clergymen the Lincolns knew, the circuit-riding Methodist Jesse Head, who had married Thomas and Nancy, was also said to be antislavery. "Tom and Nancy and Sally Bush [Thomas's second wife]," a contemporary recalled, "were just steeped full of Jesse Head's notions about the wrong of slavery and the rights of man as explained by Thomas Jefferson and Thomas Paine."

Thomas Lincoln belonged to South Fork Baptist and, later, Little Mount Separate Baptist churches in Kentucky. In Indiana, he was active in the Little Pigeon Creek Baptist Church. Opposition to slavery was a common theme in these congregations. In Kentucky, the Lincolns were part of the Baptist Licking-Locust Association Friends of Humanity, also known as an "emancipation association." This is striking and underappreciated in the popular impression of Lincoln: Abraham Lincoln grew up in a family and among neighboring churchgoers who knew antislavery preaching and subscribed to antislavery theology. Young Lincoln would recite sermons he had heard, and according to a clergyman who claimed to have found an "old, faded memorandum book" in the Little Pigeon Creek church in 1866, Lincoln had worked as a sexton in the log building. When Lincoln would later say that he was "naturally antislavery," he was not manufacturing a useful past for political purposes. He was reporting the fact of the matter.

The roots of the religious antislavery convictions that Lincoln encountered can be found on both sides of the Atlantic. Essential to the long war for emancipation was the faith of enslaved and freed Black people themselves, many of whom bravely rose against slavery and many of whom drew on religion through interminable years of captivity. Absalom Jones, Richard Allen, and Thomas Paul were leading ministers in the closing years of the eighteenth century and into the nineteenth. There were alliances and overlap with Quakers, the denomination that was home to pioneering voices for universal human liberty; figures such as Benjamin Lay made the case against slavery on the grounds that God created human beings to be equal. In the latter decades of the eighteenth century, the cause was taken up by Anglicans including the Reverend John Newton (who wrote the words of the hymn "Amazing Grace"), William Wilberforce, Granville Sharp, Thomas Clarkson, and Hannah More, as well as the Methodist John Wesley. The abolitionist motto, emblazoned with an image of a man in chains, was powerful: "Am I Not a Man and a Brother?"

An artist's rendering of the Lincolns' antislavery Little Pigeon Creek Baptist Church in Spencer County, Indiana.

It was not an uncomplicated story. The First Great Awakening of the middle of the eighteenth century had failed to confront the evils of enslavement. The legendary evangelist George Whitefield at once argued for paying attention to the souls of Black people while he himself owned enslaved people. Yet the gospel message of equality before God and the evangelical emphasis on the individual fed an antislavery strain amid the ethos of proslavery theology, particularly in Methodist and Baptist circles. In 1788, a British Baptist, the Reverend Robert Robinson, published a sermon entitled *Slavery Inconsistent with the Spirit of Christianity*. Two years later, in 1790, John Leland, a leading Baptist in Virginia, of which Kentucky was still a part,* wrote that "slavery is a violent deprivation of the rights of nature, and inconsistent with a republican government." Leland's goal for the church: "To extirpate the horrid evil from the land and pray Almighty God, that our Honorable Legislature may have it in their power, to proclaim the general jubilee, consistent with the principles of good policy."

"Slavery," the prominent Baptist John Leland wrote, "is a violent deprivation of the rights of nature."

The Lincolns' Baptist association had been founded in part through the labors of David Barrow, an antislavery Baptist minister who corresponded on the subject with Thomas Jefferson. A veteran of the Revolutionary War, Barrow was heavily influenced by Thomas Clarkson, arranging to promulgate Clarkson's 1785 *Essay on Slavery and Commerce of the Human Species* and publishing his own *Involuntary, Unmerited, Perpetual, Absolute, Hereditary Slavery Examined on the Principles of Nature, Reason, Justice, Policy, and Scripture* in 1808.

After church services on the American frontier, a Lincoln kinswoman recalled, "Abe would go out to work in the field—get up on a stump and repeat almost word for word the sermon he had heard the Sunday before." Such sermons were preached by William Downs and,

---

* Kentucky would win statehood in the spring of 1792.

later, by David Elkin, two ministers who were antislavery. Downs was thought to be "one of the most brilliant and fascinating orators in the Kentucky pulpit in his day. . . . [He] was fond of controversy and engaged in several debates. His exceeding familiarity with the Sacred Scriptures, his ready wit, keen sarcasm, and brilliant oratory attracted the attention and won the admiration of the most intelligent and refined people within the limits of his acquaintance." Yet Downs was also a creature of the rough frontier and was seen as "disorderly . . . indolent, slovenly, and self-indulgent." Polished or not, Downs had been influenced by the antislavery preacher Joshua Carman, who was described as "fanatical on the subject of slavery."

An antislavery pamphlet authored by David Barrow, a Baptist minister who helped found the Lincolns' Licking-Locust Association in Kentucky.

David Elkin was largely self-taught. When he "first went to preaching," an Elkin grandson recalled, "he did not know but one letter in the alphabet, the letter O, and he knew that because it was round. In his old age, however, he could read the Bible through by heart." Born about 1779, Elkin, who would become close to the Lincoln family in Kentucky, reportedly grew up in the Good Hope Church in Green County, Kentucky. Elkin was "a man of extraordinary natural intellect," a historian of Kentucky Baptists observed, though he was "uncultivated, being barely able to read. He was extremely poor, as to this world's goods; and . . . very indolent and slovenly in his dress. Yet it pleased the Lord to use him to good account." Elkin's voice, it was said, could carry a quarter of a mile. This was important in frontier settings. "Those ministers, with a log or fallen tree or a stump for their pulpit and the heavens their sounding board," wrote a Separate Baptist chronicler, "would dispense the word of life and salvation to a lost and ruined world."

Adam Shoemaker, known as "the Emancipation Preacher," was another figure who featured in the world of Lincoln's youth. Shoemaker reportedly "exposed the horrors of slavery and awoke the people from their stupor"; he was credited with offering a message of "Equal rights for all men: Emancipation! Let every man work for a living!" Three other ministers in Indiana—William Downs's brother Thomas, Alexander Devin, and Charles Polke—also preached a gospel of liberty for all.

The emphasis on emancipation in the Baptist world of the upper South was founded on a straightforward application of the biblical understanding of human equality. "As a political evil, every enlightened wise citizen abhors" slavery, the Licking-Locust Association declared; and "as it is a sin against God, every citizen is in duty bound to testify against it." The Baptist Carter Tarrant, an ally of David Barrow's and an influential antislavery voice in Kentucky, believed slavery "a violation of nature, reason, philosophy and the word of God." The evangelical emphasis on emancipation would be relatively short-lived as the slave-owning interest grew stronger, but it was real in a crucial moment: during the childhood and youth of Abraham Lincoln, who knew slavery, saw it, and was likely exposed to teaching and preaching that declared it wrong.

Still, there was something in the faith of his father that kept Lincoln from declaring himself a believer and joining the church in which he was raised. Perhaps he disliked following his father, a parent with whom he had a complicated relationship on the best of days. Perhaps he was uncomfortable with the Baptist expression of predestination, which held that an omnipotent God had previously determined who was to be saved and who was to be damned, a theological assertion derived from John Calvin. Perhaps he never truly felt the call to make a public assent to the claims of the frontier Baptist sect he knew. And perhaps he sensed, at some level, a discrepancy between scripture, which Lincoln was coming to know well, and religious doctrine. The stories of the Bible conveyed complexities, not sectarian certitudes. The God who created the world and declared it good was also the God who had sent the Flood. The God who parted the Red Sea was also the God who had allowed Egypt to enslave Israel. The God who claimed love to be the motive force of the universe inflicted pain on the faithful servant Job. Rather than conforming to the codes of his clan and of his neighborhood, Lincoln chose to stand alone and apart from his family.

The language and imagery of faith was nevertheless ambient, and Baptists Lincoln knew were antislavery in sentiment. Lincoln "would hear sermons preached—come home—take the children out—get on a stump or log and almost repeat it word for word," Sarah Bush Lincoln recalled. "He made other Speeches—Such as interested him and the children. His father had to make him quit sometimes as he quit his own work to speak & made the other children as well as the men quit their work."

If the children were left at home, Lincoln would organize makeshift services. "When they were gone—Abe would take down the Bible, read a verse—give out a hymn—and we would sing—we were good singers," Lincoln's stepsister Matilda Johnston Moore recalled. "Abe was about 15 years of age—he would preach & we would do the Crying—sometimes he would join the Chorus of Tears."

Religion was a complicated, elusive factor in Lincoln's upbringing. "Probably it is to be my lot to go on in a twilight," he reportedly remarked as a young man, "feeling and reasoning my way through life, as questioning, doubting Thomas did." This much is clear: Lincoln's acceptance of the moral case against slavery and his rejection of the passivity of Calvinistic predestination would help determine the course of his life, and of the nation's. "If I ever get a chance to hit" slavery, Lincoln is said to have later remarked, "I'll hit it hard."

CHAPTER TWO

Abe Was Hungry for Books

He was a Constant and I may Say Stubborn reader.
—Lincoln cousin DENNIS HANKS, on the young Lincoln

The progress of truth is slow; but it will, in the end, prevail. . . .
Let us not only declare by words, but demonstrate by our
actions, "That all men are created equal."
—WILLIAM GRIMSHAW, *History of the United States*

THE YOUNG LINCOLN was far more attracted to reading, thinking, and talking than he was to farming, rail-splitting, and hunting. He liked to make people laugh; there was, he discovered, a power in charm. His mother was an early audience. She was weaving one day when her son "quizzically asked his good mother who was the father of Zebedee's children," his cousin Dennis Hanks recalled. "She saw the drift and laughed."

Lincoln never lost his love of such moments in company with others. At house raisings and other community events, Lincoln "would say to himself and sometimes, too, to others—I don't want these fellows to work anymore and instantly he would Commence his pranks—tricks—jokes—stories—and sure Enough all would stop—gather around Abe & listen. He would sometimes mount a stump—chair or box and make speeches—Speech with stories—anecdotes & such like things: he never failed here."

Indiana was Abraham Lincoln's home for nearly a decade and a half. "It was a wild region, with many bears and other wild animals still in the woods," Lincoln recalled. Thomas Lincoln went to work—and put his son to work—in "an unbroken forest; and the clearing away of surplus wood was the great task ahead." Abraham "had an axe put into [my] hands at once; and from that till within [my] twenty-third year [I] was almost constantly handling that most useful instrument—less, of course, in plowing and harvesting seasons." The toil was grueling. In verses composed later in life, Lincoln recalled:

> *When my father first settled here,*
> *'Twas then the frontier line:*
> *The panther's scream, filled night with fear*
> *And bears preyed on the swine.*

The father was physically strong, an accomplished hunter, and good company in the limited worlds in which he moved. Unlucky in business and in farming, Thomas Lincoln struggled to provide. At the time of the move to Indiana, he built a flatboat out of yellow poplar from the Knob Creek farm, "loaded his household furniture—his tools—whisky and other Effects, including pots—vessels—rifles. &c. &c. . . . He floated on awhile on down the Rolling Fork and upset—and lost the most of the tools &c and some of his Whisky."

As a child, Lincoln appears to have had a warm relationship with his mother. She read to him from the Bible, which introduced him to the poetry of scripture. She tried to teach him more practical lessons, too. "At this place [I] took an early start as a hunter, which was never much improved afterwards," Lincoln recalled of Indiana. "A few days before the completion of [my] eighth year, in the absence of [my] father, a flock of wild turkeys approached the new log-cabin, and [I] with a rifle gun, standing inside, shot through a crack, and killed one of them. [I have] never since pulled a trigger on any larger game." His mother had loaded the gun for him.

On Monday, October 5, 1818—two years after the move to Indiana—Nancy Hanks Lincoln died. She had contracted "milk sickness." Known at first as "sick stomach," the "puking illness," and the "slows," the disease was "vegetable poisoning caused by tremetol, an alcohol found in the white snakeroot plant," medical historians have found. "Grazing animals, allowed to feed in the woods, ate the plant. Humans then acquired the disease by drinking the milk or eating the meat of affected animals." Symptoms included "a whitish coat on the tongue," a doctor recalled, "burning sensation of the stomach, severe vomiting, obstinate constipation of the bowels, coolness of the extremities, great restlessness . . . pulse rather small, somewhat more frequent than natural. . . . In the course of the disease the coat on the tongue becomes brownish and dark." Death, the doctor reported, could come as quickly as within sixty hours.

Nancy Lincoln "struggled on . . . day by day," Dennis Hanks recalled, a "good Christian woman." The disease killed her in about a week's time. "There was no physician near[er] than 35 miles," Hanks recalled. "She knew she was going to die & Called up the Children to her dying side and told them to be good & kind to their father—to one another and to the world, Expressing a hope that they might live as they had been taught by her, to love men—love—reverence and worship God."

She had done what she could as a mother. "Here in this rude house, of the Milk Sick, died one of the very best women in the whole race, known for kindness—tenderness—charity & love to the world," Hanks recalled of his aunt. "Mrs. Lincoln always taught Abe goodness—kindness—read the good Bible to him—taught him to read and spell—taught him sweetness & benevolence as well." She was buried a quarter mile from the Lincoln cabin. It took several months for a minister—David Elkin—to arrive to preach a funeral sermon. The grave remained unmarked. In the last winter of his life, Lincoln said that he hoped to visit the site once more and erect a headstone. He did not live to see the project through.

Abraham was nine when she died. His recollections of her were sparse, his ambivalence about her deep. Once she was gone she was unable to provide her son with love or with security. In memory, she was a source of insecurity and embarrassment as Lincoln absorbed the stories of her illegitimacy and of the allegations about her, or certainly her family's, promiscuity. When he needed her as he grew up, he could not have her. Later in life, when he did not want her—or did not want to share in the stigma of her and her family's origins and conduct—he could not avoid stories about her. Lincoln thus preferred to be seen a child of the frontier, not as the child of either of his parents.

He and his father were never in sympathy with each other. Abe so resented being hired out to neighbors—his father would take his wages—that the experience may have informed his hatred of slavery. "I used to be a slave"—one under his father's autocratic control, Lincoln would remark. "I have Seen his father knock him Down," Dennis Hanks recalled. Another kinsman observed, "Thos. Lincoln never showed by his actions that he thought much of his son Abraham when a boy."

The feeling was mutual. The son felt superior to his father and apparently did not try to disguise it. At supper one day, William Herndon reported, "The elder Lincoln, true to the custom of the day, returned thanks for the blessing. The boy, realizing the scant proportions of the meal, looked up into his father's face and irreverently observed, 'Dad, I call these'—meaning the potatoes—'mighty poor blessings.'"

"Sometimes Abe was a little rude," Dennis Hanks recalled. "When strangers would ride along & up to his father's fence, Abe always, through pride & to tease his father, would be sure to ask the stranger the first question, for which his father would sometimes knock him a rod. Abe was then a rude and forward boy. Abe when whipped by his father never bawled but dropt a kind of silent unwelcome tear, as evidence of his sensations—or other feelings." Yet Lincoln persisted in speaking to the broader world, seeming to insist that he had as much right, if not more of one, as his father did to represent the place and the family. "He was ambitious & determined & when he attempted to Excel [as] man or boy," Hanks recalled, "his whole soul & his Energies were bent on doing it—and he in this generally—almost always accomplished his Ends."

Lincoln had long shown signs of precocity. "He always appeared to be very quiet during playtime," a classmate, E. R. Burba, recalled, "never was rude; seemed to have a liking for solitude; was the one chosen in almost every case to adjust difficulties between boys of his age and size, and when appealed to, his decision was an end of the trouble." Even allowing for sentimental retrospection, the observation is revealing: Lincoln was a figure of authority and adjudication among his peers.

Lincoln may have sought such roles as a way to win the respectability he felt his family lacked. He could not alter his origins. He could not make his father into an educated man. He could not elevate his mother or her family above rumors of scant virtue. And so he summoned all he could from within himself to exert control on the world as he found it, casting himself as a leader and storyteller who could attract the attention and affection of others through his own merits.

He had some help in this from an unexpected quarter: a stepmother who entered his life in the winter of 1819–20. About a year after Nancy Hanks Lincoln died, Thomas Lincoln left Indiana on a visit back to Kentucky. A woman he had known years before, Sarah Bush

Johnston, had been widowed after her husband, the jailer in Elizabeth-town, died in 1816. Thomas offered his suit straightforwardly.

"Well, *Miss* Johnston, I have no wife & you have no husband," Lincoln reportedly said to her. "I came *a* purpose to marry you. I *knowed* you from a gal & you *knowed* me from a boy—I have no time to lose and if you are willing, let it be done Straight off."

"Tommy, I know you well & have no objection to marrying you," Sarah Johnston replied, "but I cannot do it straight off as I owe some debts that must first be paid."

Thomas Lincoln then "asked her for a list of [the debts], which was given," Samuel Haycraft recalled, and "he went & paid them off that same day." The next morning the couple received their marriage license, and "they were Married *Straight off* on that day & left."

Sarah Lincoln arrived in Spencer County as a kind of savior. "This [was] a new era in Abe Lincoln's life," John Helm recalled. "The Bushes were rough, uncouth, uneducated beyond anything that would seem credible now to speak of"—but, he added, "the Hanks ... were a long way below the Bushes again." As a stepmother, Sarah Bush Lincoln encouraged Abraham's interest in educating and in improving himself. "She proved a good and kind mother" to him, Lincoln recalled. When she first encountered her husband's children, she found them "wild—ragged & dirty," Dennis Hanks recalled. "She Soaped, rubbed, and washed the Children Clean so that they look[ed] pretty neat—well & clean. She sewed and mended their Clothes & the Children once more looked human as their own good mother left them."

Thomas Lincoln had been distracted in the aftermath of his first wife's death. "In [my] tenth year [I] was kicked by a horse," Lincoln recalled, "and apparently killed for a time." With Thomas Lincoln's second wife, order had come. As did three stepsiblings to the growing household: John, Sarah, Elizabeth, and Matilda. "Thos Lincoln now hurried his farming ... always ... hunting," Dennis Hanks recalled—but Lincoln's son did not share these passions. "Now at this time Abe was getting hungry for books, reading Everything he could lay his hands on.... He was a Constant and I may Say Stubborn reader, his father having Sometimes to slash him for neglecting his work by reading." John Romine, a neighboring farmer, recalled that Abraham "worked for me, but was always reading and thinking. I used to get mad at him for it.... He would laugh and talk—crack his jokes and tell stories all the time; didn't love work half as much as his pay. He said to me one day that his father taught him to work; but he never taught him to love it."

The new Mrs. Lincoln championed her stepson. "I induced my husband to permit Abe to read and study at home as well as at school," Sarah Bush Lincoln recalled. "At first he [Thomas Lincoln] was not easily reconciled to it, but finally he too seemed willing to encourage him to a certain extent. Abe was a dutiful son to me always, and we took particular care when he was reading not to disturb him—would let him read on and on till he quit of his own accord." A neighbor reported that Sarah Lincoln raised Abraham to be a "a slender well behaved quiet boy. . . . She was doubtless the first person that ever treated him like a human being."

Formal schooling was sparse. "There were some schools, so called; but no qualification was ever required of a teacher, beyond 'readin, writin, and cipherin' to the Rule of Three," Lincoln recalled. "If a straggler supposed to understand latin, happened to sojourn in the neighborhood, he would be looked upon as a wizard. There was absolutely nothing to excite ambition for education."

Yet his curiosity was innate. When he heard older people speak, Lincoln recalled, he would retreat later and spend "no small part of the night . . . trying to make out what was the exact meaning of some of their, to me, dark sayings. . . . I was not satisfied until I had repeated over and over, until I put it in language that was plain enough, as I thought, for any boy . . . to comprehend."

Books were his means of escape and of transcendence. "Abe was not Energetic Except in one thing—he was active & persistent in learning," his stepsister recalled. He absorbed standards such as Thomas Dilworth's *A New Guide to the English Tongue*, the Bible, Aesop's *Fables*, John Bunyan's *Pilgrim's Progress*, Mason Locke Weems's *The Life of Washington*, Daniel Defoe's *Robinson Crusoe*, and James Riley's *An Authentic Narrative of the Loss of the American Brig Commerce*. "Abe was a good boy: he didn't like physical labor—was diligent for Knowledge—wished to Know & if pains & Labor would get it he was sure to get it," Sarah Bush Lincoln recalled. "He read all the books he could lay his hands on." The psalms of the King James Version were favorites, as were the hymns of Isaac Watts.

His time in a classroom was limited to less than a year. "What [I have] in the way of education," Lincoln wrote, "[I have] picked up." To understand the man he became, it is illuminating to read what he read as he "picked up" an education on his own. To a correspondent shortly after Lincoln's assassination, William Herndon wrote, "I am writing Mr L's life . . . giving him in his passions—appetites—& affections— perceptions—memories—judgements—understanding . . . just as he lived, breathed—ate & laughed in this world, clothed in flesh & sinew— bone & nerve." The task was not a simple one. The origins of much of the mature Lincoln can be found in what the young Lincoln read—in those works that created his intellectual, imaginative, and moral infra- structure. By Lincoln's own account, perhaps the most important book of his life (other than the King James Bible) was Lindley Murray's *The English Reader,* which Lincoln described as "the best schoolbook ever put into the hands of an American youth."

The English Reader, an anthology published in 1799 to collect "Pieces in Prose and Poetry, Selected from the Best Writers," was hugely successful. The book's purpose was stated in the subtitle: "To Assist Young Persons to Read with Propriety and Effect; to Improve Their Language and Sentiments; and to Inculcate Some of the Most Impor- tant Principles of Piety and Virtue." The book opens with common- places about equanimity, moderation, and an appreciation of vicissitude; it is life counsel for the young as they grow into men:

> Nothing is so inconsistent with self-possession as violent anger. It overpowers reason; confounds our ideas; distorts the appearance, and blackens the color of every object.
>
> . . .
>
> In judging of others, let us always think the best, and employ the spirit of charity and candor. But in judging of ourselves, we ought to be exact and severe.
>
> . . .
>
> We should cherish sentiments of charity towards all men.
>
> . . .
>
> In seasons of distress or difficulty, to abandon ourselves to de- jection, carries no mark of a great or a worthy mind. Instead of sinking under trouble, and declaring "that his soul is weary of life," it becomes a wise and a good man, in the evil day, with firm- ness to maintain his post; to bear up against the storm; . . . and

never give up the hope that better days may yet arise.

A Pennsylvania Quaker who moved to York, England, Lindley Murray was an admirer of the late seventeenth- and early eighteenth-century English essayist, poet, and politician Joseph Addison and of Hugh Blair, a Presbyterian clergyman and Scottish Enlightenment figure whose writings and sermons form a large portion of *The English Reader.* "I consider a human soul, without education, like marble in the quarry," Addison had written in words reproduced by Murray. "The philosopher, the saint, or the hero, the wise, the good, or the great man, very often

Lindley Murray's English Reader, *which the young Lincoln loved, included these words: "We should cherish sentiments of charity towards all men."*

lies hid and concealed in a plebeian, which a proper education might have disinterred, and have brought to light."

Reading these words may have been empowering to Lincoln, even transporting, for they promised deliverance. If he was diligent in his studies, insistent on acquiring knowledge, and devoted to mercy and grace, he could become not a poor and obscure farmer but a philosopher, a saint, a hero, or a wise, good, great man.

It would not be easy. Lincoln's initial claims to distinction among his neighbors and peers were about wit and strength. The story is told that Lincoln was splitting rails one day when a man with a gun passed by and called to Lincoln to "look up—which he did, [and] the man raised his gun in an attitude to shoot." A surprised Lincoln asked the man what he was doing, and the passerby "replied that he had promised to shoot the first man he met who was uglier than himself—Lincoln asked to see the man's face & after taking a look remarked—If I am uglier than you, then blaze away."

His humor could be endearing, but his skill at sport was instrumental in his persona. He was strong, and his physical power—as well as abilities as a wrestler—earned the respect of other men. "He Could throw Down any man that took hold of him," a neighbor and friend recalled. "He Could out jump the Best of them. He Could out-Box the Best of them. . . . He was the favorite of all at home, Men & women & Children."

In quieter moments alone, reading Lindley Murray, Lincoln saw that the path to sustained success was long and arduous. "By whatever means you may at first attract the attention, you can hold the esteem, and secure the hearts of others, only by amiable dispositions, and the accomplishments of the mind," Hugh Blair wrote in a selection in *The English Reader*.

Blair also urged readers to recognize that the world would never fully conform to human wishes—a valuable lesson for Lincoln, who would long struggle with the extent to which individuals could alter history. "We find man placed in a world where he has by no means the disposal of the events that happen," Blair wrote. "Calamities sometimes befall the worthiest and the best, which it is not in their power to prevent, and where nothing is left them, but to acknowledge, and to submit to, the high hand of Heaven."

Addison offered advice for a political creature, suggesting that one's words mattered—a point Lincoln heeded all his life. The wise man, Addison observed, is one who "knows how to pick and cull his thoughts for conversation, by suppressing some, and communicating others; whereas [the foolish man] lets them all indifferently fly out." Citing the ancients, Addison added that "a man should live with his enemy in such a manner as might leave him room to become his friend. . . . [I]t is the discreet man, not the witty, nor the learned, nor the brave, who guides the conversation, and gives measures to society."

Lincoln was engaged, too, in the story of his country, reading William Grimshaw's popular *History of the United States*, first published in 1820. Grimshaw took a progressive view of history and of human nature, linking the colonization of the New World and the founding of the American republic to insights from the Scientific Revolution and the Enlightenment. The capacity of mariners to navigate more precisely; the broadening of conceptions of reality to include distant lands; and the steady hunger for individual liberty were all factors in the making of the nation—as was the notion of Manifest Destiny.

"A new era had arisen in the west," Grimshaw wrote of the American Revolution. He quoted the Declaration of Independence in its entirety—possibly the first time Lincoln had ever encountered the document. Jefferson's urgent yet elegant prose stretched out over nearly five pages of Grimshaw's book, from the majestic opening ("When, in the course of human events") to the elevating close ("with a firm reliance on the protection of Divine Providence, we mutually pledge to each other our lives, our fortunes, and our sacred honor").

For Grimshaw, the American Revolution and the creation of the constitutional order were sequential chapters in the story of a gradually rising civilization—a story that required an end to human enslavement. "Since the middle of the last century, expanded minds have been, with slow gradations, promoting the decrease of slavery in North America," Grimshaw wrote. "The progress of truth is slow; but it will, in the end, prevail. . . . Let us not only declare by words, but demonstrate by our actions, 'That all men are created equal; that they are endowed, by their Creator, with certain unalienable rights; that, amongst these, are life, liberty, and the pursuit of happiness.'" To young Lincoln, then, the cause of antislavery was presented as a necessary battle in the war for American progress and liberty.

These lessons were imbued piecemeal amid the crush of his work and duties on the frontier. "The little advance [of education] I have now . . . I have picked up from time to time under the pressure of necessity," Lincoln recalled almost thirty years later. "I was raised to farm work which I continued till I was twenty-two"—and which he took pains to escape when he joined his family in moving from Spencer County, Indiana, to Macon County, Illinois, in March 1830. It was a sad time: Lincoln's sister, Sarah, who had married Aaron Grigsby in 1826, had died giving birth in 1828.

By these years, Lincoln had already begun to travel more widely. In 1828, he was a ferryman on the Ohio and Mississippi rivers and made a trip with another man to New Orleans. They had to "linger and trade along the Sugar coast," Lincoln recalled, and "one night they were attacked by seven negroes with intent to kill and rob them. They were hurt some in the melee, but succeeded in driving the negroes from the boat, and then 'cut cable,' 'weighed anchor,' and left." On a second trip to New Orleans a few years later, Lincoln, according to a family tradition, "saw negroes chained, maltreated, whipped and scourged. Lincoln saw it. His heart bled." It is unclear whether this was an accurate recollection, for the source, Lincoln cousin John Hanks, was not with Lincoln in New Orleans. What is certain is that Lincoln saw the slave markets in New Orleans and what Alexis de Tocqueville described as "the faces with every shade of color" in the city.

For the journey from Indiana to Illinois two years later, in 1830, Lincoln drove a family wagon. He had a kindly disposition—and an active conscience. During the trip, one of the family's dogs was stranded across an icy stream. No one, apparently, wanted to go back to rescue it. "But I could not endure the idea of abandoning even a dog," Lincoln recalled. "Pulling off shoes and socks I waded across the stream and triumphantly returned with the shivering animal under my arm. His frantic leaps of joy and other evidences of a dog's gratitude amply repaid me for all the exposure I had undergone."

The family settled on the north side of the Sangamon River, roughly ten miles west of Decatur, Illinois. "Here they built a log-cabin," Lincoln recalled, "into which they removed, and made sufficient of rails to fence ten acres of ground, fenced and broke the ground, and raised a crop of sow[n] corn upon it the same year."

This undertaking would be Lincoln's last among his family. Now in his early twenties, he soon moved, by himself, to the village of New Salem, Illinois, where he worked for a year, he recalled, "as a sort of Clerk in a store." The owner was Denton Offutt, whom a contemporary remembered as "a wild, harum-scarum kind of a man, and I think not much of a businessman." Lincoln was a conscientious clerk, sleeping for a time in the store itself and then boarding with different villagers in the neighborhood.

As he had back in Indiana, Lincoln won admiration with physical feats, including wrestling. "Mr. L was very fond of out door recreations & sports, and excelled in them," the New Salem farmer James Short recalled. "He lifted 1000 pounds of shot by main strength. He never played cards, nor drank, nor hunted." He was a popular figure, challenging the great Jack Armstrong, a local legend, in a fabled wrestling match; Lincoln had also learned enough from his reading of Lindley Murray to make himself pleasant to men and women alike, presenting a congenial face to the world around him.

That world was overwhelmingly political. The America of Lincoln's young manhood was roiled by debates about democracy and public life. It was the age of Andrew Jackson, an era of expanding suffrage for white men and of growing engagement with political questions. "Scarcely have you descended on the soil of America when you find yourself in the midst of a sort of tumult; a confused clamor is raised on all sides; a thousand voices come to your ear at the same time," Tocqueville wrote. "To meddle in the government of society and to speak about it is the greatest business and, so to speak, the only pleasure that an American knows."

This was Lincoln's daily universe. Shaped by the lessons of faith at home and by the high-minded admonitions of Blair and of Addison, he found himself, by 1830, in the heart of village life in Jacksonian America—an America in which politics was not an incidental but a controlling element of life. Lincoln longed to transcend his origins and appear legitimate, respected, and vindicated in the eyes of others. As he settled into the tiny but representative universe of New Salem, then, he naturally gravitated to the sphere of public questions to try to make his mark.

He knew how to handle an axe. What the bookish young man wanted to wield was power not over nature but over human nature. Drawn to the drama of trials—an arena of action where the ability to argue was decisive—a fascinated Lincoln watched lawyers at work. In Boonville, Indiana, he observed a defense lawyer named John Brackenridge make a powerful case for his client in a murder trial. Years later, the lawyer called on President Lincoln in the White House. "If I could, as I then thought, have made as good a speech as that, my soul would have been satisfied," Lincoln told his visitor, "for it was up to that time the best speech I had ever heard."

Even before he had settled in New Salem, in the early summer of 1830, Lincoln, then twenty-one years old, had delivered his first political speech in Decatur, Illinois, one that addressed the subject of the navigation of the Sangamon River. It was the first time he offered words in public designed to move and to convince. He had found that there was something sweet about the sound of his voice, about the compliment of the attention of others, about controlling, for a moment, the reality around him. Maybe, just maybe, there might be a future in such things.

CHAPTER THREE

I Am Humble Abraham Lincoln

There was nothing of the poke about him. Whenever he went
at anything he went at it to do it. . . . Always put things
through in a hurry.

—N. W. BRANSON, a New Salem neighbor

The Continued thought & study of the man Caused—with
the death of one whom he dearly & sincerely loved—a . . .
partial & momentary derangement.

—An Illinois friend, on the death of Lincoln's fiancée Ann Rutledge

THE SPRING OF 1832 WAS A CROWDED TIME. Thirty-two days after his twenty-third birthday, Lincoln, in the pages of the Thursday, March 15, *Sangamo Journal,* announced his candidacy for the Illinois state legislature. He had, he recalled, "rapidly made acquaintances and friends" who encouraged his ambitions. Polished, candid, and eloquent, Lincoln's published statement offered a conventional Whig platform. Like Henry Clay of Kentucky, who was challenging Andrew Jackson in the presidential campaign, Lincoln favored internal improvements, arguing for a government role in creating an infrastructure for private enterprise and for social mobility. Education, Lincoln added, was "the most important subject which we as a people can be engaged in." There was something of his familial drama here, too. Thomas Lincoln is thought to have been a Jacksonian Democrat, yet his son, at the first opportunity, struck out on a different political path.

In his announcement, Lincoln spoke of his determination to win the esteem of others. "How far I shall succeed in gratifying this ambition is yet to be developed," he wrote. "I am young and unknown to many of you. I was born and have ever remained in the most humble walks of life. I have no wealthy or popular relations to recommend me. My case is thrown exclusively upon the independent voters of this county, and if elected they will have conferred a favor upon me, for which I shall be unremitting in my labors to compensate."

Just over a month later, on Thursday, April 19, 1832, word of a frontier war with the Sac and Fox tribes under Chief Black Hawk reached New Salem. In the fever of the rising conflict, Lincoln learned that he had not been foolish to offer himself for the legislature—an election scheduled for August—when his fellow militiamen selected him as their captain "by a unanimous vote against all opposition," as a friend of his recalled with pride. Lincoln had prevailed over a prominent man, William Kirkpatrick. To a neighbor, William G. Greene, Lincoln said, "I'll be damned, Bill, but I've beat him!" Lincoln's men—members of the Fourth Illinois Regiment of Mounted Volunteers—were described as "generous ruffians." Lincoln's first order to one was greeted with a cry of "Go to the devil, sir!" Still, his victory—a sign of affection and respect, two things he craved—was thrilling. It was, he recalled on the eve of his election to the presidency nearly three decades later, "a success which gave me more pleasure than any I have had since."

His experience of combat was minimal. He later joked that he fought more mosquitoes than men, but he did see the human cost of battle firsthand. On Tuesday, May 15, Lincoln and his troops buried the bloodied remains of eleven militiamen at Stillman's Run—"all scalped," an observer recalled, "some with the heads cut off. Many with their throats cut and otherwise Barbarously Mutilated." Riding up a small hill to the decimated camp, Lincoln slowly realized the horror before him. As one of his companions recalled, the bodies "were horribly mangled—heads cut off—heart taken out—& disfigured in Every way." Lincoln remembered the scene in misty, blood-red tones, as if the hilltop were otherworldly, transformed by violence. A small detail stuck with him: "One man had on buckskin breeches"—as if the pained Lincoln had averted his eyes from the carnage, seeking the comfort of the mundane in such a startling tableau.

Yet Lincoln insisted on as much magnanimity as men could muster in such moments. An aged Indian man "Came to Camp & delivered himself up, showing us an old paper written by [Secretary of War] Lewis Cass, Stating that the Indian was a good & true man," William Greene recalled. The militiamen did not care about the letter, saying, "we have come out to fight the Indians and by God we intend to do so," adding, "The Indian is a damned spy." Lincoln was having none of it.

"Men, this must not be done—he must not be shot and killed by us," Lincoln said.

"This is cowardly on your part, Lincoln," some of the company said.

"If any man thinks I am a coward," Lincoln said, "let him test it."

"Lincoln—you are larger & heavier than we are," came the reply.

"This you can guard against," Lincoln said. "Choose your weapons."

And that, William Greene recalled, "soon put to silence quickly all Charges of the Cowardice of Lincoln."

Discharged from militia duty on Tuesday, July 10, Lincoln returned to New Salem to face the voters. "Fellow Citizens, I presume you all know who I am," he told his townspeople. "I am humble Abraham Lincoln. I have been solicited by my friends to become a candidate for the Legislature. My politics are short and sweet, like the old woman's dance. I am in favor of a national bank. I am in favor of the internal improvement system and a high protection tariff. These are my sentiments and political principles."

His politics were those of Henry Clay, and Lincoln's assent to the Whig Party platform put him in the political mainstream in the age of Jackson. Lincoln was, as he recalled in 1859, "always a Whig in politics." The origins of the Whig Party—initially known as the National Republican Party—can be traced to 1824, when Clay became secretary of state after throwing his support to John Quincy Adams to defeat Andrew Jackson for the presidency. The hero of the Battle of New Orleans, Jackson had won the popular vote but failed to secure a majority in the Electoral College, thus sending the election to the House of Representatives. Jackson accepted the result of an Adams presidency but dubbed the maneuver the "corrupt bargain," a charge he would repeat as he planned a campaign in 1828.

The Adams-Clay party took a more expansive view of the central government than did Jackson's Democratic Party. From the Whig perspective, the Constitution's powers could be interpreted beyond the plain text of the document. Federally funded roads, canals, and bridges were constitutional, the Whig interest argued, as were innovations such as the Bank of the United States. Westerners, in particular need of internal improvements, were especially open to such arguments. Some

A friend said that Henry Clay of Kentucky was Lincoln's "favorite of all the great men of the nation." Lincoln himself called Clay "the beau ideal of a statesman."

white Southerners were less enamored of broad constitutional inter-pretations, not least because many of them feared attacks on slavery. "The states having no slaves may not feel as strongly as the states having slaves about stretching the Constitution," Nathaniel Macon of North Carolina observed in 1818, "because no such interest is to be touched by it." Westerners—Lincoln among them—also saw federal tariffs as a reasonable way to raise revenue for vital internal improvements. Such tariffs, though, were thought to harm Southern exporters of raw mate-rials to nations that found sending finished goods back to the Ameri-can marketplace to be prohibitively expensive.

The battles over such questions in the first half of the nineteenth century were pitched. That Lincoln ran his first election in 1832, the year of the Clay-Jackson presidential contest, was significant, for he would have absorbed the nuances of the national debate even as he sought office in local circumstances. "'THE COMMONWEALTH' is the term best expressing the Whig idea of a State or Nation," the New York editor Horace Greeley wrote, "and our philosophy regards a Government with hope and confidence, as an agency of the community through which vast and beneficent ends may be accomplished." The

Jacksonians took a different tack, believing, in the words of the motto of the leading Democratic newspaper, the *Globe* of Washington, that *"The World is governed too much."*

As an aspiring Whig politician, Lincoln said that he believed "the legitimate object of government is 'to do for the people what needs to be done, but which they can not, by individual effort, do at all, or do so well, for themselves.'" Open about his philosophy, Lincoln sought to convince others—and perhaps himself—that the election was not of paramount importance to him. "If elected, I shall be thankful," Lincoln told the public; "if not it will be all the same." He would have the chance to see whether the latter were the case, for he was defeated in the Monday, August 6, 1832, election. Unsurprisingly, he disliked losing. Years later he recalled that the New Salem campaign was "the only time" he was "ever beaten on a direct vote of the people." But Lincoln noted a mitigating factor: While he was "an avowed Clay man," his precinct went for Jackson in November.

Lincoln's disappointment was understandable. At the age of twenty-three, Lincoln was already a political creature, seeking affection from, and authority over, others. He promised that he would be back. "When I have been a candidate before you some 5 or 6 times and have been beaten every time," Lincoln remarked, "I will consider it a disgrace and will be sure never to try it again." Observers were impressed by his showing. "Lincoln," a friend recalled, "knew what he was about and . . . he had running qualities."

Lincoln pondered next steps. "[I] was now without means and out of business"—Denton Offutt's store had folded—"but was anxious to remain with [my] friends who had treated [me] with so much generosity"—adding, wittily but truly, "especially as [I] had nothing elsewhere to go." He briefly opened another store, this time with William F. Berry. "Of course," Lincoln recalled, we "did nothing but get deeper and deeper in debt." The store, he lamented, "winked out." The quest to make a living—and a life—went on. "[I] studied," Lincoln wrote, "what [I] should do—thought of learning the black-smith trade—thought of trying to study law—rather thought [I] could not succeed at that without a better education."

For a moment, oddly, the leader of the opposition party helped the young man from afar. In May 1833, President Jackson was coming to the end of a crisis with South Carolina, where radical leaders—including Jackson's first-term vice president, John C. Calhoun—were advancing the doctrine of nullification, a divisive sectional initiative designed to give states the power to "nullify" federal laws they found objectionable. The immediate occasion was a federally imposed protective tariff. But everyone knew, as Jackson put it after fending off the white Southern firebrands, that "the tariff was only the pretext, and disunion and southern confederacy the real object. The next pretext will be the negro, or slavery question."

Jackson wrote these words on Wednesday, May 1, 1833. Six days later, the president appointed the twenty-four-year-old Abraham Lincoln—defeated Whig and failed storekeeper—to be postmaster of New Salem. The office, Lincoln recalled, was "too insignificant to make [my] politics an objection." Running the post office was hardly a life-changing or life-sustaining enterprise. The county surveyor offered Lincoln work if he could master the craft. Lincoln "accepted, procured a compass and chain, studied . . . a little, and went at it." A pleasant enough interlude, it was only that: an interlude. "This procured bread, and kept soul and body together," Lincoln recalled.

He was interested not only in his body and in his soul but also in his mind. In this period, Lincoln became a devotee of Samuel Kirkham's *English Grammar,* a book that supplemented the foundation he had built in reading the King James Bible, Grimshaw's *History,* and Murray's *The English Reader.* "It may be laid down as a maxim of eternal truth, that *good sense* is the foundation of all good writing," Kirkham wrote. "Remember that 'knowledge is power'; that an enlightened and a virtuous people can never be enslaved."

Lincoln intuitively heeded Kirkham's exhortation that in knowledge there was power. Voraciously curious in the New Salem years, Lincoln read Constantin Volney's 1791 *The Ruins, or, Meditation on the Revolutions of Empires,* and Thomas Paine's 1794–95 *The Age of Reason.* Such arguments held immense appeal for Lincoln—not simply for their sensational value, though they surely had such value, but for their insistence on the individual interpretation of reality rather than on the blind acceptance of tradition.

Following Thomas Hobbes and John Locke, Volney wrote of the social contract that had rescued humankind from Hobbes's war of all against all in the state of nature. "What one seizes to-day, another takes to-morrow," Volney wrote. "Let us establish judges, who shall arbitrate our rights, and settle our differences. When the strong shall rise against the weak, the judge shall restrain him . . . and the life and property of each shall be under the guarantee and protection of all."

Such words informed Lincoln's nascent political philosophy. To contemplate American democracy was to contemplate Americans themselves, since democracies were expressions of individual worldviews. In the United States professed religious belief was foundational, for the enfranchised constituents of the republic tended to profess religious belief. "The Americans combine the notions of Christianity and of liberty so intimately in their minds," Tocqueville wrote, "that it is impossible to make them conceive the one without the other."

Thomas Paine hoped to break this bond. To Paine—as to many freethinking skeptics—democracy should be based on reason, and reason led him to reject many of the supernatural claims of religion in the same way he rejected the claims of autocracy. "I believe in the equality of man," Paine wrote; "and I believe that religious duties consist in doing justice, loving mercy, and endeavoring to make our fellow-creatures happy. I do not believe . . . in the creed of any church I know of. My own mind is my own church." In Paine's view, God had created the universe, set it in motion, and did not intervene in human affairs.

These points moved Lincoln. In New Salem, according to William Herndon, Volney and Paine's works "passed from hand to hand, and furnished food for the evening's discussion in the tavern and village store." Enamored by the case against traditional religion, Lincoln "prepared an extended essay—called by many, a book—in which he made an argument against Christianity, striving to prove that the Bible was not inspired, and therefore not God's revelation, and that Jesus Christ was not the son of God," Herndon reported. The Lincoln essay was "read and freely discussed" in New Salem circles.

Then Samuel Hill intervened. A storekeeper and protective friend of Lincoln's, Hill "snatched the manuscript and thrust it into the stove." Freethinking was fine for a frontier evening. It was not fine for a politically ambitious man who sought power in a country where so many professed the faith of their fathers. "The book went up in flames, and Lincoln's political future was secure," Herndon recalled.

Lincoln would not publicly go so far along the skeptical path as he did privately. Like Jefferson, Lincoln was pragmatic about religion. A man who aspired to lead a democracy needed to speak in a common vernacular, and the American vernacular was steeped in the language and in the imagery of Protestantism. Lincoln's was not an entirely cynical accommodation. He appreciated traditional religious belief even if he did not fully share it. "In my intercourse with Mr. Lincoln I learned that he believed in a Creator of all things," his friend I. W. Keys recalled. "As to the Christian theory that Christ is God or equal to the Creator, he said that it had better be taken for granted; for by the test of reason we might become infidels on that subject . . . ; but that the system of Christianity was an ingenious one at least, and perhaps was calculated to do good."

Influenced by writers who saw science as supreme and religion as superstitious, Lincoln charted his own course through the tides of skepticism and conviction. While the Lincoln of New Salem thought of God as a remote Creator, uninvolved in history, the Lincoln of the White House came to a different view: That the human drama on earth was bound up with the inscrutable but evident will of God. This was, after all, the lesson of the Bible itself, which Lincoln knew intimately and admired greatly. "Where wast thou," a sneering Lord says to Job out of the whirlwind, "when I laid the foundations of the earth?" Lincoln realized that life would never conform to human aspiration or submit to human design. "O the depth of the riches both of the wisdom and knowledge of God!" Saint Paul wrote. "How unsearchable are his judgments, and his ways past finding out!" The fate of mortals was to marshal reason, experience, and faith in order to realize the ideal of loving one's neighbor as oneself. "When I do good I feel good, when I do bad I feel bad, and that's my religion," an old man in Indiana had once said in Lincoln's hearing. Lincoln quoted these words to describe his own religious views.

In New Salem in the 1830s, Lincoln's postmastership and surveying paid for his daily bread—his main expenses were "board and clothing bills"—but politics remained his central interest. In 1834, two years after his initial election loss, Lincoln stood again for the legislature. This time he prevailed, he recalled with pride, "by the highest vote cast for any candidate" in the balloting on Monday, August 4. He was twenty-five, and he had found his métier. He would win three subsequent elections, serving in the Illinois state legislature for four terms, from 1834 to 1842. He borrowed $200—part of which he invested in a new suit of clothes "to make a decent appearance in the legislature"—and went to Vandalia, then the state capital.

Lincoln, a contemporary recalled, "reveled in [politics] . . . as a fish does in water, as a bird disports itself on the sustaining air." He kept a freshman's low profile in Vandalia, a village that some lawmakers believed "the dullest, dreariest place" they had ever encountered. Yet Lincoln was intrigued by his colleagues and their circles. "Lincoln had seen but very little of what might be called society and was very awkward, and very much embarrassed in the presence of ladies," Orville L. Browning, a state senator, recalled. "Mrs. Browning very soon discovered his great merits, and treated him with a certain frank cordiality which put Lincoln entirely at his ease."

To Lincoln, this was the great world to which he had long aspired. "The society of Vandalia and the people attracted thither by the Legislature made it, for that early day, a gay place indeed," Herndon recalled. "Men of capital and brains were there. . . . There were acts to incorporate banks, turnpikes, bridges, insurance companies, towns, railroads, and female academies." The most significant milestone of the ten-week session was the funding of an Illinois–Michigan canal that powered the growth of Chicago—Whig doctrine in action. The whole of the experience, both political and social, was exhilarating. "Lincoln improved rapidly in Mind & Manners after his return from Vandalia," Abner Y. Ellis, a New Salem friend, recalled.

Service in the legislature was not full-time, and one of his fellow lawmakers from Sangamon County, Major John T. Stuart, suggested that Lincoln consider the practice of law. It would be Lincoln's fifth attempt to find a moneymaking vocation, after farming, ferry work, storekeeping, and surveying. He borrowed books from Vincent A. Bogue (a copy of Blackstone), from David Turnham (*The Statutes of Indiana*), and from Stuart. Lincoln "studied with nobody," he recalled, but, as usual, "went at it in good earnest."

The legislative session interrupted Lincoln's studies ("When the Legislature met," he said, "the law books were dropped"), but he persevered. "Work, work, work, is the main thing," Lincoln would remark. He was licensed as a lawyer in the autumn of 1836. About seven months later, on Saturday, April 15, 1837, Lincoln moved from New Salem to the larger, bustling Springfield, where he entered practice with Major Stuart.

By the end of his twenties, the self-taught Lincoln had a coherent political worldview. He had come far in these New Salem years. Driven and self-educated, popular and determined, Lincoln had found a respectable way to make a living, won political office, and deepened his understandings about history and human nature. What he did not yet have was a wife.

He thought he'd found the perfect girl. Her name was Ann Rutledge, the daughter of a New Salem tavern owner, James Rutledge, with whom Lincoln had boarded in 1833. Remembered as a "beautiful and very amiable young woman," Miss Rutledge was from the western branch of a prominent South Carolina family. Her father was a gregarious man, and the Rutledges were at the center of life in New Salem. "Like other Southern people," William Herndon wrote of James Rutledge, "he was warm—almost to impulsiveness—social, and generous." There were nine children in the Rutledge clan; Ann was the third. Her "winning ways," it was said, "attached people to her so firmly that she soon became the most popular young lady in the village."

On this point testimony was unanimous. "She was amiable and of exquisite beauty, and her intellect was quick, deep, and philosophic as well as brilliant," the Menard County lawyer L. M. Greene recalled. "Miss Rutledge," Mrs. Hardin Bale said, "had auburn hair, blue eyes, fair complexion. She was pretty, slightly slender, but in everything a good hearted young woman. She was about five feet two inches high, and weighed in the neighborhood of a hundred and twenty pounds. She was beloved by all who knew her." Another recalled, "Miss Rutledge was a gentle, amiable maiden, without any of the airs of your city belles, but winsome and comely withal; a blonde in complexion, with golden hair, cherry-red lips, and a bonny blue eye."

This last assessment came from an interested party: A man known as John McNeil, a suitor for Ann's hand who had arrived in New Salem from the east "seeking his fortune in the West." As Herndon recalled, "He went to work at once, and within a short time had accumulated by commendable effort a comfortable amount of property. Within three years McNeil owned a farm, and a half interest with

Samuel Hill in the leading store." He was, in other words, a rising man—and before long he joined the quest to win the lovely seventeen-year-old Ann.

The field was not uncrowded. Samuel Hill had tried his luck but failed. Now McNeil, sensing an opportunity, swung into action. He met with more success than Hill, engaging himself to Miss Rutledge. It was a good match, even a great one, considering McNeil's prosperity. Villagers speculated that the newcomer, who was "acquiring property and money day by day," may have stored up as much as ten to twelve thousand dollars since arriving on the scene.

Then the story took an unexpected turn. In conversation with Ann, McNeil told her that he was not John McNeil, as she and all of New Salem believed, but John McNamar. He had assumed a false name, he said, with good reason. "I left behind me in New York, my parents and brothers and sisters," he told Ann. "They are poor, and were in more or less need when I left them in 1829"—some four years earlier. "I vowed that I would come West, make a fortune, and go back to help them." He had been duplicitous for "fear that if the family in New York had known where he was they would have settled down on him, and before he could have accumulated any property would have sunk him beyond recovery. Now, however, he was in a condition to help them, and he felt overjoyed at the thought." His plan was to return east, collect his people, return, and marry Ann, and all would be well.

The young lady said she understood. She would wait. She was in love, and the delay was nothing to her so long as McNeil (or now, as she knew, McNamar) came back—ideally with dispatch. He rode off to the east.

A curious interlude ensued. McNamar took ill along the way—a fever felled him in Ohio for nearly a month—and did not write to Ann, a silence that created much anxiety back in New Salem. "Her friends encouraged the idea of cruel desertion," Herndon reported. "The change of McNeil to McNamar had wrought in their minds a change of sentiment. Some contended that he had undoubtedly committed a crime in his earlier days, and for years had rested secure from apprehension under the shadow of an assumed name; while others . . . whispered in the unfortunate girl's ear the old story of a rival in her affections." By the time McNamar reached New York, he had to deal with a dying father. All of this consumed a great deal of time, and when he finally wrote to Ann he seemed to have had a change of heart about the engagement. McNamar's letters were "growing less ardent in tone, and more formal in phraseology. . . . At last the correspondence ceased altogether." The affair, it seemed, was over.

Lincoln saw his chance, and he took it. "Mr. Lincoln was not to my knowledge paying particular attention to any of the young ladies of my acquaintance when I left for my home in New York," McNamar recalled years later. "There was no rivalry between us on that score; on the contrary, I had every reason to believe him my warm, personal friend." But all's fair in love and war, and this was love. Offering himself as a live alternative to the distant McNamar, Lincoln proposed marriage.

Ann was open to her new suitor but could not quite be off with the old—at least not yet. Would Lincoln wait, she asked, until she had an explicit exchange with McNamar that unequivocally ended the previous engagement? Lincoln said yes—he could hardly have said otherwise—and found himself at the mercy of fate and of another man's will. "The slow-moving mails carried her tender letter to New York," Herndon wrote. "Days and weeks—which to the ardent Lincoln must have seemed painfully long—passed, but the answer never came." In this anxious and uncertain atmosphere, an anguished Lincoln waited.

And waited. Though the object of his affection was almost his, any day could bring a verdict that would end his hopes forever. And so he waited.

At last, Ann ended the suspense—with a happy result, but one shadowed by the unfinished business with the other man. "In a half-hearted way," Herndon recalled, "she turned to Lincoln, and her looks told him that he had won." She would be his wife. He was not her first choice, and he knew that, but he was, in the end, the choice.

He had carried the day, but only barely, and very nearly not at all. It had been a close-run thing, and he may have felt more in love with Ann than she was with him. Her evident ambivalence would have been unsettling for Lincoln, who had certainly not emerged from childhood with a healthy sense of himself. His ambition was a complicated thing: a search for a sense of legitimacy that, at some level and to some degree, he did not feel within himself. Shadowed by his mother's shameful origins—and by the rumors about his own—he was in a precarious position in the larger world he had found in New Salem. With Ann Rutledge, he was a second choice, a runner-up, an *accommodation*. Perhaps to cope with that uncomfortable reality, Lincoln taught himself to fall even more deeply in love with Ann, perhaps seeking to purge her ambivalence—and his anguish at her ambivalence—in the flames of consuming passion.

Though he could never match the fortune McNamar would have brought to marriage, Lincoln sought to secure his financial position. He asked for a bit of time to get his footing in the law. "As soon as his studies are completed," Ann told one of her brothers, "we are to be married."

Yet it was not to be. In the summer of 1835, Ann was stricken by a fever. An anxious Lincoln kept watch at a remove, but Ann, having made her decision, wanted him by her side. The attending doctor advised against callers; nevertheless, she "kept inquiring for Lincoln so continuously, at times demanding to see him," a Rutledge brother recalled, "that the family at last sent for him." It was the most difficult of hours. "I have heard mother say that Ann would frequently sing for Lincoln's benefit," the brother recalled. "She had a clear, ringing voice. Early in her illness he called, and she sang a hymn for which he always expressed a great preference." The piece was a Methodist hymn written by Joseph Hart:

> *Vain man, thy fond pursuits forbear—*
> *Repent, thine end is nigh;*
> *Death at the farthest can't be far:*
> *Oh! Think before thou die . . .*
>
> *Today, the Gospel calls, today,*
> *Sinners, it speaks to you;*
> *Let everyone forsake his way,*
> *And mercy will ensue.*

It was, her brother said, "the last thing she ever sung." Lincoln went from her house to that of a friend, the sad hymn echoing in his mind. "He was very much distressed," the friend recalled, "and I was not surprised when it was rumored subsequently that his reason was in danger." Ann deteriorated rapidly, dying on Tuesday, August 25, 1835. "Lincoln took it very hard indeed," Lynn McNulty Greene told Herndon. Ann was buried in the Concord cemetery near Petersburg. "I cannot endure the thought that the sleet and storm, frost and snow of heaven should beat on her grave," Lincoln said later.

In the *English Reader* anthology that Lincoln loved, a Roman writer reflected on the sadness of the death of an affianced young woman. "She was contracted to a most worthy youth; the wedding day was fixed, and we were all invited—How sad a change from the highest joy, to the deepest sorrow! How shall I express the wound that pierced my heart, when I heard [the bride's father] . . . ordering the money he had designed to lay out upon clothes and jewels for her marriage, to be employed in myrrh and spices for her funeral!"

Ann's death hurled Lincoln into crisis. His friends "had to lock him up and keep guard over him for some two weeks . . . for fear he might Commit Suicide," John Hill recalled. "The whole village engaged in trying to quiet him and reconcile him to the loss." Lincoln took refuge for a time with Bowling Green, a mentor and friend. "The effect upon Mr. Lincoln's mind was terrible," one of Rutledge's brothers recalled. "He became plunged in despair, and many of his friends feared that reason would desert her throne." In Herndon's opinion, "He had fits of great mental depression, and wandered up and down the river and into the woods woefully abstracted—at times in the deepest distress." Lincoln, William Greene recalled, "from the sudden shock [was] somewhat temporarily deranged. We watched during storms—fogs—damp gloomy weather Mr. Lincoln for fear of an accident."

Lincoln's depression was profound, and his gloom fed thoughts of suicide. "I [ran] off the track: it was my first," Lincoln recalled of his grief. "I loved the woman dearly & sacredly. . . . I did honestly—& truly love the girl & think often—often of her now." He lost weight—and lost himself in reading law. He "was studious—so much so that he somewhat injured his health and Constitution," an Illinois friend recalled. "The Continued thought & study of the man Caused—with the death of one whom he dearly & sincerely loved—a . . . partial & momentary derangement."

As the years went by he wrote of her not at all and spoke of her only sparingly. The pain was too real, too raw. "Long after Ann died," Greene said, "Abe and I would be alone perhaps in the grocery on a rainy night, and Abe would sit there, his elbows on his knees, his face in his hands, the tears dropping through his fingers."

The only way forward: Will himself to work. There was the law, there was surveying, and there was politics. He availed himself of all three avenues to climb out of the despair that had descended in the late summer of 1835. A special session of the legislature met on Monday, December 7, 1835, to address banking, internal improvements, and public lands. Lincoln also played a role in resolutions about the approaching presidential election. Democrats registered their support for Vice President Martin Van Buren to succeed Jackson; Lincoln went on record for Hugh L. White, a Whig from Jackson's Tennessee. For his own part, Lincoln addressed himself anew to his constituents as he prepared to seek reelection. Reading the *Sangamo Journal* of Saturday, June 11, 1836, he saw a plea signed by "Many Voters" asking candidates to "show their hands." Replying on the following Monday, June 13, Lincoln wrote, "Agreed. Here's mine!"

"I go for all sharing the privileges of the government, who assist in bearing its burthens," Lincoln wrote. "Consequently I go for admitting all whites to the right of suffrage, who pay taxes or bear arms, (by no means excluding females)." He wrote of how he saw his duty as a legislator elected by that suffrage. "If elected, I shall consider the whole people of Sangamon my constituents," Lincoln wrote. "While acting as their representative, I shall be governed by their will, on all subjects upon which I have the means of knowing what their will is; and upon all others, I shall do what my own judgment teaches me will best advance their interests."

His were commonplace insights on representation. In this campaign address, the young Lincoln—he was still not yet thirty—avoided grappling with what he might do should there be a conflict between his judgment and that of his constituents. Taken at his word, Lincoln asserted the right to form his own opinions only in cases where he did not know the will of the public. But what if he knew their will and disagreed with it? What if his conscience dictated a course at variance with popular opinion? The eighteenth-century statesman and philosopher Edmund Burke had thought much on this question. "Your representative," Burke remarked, "owes you not his industry only, but his judgment; and he betrays, instead of serving you, if he sacrifices it to your opinion."

Lincoln would come to see democracy as a work in progress, a process in which reason took its chances against prejudice and passion. Of significant issues—including emancipation—Lincoln remarked to Herndon, "All such questions must first find lodgment with the most enlightened souls who stamp them with their approval. In God's own time they will be organized into law and thus woven into the fabric of our institutions."

To be a soldier in the cause of such enlightenment required the ability to withstand the slings and arrows of political life. Adept on the stump, he did not mind the arena. In the 1836 contest for the legislature, a Democrat, Colonel Robert Allen, was hinting that he had damaging information about Lincoln and his friend N. W. Edwards. Lincoln was quick to confront Allen, writing, "I am told that . . . you passed through this place, and stated publicly, that you were in possession of a fact or facts, which, if known to the public, would entirely destroy the prospects of N. W. Edwards and myself at the ensuing election; but, that through favor to us, you should forbear to divulge them." Lincoln then went in for the kill:

> No one has needed favors more than I, and generally, few have been less unwilling to accept them; but in this case, favor to me, would be injustice to the public, and therefore I must beg your pardon for declining it. That I once had the confidence of the people of Sangamon, is sufficiently evident, and if I have since done anything, either by design or misadventure, which if known, would subject me to a forfeiture of that confidence, he that knows of that thing, and conceals it, is a traitor to his country's interest. . . .
>
> I am flattered with the personal regard you manifested for me, but I do hope that, on more mature reflection, you will view the public interest as a paramount consideration, and, therefore, determine to let the worst come.

Colonel Allen had nothing to say in return. The matter died there—with Lincoln victorious in the skirmish. Invigorated by silencing Allen, Lincoln also turned in a memorable performance at the Springfield courthouse in July 1836, wittily attacking the Democratic interest in debate. "At one fell stroke, [Lincoln] broke the ice upon which we have seen [his opponent] standing, and left him to contend with the chilling waters and merciless waves," the *Sangamo Journal* reported. "His speech became more fluent, and his manner more easy as he progressed. . . . A girl might be born and become a mother before the Van Buren men will forget Mr. Lincoln. From beginning to end Mr. Lincoln was frequently interrupted by loud bursts of applause from a generous people."

For Lincoln, the political lesson was clear: When struck, strike back—certainly, surely, and eloquently.

CHAPTER FOUR

Founded on Injustice and Bad Policy

America is more our country, than it is the whites—we have
enriched it with our *blood and tears*.

—DAVID WALKER, *Appeal to the Coloured Citizens of the World,* 1829

A people, owning slaves, are mad, or worse than mad, who do
not hold their destinies in their own hands.

—ROBERT BARNWELL RHETT, attorney general of South Carolina, 1833

I N THE CLOSING DAYS OF 1836, the Kentucky-born governor of
Illinois, Joseph Duncan, was reading his mail. Included in his correspondence were petitions and letters from white leaders and legislatures around the nation alarmed by the movement to abolish slavery.
Illinois was putatively a free state, but anti-Black prejudice predomi-
nated, and de facto slavery remained a reality after the territory's admission to the Union in 1818. An early Illinois law captured the spirit
of the times. Anyone who "should permit slaves or servants to assemble
for dancing or revelling, by night or day, were to be fined twenty dollars," a historian of the state wrote. "It was made the duty of all sheriffs,
coroners, judges, and justices of the peace . . . to commit the slaves to
jail, and to order each one of them to be whipped, not exceeding thirty-
nine stripes, on the bare back."

A territorial governor, Ninian Edwards, father of Lincoln's contemporary and friend, was, like other Illinois governors, U.S. senators, and
congressmen, a slave owner. In an advertisement published while he
was in office, Edwards announced the sale of "twenty-two slaves, among
them . . . several of both sexes between the years of ten and seventeen. . . . I have also for sale a full-blooded horse, a very large English
bull and several young ones."

Presiding over the state in these waning years of the Jackson administration, Governor Duncan understood that slavery and anti-Black prejudice were American realities—and so were the moral and political pressures to abolish the nation's system of human bondage. In 1823, the Reverend Jeremiah Gloucester, pastor of the Second African Presbyterian Church in Philadelphia, had preached: "Nay, the blissful period is just at hand, when we shall be elevated to an equal stand!"

In 1820, the struggle over slavery in the Missouri Territory had put the slaveholding South on notice: Antislavery sentiment could not be ignored or dismissed. Slaveholding Missouri was admitted to the Union but only once it was agreed that Maine would come in as a free state, preserving balance. Most ominous for the slaveholding interest was the congressional prohibition on slavery (with the exception of Missouri) north of the 36° 30′ latitude in the Louisiana Territory—a major victory for antislavery forces. The spirit and the substance of the antislavery Northwest Ordinance were at work as the national government limited the growth of slavery, effectively rendering a judgment that a dominant feature of life in the South was to be circumscribed.

The Massachusetts General Colored Association was formed in 1826 to advocate for emancipation and racial equality. The next year brought the founding, by the Reverend Samuel Cornish and John Russwurm, of *Freedom's Journal,* the nation's first Black newspaper. One of the paper's agents, David Walker, published his *Appeal to the Coloured Citizens of the World* in 1829. Black people in the United States were "the most degraded, wretched, and abject set of beings that ever lived since the world began," Walker wrote, "and I pray God that none like us ever may live again until time shall be no more." The fight for freedom must begin here, and it must begin now. On New Year's Day 1831, William Lloyd Garrison published the first edition of *The Liberator*, writing, "I am in earnest—I will not equivocate—I will not excuse—I will not retreat a single inch—AND I WILL BE HEARD." Two years later came the founding of the abolitionist American Anti-Slavery Society in Philadelphia, an organization designed to "convince all our fellow-citizens, by arguments addressed to their understandings and consciences, that slaveholding is a heinous crime in the sight of God."

Roughly put, many abolitionists called for the immediate emancipation of the enslaved; some of those abolitionists argued for a subsequent recognition of social and political equality. These claims were a radical form of a more general antislavery sentiment that had been a

David Walker's landmark Appeal to the Coloured Citizens of the World *was published in 1829.*

factor at the Constitutional Convention. Numerous compromises had been made with the slave interest in Philadelphia in 1787, but James Madison and others had also arranged to abolish the Atlantic slave trade in 1808 and prevented the document from explicitly affirming slavery's legitimacy or from recognizing "property in man" in national law. Frederick Douglass endorsed this understanding of the document— one Lincoln shared—writing that "the Constitution of the United States, standing alone and construed only in the light of its letter without reference to the opinions of the men who framed and adopted it, or to the uniform universal and undeviating practice of the nation under it, from the time of its adoption until now is not a pro-slavery instrument."

Among the stumbling blocks to abolition was the fact that most antislavery advocates (including Lincoln) believed the federal government had no constitutional power to abolish slavery in states where it existed. From the framing of the Constitution until the Civil War, this "federal consensus," as it has been called, held that the national government was prohibited from forcing outright emancipation in slavery's present spheres. Even the antislavery Republican Party's platforms in 1856 and in 1860 accepted that the existing slave states were sovereign on the matter. In the first Federal Congress, a committee of congress-men declared that "Congress have no authority to interfere in the emancipation of slaves, or in the treatment of them within any of the States; it remaining with the several States alone to provide any regula-tions therein, which humanity and true policy may require." The *states* could emancipate, but not the federal government.

The "Federal Government was one of delegated, not of inherent, powers," Senator Lyman Trumbull, Republican of Illinois, said in the Secession Winter of 1860–61. Control of slavery was not delegated to the national authority in the Constitution; therefore, Trumbull added, "there is no man of any party who contends that Congress has author-ity to interfere with slavery in the States." Thus the focus for Lincoln and the Republicans until well into the Civil War was less about de-ploying federal power to free the currently enslaved—which was viewed as a constitutional impossibility—and more about creating the condi-tions for ultimate abolition. And they believed the work to bring about those conditions should begin immediately, with the prohibition of slavery in the territories.

Lincoln subscribed to what some called the "scorpion's sting" strat-egy. The idea was that a "cordon of freedom" would surround the South until, in the 1847 words of the Massachusetts Anti-Slavery Society, the antislavery "circle of fire . . . around the scorpion will grow hotter and hotter, and close nearer and nearer, until it will be compelled to bury its sting in its own brain, and rid the world, by a blessed suicide, of its mon-strous existence." The Lincoln antislavery strategy envisioned not a forcible federal intervention but rather a day when the states themselves would agree to emancipation—which would, like the British experi-ence, probably be gradual and compensated. Preventing the extension of slavery into the territories—the Constitution gave the Congress au-thority over such questions—was a crucial step and was at once the means of Lincoln's rise and the immediate occasion of secession, for the slave-owning South saw his presidential victory as the triumph of anti-slavery forces. In the end, only in the crucible of the Civil War would resolution come. And when it came, it was in the form of the abolition-ist Thirteenth Amendment, which did not win congressional approval until 1865—at last making the Constitution explicitly antislavery.

The energized movement for immediate abolition in the 1830s came amid a revolution in communications. In 1830, it is estimated, there were 906 newspapers in the United States, 100 of which were published daily. In 1840, the number of publications had risen by 74 percent, to 1,577, and dailies had doubled, to 209. More efficient printing presses and readier distribution made national conversations possible. The introduction of the telegraph in 1844 would further collapse the great distances that had so long defined the country and the world.

The opinions of an editor in Massachusetts, or a minister in New York, could now more easily reach the planter in South Carolina, the enslaved person in Georgia, the governor in Illinois, or the anxious free Black person in Ohio. It was unifying in the sense of creating a common political and cultural sphere. It was divisive in that Massachusetts or New York could challenge and indict the accepted realities of life in South Carolina or Georgia or Illinois or Ohio. More than ever before, what was said and thought and done in one part of the nation might affect what was said and thought and done in other parts.

In many quarters, abolitionists were viewed as disruptive radicals— and their actions were swiftly met by the forces of reaction. In Illinois, Governor Duncan said he opposed "any attempt . . . to agitate the question of abolishing slavery in this country, for it can never be broached without producing violence and discord, whether it be in a free or slave State." Several states—including Mississippi, Connecticut, and New York—had ratified resolutions to prevent abolitionists from "writing, speaking, printing or publishing sentiments and opinions . . . calculated in temper and spirit . . . to endanger our right of property or domestic repose."

In Vandalia, the governor referred the issue to the legislature, where Lincoln was serving his second term. The lawmakers passed resolutions to reassure their slaveholding brethren in other states by condemning abolitionists, expressing support for colonization, and defending slavery in the District of Columbia. The vote in the House was 77–6. Abraham Lincoln was one of the few dissenters.

Slave owners and white racists were afraid that the world they had always known was slipping away from them. Fear was a great motivator— fear of change, fear of losing power, fear of being told that they were wrong. The roots of white anxiety over threats to enslavement and to legalized white supremacy ran deep.

Before the mid-1830s, many white Southerners and their allies in the North had quietly recognized the system's evils even while they perpetuated that system. In 1818, the Committee of the General Assembly of the Presbyterian Church, which included commissioners from the South, wrote: "We consider the voluntary enslaving of one part of the human race by another, as a gross violation of the most precious and sacred rights of human nature; as utterly inconsistent with the law of God, which requires us to love our neighbour as ourselves, and as totally irreconcilable with the spirit and principles of the gospel of Christ."

In moments of clarity, white Americans saw the conflict between the rhetoric of liberty and the durability of slavery. "To sum up all, it is evident, that the bondage we have imposed on the Africans, is absolutely repugnant to justice," Arthur Lee of Virginia wrote in 1764. To many white Southerners before, during, and after the American Revolution, slavery was acknowledged to be an evil, but a necessary one. Abolition was impractical. There was nothing to be done.

In Vandalia, the resolutions that had come to the floor of the Illinois legislature in 1837 were partly the result of a hardening white Southern view, born in the furnace of anxiety, that slavery should be defended and spread without embarrassment. "[L]et me not be understood as admitting, even by implication, that the existing relations between the races in the slaveholding States is an evil:—far otherwise; I hold it to be a good—a positive good," John C. Calhoun told the United States Senate that same year. *"Slavery is not a national evil,"* Governor Stephen D. Miller of South Carolina said in 1829; *"on the contrary, it is a national benefit."* The case of Basil Manly, Sr., an influential white Southern Baptist minister, was revealing. In 1821 he saw slavery as "an evil under which this country has long groaned" and said it "seems to be utterly repugnant to the spirit of republican institutions." By 1837, Manly, who also served as the president of the University of Alabama, was preaching a different gospel, arguing that slavery was divinely sanctioned and should be defended out of a duty to God.

Why the change? After the Missouri Compromise put the federal government on record against the unchecked spread of slavery across the continent, the slave-owning interest grew ever more defensive and ever more strident. Defending a necessary evil was intrinsically difficult, for a necessary evil was still an evil. Defending a "good," in Calhoun's formulation, and a "benefit," in Miller's, was infinitely easier, particularly if the argument invoked, as Manley's did, biblical authority.

The Missouri Compromise: 1820

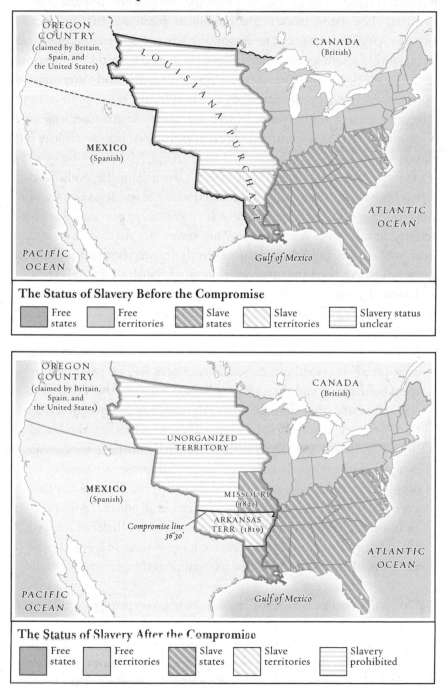

The Status of Slavery Before the Compromise

- Free states
- Free territories
- Slave states
- Slave territories
- Slavery status unclear

The Status of Slavery After the Compromise

- Free states
- Free territories
- Slave states
- Slave territories
- Slavery prohibited

The fear was fueled by threats from within and without. The debates over Missouri and the rise of abolitionism were thought to have inspired slave conspiracies and rebellions from South Carolina in 1822 to Virginia in 1831. The lesson for white Southerners: Even *debating* slavery could lead to chaos, bloodshed, and revolt. From 1829 to 1837, Kentucky, Louisiana, Mississippi, Missouri, and Virginia reported actual or allegedly planned slave rebellions. From 1830 to 1835, Alabama, Georgia, Louisiana, North Carolina, South Carolina, and Virginia passed laws criminalizing the teaching of literacy to the enslaved.

Andrew Jackson's victory over South Carolina in the Nullification Crisis of the early 1830s also exacerbated white fears. To many, submission to the federal tariff was a prelude to emancipation and was to be resisted at all costs. "A people, owning slaves, are mad, or worse than mad, who do not hold their destinies in their own hands," said Robert Barnwell Rhett, then the attorney general of South Carolina.

Iveson Brookes, a slaveholding Southern clergyman, recounted what he described as a "plausible dream" in February 1836:

> The substance of it was that in some twenty or thirty years a division of the Northern & Southern States will be produced by the Abolitionists and then a war will issue between the Yankees & slave-holders—that the Army of Yankees will be at once joined by the N[egroe]s who will shew more savage cruelty than the blood thirsty Indians—and that Southerners with gratitude for having escaped alive will gladly leave their splendid houses & farms to be occupied by those who once served them.—This all looks so plausible that I have been made to conclude that all who act with judicious foresight should within two years sell every [half] of a negro & land & vest the money in Western lands—so as to have a home and valuable possessions to flee to in time of danger.

To justify themselves, slave owners sought sanction from the realm of religion. Lincoln understood what was afoot. In the late 1850s, he would read an unambiguously titled book by the Reverend Frederick A. Ross, a Presbyterian minister: *Slavery Ordained of God*. As Lincoln described Ross's argument, if the proslavery Christian "decides that God wills Sambo to continue a slave, he thereby retains his own comfortable position; but if he decides that God wills Sambo to be free, he thereby has to walk out of the shade, throw off his gloves, and delve for his own bread."

The Ross argument was abroad in the land in the middle of the nineteenth century, a time when the nation was widely and deeply churched. In its sundry manifestations, organized Christianity had an unmatched reach in the America of the time. From about 1800 into the 1830s, the Second Great Awakening made religious faith a vital element as the debates over slavery and freedom grew. Abolitionists and antislavery advocates invoked the spirit of a loving God and the common humanity of all creatures; slave owners and their allies advanced biblical arguments designed to prove that slavery was divinely ordained.

What was known as the curse of Ham was foundational to proslavery theology. In the story, from the ninth chapter of the Book of Genesis, a drunken Noah is lying naked in his tent after the Flood. Ham, whom the scripture calls "the father of Canaan," finds him and brings his two brothers, Japheth and Shem, to see Noah.

> And Shem and Japheth took a garment, and laid it upon both their shoulders, and went backward, and covered the nakedness of their father; and their faces were backward, and they saw not their father's nakedness.
>
> And Noah awoke from his wine, and knew what his younger son had done unto him.
>
> And he said, Cursed be Canaan; a servant of servants shall he be unto his brethren.
>
> And he said, Blessed be the Lord God of Shem; and Canaan shall be his servant.
>
> God shall enlarge Japheth, and he shall dwell in the tents of Shem; and Canaan shall be his servant.

Canaan was Africa; the sons of Ham were therefore to be enslaved by Noah's decree. "The prophecy of Noah . . . was to be fulfilled, not in the individuals named, but nationally in their descendants," the Reverend Frederick Dalcho, a Charleston, South Carolina, Episcopal clergyman, wrote in his 1823 *Practical Considerations Founded on the Scriptures, Relative to the Slave Population of South Carolina by a South-Carolinian.* "Canaan's whole race were under the malediction" of consignment to "the lowest state of servitude, *slaves*." Abraham held slaves, which was itself taken as sanction for the practice, and the Book of Leviticus was oft quoted:

> Both thy bondmen, and thy bondmaids, which thou shalt have, shall be of the heathen that are round about you; of them shall ye buy bondmen and bondmaids.
>
> Moreover of the children of the strangers that do sojourn among you, of them shall ye buy, and of their families that are with you, which they begat in your land: and they shall be your possession.
>
> And ye shall take them as an inheritance for your children after you, to inherit them for a possession; they shall be your bondmen for ever.

The New Testament, particularly quotations from the epistles urging slaves and servants to obey their masters, was also deployed. Paul's letter returning the converted slave Onesimus to Philemon was crucial, as was Jesus's silence on the subject.

Such proslavery thinking helped lead to schisms among Methodists, Presbyterians, and Baptists—splits that contemporary observers believed foreshadowed a severing of the Union itself. In 1844, the Methodists broke into sectional churches after a dispute over Bishop James Andrew of Georgia's ownership of slaves. The next year, American Baptists divided over slavery, with slave owners and their sympathizers meeting in Augusta, Georgia, to form the proslavery Southern Baptist Convention. Presbyterians, too, were roiled by the tensions between slavery and freedom. A Methodist Virginian worried that the "division of our church" might be followed by "a civil division of this great confederacy" that would lead to "civil war and far-reaching desolation." The churches were failing to reconcile slavery and scripture, custom and justice. Would the Union be far behind?

In Vandalia, Governor Duncan's proslavery resolutions had passed in January 1837. On Friday, March 3, Lincoln and the Vermont-born and -educated Daniel Stone, a Springfield Whig who was leaving the legislature, weighed in with an official protest. It was no call for abolition, but it was nonetheless remarkable. In clear, sparse language, Lincoln and Stone wrote:

They believe that the institution of slavery is founded on both injustice and bad policy; but that the promulgation of abolition doctrines tends rather to increase than to abate its evils.

They believe that the Congress of the United States has no power, under the constitution, to interfere with the institution of slavery in the different States.

They believe that the Congress of the United States has the power, under the constitution, to abolish slavery in the District of Columbia; but that that power ought not to be exercised unless at the request of the people of said District.

There was no evident political gain to be had for Lincoln; quite the opposite. So why did he—still in his twenties—state so clearly that slavery was unjust?

"I am naturally anti-slavery," he would write in 1864. "If slavery is not wrong, nothing is wrong. I can not remember when I did not so think, and feel." As a child in Kentucky he may have seen that human traffic—the enslaved in chains—on the Cumberland Road. As a youth he had lived in antislavery Baptist circles. And he had disturbing recollections of working along the Ohio and the Mississippi rivers and in New Orleans.

"Slavery ran the iron into him then and there," John Hanks recalled. Hanks's recollections are likely embellished—he was not with Lincoln in New Orleans—but are perhaps rooted in remarks Lincoln may have made afterward. As Herndon wrote after conversations with both Hanks and Lincoln, "One morning in . . . the city [Lincoln] passed a slave auction. A vigorous and comely mulatto girl was being sold. She underwent a thorough examination at the hands of the bidders; they pinched her flesh and made her trot up and down the room like a horse, to show how she moved, and in order, as the auctioneer said, that 'bidders might satisfy themselves' whether the article they were offering to buy was sound or not. The whole thing was so revolting that Lincoln moved away from the scene with a deep feeling of 'unconquerable hate.' Bidding his companions follow him he said, 'By God, boys, let's get away from this.'" Experience formed one element of Lincoln's reaction, if not the main one. "The slavery question often bothered me as far back as 1836–1840," Lincoln recalled in 1858. "I was troubled and grieved over it."

The surest source of his landmark 1837 statement was probably a distant and, to him, inspirational figure: Henry Clay, who, as early as 1798, had said, "All America acknowledges the existence of slavery to be an evil" and called for its ultimate extinction: "The sooner we attempt its destruction the better." We know from his family and early friends that Lincoln "always Loved" Clay's speeches—a volume of them had appeared nearly a decade earlier, in 1827—and Lincoln later said that he considered the Kentuckian "the beau ideal of a statesman." A Lincoln friend recalled, "Henry Clay was his favorite of all the great men of the Nation. He all but worshipped his name." "He ever was, on principle and in feeling, opposed to slavery," Lincoln said of Clay in an 1852 eulogy. "He did not perceive, that on a question of human right, the negroes were to be excepted from the human race."

From his childhood Lincoln had known slavery was wrong. He believed, too, that what Clay had called "universal emancipation" and the creation of a racially egalitarian America were, at the time, impossibly remote. One answer to the conundrum in the climate of the time: the voluntary removal of Black Americans from the United States—the project of the American Colonization Society, founded in 1816. Under the titular leadership of James Madison and James Monroe, the organization promoted the voluntary removal of free Black Americans and the establishment of colonies that would accept them. Colonization was also linked to emancipation, the idea being that the enslaved could be liberated and then emigrate as well. Then and later, some Black leaders favored different colonization efforts as a means to create a secure nation for Black Americans away from enslavement and subjugation. Captain Paul Cuffe, who led a trip to Sierra Leone, was one such figure, but the chief support for the decades-long campaign came from white Americans.

There were white Southerners who believed colonization was the tip of an abolitionist spear; many other Americans, Black and white, saw such colonization proposals not as an antislavery project but as a proslavery device. For one thing, it was thought that the removal of free Black people would in fact aid the slave-owning cause by silencing Black abolitionist voices, or at least dispatching such voices to far distances. For another, the expense and complexity of exiling millions of Black people was staggering, and it was argued that the colonizers' linkage of emancipation with emigration was a ruse to make even gradual abolition seem impossible. If one couldn't send the Black race elsewhere—to Africa, to Haiti, to Canada, all of which were bruited as possibilities—then one couldn't emancipate the enslaved, the argument went, and therefore the status quo would necessarily prevail.

To chart Lincoln's lifelong moral and political course on slavery and equality is not to sing his praises as if he were the hero of an epic poem. In publicly declaring slavery unjust in the Illinois and in the America of the late 1830s, however, Lincoln was taking a notable moral stand for a white politician in the context of the time. "Lincoln was talking and men were standing up around him listening to the conversation," a friend recalled. "One of them asked him if he was an abolitionist. Mr. Lincoln in reply, reached over and laid his hand on the shoulder of Mr. [Thomas] Alsopp who was a strong abolitionist and said, 'I am mighty near one.'" Not near enough, but nearer than many. That would have to suffice for the time being.

Newly admitted to the bar, Lincoln moved from New Salem to Springfield, the county seat soon to be the state capital, shortly after filing his slavery protest in March 1837. He had fought to locate the capital in central Illinois; his constituents stood to benefit from the move. As the *Sangamo Journal* wrote in March 1837, "The owner of real estate sees his property rapidly enhancing in value; the merchant anticipates a large accession to our population and a corresponding additional sale for his goods; the mechanic already has more contracts offered him for building and improvement than he can execute; the farmer anticipates, in the growth of a large and important town, a market for the varied products of his farm; indeed every class of our citizens look to the future with confidence that we trust will not be disappointed."

Still, life in Springfield was "rather a dull business" for Lincoln. He liked an old joke about a minister who visited to preach on "The Second Coming of the Lord." As Lincoln remarked, "It is my private opinion that, if the Lord has been in Springfield once, he will never come the second time."

The Lincoln who came to the new state capital had been broken by the loss of Ann Rutledge and seasoned by his years at Vandalia. Joshua Speed, who was to become his closest friend, met him shortly after Lincoln arrived in town. "The tone of his voice was so melancholy that I felt for him," Speed, then a merchant, recalled. "I looked up at him and I thought then, as I think now, that I never saw so gloomy and melancholy a face in my life." Lincoln took some getting to know, but those who did so found him engaging. "He was the most uncouth looking young man I ever saw," H. E. Drummer, a law partner of John T. Stuart's in Springfield, recalled of Lincoln. "He seemed to have but little to say; seemed to feel timid, with a tinge of sadness visible in the countenance, but when he did talk all this disappeared . . . and he demonstrated that he was both strong and acute. He surprised us more and more at every visit."

Speed was surprised, too, by his own innate fondness for Lincoln. "He had ridden into town on a borrowed horse," Speed recalled, "and engaged from the only cabinet-maker in the village a single bedstead. He came into my store, set his saddlebags on the counter, and inquired what the furniture for a single bedstead would cost." Told the figure, Lincoln blanched: It seemed out of reach. "It is probably cheap enough; but I want to say that, cheap as it is, I have not the money to pay," Lincoln said. "But if you will credit me until Christmas, and my experiment here as a lawyer is a success, I will pay you then. If I fail in that I will probably never pay you at all." Speed wasn't quite sure why, but he was moved. He offered Lincoln accommodations in his own room— one "with a very large double bed in it," Speed said, "which you are perfectly welcome to share with me if you choose."

"Where is your room?" Lincoln asked.

"Upstairs," Speed replied.

Lincoln accepted, dropped off his bags, and returned downstairs.

"Well, Speed," he said, "I'm moved."

It was the kind of fortuitous thing that seemed to happen to Lincoln often. "No man ever had an easier time of it in his early days than Lincoln," William Herndon recalled. "He had . . . influential and financial friends to help him; they almost fought each other for the privilege of assisting Lincoln. . . . Lincoln was a pet . . . in this city."

Lincoln was always watching the world beyond New Salem and Vandalia and Springfield. A devotee of newspapers, he followed events near and far, and he was disturbed as 1837 gave way to 1838. It was a chaotic season, with reports of violence, mobs, and lynchings, some close to hand. "Accounts of outrages committed by mobs, form the every-day news of the times," Lincoln observed. "They have pervaded the country, from New England to Louisiana." Difficult economic times, for instance, had contributed to unrest in New York, where a meeting called to protest "the price of flour, meat, rent, and fuel" descended into the sacking of several stores. Newspapers deplored "these lawless, high-handed measures" as well as an incident in which a group of Black New Yorkers sought to liberate a captured alleged fugitive slave in Manhattan. "This outrage alone should be a lesson to the fanatics of abolitionism," the New Orleans *Daily Picayune* wrote in April 1837. "Who is happiest, the free negro of New York, sometimes half starved, or the slave of Louisiana, whose master clothes and feeds him?"

Racial violence, then, was very much on Lincoln's mind. In Alton, Illinois, about ninety miles southwest of New Salem on the Missouri border, an abolitionist editor, Elijah Lovejoy, was murdered on Tuesday, November 7, 1837, after he helped found an Illinois chapter of Garrison's American Anti-Slavery Society. Lovejoy had already been hounded out of St. Louis for his views on slavery. THE FIRST MARTYR HAS FALLEN IN THE HOLY CAUSE OF ABOLITION! wrote the *Vermont Telegraph*. Calling Lovejoy an "infatuated editor" who had "at length fallen a victim to his obstinacy in the cause of the abolitionists," the antiabolitionist *Missouri Argus* celebrated the murder. "Disregarding the known and expressed sentiments of a large portion of the citizens of Alton, in relation to his incendiary publication, and, as it would seem, bent upon his own destruction," Lovejoy for "his temerity has received awful retribution from the hands of an infuriated and lawless mob." A piece in *The Liberator* mourned the attack on Lovejoy: "He has fallen a victim to the wicked spirit of slavery—a martyr to the cause of human rights, of freedom of speech and of the Press."

There was more. In St. Louis, a Black man, Francis L. McIntosh of Pittsburgh, Pennsylvania, a cook aboard the steamboat *Flora,* had been lynched after reportedly stabbing a deputy sheriff to death and wounding a deputy constable. McIntosh, Lincoln recalled, "was seized in the street, dragged to the suburbs of the city, chained to a tree, and actually burned to death." And in Mississippi, "negroes, suspected of conspiring to raise an insurrection, were caught up and hanged in all parts of the State," Lincoln said. "Then, white men, supposed to be leagued with the negroes; and finally, strangers, from neighboring States, going thither on business, were, in many instances, subjected to the same fate.... [T]ill, dead men were seen literally dangling from the boughs of trees upon every road side; and in numbers almost sufficient, to rival the native Spanish moss of the country, as a drapery of the forest."

In a prescient address to the Young Men's Lyceum in Springfield in 1838, Lincoln meditated on this violence as he explored the fragility of the republic and the centrality of union. A "mobocratic spirit" posed a threat to "the *attachment* of the People" to their government. The principles of the Declaration and the balance of the Constitution were essential, Lincoln said, even holy:

> We find ourselves under the government of a system of political institutions, conducing more essentially to the ends of civil and religious liberty, than any of which the history of former times tells us. . . . As the patriots of seventy-six did to the support of the Declaration of Independence, so to the support of the Constitution and Laws, let every American pledge his life, his property, and his sacred honor—let every man remember that to violate the law, is to trample on the blood of his father, and to tear the [charter] of his own, and his children's liberty. Let reverence for the laws, be breathed by every American mother, to the lisping babe, that prattles on her lap—let it be taught in schools, in seminaries, and in colleges;—let it be written in Primmers, spelling books, and in Almanacs—let it be preached from the pulpit, proclaimed in legislative halls, and enforced in courts of justice. And, in short, let it become the *political religion* of the nation; and let the old and the young, the rich and the poor, the grave and the gay, of all sexes and tongues, and colors and conditions, sacrifice unceasingly upon its altars.

The danger to America came from within America—from "wild and furious passions" that might overwhelm the Union and its constitutional order. "At what point shall we expect the approach of danger?" Lincoln asked. "Shall we expect some transatlantic military giant, to step the Ocean, and crush us at a blow? Never! . . . I answer, if it ever reach us, it must spring up amongst us. . . . If destruction be our lot, we must ourselves be its author and finisher. As a nation of freemen, we must live through all time, or die by suicide."

The allusion to suicide was striking for a man who struggled with depression. Lincoln saw the republic as a living being, its fate uncertain.

Passion could fray the bonds of union, divide one from another, and fatally wound the American experiment in democracy that Lincoln defined as *"the capability of a people to govern themselves."* He worried about trouble coming from the many as well as the few—or even the one, in the form of a demagogue who might try to profit from lawlessness and distrust.

"Towering genius disdains a beaten path," Lincoln said of aspiring autocrats. "It seeks regions hitherto unexplored. . . . It *denies* that it is glory enough to serve under any chief. It *scorns* to tread in the footsteps of *any* predecessor. . . . It thirsts and burns for distinction. . . . Is it unreasonable then to expect, that some man possessed of the loftiest genius, coupled with ambition sufficient to push it to its utmost stretch, will at some time, spring up among us?"

Lincoln feared that the power of the story of the American Revolution and of the early Republic was ebbing. The people of the Founding era *"were* the pillars of the temple of liberty; and now, that they have crumbled away, that temple must fall, unless we, their descendants, supply their places with other pillars, hewn from the solid quarry of sober reason. . . . Upon these let the proud fabric of freedom rest, as the rock of its basis; and as truly as has been said of the only greater institution, *'the gates of hell shall not prevail against it.'"*

The concerns the young man elucidated in the Lyceum address were ones that would shape his public life: Union, violence, passion, power, faith, slavery, order. Lincoln, John T. Stuart said, "loved principles and such like large political & national ones, Especially when it leads to his own Ends—paths—Ambitions—Success—honor &c. &c." Stuart was right on both counts: Lincoln was engaged by the lofty and invigorated by the fight.

I n his Springfield address, Lincoln had called for an American ethos of liberty and of reason. In Washington, the slaveholding interest was in full flight from both. Beginning in 1836, a proslavery majority in the House worked to shut down petitions to Congress touching on slavery. Congressman Henry L. Pinckney of South Carolina drafted a "gag" resolution to prevent discussion of any resolution regarding slavery. By the early 1840s, Rule 21 of the House of Representatives read: "No petition, memorial, resolution, or other paper praying the abolition of slavery . . . shall be received by this House, or entertained in any way whatever." In short, white Southern insecurities regarding their long-term position led them to prevent even the *reception* of antislavery petitions in the House. To stifle free speech out of fear of what that speech might lead to ran counter to everything Lincoln had spoken of to the Lyceum.

To make matters worse, President Jackson had proposed legislation prohibiting the federal postal service from circulating publications that might "instigate the slaves to insurrection." (It failed to pass.) For the Anti-Slavery Society, this effort, too, was a troubling sign of the strength of the Slave Power. "When *mail-robbing* is honored and sanctioned, in support of slavery," the society said, "it is time to inquire whether we are not mistaken in our hope that slavery will be removed by the spontaneous action of slaveholders; whether free states can any longer be safe by the side of such an 'evil.'"

An interest willing to suppress speech was an interest willing to put its own power ahead of democracy. The proslavery bids to curb abolition, both in Congress and in the mails, were a form of tyranny, a nascent dictatorship of opinion—the kind of tyranny and dictatorship against which Lincoln had warned. As the 1830s ended, the proslavery forces were engaged, energized, and hypersensitive. Their world was under assault, and they hated it.

Allegiance to William Henry Harrison, the war hero known as "Old Tippecanoe," would offer Lincoln his first sustained exposure to national politics in 1840. "Lincoln as early as 1830 began to dream of a destiny—I think it grew & developed & bloomed with beauty &c in the year 1840 *Exactly*," Herndon recalled. "Mr. Lincoln told me that his ideas of [becoming] something—burst on him in 1840."

Presidential politics as popular drama burst in on the American people themselves in 1840. Foreshadowed by Andrew Jackson's campaigns in 1828 and 1832, when "Old Hickory" dominated a national political narrative—with torchlight parades and large campaign events—the 1840 race pitted William Henry Harrison against the incumbent President Van Buren. A veteran of the Indian wars of the Northwest Territory, Harrison, a Virginian by birth, held more mass appeal than his rivals Clay or Winfield Scott. Lincoln accepted the political argument in favor of the war hero; he believed that "the people—the bone and sinew of the country—the main pillar of the republic—I mean the farming and laboring classes" were likelier to rally to Harrison than to the alternatives.

It was a wild campaign. "The whole country is in a state of agitation upon the approaching Presidential election such as was never before witnessed," John Quincy Adams wrote in his diary in September 1840. "Here is a revolution in the habits and manners of the people. Where will it end? These are party movements, and must in the natural progress of things become antagonistical. . . . Their manifest tendency is to civil war." A Harrison supporter, Lincoln took full-throated part in the campaign. His speeches for the Whig cause, the *Sangamo Journal* reported, were "characterized by that great force and point for which he is so justly admired."

Within three weeks of Harrison's nomination for president, Lincoln rose in the hall of the State House in Springfield—it was the day after Christmas 1839, a winter Thursday—to make the case against Van Buren. The lawyer Josiah Lamborn, a Democrat who would become the attorney general of Illinois the next year, had just predicted that "every state in the Union will vote for Mr. Van Buren at the next Presidential election."

Lincoln begged to differ. "Address *that* argument to *cowards* and to *knaves;* with the *free* and the *brave* it will effect nothing," Lincoln told the audience. Swept up in the fervor of the moment, Lincoln concluded, "Let none falter, who thinks he is right, and we may succeed. But, if after all, we shall fail, be it so. We still shall have the proud consolation of saying to our consciences, and to the departed shade of our country's freedom, that the cause approved of our judgment, and adored of our hearts, in disaster, in chains, in torture, in death, we NEVER faltered in defending."

Lincoln fed racial fears to make his points in 1840. In 1821, in New York, Van Buren had supported Black voting rights—a political hour that Lincoln and others exploited to attract white voters first in 1836 and now again in 1840. In a springtime speech that "reviewed the political course of Mr. Van Buren, and especially his votes in the New York Convention in allowing Free Negroes the right of suffrage," Lincoln was reported to have been "particularly felicitous, and the frequent and spontaneous bursts of applause from the People, gave evidence that their hearts were with him."

In spite of their forebodings about the future, the slaveholders were powerful in both the Democratic and Whig parties—so much so that a group of abolitionists met at Arcade, New York, in January 1840 to launch the Liberty Party, which nominated James G. Birney for president. It was a noble but ineffective effort. Birney polled .031 percent of the popular vote as Harrison and John Tyler defeated Van Buren and Richard M. Johnson, with a margin of 234 to 60 in the Electoral College. The Whigs won 52.9 percent of the popular vote to the Democrats' 46.8 percent.

Lincoln was reelected that year to a fourth term in the legislature. In the December session, the Democrats tried to lock in the Whigs on the floor, Lincoln among them, as part of a parliamentary maneuver to create a quorum. Not to be outwitted, Lincoln climbed out the window of the chamber. The sergeant at arms despaired of obeying Democratic commands to give chase. "My God! Gentlemen, do you know what you ask?" the sergeant at arms said. "Think of the length of Abe's legs, and then tell me how I am to catch him."

By the end of 1840, Lincoln had made a mark with his campaigning for Harrison throughout Illinois. "He was ambitious & determined & when he attempted to Excel by man or boy his whole soul & his Energies were bent on doing it," a kinsman recalled. "And he in this generally—almost always accomplished his Ends." Politics had put Lincoln before audiences, earned him applause, and given him the means to rise—and he meant to keep at it.

CHAPTER FIVE

She Had the Fire, Will, and Ambition

Mary, I agree with you—Mr. Lincoln is talented and will be an
influential man, a leader among men.

—NINIAN W. EDWARDS to Mary Todd, on her marriage to Lincoln

She loved show and power, and was the most ambitious
woman I ever knew. She used to contend when a girl, to her
friends in Kentucky, that she was destined to marry a
President.

—ELIZABETH TODD EDWARDS, a sister of Mary Lincoln

HE WAS NOT LUCKY IN LOVE. Skilled at winning over audiences, Lincoln was less adept with the women of his acquaintance. Standing six feet four, he was, as William Herndon observed, "wiry, vigorous, and strong. His feet and hands were large, arms and legs long and in striking contrast with his slender trunk and small head." Lincoln always retained vestiges of the frontier, compensating for his lack of traditional social grace with his sense of humor and his quiet charm. He told stories and jokes not only to illustrate his points but also to win with wit that which he could not gain with physical attractiveness or with elegance: the hearts of others.

Though he had reservoirs of kindliness, Lincoln was not notably thoughtful or solicitous in a social sense. Perhaps he dwelt too much in his mind. Perhaps his ambition, which would have been better served had he been more, not less, attuned to the needs of others, was too consuming. Whatever the reasons, in his longing and in his drive for legitimacy and for place, Lincoln most often pursued fulfillment in the public rather than in the private sphere—an understandable tendency given that he had lost his mother and had found his relationship with his father wanting. His primary attachments had proven unsatisfactory. In reaction, he turned his gaze outward, to the larger world. "His habits, like himself, were odd and wholly irregular," his sister-in-law Eliza-beth Todd Edwards recalled. "He would move around in a vague, abstracted way, as if unconscious of his own or anyone else's existence."

After Ann Rutledge, Lincoln would fail several more times in love before finally—and barely—marrying Mary Todd of Lexington, Ken-tucky. In 1836, Mary S. Owens, the sister-in-law of Bennett Abell of New Salem, arrived in Lincoln's neighborhood on a visit. He had first met her three years before. She was recalled as having "fair skin, deep blue eyes, and dark curling hair; height five feet, five inches; weight about a hundred and fifty pounds." The child of a prosperous family, she was an educated young woman. "They talked the matter of Mar-riage over quite freely but as I understand it never made a contract or agreement to marry," recalled Lynn McNulty Greene, a Lincoln friend from New Salem. "She was a very superior woman but like some other pretty women (God bless them) she loved Power & conquest."

Lincoln worried that Miss Owens might love money too much, for he had very little of it. Fretful, he started and discarded two letters to her on the question. At last he got the words out. "I am often thinking about what we said of your coming to live at Springfield," Lincoln wrote to her on Sunday, May 7, 1837. "I am afraid you would not be satisfied. There is a great deal of flourishing about in carriages here, which it would be your doom to see without sharing in it. You would have to be poor without the means of hiding your poverty. Do you believe you could bear that patiently? Whatever woman may cast her lot with mine . . . it is my intention to do all in my power to make her happy and contented; and there is nothing I can imagine that would make me more unhappy than to fail in the effort."

That the marriage did not come off may have had more to do with Lincoln's manners than with his means. "I thought Mr. Lincoln was deficient in those little links which make up the chain of [a] woman's happiness—at least it was so in my case," Mary Owens recalled. On an outing, she was annoyed when he neglected to offer to help carry a young mother's baby—an omission she saw as ill-mannered. At an-other point, Lincoln failed to make sure that she made it across a treacherous branch of water on a riding trip. "The other gentlemen were very officious in seeing that their partners got safely over," Mary Owens recalled. "We were behind, he riding [ahead], never looking back to see how I got along. When I rode up beside him, I remarked,

'You are a nice fellow! I suppose you did not care whether my neck was broken or not.' He laughingly replied (I suppose by way of compliment), that he knew I was plenty smart to take care of myself."

Lincoln was not trying to signal that he had lost interest. "Write back as soon as you get this," he wrote to her, "and if possible say something that will please me, for really I have not [been] pleased since I left you."

He could be charming when he felt moved to be, but playful affection was too rare with him to win Mary Owens. "I want in all cases to do right, and most particularly so, in all cases with women," he wrote to her on Wednesday, August 16, 1837. "I want, at this particular time, more than anything else, to do right with you, and if I knew it would be doing right, as I rather suspect it would, to let you alone, I would do it. . . . I now say, that you can now drop the subject, dismiss your thoughts (if you ever had any) from me forever . . . without calling forth one accusing murmur from me."

She declined his proposal when he made it. "We never had any hard feelings towards each other that I know of," Mary Owens recalled. The last communication between the two was couched in self-protective irony. "Tell your sister," Lincoln remarked to Mrs. Abell about a year after the affair ended, "that I think she was a great fool because she did not stay here and marry me!" "Characteristic of the man!" was Mary Owens's verdict on hearing the message.

Stung by Mary Owens's refusal, Lincoln assuaged his feelings of rejection in an acidic letter to his friend Mrs. Eliza Caldwell Browning. "I knew she was over-size," Lincoln wrote of seeing Mary for the second time, "but she now appeared a fair match for Falstaff." When he looked on her, he said, he "could not for my life avoid thinking of my mother; and this, not from withered features, for her skin was too full of fat . . . but from her want of teeth, weather-beaten appearance in general, and from a kind of notion that ran in my head, that *nothing* could have . . . reached her present bulk in less than thirty five or forty years; and, in short, I was not all pleased with her."

Still, he was hurt by his failure to win her. "My vanity was deeply wounded . . . that she whom I had taught myself to believe nobody else would have, had actually rejected me with all my fancied greatness; and to cap the whole, I then, for the first time, began to suspect that I was really a little in love with her," Lincoln told Mrs. Browning. "But let it all go. I'll try and out live it. . . . I have now come to the conclusion never again to think of marrying; and for this reason, I can never be satisfied with anyone who would be block-head enough to have me."

Such resolutions were easily professed but rarely kept. As a politician, Lincoln knew that marriage could be useful as well as desirable. "The sober truth is that Lincoln was inordinately ambitious," Herndon recalled. "Conscious . . . of his humble rank in the social scale, how natural that he should seek by marriage in an influential family to establish strong connections and at the same time foster his political fortunes!" The Rutledges had been important in the village where he lived; Mary Owens had also come from an established family.

The Todd clan of Lexington, Kentucky, ranked higher than any other that Lincoln had encountered. A child of the family, Elizabeth Todd, had come to Springfield in 1833 with her husband, the legislator and lawyer Ninian W. Edwards, a son of the former governor. There, in the Edwardses' hilltop house on Second Street, Elizabeth's younger sister Mary Todd arrived for a visit in the middle of 1837.

Born on Sunday, December 13, 1818, in Lexington, Mary Todd had a notable ancestry. She was the great-granddaughter of Revolutionary-era officer Andrew Porter, who served with George Washington and with Henry Knox, who became the nation's first secretary of war. Her grandfathers, Levi Todd and Robert Parker, were among the founders of Lexington. They had both fought in the Revolutionary War; long afterward they were still known as General Todd and Major Parker. "I am County Lt of a Populous County, Clerk of the Court in the same, a farmer, and at the head of a large family and in addition to this, practice as an attorney in an adjacent county," Levi Todd once wrote. The two men owned slaves, built fine houses, furnished them with imported goods, and educated their children at private institutions.

Their families joined forces in 1812 with the marriage of Eliza Parker (described as "a rising beauty") and Robert Smith Todd, who had been educated at Transylvania University in Lexington and become clerk of the state house of delegates, a state assemblyman, and a state senator. The couple had seven children (one son died at fourteen months), of whom Mary (initially named Mary Ann) was the fourth. At the age of thirty-one, Eliza Parker Todd died of complications from giving birth to a son, George, in the summer of 1825. With six children on his hands, Robert Smith Todd needed a new wife.

He set his sights on Elizabeth Humphreys. From a Frankfort, Kentucky, family that included two United States senators—James Brown of Louisiana and John Brown of Kentucky—Miss Humphreys needed some persuading to accept Robert Smith Todd's offer to move to Lexington. "As your feelings in this matter are involved I am determined to be regulated by your decision," Todd wrote to Elizabeth, "but at the same time trust that the period will not be more remote than the one named, nor our marriage postponed one moment longer than you may deem absolutely necessary. I hope it is not necessary to tell you that my situation is irksome."

When she did accede to the proposal and move into the Todd household—the wedding took place on Wednesday, November 1, 1826—the new Elizabeth "Betsey" Todd became stepmother to a highly skeptical young Mary, then about to mark her eighth birthday. Devastated by the death of her mother and unhappy about the new Mrs. Todd, Mary looked back on her childhood with sadness and anger. Her upbringing, she would recall, was "desolate." In his second marriage Robert Smith Todd fathered no fewer than nine more children, adding new burdens and creating new sources of competition for attention in his ever-sprawling family. "I wish I could forget myself," Mary once said.

One reprieve from her stepmother's house came at school, where Mary was educated from 1827 until about 1837. A copy of Mary Wollstonecraft's *A Vindication of the Rights of Woman,* a 1792 treatise that argued, among other things, for the education of women, was in the library of the house where her father grew up. Mary devoted herself to her studies. She was remembered as being "far in advance over other girls in education; she had a retentive memory and mind that enabled her to grasp and understand thoroughly that lesson she was required to learn."

The Mary Todd who escaped Kentucky for a time in 1837 for her sojourn with her sister in Springfield had, a friend said, "clear blue eyes, long lashes, light brown hair with a glint of bronze and a lovely complexion." William Herndon acknowledged Mary's virtues on her arrival in Illinois. "In her bearing she was proud but handsome and vivacious," he recalled. "She was a good conversationalist, using with equal fluency the French and English languages. When she used a pen, its point was sure to be sharp, and she wrote with wit and ability. She not only had a quick intellect but an intuitive judgment of men and their motives."

She brought something else, too, beyond a pleasing countenance, the most talkative of dispositions, and important family connections: a love of politics. Vote getting, speechmaking, editorial writing, and governing had long been familiar to her. From her father's work in Frankfort to the ambitions of Todd family friend Henry Clay, whose house, Ashland, was near the Todd place in Lexington, Mary Todd had grown up surrounded by electioneering. Family lore was intertwined with the story of American politics. Between the Todds and the Parkers, Mary could boast of connections to officers of the Continental Army in the Revolution, veterans of the War of 1812, a governor of Michigan, a governor of Pennsylvania, and a secretary of the Navy.

She had, therefore, much to discuss with the politically obsessed young men of Springfield—a company that included Lincoln. Yet their courtship would not begin in earnest on this first visit. In the autumn of 1837, Mary went home to Kentucky, returning to Springfield in the summer of 1839. "We expect a very gay winter," she wrote to a friend in 1840, "evening before last my sister gave a most agreeable party, upwards of a hundred graced the festive scene." The Harrison–Van Buren campaign that so consumed Lincoln consumed Mary, too. She joined Lincoln in evening conversation about politics in the offices of the *Sangamo Journal,* telling a friend that she was now "quite a politician, rather an unladylike profession, yet at such a crisis whose heart could remain untouched[?]" "Lincoln went into the Southern part of the State as Elector [—] Canvasser [—] debator [—] Speaker," Joshua Speed recalled. "Here first wrote his *Mary*—She darted after him—wrote him."

To the outside world—even to those closest to them—they were not evenly matched. "I have often happened in the room where they were sitting, and Mary invariably led the conversation," Elizabeth Edwards recalled. "Mr. Lincoln would sit at her side and listen. He scarcely said a word, but gazed on her as if irresistibly drawn towards her by some superior and unseen power. He could not maintain himself in a continued conversation with a lady reared as Mary was." Mrs. Edwards continued:

> He was not educated and equipped mentally to make himself either interesting or attractive to the ladies. He was a good, honest, and sincere young man whose rugged, manly qualities I admired; but to me he somehow seemed ill-constituted by nature

and education to please such a woman as my sister. Mary was quick, gay, and in the social world somewhat brilliant. She loved show and power, and was the most ambitious woman I ever knew. She used to contend when a girl, to her friends in Kentucky, that she was destined to marry a President. I have heard her say that myself, and after mingling in society in Springfield she repeated the seemingly absurd and idle boast. Although Mr. Lincoln seemed to be attached to Mary, and fascinated by her wit and sagacity, yet I soon began to doubt whether they could always be so congenial. In a short time I told Mary my impression that they were not suited, or, as some persons who believe matches are made in heaven would say, not intended for each other.

Mrs. Edwards was on to something, for both parties had difficulty committing to the match though they seemed to have a private understanding. (Herndon believed they had reached "the point of engagement.") Life unfolded amid the swirl of society in the Edwards circle. Members reportedly called it "the Coterie"; the resentful derided it as "the Edwards clique."

As he pondered life with Mary, Lincoln appears also to have thought much of Mathilda Edwards, a cousin of Ninian W. Edwards who was visiting Springfield in 1840. One witness, Jane D. Bell, reported that Lincoln "fell desperately in love" with Mathilda. The young lady, however, later said that Lincoln "never mentioned Such a Subject to me: he never even stooped to pay me a Compliment."

And there was Sarah Rickard, the sister of a family with whom Lincoln had boarded. "Mr. Lincoln did Propose marriage to me in the winter of 1840 and '41," Rickard, who had become Sarah Barret, recalled to Herndon in 1888. "My reasons for refusing his Proposal was that I was young only 16 years old and had not thought much about matrimony. I had the highest Regard for Mr. Lincoln [but] he seemed almost like an older Brother being as It were one of my Sister's family." There was something else: "His peculiar manner and his General deportment," Sarah recalled, "would not be likely to fascinate a young girl just entering the society world."

Mary, too, was keeping her options open. "Miss Todd is flourishing largely," it was reported. "She has a great many beaux." Stephen Douglas, "dashing and handsome," was a suitor; a relative of Mary's claimed "she loved Douglas, and but for her promise to marry Lincoln would have accepted him." Edwin B. Webb (his friends called him "Bat"), a widowed lawyer and legislator who had studied at Transylvania in Mary's Lexington, was another prospect. Mary thought him her "principal lion" in 1840. Observers believed that Mary had made her choice and that Webb, not Lincoln, had won the contest.

The Harrison–Van Buren campaign was drawing to a close, and Mary Todd and Abraham Lincoln circled each other with varying degrees of wariness amid a shifting cast of marital candidates. Then Christmas came. As did a crisis.

On Friday, January 1, 1841—Lincoln called it "that fatal first"—he visited Mary Todd at the Edwardses' house on Second Street. At this distance the sequence of events is muddled—and, given the emotions of the hour, things may have seemed muddled even then—but the engagement was clearly off. "I had it from good authority," Lincoln friend Abner Y. Ellis recalled, "that after Mr. Lincoln was engaged to be married to his wife Mary that she a short time before they were to be married backed out from her engagement with him." It is likelier, however, that Lincoln instigated the break. "When I told Mary that I did not love her," Lincoln told Joshua Speed, "she burst into tears and almost springing from her chair and wringing her hands as if in agony, said something about the deceiver being himself deceived." This last was possibly an allusion to her own flirtations with Douglas and Webb.

"Go," she is said to have exclaimed, "and never, never come back."

That evening, Lincoln recounted the scene.

"What else did you say?" Speed asked Lincoln.

"To tell you the truth, Speed, it was too much for me," Lincoln replied. "I found the tears trickling down my own cheeks. I caught her in my arms and kissed her."

"And that's how you broke the engagement," a skeptical Speed said. "You not only acted the fool, but your conduct was tantamount to a renewal of the engagement, and in decency you cannot back down now."

"Well," Lincoln said, "if I am in again, so be it. It's done, and I shall abide by it."

The "world had it that Mr L backed out," Elizabeth Edwards recalled, "and this placed Mary in a peculiar Situation & to set herself right and to free Mr. Lincoln's mind She wrote a letter to Mr L Stating that She would release him from his Engagements." There was an important proviso: "She would hold the question an open one," Mrs. Edwards said, and "had not Changed her mind, but felt as always."

For Lincoln, depression ensued—perhaps his darkest period since the death of Ann Rutledge five years before. Though he had broken the engagement, he felt the turmoil of the time deeply. He may have experienced pangs of guilt. Whatever the reason, Lincoln spiraled into shadow. "Restless, gloomy, miserable, desperate, he seemed an object of pity," Herndon wrote. "The doctors say he came within an inch of being a perfect lunatic for life," Jane Bell reported. "He was perfectly crazy for some time, not able to attend to his business at all. They say he does not look like the same person." Lincoln, according to Ninian W. Edwards, "in his Conflicts of duty—honor & his love went as Crazy as a *Loon*."

Suicide was thought to be a possibility. "Knives and razors, and every instrument that could be used for self-destruction, were removed from his reach," Speed recalled. As he had in the past, Lincoln lost weight, his appetite a victim of his melancholy. He was, an observer wrote, "reduced, and emaciated in appearance and seems scarcely to possess strength enough to speak above a whisper." He missed a number of votes in the legislature—unusual for him—but willed himself to remain in Springfield until the end of the session. "I am now the most miserable man living," Lincoln wrote to John T. Stuart on Saturday, January 23, 1841. "If what I feel were equally distributed to the whole human family, there would not be one cheerful face on the earth. Whether I shall ever be better I can not tell; I awfully forebode I shall not. To remain as I am is impossible; I must die or be better, it appears to me."

He would get better in time. Joshua Speed invited him for a respite at the Speed family place near Louisville. There, Lincoln read the Bible and waited out his demons. "He was much depressed," Joshua Speed recalled. "At first he almost contemplated suicide. In the deepest of his depression he said one day he had done nothing to make any human being remember that he had lived; and to connect his name with the events transpiring in his day and generation, and so impress himself upon them as to link his name with something that would redound to the interest of his fellow-men, was what he desired to live for."

The way out of his personal hell was a public life. Joshua Speed's brother James, a lawyer, remembered Lincoln's calling on him in his office on this visit. "He read my books," James Speed said, "talked with me about his life, his reading, his studies, his aspirations."

I n the winter of 1842, just after his thirty-third birthday, Lincoln shared some of the fruits of his study. In the Second Presbyterian Church of Springfield to address a temperance society meeting on Washington's birthday, he offered a profound vision of human nature, arguing that previous generations of religiously driven temperance ad-vocates had pursued their cause in the wrong way. "When the dram-seller and drinker, were incessantly told," Lincoln said, "not in the accents of entreaty and persuasion, diffidently addressed by erring man to an erring brother; but in the thundering tones of anathema and de-nunciation . . . I say, when they were told all this, and in this way, it is not wonderful that they were slow, *very slow,* to acknowledge the truth of such denunciations, and to join the ranks of their denouncers, in a hue and cry against themselves."

To be hectored and condemned; to be told that they were wholly wrong; to be told that preachers were in full possession of the truth: Lincoln believed that was a path not to reform but to intransigence. Self-righteousness and certitude were the enemies of conciliation and conversion. "When the conduct of men is designed to be influenced, *persuasion,* kind, unassuming persuasion, should ever be adopted," Lin-coln said. "It is an old and a true maxim, that a 'drop of honey catches more flies than a gallon of gall.' So with men." He continued:

> If you would win a man to your cause, *first* convince him that you are his sincere friend. Therein is a drop of honey that catches his heart, which, say what he will, is the great high road to his reason, and which, when once gained, you will find but little trouble in convincing his judgment of the justice of your cause. . . . On the contrary, assume to dictate to his judgment, or to command his action, or to mark him as one to be shunned and despised, and he will retreat within himself, close all the avenues to his head and his heart; and tho' your cause be naked truth itself, transformed to the heaviest lance, harder than steel, and sharper than steel can be made, and tho' you throw it with more than Herculean force and precision, you shall no more be able to pierce him, than to pene-trate the hard shell of a tortoise with a rye straw.

Such is man, and so *must* he be understood by those who would lead him.... Happy day, when, all appetites controlled, all passions subdued.... Hail fall of Fury! Reign of Reason, all hail!

On the Fourth of July, 1842, Lincoln signaled a sense of calm about his own prospects. "Whatever [God] designs, he will do for *me* yet," he wrote to Joshua Speed. "'Stand *still* and see the salvation of the Lord' is my text just now." The quotation is from Moses's address to the Israelites just before the crossing of the Red Sea—an allusion that suggests Lincoln believed a decisive hour had come.

About the same time that Lincoln was writing to Speed, Mary told a friend that Lincoln "deems me unworthy of notice, as I have not met him in the gay world for months." It was Eliza Francis who mended the breach between Lincoln and Mary. In 1842, more than a year after the couple had parted ways in the Edwards parlor, Mrs. Francis, the wife of *Sangamo Journal* editor Simeon Francis, invited the estranged pair to a party. Though they arrived separately, they were thrown together by Mrs. Francis with an injunction: "Be friends again."

Things moved with dispatch as the two renewed the suspended courtship. They were quiet about it, and quick—so quiet and so quick that Mary's sister Elizabeth Edwards was surprised when she learned about the reconciliation. "I asked Mary why she was so secretive about it," Mrs. Edwards recalled. "She said evasively that after all that had occurred, it was best to keep the courtship from all eyes and ears. Men and women and the whole world were uncertain and slippery, and if misfortune befell the engagement all knowledge of it would be hidden from the world."

The class divide was real. "Lincoln had poor judgment of the fitness and appropriateness of things," Herndon recalled. "He would wade into a ballroom and speak aloud to some friend: 'How clean these women look!'" To Mary Todd, Lincoln said, "I want to dance with you in the worst way." When they were done, Mary remarked, "Mr. Lincoln, I think you have literally fulfilled your request—you have danced the worst way possible." She would complain for years to come that he failed to use the proper knife to cut the butter, that he greeted callers at the door in shirtsleeves, that his clothes were tattered, and that his socks failed to match. "Why don't you dress up and look like somebody?" Mary would say.

Yet she could be loving and affectionate. "How much I wish instead of writing, we were together this evening," she told him in 1848. "I feel very sad away from you. With love I must bid you good night." Lincoln reciprocated. "Then come along, and that as soon as possible," he wrote to her. "I shall be impatient till I see you. . . . Come on just as soon as you can."

In the first days of November 1842, Lincoln, who had begun to call Mary "Molly," arranged to marry. "I now suggest and insist upon our marriage at once," he reportedly said. "We will live at the Globe Tavern for the present. Now we must go, very quietly without fuss and feathers, at ten o'clock tomorrow morning, before the magistrate, and ask him to marry us."

Mary was delighted. She told her sister Elizabeth about the plans, but Mrs. Edwards had other ideas. "Do not forget that you are a Todd," she told her sister, dismissing the thought of a civil ceremony. "But, Mary, if you insist on being married today, we will make merry, and have the wedding here this evening. I will not permit you to be married out of my house."

For his part, Ninian W. Edwards was pleased. Hearing Mary praise her soon-to-be husband, Edwards replied, "Mary, I agree with you—Mr. Lincoln is talented and will be an influential man, a leader among men. And now, ask all of your friends to be present at your wedding." The service would be held that evening in the parlor of the house on Second Street.

Friday, November 4, a Todd kinswoman recalled, was "a hurly-burly day. How we hustled! I had a whole boiled ham which I took over for the wedding supper, and made the bride's and groom's cake. It was a very pretty and gay wedding." The Episcopal rector of St. Paul's Church in Springfield, the Reverend Charles Dresser, vested and presided "with much and impressive ceremony." Afterward the party "danced until midnight in those spacious parlors of the Ninian Edwards home."

What did Mary see in Lincoln? *Possibilities.* To Elizabeth Edwards, Mary had mused about the kind of man she would like to marry—"a good man, with a head for position, fame and power, a man of mind with a hope and bright prospects rather than all the houses and gold in the world." What did Lincoln see in Mary? *Possibilities.* He was clearly in a marrying mood—after Ann Rutledge and Mary Owens had passed from the scene, Mary Todd was, after all, one of several women he pursued in a brief space of time—and she offered him social respectability and possible advancement. She was a woman of connections and culture who was interested in what he was interested in: the amassing and wielding of power. The Lincoln-Todd marriage was "a policy Match all around," Mary's cousin and former Lincoln law partner John T. Stuart observed. "His wife made him Presdt: She had the fire—will and ambition—Lincoln's talent & his wife's Ambition did the deed.... Lincoln needed driving—(well he got that)."

William Herndon thought "Lincoln's married life was a domestic hell on earth." Mary physically struck Lincoln and had what observers called a "very violent temper" that Herndon said made her "as mad as a disturbed hornet." "Mrs. Lincoln often gave L Hell in general," recalled James H. Matheny, a Springfield friend of Lincoln's. "*Ferocity*—describes Mrs. L's conduct to L." Historians, scholars, and doctors have long speculated that Mary suffered from mental illness, perhaps bipolar disorder, or possibly a form of anemia that manifested itself in erratic behavior. There were other instances of behaviors consistent with a bipolar diagnosis in the Todd family—manic episodes as well as depressive ones. "One of Mary's brothers, Dr. George Todd, was 'given to moods of deep melancholy,'" wrote a psychiatrist who studied Mary's history, "while another brother, Levi Owen Todd, died in an insane asylum. Also institutionalized were niece Mattie Todd and a grandniece.... Another grandniece ... committed suicide, and fourteen members of her family were said to have been in asylums."

A half sister of Mary's, Elodie, once bluntly described her own personality. "I cannot govern my temper or tongue, and when I am angry say much that I am very sorry for afterwards and altho' [I] speak my feelings at the time, [and] change them when I get a little cooler, but it is just the same next time.... I am one of the most unforgiving creatures you ever knew in my disposition, and if a wrong is done me and I am angered, I can never again be reconciled to the offender." As the historian Michael Burlingame observed, "If Mary Lincoln had been as self-aware and candid as Elodie, she might well have described herself in similar terms."

"Mary Todd made Lincoln's life miserable" was a common view in Lincoln family and political circles. Still, he tried to be stoic. In search of a domestic life that he himself had never truly known, he was ready for a family. Her devotion to their children makes it clear that she shared that hunger. Just as he wanted never to replicate Thomas Lin-

*The daughter of a prominent Kentucky family,
Mary Todd was well educated, politically
curious—and erratic.*

coln's household, she was trying to redeem the unhappiness of her
stepmother's reign. And they were physically attracted to each other.
On once seeing his wife in a low-cut gown, Lincoln was quoted as ap-
preciatively saying, "Our cat has a long tail tonight." Their first child
was born not quite nine months after the wedding, provoking speculation that Mary had seduced Lincoln before the wedding and he had
agreed to the marriage out of honor. Whatever the truth, between their
exchanging vows in the Edwardses' house and their last night together
at Ford's Theatre, the Lincolns would be joined together amid the
most profound hours of American history.

For the Lincolns, married life began at the Globe Tavern, a Springfield boardinghouse on the north side of Adams Street between
Third and Fourth. For $4 a week, the couple rented a room that mea-
sured twelve by fourteen feet. In the *Sangamo Journal* the week before the
wedding, C. G. Saunders, who then owned the establishment, had advertised that his house, "having undergone considerable repairs," was

ready to "furnish the weary with a comfortable resting place—and the hungry shall always find the best table the market will afford." And not just travelers. "A few families can be accommodated with pleasant and convenient rooms as boarders if application is made soon." And so the Lincolns came, moving into the same quarters where a brother-in-law of Mary's, Dr. William S. Wallace, had once lived.

Their lives were enmeshed in politics from the start. On Monday, February 20, 1843, the War of 1812 general William F. Thornton, a leading Illinois Whig, hosted a large party at the Globe Tavern. All of Springfield, social, official, and in between, was there. "There was a sound of revelry by night," a reporter wrote, "and Springfield's capital had gathered. . . . Her beauty and her chivalry. . . . The lamps shone o'er fair women and brave men—"

Lincoln was maneuvering for the district's nomination to the U.S. House of Representatives. "Now if you should hear anyone say that Lincoln don't want to go to Congress, I wish you as a personal friend of mine, would tell him you have reason to believe he is mistaken," Lincoln wrote to a correspondent in February 1843. "The truth is, I would like to go very much. Still, circumstances may happen which may prevent my being a candidate." His main rival, his friend Edward Baker, prevailed after Lincoln's opponents cast the son of impoverished Knob Creek, Kentucky, as a tool of the Todds of prosperous Lexington. "It would astonish if not amuse, the older citizens . . . who twelve years ago knew me a strange, friendless, uneducated, penniless boy, working on a flat boat—at ten dollars per month—to learn that I have been put down here as the candidate of pride, wealth, and aristocratic family distinction," Lincoln wrote afterward. The Todd question would be a recurring feature of his political life. "I must confess I am afraid of 'Abe,'" Chicago editor Charles H. Ray would write in 1854. "He is Southern by birth, Southern in his associations, and Southern, if I mistake not, in his sympathies. I have thought that he would not come squarely up to the mark in a hand to hand fight with Southern influence and dictation. His wife, you know, is a Todd, of a pro-slavery family, and so are all his kin."

Religion also played a role in the congressional loss. "There was . . . the strangest combination of church influence against me," Lincoln recalled. "My wife has some relatives in the Presbyterian and some in the Episcopal churches, and therefore, wherever it would tell, I was set down as either the one or the other, whilst it was everywhere contended that no christian ought to go for me, because I belonged to no church, was suspected of being a deist. . . . [T]hose influences levied a tax of a considerable per cent upon my strength throughout the religious community."

Resolute in defeat—he knew the vicissitudes of politics well—he practiced law, campaigned for the Whigs, and enjoyed the first months together with Mary. In mid-April 1843, James C. Conkling encountered Lincoln in Bloomington, Illinois, on legal business. Lincoln was "desperately homesick and turning his head frequently towards the south." Marriage, Lincoln wrote, was "a matter of profound wonder."

On Tuesday, August 1, 1843, at the Globe Tavern, Mary gave birth to the son she named Robert Todd Lincoln. "Young Bob Lincoln was possessed of a pair of powerful lungs," an observer recalled. "He cried lustily." Soon the Lincolns moved to 214 South Fourth Street and ultimately took up residence at Eighth and Jackson in a house purchased from Charles Dresser, the Episcopal rector. A second son, Edward Baker Lincoln, called Eddy (sometimes spelled "Eddie"), arrived in March 1846.

Lincoln was an indulgent father. "He talks very plainly—almost as plainly as anybody," Lincoln told Joshua Speed in a letter describing young Robert as a toddler. "He is quite smart enough. . . . He has a great deal of that sort of mischief, that is the offspring of much animal spirits." Lincoln approved of such a restless disposition. Disappointed in his bid for Congress, he remained in the arena as a Whig campaigner.

In a political circular that had been published on Saturday, March 4, 1843, Lincoln and two co-authors drew on Aesop and the Bible to argue that "union is strength"—"a truth," they wrote, "that has been known, illustrated and declared, in various ways and forms in all ages of the world. That great fabulist and philosopher, Aesop, illustrated it by his fable of the bundle of sticks; and he whose wisdom surpasses that of all philosophers, has declared that 'a house divided against itself cannot stand.'"

John Tyler had become president when William Henry Harrison died a month after the 1841 inauguration. Dismissed as "His Accidency," Tyler had lost Whig support, and Henry Clay was once more the party's choice in the general election. Clay faced Democrat James K. Polk of Tennessee, known as "Young Hickory." The election was fought in part over the annexation of Texas, which would mean that additional slave land would enter the Union. To observers, the contest came down to *"Polk, slavery, and Texas"* or *"Clay, Union, and liberty,"* and Polk emerged victorious.

Lincoln had stood by his man in the campaign. Believing the Clay platform on economics—including currency, tariffs, and internal improvements—to be sound, Lincoln was a loyal campaigner, speaking for the Whig ticket in Illinois and in Indiana. The popular Lincoln also attracted partisan hostility. "Lincoln is a long-legged varmint," an opposition newspaper wrote. "He can make a speech which is all length and height like himself, and no breadth or thickness."

It was all part of the great game. The spectacle of the race was entertaining and invigorating; everyone believed they were taking part in a campaign that was both exciting and grave. After a procession in which Lincoln marched, an observer wrote, "Old Sangamon . . . sent on a noble corps of choice spirits who, accompanied by an unsurpassable glee club, called forth thundering cheers as they passed."

Polk narrowly defeated Clay. The Whig nominee's failure to reassure antislavery voters, particularly in New York, which Polk carried, was probably decisive. The Lincolns consoled themselves with holiday cheer. "The night was one of great hilarity and enjoyment in Springfield," the *Daily Missouri Republican* reported of New Year's Eve. "A large and very general party at the State House and a select party by Mrs. Young at the American House [a rival of the Lincolns' old Globe Tavern]. Ladies of [the] Episcopal Church also gave a supper—proceeds for religious purposes. It was one of the handsomest things I ever attended. . . . A very large number in attendance, and all expressed themselves gratified." Elizabeth and Ninian W. Edwards followed on with a party for four hundred.

With Mary by his side, handling callers and helping with his correspondence, Lincoln entered the middle of the decade a seasoned, thoughtful man who knew his way around Sangamon County, around Springfield, indeed around the whole of Illinois. It was time to try a turn on a larger stage. His new wife believed he would do well there. "She was an Extremely Ambitious woman and in Ky often & often Contended that She was destined to be the wife of some future President," Elizabeth Todd Edwards recalled. Mary had pursued him with a goal in mind: She wanted to marry, she said, the man "who has the best prospects of being President." And she had married Lincoln.

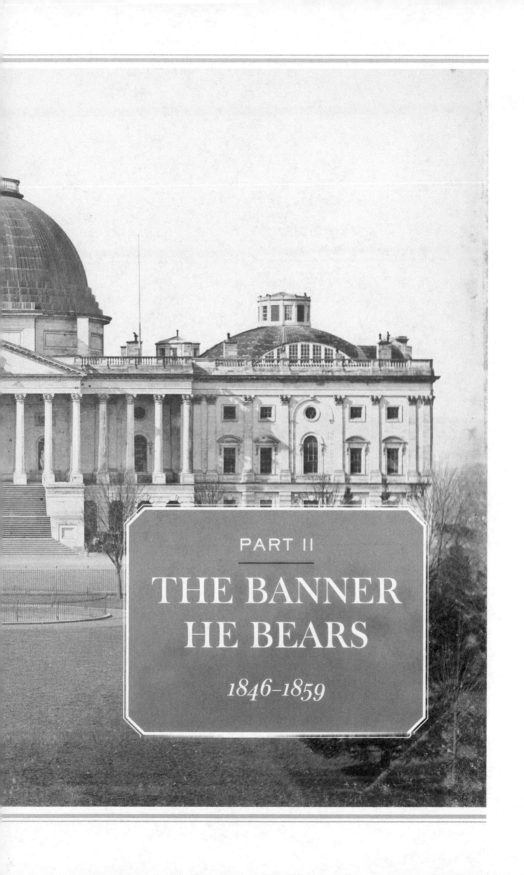

PART II

THE BANNER
HE BEARS

1846–1859

CHAPTER SIX

From the Very Depths of Society

He will find many men in Congress who possess twice the
good looks, and not half the good sense, of our own
representatives.

—The *Illinois Journal,* on Lincoln's election to Congress

It is like the plague of frogs—everywhere.

—Senator Thomas Hart Benton of Missouri,
on the slavery question

H E LONGED FOR WASHINGTON. Lincoln had not held an elective post for four years, since 1842. Campaigning for Clay had
been engaging but had not fulfilled him in the way that he
hoped a victory of his own would. As the 1846 election for the U.S.
House approached, Lincoln prepared to seek the Whig nomination in
Illinois's Seventh Congressional District. "I would rejoice to be spared
the labour of a contest," he wrote, "but 'being in' I shall go it thoroughly, and to the bottom."

His Whig opponent was John J. Hardin, who was described as "a tall
man with a bold face"—and, Lincoln believed, a consuming ambition.
"Hardin is a man of desperate energy and perseverance; and one that
never backs out," Lincoln wrote. That Hardin was in the race at all violated a long-standing arrangement among the district's Whigs. Three
years earlier, in 1843, three leading figures—Hardin, Lincoln, and Edward Baker—had agreed to a sequential succession. Hardin would
serve, then Baker, and then Lincoln. Hardin and Baker had had their
turns. Now it was Lincoln's—and yet Hardin refused to stand down.

Lincoln campaigned with energy and care. "When this [state] Supreme court shall adjourn," he wrote to an ally on Wednesday, January 14, 1846, "it is my intention to take a quiet trip through the towns
and neighbourhoods of Logan county, Delevan [*sic*], Tremont, and on

to & through the upper counties" of the district. His political calculus about the district's counties was precise. "Morgan & Scott are beyond my reach," he wrote. "Menard is safe to me. Mason—neck and neck. Logan is mine. To make the matter sure, your entire Senatorial District must be secured. Of this I suppose Tazewell is safe; and I have much done in both the other counties. . . . Still I wish you all in Tazewell, to keep your eyes continually on Woodford and Marshall. Let no opportunity of making a mark escape. When they shall be safe, all will be safe—I *think*."

He was indeed safe, and Hardin withdrew from the race. Lincoln was officially nominated in Petersburg on Friday, May 1, 1846. "Mr. Lincoln, we all know, is a good Whig, a good man, an able speaker and richly deserves the confidence of Whigs in District and State," the *Sangamo Journal* wrote.

In the general election Lincoln faced the Reverend Peter Cartwright, a popular Methodist preacher. Born in Virginia in 1785, Cartwright rode circuit, it was said, "with Bible and rifle; if a sinner came in drunk and interrupted the sermon Cartwright jumped from the pulpit and personally threw him out." The people of the district and of the day loved Cartwright's speeches and sermons. The story is told of an elderly lady in Henderson County, Illinois, who, when asked whether she had ever ventured out for a Lincoln appearance, replied, "No, we never took the trouble to go hear him, but we always drove across the county to hear Peter Cartwright!"

Lincoln preached his own Whig gospel. In an oft-repeated tale, he once attended a Cartwright revival during the race. When Cartwright came to the altar call, summoning sinners to accept the Lord and be saved, he saw Lincoln sitting in the audience, declining to rise.

"If you are not going to repent and go to Heaven, Mr. Lincoln," Cartwright cried, "where are you going?"

"I am going to Congress, Brother Cartwright," Lincoln replied.

In the campaign, Cartwright used the means at hand, and Lincoln's views on religion were one such means. "Mr. Lincoln had no faith and no hope in the usual acceptation of those words," Mary Lincoln recalled. "He never joined a Church; but still, as I believe, he was a religious man by nature." Uninterested in the nuances of the matter, Cartwright had an election to win. Lincoln believed that the minister and his forces were "slyly sow[ing] the seed" of Lincoln as infidel "in select spots" in the district by "whispering the charge of infidelity against me."

Such whispers about Lincoln were not unusual. The Springfield lawyer and Lincoln friend James Matheny recalled that his father, Charles Matheny, who was "a strong Methodist—a Kind of minister and loving Lincoln with all his soul," nevertheless "hated to vote for him because he heard that Lincoln was an Infidel." As the younger Matheny remembered it, "I have often heard Mr. Lincoln talk of the miraculous Conception, inspiration—Revelation—Virgin Mary... &c. His was the language of respect yet it was from the point of ridicule—not scoff. ... Many religious—Christian whigs hated to vote for Lincoln on that account—had to argue the question &c. with them."

Striking back in a handbill addressed to his "Fellow Citizens" on Friday, July 31, 1846, Lincoln defended himself. He was not "an open scoffer at Christianity," Lincoln wrote. "That I am not a member of any Christian Church, is true; but I have never denied the truth of the Scriptures; and I have never spoken with intentional disrespect of religion in general, or of any denomination of Christians in particular." He recognized the utility—and the ubiquity—of Christianity.

The most compelling of moral issues—the future of American slavery—featured in only a symbolic way in the Seventh District in 1846. Both antislavery, Lincoln and Cartwright competed in a field that included one other candidate: Elihu Walcott, a nominee of the Liberty Party, the organization created in 1840. "The Liberty Party... deem it due to themselves as well as to humanity, to use their political power to overthrow slavery," wrote the *Emancipator Extra,* an abolitionist publication.

Lincoln won the election to Congress, 6,340 to 4,829—55.5 percent to 42.3 percent, with Walcott polling just over 2 percent. "We had hoped better results would have followed the nomination of Mr. Cartwright," the Democratic *Illinois State Gazette* wrote. "Better luck next time."

The winner was relieved but restless. "Being elected to Congress, though I am very grateful to our friends, for having done it, has not pleased me as much as I expected," Lincoln wrote to his friend Joshua Speed. Vulnerable to depression and a striver for an elusive sense of legitimacy, Lincoln may have feared that no external glory could ever fill the inner needs he felt. That was the tragedy of the driven man: To seek vindication in the world but to suspect that no trumpets could totally drown out the uncertain notes of the boy who doubted his place in the world.

Yet Lincoln could not rest. He could not stop. He ran the race. He could do no other.

His election came as the United States fought the Mexican-American War, a consequential conflict that put slavery at the center of national debate. Swaths of Mexican-owned Western land stretching to the Pacific coast were in play, as was sprawling Texas, which had declared a disputed independence from Mexico in 1836. Eyeing Texas as an addition to the slave-owning interest, Governor James Henry Hammond of South Carolina said, "If the Union is to break there could not be a better pretext. With Texas, the slave states would form a territory large enough for a *first rate power* . . . that would flourish beyond any on the Globe." Lincoln opposed the acquisition of Texas on just these grounds.

He and his party lost that battle. On Friday, July 4, 1845, Texas accepted the United States' offer of statehood. In addition, there were expansionist designs on Mexican-owned land that would come to comprise all or parts of Arizona, California, Colorado, Kansas, Nevada, New Mexico, Oklahoma, Utah, and Wyoming. Eager for the extensive Mexican holdings, President Polk moved, often covertly and deceptively, toward war. Armed conflict and a declaration of war came after a controversial April 1846 skirmish between U.S. and Mexican troops in territory along the Rio Grande. "Hostilities may now be considered as commenced," reported General Zachary Taylor.

By late 1847, U.S. forces had prevailed, and Polk arranged for a $15 million purchase price for the territory that became known as the Mexican Cession. The sphere of conflict over slavery was now significantly larger than it had been even a year and a half before. "Our nation seems resolved to rush on in her wicked career, though the road be ditched with human blood, and paved with human skulls," Frederick Douglass wrote in an editorial for his *North Star* newspaper. "Well, be it so."

Not due in Washington for his first session as a member of Congress until December 1847, Lincoln had traveled to Chicago in the summer of that year. The occasion: the River and Harbor Convention called to protest President Polk's August 1846 veto of a large internal improvements bill. The meeting was a grand undertaking—so grand that it overwhelmed Chicago. "Not a single line of railroad had yet reached the city," James Shaw, the director of the Aurora, Illinois, public library, reported to the journalist Ida M. Tarbell. "Entrance into and exit from it had to be made by sail or steam on the lake, or by carriage and horseback on land." The influential New York editors Horace Greeley and Thurlow Weed were among the twenty thousand convention-goers.

Lincoln remained an unpolished figure. "Tall, angular, and awkward," Elihu B. Washburne of Galena, Illinois, recalled, "he had on a short-waisted, thin swallow-tail coat, a short vest of the same material, thin pantaloons, scarcely coming to his ankles, a straw hat and a pair of brogans with woolen socks."

Yet he could charm and impress. Horace Greeley approvingly called him the "Hon. Abraham Lincoln, a tall specimen of an Illinoisan" who spoke "briefly and happily," and the Whig *Chicago Daily Journal* puffed the young congressman-to-be. "We expect much from him as a representative in Congress," the paper wrote, "and we have no doubt our expectations will be more than realized, for never was reliance placed in a nobler heart and a sounder judgment. We know the banner he bears will never be soiled."

Three and a half months later, on Saturday, October 23, Lincoln leased the house at Eighth and Jackson in Springfield to Cornelius Ludlum for $90 a year, payable in quarterly installments and setting "the North-up-stairs room" aside to store the Lincolns' family furniture. (The lease agreement included an exhortation for Ludlum "to be especially careful to prevent any destruction by fire.") Their belongings packed, Mary and Abraham Lincoln, with Robert and Eddy in tow, left Springfield for Washington on Monday, October 25. Wives and families did not often join congressmen in the capital, but Mary Lincoln wanted to go. "She wishes to loom largely," the lawyer and Lincoln friend David Davis remarked. For both Lincolns, the Thirtieth Congress awaited.

His constituents knew their man. "Mr. Lincoln, the member of Congress elect from this district, has just set out on his way to the city of Washington," the *Illinois Journal* reported. "He will find many men in Congress who possess twice the good looks, and not half the good sense, of our own representatives."

The Lincolns stopped in Lexington for a visit to Mary's ancestral home in early November. A half sister of Mary's, Emilie, was among those who gathered to greet the Springfield relatives. "Mary came in first with little Eddie, the baby, in her arms," Emilie recalled. "To my mind she was lovely; clear, sparkling blue eyes, lovely smooth white skin with a faint, wild rose color in her cheeks, and glossy light brown hair, which fell in soft short curls behind each ear." To the nearly eleven-year-old Emilie the figure who came through the door after Mary was very different.

"Mr. Lincoln followed her into the hall with his little son, Robert Todd, in his arms," Emilie recalled. "He put the little fellow on the floor, and as [Lincoln] arose, I remember thinking of 'Jack and the Bean Stalk,' and feared he might be the hungry giant of the story—he was so tall and looked so big with a long, full black cloak over his shoulders, and he wore a fur cap with ear straps which allowed but little of his face to be seen. Expecting to hear the 'fe, fi, fo, fum,' I shrank closer to my mother and tried to hide behind her voluminous skirts." Lincoln noticed the shy little girl, lifted her up, and said, "So this is little sister." To Emilie, all was now well: "His voice and smile banished my fear of the giant."

While in Lexington, Lincoln browsed through the Todds' library, memorizing a poem of William Cullen Bryant's, "Thanatopsis." The poem speaks of the world's dead in a reassuring way, urging the living to see the present as a challenge to be met:

> *So live, that when thy summons comes to join*
> *The innumerable caravan, which moves*
> *To that mysterious realm, where each shall take*
> *His chamber in the silent halls of death,*
> *Thou go not, like the quarry-slave at night,*
> *Scourged to his dungeon, but, sustained and soothed*
> *By an unfaltering trust, approach thy grave,*
> *Like one who wraps the drapery of his couch*
> *About him, and lies down to pleasant dreams.*

The present—and the future—were the subjects of a speech of Henry Clay's that Lincoln attended in the Todds' Lexington. Venturing from his home, Ashland, to Market Square at eleven o'clock on the morning of Saturday, November 13, 1847, Clay denounced President Polk's war with Mexico. Lincoln's father-in-law, Robert S. Todd, was a vice president of the meeting. "It had rained all the morning, and everything looked Novemberish," a reporter noted.

"The day is dark and gloomy, unsettled and uncertain, like the condition of our country, in regard to the unnatural war with Mexico," Clay said in his two-and-a-half-hour speech. To Clay—and to Lincoln— balance between slave and free states was essential. And he made a moral point: "I have ever regarded slavery as a great evil, a wrong, for the present, I fear, an irremediable wrong to its unfortunate victims."

To Clay, the end of slavery would take time, and he advocated colonization. "It may be argued, that, in admitting the injustice of slavery, I admit the necessity of an instantaneous reparation of that injustice," Clay said. "Unfortunately, however, it is not always safe, practicable or possible, in the great movements of States and public affairs of nations, to remedy or repair the infliction of previous injustice." Clay's vision was Lincoln's vision: Slavery was wrong. The United States must not allow its expansion. Yet for now, custom, racial prejudice, and constitutional consensus protected the institution where it existed from federal action, and a multiracial democracy was not thought feasible. Lamentable, yes, but such was life. Such was America.

The Lincolns reached Washington late on the evening of Thursday, December 2. The Scottish writer Alexander Mackay, who visited the capital in this same period, recalled his own first impressions of an evening arrival: "The night was cloudy and dark, and as we approached the town, the outline of the Capitol was barely discernible, on our left, looming up against the dull heavy sky." The Capitol was the city's focal point. "I have seen it when its milk-white walls were swathed in moonlight," Mackay observed, "and when, viewed from amid the fountains and shrubbery which encircle it, it looked more like a creation of fairyland than a substantial reality."

The Lincolns boarded briefly at Brown's Indian Queen Hotel on the northwest corner of Sixth and Pennsylvania before moving to Mrs. Ann Sprigg's lodging on First Street, S.E., on Capitol Hill. The Sprigg house, which faced the East Front of the Capitol, sat along what was called Carroll Row. The old Jacksonian editor Duff Green was a neighbor. "I will tell you how I am situated," a boarder, Theodore Weld, had written in 1842. "The iron railing around the Capitol Park comes within fifty feet of our door. Our dining room overlooks the whole Capitol Park which is one mile around and filled with shade trees and shrubbery. I have a pleasant room on the second floor with a good bed, plenty of covering, a bureau, table, chairs, closets and clothes press, a good fireplace."

A number of antislavery men also boarded along the Lincolns' Carroll Row, among them Joshua Giddings of Ohio; John Dickey, John Blanchard, James Pollock, and Abraham R. McIlvaine of Pennsylvania; and Nathan Sargent of Vermont, the House sergeant at arms. Known as the "Abolition House," Mrs. Sprigg's establishment is thought to have been part of the Underground Railroad, the informal network associated with figures such as Harriet Tubman who helped arrange escapes for the enslaved. Antislavery sentiment, then, was part of the air Lincoln was breathing at home in Washington.

Breakfast was served at eight at Mrs. Sprigg's. Afterward Lincoln would go to the Capitol, returning for dinner at three P.M. To reach the House of Representatives, Lincoln would walk out of Mrs. Sprigg's house, cross First Street, traverse the park, and climb the Capitol steps on the East Front. There were pedestals along the ascent, but in Lincoln's day only one statue was in place: one of Christopher Columbus. Representations of Peace and War flanked the east doors to the Rotunda, where the grand paintings of John Trumbull had hung since 1826. The Hall of the House (now Statuary Hall) was to the left of the Rotunda. Lincoln's desk, No. 191, was in the farthest row from the Speaker's raised platform.

A statue of Clio, the Muse of History, presided over the room. Twenty-two pillars encircled the chamber; they had been quarried by enslaved laborers near Point of Rocks in Maryland. There was a visitors' gallery, but those who came to the hall—as well as members themselves—had trouble hearing what was said. "The confusion and noise of the House of Representatives is wearying, you can have no conception of it," the wife of a congressman from New York wrote; "I never saw a district school dismissed at noon so rude and noisy."

Lincoln was unintimidated by the capital; like him, many of his colleagues were, in Henry Clay's term, "self-made." "The political arena is filled with those who plunge into it from the very depths of society," Alexander Mackay observed. Politics and governance gave "them a shorter road to consideration than that which they would have to pursue in the accumulation of property."

In his annual message, President Polk had accused Mexico of "invading the territory of the State of Texas, striking the first blow, and shedding the blood of our citizens on our own soil." It was widely believed, particularly among Whigs like Lincoln, that the president, intent on war, had misled the United States. On Wednesday, January 12, 1848, Lincoln delivered a forty-five-minute speech on the justice of the conflict. It was true, he allowed, that "any people anywhere, being inclined and having the power, have the *right* to rise up, and shake off the existing government, and form a new one that suits them better. This is a most valuable—a most sacred right—a right, which we hope and believe, is to liberate the world." Standing in the House chamber, he said he was not here to debate that. Asserting that Polk had misled the public by going to war after claiming that American blood had been spilled on American territory, Lincoln said that he wanted to know "whether the particular spot of soil on which the blood of our *citizens* was so shed, was, or was not, *our own soil*, at that time."

Worried that observers back home thought his position unpatriotic—his resolutions were dismissed, in an allusion to his "spot" critique, as "spotty"—Lincoln wrote to Herndon to explain that "This vote has nothing to do in determining my votes on the questions of supplies. I have always intended, and still intend, to vote supplies." Lincoln underscored that he was defending a fundamental constitutional principle on war making. "Allow the President to invade a neighboring nation, whenever *he* shall deem it necessary to repel an invasion, and you allow him to do so, *whenever he may choose to say* he deems it necessary for such purpose—and you allow him to make war at pleasure."

Lincoln's demands of the president were eloquent and impassioned. "Let him answer, fully, fairly, and candidly," Lincoln said of Polk. "Let him answer with *facts*, and not with arguments. Let him remember he sits where Washington sat, and so remembering let him answer, as Washington would answer. As a nation *should* not, and the Almighty *will* not, be evaded, so let him attempt no evasion—no equivocation." The appeal to George Washington's memory was of a piece with the Lincoln conviction that the Founders held a sacred place in American life and that the present could profit from their example. "Their *all* was staked upon" the American experiment, Lincoln had said in 1838, and "their destiny was *inseparably* linked with it. . . . If they succeeded, they were to be immortalized. . . . If they failed, they were to be called knaves and fools, and fanatics for a fleeting hour; then to sink and be forgotten." In 1842, in his address to the temperance society in Springfield, Lincoln had said, "Washington is the mightiest name of earth—*long since* mightiest in the cause of civil liberty." The Founders, Lincoln believed, were "iron men."

Lincoln served in the House with John Quincy Adams, the personification of the nation's story.

Lincoln was in the Capitol when John Quincy Adams, one of the last living monuments of the Revolutionary era, collapsed and died. On Monday, February 21, 1848, the Speaker of the House, Robert C. Winthrop of Massachusetts, was cut off in midsentence when the aged Congressman Adams of the Twelfth District of Massachusetts, the sixth president of the United States, "was observed to be sinking from his seat in what appeared to be the agonies of death."

The son of the second president, John Quincy Adams embodied the national history that Lincoln had read of by firelight on the frontier. The seven-year-old Adams had watched the Battle of Bunker Hill. In 1781, at the age of fourteen, he had traveled to Russia as secretary to the diplomat Francis Dana. Defeated for a second presidential term by Andrew Jackson in 1828, Adams had told his diary, "The sun of my political life sets in the deepest gloom." Yet he could not stay out of the political fray that had been his métier for a lifetime, and Adams won election to the House of Representatives in 1830. Over the next decade and a half, Adams would become a persistent antislavery voice in the debate he had once dismissed as the "Slave and Abolition whirligig." Southerners attacked him as "the madman from Massachusetts." To his admirers he was "Old Man Eloquent."

On the floor of the chamber where young Lincoln also sat, the eighty-year-old Adams reached to his right and slouched to his left. "Mr. Adams is dying!" an observer called out. Adams was carried to Speaker Winthrop's office. "This is the end of earth," Adams said as the light faded, "but I am composed." Two days later, at seven thirty on the evening of Wednesday, February 23, 1848, Adams died.

Congressman Lincoln was appointed to the committee to "superintend the funeral solemnities" in the Capitol for the former president. The old man's desk was covered in mourning drapery. At the service on Saturday the twenty-sixth, the House chaplain read from the Book of Job: "And thine age shall be clearer than the noonday: thou shalt shine forth, thou shalt be as the morning." It was, President Polk observed, "a splendid pageant."

Slavery, which had consumed John Quincy Adams's last years, pervaded Lincoln's term in Congress. This "black question," Senator Thomas Hart Benton of Missouri complained, "rises forever on the table. It is like the plague of frogs—everywhere." Slavery, slavery, slavery—there seemed no other topic.

CHAPTER SEVEN

We Have Got to Deal with This Slavery Question

The true rule, in determining to embrace, or reject anything, is not whether it have *any* evil in it; but whether it have more of evil, than of good.
—ABRAHAM LINCOLN, 1848

He has a very tall and thin figure, with an intellectual face, showing a searching mind, and a cool judgment.
—*The Boston Advertiser,* on the Lincoln of 1848

THE CONTRASTS OF AMERICAN LIFE were on display within the Capitol itself. Entering the Senate balcony one day, the Scottish writer Alexander Mackay saw "an aged negro, his hair partially whitened with years, and his fingers crooked with toil" on the staircase off the gallery. "The ceiling of the chamber was visible to him, and the voices of the speakers came audibly from within," Mackay recalled. "I listened and recognized the tones of one of the representatives of Virginia, the great breeder of slaves, dogmatizing upon abstract rights and constitutional privileges.... To think that such words should fall upon such ears; the freeman speaking, the slave listening, and all within the very sanctuary of the constitution."

Lincoln's antislavery sympathies had been evident since his protest in the Illinois legislature nearly a dozen years before. During the congressional campaign against Peter Cartwright, Lincoln had impressed a delegation of antislavery advocates. The callers, a contemporary recalled, were "so well pleased with what he said on the subject that we advised that our anti-slavery friend[s] throughout the district should cast their vote for Mr. Lincoln: which was generally done."

As a congressman, Lincoln voted in favor of the Wilmot Proviso, the

1846 proposal, authored by David Wilmot of Pennsylvania, banning slavery from any territory obtained from Mexico. The legislation failed to become law, but Lincoln was a consistent supporter. "I think I may venture to say," Lincoln recalled, "I voted for it at least forty times." A reaction to the annexation of Texas and the Mexican Cession, the Wilmot Proviso illuminated a widening chasm on slavery, if not on race, for the country was dominated by white prejudice. John C. Calhoun's arguments for slavery as "a good—a positive good" had taken hold in slaveholding circles. Antislavery legislators saw Calhoun, whom many white Southerners revered as the sage of Fort Hill, South Carolina, as the tribune of white Southern implacability.

The issue of slavery extension suffused not just life in the Capitol but life at Mrs. Sprigg's. "The Wilmot Proviso was the topic of frequent conversation and the occasion of very many angry controversies," recalled Samuel Clagett Busey, a fellow boarder. Some of the antislavery congressmen were more combative than others. John Dickey, for instance, was said to be "a very offensive man in manner and conversation, and seemed to take special pleasure in ventilating his opinions and provoking unpleasant discussions with ... [those] who held adverse opinions on the Wilmot Proviso."

Lincoln was subtler—and better company. He "may have been as radical [but] ... was so discreet in giving expression to his convictions on the slavery question as to avoid giving offence to anybody, and was so conciliatory as to create the impression, even among the proslavery advocates, that he did not wish to introduce or discuss subjects that would provoke a controversy," Busey recalled. "When such conversa-

The abolitionist Harriet Tubman, a key figure in the Underground Railroad. Lincoln's boardinghouse in Washington is thought to have been part of the network devoted to helping enslaved people escape to freedom.

tion would threaten angry or even unpleasant contention, he would interrupt it by interposing some anecdote, thus diverting it into a hearty and general laugh, and so completely disarrange the tenor of the discussion that the parties engaged would either separate in good humor or continue conversation free from discord." It was a useful skill, honed in the courtrooms and taverns of Illinois, brought to the seat of American power.

On Tuesday, December 21, 1847—not yet a month after his arrival in the capital—Lincoln stood with abolitionists to support the acceptance of antislavery petitions from the District of Columbia.* He voted the same principle—that refusing to consider such petitions was wrong—on two other occasions that month, declining to "table," or ignore, antislavery pleas from Indiana and from Philadelphia.

Yet he was not entirely consistent. He did oppose an antislavery resolution of Representative Amos Tuck of New Hampshire. And in mid-January 1848, the evils of slave catching—the hunting down of fugitives from enslavement—had come within the walls of the house where Lincoln lived. A Black man who worked for Mrs. Sprigg, Henry Wilson, was only $60 away from buying his liberty when his owner decided to seize him and bring him back into bondage. Three men reportedly "gagged" Wilson, "placed him in irons, and, with loaded pistols, forced him into one of the slave prisons" in the capital.

While Lincoln said nothing publicly, Joshua Giddings went to the House floor to call for a committee to explore "the propriety of repealing such acts of Congress as sustain or authorize the slave trade in this District, or to remove the seat of Government to some free State." The resolution created chaos in the House chamber. "The Speaker was much troubled to preserve order," a journalist noted, "having frequently to rap with his hammer and call the House to order in an imperative manner." Though he took no part in the debate, Lincoln voted in support of the House's taking up Giddings's resolution—a motion that lost. Giddings organized the raising of a fund to help secure Wilson's freedom.

A few months later, in mid-April 1848, a sailor and abolitionist, Daniel Drayton, and Edward Sayres, the captain of the schooner *Pearl*,

---

* The proslavery gag rule had been repealed in 1844, but the House could still choose not to accept abolitionist petitions.

set off from the Seventh Street wharf in Washington with seventy or so enslaved people who were seeking freedom farther north. The *Pearl* was captured on the Potomac. The enslaved were returned to Washington and were imprisoned while a proslavery "lawless mob" attacked the office of *The National Era,* a Washington abolitionist newspaper.

On Capitol Hill, the *Pearl* affair roiled the Congress. "History will record the fact that . . . *we,* the members of this House, at this age of light and knowledge, and of civil liberty, maintain and keep in force a law for selling fathers and children, mothers and tender babies," Giddings said. The debate opened with a Giddings resolution to investigate the use of a jail within the Federal City to incarcerate those fleeing bondage. Such detention, Giddings said, was "derogatory to our National Character, incompatible with the duty of a civilized and Christian people, and unworthy of being sustained by an American Congress." The storm continued when Representative John Palfrey of Massachusetts used Giddings's exposure to danger during the episode—Giddings had gone to the jail and been harassed by the proslavery mob—to ask whether federal lawmakers were sufficiently protected from violence. In the House, the Giddings-Palfrey arguments were seen as abolitionist extremism, and Lincoln voted with the proslavery majority to move on.

In August 1848, Lincoln cast an antislavery vote against a bill concerning the organization of the Oregon Territory that would have extended the Missouri Compromise line to the Pacific, authorizing slavery south of the 36° 30′ latitude. The measure was defeated, and Lincoln backed an Oregon-specific bill that banned slavery in the language of the Northwest Ordinance. In character, however, he soon declined to support calls to end slavery in the national capital without compensation for slave owners. George W. Julian, Giddings's son-in-law, observed that Congressman Lincoln was "a moderate . . . man"—a man whose "anti-slavery education had scarcely begun."

In the 1848 presidential race among the Whigs' Zachary Taylor, the Democrats' Lewis Cass, and Martin Van Buren, who was the nominee of the new antislavery Free Soil Party, Lincoln took his rhetoric on the road. In New England to campaign for the Whig ticket in the fall, he impressed his audiences. "He has a very tall and thin figure, with an intellectual face, showing a searching mind, and a cool judgment," the

Boston Advertiser wrote. "He spoke in a clear and cool, and very eloquent manner, for an hour and a half, carrying the audience with him in his able arguments and brilliant illustrations."

He was moving in grand circles. "I had been chosen to Congress then from the wild West," Lincoln recalled, "and with hayseed in my hair I went to Massachusetts, the most cultured State in the Union, to take a few lessons in deportment." After a memorable dinner hosted by a distant cousin from the Hingham line, former Massachusetts governor Levi Lincoln, on Wednesday, September 13, 1848, Congressman Lincoln "remarked upon the beauty of the china, the fineness of the silverware and the richness of all the table appointments, and spoke of the company of distinguished and thoroughly educated men whom he met there in the animated, free and intimate conversation inspired by such an accomplished host as Governor Lincoln."

In Boston on Friday, September 22, he shared a platform with William H. Seward at the Tremont Temple, a Greek Revival former theater now serving as home to a Baptist congregation. Faneuil Hall was unavailable because of a horticultural exhibit, and the Tremont postponed a scheduled lecture about—and showing of—Rembrandt Peale's enormous painting *The Court of Death* to host the political meeting.

Seward's speech was the main event. Born in 1801, a lion of New York politics, he was firmly antislavery. On stage with Lincoln, Seward said that he "believed in the force of moral power, and . . . believed that the time would come, and that too in his day, when the free people would free the slaves in this country. This is to be accomplished by moral force." Seward, however, was a practical man. "It was to be done without injustice," he added; "it was to be done by paying a full remuneration for so great a blessing." On the day after their joint appearance, Lincoln reportedly told Seward: "I have been thinking about what you said in your speech. I reckon you are right. We have got to deal with this slavery question, and got to give more attention to it hereafter than we have been doing."

Mary Lincoln had taken the children back to Lexington in the spring of 1848. The Lincolns' marriage was rarely placid. "Lincoln & his wife got along tolerably well, unless Mrs L got the devil in her: Lincoln paid no attention—would pick up one of his Children & walked off—would laugh at her—pay no Earthly attention to her when in that wild furious Condition," the Lincolns' Illinois neighbor James

Gourley recalled. "I don't think that Mrs Lincoln was as bad a woman as She is represented: She was a good friend of mine. She always Said that if her husband had stayed at home as he ought to, that She could love him better." Though Mary liked the bustle of Washington, she was underwhelmed by boardinghouse life. With her husband consumed by business on the floor—and by telling jokes to the Capitol crowd in the little House post office, where he whiled away some time—she decided to visit her family in Kentucky.

He missed her and the children. "In this troublesome world, we are never quite satisfied," Lincoln wrote to Mary in April 1848. "When you were here, I thought you hindered me some in attending to business; but now, having nothing but business—no variety—it has grown exceedingly tasteless to me. I hate to sit down and direct documents, and I hate to stay in this old room by myself. You know I told you in last Sunday's letter, I was going to make a little speech during the week; but the week has passed away without my getting a chance to do so; and now my interest in the subject has passed away too." His fondness for the boys was evident. "I went yesterday to hunt the little plaid stockings, as you wished," he wrote, "but found that McKnight has quit business, and Allen had not a single pair of the description you give, and only one plaid pair of any sort that I thought would fit 'Eddy's dear little feet.' I have a notion to make another trial to-morrow morning."

He knew she could be too much for others (and often for himself), but he had made his bargain. He would keep it. "All the house—or rather, all with whom you were on decided good terms—send their love to you," he told her of Mrs. Sprigg's. "The others say nothing." An Illinois acquaintance, Turner R. King, recalled, "Lincoln's wife was a hellion—a she devil—vexed—& harrowed the soul out of that good man . . . drove him from home &c—often & often."

Whatever the world thought, Lincoln was solicitous. "And you are entirely free from head-ache?" he asked Mary. "That is good—good—considering it is the first spring you have been free from it since we were acquainted. I am afraid you will get so well, and fat, and young, as to be wanting to marry again. . . . Don't let the blessed fellows forget father." Mary took care to reassure him on this score. "Even E[ddy]'s eyes brighten at the mention of your name," Mary told her husband.

Writing to him on a warm late spring Saturday from Buena Vista, the Todd retreat near Lexington, Mary, refreshing herself with ice cream, filled him in on family news. "Bobby" had found a kitten that day and brought it indoors, where "Eddy" made much of it. The younger child's "*tenderness*, broke forth," Mary said, and he "made them bring it *water*, fed it with bread himself, with his *own dear hands*, he was a delighted creature over it." (The "them" who fetched the water were presumably enslaved people owned by the Todds.) No fan of cats, Mary's stepmother ordered, "in a very unfeeling manner," that the creature be taken outdoors. Eddy's resulting cries were "long & loud," but Mrs. Todd prevailed. "Tis unusual for her *now a days* to do anything quite so striking," Mary confided to Lincoln. "She is very obliging & accommodating"—perhaps Lincoln's ascent in the political world helped with that—though Mary was certain of this much: "If she thought any of us were on her hands again, I believe she would be *worse* than ever."

On Monday, June 12, 1848, he wrote to her from his desk in the House chamber. Worn out from his journey the day before from the Whig convention in Philadelphia that nominated Zachary Taylor for president and Millard Fillmore for vice president, Lincoln apologized for waiting overnight to reply. "I was so tired and sleepy, having ridden all night, that I could not answer . . . til to-day," he told her. She wanted to come back to Washington, and he responded flirtatiously.

"The leading matter in your letter, is your wish to return to this side of the Mountains," Lincoln wrote. "Will you be a *good girl* in all things, if I consent? Then come along, and that as *soon* as possible. Having got the idea in my head, I shall be impatient till I see you."

Sexual allusions were not foreign to the Lincolns—a suggestion that their physical connection formed a bond that neighbors startled by Mrs. Lincoln's temper could not appreciate. "The music in the Capitol grounds on Saturdays, or, rather, the interest in it, is dwindling down to nothing," Lincoln wrote to Mary in early July. "Yesterday evening the attendance was rather thin." But not wholly thin: A pair of presumed prostitutes, "whose peculiarities were the wearing of black fur bonnets, and never being seen in close company with other ladies," were there. "One of them was attended by their brother, and the other had a member of Congress in tow. He went home with her; and if I were to guess, I would say, he went away a somewhat altered man—most likely in his pockets, and in some other particular," Lincoln said. He closed warmly: "Father expected to see you all sooner; but let it pass; stay as long as you please, and come when you please. Kiss and love the dear rascals."

Mary could parry on sexual matters, too. Alluding to her old beau Edwin Webb, whom she had rejected for Lincoln, she wrote, "*Patty Webb's* school in S[helbyville] closes the first of July, I expect *Mr Webb* will come on for her," Mary wrote. "I must go down about that time & carry on quite a flirtation, you know *we* always had a *penchant* that way." By midsummer, Mary and the boys had returned to Mrs. Sprigg's.

Lincoln spent the winter of 1848–49 on the slavery question in Washington itself. He saw the truth in a remark of Horace Mann's: "This District is the common property of the nation. . . . While slaves exist in it, therefore, it can be charged upon the North that they uphold slavery." On Monday, January 8, 1849, Joshua Giddings wrote in his diary, "Mr. Dickey [of Pennsylvania] . . . and Mr. Lincoln of Illinois were busy preparing resolutions to abolish slavery in the D[istrict of] C[olumbia] this morning."

On Wednesday, January 10, Lincoln rose to offer "an act to abolish slavery in the District of Columbia, by the consent of the free white people of said District, and with compensation to owners." It was a gradualist plan, rife with caveats. Enslaved people currently in the District could be freed only if their owners applied for, and accepted, compensation amounting to the "full value of his or her slave," a figure that would be determined by a board—which was to meet on the first Monday of each month—comprised of the president of the United States and the secretaries of state and of the Treasury. Once compensation was assessed and paid, the enslaved would be "forthwith and forever free."

Federal officials who were slave owners could still bring enslaved people into the District while on "public business," and the municipal authorities were "required to provide active and efficient means to arrest, and deliver up to their owners, all fugitive slaves escaping into said District." To ratify or reject the plan, Lincoln called for a referendum of "every free white male citizen" who had lived in the District for the preceding year. Should a majority approve, the president himself would be compelled to issue a proclamation giving the law "full force and effect."

Lincoln told the House that he was "authorized to say, that of about fifteen of the leading citizens of the District of Columbia to whom this proposition had been submitted, there was not one but who approved of the adoption of such a proposition."

"Who are they?" came the cries in the chamber. "Give us their names!" Lincoln, it was reported, said nothing in reply. And there was an end to it. The effort failed.

Lincoln thought he had prepared the ground for the legislation. He had called on the mayor of Washington, William Seaton, who also owned the *National Intelligencer* newspaper, "and others whom I thought best acquainted with the sentiments of the people, to ascertain if a bill such as I proposed would be endorsed by them," Lincoln recalled. "Being informed that it would meet with their hearty approbation I gave notice in Congress that I should introduce a Bill. Subsequently I learned that many leading southern members of Congress, had been to see the Mayor, and the others who favored my Bill and had drawn them over to their way of thinking. Finding that I was abandoned by my former backers and having little personal influence, I *dropped* the matter knowing that it was useless to prosecute the business at that time."

Purists were unimpressed in any event. In the abolitionist world, Wendell Phillips would dismiss the 1849 effort as "no credit to any man, being one of the poorest and most confused specimens of pro-slavery compromise." There was more from Phillips, who would call Lincoln "the Slave-Hound of Illinois" for the bill's provisions on fugitive slaves.

Lincoln's emphasis on compromise and compensation would recur. "Our whole mess remained in the dining-room after tea, and conversed upon the subject of Mr. Lincoln's bill to abolish slavery," Giddings wrote on Thursday, January 11. "It was approved by all; I believe it as good a bill as we could get at this time, and am willing to pay for slaves in order to save them from the Southern market." The press took note as well. "He is a strong but judicious enemy to Slavery," the *New York Tribune* wrote after the session, "and his efforts are usually very practical, if not always successful." Looking back on the legislation in 1860, Lincoln told an interviewer, "My mind has been in process of education since that time. [I] do not know that I would now approve of the Bill, but in the main, *think* that I would." Like his 1837 protest in Illinois, his 1849 proposal in Congress was a signpost on a longer journey—though no one knew where, exactly, that journey might end.

According to Whig custom in his district, Lincoln did not seek re-election to the House. The previous fall he had campaigned hard for General Taylor, who won 47.3 percent of the popular vote to Cass's 42.5 percent and Van Buren's 10.1 percent, with a margin of 163–127 in the

Electoral College. Van Buren's Free Soilers carried no state outright, but the party's performance far outpaced the Liberty Party's in previous elections, and the Free Soilers were instrumental in electing a number of legislators, including Salmon P. Chase, who won a Senate seat from Ohio on the party's ticket.

After the 1848 elections, Lincoln unsuccessfully lobbied to become commissioner of the General Land Office, a highly compensated federal appointment. "In these days of Cabinet making, we out West are awake as well as others," he wrote in February. To Duff Green, Lincoln implored, "Now cannot you get the ear of Gen. Taylor?" He remembered, bitterly, "almost sweating blood to have Genl. Taylor nominated." Making a case for his suitability in terms of geography within the state, Lincoln planned to ask Taylor, "I am in the center. Is the center nothing?—that center which alone has ever given you a Whig representative?" It was to no avail.

On the evening of Taylor's swearing-in as the twelfth president, Lincoln stayed at the inaugural ball until the wee hours. "When we went to the cloak and hat room," his friend E. B. Washburne wrote, "Mr. Lincoln . . . was unable to find his hat . . . and after an hour . . . started off bareheaded for his lodgings." It had been that kind of season. And it got a bit worse than a lost hat: Two days later, Lincoln was admitted to the bar of the U.S. Supreme Court to argue a case over procedure involving Illinois. Within a week the justices issued their ruling. Lincoln had lost.

He was ready to go, setting off for Springfield on Tuesday, March 20. In due course, the new Taylor administration offered Lincoln first the secretaryship of the Oregon Territory, which he declined, and then the territorial governorship, which he considered. Lincoln asked John T. Stuart what he thought of the Oregon possibility. Stuart was in favor, observing that Lincoln "could go out there and in all likelihood come back from there as a Senator when the state was admitted." It was tempting, and "Mr. Lincoln finally made up his mind that he would accept the place if Mary would consent to go," Stuart recalled to John G. Nicolay. "But Mary would not consent to go out there." Lincoln would instead practice law "with greater earnestness than ever before."

What had Lincoln learned in his two years in the national capital? At Mrs. Sprigg's table with Joshua Giddings and their fellow boarders, he had developed a deepening awareness of the slavery issue.

On the House floor and in the byways of the Capitol, he had seen and gotten to know the Republic's good and great—as well as its cynics and its cranks—and likely realized that human nature is constant across geography and gradations of power. On the road for Taylor, he had experienced the mechanics of a presidential campaign in different regions. He'd always understood politics as a matter of compromise rather than of conquest, and his sense of statecraft was keener than ever.

"The true rule, in determining to embrace, or reject anything, is not whether it have *any* evil in it; but whether it have more of evil, than of good," Lincoln had told the House. "There are few things *wholly* evil, or *wholly* good. Almost everything, especially of governmental policy, is an inseparable compound of the two; so that our best judgment of the preponderance between them is continually demanded."

That, Lincoln understood, was the moral work of politics: to make the good outweigh the bad.

CHAPTER EIGHT

The Conscience of the Nation Must Be Roused

RIGHT IS OF NO SEX—TRUTH IS OF NO COLOR—GOD IS
THE FATHER OF US ALL, AND ALL WE ARE BRETHREN.
—Motto of Frederick Douglass's *North Star* newspaper

The spirit of our age is democracy. All for the people, and all
by the people. Nothing about the people without the people.
—Hungarian reformer LOUIS KOSSUTH, 1852

THOUGH FAR FROM THE PINNACLE OF POWER, Lincoln was thinking widely and deeply—even lyrically. He once stopped on a trip home to take in Niagara Falls—a visit that prompted a philosophic, if unfinished, essay. Niagara's wonder, Lincoln wrote, lay in its "power to excite reflection, and emotion. It calls up the indefinite past. When Columbus first sought this continent—when Christ suffered on the cross—when Moses led Israel through the Red-Sea—nay, even, when Adam first came from the hand of his Maker—then as now, Niagara was roaring here. . . . In that long—long time, never still for a single moment. Never dried, never froze, never slept, never rested," The reflections ended not with a period, but with that comma.

Lincoln may as well have been describing history itself. A paraphrase of Psalm 90 he knew from the hymns of Isaac Watts touches on the same themes:

> *Time, like an ever-rolling stream,*
> *Bears all its sons away;*
> *They fly, forgotten, as a dream*
> *Dies at the opening day.*

Lincoln aimed not to be forgotten. He knew it wouldn't be easy, or even possible. "With *me,* the race of ambition has been a failure—a flat failure," he would write in 1856. Yet he endured. In the eleven years between his service in Congress and his bid for the presidency in 1860, Lincoln considered the works of Theodore Parker and Ralph Waldo Emerson, engaged with the words of the Founders, and absorbed Euclidean geometry. He combined the pursuits in applying Euclid's notion of the existence of "axioms," or propositions that are self-evidently true, to the American promise of liberty. For Lincoln, the path to power in the present lay in mastering—and reinterpreting—the past as he explored ideas about power, faith, equality, and slavery.

His intellectual and political odyssey through the 1850s opened in gloom. The first day of summer in June 1849 found him in Washington, still seeking the commissionership of the General Land Office. On learning he had lost the appointment, Lincoln reportedly hurled himself on his boardinghouse bed and lay still for "an hour or more."

Back in Illinois, in small inns and taverns, trying cases, Lincoln took refuge in reading. His legs too long for the small beds of the era, his naked shinbones evident to his companions, he would pick up a volume of Shakespeare or Robert Burns and read by candlelight. Lincoln's fellow lawyers were impressed at his concentration as they "filled the air with our interminable snoring."

He had been pondering the best way of lawyering now that he was home again. In a set of "Notes for a Law Lecture," Lincoln had advised younger members of the bar to work hard ("The leading rule for the lawyer, as for the man of every other calling, is diligence"); to communicate clearly ("Extemporaneous speaking should be practiced and cultivated. It is the lawyer's avenue to the public. However able and faithful he may be in other respects, people are slow to bring him business if he cannot make a speech"); and to find common ground ("Discourage litigation. Persuade your neighbors to compromise whenever you can").

Lincoln practiced law for almost a quarter of a century. His cases included mundane rural disputes, fugitive slave cases, and corporate matters involving large railroad interests. Scholars from the Lincoln biographer Benjamin P. Thomas to Mark E. Steiner have seen Lincoln's legal years as "an educational process," as Thomas wrote, in which "he further developed his political astuteness, learning the thought-processes of the people." In 1847, Lincoln unsuccessfully represented a slave owner who tried to hold several enslaved people in bondage after bringing them from Kentucky to work on a property of the slave owner's in Illinois. Lincoln felt an ethical obligation to argue his client's case, reportedly remarking that "as a lawyer, he must represent and be faithful to those who counsel with and employ him." On another occasion he won an 1845 case defending "an abolitionist who had been charged with aiding fugitive slaves." His legal career was good training for politics and for governing. Lincoln learned how to marshal facts, frame arguments, and deploy precedents—all while knowing he had to convince the human tribunals of judges and juries.

He spent his days in his messy law office or on the road, riding circuit as his mind worked through the global and the universal as well as the parochial and the practical. The Hungarian patriot and reformer Louis Kossuth was touring America, and Lincoln, moved as so many were by the European revolutions of 1848, supported Kossuth's cause. "The spirit of our age is democracy," Kossuth declared. "All for the people, and all by the people. Nothing about the people without the people."

As a player in the Old World revolutions of 1848 that challenged inherited privilege, Hungary was top of mind in the first years of the 1850s. Americans thrilled to the struggle for democracy abroad, and Lincoln authored resolutions to be published and sent to Kossuth as well as to the Illinois congressional delegation. The American people, Lincoln's resolutions declared, "cannot remain silent" on democratic aspirations in other lands "without justifying an inference against our continued devotion to the principles of our free institutions"—implying that a failure to support democracy elsewhere undermined democracy at home and opened the country to the charge of hypocrisy.

Talk of democratic revolution took Lincoln back to the American exercise of that right. He had read one version of the Founding in Mason Weems's hagiographic *Life of Washington*, a book that owed as much to fantasy as to fact. A committee had been formed in the Second Continental Congress to draft a Declaration of Independence: Jefferson, Franklin, John Adams, Robert Livingston, and Roger Sherman. In Weems's telling, all agreed to write a separate draft. This did not happen; Jefferson did virtually all of the writing, and the others offered editorial comments.

Weems got the details wrong, but the young Lincoln, reading about the heroic events, could not have known that. It probably would not have mattered if he had. The tale was all. Jefferson was said to have asked to read his draft first—and history was made. According to Weems, Jefferson's version gave "such complete satisfaction, that none other was read." It was as though Moses had come down from Sinai with the tablets, only in this case the words were on parchment, not stone.

Lincoln was reading Jefferson in the 1850s, drawing on his imagery and sometimes quoting him directly. In his first inaugural address, Jefferson had included a poetic phrase that stayed in Lincoln's mind. The United States, Jefferson had said, was "the world's best hope." Lincoln used the same words in a eulogy for Henry Clay, who had died of tuberculosis in the summer of 1852 at the age of seventy-five. "Feeling, as he did, and as the truth surely is, that the world's best hope depended on the continued Union of these States, he was ever jealous of, and watchful for, whatever might have the slightest tendency to separate them," Lincoln said on Tuesday, July 6, 1852. His words on Clay, delivered in Springfield, were heartfelt. "With other men, to be defeated, was to be forgotten; but to him, defeat was but a trifling incident, neither changing him, or the world's estimate of him."

Politics was a cruel business; even the most successful experienced hours of suffering and of shadow. "The Presidency, even to the most experienced politicians, is no bed of roses; and Gen. Taylor like others, found thorns within it," Lincoln said in another eulogy, this one for Zachary Taylor, who had died in office in 1850. "No human being can fill that station and escape censure."

This realistic view of the price of power was reminiscent of one offered by Jefferson. In his first inaugural address, the third president had pleaded for forbearance: "I repair, then, fellow-citizens, to the post you have assigned me. . . . I have learnt to expect that it will rarely fall to the lot of imperfect man to retire from this station with the reputation and the favor which bring him into it." Like Jefferson, though, Lincoln was made for the public realm and believed the times required him. The American Revolution, Jefferson said, had been a "bold and doubtful election . . . for our country, between submission, or the sword." And Jefferson's contribution, in the beginning, had been to write the words that gave meaning to everything that followed—a task that would also one day fall to Lincoln.

"The principles of Jefferson are the definitions and axioms of free society," Lincoln said—chief among which was that all men were created equal. "All honor to Jefferson—to the man who, in the concrete pressure of a struggle for national independence by a single people, had the coolness, forecast, and capacity to introduce into a merely revolutionary document, an abstract truth, applicable to all men and all times, and so to embalm it there, that to-day, and in all coming days, it shall be a rebuke and a stumbling-block to the very harbingers of re-appearing tyranny and oppression."

Lincoln firmly believed this. "I have never had a feeling politically that did not spring from the sentiments embodied in the Declaration of Independence," he would remark at Independence Hall in 1861. "I have often pondered over the dangers which were incurred by the men who assembled here. . . . It was not the mere matter of the separation of the colonies from the mother land; but something in that Declaration giving liberty, not alone to the people of this country, but hope to the world for all future time." Everything—*everything*—came back to Jefferson: "All men are created equal."

The idea was deeply rooted in the Atlantic world. "No man . . . can be so stupid to deny that all men naturally were born free, being the image and resemblance of God himself," John Milton wrote in his 1649 *The Tenure of Kings and Magistrates*. In 1689, in his *Second Treatise*, John Locke wrote, "To understand political power right, and derive it from its original, we must consider what state all men are naturally in, and that is, a state of perfect freedom to order their actions, and dispose of their possessions and persons, as they think fit, within the bounds of the law of nature; without asking leave, or depending upon the will of any other man." Within a decade, Algernon Sidney, in his 1698 *Discourses Concerning Government*, expanded the thought by compressing it: "The Liberty of a People is the gift of God and Nature." In his first draft of the 1776 Virginia Declaration of Rights, George Mason wrote, "all men are born equally free and independent, and have certain inherent natural rights, of which they cannot, by any compact, deprive or divest their posterity; among which are, the enjoyment of life and liberty, with the means of acquiring and possessing property, and pursuing and obtaining happiness and safety." The next month, Jefferson would write his crisper version of the sentiment, the one adopted by the Second Continental Congress on Thursday, July 4, 1776.

Not that all were considered equal. The institution of slavery had been protected by the Constitution. There were antislavery elements: the 1808 abolition of the Atlantic slave trade and the document's failure to explicitly assert that there could be "property in man." And there had been the Northwest Ordinance of 1787. Still, the Founding era's concessions to the slave order had been numerous, notably the Constitution's three-fifths provision that gave white Southern slave owners disproportionate political power in Washington. And the federal consensus that the national government had no power to abolish slavery where it existed—a consensus long shared by Lincoln—enabled the slave order to maintain its grip on the lives and liberty of millions.

Lincoln argued, however, that the Founders' notion of equality gave the nation a goal to seek, an ideal to realize, a promise to fulfill. The Founders, Lincoln said in 1857, had deployed the Declaration as "a standard maxim for free society, which should be familiar to all, and revered by all; constantly looked to, constantly labored for, and even though never perfectly attained, constantly approximated, and thereby constantly spreading and deepening its influence, and augmenting the happiness and value of life to all people of all colors everywhere."

Yet until the Civil War years, Lincoln did not follow the logic of his argument about liberty to its just conclusion. If all men were created equal, then the distinction of color should not matter—*at all*. If one believed, as Lincoln said he did, that all men were created equal, then why were not all men, regardless of color, entitled to the ensuing Jeffersonian rights to life, liberty, the pursuit of happiness—and citizenship? If, as Lincoln argued, slavery should fall under the weight of the Declaration, then why not insist that egalitarianism rise in its place?

Lincoln's position—that the Declaration applied to all, but not all were to be treated equally by law and by custom—fell short of the egalitarian goals articulated by many abolitionists. The Founders, he said, "meant simply to declare the *right*, so that the *enforcement* of it might follow as fast as circumstances should permit. . . . The assertion that 'all men are created equal' . . . was placed in the Declaration . . . for future use." For Black Americans, assurances about the future were of little use in the present. Emancipation was not inevitable, nor was racism merely incidental to the American experience. The antislavery tradition did make progress possible, but only in concert with decades of activism and agitation as well as four years of war.

"The hypocrisy of the nation must be exposed,"
said Frederick Douglass, who had been born
into slavery in Maryland.

Lincoln died as he brought about a nation that would ratify the Thirteenth and Fourteenth Amendments to abolish slavery and make citizenship for Black Americans a federal constitutional right. In his lifetime, however, he would never fully put into practice the principles summed up in the motto of a newspaper founded in Rochester, New York, in 1847: RIGHT IS OF NO SEX—TRUTH IS OF NO COLOR— GOD IS THE FATHER OF US ALL, AND ALL WE ARE BRETHREN.

That paper, *The North Star*, was edited by Frederick Douglass and, initially, Martin R. Delany. Born into enslavement in Maryland in 1818, Douglass had escaped to freedom, published a widely read memoir, *Narrative of the Life of Frederick Douglass, an American Slave,* and become an eloquent advocate of abolition and of racial equality. "This, to you, is what the Passover was to the emancipated people of God," Douglass said in an 1852 Fourth of July oration in Rochester, New York, directing his words to white Americans. "The sunlight that brought life and healing to you, has brought stripes and death to me," he said. "This Fourth of July is *yours*, not *mine. You* may rejoice, *I* must mourn." It profited no one, Douglass argued, to mince words. "The feeling of the nation must be quickened; the conscience of the nation must be roused; the propriety of the nation must be startled; the hypocrisy of the nation must be exposed; and its crimes against God and man must be proclaimed and denounced."

For all this, Douglass worked in hope as he combated fear. "There are forces in operation which must inevitably work the downfall of slavery," he said in Rochester. "While drawing encouragement from the 'Declaration of Independence,' the great principles it contains, and the genius of American Institutions, my spirit is also cheered by the obvious tendencies of the age." Technology, literacy, and the emergence of a common public square had all contributed to the movement for abolition. "Nations do not now stand in the same relation to each other that they did ages ago," Douglass said, continuing:

> No nation can now shut itself up from the surrounding world and trot round in the same old path of its fathers without interference. The time was when such could be done. Long established customs of hurtful character could formerly fence themselves in, and do their evil work with social impunity. Knowledge was then confined and enjoyed by the privileged few, and the multitude walked on in mental darkness. But a change has now come over the affairs of mankind. Walled cities and empires have become unfashionable. The arm of commerce has borne away the gates of the strong city. Intelligence is penetrating the darkest corners of the globe. It makes its pathway over and under the sea, as well as on the earth. Wind, steam, and lightning are its chartered agents. Oceans no longer divide, but link nations together.

Justice, reason, and the logic of American ideals were all with Douglass and his allies. Voices like Douglass's sought to prick the conscience and show the way—and Douglass knew this was the work not of a day but of an era. The nation's common texts—the Bible and the Declaration—offered a path forward, though it was a path that many white Americans, including Abraham Lincoln, now practicing law in Illinois, had not yet traveled.

It was a dark time at the Lincolns' home on Eighth and Jackson. In late 1849, little Eddy Lincoln, aged three, fell ill. "He was sick fifty-two days," Lincoln recalled. Inexorably declining, the child died, likely of pulmonary tuberculosis, on the cold morning of Friday, February 1, 1850. Mary, it was recalled, "lay prostrated, stunned, turning away from food, completely unable to meet this disaster." She would never fully recover. "I grieve to say," Mary wrote three years afterward, "that even at this day I do not feel sufficiently submissive to our loss." Lincoln tried to comfort her, saying, gently, "Eat, Mary, for we must live."

His own grief was profound. On returning from Eddy's burial in Hutchinson's Cemetery (likely in lot 490, for which Lincoln paid $15) presided over by the Reverend James Smith, the pastor of Springfield's First Presbyterian Church, Lincoln "came into the room and picked up a card which lay on the table," an observer recalled. "It was the last prescription written by the doctor for the child. He looked at it—then threw it from him and bursting into tears left the room."

The funeral took place on Saturday, February 2. On the following Thursday, the *Illinois Journal* published, "By Request," a poem entitled "Little Eddie." Often thought to have been composed by one of the Lincolns, the verses were in fact authored by Ethel Grey (a pseudonym for the poet Mary E. Chamberlain) of St. Louis. They were published in Springfield in the wake of the Lincoln child's death:

> *Eddie, meet blossom of heavenly love,*
> *Dwells in the spirit-world above.*
> *Angel boy—fare thee well, farewell*
> *Sweet Eddie, we bid thee adieu!*
> *Affection's wail cannot reach thee now,*
> *Deep though it be, and true.*
> *Bright is the home to him now given,*
> *For "of such is the kingdom of Heaven."*

"We miss him very much," Lincoln wrote in late February. Lincoln and Mary found comfort with each other. Ten and a half months after Eddy's death, on Saturday, December 21, 1850, the Lincolns' third child, William Wallace Lincoln, or "Willie," was born, which puts his likely conception within ten weeks of his brother's death.

Thomas Lincoln, meanwhile, was dying. The son's alienation from the father was illustrated by Lincoln's failure to reply to not one but two letters on the subject from a stepbrother, John D. Johnston. He had not responded, he explained, "because it appeared to me I could write nothing which could do any good." Dispassionately, Lincoln went on: "You already know I desire that neither Father or Mother shall be in want of any comfort either in health or sickness while they live; and

I feel sure you have not failed to use my name, if necessary, to procure a doctor, or anything else for Father in his present sickness. My business is such that I could hardly leave home now, if it were not, as it is, that my own wife is sick-abed. (It is a case of baby-sickness, and I suppose is not dangerous.)"

The breach between father and son never healed. Why Lincoln felt so strongly about his father remains a mystery. If Lincoln believed the rumors that he was not Thomas's biological son, he may have thought Thomas weak, even contemptible. It is possible, too, that Lincoln saw Thomas's insistence on his son's working at manual labor as a form of slavery—the term was one Lincoln used to describe not only the chattel system in the South but any form of powerless servitude—and therefore viewed his father as a tyrannical master from whom he had escaped. Even as an adult, after a visit to Indiana to campaign for Clay for president, Lincoln described the scene of his upbringing "as unpoetical as any spot of the earth." One suspects he was not just referring to the landscape.

"I sincerely hope Father may yet recover his health; but at all events tell him to remember to call upon, and confide in, our great, and good, and merciful Maker; who will not turn away from him in any extremity," Lincoln wrote to John Johnston. "He notes the fall of a sparrow, and numbers the hairs of our heads; and He will not forget the dying man, who puts his trust in Him. Say to him that if we could meet now, it is doubtful whether it would not be more painful than pleasant; but that if it be his lot to go now, he will soon have a joyous [meeting] with many loved ones gone before; and where [the rest] of us, through the help of God, hope ere-long [to join] them." Thomas Lincoln died on Friday, January 17, 1851, in Coles County, Illinois. His son did not attend the funeral.

The Christian language in Lincoln's letter came at a time when he was pondering traditional religion with some seriousness. Eddy's death had been a catalyst. After the boy's funeral, the Reverend James Smith had given Lincoln a copy of his own apologetic, *The Christian's Defense,* and later claimed, unconvincingly, that Lincoln had embraced orthodox Christianity. Lincoln's words to Johnston may have been in keeping with the son's political character of respecting his opponent's views. Thomas Lincoln was a Bible-believing Baptist, so Lincoln could have been reassuring his father from afar in terms he knew his father would welcome. In this light, Lincoln's letter was at least informed by generosity.

"Mr Lincoln," James Matheny said, "grew more . . . Contemplative—&c. as he grew older." Lincoln was always grappling with matters of faith and reason. "Mr Lincoln believed in God—and all the great substantial groundworks of Religion—Believed in the progress of man and of nations—He believed that nations like individuals were punished for their Sins—their violations of fundamental rights—&c.," Lincoln friend Isaac Cogdal recalled. "He was a Universalist tap root & all in faith and sentiment."

His views were fluid. "It is true," Lincoln had said in his campaign against Peter Cartwright in 1846, "that in early life I was inclined to believe in what I understand is called the 'Doctrine of Necessity'—that is, that the human mind is impelled to action, or held in rest by some power, over which the mind itself has no control; and I have sometimes (with one, two or three, but never publicly) tried to maintain this opinion in argument. The habit of arguing thus however, I have, entirely left off for more than five years."

He may have left off arguing the point because it undercut the work of his life. Lincoln sometimes seemed so resigned about human agency that he could sound nihilistic.* "What is to be will be," Mary Lincoln heard her husband say, "and no cares of ours can reverse the decree." Except that Lincoln *did* care. Herndon argued that Lincoln believed "the will to a very limited extent, in some fields of operation, was somewhat free." To want to change the world implies a conviction that the world is changeable. In an incisive discussion of these matters, the historian Richard Carwardine observed, "The fatalist and activist were thus fused in Lincoln."

According to Herndon, Lincoln thought that "all things were fixed, doomed one way or the other, from which there was no appeal." Yet as he grew older, Lincoln came to appreciate that individual efforts could affect the course of things. "That the Almighty does make use of human agencies and directly intervenes in human affairs, is one of the plainest statements of the Bible," Lincoln once said "I have had so many evi

---

* "In the most general sense," the historian Allen C. Guelzo observed, "the paradox of Lincoln's fatalism falls into a pattern that has reapppeared throughout modern Western history, and it arises from the peculiar tendency of determinists, from Oliver Cromwell to Karl Marx, to preach divine or material inevitability at one moment and then turn into the most avowed revolutionary activists at the next."

dences of his direction, so many instances when I have been controlled by some other power than my own will, that I cannot doubt that this power comes from above." The common term for the divine governance of the world was "providence," which literally means "seeing ahead," and to some the word did mean that everything was predestined.

In practice, to believe in the role of providence did not necessarily mean that one was passive. *Providence* might know the decision someone was to make—to turn left instead of right, and thus meet his doom; to go to this party instead of that one, and thus meet a mate; to seek office or not, and thus meet a historical moment—without that *person's* knowing in advance what that decision or its results would be. Even if actions, choices, and decisions were foreordained, the individual was still acting, choosing, and deciding. If one did not believe that—did not believe in the power of conscience and of character to reach a certain conclusion to conduct oneself in a certain way over and against another way—then one was hardly likely to run life's great race with the energy that Abraham Lincoln did. One would not, in all likelihood, *run* at all, for why bother? If what will be will be, then what was the imperative to do more than seek the barest necessities of life, and wait for fate to do the rest?

Lincoln's darker musings about fate and fatalism were doubtless reflective of what he was thinking and how he was feeling when the world seemed unmanageable. One would have to be particularly unperceptive—and Abraham Lincoln was among the most perceptive of men—not to wonder at times whether history could be bent or justice achieved. Despite his doubts, he demonstrated a belief in the role individuals could play in the world. Skeptical about human agency, Lincoln was nevertheless determined to be one of history's greatest human agents.

CHAPTER NINE

To Understand the Moral Universe

We know that we are right; we are sure to prevail. But in
times present and future, as in times past, we need heroism,
self-denial, a continual watchfulness, and an industry
which never tires.

—THEODORE PARKER, 1850

We were thunderstruck and stunned; and we reeled and fell
in utter confusion. But we rose each fighting, grasping
whatever [we] could first reach—a scythe—a pitchfork—a
chopping axe, or a butcher's cleaver.

—ABRAHAM LINCOLN, on the 1854 repeal of
the Missouri Compromise

LINCOLN WAS A REPRESENTATIVE FIGURE in the struggle, as Alexander Pope had written in 1733, in an echo of John Milton, to "vindicate the ways of God to man." The middle of the nineteenth century—the era of Lincoln—was an age of doubt about familiar religious belief. People on both sides of the Atlantic sought to reconcile faith with modernity amid a new debate over the origins of life in the wake of the Scientific Revolution.

A Springfield acquaintance gave Lincoln a copy of Robert Chambers's 1844 *Vestiges of the Natural History of Creation,* which, William Herndon recalled, "interested [Lincoln] so much that he read it through." Initially published anonymously in Great Britain, *Vestiges* was an epochal work that fascinated popular, scientific, and theological audiences with its argument that the solar system and humankind were products of evolution. Prince Albert read the book aloud to Queen Victoria. On seeing a review, Alfred, Lord Tennyson immediately sent for a copy.

In distant Illinois, Lincoln was intrigued. As with Charles Darwin's *On the Origin of Species,* which appeared in 1859, Chambers's work gave the world new perspectives on reality. Progress and change were possible. The world need not remain static. The story was not finished, but unfolding. To borrow from the verses of Shakespeare that Lincoln carried around his judicial circuit, reading in snatches on stagecoaches and by candlelight amid his snoring legal brethren, it was a brave new world. Old certitudes were cracking, familiar truths unraveling. Like Lincoln, the poet Matthew Arnold was struggling with modernity and was inclined toward a tragic view of human nature. In "Dover Beach," Arnold wrote:

> *The Sea of Faith*
> *Was once, too, at the full, and round earth's shore*
> *Lay like the folds of a bright girdle furled.*
> *But now I only hear*
> *Its melancholy, long, withdrawing roar,*
> *Retreating, to the breath*
> *Of the night-wind, down the vast edges drear*
> *And naked shingles of the world.*
>
> *Ah, love, let us be true*
> *To one another! For the world, which seems*
> *To lie before us like a land of dreams,*
> *So various, so beautiful, so new,*
> *Hath really neither joy, nor love, nor light,*
> *Nor certitude, nor peace, nor help for pain;*
> *And we are here as on a darkling plain*
> *Swept with confused alarms of struggle and flight,*
> *Where ignorant armies clash by night.*

With Arnold, Lincoln worried, too, that the world had too little joy, love, and light. Yet the rising American politician did not retreat from the "darkling plain." Among the figures whom he read were John Stuart Mill and Francis Wayland. He also appears to have encountered Thomas Brown's *Lectures on the Philosophy of the Human Mind* and perhaps William Paley's *Principles of Moral and Political Philosophy*. Mill and Wayland wrote searchingly about human nature and about how society could be arranged, in Mill's phrase, to achieve the greatest good for the greatest number. As political economists, Mill and Wayland explored motive and self-interest, concepts the pragmatic Lincoln understood and appreciated.

Less noted is another work that Lincoln cited as important to him: Joseph Butler's *Analogy of Religion*, first published in 1736. A bishop in the Church of England, Butler argued that conscience could ameliorate avarice and appetite. On this Butler and Mill agreed. "It is not because men's desires are strong that they act ill," Mill wrote; "it is because their consciences are weak." Conscience was therefore indispensable. Without it there would be only perpetual war. Butler argued, too, that a theocentric universe encouraged moral action in light of the possibility of reward or punishment after death.

Lincoln's specific religious beliefs remain shrouded in speculation. It is clear that he thought proslavery theology was "not the sort of religion upon which people can get to heaven!" Beyond that, intimates were left to make educated guesses about Lincoln's theological convictions. "His religious views were eminently practical, and are summed up, as I think, in these two propositions: The Fatherhood of God, and the brotherhood of man," longtime Lincoln friend Jesse W. Fell wrote. "No religious views with him seemed to find any favor except of the practical and rationalistic order; and if . . . I was called upon to designate an author whose views most nearly represented Mr. Lincoln's on this subject, I would say that author was Theodore Parker."

A contemporary of Lincoln's, Theodore Parker was born in 1810 in Lexington, Massachusetts, and graduated from Harvard Divinity School in 1836. As a child, Parker had heard an inner voice cry out "It is wrong!" when he'd been about to poke "a little spotted tortoise sunning himself in the shallow water" of a stream.

What had just happened? He asked his mother.

"Some men call it conscience," she replied, "but I prefer to call it the voice of God in the soul of man. If you listen and obey it, then it will speak clearer and clearer, and always guide you right, but if you turn a deaf ear and disobey it will fade out little by little, and leave you all in the dark and without a guide." He never forgot the conversation, or its implications.

Inspired by William Ellery Channing of the Federal Street Church and by Lyman Beecher of the Hanover Street Church, Parker pursued the ministry. He married a daughter of the prominent Cabot family, but the match was a rocky one. He found his greatest fulfillment not at home—the Parkers lived with a Cabot aunt, an unhappy arrangement—but in public, both in his congregations and in the battle for abolition. After divinity school, Parker was called to a church in West Roxbury, Massachusetts; John Quincy Adams attended his ordination. Untethered by orthodoxy or by settled opinion, Parker explored the deepest of questions. In *A Discourse on the Transient and the Permanent in Christianity*, he argued that debates over atonement and sacraments, doctrine and authority, were distractions, for believers themselves were forever disagreeing.

To Parker, the Bible was not the end of the conversation, but the beginning. To ground a claim about reality solely on scripture absent reason and conscience was, for Parker, risible and wrong. "The Bible or the New Testament is not the sole and exclusive foundation of Christianity," he said. "Its truths are laid in human nature; they live with the Soul. They are the soul's law." God, in other words, gave us mind and conscience, and they were to be engaged in guiding the lives of individuals and of nations. Parker's views were shaped, too, by Ralph Waldo Emerson's July 1838 address to the Harvard Divinity School in which Emerson argued that there was a natural order, divinely created and expressed in laws accessible by reason and by conscience. "These laws refuse to be adequately stated," Emerson said. "They will not by us or for us be written out on paper, or spoken by the tongue. . . . [Y]et we read them hourly in each other's faces, in each other's actions, in our own remorse."

Parker was transfixed and transported on that Cambridge summer evening. "So beautiful, so just, so true, & terribly sublime," Parker wrote in his diary after hearing Emerson. "My soul is roused." Informed by the intellectual and cultural atmosphere of New England, Parker became an eloquent thinker, preacher, and writer, and his worldview held appeal for Abraham Lincoln.

One element of Parker's creed was an appreciation of reality itself. "There are some things which are true, independent of all human opinion," Parker preached in 1850. "Such things we call facts. Thus it is true that one and one are equal to two, that the earth moves round the sun, that all men have certain natural unalienable rights. . . . No man made these things true; no man can make them false." To wish away uncomfortable facts was appealing—but counterproductive.

And there was Parker's conviction about what he called the "moral universe." In this understanding, life need not be, in Thomas Hobbes's dark formulation, "solitary, poor, nasty, brutish, and short." There were, rather, principles of justice and of good, of divine origin, that could guide human conduct. People could discern those principles through reason and interpret them through conscience. History was the story of the degree to which mortals might close the gap between the ideal and the real, between the transcendent and the actual. And politics was a central arena in which that gap was either narrowed or widened.

Parker's conscience did not lead him to advocacy for racial equality— something he had in common with many white abolitionists who opposed slavery but who failed to profess egalitarian views. Attracted to works asserting Anglo-Saxon superiority, Parker once remarked that "in respect to the power of civilization, the African is at the bottom, the Indian is next." In January 1858, Parker publicly said that "the African is the most docile and pliant of all the races."

Still, he was firmly antislavery. Parker was in correspondence with William Herndon in the 1850s, and a Parker sermon in 1850 in Boston, to the New England Anti-Slavery Convention, brought together tributaries of thought and of action that Herndon and his law partner were considering about slavery and freedom. "There must be unity of action in a nation, as well as in a man, or there cannot be harmony and welfare," Parker had said in that sermon. "As a man 'cannot serve two masters' antagonistic and diametrically opposed to one another, as God and Mammon, no more can a nation serve two opposite principles at the same time." He had continued:

> There is what I call the American idea. . . . The idea that all men have unalienable rights; that in respect thereof, all men are created equal; and that government is to be established and sustained for the purpose of giving every man an opportunity for the enjoyment and development of all these unalienable rights. This idea demands . . . a democracy, that is, a government of all the people, by all the people, for all the people; of course, a government after the principles of eternal justice, the unchanging law of God; for shortness' sake, I will call it the idea of freedom.
>
> That is one idea; and the other is, that one man has a right to hold another man in thralldom, not for the slave's good, but for

the master's convenience; not on account of any wrong the slave has done or intended, but solely for the benefit of the master. This idea is not peculiarly American. For shortness' sake, I will call this the idea of slavery. It demands . . . an aristocracy, that is, a government of all the people by a part of the people—the masters; for a part of the people—the masters; against a part of the people— the slaves; a government contrary to the principles of eternal justice, contrary to the unchanging law of God. These two ideas are hostile, irreconcilably hostile, and can no more be compromised and made to coalesce in the life of this nation, than the worship of the real God and the worship of the imaginary devil can be combined and made to coalesce in the life of a single man. . . . So there must be war between them before there can be peace.

Lincoln found such thinking illuminating. So did Frederick Douglass. Invited to address Parker's church, Douglass wrote, "To speak in the pulpit of Mr. Parker is a huge undertaking. I shall come to the work with fear and trembling, but shall come nonetheless."

In 1850, Congress undertook a landmark effort to protect both slavery and Union. The issues had been precipitated by the Mexican War and the nation's acquisition of sweeping portions of the continent. The terms of California's admission to the Union—would slavery be allowed there?—had prompted a crisis. "I have witnessed many periods of great anxiety, of peril, and of danger even to the country," Henry Clay said in February 1850, "but I have never before arisen to address any assembly so oppressed, so appalled, so anxious."

In this charged climate the debate unfolded. "It is a great mistake to suppose that disunion can be effected at a single blow," John C. Calhoun argued to the Senate on Monday, March 4, 1850. If California were to come in as a free state, Calhoun said, there would be an end of the precarious balance between North and South.

In his search for solutions to preserve slavery, Calhoun had pondered a dual executive. "The nature of the disease is such that nothing can reach it, short of some organic change—a change which shall so modify the constitution, as to give the weaker section, in some one form or another, a negative on the action of the government," Calhoun had written. Perhaps such an arrangement "might be effected through a reorganization of the executive department; so that its powers, instead of being vested, as they now are, in a single officer, should be vested in two." Short of such a seismic shift, Calhoun believed, the question now was one of "submission or resistance."

The battle over compromise in the Capitol in 1850 was long, difficult, and wordy. Southerners echoed Calhoun's 1837 declaration that slavery was "a good—a positive good." The antislavery forces found a voice in William Seward: "We cannot, in our judgment, be either true Christians or real freemen, if we impose on another a chain that we defy all human power to fasten on ourselves." The Constitution might allow for the evil, Seward added, "but there is a higher law than the Constitution." Senator George Edmund Badger, a North Carolina Whig, was horrified by Seward's thought. Such ideas, Badger said, "give us a fanatical and wild notion, that every man in civilized society has a right, as a citizen, to make his own judgment a rule of conduct paramount to, and overruling, the law of his country."

Badger went further still, insisting that slavery was divinely ordained. "Whether the institution of slavery be considered as an evil or not, it is not a sin—it is not in itself a violation of the divine law," Badger argued. "Nothing could be easier than for St. Paul to have said, 'Slaves, be obedient to your heathen masters; but I say to you, believing masters, emancipate your slaves: the law of Christ is against that relation, and you are bound, therefore, to set them at liberty.' No such word is spoken."

Theodore Parker was wittily dismissive of such assertions. "If the Bible defends slavery," he said, "it is not so much the better for slavery, but so much the worse for the Bible." Parker claimed mighty allies in the struggle. "The American idea is with us. . . . The religion of the land, also, is on our side; the irreligion, the idolatry, the infidelity thereof, all of that is opposed to us. Religion is love of God and love of man: surely, all of that, under any form, Catholic or Quaker, is in favor of the unalienable rights of man," he said. "We know that we are right; we are sure to prevail. But in times present and future, as in times past, we need heroism, self-denial a continual watchfulness, and an indus try which never tires. . . . There is no attribute of God which is not on our side; because, in this matter, we are on the side of God." The task of the conscientious, then, was to bear witness, to persist, to keep the faith.

The Compromise of 1850 allowed California to join the Union as a free state; left the question unresolved for now in the territories that were to later become Arizona, Nevada, New Mexico, and Utah; abolished the slave trade in the District of Columbia; and included a strengthened Fugitive Slave Act that outraged free states by ending due process for escaped enslaved persons, authorizing penalties for people found guilty of aiding those seeking freedom, and creating a financial incentive for the federal commissioners—known more widely as "slave catchers"—who captured and returned the enslaved to captivity. In sum, the Fugitive Slave Act of 1850 explicitly deployed the power of the federal government in the service of slaveholders.

For the Lincolns things were busy at home. On Monday, April 4, 1853, they welcomed a new child, another boy, Thomas, known as Tad. Devoted as she was to her children—and she was an attentive mother—Mary Lincoln still missed Washington and encouraged her husband to think again of seeking office. "Wife is a woman of fine intellect," John T. Stuart said of Mary; "very ambitious."

Lincoln's mind was always turning over politics, law, and human nature. "He was still the center of interest of every social group he encountered, whether on the street or in the parlor," his White House secretaries John M. Hay and John G. Nicolay recalled in their multivolume *Abraham Lincoln: A History*. "Wherever he went he left an ever-widening ripple of smiles, jests, and laughter.... But it became noticeable that he was less among the crowd and more in the solitude of his office or his study, and that he seemed ever in haste to leave the eager circle he was entertaining."

His intellectual and practical interests came together in early 1853, in the statehouse in Springfield on Tuesday, January 11, when Ralph Waldo Emerson delivered a lecture on a subject close to Lincoln's heart and much on Lincoln's mind: power. "There are men, who, by their sympathetic attractions, carry nations with them, and lead the activity of the human race," Emerson said. Human action mattered, and all things were connected. "All successful men have agreed in one thing, they were *causationists*," Emerson said. "A belief in causality, or strict connection between every pulse-beat and the principle of being . . . characterizes all valuable minds." For Lincoln, who wanted to carry nations with him, the words resonated.

A fellow writer of Emerson's, Harriet Beecher Stowe, had recently put words into action. Beginning in June 1851, Stowe's *Uncle Tom's Cabin or Life Among the Lowly* had been serialized in Washington's *National Era.* Published as a stand-alone novel in March 1852, Stowe's book, which became a widely performed play, was a sensation. "Never since books were first printed has the success of *Uncle Tom* been equaled; the history of literature contains nothing parallel to it, nor approaching it," *Putnam's Monthly* wrote in 1853. After a trip to Italy, the English politician and historian Thomas Babington Macaulay told Mrs. Stowe that "your fame seems to throw that of all other writers into the shade. There is no place where Uncle Tom (transformed into 'Il Zio Tom') is not to be found."

Another, lesser-known novel shed light on the white Southern mind in the decades before the Civil War. Written by the Virginian Nathaniel Beverley Tucker, *The Partisan Leader: A Tale of the Future,* published in 1836, imaginatively invented a Southern confederacy. "If we will not *have* slaves, we must *be* slaves," Tucker remarked. One of the book's epigraphs was the motto of Virginia: Sic Semper Tyrannis.

Tucker's book appeared three years before *American Slavery as It Is: Testimony of a Thousand Witnesses,* by the abolitionists Theodore Dwight Weld, Angelina Grimké, and Sarah Grimké. A project of the American Anti-Slavery Society, the book detailed enslavement in vivid terms. Literature inspired by the experiences of enslaved people grew through the 1850s. There were novels by William Wells Brown, Frank J. Webb, and Martin Delany, and poetry by Joseph C. Holly, James Madison Bell, James M. Whitfield, and Frances Ellen Watkins Harper, who followed in the tradition of Phillis Wheatley. Especially profound were accounts of sexual violence against enslaved women and girls. In a letter to Horace Greeley's *New York Tribune* in 1853, Harriet A. Jacobs, who later published the book *Incidents in the Life of a Slave Girl, Written by Herself,* wrote in response to a self-serving and sentimental portrait of slavery published by former First Lady Julia Tyler. In wrenching prose, Jacobs reported the fate of a young enslaved woman who had been forced to bear two children fathered by her owner, a man driven by "brutal passion." The owner's wife was furious and jealous. The children "bore too strong a resemblance to him who desired to give them no other inheritance save Chains and Handcuffs," and they were sold. "And such," Jacobs wrote, "are the peculiar circumstances of American Slavery—of all the evils in

Harriet A. Jacobs's book Incidents in the Life of a Slave Girl, Written by Herself *detailed the horrifying reality of enslavement.*

God's sight the most to be abhorred." Stowe's novel, Jacobs added, "has not told the half."

A decade after *Uncle Tom's Cabin*, Lincoln received Stowe in the White House. "Is this the little woman who made this great war?" he reputedly asked.

That great war was becoming more likely in the mid-1850s. The latest realm of contention: the Nebraska Territory, which ranged from modern-day Kansas to the Canadian border and east to west from the Missouri River to the Rocky Mountains. Out of the Nebraska Territory would come all or parts of Nebraska, Colorado, Montana, Wyoming, and North and South Dakota. To organize the territory—and to lay plans for a transcontinental railroad that would take a more northerly than southerly route—Stephen Douglas proposed repealing the Missouri Compromise, which had banned slavery north of the 36° 30′ latitude, in favor of allowing new states to decide the issue for themselves through popular sovereignty. He had tried to avoid explicitly taking on the 1820 agreement, but the price of vital Southern votes was undoing the Missouri Compromise by allowing the possibility of slavery above the compromise line. The bill, Douglas knew, would "raise a hell of a storm."

The 1854 debate over slavery in the West was a front in the long-running battle between North and South. As Stowe's novel swept the world, slave owners felt ever more isolated. The Compromise of 1850 had been designed to relieve the sectional tension, but what abolitionists called the "slave power" was never really at ease. As a student of human nature, James Madison had sensed what was coming. "The great danger to our general government," Madison had said during the Constitutional Convention in 1787, *"is the great southern and northern interests of the continent, being opposed to each other."* The answer to the white Southern conundrum of how to preserve slavery was the amassing of *power*—raw, brutal power. Control land and people and one controlled politics and economy and culture, unless—and this was the slaveholders' fear—ideas and moral convictions contrary to the ideas and moral convictions held by the prevailing interest permeated the borders of a closed system. This anxiety helped give rise to white Southern nationalism, a sense of white Southern identity as a force independent from the opinions, laws, customs, and claims of the North and of much of the rest of the world.

In Congress, the House had voted to recognize Nebraska as a territory, but the South blocked the measure in the Senate due to Nebraska's lying wholly north of the 1820 Missouri Compromise line. Then Douglas called for popular sovereignty, barring slavery until the territorial legislature could vote on the issue. But Douglas's bill also proposed creating a new, second territory—Kansas, which was still north of the 1820 line—so that slaveholders had a better chance of controlling one new territory.

The legislation provoked an "Appeal of the Independent Democrats," a fiery response from antislavery lawmakers such as Salmon

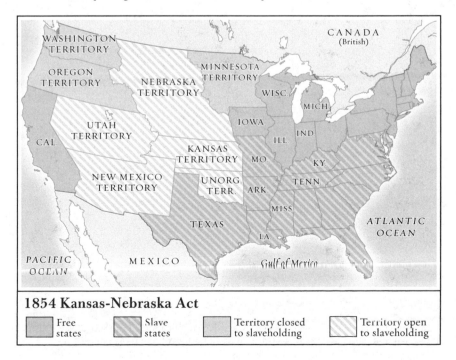

1854 Kansas-Nebraska Act

▨ Free states	▨ Slave states
▨ Territory closed to slaveholding	▨ Territory open to slaveholding

P. Chase and Joshua Giddings of Ohio, Charles Sumner of Massachusetts, and others. "We arraign this bill as a gross violation of a sacred pledge," the group declared; "as a criminal betrayal of precious rights; as part and parcel of an atrocious plot to exclude from a vast unoccupied region immigrants from the Old World, and free laborers from our own States, and convert it into a dreary region of despotism, inhabited by masters and slaves."

Yet the bill passed. On Tuesday, May 30, 1854, President Franklin Pierce* signed the Kansas-Nebraska Act, opening the West to slavery. A principle of more than three decades' standing had fallen.

The death of the Missouri Compromise, Lincoln said, "took us by surprise—astounded us. . . . We were thunderstruck and stunned; and we reeled and fell in utter confusion. But we rose each fighting, grasping whatever [we] could first reach—a scythe—a pitchfork—a chopping axe, or a butcher's cleaver." He was "aroused," he added, as he "had never been before."

---

* Millard Fillmore had become president when Zachary Taylor died in 1850; a New England Democrat, Franklin Pierce had succeeded Fillmore in the White House in 1853.

CHAPTER TEN

If All Earthly Power Were Given Me

> If the negro is a *man,* why then my ancient faith teaches me that
> "all men are created equal"; and that there can be no moral
> right in connection with one man's making a slave of another.
>
> —ABRAHAM LINCOLN at Peoria, Illinois, 1854

L INCOLN'S PART IN THE FIGHT: a campaign for a seat in the United States Senate. "I have always hated" slavery, Lincoln remarked in the summer of 1854, "but I have always been quiet about it until this new era of the introduction of the Nebraska Bill began." The Lincoln who occasionally spoke abstractly of fatalism, of the inevitability of all things, and of the hopelessness of individual action was stepping forward to shift the course of human events by efforts of his own will.

The capacity of American democracy to achieve justice was the subject of stark debate in these years. William Lloyd Garrison had long argued that the Constitution was "a covenant with death, and an agreement with hell." His belief that the Union was fatally flawed had led him and his allies, including Wendell Phillips, to eschew electoral politics. On the Fourth of July 1854, during a meeting at Harmony Grove in Framingham, Massachusetts, that included speeches by Sojourner Truth, Lucy Stone, and Henry David Thoreau, Garrison publicly burned copies of the 1850 Fugitive Slave Act and of the Constitution, a manifestation of his conviction that the nation's founding governmental document was irredeemably proslavery. "The law will never make men free," Thoreau had told the crowd; "it is men who have got to make the law free." The Constitution, Garrison cried, was "the source and parent of the other atrocities," adding, "So perish all compromises with tyranny!" before calling out, "And let all the people say, 'Amen.'" Sojourner Truth was blunt, too: The Lord, she said, "would yet execute his judgments upon the white people for their oppression and cruelty." A decade earlier, Garrison's American Anti-Slavery Society had resolved that "secession from the present United States govern-ment is the duty of every abolitionist; since no one can take office, or . . . vote for another to hold office, under the United States Constitution, without violating his anti-slavery principles, and rendering himself an abettor of the slaveholder in his sin." Yet this was not Frederick Doug-lass's view. He amended Garrison's cry of "No union with slaveholders" to "No union with slaveholding"—a crucial distinction that suggested an emancipated Union was indeed possible.

Lincoln agreed, and he was plotting a return to Washington in part to pursue such a Union. While Lincoln shared the view that the Con-stitution prohibited federally mandated abolition where slavery cur-rently existed, he opposed slavery's extension and articulated moral objections to human bondage with eloquence. In a polarized nation, the Lincoln of the mid-1850s held an antislavery ground that foresaw a ban on slavery in new states and, in the current Union, gradual eman-cipation, with compensation for slave owners, that could be followed by the voluntary removal of Black people from the United States.

On Monday, July 10, 1854, the formidably named Cassius Marcellus Clay of Lexington, Kentucky, founder of the antislavery newspaper *The True American*, commanded a crowd of about fifteen hundred in a grove in Springfield. Lincoln, accompanied by his friend Orville Browning, was there. "Whittling sticks, as he lay on the turf, Lincoln gave me a most patient hearing," Clay recalled. "I shall never forget his long, un-gainly form, and his ever sad and homely face."

Clay argued that America should "strike at the monster aggressor" of slavery "whenever it could be reached under the Constitution." All his life, Clay once remarked, "I have been between two fires—the Slave-power on one side, and the Abolition cranks on the other." Lin-coln understood. But he also understood slavery was wrong. "Yes, I al-ways thought," Clay recalled Lincoln's saying, "that the man who made the corn should eat the corn."

Before the 1913 ratification of the Seventeenth Amendment, sena-tors were chosen not by the voters at large but by state legislatures; the contests in which Lincoln took part in 1854 and again in 1858 were designed to elect sympathetic state lawmakers and to build support for the final selection that would be made when the new legislature con-vened in the new year. This was standard constitutional practice. What was less standard was the intensity of the Stephen Douglas–Lincoln rivalry. "It was a peculiarity of the early West—perhaps it pertains to all primitive communities—that the people retained a certain fragment of the chivalric sentiment, a remnant of the instinct of hero-worship," Hay and Nicolay wrote. "As the ruder athletic sports faded out, as shooting-matches, wrestling-matches, horse-races, and kindred games fell into disuse, political debate became, in a certain degree, their substitute." Given Douglas's and Lincoln's diametrically opposed positions on slavery, their campaigns against each other had an elemental feel.

Born in 1813 in Vermont, Stephen Douglas had come to Illinois and had, like Lincoln, become a lawyer in the early 1830s and later a state legislator. Called the "Little Giant" because of his five-foot-four height, Douglas had been a familiar figure in and around Springfield. A Democrat, he served on the state supreme court (thus earning his lifelong honorific of "Judge Douglas") before being elected to the U.S. House and, in 1847, to the U.S. Senate. Douglas had "excellent prize fighting qualities," a New England journalist noted. "Pluck, quickness and strength; adroitness in shifting his positions, avoiding his adversary's blows, and hitting him in unexpected places in return." Douglas embodied the Democratic order of the day. "No man of his time," Frederick Douglass remarked of the Illinois senator, "has done more to intensify hatred of the negro."

On arriving in Illinois in 1854, Douglas is said to have enunciated the key issue "slowly, measuredly, distinctly": "Neither—to legislate—slavery—into—a territory—nor to exclude it—therefrom—but—to leave—the peo-ple—perfectly free—to form—and regulate—their—domestic institutions—in their own way—subject—only—to the—Constitution—of—the United States: that—all—there is—of the Nebraska Bill," Douglas said. "That is 'popular sovereignty'—upon which—I am to speak—tomorrow at the Statehouse."

Lincoln mounted an opposition case. The *Illinois Register* noted that he "had been nosing for weeks in the State Library, and pumping his brains and his imagination for points and arguments with which to demolish the champion of popular sovereignty." At Bloomington on Tuesday, September 26, 1854, Lincoln recalled scenes of slavery in Washington: "The famous Georgia Pen, in Washington, where negroes were bought and sold within sight of the National Capitol, began to grow offensive in the nostrils of all good men, Southerners as well as

Springfield, Illinois, as it was in the years of Lincoln's practice of law and campaigns for the Senate in the 1850s.

Northerners." In Springfield, he said Americans "were proclaiming ourselves political hypocrites before the world, by thus fostering Human Slavery." He expanded on the theme on October 16, in the early evening hours of an autumn Monday near the banks of the Illinois River, in Peoria.

The village's bluffs, it was remembered, were "covered with oak and hickory—undergrowth of hazel brush and wild blackberry—ravines in which the wolf still lingered. . . . Clouds of black birds darkened the skies. The honk of wild geese winging . . . in endless file the whole day long foretold the season's change."

Senator Douglas had entered Peoria with all the panoply of state; reporters noted his arrival in a carriage "drawn by four beautiful white palfreys" as a band played and cannons boomed.

Lincoln arrived alone, in darkness, about two o'clock in the morning, and checked in to room 84 of the Peoria House hotel.

The two men met at two o'clock in the afternoon on the courthouse square. Douglas spoke first, delivering a three-hour defense of the repeal of the Missouri Compromise.

He finished at just past five o'clock. The crowd had been there for several hours.

Lincoln read the moment well. "I do not arise to speak now, if I can stipulate with the audience to meet me here at half past 6 or at 7 o'clock," he said. "It will take me as long as it has taken him. That will carry us beyond eight o'clock at night. Now every one of you who can remain that long, can just as well get his supper, [and] meet me at seven."

He knew what he was doing. A hungry audience would be a poor audience. The crowd drifted off to fortify themselves for the evening session.

Two hours later, in the gathering darkness, Lincoln stood before them again. "I do not propose to question the patriotism, or to assail the motives of any man, or class of men; but rather to strictly confine myself to the naked merits of the question," he said in a review of the history of slavery and freedom in which he noted how judicious the Founders had been to proscribe the institution to the geographic bounds where it existed at the framing of the Constitution. He cast back to the world of Parson Weems and Lexington and Concord and Bunker Hill and Yorktown, praising the banning of slavery in the Northwest Ordinance of 1787. Yet everything would have changed, Lincoln warned, if the principles of Douglas's Kansas-Nebraska Act had been in place. Had that been the case, Illinois, Ohio, Michigan, Indiana, Wisconsin, and Minnesota—which had long inhaled "the pure, fresh, free breath of the revolution"—could have been slave states.

Lincoln attacked the "*declared* indifference" of popular sovereignty as in fact "covert *real* zeal for the spread of slavery." This, he said, "I can not but hate. I hate it because of the monstrous injustice of slavery itself. I hate it because it deprives our republican example of its just influence in the world—enables the enemies of free institutions, with plausibility, to taunt us as hypocrites—causes the real friends of freedom to doubt our sincerity, and especially because it forces so many really good men amongst ourselves into an open war with the very fundamental principles of civil liberty—criticizing the Declaration of Independence, and insisting that there is no right principle of action but *self-interest*."

It was a firm point, but he hastened to be empathetic, understanding, *reasonable*. "I have no prejudice against the Southern people," Lincoln said. "They are just what we would be in their situation." He continued:

If all earthly power were given me, I should not know what to do, as to the existing institution. My first impulse would be to free all the slaves, and send them to Liberia—to their own native land. But a moment's reflection would convince me, that whatever of high hope, (as I think there is) there may be in this, in the long run, its sudden execution is impossible. If they were all landed there in a day, they would all perish in the next ten days; and there are not surplus shipping and surplus money enough in the world to carry them there in many times ten days. What then? Free them all, and keep them among us as underlings? Is it quite certain that this betters their condition? I think I would not hold one in slavery, at any rate; yet the point is not clear enough for me to denounce people upon. What next? Free them, and make them politically and socially, our equals? My own feelings will not admit of this; and if mine would, we well know that those of the great mass of white people will not. Whether this feeling accords with justice and sound judgment, is not the sole question, if indeed, it is any part of it. A universal feeling, whether well or ill-founded, can not be safely disregarded. We can not, then, make them equals. It does seem to me that systems of gradual emancipation might be adopted; but for their tardiness in this, I will not undertake to judge our brethren of the south.

He returned to the Founding. "When the white man governs himself that is self-government," Lincoln said; "but when he governs himself, and also governs *another* man, that is *more* than self-government—that is despotism. If the negro is a *man*, why then my ancient faith teaches me that 'all men are created equal'; and that there can be no moral right in connection with one man's making a slave of another."

Lincoln's key point: The nation's foundational document applied to all humankind. "Let us re-adopt the Declaration of Independence, and with it, the practices, and policy, which harmonize with it. Let north and south—let all Americans—let all lovers of liberty everywhere—join in the great and good work," he said. "If we do this, we shall not only have saved the Union; but we shall have so saved it, as to make, and to keep it, forever worthy of the saving."

To Lincoln, slavery was a moral wrong, but he did not always base his argument solely on appeals to conscience. Lands owned and worked by the enslaved could not be owned and worked by white settlers; capital controlled by a slave-owning elite was capital that would be inaccessible to the mass of white people. "The whole nation is interested that the best use shall be made of these territories," Lincoln said at Peoria. "We want them for the homes of free white people. . . . Slave States are places for poor white people to remove FROM; not to remove TO."

Lincoln's pleas to the white South: Abandon the effort to baptize slavery as divinely ordained. Give up the arguments from scripture and the contortions of selective biblical interpretation. Stop insisting that Black people were not human. Keep the territories free of slavery, and he was willing to go along with even the Fugitive Slave Act. "I confess I hate to see the poor creatures hunted down, and caught, and carried back to their stripes, and unrewarded toils," Lincoln wrote, "but I bite my lip and keep quiet." The forces arrayed against Lincoln's understanding of human liberty were many and powerful. "I do not question Mr. Lincoln's conscientious belief that the negro was made his equal, and hence is his brother," Stephen Douglas would remark. "But, for my own part, I do not regard the Negro as my equal, and I positively deny that he is my brother, or any kin to me whatever."

In the short run, Lincoln lost the campaign for the Senate when the legislature voted in early 1855. "I regret my defeat moderately," Lincoln wrote to a friend, "but I am not nervous about it"—and by "nervous," he meant depressed. An entirely political man might have moderated his antislavery views, or altered them, in the 1850s. Lincoln, however, kept faith with the Lincoln of childhood, of the Lyceum address, of the Illinois legislative protest, and of the bid while in Congress to abolish slavery in the District of Columbia. He would not give up on what he called his "political religion" or his "ancient faith"—that all men were created equal. The ground Lincoln occupied was not radically abolitionist ground—but it was ground that had to be held before further advances could be made in the long war for a more perfect Union.

An important element in that struggle—the Republican Party—began to take form on Tuesday, February 28, 1854, in Ripon, Wisconsin. Free Soilers, Whigs, anti-Nebraska Democrats, and sundry antislavery advocates had gathered to create a new political party; a second meeting followed on Monday, March 20. Then, on Thursday, July 6, in Jackson, Michigan, leaders met and adopted a platform: "That in view of the necessity of battling for the first principles of republican government, and against the schemes of aristocracy the most revolting and oppressive with which the earth was ever cursed, we will co-operate and be known as Republicans until the contest is terminated." The issue, the new party said, had been "forced upon us by the slave power."

Lincoln's thinking and that of the emerging Republicans were largely congruent. Equality, Lincoln wrote in a fragment on slavery found in his papers, had been "made so plain by our good Father in Heaven, that all feel and understand it, even down to brutes and creeping insects. The ant, who has toiled and dragged a crumb to his nest, will furiously defend the fruit of his labor. . . . So plain that no one, high or low, ever does mistake it, except in a plainly *selfish* way; for although volume upon volume is written to prove slavery a very good thing, we never hear of the man who wishes to take the good of it, *by being a slave himself.*"

In a letter to his friend Joshua Speed, a slaveholder, Lincoln frankly expressed his visceral opposition to slavery. Through the years Lincoln had come to recall his 1841 river trip with Speed in ever grimmer terms. "You may remember, as I well do, that from Louisville to the mouth of the Ohio there were, on board, ten or a dozen slaves, shackled together with irons," Lincoln wrote to Speed in August 1855. "That sight was a continual torment to me; and I see something like it every time I touch the Ohio, or any other slave-border. It is hardly fair for you to assume, that I have no interest in a thing which has, and continually exercises, the power of making me miserable. You ought rather to appreciate how much the great body of the Northern people do crucify their feelings, in order to maintain their loyalty to the constitution and the Union." "Crucify" is a strong word. That Lincoln was using it in a private letter suggests that his antislavery convictions were deep and genuine.

Black people were not the only targets in American politics. In a trend that worried Lincoln, anti-immigrant nativists were numerous and influential. In reaction to rising numbers of Irish and German immigrants, nativists formed secret societies (they were instructed, if asked about their associations or agenda, to say "I know nothing") devoted to the principle that "Americans must rule America." The movement had gained force in 1853 in the aftermath of Winfield Scott's loss to Franklin Pierce. Scott had unsuccessfully reached out to Catholic voters, alienating Protestant extremists. Two societies, the Order of

United Americans and the Order of the Star-Spangled Banner, took the lead in marshaling nativists. "At the bottom of all this," a Pennsylvania Democrat said, "is a deep-seated religious question—prejudice if you please, which nothing can withstand." A key text was Thomas Whitney's *A Defense of the American Policy, as Opposed to the Encroachments of Foreign Influence, and Especially to the Interference of the Papacy in the Political Interests and Affairs of the United States.*

Lincoln disliked nativism. On the road to Quincy, he heard disturbing reports about his ally Richard Yates. "On my way down I heard at Jacksonville a story which may harm you if not averted—namely, that you have been a Know-Nothing," Lincoln wrote to Yates. "I suggest that you get a denial . . . into the hands of a safe man in each precinct." In the summer of 1855, Lincoln wrote to Joshua Speed: "I am not a Know-Nothing. That is certain. How could I be? How can anyone who abhors the oppression of negroes, be in favor of degrading classes of white people? Our progress in degeneracy appears to me to be pretty rapid. As a nation, we began by declaring that '*all men are created equal.*' We now practically read it 'all men are created equal, *except negroes.*' When the Know-Nothings get control, it will read 'all men are created equal, except negroes, *and foreigners, and catholics.*' When it comes to this I should prefer emigrating to some country where they make no pretense of loving liberty—to Russia, for instance, where despotism can be taken pure, and without the base alloy of hypocrisy." Anti-immigrant sentiment among antislavery advocates didn't make sense to him. "Indeed I do not perceive how any one professing to be sensitive to the wrongs of the negroes," Lincoln remarked, "can join in a league to degrade a class of white men."

The Know-Nothing interest had its own home, the American Party, and Lincoln urged Republicans in Illinois to stay clear of nativist influence. "I have no objection to 'fuse' with anybody provided I can fuse on ground which I think is right; and I believe the opponents of slavery extension could now do this, if it were not for this K. N. ism." The key, Lincoln believed, was to keep politics focused not on immigration but on slavery.

In Illinois, Lincoln pursued the antislavery theme. The "great mass of mankind . . . consider slavery a great moral wrong; and their feelings against it, is not evanescent, but eternal," Lincoln had said at Peoria. "It lies at the very foundation of their sense of justice; and it cannot be trifled with. It is a great and durable element of popular action, and, I think, no statesman can safely disregard it." Nor, he hoped, would the new Republican interest ever do so. The Republican Party "is, to-day, the best hope of the nation, and of the world," Lincoln remarked in the winter of 1857. "Their work is before them; and from which they may not guiltlessly turn away."

CHAPTER ELEVEN

The Hateful Embrace of Slavery

It would not take much to have the throats of
every Abolitionist cut.
—PRESTON BROOKS of South Carolina, 1856

Judge Taney can do many things, but he cannot perform
impossibilities. . . . He cannot change the essential nature of
things—making evil good, and good evil.
—FREDERICK DOUGLASS, on the *Dred Scott* decision, 1857

I clearly see, as I think, a powerful plot to make slavery
universal and perpetual in this nation.
—ABRAHAM LINCOLN, 1858

IN MIDSUMMER 1855, Judge George Robertson of Lexington, Kentucky, a friend of the Todd family who had served in Congress at the time of the Missouri Compromise, gave Lincoln a copy of his *Scrap Book on Law and Politics, Men and Times*. After reading remarks Robertson had made on the Missouri question, Lincoln wrote the judge a thoughtful letter. "In that speech you spoke of *'the peaceful extinction of slavery,'*" Lincoln said. "Since then we have had thirty six years of experience; and this experience has demonstrated, I think, that there is no peaceful extinction of slavery in prospect for us." Popular sovereignty was on the march. Slavery could spread. Lincoln knew the questions. What he did not have were the answers. "Our political problem now is 'Can we, as a nation, continue together *permanently—forever*—half slave, and half free?'" Lincoln wrote to Robertson. "The problem is too mighty for me. May God, in his mercy, superintend the solution."

The Lord appeared to be taking His time, for the mid-1850s were years of deepening division. There were dreams of white Southern expansion. Violence in Kansas. A brutal physical attack on Charles Sumner in the Senate. The election of the Democrat James Buchanan as president. The *Dred Scott* decision of the Supreme Court. Amid these cascading events, Abraham Lincoln was engaged, thoughtful, and working to win a place in the arena not only of debate but of decision.

The slave interest was eyeing much more than Kansas and Nebraska. Writing to Lincoln in late 1854, an Illinois legislator wondered "whether by the annexation of Cuba . . . & by the conquest of Mexico or other territory," the slave-owning South would "extend the area of slavery indefinitely." President Pierce had tried to purchase Cuba from Spain as early as 1854, when there was also a threat of the United States' taking the island by force in the Ostend Manifesto, a diplomatic assertion that America had a direct interest in acquiring Cuba. Later in the decade, President James Buchanan revived efforts to bring Cuba under American—and slaveholding—control. That those debating the future of slavery were thinking of the white American South as the beginning of slave territory, not the end, casts the arguments of Lincoln's time in a stark light. An armed and emboldened slave-owning South was not just a problem to be endured, but a hemispheric threat to confront.

Expansionists raised money, arms, and men to acquire slave territory in Mexico, the Caribbean, and other parts of Latin America. "We anticipate no terminus to the institution of slavery," William H. Holcombe of New Orleans wrote in 1860. "We are looking out toward Chihuahua, Sonora, and other parts of Mexico—to Cuba, and even to Central America," Alexander Stephens, who would become vice president of the Confederacy, said in July 1859. "Where are to be our ultimate limits, time alone can determine." "The only possible way by which the South can indemnify itself for its concessions to the antislavery fanaticism is by the acquisition of additional slave territory," the *Richmond Enquirer* argued.

One means of conquest: filibusters. Derived from Spanish, French, and Dutch words for "freebooter" and "pirate," the term applied to private citizens who armed themselves and launched military operations to subdue and then control lands outside the United States. Some filibustering expeditions were designed from the start to spread slavery; some were rooted in other motives but soon cast themselves as agents of white Southern expansion. John A. Quitman of Mississippi, a former governor and a disciple of the John C. Calhoun school of states' rights, took up the cause of acquiring Cuba. "As a Southern[er]," Quitman reportedly said, he saw "the obvious gain to the Slave States, by including amongst them a country peopled by the white Caucasian race, and acknowledging the peculiar institution which it has become our duty to defend."

Cuba was also affixed to the center of a projected slave empire envisioned by a secretive order known as the Knights of the Golden Circle. Led by a proslavery Southerner based in Cincinnati, George Bickley, the KGC aimed to make conquered parts of Latin America the bulwark of a slave-based nation that would include the American South. It was the age of adventurers such as William Walker, a nineteenth-century celebrity often referred to as "the Grey-Eyed Man of Destiny." Born in Tennessee in 1824, Walker was a restless young man. He studied medicine, then law, and then took up journalism. Fond of power, Walker was drawn to the drama of the filibuster. He tried and failed in Baja California Sur in 1853–1854. The next year, Walker seized control of Nicaragua, a crossroads nation between the Pacific and the Gulf of Mexico.

Led by George Bickley, the secretive Knights of the Golden Circle sought a slavery-based hemispheric empire.

On Monday, September 22, 1856, Walker reinstituted slavery in Nicaragua. "If we look at Africa in the light of universal history, we see her . . . a mere waif on the waters of the world, fulfilling no part in its destinies, and aiding in no manner the progress of general civilization," he wrote. "But America was discovered, and the European found the African a useful auxiliary in subduing the new continent. . . . The white man took the negro from his native wastes, and teaching him the arts of life, bestowed on him the ineffable blessings of a true religion." Though he would fall from power in 1857, Walker positioned his experiment in Nicaragua as a model for the slave-owning class, urging the "men of the South" to "strike a blow . . . ere the blast of the enemy's bugle calls upon you to surrender your arms to an overwhelming force."

The late South Carolina lawyer, judge, and politician William Harper, a leading nullifier in the age of Jackson, had worried that "the inhabitants of the slaveholding States of America" were "cut off, in some degree, from the communion and sympathies of the world." That was just it. In their sense that the life they had long known was under attack, they were growing more nervous, more extreme—and more warlike.

Bloodshed in Kansas and on the floor of the United States Senate was bringing the conflict over slavery from the realm of words to that of deeds. Pro- and antislavery forces had been flocking to the Kansas and Nebraska territories. The *New York Tribune* disapprovingly wrote that Stephen Douglas's "Nebraska bill," as it was known, was "but the first . . . step in this comprehensive plan of Africanizing the whole of the American hemisphere, and establishing Slavery upon what its advocates regard as an impregnable basis." Slave owners were ready for battle. Should antislavery voters gain the advantage, the proslavery Missouri senator David Atchison said, "We will be compelled to shoot, burn & hang, but the thing will soon be over."

To Lincoln, the conflict on the ground was no less deplorable for its predictability. He knew self-interest was nearly impossible to overcome. "You say if Kansas fairly votes herself a free state, as a christian you will rather rejoice at it," Lincoln wrote to Joshua Speed. "All decent slave-holders *talk* that way; and I do not doubt their candor. But they never *vote* that way." In Lawrence on Wednesday, May 21, 1856, proslavery "border ruffians" said to be "breathing loud-mouthed threats" destroyed Free Soil newspaper offices and attacked the town's hotel with cannon fire. After the sun set, fires "lit up the evening sky as the army of desperadoes, now wild with plunder and excesses, and maddened with drink, retired from the pillaged city."

Within hours blood was also shed in Washington. On Capitol Hill, Senator Charles Sumner of Massachusetts had risen to speak on "The Crime Against Kansas"—caused, he said, by *the One Idea*, that Kansas, at all hazards, must be made a slave State." Born in Boston in 1811, Sumner, who had taken his seat in the Senate in 1851, had grown up the son of a struggling but well-read lawyer who became sheriff of Suffolk County. Raised in a house he described as "respectable, and yet only above being humble," Charles was known as "Gawky Sumner"—bright but awkward. Intense and scholarly, Sumner was educated at Harvard College and Harvard Law School and became a key figure in Boston's elite legal and intellectual worlds. "He was tall, thin, and ungainly in his movements, and sprawled rather than sat on a chair or sofa," a contemporary recalled. "Nothing saved his face from ugliness but his white gleaming teeth and his expression of bright intelligence and entire amiability." Sumner's devotion to abolition and to egalitarianism was eloquent and unwavering.

In the Kansas debate, with a large audience in the chamber and the galleries full, Sumner denounced the opening of the great West to the white Southern interest. "It is the rape of a virgin territory," he said, "compelling it to the hateful embrace of slavery." Sumner eviscerated both Stephen Douglas and Senator Andrew P. Butler of South Carolina, even mocking Butler's labial paralysis—a form of palsy. On Thursday, May 22, 1856, the day after the chaos in Lawrence, a kinsman of Butler's, Representative Preston S. Brooks, decided that it was his "duty to relieve Butler and avenge the insult to my State." How to do so? "I . . . speculated somewhat as to whether I should employ a horsewhip or a cowhide," Brooks recalled, but settled on a gold-headed cane made of gutta-percha, a somewhat flexible material.

Brooks walked into the Senate and approached Sumner, who was seated at his desk. "Mr. Sumner," Brooks said, "I have read your speech twice over carefully. It is a libel on South Carolina, and Mr. Butler, who is a relative of mine—" The congressman did not finish his sentence; he began to strike the senator—repeatedly. "Every lick went where I intended," Brooks recalled. "I . . . gave him about 30 first rate stripes. Towards the last he bellowed like a calf. I wore my cane out completely but saved the Head which is gold." Briefly unconscious, soaked in blood, Sumner was helped to his lodgings.

Vilified in the North, Brooks was celebrated in the South. "It would not take much to have the throats of every Abolitionist cut," Brooks mused. The facts of the case did not matter in the aftermath; ideology did. Antislavery members supported Sumner; proslavery members stood by Brooks.

Blood kept flowing. Lawrence had been sacked on Wednesday. Brooks had attacked Sumner on Thursday. Two days later, on Saturday, May 24, the militant abolitionist John Brown led assaults on the houses of several men (and their families) who were officials of (or associated with) the territorial district court near Pottawatomie Creek. The bodies of the victims—five in all—were mutilated. Several had died of wounds inflicted when Brown and his company split open their skulls with broadswords. "Bleeding Kansas" became a national watchword.

The following Thursday, in relatively peaceful Bloomington, Illinois, Abraham Lincoln was chosen as a Republican presidential elector for the general election of 1856. The news from Kansas and from Washington gave his theme that season urgency and force: As the *Illinois Journal* put it, Lincoln was speaking frequently of "the evils to be apprehended from the continued aggressions of the slave power."

The Lincoln of the summer of 1856 was making a national reputation for himself—not through legislation, for he had not held office since returning from Washington seven years before, but through his ideas and the way he framed them. "He is about six feet high," a newspaper reported in July, "crooked-legged, stoop-shouldered, spare-built, and anything but handsome in the face." Still, "as a close observer and cogent reasoner, he has few equals and perhaps no superior in the world. His language is pure and respectful, he attacks no man's character or motives" (unlike, say, Charles Sumner) "but fights with arguments" (unlike, say, Preston Brooks, the border ruffians, or John Brown).

Evidence of Lincoln's prominence in the new Republican Party came on Thursday, June 19, when his name was placed in nomination for the vice presidency at the first Republican National Convention. Held in Philadelphia's Musical Fund Hall on Locust Street, not far from Independence Hall, the convention had chosen the explorer John C. Frémont of California for president. William L. Dayton of New Jersey led Lincoln 253–110 on the first ballot; Lincoln's total more than doubled that of his nearest competitor, the third-place Nathaniel P. Banks of Massachusetts, the Speaker of the House. Then Dayton ran away with the vote on the second ballot. Lincoln was in Urbana, Illinois, when he learned about the encouraging, if unsuccessful, reception that his name had drawn in Philadelphia. With good humor (and perhaps recalling his glittering evening with Levi Lincoln some years before) he said that "there must be some mistake—there is a great man named Lincoln in Massachusetts, and *he* must be the one for whom votes were cast."

At Cincinnati's Smith and Nixon's Hall in June, the Democrats had nominated James Buchanan of Pennsylvania for president and John C. Breckinridge of Kentucky for vice president. The Democrats took to referring to the opposition as "Black Republicans" and warned that the new party was determined to destroy the country. Lincoln ventured into this sulfurous atmosphere to campaign for Frémont. "All this talk about the dissolution of the Union is humbug—nothing but folly," he said. "*We* WON'T dissolve the Union, and *you* SHAN'T."

In notes he wrote out on sectionalism, Lincoln pondered a crucial question: Why were Republicans able to attract votes only in free states while Democrats, who wanted to see slavery expanded, were winning support not only in slave states but also in free ones? Race was the obvious answer. The task for Lincoln and his party was much more difficult than the one facing the Democrats, who could rely on a white Southern base and also garner the votes of Northern white people uncomfortable with the Republicans' antislavery vision and its theoretical egalitarian implications. In response, Lincoln tried to appeal to white voters who seemed impervious to moral argument. "Have we no interest in the free Territories of the United States—that they should be kept open for the homes of free white people?" he asked in late August at Kalamazoo, Michigan.

Proslavery advocates, Lincoln said, had it wrong. "They insist that their slaves are far better off than Northern freemen," he said. "What a mistaken view . . . ! They think that men are always to remain laborers here—but there is no such class. The man who labored for another last year, this year labors for himself, and next year he will hire others to labor for him." Proslavery Democrats weren't interested in hearing Lincoln out on the merits. The *Illinois Register* dismissed him as a "great high-priest of abolitionism" and attacked him as "the depot master of the underground railroad, the great Abram Lincoln."

November brought bad news: James Buchanan defeated John Fré-mont, 45 percent to 33 percent; former president Millard Fillmore's Know-Nothings netted 21 percent. From the White House, the Democratic incumbent, Franklin Pierce, interpreted Buchanan's victory as a commendable verdict against the Republicans' antislavery campaign. The president saw the North, not the South, as the gravest threat to the Union. "Extremes beget extremes," Pierce wrote in his annual message in December. "Violent attack from the North finds its inevitable consequence in the growth of a spirit of angry defiance at the South." The country, the president argued, had accepted a white Southern idea: that "the imprescriptible right of equality of the several States" was more important than the rights of human equality.

Lincoln critiqued that Democratic worldview in a post-election speech to a Republican banquet in Chicago. "Our government rests in public opinion," he said. "Whoever can change public opinion, can change the government. . . . Public opinion, [on] any subject, always has a *'central idea,'* from which all its minor thoughts radiate. That 'central idea' in our political public opinion, at the beginning was, and until recently has continued to be, 'the equality of men.'" Buchanan's triumph and Pierce's message, Lincoln believed, were lost battles, but not a lost war. "Can we not come together, for the future?" Lincoln asked in Chicago. "Let past differences, as nothing be; and with steady eye on the real issue, let us reinaugurate the good old 'central ideas' of the Republic. We *can* do it. The human heart *is* with us—God is with us."

God might be. But at this juncture the voters were not.

Despite Frémont's loss in the presidential race, the winter season in Springfield was a diverting one. The Lincolns entertained and were entertained. A night at the governor's mansion was described as "delightful and magnificent. . . . Throughout the evening, a fine brass and string band discoursed most delicious music and the dancers kept the cotillions filled until a late hour." Writing to her half sister Emilie, Mary Lincoln reported that "within the last three weeks there has been a party almost every night and some two or three grand fetes are coming off this week."

The political work before Lincoln—the limitation of slavery to its existing sphere—grew monumentally more difficult in the space of forty-eight hours in the first week of March 1857. On Wednesday, March 4, Buchanan was sworn in as president on the East Front of the Capitol. The new president urged the nation to accept the possible extension of slavery. His election, he said, had shown that "the will of the majority" had led to "the settlement of the question of domestic slavery in the Territories." History seemed to be moving in Buchanan's direction. Among those listening to the new president's words was Roger Brooke Taney, the chief justice of the United States, who, two days later, on Friday, March 6, in the Supreme Court chamber on the ground floor of the Capitol, announced the opinion of the court in the case of Dred Scott.

For a decade, from 1833 to 1843, Scott, an enslaved man, had been taken from Missouri to military posts in Illinois and in the Wisconsin Territory—both of which were above the line established by the Missouri Compromise—before being brought back south of the line. (Scott had married and had two children while on free land.) Upon his forcible return to a slave state, Scott sued for his and his family's freedom in the St. Louis Circuit Court. Under a legal principle established in Missouri known as "once free, always free," a lower court agreed with Scott. In a major victory for the proslavery cause, however, the state supreme court ruled against him on Monday, March 22, 1852.

In the state court's majority opinion, Missouri justice William Scott acknowledged the decision was in reaction to rising antislavery sentiment—what he alluded to as the "dark and fell spirit" of abolition. The proslavery line had to be held, and he was going to hold it. That meant the "once free, always free" principle had to be struck down. The case made its way to the U.S. Supreme Court, which heard the case in February 1856.

The justices on Taney's court were hardly diverse in their political viewpoints. Seven were Democrats; five, including Taney of Maryland, were from slave states. In the decision announced in March 1857, by seven votes to two, a majority essentially ruled that the Declaration of Independence's assertion of equality did not include Black people, that Black people were not citizens, and that the Missouri Compromise—

and any future restrictions on slavery—was unconstitutional. Dred
Scott had no standing in court, for he had no standing in the American
order other than the fact of his enslavement. In Taney's words, Black
people "are not included, and were not intended to be included, under
the word 'citizens' in the Constitution.... On the contrary, they were
at that time considered as a subordinate and inferior class of beings,
who had been subjugated by the dominant race, and, whether emancipated or not, yet remained subject to their authority." Black people,
Taney went on, "had for more than a century before been regarded as
beings of an inferior order, and altogether unfit to associate with the
white race, either in social or political relations; and so far inferior, that
they had no rights which the white man was bound to respect."

The seven justices were deploying the power of the judiciary to re-
order American reality by declaring the antislavery cause unconstitutional. The great debate in the nation—a debate in which Lincoln was
playing his part—turned on whether *all* were included in Jefferson's assertion that "all men are created equal," and therefore whether slavery
was in keeping with the aspirations of the Republic. The Taney court
wanted to end that conflict of ideas in a single blow.

In New York, Frederick Douglass reacted with passion and proportion: "You will readily ask me how I am affected by this devilish
decision—this judicial incarnation of wolfishness?" Douglass said. "My
answer is, and no thanks to the slave-holding wing of the Supreme
Court, my hopes were never brighter than now," continuing:

> I have no fear that the National Conscience will be put to sleep by
> such an open, glaring, and scandalous tissue of lies as that decision
> is, and has been, over and over, shown to be.
>
> The Supreme Court of the United States is not the only power
> in this world. It is very great, but the Supreme Court of the Al-
> mighty is greater. Judge Taney can do many things, but he cannot
> perform impossibilities.... He cannot change the essential na-
> ture of things—making evil good, and good evil.

In Illinois, Lincoln found the ruling "erroneous" and was determined to peaceably "over-rule" it. "Chief Justice Taney, in delivering
the opinion of the majority of the Court, insists at great length that
negroes were no part of the people who made, or for whom was made,

the Declaration of Independence, or the Constitution of the United States," Lincoln remarked in a speech in Springfield in June. In this, Lincoln said, the chief justice was wrong. As Justice Benjamin Curtis argued in his *Dred Scott* dissent, in at least five of the thirteen original states (New Hampshire, Massachusetts, New York, New Jersey, and North Carolina) free Black people could and did vote.

New Jersey and North Carolina had since revoked Black suffrage; New York had "greatly abridged" it. State legislatures had made emancipation more difficult. The enslaved had virtually no grounds for hope. "All the powers of earth seem rapidly combining against [the enslaved person]," Lincoln said. "Mammon is after him; ambition follows, and philosophy follows, and the Theology of the day is fast joining the cry. They have him in his prison house; they have searched his person, and left no prying instrument with him. One after another they have closed the heavy iron doors upon him, and now they have him, as it were, bolted in with a lock of a hundred keys."

Parrying Democratic claims that the Republicans were undermining the rule of law in criticizing the decision, Lincoln replied: "It is not resistance, it is not factious, it is not even disrespectful, to treat it as not having yet quite established a settled doctrine for the country." It was a politically realistic reply, for Lincoln was attentive to tactics and to public opinion. In early April 1857 he was already in conference in his law office about "Republicanism in border states in 1860" and discussing newspaper party endorsements. "The vicissitudes of a political campaign brought into play all his tact and management and developed to its fullest extent his latent industry," William Herndon recalled. "In common with other politicians he never overlooked a newspaperman who had it in his power to say a good or bad thing of him." The *Chicago Daily Journal* offered a kind word in May 1857, referring to Lincoln as "the successor of Stephen A. Douglas in the U.S. Senate" in the approaching 1858 contest.

"I claim," Lincoln said, "no extraordinary exemption from personal ambition"—which was good, for he was deeply and evidently ambitious. "I clearly see, as I think, a powerful plot to make slavery universal and perpetual in this nation. . . . I enter upon the contest to contribute my humble and temporary mite in opposition to that effort."

In the summer of 1857, probably financed on the "strength of a large fee won from Illinois Central," the Lincolns traveled east. "The summer has so strangely and rapidly passed away," Mary Lincoln wrote. "Some portion of it was spent most pleasantly in traveling East. We visited Niagara, Canada, New York and other points of interest." She had loved New York, especially the shopping. "I often laugh & tell Mr. Lincoln that I am determined my next husband shall be rich," she wrote to a sister.

Back at home, Lincoln prepared for the 1858 challenge to Senator Douglas. As he traveled around the state, the story is told, a woman on horseback once approached Lincoln appraisingly on the road.

"Well, for the land's sake, you are the homeliest man I ever saw," she said.

"Yes, ma'am, but I cannot help that."

"No, I suppose not," she replied, "but you might stay at home."

That was something he could not do.

CHAPTER TWELVE

By White Men for the Benefit of White Men

Now, I do not believe that the Almighty ever intended the
negro to be the equal of the white man.
—STEPHEN A. DOUGLAS, 1858

I have an abiding faith that we shall beat them in the long run.
—ABRAHAM LINCOLN, on losing the 1858 Senate race to Douglas

L INCOLN'S NOMINATION FOR THE SENATE was set for the state
Republican convention in June 1858. In the weeks leading up to
the gathering, he worked on a speech, jotting thoughts, William
Herndon recalled, "on stray envelopes and scraps of paper, as ideas suggested themselves, putting them into that miscellaneous and convenient
receptacle, his hat." In private, Lincoln read the speech to Herndon and
to other advisers. In one session in the library of the statehouse, several
fastened onto a single line, one drawn from these words of Jesus: "Every
kingdom divided against itself is brought to desolation; and every city or
house divided against itself shall not stand." Herndon articulated the
common objection: The "house divided" image pointed toward a new
order beyond the status quo of slave states and free states under the
Constitution.

"It is true," Herndon asked Lincoln, "but is it wise or politic to
say so?"

"That expression," Lincoln replied, "is a truth of all human experience. . . . I would rather be defeated with this expression in the speech,
and uphold and discuss it before the people, than be victorious without it."

On the afternoon of Wednesday, June 16, 1858, the Illinois Republican convention was unanimous: "Abraham Lincoln is the first and only choice of the Republicans of Illinois for the U.S. Senate." At eight o'clock that evening, the nominee addressed the delegates. He spoke simply:

> If we could first know *where* we are, and *whither* we are tending, we could then better judge *what* to do, and *how* to do it.
>
> We are now far into the *fifth* year, since a policy was initiated, with the *avowed* object, and *confident* promise, of putting an end to slavery agitation.
>
> Under the operation of that policy, that agitation has not only, *not ceased*, but has *constantly augmented*.
>
> In *my* opinion, it *will* not cease, until a *crisis* shall have been reached, and passed.
>
> "A house divided against itself cannot stand."
>
> I believe this government cannot endure, permanently half *slave* and half *free*.
>
> I do not expect the Union to be *dissolved*—I do not expect the house to *fall*—but I *do* expect it will cease to be divided.
>
> It will become *all* one thing, or *all* the other.

Lincoln's Springfield convention speech, Frederick Douglass remarked, was "well and wisely said.... Liberty or slavery must become the law of the land."

"I have always hated slavery, I think as much as any Abolitionist," Lincoln said in a speech in Chicago in July 1858. "Let us discard all this quibbling about this man and the other man—this race and that race and the other race being inferior, and therefore they must be placed in an inferior position.... Let us discard all these things, and unite as one people throughout this land."

Stephen Douglas was ready, and he was not subtle. "Do you desire to turn this beautiful State into a free negro colony?" Douglas cried across Illinois. "If you desire negro citizenship, if you desire to allow them to come into the State and settle with the white man, if you desire them to vote on an equality with yourselves, and to make them eligible to office, to serve on juries, and to adjudge your rights, then support Mr. Lincoln and the Black Republican party." A Democratic newspaper in Illinois, the *Register,* wrote that Lincoln's "n——rism has as dark a hue as that of Garrison or Fred Douglass." The same paper dismissed a Lincoln speech as "all about 'freedom,' 'liberty' and n——rs." Douglas could not make the point enough. "I believe this Government was made on the white basis," he said. "I believe it was made by white men for the benefit of white men and their posterity for ever."

Remembering that he had once seen Frederick Douglass riding through the streets of Freeport, Illinois, in company with a white woman, Senator Douglas sneered: "[T]hose of you who believe that the negro is your equal and ought to be on an equality with you socially, politically, and legally; have a right to entertain those opinions, and of course will vote for Mr. Lincoln." Lincoln had anticipated Douglas's race-baiting. "There is a natural disgust in the minds of nearly all white people, to the idea of an indiscriminate amalgamation of the white and black races; and Judge Douglas evidently is basing his chief hope, upon the chances of being able to appropriate the benefit of this disgust to himself," Lincoln had said the year before. Lincoln had continued:

> Now I protest against that counterfeit logic which concludes that, because I do not want a black woman for a *slave* I must necessarily want her for a *wife*. I need not have her for either, I can just leave her alone. In some respects she certainly is not my equal; but in her natural right to eat the bread she earns with her own hands without asking leave of anyone else, she is my equal, and the equal of all others.

Douglas was a difficult foe. "Senator Douglas is of world wide renown," Lincoln said in July 1858. "We have to fight this battle upon principle, and upon principle alone." Yet principle could be vulnerable to politics. In midsummer, Lincoln and his fellow Republicans worried that Douglas's showmanship was carrying the day. "The fame and prestige of the 'Little Giant' was beginning to incline the vibrating scale," Hay and Nicolay recalled. On Saturday, July 24, Lincoln challenged Douglas to a series of debates: "Will it be agreeable to you to make an arrangement for you and myself to divide time, and address the same audiences during the present canvass?"

Lincoln was confident that he could hold his own. He had come this far by dint of his own effort. Why not go farther now, in an hour of maximum drama? Douglas accepted and proposed seven meetings—one in each of the state's congressional districts. The incumbent would open for an hour at Ottawa, Jonesboro, Galesburg, and Alton. Lincoln would have ninety minutes thereafter; and Douglas would have a half hour to reply. They would reverse roles at Freeport, Charleston, and Quincy.

The Lincoln-Douglas debates mattered because, as Lincoln knew, words mattered. "In this and like communities, public sentiment is everything," Lincoln remarked in the summer. "With public sentiment, nothing can fail; without it, nothing can succeed." He feared that Douglas's words could create a climate where slavery would not only survive but thrive, for Douglas spoke of the enslaved not as human beings but as any other kind of property. Lincoln spoke the way he did, he said, to fight against the "tendency to dehumanize the negro—to take away from him the right of ever striving to be a man."

Elements of his debates with Douglas make for painful reading. In speaking to a white electorate in 1858, Lincoln offered a morally informed antislavery argument but did not assert that Black people could become fully empowered citizens. He was a campaigner who believed that the public sentiment he so respected tended to be best shaped gradually. Not a preacher but a politician, not a full-time reformer but an office-seeker, he calibrated his case in 1858 with care.

Lincoln's challenge was how to appeal to antislavery Republicans while still attracting moderates who worried that he was too much of a radical. The tensions were real, the calculations precise. The two candidates maneuvered through the senatorial campaign with another expectation: that both men were trying out for their parties' 1860 national tickets. A vote for Douglas was a vote for the possible spread of, and a durable future for, slavery. A vote for Lincoln was a vote for limiting slavery and, "in God's own good time," as he put it, seeing it to "ultimate extinction." A vote for Douglas was a vote for white supremacy—world without end. A vote for Lincoln was a vote for a vision that threatened white supremacy—for Lincoln saw Black people not as chattel but as human beings.

Douglas and Lincoln met at Ottawa on Saturday, August 21, for their first official debate. Douglas spoke of his long association with Lincoln. "We were both comparatively boys, and both struggling with poverty in a strange land," he said to the boisterous crowd. "I was a school-teacher in the town of Winchester, and he a flourishing grocery-keeper in the town of Salem." At this—"grocery-keepers" were basically saloonkeepers—there was "applause and laughter." Douglas traced Lincoln's political career, attacking him for "taking the side of the common enemy against his own country" in the Mexican War. "He came up again in 1854, just in time to make this Abolition or Black Republican platform."

Race was Douglas's theme. "Now, I do not believe that the Almighty ever intended the negro to be the equal of the white man," he said. "If he did, he has been a long time demonstrating the fact. For thousands of years the negro has been a race upon the earth, and during all that time, in all latitudes and climates, wherever he has wandered or been taken, he has been inferior to the race which he has there met. He belongs to an inferior race, and must always occupy an inferior position." Douglas homed in on Lincoln's "house divided" image. "Why should Illinois be at war with Missouri, or Kentucky with Ohio, or Virginia with New York, merely because their institutions differ?" Douglas asked. "I believe that this new doctrine preached by Mr. Lincoln and his party will dissolve the Union if it succeeds."

Lincoln rose to reply. He leaned forward slightly when he addressed an audience, his feet parallel. "He never ranted," Herndon recalled, "never walked backward and forward on the platform." Lincoln's voice, at the beginning of a debate, was "shrill, piping, and unpleasant. His manner, his attitude, his dark, yellow face, wrinkled and dry, his oddity of pose, his diffident movements—everything seemed to be against him, but only for a short time." His hands behind his back, "the back of his left hand in the palm of his right, the thumb and fingers of his right hand clasped around the left arm at the wrist," he emphasized his points with his head—"throwing it with vim this way and that." As Lincoln settled into his speech, he became ever more compelling, and his voice "lost in a measure its former acute and shrilling pitch, and mellowed into a more harmonious and pleasant sound." At his most animated, "to express joy or pleasure, he would raise both hands at an angle of about fifty degrees, the palms upward, as if desirous of embracing the spirit of that which he loved," Herndon recalled. "If the sentiment was one of detestation—denunciation of slavery, for example—both

The Lincoln-Douglas debates of 1858 explored issues of freedom and slavery. "In this and like communities," Lincoln said, "public sentiment is everything."

arms, thrown upward and fists clenched, swept through the air, and he expressed an execration that was truly sublime."

At Ottawa and later at Charleston, Illinois, Lincoln positioned himself against racial egalitarianism as defined by abolitionists such as Douglass and Garrison. "I have no purpose to introduce political and social equality between the white and the black races," he told the audience. "There is a physical difference between the two, which in my judgment will probably forever forbid their living together upon the footing of perfect equality, and inasmuch as it becomes a necessity that there must be a difference, I, as well as Judge Douglas, am in favor of the race to which I belong, having the superior position."

That he did not seek political or social equality between whites and Blacks, and his occasional use of the N-word including in the debates with Douglas, raise difficult questions about Lincoln's own views on race. However deep his antislavery commitment, he was a white man in a white-dominated nation shaped by anti-Black prejudice that he to some extent shared. As his defenders have noted, Lincoln had respectful dealings with free Black people in Springfield, including representing Black clients, and he would welcome Black callers to the White House—details that suggest more of an egalitarian attitude than many of his white contemporaries shared. Still, he was pessimistic about combating racist feeling in the United States. Like many others of the era, including figures such as the Black abolitionist Martin Delany, Lincoln chose to believe that racial prejudice among whites was of such scope that the practical course was to acknowledge it and accommodate it (which partially fueled Lincoln's support for voluntary colonization).

Simultaneously, Lincoln advanced an argument in direct conflict with the racist consensus of the age: that, as human beings, Black people were included in Jefferson's assertions about innate equality. There was, Lincoln said at Ottawa, "no reason in the world why the negro is not entitled to all the natural rights enumerated in the Declaration of Independence, the right to life, liberty and the pursuit of happiness."

Interrupted by "Loud cheers," he continued: "I hold that he is as much entitled to these as the white man. I agree with Judge Douglas that he is not my equal in many respects—certainly not in color, perhaps not in moral or intellectual endowment. But in the right to eat the bread, without leave of anybody else, which his own hand earns, *he is my equal and the equal of Judge Douglas, and the equal of every living man.*"

Lincoln's partisans greeted the words with "Great applause."

"Douglas and I, for the first time this canvass, crossed swords here yesterday," Lincoln wrote on Sunday, August 22; "the fur flew some, and I am glad to know I am yet alive."

There were six more debates. Throughout, Lincoln articulated his moral commitment against slavery and yet professed a willingness to leave a white-dominated society intact. To make his points to white audiences, Lincoln insisted that Douglas's arguments for the spread of slavery to the territories foreshadowed a tyranny based not only on race but on rank and wealth—a tyranny that should be a source of fear to white Americans who were not among the slave-owning class. In notes for the campaign, Lincoln wrote:

> If, by all these means, [Douglas] shall succeed in moulding public sentiment to a perfect accordance with his own . . . in bringing all tongues to as perfect a silence as his own, as to there being any

wrong in slavery—in bringing all to declare, with him, that they care not whether slavery be voted down or voted up—that if any people want slaves they have a right to have them—that negroes are not men—have no part in the declaration of Independence—that there is no moral question about slavery—that liberty and slavery are perfectly consistent—indeed, necessary accompaniaments— that for a strong man to declare himself the *superior* of a weak one, and thereupon enslave the weak one, is the very *essence* of liberty— the most sacred right of self-government—when, I say, public sentiment shall be brought to all this, in the name of heaven, what barrier will be left against slavery being made lawful everywhere? . . .

And then, the negro being doomed, and damned, and forgotten, to everlasting bondage, is the white man quite certain that the tyrant demon will not turn upon him too?

In debate, Lincoln pressed this case again and again and again. In private, he went further, writing:

If A. can prove, however conclusively, that he may, of right, enslave B.—why may not B. snatch the same argument, and prove equally, that he may enslave A?—

You say A. is white, and B. is black. It is *color*, then; the lighter, having the right to enslave the darker? Take care. By this rule, you are to be slave to the first man you meet, with a fairer skin than your own.

You do not mean *color* exactly?—You mean the whites are *intellectually* the superiors of the blacks, and, therefore have the right to enslave them? Take care again. By this rule, you are to be slave to the first man you meet, with an intellect superior to your own.*

---

* Lincoln quoted an 1849 letter of Henry Clay's to underscore the point. "I know there are those who draw an argument in favor of slavery from the alleged intellectual inferiority of the black race," Clay had written. "Whether this argument is founded in fact or not, I will not now stop to inquire, but merely say that if it proves anything at all, it proves too much. It proves that among the white races of the world any one might properly be enslaved by any other which had made greater advances in civilization. And, if this rule applies to nations there is no reason why it should not apply to individuals; and it might easily be proved that the wisest man in the world could rightfully reduce all other men and women to bondage."

The antislavery appeal to white self-interest was an understandable tactic. "It is far easier to convince the multitude that Slavery is a baleful evil to them than to possess them with the idea that it is a cruel wrong to the enslaved," the *Chicago Tribune* wrote in a comment headlined A WHITE MAN'S PARTY. "So inveterate are the prejudices of color; so deep rooted . . . is the conviction that the African is a being of an inferior order; so intolerant is the Caucasian of the African assertion of equality; so low, under the depressing influence of 'the institution,' has the national morality descended, that this method, narrow and incomplete as it is, holds out the only promise of success."

Douglas's advocacy of democratic means ("popular sovereignty") to perpetuate slavery was politically potent. Lincoln's vision of America differed in important ways, and he often repeated himself to counteract Douglas's influence over "public sentiment." Slavery ought to be contained, Lincoln said, because slavery was immoral, and such containment would circumscribe the power of the slave-owning interest so "that white men may find a home . . . where they can settle upon new soil and better their condition in life. I am in favor of this not merely . . . for our own people who are born amongst us, but as an outlet for *free white people everywhere, the world over.*"

Slavery, Lincoln was saying, need not be forever race-based. What if the aristocracy enriched by human chattel were to enslave white people as well as Black? "Now, when . . . you have succeeded in dehumanizing the negro," Lincoln said; "when you have put him down, and made it forever impossible for him to be but as the beasts of the field; when you have extinguished his soul, and placed him where the ray of hope is blown out in darkness like that which broods over the spirits of the damned; are you quite sure the demon which you have roused *will not turn and rend you?*"

A t Jonesboro in southern Illinois in mid-September 1858, Lincoln quoted an editor and judge from DeKalb County who had written: "Our opinion is that it would be best for all concerned to have the colored population in a State by themselves."

Lincoln interjected: "In this I agree with him."

As the aside made clear, Lincoln was advocating racial separatism. "I have said that the separation of the races is the only perfect preventive of amalgamation. . . . Such separation, if ever effected at all, must be effected by colonization," he had said in Springfield in June 1857. "The enterprise is a difficult one; but 'when there is a will there is a way'; and what colonization needs most is a hearty will. Will springs from the two elements of moral sense and self-interest. Let us be brought to believe it is morally right, and, at the same time, favorable to, or, at least, not against, our interest, to transfer the African to his native clime, and we shall find a way to do it, however great the task may be." To allow slavery to expand was to snuff out such hopes. "It will be ever hard to find many men who will send a slave to Liberia, and pay his passage," Lincoln said, "while they can send him to a new country, Kansas for instance, and sell him for fifteen hundred dollars."

With such talk Lincoln was acting within an American tradition. The American Colonization Society had been part of the slavery conversation in the United States for four decades, and even some Black Americans supported at least the idea of emigration as means of empowerment. In 1852, the abolitionist Martin Delany had published *The Condition, Elevation, Emigration, and Destiny of the Colored People of the United States, Politically Considered,* an effort to build support for an all-Black nation. (He followed this up with a convention on the topic in Cleveland in 1854.) Delany, Henry Highland Garnet, and other Black abolitionists weighed the question through the 1850s and even into the Civil War years.

At Charleston, Illinois, Lincoln staked out a pro-white ground without nuance. "While I was at the hotel to-day, an elderly gentleman called upon me to know whether I was really in favor of producing a perfect equality between the negroes and white people," Lincoln said, to "great Laughter," continuing:

> I will say . . . that I am not nor ever have been in favor of making voters or jurors of negroes, nor of qualifying them to hold office, nor to intermarry with white people; and I will say in addition to this that there is a physical difference between the white and black races which I believe will forever forbid the two races living together on terms of social and political equality. And inasmuch as they cannot so live, while they do remain together there must be the position of superior and inferior, and I as much as any other man am in favor of having the superior position assigned to the white race.

On his next sentence hung much: "I say upon this occasion," Lincoln went on, that "I do not perceive that because the white man is to have the superior position the negro should be denied everything." That such a sentiment was even remotely progressive in its time was grim evidence of the ruling racism of the era. The laughter of the Charleston crowd at just the mention of equality was cruel. Lincoln shared the then commonly held view that the federal government had little or no power to regulate individual rights within the separate states. And he plainly stated that he would not favor Black citizenship in Illinois. "Now my opinion is that the different States have the power to make a negro a citizen under the Constitution of the United States if they choose," Lincoln said. "The Dred Scott decision decides that they have not that power. If the State of Illinois had that power I should be opposed to the exercise of it."

The states were the controlling authorities on civil and political equality, not Washington. (This would be true until the passage of the Fourteenth Amendment, which defined national citizenship, and the Fifteenth Amendment, which theoretically protected the right of all male citizens to vote.) "I do not understand there is any place where an alteration of the social and political relations of the negro and the white man can be made except in the State Legislature—not in the Congress of the United States," Lincoln said, "and as I do not really apprehend the approach of any such thing myself, and as Judge Douglas seems to be in constant horror that some such danger is rapidly approaching, I propose as the best means to prevent it that the Judge be kept at home and placed in the State Legislature to fight the measure."

At this there was reportedly "uproarious laughter and applause."

"I do not propose dwelling longer at this time on this subject," Lincoln said, probably drolly, and moved on.

On a rare September evening at home in Springfield, Lincoln greeted a crowd of Republican well-wishers who brought along a band. The musicians, the *Illinois Journal* reported, played "a few lively airs in front of his house," and Lincoln stepped out to thank them all. He projected confidence, telling his friends that "wherever he has been the skies are bright and the prospects good for the triumph of those principles which are dear to us all." He went back inside "amid deafening cheers."

The skies were not bright enough. On Tuesday, November 2, 1858, the voters of Illinois sided with legislators who would choose Douglas for the Senate, dealing Lincoln yet another electoral defeat. Though the Republicans won a popular plurality of about four thousand votes, the existing districts were such that the Democrats had the upper hand in the state legislature. Douglas won the senatorial vote in Springfield in January 1859, 54 to 46.

"I am glad I made the late race," Lincoln wrote to his friend A. G. Henry in mid-November 1858. "It gave me a hearing on the great and durable question of the age, which I could have had in no other way; and though I now sink out of view, and shall be forgotten, I believe I have made some marks which will tell for the cause of civil liberty long after I am gone." "I write merely to let you know that I am neither dead nor dying," Lincoln told another friend, Alexander Sympson, in mid-December 1858. "I have an abiding faith that we shall beat them in the long run. Step by step the objects of the leaders will become too plain for the people to stand them." To the *Chicago Tribune*'s Charles H. Ray, he wrote, "Another 'blow-up' is coming; and we shall have fun again."

As he recovered from the campaign, Lincoln believed that the point with which he had begun remained true: A house divided could not stand. "Well, the election is over; and, in the main point, we are beaten," he told a correspondent. "Still, my view is that the fight must go on. Let no one falter. The *question* is not half settled."

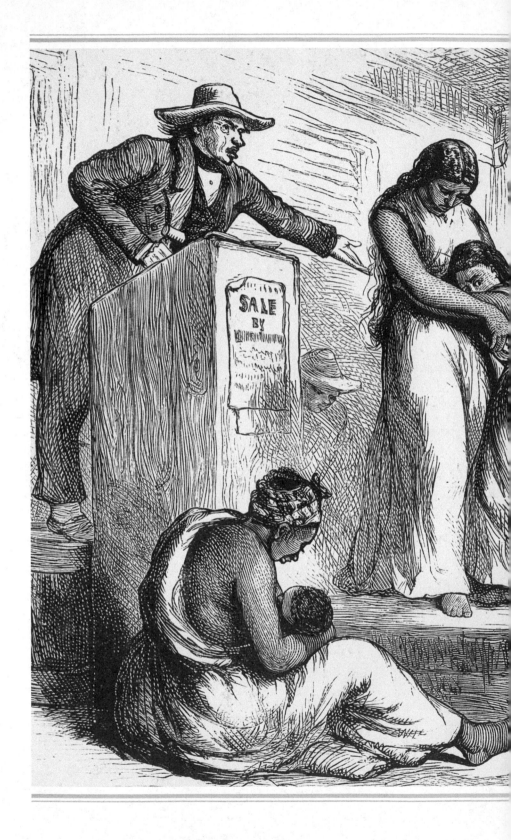

PART III

RIGHT MAKES MIGHT

1859–1861

CHAPTER THIRTEEN

Let Us Dare to Do Our Duty

The question recurs, what will satisfy them? . . . This, and
this only: cease to call slavery *wrong*, and join them in
calling it *right*.

—ABRAHAM LINCOLN, on white Southerners, Cooper Union,
February 1860

Is it not time we were arming for our defense?

—REPRESENTATIVE REUBEN DAVIS of Mississippi, after John Brown's
raid at Harpers Ferry

WINTERS IN SPRINGFIELD COULD BE BLEAK. Wednesday,
February 2, 1859, was a "cloudy, foggy, muddy, dismal day,"
Orville Browning told his diary. The only bright spot was a
"large party at Lincoln's" at Eighth and Jackson in the evening. The
Lincolns were carrying on with good cheer after the Senate defeat, but
it was a long, difficult season across the nation, for Lincoln had been
right the year before: The slavery question was open and urgent. The
victorious Senator Douglas was on the road in the South in the winter
months of 1858–59. "It is a law of humanity, a law of civilization, that
whenever a man or a race of men show themselves incapable of managing their own affairs, they must consent to be governed by those who
are capable," Douglas said in New Orleans. "It is on this principle that
you establish those institutions of charity for the support of the blind,
or the deaf and dumb, or the insane. . . . I assert that the negro race,
under all circumstances, at all times, and in all countries, has shown itself incapable of self-government."

Lincoln was thinking different thoughts in the Illinois cold. At a Republican gathering in Chicago, he spoke in moral and national terms. If
slavery could be declared right and just on one side of a geographic line,
Lincoln asked, then what was to stop it from being declared right and

just on the other? Right and wrong were not situational realities, but eternal ones. "Stand by your principles," Lincoln told his Republican brethren in Chicago; "stand by your guns; and victory complete and permanent is sure at the last."

Mrs. Lincoln wrote during this Chicago trip with worrying news from Springfield. "If you are going up to Chicago today, & should meet Mr L there, will you say to him, that our *dear little Taddie* is quite sick," Mary told Ozias M. Hatch, the Illinois secretary of state. "The Dr thinks it may prove a *slight* attack of *lung* fever. I am feeling troubled & it would be a comfort to have him *at home*. [Tad] passed a bad night, I do not like his symptoms, and will be glad if he hurries home." The specter of the lost Eddy must have loomed large for Mary amid the sickness in the house. Lincoln was home within two days, and the boy recovered.

Lincoln was a man with national ambitions. "We must hold conventions, adopt platforms, select candidates, and carry elections," he said. "At every step we must be true to the main purpose." He published his 1858 debates with Douglas, cultivated journalists, and delivered major speeches in Illinois, Ohio, Wisconsin, Kansas, and beyond. The Republican political world had taken note of the defeated senatorial candidate. "You are like Byron, who woke up one morning and found himself famous," the editor Charles H. Ray had written to him. "People wish to know about you." Lincoln's friend David Davis agreed: "You have made a noble canvass, which, if unavailing in this State, has earned you a national reputation, and made you friends everywhere." In the fall of 1859, the Republican boss Thurlow Weed dispatched a simple telegram: "Send Abraham Lincoln to Albany immediately." The 1858 Senate defeat became ever more distant as the world looked forward to 1860.

To defeat the Democrats in 1860, Lincoln told his old Carroll Row messmate Nathan Sargent, "it has to be done by the North; no human invention can deprive them of the South." He was right: The white Southern interest was defiant and self-absorbed. "Last of all, in this great struggle, *we defend the cause of God and religion*," said the Reverend Benjamin M. Palmer, who was to become the first moderator of the first General Assembly of the Presbyterian Church in the Confederate States of America. "The abolition spirit is undeniably atheistic."

Palmer's words were part of the ethos of white Southern nationalism. Slave owners must learn to shape "the mind and heart of the age,"

the Episcopal bishop of Louisiana, Leonidas Polk, wrote in the second half of the 1850s. "We must either receive or make impressions. We have done our share of receiving. And the time has fully come when we should enter upon the work of mak-
ing." Polk's plan: a Southern university and seminary. "There ought to be enough of a love of learning and religion in the Church itself to found and endow the institution we would establish, amply," Polk wrote to the bishop of Georgia, Stephen Elliott. "I think there is a large amount at our disposal, enough perhaps for our purposes. If not, we have happily another influence at our disposal.... *The negro question will do the work.* It is an agency of tremendous power, and in our circumstances needs to be delicately managed. But it is in hand and in great force to be used by somebody. It will be used. *It insists upon being used.*"

The Louisiana bishop Leonidas Polk, who would become a Confederate general.

T he fall of 1859 also brought news from Harpers Ferry, Virginia, where John Brown, the architect of some of the most notorious violence in "Bleeding Kansas," had attempted to inspire a rebellion of the enslaved by seizing a federal arsenal. Consumed by biblical fervor and a sense of destiny, Brown, who had been born in 1800, saw visions others did not see and believed that he could light a conflagration that would destroy slavery. "I expect nothing but to endure hardness," he wrote before Harpers Ferry, "but I expect to effect a mighty conquest, even though it be like the last victory of Samson."

The allusion was telling. In the Book of Judges, Samson conquers in the last instance only in bringing about his own death. Blinded by the Philistines, Samson stands next to two pillars in a temple where his foes are gathered. "And Samson said, Let me die with the Philistines. And he bowed himself with all his might; and the house fell upon the lords, and upon all the people that were therein. So the dead which he slew at his death were more than they which he slew in his life."

Late on the night of Sunday, October 16, 1859, Brown and his twenty or so confederates captured the federal armory and a nearby rifle factory at Harpers Ferry. Word of the attack—which failed to prompt a widespread, or even a local, revolution—brought a force of marines from Washington under the command of Colonel Robert E. Lee. A brief assault ended the affair. One marine was killed. Half of Brown's force were dead; of the rest, seven—including Brown—were arrested, and five made their escapes. Brown was quickly tried, convicted, and hanged.

The particular had universal implications. The Harpers Ferry raid itself was brief. Its power, it turned out, was not in the actual but in the symbolic. From New England, Henry David Thoreau saw Brown as a noble martyr. "Some eighteen hundred years ago, Christ was crucified," Thoreau wrote. "This morning, perchance, Captain Brown was hung. These are two ends of a chain which is not without its links." In Virginia, the *Richmond Enquirer* saw Harpers Ferry as the end of the Union. "We must separate, unless we are willing to see our daughters and wives become the victims of a barbarous passion and worse insult," the paper said in November. On Capitol Hill, three Democratic members of a Senate investigating committee—Jefferson Davis of Mississippi, James Mason of Virginia, and Graham Fitch of Indiana—"sought diligently but unsuccessfully to find grounds to hold the Republican party at large responsible for Brown's raid," Hay and Nicolay recalled. In December, Representative Reuben Davis of Mississippi put the question on the Southern mind frankly: "Is it not time we were arming for our defense?"

On a speaking trip in Kansas, Lincoln tried to calm the storm. John Brown's attack "was a violation of law and it was, as all such attacks must be, futile as far as any effect it might have on the extinction of a great evil," Lincoln said. "We have a means provided for the expression of our belief in regard to Slavery—it is through the ballot box—the peaceful method provided by the Constitution."

In late 1859, with an eye on the presidential nomination, Lincoln was seeking to inform what he liked to call "public sentiment" with arguments rooted in history, reason, and faith. He did so because, as a practical man, he knew that history, reason, and faith were forever contending for dominion in the American arena. They did not always, or all that often, prevail. Partisan passion, economic interest, and cultural prejudice, whether against Black people or immigrants, were mighty, and frequently successful, forces. To contain human enslavement—and to fulfill his moral antislavery commitment—while preserving the American Union, he framed the question as one of fealty to the Founding versus fueling the fires of disunion.

Lincoln insisted that he and his party were the reasonable ones. "Your own statement of it is, that if the Black Republicans elect a President, you won't stand it," he said to critics in Kansas. "You will break up the Union. That will be your act, not ours." He then deftly deployed the news of the hour. "Old John Brown has just been executed for treason against a state. We cannot object, even though he agreed with us in thinking slavery wrong. That cannot excuse violence, bloodshed, and treason." Then he put the opposition on notice. "So, if constitutionally we elect a President, and therefore you undertake to destroy the Union, it will be our duty to deal with you as old John Brown has been dealt with."

Lincoln's words came as proslavery forces were seeking to curb the circulation of antislavery arguments. This was old and familiar ground: Gag rules and attempts at suppressing abolitionist mail dated from the age of Jackson. John Brown's raid and Hinton Rowan Helper's 1857 antislavery book *The Impending Crisis of the South: How to Meet It*—a Republican favorite—gave the issue fresh force. Mischaracterizing Helper's argument, Senator Alfred Iverson of Georgia charged that it called on "our slaves to fire our dwellings and put their knives to our throats." As a result, white Southerners "ought to hang every man who has approved or endorsed it." Democratic newspapers even called it "The Text Book of Revolution."

For decades the antislavery war had provoked proslavery reaction. In just the preceding thirty years, David Walker's *Appeal to the Coloured Citizens of the World,* the founding of Garrison's *Liberator,* and the publication of *American Slavery as It Is: Testimony of a Thousand Witnesses* in 1839, among other works, including *Uncle Tom's Cabin,* had forced the slaveholding South to field its own rhetorical armies. Slavery's defenders had long advanced their arguments, but they feared, in the words of South Carolina's William Harper, "the indisposition of the rest of the world to hear anything more on this subject."

In frustration and fear, the slave-owning interest caricatured their foes, affirmed their own virtue, and preached their own gospel. "The parties in this conflict are not merely abolitionists and slaveholders— they are atheists, socialists, communists . . . on the one side, and friends of order and regulated freedom on the other," the Presbyterian clergyman James Henley Thornwell, a defender of slavery from South Carolina, said in a representative sermon, "The Rights and the Duties of Masters," in 1850. "In one word, the world is the battleground—Christianity and Atheism the combatants; and the progress of humanity the stake." To Thornwell, slave owners were true Christians and adherents to the "ordinance of God." To defend slavery, then, was to defend Christianity itself. When the issue was framed so starkly, compromise was impossible, for to compromise was to sin. Reason did not enter into it. Minds could not be changed, nor hearts altered.

Talk of Lincoln's presidential prospects intensified. Lincoln was, after all, a voice of reason, or at least of reasonableness. In his debates with Douglas, he had proven a sensible advocate for the Republican position. He was firm in his antislavery convictions but not radical; clearheaded but not unnecessarily contentious or censorious. He was, in sum, an attractive prospect to take the Republican case to a divided nation.

Early in the year, in the library of the state supreme court, Jackson Grimshaw, Ozias Hatch, and several other Illinois friends asked Lincoln to an informal meeting upstairs in a private room Hatch sometimes used in the statehouse. "We all expressed our personal preference for Mr. Lincoln as the Candidate for the Presidency and asked him if his name might be used at once in Connection with the Coming Nomination and election," Grimshaw recalled. "Mr. Lincoln . . . doubted whether he could get the Nomination even if he wished it and asked until the next morning to answer us."

Lincoln returned the next day. He had an answer. It was yes.

In Washington, Senator Jefferson Davis of Mississippi was busy. On Thursday, February 2, 1860, he introduced resolutions asking his colleagues to declare that "no change of opinion or feeling on the part of the non-slaveholding States of the Union . . . can justify them or their citizens in open and systematic attacks thereon, with a view to its overthrow."

Born in Kentucky in 1808, Davis had grown up in Mississippi, at a house near Woodville called Poplar Grove. Tall and angular in the manner of Lincoln, Davis was well educated, attending a Roman Catholic school as a boy, spending time at Transylvania University in Lexington, and graduating from West Point. A Mississippi planter who owned about a hundred enslaved persons, Davis served in the U.S. House, as an officer in the Mexican War, and in the U.S. Senate before becoming Franklin Pierce's secretary of war. Davis returned to the Senate in 1857.

As Senator Davis's resolutions sat before the Senate in the late winter and spring of 1860, Lincoln left Springfield for the East. A highlight of the trip: a scheduled lecture at Henry Ward Beecher's Plymouth Church in Brooklyn. The Democratic *Illinois Register* commented: "Subject, not known. Consideration, $200 and expenses. Object, presidential capital." As it turned out, the venue was shifted across the East River to Manhattan. And so, on Monday, February 27, 1860, Abraham Lincoln would rise to address those gathered in the Great Hall of the Cooper Union for the Advancement of Science and Art, the brainchild of the inventor Peter Cooper to offer free classes for working people.

"No former effort in the line of speech-making had cost Lincoln so much time and thought as this one," William Herndon recalled of the Cooper Union address. Lincoln had received the invitation the previous October. He asked Herndon's "advice and that of other friends as to the subject and character of his address," Herndon recalled. "We all recommended a speech on the political situation." In the state library, Lincoln "searched through the dusty volumes of congressional proceedings" and spent time with the historian Jonathan Elliot's edition of *The Debates in the Several State Conventions on the Adoption of the Federal Constitution*, which he owned.

In New York in late February, Lincoln polished the text in his quarters at Astor House, the grand hotel next to St. Paul's Chapel at Broadway and Vesey. This was not an ordinary rally or even an ordinary campaign occasion. The Cooper audience was learned, influential, and exacting. Worried about the impression he was to make, Lincoln had brought a new suit from Illinois, but it was wrinkled from the journey and in any event didn't quite fit. "The collar of his coat on the right side had an unpleasant way of flying up whenever he raised his arm to gesticulate," Herndon recalled. The editor and poet William Cullen Bryant presided over the evening, and Lincoln fretted that the crowd might note "the contrast between his Western clothes and the neatfitting suits of Mr. Bryant and others who sat on the platform."

All such concerns evaporated as Lincoln said what he had come to say. It was a lawyerly address, rooted in fact. The frontier politician forwent stories and jokes, as if to make absolutely clear to the sophisticates of New York that he was a man to be taken seriously.

Lincoln made his case with precision. The nation lived under a Constitution framed by those who intended for the federal government to prevent the spread of slavery—the same framers who had prohibited the institution in the Northwest Ordinance. *"This is all Republicans ask— all Republicans desire—in relation to slavery,"* Lincoln said. *"As those fathers marked it, so let it be again marked, as an evil not to be extended, but to be tolerated and protected only because of and so far as its actual presence among us makes that toleration and protection a necessity. Let all the guaranties those fathers gave it, be, not grudgingly, but fully and fairly maintained."*

He was talking not only slavery versus freedom, but reason versus unreason, nationhood versus sectionalism. "I do not mean to say we are bound to follow implicitly in whatever our fathers did," Lincoln said. "To do so, would be to discard all the lights of current experience—to reject all progress—all improvement. What I do say is, that if we would supplant the opinions and policy of our fathers in any case, we should do so upon evidence so conclusive, and argument so clear, that even their great authority, fairly considered and weighed, cannot stand."

There was no such evidence, no such argument, when it came to slavery's expansion. As Lincoln saw it, white Southerners were staking everything on a defensive and belligerent worldview. It was all or nothing. "You will grant a hearing to pirates or murderers, but nothing like it to 'Black Republicans,'" Lincoln said, addressing white Southerners. "Indeed, such condemnation of us seems to be an indispensable prerequisite—license, so to speak—among you to be admitted or permitted to speak at all." Such was not the path to democratic deliberation, but to total war. Lincoln saw this. He knew this. And he warned his audience about this. To blindly and repeatedly assert one's own position, one's own righteousness, and one's own rectitude in the face of widely held opinion to the contrary was not democracy. It was an attempt at autocracy—a bid, as Lincoln said, to "rule or ruin in all events."

Democracies could not endure if absolutists prevailed. "A few words now to Republicans," Lincoln said. *"Even though the southern people will not so much as listen to us, let us calmly consider their demands, and yield to them if, in our deliberate view of our duty, we possibly can.* Judging by all they say and do, and by the subject and nature of their controversy with us, let us determine, if we can, what will satisfy them." He continued:

> The question recurs, what will satisfy them? . . . This, and this only: cease to call slavery *wrong,* and join them in calling it *right.* And this must be done thoroughly—done in *acts* as well as in *words.* Silence will not be tolerated—we must place ourselves avowedly with them.

Lincoln noted that the slave-owning interest wanted to suppress "all declarations that slavery is wrong, whether made in politics, in presses, in pulpits, or in private. We must arrest and return their fugitive slaves with greedy pleasure. We must pull down our Free State constitutions. The whole atmosphere must be disinfected from all taint of opposition to slavery, before they will cease to believe that all their troubles proceed from us." He made a critical point as he moved toward his conclusion. "Most of them would probably say to us, 'Let us alone, *do* nothing to us, and *say* what you please about slavery,'" Lincoln said. "But we do let them alone—have never disturbed them—so that, after all, it is what we say, which dissatisfies them."

"It is what we say": The very assertion of the rightness or wrongness of slavery was a source of agitation. "Their thinking it right, and our thinking it wrong," Lincoln noted, "is the precise fact upon which depends the whole controversy." Little wonder, then, that the white South reacted out of fear and pride and anger when it heard words of those, like Lincoln, who saw an entire way of life as founded not on a good but on an evil. He closed nobly:

> Wrong as we think slavery is, we can yet afford to let it alone where it is . . . but can we, while our votes will prevent it, allow it to spread into the National Territories, and to overrun us here in

these Free States? If our sense of duty forbids this, then let us stand by our duty, fearlessly and effectively. . . . LET US HAVE FAITH THAT RIGHT MAKES MIGHT, AND IN THAT FAITH, LET US, TO THE END, DARE TO DO OUR DUTY AS WE UNDER-STAND IT.

"Since the days of Clay and Webster, no man has spoken to a larger assemblage of the intellect and mental culture of our city," Horace Greeley's *New York Tribune* reported. "No man ever before made such an impression on his first appeal to a New York audience."

Lincoln did not rest. He spoke the next day in Providence, Rhode Island, to a crowd in the city's Railroad Hall that had come, as a journalist put it, "to hear the great champion of Republicanism in Illinois," then spent much of the ensuing Wednesday traveling by train to see Robert at school in Exeter, New Hampshire. Over the next two weeks Lincoln greeted voters and addressed audiences in Concord, Manchester, Dover, Exeter, Hartford, New Haven, Meriden, New London, Woonsocket, Norwich, and Bridgeport before returning to New York. "I have been unable to escape this toil," Lincoln wrote to his wife from Exeter on Sunday, March 4. "If I had foreseen it, I think I would not have come east at all."

This last point was that of a man who was tired, not one who truly regretted his many large and appreciative audiences. "The speech at New York, being within my calculation before I started, went off passably well and gave me no trouble whatever. The difficulty was to make nine others, before reading audiences who had already seen all my ideas in print." That was the price of the political life: to repeat himself many times over; to greet each new person in each new city as if the world revolved around that person and that city; to worry about the polish of each performance.

Lincoln left New York for home on the morning of Monday, March 12, boarding the Erie Railroad. "Mr. Lincoln has done a good work and made many warm friends," the *Tribune* wrote. He would need them all, and more, as attention moved to the Republican National Convention in Chicago, set for May. His ambition was evident. "The taste *is* in my mouth a little," Lincoln confessed to a friend in April. He liked his chances. After Cooper Union, he wasn't alone. "We hazard nothing in saying that no man," the *Chicago Press and Tribune* wrote, "has ever risen so rapidly to political eminence in the United States."

Politics being politics, Lincoln received, and rejected, suggestions that he buy support among the Republican delegates in Chicago. "I cannot enter the ring on the money basis—first, because, in the main, it is wrong; and secondly, I have not, and cannot get, the money," he wrote to a Republican correspondent in Kansas in March. Another man, E. Stafford, apparently proposed that a large sum would help secure votes. "I could not raise ten thousand dollars if it would save me from the fate of John Brown," Lincoln replied. "Nor have my friends, so far as I know, yet reached the point of staking any money on my chances of success. I wish I could tell you better things, but it is even so."

In the 1860 Republican contest, Lincoln believed he stood the best chance of uniting his party. William Seward of New York was seen as the strongest candidate as delegates gathered in Chicago. Other contenders included Salmon P. Chase of Ohio, Simon Cameron of Pennsylvania, and Edward Bates of Missouri. "My name is new in the field; and I suppose I am not the *first* choice of a very great many," Lincoln wrote on Saturday, March 24, 1860. "Our policy, then, is to give no offense to others—leave them in a mood to come to us, if they shall be compelled to give up their first love."

He had the politics just about perfect. The other contenders seemed to have more support—but they also had more opposition. Lincoln's advice to his allies in Chicago: "Give no offense, and keep cool under all circumstances." In a stormy time, a steadying hand might be welcome. *"Make no contracts that will bind me,"* he ordered his lieutenants.

Articulate and without an inordinate number of enemies, Lincoln emerged as the nominee at Chicago, winning on the convention's third ballot on Friday, May 18, 1860. Word of his victory was telegraphed to Springfield by noon. After the second ballot, Lincoln had left the telegraph office to pay a call at the *Illinois Journal*. When the news came, the telegraph operator scribbled: "Mr. Lincoln, you are nominated on the third ballot." A messenger scurried to the newspaper and gave the note to Lincoln, who pocketed it, thought of Mary, and said, "There's a little woman down at our house [who] would like to hear this. I'll go down and tell her."

"How gratified . . . Mary must feel, at Mr. Lincoln's nomination," her sister Elizabeth Todd Edwards wrote in May. "I do hope that her ambition may be fully satisfied in November next."

After an evening rally at the statehouse, friends and supporters swarmed the Lincolns' home at Eighth and Jackson. "To-night the City is in a blaze of excitement," *The New York Times* reported from Springfield. In remarks to the throng outside the house, Lincoln "said he would invite the whole crowd into his house if it was large enough to hold them"; a voice called out, "We will give you a larger house on the fourth of next March[!]" A delegation from Chicago led by George Ashmun of Massachusetts, the president of the convention, called at the house the next day. During the pleasantries, Lincoln singled out the tall Judge William D. Kelley of Pennsylvania.

"What's your height?" Lincoln asked.

"Six feet three; what is yours, Mr. Lincoln?"

"Six feet four."

"Then," Kelley said, "Pennsylvania bows to Illinois. My dear man, for years my heart has been aching for a President that I could *look up to*, and I've found him at last in the land where we thought there were none but *little* giants." A New England delegate praised the nominee to the *Chicago Daily Journal*: "I was afraid I should meet a gigantic railsplitter, with the manners of a flat-boatman, and the ugliest face in creation; and he's a complete gentleman."

Springfield was jubilant. Reporters noted "the sky blazing with rockets, cannon roaring at intervals, bonfires blazing at the street corners, long rows of buildings brilliantly illuminated, the State-House overflowing with shouting people."

Lincoln, who was to stand for election on a ticket with Hannibal Hamlin of Maine as the vice presidential nominee, looked forward, not backward. "Holding myself the humblest of all whose names were before the convention, I feel in especial need of the assistance of all," he wrote to Salmon P. Chase. "I shall, in the canvass, and especially afterwards, if the result shall devolve the administration upon me, need the support of all the talent, popularity, and courage, North and South, which is in the party," Lincoln told Cassius M. Clay. "May the Almighty grant that the cause of truth, justice, and humanity, shall in no wise suffer at my hands," Lincoln wrote to his old friend Joshua Giddings.

What a victory for truth, justice, and humanity would look like was at issue, for Lincoln's definition of truth, his grasp of justice, and his vision of what would best serve humanity was far from universally shared. The Democratic press derided Lincoln as "a third-rate, slang-whanging lawyer; a man, well enough in his way, but possessing no proper qualification for the place for which he is nominated . . . put forward as 'Old Abe Lincoln'—'Old Uncle Abe'—'Honest Old Abe'—and the people are expected to accept a slang nickname, in lieu of fitness, and 'go it blind.' "

He was seeking the presidency of a country riven not only by competing interests but by incompatible understandings of reality. Lincoln saw democracy as an essential good; his foes saw it as a threat to an aristocracy of power. Lincoln saw slavery as an evil to be eradicated; his foes saw it as a necessary and divinely ordained fact of life. To defend that aristocracy, and that fact of life, those foes of the Republican railsplitter of Illinois had gathered in Charleston, South Carolina, to marshal their forces, and to take their stand.

CHAPTER FOURTEEN

God Help Me, God Help Me

Lincoln is President-elect of these United States.
—Washington Republican BENJAMIN BROWN FRENCH,
November 1860

If there is sufficient manliness at the South to strike for our
rights, honor, and safety, in God's name let it be done before
the inauguration of Lincoln.
—GOVERNOR MADISON PERRY of Florida, autumn 1860

The triumph of the principles which Mr. Lincoln is pledged to
carry out is the death-knell of slavery.
—JAMES HENLEY THORNWELL of South Carolina, 1861

T
HE VISION OF AMERICA in Charleston was not the vision of
America in Chicago. The theological, historical, and intellectual
perspectives that led Abraham Lincoln to stand against the
spread of slavery were inverted in the white South, which defended
enslavement through its own theological, historical, and intellectual
lenses. In many of the planter states, especially in the lower South, slavery was not to be endured as a temporal evil protected by the Constitution (Lincoln's position) but was to be celebrated as an eternal good, as
a gift of God, and as a wholly rational institution.

At noon on Monday, April 23, 1860, the Honorable David A. Smal-
ley, the United States district judge for Vermont and chairman of the
Democratic National Committee, called the party's 1860 convention
to order in the Grand Hall of Charleston's South Carolina Institute
on Meeting Street. Within minutes—after a prayer by an Episcopal
clergyman—the delegates fell into procedural squabbles. No one seems
to have been in a particularly good humor. Charleston in the late spring
was already brutally hot, and a cold rain shower just before the convention convened brought suffocating humidity.

On the floor, William Lowndes Yancey of Alabama spoke for the fractious, defensive, wary, martial spirit of white Southerners who believed the present and the future were slipping from their accustomed control. "Ours is the property invaded; ours are the institutions which are at stake; ours is the peace that is to be destroyed; ours is the property that is to be destroyed; ours is the honor at stake," Yancey said. They would, he added, "yield no position here until we are convinced we are wrong."

A revealing phrase: *"Until we are convinced we are wrong."* By the spring of 1860, it was as though the slaveholder interest could hear nothing more—could absorb nothing more—once it was told that the rest of the nation had found its way of life morally wanting. It felt *judged*, and it hated it.

I n Charleston, a majority report of the 1860 Democratic platform committee was unambiguously proslavery, asserting that "Congress has no power to abolish slavery in the Territories." "We shall go to the wall upon this issue if events shall demand it, and accept defeat upon it," Yancey said. In Washington, Jefferson Davis told the Senate, "We want nothing more than a simple declaration that negro slaves are property, and we want the recognition of the obligation of the Federal Government to protect that property like all other."

A minority report in the Democratic convention was more moderate, calling for the party to avoid congressional action on slavery and to support popular sovereignty. Northern Democrats were strong—but not strong enough to reach the two-thirds threshold needed to secure the presidential nomination for Stephen Douglas, whom the party's Southern wing saw as too soft on slavery. Driven by passion and pride, many of the more radical Southern Democrats, losing the platform vote 165 to 138, left the convention. Alabama, Florida, Mississippi, and Texas withdrew outright. A majority of delegates from Arkansas, Georgia, South Carolina, and Virginia followed as well. "Perhaps even now the pen of the historian is nibbed to write the story of a new revolution," Yancey cried.

In Washington, Benjamin Brown French reported, the city's Republicans were in "high glee" at the "broken" Democratic convention. Born in New Hampshire in 1800, French was a longtime Washington figure, a former commissioner of public buildings and former clerk of the U.S. House who had joined the Republican ranks. At a three-hour Republican meeting after the Democratic collapse in Charleston, Representative Charles Case of Indiana read the preamble of Pennsylvania's 1780 act for gradual abolition. Regardless of race, the Pennsylvanians had declared, "all are the work of an Almighty Hand. We find in the distribution of the human species, that the most fertile as well as the most barren parts of the earth are inhabited by men of complexions different from ours, and from each other; [and] . . . He who placed them in their various situations, hath extended equally his care and protection to all, and that it becometh not us to counteract his mercies." French articulated the core Republican view: "It is strong, and shows how determined our fathers were that the Declaration of Independence should not be a farce of mere words!"

The regular Democrats soon reconvened in Baltimore. Douglas secured the nomination, but it was a Pyrrhic victory. The Yancey-led forces had broken away for good and selected Vice President John C. Breckinridge of Kentucky as their man for president. Aside from Lincoln, there was yet a fourth candidate, John Bell of Tennessee, a "Constitutional Unionist" moderate who represented the Whig remnant.

No fire-eater, the young, attractive Breckinridge came from Mary Lincoln's Lexington. It was speculated at the time that his nomination was motivated more by anti-Douglas animus among white Southern Democrats than by genuine enthusiasm for Breckinridge. Observers then (and scholars since) believe that the idea was to divide the Democrats so deeply that Douglas, Breckinridge, and Bell would withdraw in favor of former President Franklin Pierce. The ploy failed. The incumbent vice president stayed in the race. "Breckinridge may not be for disunion," Stephen Douglas remarked, "but all the disunionists are for Breckinridge."

On Monday, June 4, 1860, Charles Sumner spoke in the Senate. "Barbarous in origin; barbarous in its law; barbarous in all its pretensions; barbarous in the instruments it employs; barbarous in consequences; barbarous in spirit; barbarous wherever it shows itself," Sumner said, "Slavery must breed barbarians." *The New York Times* reported the remarks, entitled "Charles Sumner on the Barbarism of Slavery," in full. "It is pronounced the most ultra violent and offensive speech ever delivered in either branch of Congress," the *Times* wrote, and Sumner had the text reprinted and distributed widely. He sent

Lincoln a copy that week. "I have not yet found time to peruse the speech," Lincoln replied, "but I anticipate much both of pleasure and instruction from it."

In the white South, Sumner's words foreshadowed a Republican reign of terror. "I cannot possibly be enlightened or in any way be used by you & your associates to subserve your impious & treasonable designs against the religion of the Bible, & the Government of our Country," the Episcopal clergyman Edward Fontaine of Jackson, Mississippi, wrote to Sumner on Saturday, August 25, 1860. "Your speech is calculated to produce the impression that your caning has to some extent crazed your wit, & entirely destroyed your charity. You seem to regard every Southern Slaveholder as a 'bloody-minded' Brooks; and every negro-slave as a poor wretch flogged like yourself. But you are entirely mistaken, & you deceive your constituents."

To question slavery was to question the white South's values, faith, and intelligence—and such questions solicited not thoughtful replies but raw anger. For slavery was not incidental to the white Southern way of life; it was essential to white Southern power in terms of creating wealth, of maintaining white hegemony, and of holding sway in national politics. Limit slavery and you limited the reach of white Southerners; allow freedom to grow in the West and you put slavery in danger where it existed. When everything was at stake, nothing could be conceded.

As the four-way presidential field prepared to face voters, Lincoln remained in Springfield. "I trust that Mr. Lincoln is safe, but the Democrats about here express a strong faith in some combination that will make Douglas the next President," Elizabeth Todd Edwards wrote to her son Edward in August. The nominee understood how the slave states, including Kentucky, felt about him. When a visit to his native state was suggested, Lincoln replied, "Would not the people Lynch me?" Tennessee seemed equally inhospitable. A campaign broadside for John Bell referred to Lincoln as "Traitor Lincoln," "Tory Lincoln," and "N——r Lincoln." The election, for Lincoln, would be decided in the North.

"Lincoln bears his honors meekly," Orville Browning noted in June. "As soon as other company had retired after I went in he fell into his old habit of telling amusing stories, and we had a free and easy talk of an hour or two." Lincoln declined to weigh in on issues beyond what he had already said in the public record. "Tell him my motto is 'Fairness to all,'" Lincoln instructed his new secretary, the former Illinois editor John G. Nicolay, who was about to meet with an old congressional friend. "But commit me to nothing." Lincoln was cautiously optimistic about the campaign. "The prospect of Republican success now appears very flattering, so far as I can perceive," the presidential nominee wrote to Hannibal Hamlin in July.

The Lincoln-Hamlin ticket looked strong. "We know not what a day may bring forth"—the phrase was an allusion to Proverbs—"but, to-day, it looks as if the Chicago ticket will be elected," Lincoln confided to a friend on the Fourth of July. He was writing in some personal distress. Willie had been sick, and Lincoln himself was under the weather. "Our boy, in his tenth year (the baby when you left), has just had a hard and tedious spell of scarlet-fever; and he is not yet beyond all danger. I have a head-ache, and a sore throat upon me now, inducing me to suspect that I have an inferior type of the same thing." There was more family news: "Our eldest boy, Bob, has been away from us nearly a year at school, and will enter Harvard University this month," Lincoln wrote. "He promises very well, considering we never controlled him much."

The press of business did not prevent Lincoln from reassuring a Phillips Exeter classmate of Bob's, George Latham, another Springfield boy, who had been rejected by Harvard College. It was a generous note, grounded in Lincoln's own disappointments along the way. "In your temporary failure there is no evidence that you may not yet be a better scholar, and a more successful man in the great struggle of life, than many others, who have entered college more easily." He did not say—and did not need to—that such counsel came from a man who knew of what he spoke: A single-term congressman and failed would-be senator now likely to become the next president of the United States.

A terrible storm struck Springfield in the first days of August, bringing down a brick wall at William and George Withey's carriage and wagon manufacturing shop. Lincoln reported the storm's "considerable damage" to a friend, then moved quickly on to the electoral map: "I hesitate to say it, but it really appears now as if the success of the Republican ticket is inevitable. We have no reason to doubt any of the states which voted for Frémont. Add to these, Minnesota, Pennsylvania, and New-Jersey, and the thing is done."

"Well, boys, your troubles are over now," Lincoln told friends after he and Hannibal Hamlin won the 1860 election, "but mine have just commenced."

A correspondent for *The New York Herald* called at Eighth and Jackson on Tuesday, August 7. "The ladies were especially entertaining, while 'Old Abe' and your correspondent took a chair together and talked upon almost every topic now attracting the attention of the public," the *Herald* wrote. Lincoln spoke of slavery, repeating his assurances that he would not interfere with it where it existed. "The Southern mind, he said, was laboring under the delusion that the Republicans were to liberate the slaves, who were to apply firebrands to the fields and dwellings of their masters, massacre old and young, and produce a state of general anarchy and bloodshed in the South," the *Herald* reported. He would like to be able to explain himself directly to those white Southerners, he added, "were it not that the minds of some were so inflamed against him that they would not listen to his reasoning" and "might be inclined to inflict Lynch law upon his person should he appear among them."

Another caller at the house recorded a homey domestic scene. "It was a plain, comfortable frame structure, and the supper was an old-fashioned mess of indigestion, composed mainly of cake, pies and chickens, the last evidently killed in the morning, to be eaten, as best they might, that evening," the Ohio diplomat and editor Donn Piatt recalled. Mary was the center of energy, Lincoln a large and welcoming presence. "His body seemed to me a huge skeleton in clothes," Piatt recalled. "Tall as he was, his hands and feet looked out of proportion, so long and clumsy were they. Every movement was awkward in the extreme. He sat with one leg thrown over the other, and the pendent foot swung almost to the floor. And all the while, two little boys, his sons, clambered over those legs, patted his cheeks, pulled his nose, and poked their fingers in his eyes, without causing reprimand or even notice."

Lincoln played his part as husband well and wryly. "Mrs. L. declares it is a superb article," he wrote to a correspondent in thanks for a gift of soap. "She at the same time protests that *I* have never given sufficient attention to the 'soap question' to be a competent judge." Mary talked a good deal. "This good lady injected remarks into the conversation with more force than logic," Piatt recalled, "and was treated by her husband with about the same good-natured indifference with which he regarded the troublesome boys."

Lincoln's only public remarks of the campaign came at the fairgrounds in Springfield. Arriving by carriage, Lincoln was swarmed. He spoke less as a candidate and more as a president, as a leader of all, not as the favorite of some. The cheering reception was "evidence that four years from this time you will give a like manifestation to the next man who is the representative of the truth on the questions that now agitate the public," Lincoln said. "And it is because you will then fight for this cause as you do now, or with even greater ardor than now, though I be dead and gone."

Death was on his mind as threats of assassination reached Springfield. On Saturday, October 20, Major David Hunter, a West Point graduate stationed at Fort Leavenworth, Kansas, wrote that "a number of young men in Virginia had bound themselves 'by oaths most solemn' to assassinate Lincoln if he were elected." It was likely just talk, but Hunter noted that on "'the *institution*'"—slavery—"these good people are most certainly demented."

"We are hovering over a volcano ready to burst at any moment," Robert H. Cartmell, a Madison County, Tennessee, slave-owning farmer, wrote in his diary in October 1860. "*What a pity!* To sever, tear up and destroy the best Government ever devised by the ingenuity of man or revealed by heaven, except for the slavery question I believe no other question could sever the bands of Union."

The Lincoln circle watched the race nervously. "I presume . . . Mary is still alternating between hope and fear, and will scarcely be calmed after Mr. Lincoln's election which seems to be a thing decided upon," Elizabeth Todd Edwards wrote on the first day of November. "A few more days, I hope, will furnish us the pleasing assurance."

Election Day—Tuesday, November 6, 1860—was reported to be "cool . . . clear and . . . fine." Lincoln spent much of the day in his borrowed offices at the statehouse, voting at about three thirty in the afternoon. In the evening he took up headquarters in the city's telegraph office at 121 South Fifth Street—it was located above Chatterton's jewelry store—to monitor the returns.

Results trickled in through the early-morning hours of Wednesday; Mary Lincoln was asleep at the Lincolns' house when the returns added up to a Republican victory. Her husband then walked the roughly eight blocks home to Eighth and Jackson. "Mary, Mary!," Lincoln reputedly told his drowsy wife, *"we are elected!"* The vote reflected the nation's fractures. Lincoln won 53.9 percent of the popular vote in the eighteen states that comprised the North, running up majorities in Connecticut, Illinois, Indiana, Iowa, Maine, Massachusetts, Michigan, Minnesota, New Hampshire, New York, Ohio, Pennsylvania, Rhode Island, Vermont, and Wisconsin. He won California, New Jersey, and Oregon with pluralities of the popular vote.

In the slave states, Lincoln won only 2.1 percent of the votes—a nearly negligible performance—as Breckinridge carried the region with 44.7 percent. (Bell was second, with 40.4 percent; Douglas third with 12.8 percent.) Lincoln's name was not even on the ballot in Alabama, Arkansas, Florida, Georgia, Louisiana, Mississippi, North Carolina, South Carolina (which did not bother to hold a vote at all, choosing to give their electors to Breckinridge), Tennessee, and Texas. He had some support in the border states of Delaware, Kentucky, Maryland, and Missouri, and managed a 1.2 percent showing in Virginia.

"Lincoln is President-elect of these United States," Benjamin Brown French told his diary. "My political hopes so far are realized, but my fears that the threats of the South are really to bring trouble upon the whole Union, by being carried into stern action[,] almost render me joyless at the grand result. But if Disunion is to come merely because the South cannot have *all* the old sow's teats to suck, then I say in John Quincy Adams's words[,] 'Let it come!'"

On the whole, Frederick Douglass thought the news good. "For fifty years the country has taken the law from the lips of an exacting, haughty and imperious slave oligarchy," Douglass observed. "Lincoln's election has vitiated their authority, and broken their power."

Which was precisely what the rebel South feared—and would fight against.

Lincoln was the focus of all attention. Seventy years before, in the first days of the government under the Constitution, John Adams had foreseen how central the president would be in American life. "His person, countenance, character, and actions, are made the daily contemplation and conversation of the whole people," Adams wrote in 1790. Now it was Lincoln's turn.

A young girl from upstate New York, Grace Bedell, had written Lincoln an amusing but important letter. "I am a little girl only eleven years old, but want you should be President of the United States very much so I hope you won't think me very bold to write to such a great man as you are.... I have got 4 brothers and part of them will vote for you anyway and if you will let your whiskers grow I will try and get the rest of them to vote for you. You would look a great deal better for your face is so thin. All the ladies like whiskers and they would tease their husbands to vote for you and then you would be President."

Lincoln replied with caution—"As to the whiskers, having never worn any, do you not think people would call it a piece of silly affection if I were to begin it now?"—but soon appeared in public just as Grace Bedell had envisioned.

For Lincoln, the election marked not an end, but a beginning—of stress and strain, of crisis and anguish, of uncertainty and obligation. He constructed his cabinet in order to bring all the elements of his party into his official family. Seward accepted the Department of State; Chase the Treasury; Bates became attorney general. Reaching out to the powerful Blair family, Lincoln appointed Montgomery Blair postmaster general. The Blairs had been a force in American politics since the days of Jackson. Based in Washington, with a country house at Silver Spring, Maryland, the clan included Francis Preston Blair, Sr., and Francis Blair, Jr., a congressman from Missouri. Antislavery but not egalitarian, they—as well as Lincoln at this point—favored emancipation and colonization. Hour to hour and day to day, Lincoln understood the enormity of what awaited him. "I feel a great responsibility," he remarked. "God help me, God help me." "Well, boys, your troubles are over now," he said after the election, "but mine have just commenced."

As he spoke, those troubles were multiplying with speed and force. Within three days of the election, Lincoln was hanged in effigy in Pensacola, Florida. "If there is sufficient manliness at the South to strike for our rights, honor, and safety," Governor Madison Perry of Florida wrote, "in God's name let it be done before the inauguration of Lincoln." South Carolina's two United States senators, James Henry Hammond and James Chesnut, Jr., resigned their seats in the Congress less than a week after the presidential election. The state called for a secession convention to meet in Columbia on Monday, December 17.

At the one-week mark after his election, Lincoln was discovered reading Andrew Jackson's proclamation to the people of South Carolina of Monday, December 10, 1832. Armed with a steel-tipped pen in his office on the second floor of the White House, Jackson had drafted the proclamation so quickly that the pages glistened with ink as he wrote. To Jackson, it was a great truth that the Constitution "forms a *government*, not a league. . . . Disunion by armed force is *treason*." The people, not the states, were paramount. The ballot box, the courts, and the process of amendment were the proper avenues of reform. All else led to what Jackson called "the mad project of disunion."

The rights of nullification and secession, Lincoln believed, had been thus settled. Henry Clay had helped resolve the crisis of 1832–33, and the Union had endured. The same had happened in 1820 and in 1850. History therefore suggested that a resolution short of war was within the realm of possibility. "My own impression is at present (leaving myself room to modify the opinion if upon a further investigation I should see fit to do so) that this government possesses both the authority and the power to maintain its own integrity," the president-elect observed. Lincoln hoped for the best. "I am told that Mr. Lincoln considers the feeling at the South to be limited to a very small number, though very intense," the *New York Tribune* wrote. White Southerners "won't give up the offices," Lincoln remarked in November. "Were it believed that vacant places could be had at the North Pole, the road there would be lined with dead Virginians."

The Lincolns left Springfield for a visit to Chicago on Wednesday,

November 21. "Old Abe looks as though the campaign had worn lightly upon him," the Lexington, Illinois, *Weekly Globe* reported. "He is commencing to raise a beautiful pair of whiskers, and looks younger than usual." In Chicago, the president-elect met Hannibal Hamlin at the Tremont House, and they conferred over the next several days, dining with Lyman Trumbull and meeting at Ebenezer Peck's mansion, Lake View, on the city's North Side. At dinner one evening, Donn Piatt, the Ohio Republican, grew heated on hearing Lincoln insist that the South was unlikely to secede and to fight. "I became somewhat irritated and told him that in ninety days the land would be whitened with tents," Piatt recalled.

"Well, we won't jump that ditch until we come to it," Lincoln said.

Lincoln was wrong about the scope and scale of secessionist sentiment. "Our fathers made this a government for the white man, rejecting the negro, as an ignorant, inferior, barbarian race, incapable of self-government, and not, therefore, entitled to be associated with the white man upon terms of civil, political, or social equality," the secessionist leader William L. Harris of Mississippi remarked. "This new administration comes into power, under the solemn pledge to overturn and strike down this great feature of our Union . . . and to substitute in its stead their new theory of the universal equality of the black and white races." Lincoln's election was understood to be what the South Carolina Presbyterian divine James Henley Thornwell called "the death-knell of slavery." The white power structure with the most to lose—or to gain—believed the president-elect embodied their deepest fear: the destruction of slavery.

CHAPTER FIFTEEN

He Has a Will of His Own

Too many of us forget that when this Union was formed,
Slavery was the RULE—Freedom the EXCEPTION.

—Republican editor THURLOW WEED, December 1860

It is demanded of us that we shall consent to change the
Constitution into a genuine proslavery instrument, and to
convert the Government into a great slave-breeding, slavery-
extending empire.

—SENATOR JAMES GRIMES, Republican of Iowa

O N SUNDAY, NOVEMBER 25, 1860, Lincoln attended services at
Chicago's St. James Episcopal Church. Seated in what was
called the Arnold pew, halfway up the center aisle on the right
side of the sanctuary, the president-elect "was very attentive to the service," an observer recalled, "but during the sermon . . . he became lost
in thought and leaned forward to 'play' with a large tassel that hung on
the hood of a cloak worn by a lady sitting in front of him." As the
preacher droned on and Lincoln worked things through in his mind,
the readers of the *Albany Evening Journal* were absorbing a new line of
argument from its editor, the Republican Thurlow Weed. Born in 1797,
Weed, a close ally of William Seward's, had become a fixer and fixture
in New York politics. Lincoln appreciated the editor's perspective—
and his power.

In the Saturday, November 24, 1860, edition of the *Evening Journal,*
Weed raised the possibility of compromise with the slaveholding South.
Of the "vexed question" of "the right of going into the Territories with
Slaves," Weed wrote, "why not restore the Missouri Compromise
Line?" This was something striking: An overture from the Republican
side signaling that the crucial tenet on which Lincoln had run—the
containment of slavery—could be negotiable. *The New York Times* re-

On a mission to Springfield, Thurlow Weed of the Albany Evening Journal *urged the president-elect to compromise on slavery.*

ported that "leading men" in Washington were talking about opening the southern portions of the Western territories—and perhaps future acquisitions below the 36° 30′ latitude—to slavery. "Too many of us forget that when this Union was formed, Slavery was the RULE—Freedom the EXCEPTION," Weed argued that winter. "It will, and may be said, that we are forgetting the wrongs, encroachments, aggressions, and outrages of Slavery. True. We choose to do so just now."

A compromise in the winter of 1860–61 could have enshrined slavery across the continent—and perhaps across the hemisphere—across the century. The pressure was great; what was America, after all, but an exercise in compromise? The Founders whom Lincoln revered were masters of the art. Henry Clay had built his reputation upon give-and-take. Crises were always presenting themselves, from Missouri in 1820 to nullification in 1832–33 to the crises of 1850 and 1854.

Presidents, senators, business leaders, and editors counseled Lincoln to consider another such accommodation. Even William Seward, the incoming secretary of state, privately retracted his assertion that the struggle between slavery and freedom was an "irrepressible conflict." It might well be repressible, and indeed repressed, Seward admitted to a friend, should the new president agree to a compromise. The "irrepressible conflict" rhetoric, Seward told William C. Rives of Virginia, had been "intended for effect at home, and not designed for the ears of the South."

For Lincoln, the Union, the fate of slavery, and the viability of democracy were always entwined. He could not put his antislavery principles into practice without the Union, for the enslaved would have been at the mercy of the Confederacy in a dismembered American Republic. And a dismembered American Republic would have jeopardized the cause of democracy worldwide. To Lincoln, maintaining the Union, sustaining self-government, and eradicating slavery were one and the same cause. The white South understood this; that is why secession and war came.

If the image of Lincoln as Father Abraham, the Great Emancipator, is sometimes overdrawn, Lincoln courageously resisted compromising on slavery in an hour when such compromise was within the realm of acceptable opinion. The president-elect's steadfastness in the winter of 1860–61 helped make the end of slavery possible. In these cold and complex months, Abraham Lincoln was both statesman and moral being, choosing the difficult over the easy, the catastrophic over the convenient, the right over the wrong.

S eward harbored hopes for a deal. "If southern members will be for once cautious and forbearing," he wrote in early December, "if we can keep peace and quiet for a time, the temper will be favorable on both sides to consultation." In the North, many business leaders believed secession was bad for commerce. On Saturday, December 15, two thousand merchants gathered at 33 Pine Street in New York to "urge the South to postpone disunion," *The New York Times* reported, until a committee of businessmen could intervene and help protect slavery in the territories. "The mercantile world is in a ferment, even some good reliable Republicans are alarmed and wish something done. . . . I do fear that this Republican alarm may extend even to Springfield," wrote Senator Zachariah Chandler of Michigan, a firm Republican.

It was a reasonable anxiety—and it was one that an aging lawmaker from Kentucky hoped to exploit as he rose in the Senate on Tuesday, December 18, 1860. A familiar figure in the national capital, the elderly John Jordan Crittenden—he was seventy-three in the winter of 1860–61—had been in public service since 1809, the year Lincoln had been born. Attorney for the Illinois Territory under the governorship of the elder Ninian Edwards, Crittenden had been first elected to office in 1811, when he began a series of terms in the Kentucky House of Representatives. A veteran of the War of 1812 and a friend of the Todd family in Lexington, Crittenden had been born in 1787 and educated at Washington College (later Washington & Lee) and at William and Mary. For decades he moved between politics and the practice of law, serving in the U.S. Senate, as attorney general, and as governor of Kentucky. The end of the 1850s found him again in the Senate.

Crittenden was seeking to avert war and defend slavery with a sweeping set of constitutional amendments and legislative proposals. Slavery would be protected in the District of Columbia ("so long as it exists in the adjoining States of Virginia and Maryland") and on federal installations in slave-owning states. Enforcement of the Fugitive Slave Act would be strengthened. The keystone: the extension of the Missouri Compromise line west—including in territory "hereafter acquired," which made Cuba, Mexico, and the rest of Latin America fertile ground for slaveholders. States could join the Union free or slave—and a final Crittenden amendment would have declared that Congress could never again interfere with slavery.

It was a breathtakingly proslavery package. And it was popular. Petitions calling for passage poured into Washington; Crittenden estimated that a quarter of a million people had gone on record in favor of a deal. "There can be no doubt that Crittenden's plan of adjustment, if submitted to a direct vote of the people, would be adopted by such a vote as never was polled in this country," *The Richmond Whig* wrote. *New York Tribune* editor Horace Greeley agreed, recalling that the Crittenden plan "claimed a large majority of the people in its favor."

As many in the North saw it, Crittenden was asking the world of them and precious little of the South. "It is demanded of us that we shall consent to change the Constitution into a genuine proslavery instrument, and to convert the Government into a great slave-breeding, slavery-extending empire," said Senator James Grimes of Iowa. Crittenden's plan "means the dismemberment of Mexico," argued Representative James Wilson of Indiana. "It means Cuba. It means Central America. It means an empire of slavery, such as the world has never before witnessed." To his white Southern colleagues, Representative Charles Van Wyck of New York was blunt: "Your unholy crusade, therefore, against the Union, is to extend the area of slavery."

In the House, Representative Alexander Boteler of Virginia had suggested that a "Committee of Thirty-Three" be formed—each state was to receive one seat—to seek a way out of the crisis. The Senate did the same, but with thirteen members, including Seward. "There must be some tangible point presented & this has been done by Mr. Crittenden in his Missouri Compromise Resolutions," President Buchanan wrote to a correspondent in December.

So began a debate over whether the United States could remain a single nation. South Carolina was hurtling toward secession. Its convention would vote unanimously, 169 to 0, to do just that on Thursday, December 20. The Cotton States seemed likely to follow. But other slaveholding states—Virginia, Maryland, Delaware, Tennessee, Kentucky, and Missouri—appeared reachable if a reasonable compromise could be found.

On the same day that South Carolina voted to secede, the pro-compromise Thurlow Weed reached Springfield to confer with the president-elect. "Lincoln was six feet three and a half in height, and Mr. Weed more than six feet," the Lincoln adviser Leonard Swett recalled. "Both had rough, strongly marked features, and both had risen by their own exertions from humble relations to the control of a nation whose destinies they were then shaping."

Lincoln read Weed's editorial endorsing a settlement while the two men were together. "The prevalent sentiment . . . rejects all 'compromises,'" Weed had written, "and that, if it is to be accepted as our ultimatum, terminates the controversy." The piece continued:

> And yet what matter of difference between individuals, families, communities, States, or nations, was ever settled except by "compromise"? . . . Admit that, while threatening treason, while organizing armies to overthrow the Government, they have passed the boundary of negotiation, [but] let us remember that they are blinded by passion, and endeavor to reason both for them and ourselves.

Weed was sure of this much: that the North would fight for the Union, but not for abolition. Even if it came to nothing, backing the Crittenden plan would show the whole North that Lincoln had tried to prevent war and would bolster Northern support for an eventual conflict. And if the plan did come to pass, so much the better. There would be no war.

"This is a heavy broadside," the president-elect said to Weed. "You have opened your fire at a critical moment, aiming at friends and foes alike. It will do some good or much mischief. Will the Republicans in New York sustain you in this view of the question?" It did not seem so. "What calamity might not spring from making to slavery this golden promise of a shadowy and eternal by-and-by?" said Representative Roscoe Conkling, a New York Republican. "Why, sir, it would amount to a perpetual covenant of war against every people, tribe, and State owning a foot of land between here and Terra del Fuego. It would make the Government the armed missionary of slavery."

Lincoln's position was closer to Conkling's than it was to Weed's. "The most we can do now is to watch events, and be as well prepared as possible for any turn things may take," the president-elect wrote on Saturday, December 22. Lincoln urged his party to stand strong. "Let there be no compromise on the question of extending slavery," he had written to Lyman Trumbull on Monday, December 10. "If there be, all our labor is lost, and, ere long, must be done again. The dangerous ground—that into which some of our friends have a hankering to run—is Pop. Sov. Have none of it. Stand firm. The tug has to come, & better now, than any time hereafter."

Yet the impulse for compromise would not die. Seward reportedly allowed that Republicans would take a deal in which "the territorial question [was] settled by the Missouri Compromise Bill running to the Pacific." Despite his doubts, Lincoln sent Weed back East with a bit of encouragement. "Thurlow Weed was with me nearly all day yesterday, & left at night with three short resolutions which I drew up," Lincoln wrote to Lyman Trumbull. Lincoln's suggested language touched on enforcement of the Fugitive Slave Act and asserted in general terms that the Union had to be protected, nothing more. The resolutions were not particularly interesting. What is intriguing is that Lincoln did not dispatch Weed with the unambiguous conviction that the president-elect was not going to compromise in the least. As Weed recalled, Lincoln told him that "while there were some loud threats and much muttering in the cotton States, he hoped that by wisdom and forbearance the danger of serious trouble might be averted, as such dangers had been in former times." To think of compromise at all, Weed wrote that winter, "is a new and novel position, for we have been all our life showing up the dark side of the Slavery Picture. But in view of a fearful calamity, there is no want of consistency or of fidelity, in going to the verge of conciliation with the hope of averting it." Lincoln does not appear to have disagreed.

The campaign to bring Lincoln to be forbearing—to compromise in some fundamental way—continued. In late December 1860, President

Buchanan sent the editor and politician Duff Green, whom Lincoln had known of old in Washington at Mrs. Sprigg's (and who was married to a kinswoman of Mary Lincoln's), on an unpublicized mission to Springfield. A key issue was whether Lincoln would support constitutional amendments to codify the proposals of the Crittenden Compromise.

In a letter to Buchanan, Green reported that Lincoln said "he believed that the adoption of the [Missouri Compromise] line proposed would quiet *for the present* the agitation of the Slavery question, but believed it would be renewed by the seizure and attempted annexation of Mexico. He said that the real question at issue between the North & the South, was Slavery 'propagandism' [meaning growth] and that upon that issue the Republican Party was opposed to the South and that he was with his own party; that he had been elected by that party and intended to sustain his party in good faith, but added that *the question of the Amendments to the Constitution and the questions submitted by Mr. Crittenden, belonged to the people & States in legislatures or Conventions & that he would be inclined not only to acquiesce, but give full force and effect to their will thus expressed.*"* The words gave the compromisers grounds for hope. It was not a no. In a draft letter, Lincoln wrote:

> I declare that the maintenance inviolate of the rights of the States, and especially the right of each state to order and control its own domestic institutions . . . is essential to that balance of powers on which the perfection, and endurance of our political fabric depends—and I denounce the lawless invasion, by armed force, of the soil of any State or Territory, no matter under what pretext, as the gravest of crimes.
>
> I am greatly averse to writing anything for the public at this time; and I consent to the publication of this, only upon the condition that six of the twelve United States Senators for the States of Georgia, Alabama, Mississippi, Louisiana, Florida, and Texas shall sign their names to what is written on this sheet below my name, and allow the whole to be published together.

The language for the senators was straightforward: "We recommend to the people of the States we represent respectively, to suspend all ac-

---

* Italics mine.

tion for dismemberment of the Union, at least, until some act, deemed to be violative of our rights, shall be done by the incoming administration." The letter and the resolutions went nowhere. In acknowledging the primacy of the Constitution and of any amendments that might be duly ratified, Lincoln was not wavering on principle. He was, rather, signaling that those who remained within the constitutional order had nothing to fear from him—at least not in the near term. In this period, Lincoln's antislavery project was not about unilaterally striking at slavery where it existed, but about slowly strangling it.

Such details did not matter to the secessionist states. They were not listening; they had largely made their decisions. They *did* fear Lincoln. They hated his antislavery platform. They believed him an instrument of abolition and of egalitarianism—two things they were choosing to fight with all their strength. In January, South Carolina would be joined in secession by Mississippi, Florida, Alabama, Georgia, and Louisiana. In February, Texas seceded; in April, Virginia; in May, Arkansas and North Carolina; and finally, in June 1861, Tennessee.

The slaveholders' views were clear. "We know what is coming in this Union," Senator Alfred Iverson of Georgia said in December 1860. "It is universal emancipation and the turning loose upon society in the Southern States of the mass of corruption which will be made by emancipation. We intend to avoid it if we can. . . . We are obliged to have African slavery to cultivate our cotton, our rice, and our sugar fields. African slavery is essential not only to our prosperity, but to our existence as a people." "I am of the opinion that our beloved Union is drawing to an ignominious end," a Nashville diarist wrote on Christmas Day. "Lincoln has been elected President & the whole South is shaken from center to circumference." "For the North to undertake to force obedience, on the part of the South, to the views of the North, would be absolute folly," John S. Brien of Nashville wrote to a correspondent in Cincinnati on New Year's Eve 1860. "The North, perhaps, by force of its superior numbers and munitions of war, might exterminate the South—conquer it, they never could. You know this is the Southern character."

Jefferson Davis argued that the Confederacy was a restoration of the original Constitution, but Alexander Stephens saw the secessionist enterprise as an explicitly white supremacist one. The Declaration of Independence, Stephens said, was not their declaration. "Our new government is founded upon exactly the opposite idea" to that of "all men are created equal"; instead, Stephens announced, the Confederacy's "foundations are laid, its corner-stone rests, upon the great truth that the negro is not equal to the white man; that slavery subordination to the superior race is his natural and normal condition. This, our new government, is the first, in the history of the world, based upon this great physical, philosophical, and moral truth."

That the nation was dealing with emotion as well as fact on secession was evident in an exchange between Lincoln and Stephens in December. The two had known each other in Congress in the late 1840s. In a Saturday, December 22, 1860, letter to Stephens, headed "For your own eye only," Lincoln asked, "Do the people of the South really entertain fears that a Republican administration would, *directly,* or *indirectly,* interfere with their slaves, or with them, about their slaves? If they do, I wish to assure you, as once a friend, and still, I hope, not an enemy, that there is no cause for such fears. . . . You think slavery is *right* and ought to be extended; while we think it is *wrong* and ought to be restricted. That I suppose is the rub."

"When men come under the influence of fanaticism, there is no telling where their impulses or passions may drive them," Stephens replied. "This is what creates our discontent and apprehensions, not unreasonable when we see . . . such reckless exhibitions of madness as the John Brown raid into Virginia. . . . A word fitly spoken by you now would be like 'apples of gold in pictures of silver.' "

This last phrase, from the Book of Proverbs, prompted Lincoln to think about how he would address the country once he took office. In fragmentary notes on "the Constitution and the Union," he wrote:

> Without the *Constitution* and the *Union*, we could not have attained [the creation and maintenance of a great nation]; but even these, are not the primary cause of our great prosperity. There is something back of these, entwining itself more closely about the human heart. That something, is the principle of "Liberty to all"—the principle that clears the *path* for all—gives *hope* to all—and, by consequence, *enterprise,* and *industry* to all.
>
> The *expression* of that principle, in our Declaration of Independence, was most happy, and fortunate. *Without* this, as well as *with*

it, we could have declared our independence of Great Britain; but *without* it, we could not, I think, have secured our free government, and consequent prosperity. No oppressed people will *fight*, and *endure*, as our fathers did, without the promise of something better, than a mere change of masters.

The assertion of that *principle*, at *that time*, was *the* word, *"fitly spoken"* which has proved an "apple of gold" to us. The *Union*, and the *Constitution*, are the *picture* of *silver*, subsequently framed around it. The picture was made, not to *conceal*, or *destroy* the apple; but to *adorn*, and *preserve* it. The *picture* was made *for* the apple—*not* the apple for the picture.

So let us act, that neither *picture*, or *apple* shall ever be blurred, or bruised or broken.

To defend that principle of "Liberty to all," Lincoln opposed the Crittenden Compromise. "We have just carried an election on principles fairly stated to the people," he wrote in January 1861. "Now we are told in advance, the government shall be broken up, unless we surrender to those we have beaten, before we take the offices. In this they are either attempting to play upon us, or they are in dead earnest. Either way, if we surrender, it is the end of us, and of the government. They will repeat the experiment upon us *ad libitum*. A year will not pass, till we shall have to take Cuba as a condition upon which they will stay in the Union. They now have the Constitution . . . and acts of Congress of their own framing, with no prospect of their being changed; and they can never have a more shallow pretext for breaking up the government, or extorting a compromise, than now."

Lincoln would not bend. "I know him as well as he does himself," William Herndon wrote of the president-elect in January 1861, "and I say to you, that he is a man of broad deep good heartedness: but he has a *will* of his own. . . . on the questions of Justice—Right—Liberty he rules himself." And so Lincoln was resolute. "Prevent, as far as possible, any of our friends from demoralizing themselves, and our cause, by entertaining propositions for compromise of any sort, on 'slavery extension,' " Lincoln had written to Elihu B. Washburne in mid-December. "There is no possible compromise upon it, but which puts us under again, and leaves all our work to do over again." When George Sumner, a younger brother of Charles Sumner, visited Lincoln to warn him against compromise, Lincoln agreed: "By no act or complicity of mine shall the Republican party become a mere sucked egg, all shell and no principle in it."

Lincoln's ultimate refusal to compromise steeled Republicans. In December, things had not been so certain. "The Thirty-Three committee is sitting now every day and all day, and they'll be reporting some damned nonsense or other soon," Henry Adams, a son of Representative Charles Francis Adams, Sr., a Massachusetts Republican, had written to one of his brothers in mid-December. "I only speak exact truth when I tell you to prepare yourself for a complete disorganization of our party."

January brought a different impression. "Mr. Weed . . . who came . . . here with various compromise measures . . . has gone back today," Henry Adams wrote on Monday, January 7, "without having found the first Republican to give them countenance." What changed between the young Adams's despondent words in December and his more hawkish ones in January? The will of the president-elect had become clear—or clear enough. Neither the resolutions he gave Weed nor the reply he provided Green was sufficient to appease the white South. Lincoln would take what came.

On Wednesday, January 16, 1861, by a vote of 25 to 23, the Senate declined to put the Crittenden proposals on the floor. Still, it was a fluid and complicated time. Compromise overtures continued to proliferate. There was a bid to ask the four living former presidents— Martin Van Buren, John Tyler, Millard Fillmore, and Franklin Pierce—to come to Washington to adjudicate the sundry disputes. Virginia, which was still considering whether to join its southernly neighbors in secession, called for a Peace Conference to be held in Washington. And Charles Francis Adams sponsored resolutions designed to bring New Mexico into the Union as a slave state.

It was a tactical gesture. Along with Seward, Congressman Adams believed that the Republicans needed to appear reasonable in order to prevent the secession of the border South—chiefly Virginia and Maryland. To be seen as willing to concede New Mexico, whose terrain was thought to be unfriendly to slavery, would, they believed, accomplish this end. The maneuver worked: The proposal failed to pass the Congress and convinced the border South, for a time, that immediate secession was not essential. Lincoln understood the game and reluctantly approved of how his allies in Washington were playing it. "As to fugitive slaves, District of Columbia, slave trade among the slave states, and whatever springs of necessity from the fact that the institution is amongst us, I care but little, so that what is done be comely, and not altogether outrageous," the president-elect wrote to Seward on the first day of February 1861. "Nor do I care much about New-Mexico, if further extension were hedged against."

At Willard's, under the chairmanship of former president John Tyler, the Peace Conference convened by Virginia brought scores of politicians to Washington beginning in the first week of February. As the Virginia legislature put it, the goal was to "adjust the present unhappy controversies, in the spirit in which the Constitution was originally formed." Talk was plentiful, action limited. Resolution, if resolution there would be, would not come from a conference but from the secessionist South's reaction to the administration of a man who was about to board a train to come east from Springfield, into the storm. "The political horizon looks dark and lowering; but the people, under Providence, will set all right," Lincoln wrote. Providence, alas, worked on its own terms and in its own time.

CHAPTER SIXTEEN

To Take the Capitol by Violence

Treason is all around you.

—A Nashville correspondent, warning of insurrection in Washington

Mr. Lincoln entered the Capital as the poor, hunted fugitive
slave reaches the North, in disguise, seeking concealment,
evading pursuers.

—FREDERICK DOUGLASS, on Lincoln's surreptitious arrival
in Washington

WASHINGTON WAS RIVEN WITH RUMORS as the new year
began. Secession was a fact; insurrection, a consuming fear.
"The terror here among the inhabitants is something wonderful to witness," Henry Adams wrote from the capital. Henry Wise,
the former governor of Virginia, was said to be raising a twenty-five-
thousand-man army to march on the capital to prevent Lincoln's taking office. Others reported plots "to poison horses of the military,"
destroy the Capitol building, and hang loyal members of Lincoln's
party. Another rumor had several thousand secessionists arriving with
concealed arms, bribing federal troops, and seizing government buildings. The conspirators would cut the telegraph wires, sabotage the rail
lines, and install either John Breckinridge or Jefferson Davis as president of a new Southern republic before the Northern states could
mobilize. "Treason," a Nashville correspondent warned officials in
Washington, "is all around you."

It was a season of secrets, uncertainty, and threats. Newspapers reported and the House investigated, sundry scenarios. *The New York Herald* said there could be plans "to take the Capitol by violence." The
counting of the Electoral College votes, scheduled for Wednesday, February 13, might be stopped. Or Lincoln would be assassinated, either en
route to Washington or at the time of the March 4 inauguration. Representative Elihu B. Washburne of Illinois warned the president-elect

of "a widespread and powerful conspiracy." The attorney general of the United States, Edwin Stanton, thought it *"not . . . probable, hardly possible"* that the Union would still control Washington by March 4. Simon Cameron told Lincoln that "our friends are hopeful, but there is still much trouble & some danger." In a letter to Lincoln dated Saturday, December 29, 1860, William Seward reported the prevalent fears of violence or assassination. "I am not giving you opinions and rumors," Seward wrote to Lincoln. "Believe that I know what I write."

A committee of five members of the House was commissioned to "inquire whether any secret organization hostile to the government of the United States exists in the District of Columbia," and if there were, whether any municipal or federal officials were "members thereof." In closed-door hearings, the committee investigated whether "a conspiracy had been formed to seize the Capitol and Treasury, to get possession of the archives of the government, and to prevent the counting of the electoral vote and the declaration of the election of Lincoln," Representative Henry L. Dawes of Massachusetts wrote, "thereby creating chaos and anarchy, out of which might come the establishment of the Confederacy as the government *de facto* in the very halls of the national Capitol."

The committee had a secret source within the Buchanan administration: Edwin Stanton, the Unionist who had become attorney general in December. At night, Stanton would slip into the darkened streets of Washington to share documents with congressmen. As a high official, the attorney general was privy to the cabinet's deliberations—deliberations that sometimes served the interests not of the Union but of the secessionists. "Mr. Cobb believes that the time is come for resistance; that upon the election of Lincoln, Georgia ought to secede from the Union," W. H. Trescott, the assistant secretary of state, wrote of Treasury Secretary Howell Cobb of Georgia. The secretary of war, John Floyd of Virginia, attempted to move arms from Pittsburgh to the South and authorized the sale of muskets to South Carolina. The secretary of the Navy, Isaac Toucey, surrendered the Navy Yard at Pensacola to the governor of Florida and to Alabama militia. "There is a . . . traitor in the cabinet," Stanton told members of the select committee. "Pensacola has been given up." In the last days of the Buchanan administration, the House censured Toucey for failing to prepare the navy to defend Union positions and property.

The committee also received a delegation from the seceded South Carolina. The representatives of the rebel state headquartered themselves on K Street in a "fine house . . . the rent of which, it is said, they never paid," and lobbied for diplomatic recognition. President Buchanan referred the matter to Congress, and Henry Dawes recalled the young South Carolinian who presented himself to the panel. "He was a very young man for one representing in his person the majesty of an independent government, seemingly having hardly attained his majority, with light hair, boyish face, and a mustache trained after the imperial order, rare in those days, which was a surprising success upon a face otherwise so downy," Dawes wrote. "He wore patent-leather shoes and light-colored trousers in very large plaids, twirled on the tips of his fingers a cane with an apparently golden head turned over and finished in the hoof of a horse; in short, he was a dude of the dudes of that day, and fit to be a prototype of the race."

The rebels longed to be seen as legitimate, justified, even noble. After South Carolina's withdrawal from the Union, the secessionist Robert Barnwell Rhett imagined how a historian, writing in the new millennium, might describe the South: "Extending their empire across this continent to the Pacific, and down through Mexico to the other side of the great gulf, and over the isles of the sea, they established an empire and wrought out a civilization which has never been equaled or surpassed." "We shall have new and original thought; negro slavery will be its great controlling and distinctive element," the white Southern journal *De Bow's Review* wrote in July 1861; "but we should compound it of as many elements as possible—Greek, Roman, Hebrew, Christian, English, French, Spanish and Italian." To Dawes in the Capitol hearing room, the South Carolinian said, "You cannot be ignorant, sir, that the new sovereign state of South Carolina has sent ambassadors to negotiate a treaty of friendship and alliance with this neighboring government of the United States." The emissary lectured the committee: "South Carolina, when she consented to be one of the United States, gave up no part of her sovereignty, but only laid it away for future use whenever it seemed meet to her. She now decrees to resume it, and that is sufficient." As Dawes recalled, wryly, "It was so simple and easy a process that he expressed astonishment at our ignorance." At the heart of the argument: "He went on, without specific questions, to expound more at length the theory which had given birth to his government, and expatiated upon the enormity of the outrages his 'people' expected would happen . . . when Lincoln should be inaugurated."

There was the central issue: the Lincoln presidency. A window of vulnerability, Lincoln knew, was the certification of the election in mid-February. "It seems to me the inauguration is not the most dangerous point for us," the president-elect told Seward. "Our adversaries have us more clearly at disadvantage" if they could disrupt or delay the Electoral College count. "It is, or is said to be, more than probable," Henry Adams wrote, "that some attempt or other will be made to prevent the counting of votes and the declaration of Lincoln's election"—and thus to prevent his presidency.

Winfield Scott, the aged commanding general of the U.S. Army, stepped into the breach. "I have seen Genl. Scott, who bid me say he will be glad to act under your orders, in all ways to preserve the Union," Simon Cameron told Lincoln. "That, for this purpose, he has ordered here 2 companies of flying artillery; and that he will organize the militia—and have himself *sworn in as constable*." Deploying federal troops throughout the capital, Scott left no doubt about his intentions. Anyone "who attempted by force or unparliamentary disorder to obstruct or interfere with the lawful count," the general declared, would be "lashed to the muzzle of a twelve-pounder and fired out a window of the Capitol."

Much came down to a single man, and a single moment: the vice president of the United States, John Breckinridge, and the transfer of the Electoral College votes from the Senate to the House, where he was to preside and certify the election. Defeated for president, sympathetic to the Southern cause, yet constitutionally charged with being an honest broker, Breckinridge was the object of all eyes on Wednesday, February 13. "The certificates of the electoral vote from each State are kept till the appointed day in two boxes in the sole custody of the Vice-President, who, on that day, with a messenger carrying the two boxes, and followed by the Senators, two and two, proceeds from the Senate Chamber, through the corridors and rotunda, always crowded and pressed upon on either side by people following to witness the ceremony, to the House of Representatives," Dawes recalled. "There, in the Speaker's chair, and in the presence of the two Houses and a crowded gallery, he opens the certificates, counts the votes, and declares the result."

Anyone who sought to disrupt the certification of
Lincoln's lawful election, Winfield Scott declared,
would be "lashed to the muzzle of a twelve-pounder
and fired out a window of the Capitol."

Dawes captured the fears of the hour. "The ease with which desperadoes, mingling with the crowd, might fall upon the messenger as
he passed through the corridors or rotunda, and violently seize the
boxes, or from the galleries of the House might break up the proceedings, was apparent." A hundred plainclothes police from New York and
Philadelphia were stationed along the route from the Senate to the
House, and in the House gallery, "prepared for any emergency." The
chamber was "filled to overflowing with spectators," the Baltimore *Sun*
reported, and the "immense throng strained its ears to catch . . . every
word."

Breckinridge did his duty, Dawes recalled, "with Roman fidelity . . .
and the nation was saved." As a Kentuckian, though he would later become a Confederate general, Breckinridge opposed secession at this
juncture. "I would prefer to see these States all reunited upon true constitutional principles," Breckinridge would say in August 1861—and as

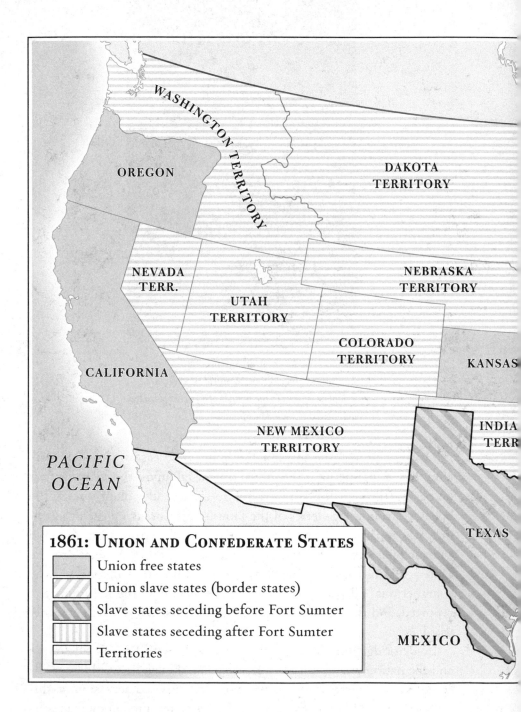

WASHINGTON TERRITORY

OREGON

DAKOTA
TERRITORY

NEVADA
TERR.

UTAH
TERRITORY

NEBRASKA
TERRITORY

COLORADO
TERRITORY

KANSAS

CALIFORNIA

INDIA
TERR

NEW MEXICO
TERRITORY

PACIFIC
OCEAN

TEXAS

1861: Union and Confederate States

Union free states

Union slave states (border states)

Slave states seceding before Fort Sumter

Slave states seceding after Fort Sumter

Territories

MEXICO

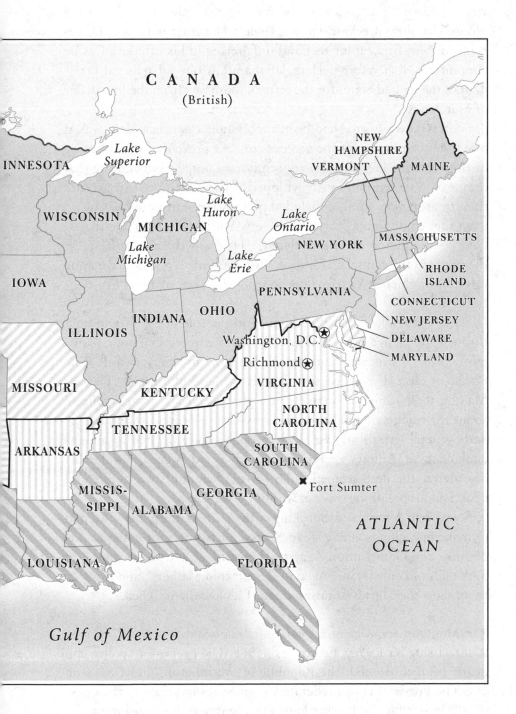

CANADA
(British)

MINNESOTA
Lake Superior
WISCONSIN
IOWA
MISSOURI
ARKANSAS
LOUISIANA

MICHIGAN
Lake Huron
Lake Michigan
ILLINOIS
INDIANA
OHIO
KENTUCKY
TENNESSEE
MISSIS-SIPPI
ALABAMA

Lake Ontario
Lake Erie
NEW YORK
PENNSYLVANIA
Washington, D.C.
Richmond
VIRGINIA
NORTH CAROLINA
SOUTH CAROLINA
GEORGIA
FLORIDA

NEW HAMPSHIRE
VERMONT
MAINE
MASSACHUSETTS
RHODE ISLAND
CONNECTICUT
NEW JERSEY
DELAWARE
MARYLAND

Fort Sumter

ATLANTIC OCEAN

Gulf of Mexico

vice president, he acted according to those principles. In the crowded House chamber, Breckinridge was "pale and a little nervous," Dawes recalled, "but firm on his feet and unfaltering in his utterance" as he announced: "I therefore declare Abraham Lincoln duly elected President of the United States for the term of four years from the fourth day of March next."

Scott's show of force had been successful. "*Unquestionably* it was at one time the purpose of the seceders to have prevented the counting of the votes for President," a contemporary noted, "but finding that they would be ignominiously whipped if they attempted to execute their treason, they wisely concluded that it were better not to essay . . . what they could not perform." The New York City lawyer and diarist George Templeton Strong declared, "This was the critical day for the peace of the capital. A foray of Virginia gents . . . could have done infinite mischief by destroying the legal evidence of Lincoln's election."

Scott was resolute that the Union, and the rule of law, would hold through the inauguration. "The old warrior is roused," Simon Cameron wrote to Lincoln, "and he will be equal to the occasion." The president-elect dispatched the adjutant general of Illinois, Thomas Mather, to Washington with a letter that asked for Scott's opinion about the rumors of conspiracy and of violence. Mather found the elderly general "grizzly and wrinkled, propped up in the bed by an embankment of pillows. . . . His hair and beard were considerably disordered, the flesh seemed to lay in rolls across his warty face and neck, and his breathing was not without great labor."

Scott's hands trembled. Speaking with emotion, the general wanted to make himself absolutely clear: Secessionists were not going to undermine the Constitution. "Say to [Lincoln] . . . 'I'll plant cannon at both ends of Pennsylvania Avenue,'" Scott told Mather, "'and if any of them show their heads or raise a finger I'll blow them to hell.'"

I n Montgomery, Alabama, the Confederate States of America came into being on Friday, February 8, 1861. The breakaway polity had nearly been christened "the Republic of Washington," but CSA won out. The Provisional Confederate Congress soon turned to the question of leadership. "Who should be President, was the absorbing question of the day," Duncan F. Kenner of Louisiana recalled. Jefferson

Davis was the clear choice, with Lincoln's old colleague Alexander Stephens of Georgia winning the vice presidency.* The election was held on Saturday, February 9; two days later, on Monday, February 11, 1861, Abraham Lincoln embarked on his journey to Washington. This was the schedule he had hoped to follow; he had resisted entreaties to come to the capital earlier in the winter. "I don't want to go before the middle of February, because I expect they will drive me insane after I get there, and I want to keep tolerably sane, at least until after the inauguration." Lincoln now set off on what he modestly called "an errand of national importance." Scheduled to speak along the route, Lincoln asked organizers to be efficient, writing, "Please arrange no ceremonies which will waste time." To borrow a phrase from one of his twentieth-century successors, Franklin D. Roosevelt, Lincoln's remarks en route to Washington formed a kind of rolling Fireside Chat—a presidential conversation with the country about the country. As he left from the Great Western depot in Springfield, Lincoln struck elegiac notes:

> For more than a quarter of a century I have lived among you, and during all that time I have received nothing but kindness at your hands. Here I have lived from my youth until now I am an old man. Here the most sacred ties of earth were assumed; here all my children were born; and here one of them lies buried. To you, dear friends, I owe all that I have, all that I am. All the strange, chequered past seems to crowd now upon my mind. Today I leave you; I go to assume a task more difficult than that which devolved upon General Washington. Unless the great God who assisted him, shall be with and aid me, I must fail. But if the same omniscient mind, and Almighty arm that directed and protected him, shall guide and support me, I shall not fail, I shall succeed. Let us all pray that the God of our fathers may not forsake us now. To him I commend you all—permit me to ask that with equal security and faith, you all will invoke His wisdom and guidance for me.

---

* Davis and Stephens were chosen by the Provisional Confederate Congress. They also won a general election held in November 1861. Had the Confederacy survived, their six-year terms would have ended in early 1868.

Among the scenes of the "strange, chequered past" that passed through his mind as he moved east were of his own half century of life, and of the vagaries and vicissitudes of a world that had propelled him, improbably, to his present place. Before he had left Springfield, he had spent a day with his stepmother, Sarah, and his cousin John Hanks.

The encounter had left him thinking about the past. As ever with Lincoln, such reflections were not an unmixed pleasure: The uncertain legitimacy of his mother's birth, and possibly of his own, was on his mind. "I cannot but know what you all know, that, without a name, perhaps without a reason why I should have a name, there has fallen upon me a task such as did not rest even upon the Father of his country," Lincoln told the Ohio legislature in Columbus on Wednesday, February 13, 1861—the day after his fifty-second birthday. "I turn, then, and look to the American people and to that God who has never forsaken them." A human admission in the throes of historical circumstance: The man who at some level doubted his own parentage was steeling himself, and summoning temporal and divine help, as he tried to put the national family back together again.

Lincoln spoke gently to the country's agitated elements. "We mean to remember that you are as good as we; that there is no difference between us, other than the difference of circumstances," he said in Cincinnati, addressing his words to white Southerners across the river in Kentucky. "We mean to recognize, and bear in mind always, that you have as good hearts in your bosoms as other people, or as we claim to have, and treat you accordingly."

In notes for remarks to the people of Kentucky, Lincoln delineated his perspective. "During the winter just closed, I have been greatly urged, by many patriotic men, to lend the influence of my position to some compromise, by which I was, to some extent, to shift the ground upon which I had been elected," Lincoln wrote. "This I steadily refused. . . . I thought such refusal was demanded by the view that if, when a Chief Magistrate is constitutionally elected, he cannot be inaugurated till he betrays those who elected him, by breaking his pledges, and surrendering to those who tried and failed to defeat him at the polls, this government and all popular government is already at an end."

Noble words, and by and large Lincoln acted accordingly. "I will suffer death," Lincoln wrote in remarks published in the nation's newspapers in late January and early February, "before I will consent or will advise my friends to consent to any concession or compromise which looks like buying the privilege of taking possession of this government to which we have a constitutional right." He was anxious to make clear that the Deep South's defections need not lead to further disunion, much less to war. "I repeat it, then—*there is no crisis*, excepting such a one as may be gotten up at any time by designing politicians," Lincoln said at Pittsburgh on Friday, February 15. "My advice, then, under such circumstances, is to keep cool."

In Westfield, New York, he alluded to Grace Bedell's letter about his whiskers. "'Some three months ago, I received a letter from a young lady here; it was a very pretty letter, and she advised me to let my whiskers grow, as it would improve my personal appearance; acting partly upon her suggestion, I have done so; and now, if she is here, I would like to see her,'" *The Philadelphia Inquirer* quoted Lincoln as saying. "A small boy," the report went on, "mounted on a post, with his mouth and eyes both wide open, cried, 'there she is, Mr. Lincoln,' pointing to a beautiful girl, with black eyes, who was blushing all over her fair face. The President left the car, and the crowd making way for him, he reached her, and gave her several hearty kisses, and amid the yells of delight from the excited crowd, he bade her good-bye, and on we rushed."

Lincoln extended a hand to Northern Democrats. "I suppose that here, as everywhere, you meet me without distinction of party, but as the people," he said to an energetic crowd at Poughkeepsie, New York, on Tuesday, February 19. "I see that some, at least, of you are of those who believe that an election being decided against them is no reason why they should sink the ship. I believe with you, I believe in sticking to it, and carrying it through; and, if defeated at one election, I believe in taking the chances next time. I do not think that they have chosen the best man to conduct our affairs, now—I am sure they did not—but acting honestly and sincerely, and with your aid, I think we shall be able to get through the storm."

Lincoln talked so much that he had become "quite hoarse." He made his excuses at different stops, saying, "I have lost my voice and cannot make a speech, but my intentions are good." Still, he managed to speak when he wanted to. "The man does not live who is more devoted to peace than I am," Lincoln told the New Jersey legislature. "None who would do more to preserve it. But it may be necessary to put the foot down firmly."

At this, the *New York Tribune* reported, "the audience broke out into cheers so loud and long that for some moments it was impossible to hear Mr. L.'s voice."

"And if I do my duty, and do right, you will sustain me, will you not?"

There were, the *Tribune* said, "Loud cheers, and cries of 'Yes,' 'Yes,' 'We will.'"

Satisfied, Lincoln added, "Received, as I am, by the members of a Legislature the majority of whom do not agree with me in political sentiments, I trust that I may have their assistance in piloting the ship of State through this voyage, surrounded by perils as it is; for if it should suffer attack now, there will be no pilot ever needed for another voyage."

At Independence Hall on Washington's birthday, Lincoln reflected on the Founders and on the price of protecting their work. To defend the Declaration was a sacred charge. If the country "cannot be saved without giving up that principle—I was about to say I would rather be assassinated on this spot than to surrender it," Lincoln said. "The Government will not use force unless force is used against it. . . . I have said nothing but what I am willing to live by, and in the pleasure of Almighty God, die by."

He believed in the sanctity of his task, and of the task facing the American populace. "I am exceedingly anxious that this Union, the Constitution, and the liberties of the people shall be perpetuated in accordance with the original idea for which that struggle was made," Lincoln had said in New Jersey, "and I shall be most happy indeed if I shall be an humble instrument in the hands of the Almighty and of this, his almost chosen people, for perpetuating the object of that great struggle."

Lincoln arrived in Washington in secrecy. Rumors of a plan to assassinate the president-elect in Baltimore compelled Samuel M. Felton, the president of the Philadelphia, Wilmington, and Baltimore Railway, to engage Allan Pinkerton, the Chicago detective, to investigate. "It was made as certain as strong circumstantial and positive evidence could make it," Felton recalled, "that there was a plot to burn the bridges and destroy the road, and murder Mr. Lincoln on his way to

Washington." From Rochester, Frederick Douglass observed, "Mr. Lincoln entered the Capital as the poor, hunted fugitive slave reaches the North, in disguise, seeking concealment, evading pursuers, by the underground railroad . . . not during the sunlight, but crawling and dodging under the sable wing of night."

When Lincoln arrived, he checked in to Willard's. Mary, who joined him via a different train, had vetoed staying at the National Hotel "on account of the sickness four years ago"—President-elect Buchanan had become ill at the National Hotel in 1857. General Scott was still monitoring the threats against the president-elect and briefed the marshal of the inauguration, Benjamin Brown French, and others about "the information, anonymous and otherwise, that he had recd. threatening the assassination of the President-elect." According to French, Scott also detailed his "theory of what the assassins expected to gain. . . . Which was, briefly, that all who could act as President of the U.S. should be got out of the way, thus leaving the U.S. Govt. without any head, when the Southern Confederacy was to step in and assume the Government of the whole Country."

"I told him," French recalled, "I thought if any such effort should be made I thought that the Southern President would not be very likely to reach Washington alive."

As French and Scott conferred, the president-elect was becoming the center of attention. On the afternoon of Monday, February 25, Lincoln visited the House and Senate floors to pay his quiet respects. While at the Capitol, the place in the city he knew best, he walked down to the Supreme Court chamber to greet Chief Justice Taney, who received the president-elect coldly but civilly. Senator Crittenden called at Willard's, as did President Buchanan and a delegation from the still unfolding Peace Conference.

The inauguration only days away, the Peace Conference issued a proposed Thirteenth Amendment to the Constitution that restored the Missouri Compromise line and directed that "no future territory could be acquired, even by treaty, without separate majority votes by free- and slave-state senators alike." Crittenden embraced the amendment, which was defeated. Another version, named for its Republican sponsor, Representative Thomas Corwin of Ohio, aimed to put the federal consensus view into the Constitution in amendment form: "No amendment shall be made to the Constitution which will authorize or give to Congress the power to abolish or interfere, within any State, with the domestic institutions thereof, including that of persons held to labor or service by the laws of said State."*

For many Republicans, the Corwin proposal offered an opportunity to appear conciliatory toward the slave-owning South without giving up real ground. Essentially, the amendment would make explicit and formal what virtually everyone agreed the Constitution already implied: that the federal government was powerless to interfere with slavery inside the states where it already existed. Nothing in the measure would prevent the states themselves from abolishing slavery—a remote prospect, but still the prospect that most observers in early 1861, including Lincoln, believed would have to be realized if slavery where it currently existed were to end. Such abolition had occurred before, though involving many fewer enslaved people, many years earlier: Pennsylvania, Connecticut, Rhode Island, New York, and New Jersey had all undertaken gradual emancipation. For Lincoln, who said he had no objection to the proposal, the Corwin Amendment did nothing to undercut his driving strategy of leading the states to agree to emancipation, however far off that day seemed in the winter of 1860–61. Most of all, support for this proposed Thirteenth Amendment fitted within the Republican strategy of seeking to stem the spread of secession—to provide evidence, in the final hours of the Buchanan administration, that the incoming Lincoln regime was hardly threatening summary abolition. In the end, it did not matter. Corwin's amendment passed both houses of Congress but was never ratified by the states.

Watching the president-elect from a distance that winter, Frederick Douglass was on the mark. "Will he compromise?" Douglass asked about Lincoln. "Time and events will soon answer this question. For the present, there is much reason to believe that he will not consent to any compromise which will violate the principle upon which he was elected. . . . Let the conflict come, and God speed the Right, must be the wish of every true-hearted American, as well as that of an onlooking world."

---

* Despite the language of the amendment and the rhetoric around the issue, however, no amendment could be irrevocable. "The idea that this shall never be altered," argued Senator Benjamin Wade, Republican of Ohio, "I do not think means anything."

A s it had been in the beginning, so it was even now. After all the fits
and starts, the overtures and the hints, Lincoln was determined to
prevent slavery from taking root in the territories or spreading to new
lands that might be added to the nation. While never an overt player in
the compromise talks, Lincoln could have sought to strike a deal to
avoid bloodshed and widespread secession. He would not have feared
impeachment, for a deal to extend slavery would have brought sufficient Democratic votes to secure his place in office even if the Republicans had turned on him in part or en masse. Nor was he apparently
thinking about reelection. "I think when the clouds look as dark as they
do now," Lincoln remarked, "one term might satisfy any man." He
often spoke of the "four years" he was to spend in the nation's service,
and in any event no president since Jackson, nearly three decades before, had won a second term.

There was surely some pride involved. Lincoln did not want to ca-
pitulate to his foes after defeating them at the polls. His own party, or
large parts of it, would have reviled him for compromising, but in the
politics of the time, they would have been thrown back to the broadly
unpopular position of defending abolition against a president who
would be seen by much of the nation as having done the rational thing.

So why did Lincoln hold the line? *Because he thought it was the right, just,
and morally sound thing to do.* Surely it was a decision rooted in political reality, but political reality has a way of quickly changing. The most powerful Republican in the country other than the president-elect, William
Seward, had been inclined to compromise, and Lincoln could have
found succor and political cover in allying himself with the New Yorker
on the issue. The most convincing explanation for Lincoln's adherence
to the principles of his Cooper Union address, which were also the
principles of the Republican platform of 1860, is that he truly believed
slavery was wrong and should be ultimately eradicated, over and against
the many who believed it was right and should be perennially protected.

Why did Lincoln think this? Why did he render a moral judgment—
for that is what it was, a moral judgment—that he then enforced in the
realm of politics? Religious tradition provided much of the language in
which he spoke of the subject ("a house divided"). But his was not a
decision that grew out of conventional Christian understandings of the
world. He did not oppose the extension of slavery only because Jesus

had instructed believers to love their neighbors as themselves, or because Saint Paul had said "There is neither Jew nor Greek, there is neither bond nor free, there is neither male nor female: for ye are all one in Christ Jesus." Such words and such thought were not unimportant to Lincoln, but his insight on the wrongness of slavery came more from an intuitive moral sensibility and a conviction that there were universal goods to be discerned and acted upon. "God," in Lincoln's vernacular, was the God of Abraham as well as the designation assigned to describe the source of the intimations of justice and of kindness that found expression in acts of conscience.

As he had made his way to Washington, Lincoln had frequently spoken of "God" and "Providence." He never stopped to define his terms, leaving his listeners to interpret his invocations of the Almighty as they would. In churchgoing America, those well-wishers heard what they wanted to hear, and he took no pains to enlighten them as to his less-than-orthodox understandings of familiar concepts. There is no doubt, however, that the Lincoln of the White House years became more religiously inclined, attending services with some regularity and meeting with ministers and congregants. In his reported remarks and in the written record, he left us evidence of a man grappling with the most fundamental of questions, the one that had consumed mortals since the first man first raised his fist to the skies and cried, "Why?"

Lincoln's theological quest is no small part of the story of his presidency, for, as in his Illinois years, his term in Congress, and in the Secession Winter, his moral calculus had a discernible influence on public affairs. A politician unburdened by conscience could have made different decisions and left us a different nation. "I may not be a great man," he once remarked. "I know I am not a great man—and perhaps it is better that it is so—for it makes me rely upon One who is great and who has the wisdom and power to lead us safely through this great trial."

A true portrait of Lincoln as president must include our best—if necessarily imperfect and incomplete—effort to capture how he understood the concepts of God and Providence. For if we take him at his word—and we should, for few presidents chose his words with more care—the mature Lincoln viewed the history of the American people and nation as mysteriously but inexorably intertwined with the will and the wishes, the vengeance and the mercy, and the punishments and the rewards of a divine force beyond time and space.

At Rochester, Pennsylvania, on his journey to Washington, Lincoln had promised a full exposition of policy come Inauguration Day— Monday, March 4, 1861.

"What will you do with the secessionists then?" a voice in the crowd called out.

"My friend," Lincoln had replied, "that is a matter which I have under very grave consideration."

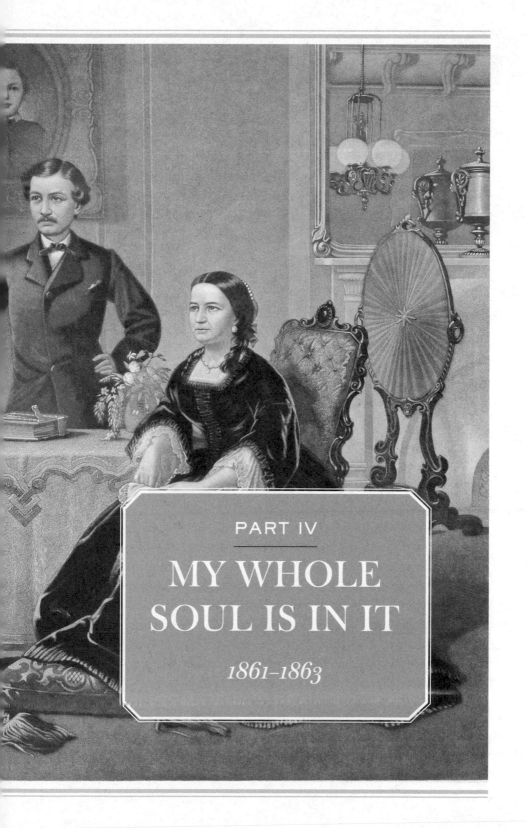

PART IV

MY WHOLE
SOUL IS IN IT

1861–1863

PREVIOUS SPREAD: *The president and his family in the White House, which Lincoln once denounced as this* "damned old house."

CHAPTER SEVENTEEN

The Momentous Issue of Civil War

Why should there not be a patient confidence in the
ultimate justice of the people? Is there any better or
equal hope in the world?

—ABRAHAM LINCOLN, First Inaugural Address

Now we are to have *war*—yes! Let it come
and God sustain the right.

—WILLIAM JONES RHEES, chief clerk of
the Smithsonian Institution, 1861

A T ABOUT TEN PAST NOON on Monday, March 4, 1861—a day
that observers noted had dawned "cloudy and raw" but turned
bright and warm—Abraham Lincoln emerged from the Fourteenth Street door of Willard's, accompanied by President Buchanan.
The two men rode in an open carriage up Pennsylvania Avenue, bound
first for the Senate chamber, where Hannibal Hamlin would be sworn
in as vice president, and then for the covered platform that had been
erected on the East Front for the presidential inauguration. Double
files of cavalrymen escorted the procession to the Capitol. Sharpshooters were stationed on rooftops along the avenue, "with orders," a federal officer recalled, "to watch the windows on the opposite side, and to
fire upon them in case any attempt should be made to fire from those
windows upon the Presidential carriage."

An hour later, hatless and adjusting his eyeglasses, Lincoln, the text of
his inaugural address in hand, stood and gazed out across a large audience. To his right were his old quarters on Carroll Row. Federal artillery
was deployed nearby. "Apprehension seems to exist among the people of
the Southern States, that by the accession of a Republican Administration, their property, and their peace, and personal security, are to be endangered," Lincoln said as he opened his remarks. "There has never

Lincoln insisted on completing the Capitol dome during the war.
"If people see the Capitol going on," he said, "it is a sign we
intend the Union shall go on."

been any reasonable cause for such apprehension. Indeed, the most ample evidence to the contrary has all the while existed, and been open to their inspection. It is found in nearly all the published speeches of him who now addresses you."

The inaugural address had been long in the making. Lincoln had slipped away from office seekers at the state capitol building in Springfield to work on the speech in a "dingy, dusty, and neglected back room" of his brother-in-law's brick general store, Yates and Smith, near the corner of Sixth and Adams. He had asked Herndon for a few documents—very few. Lincoln wanted Henry Clay's speech on the Compromise of 1850, Andrew Jackson's 1832 Nullification Proclamation, and the Constitution. As he wrote, he asked for one other—Daniel Webster's 1830 Second Reply to Hayne, with its paean to Union: "Liberty and Union, now and forever, one and inseparable!"

In Springfield, Lincoln had the draft typeset and printed to show to allies. "I have the document already blocked out," he wrote in early February; "but in the now rapidly shifting scenes, I shall have to hold it subject to revision up to near the time of delivery." At the Capitol, Lincoln appeared "slightly pale and nervous," and with good reason. No other American president had faced a task as complex as the one he now took up. The nation's divisions were familiar, but their degree and force had never been more profound. Sixty percent of voters the previous fall had supported someone else. Yet Lincoln saw himself—and longed for others to see him—as the president of all.

Much of the South was where it was—either in secession or contemplating secession—not least because it believed the North, embodied by Lincoln, held it in moral contempt. One leading Virginian, Wyndham Robertson, had called antislavery a "religion of hate" based on the "Northern crusade aimed at the sin of Southern slavery." Why was the South so intransigent? Because, Robertson observed, measures restricting slavery to its existing realm *"deny to us equality of rights, and imply, on the part of those who meditate them, a pretension of moral superiority."*

Lincoln tried to calm their fears. Citing his record, the president said, "I do but quote from one of those speeches when I declare that 'I have no purpose, directly or indirectly, to interfere with the institution of slavery in the States where it exists. I believe I have no lawful right to do so, and I have no inclination to do so.' . . . I now reiterate these sentiments."

Lincoln's First Inaugural is often remembered for its closing appeal. Seward had recommended language that referred to the "guardian angel of the nation," but Lincoln improved upon the new secretary of state's version. "We are not enemies, but friends," Lincoln wrote in his clear hand on a printed copy of the address. "We must not be enemies. Though passion may have strained, it must not break our bonds of affection. The mystic chords of memory, stretching from every battlefield, and patriot grave, to every living heart and hearthstone, all over this broad land, will yet swell the chorus of the Union, when again touched, as surely they will be, by the better angels of our nature." The brilliant final phrase about better angels was likely drawn, in part, from Shakespeare's Sonnet 144 and from *Othello*; Charles Dickens had also used a form of it in the novel *Barnaby Rudge*.

Lincoln's words about Union were precise, sober, and moving. "Plainly, the central idea of secession, is the essence of anarchy. . . . Why should there not be a patient confidence in the ultimate justice of the people? Is there any better, or equal hope, in the world?" He continued:

> In *your* hands, my dissatisfied fellow countrymen, and not in *mine*, is the momentous issue of civil war. The government will not assail *you*. You can have no conflict, without being yourselves

the aggressors. *You* have no oath registered in Heaven to destroy the government, while *I* shall have the most solemn one to "preserve, protect and defend" it.

After the address, Chief Justice Taney—who had, an observer thought, "the face of a galvanized corpse"—rose and administered the oath of office to Lincoln. "Old Abe delivered the greatest speech of the age," the engineer and future Union officer Grenville M. Dodge of Iowa wrote. "It is backbone all over. The city bristles with bayonets." Thurlow Weed encountered General Scott, who had missed the actual proceedings in order to lead any action that might be necessary to quell secessionist violence.

How was the ceremony? the general asked Weed.

"It is a success," the editor replied.

"God be praised!" Scott said. "God in His goodness be praised."

Not everyone was as enthused or as grateful. Reading the inaugural address, Frederick Douglass, so recently hopeful, was unhappy. The speech was "little better than our worst fears," Douglass remarked. That the president continued to express respect for slavery where it existed was crushing; by pledging to enforce the Fugitive Slave Acts, Douglass said, Lincoln had portrayed himself as "an excellent slave hound." Douglass had been considering immigrating to Haiti, and he saw nothing in Lincoln's inaugural address to change his mind—in fact, quite the opposite. "The United States is in great trouble," Douglass wrote in March. "Slavery, vengeance, and settled hate frown and threaten the free colored people."

During the Secession Winter, a Mississippi state legislator, William C. Smedes of Vicksburg, had written a hot letter to Henry J. Raymond of *The New York Times*, a leading Republican. Smedes declared that he "would regard death by a stroke of lightning to Mr. Lincoln as but a just punishment from an offended deity." Raymond shared the letter with Lincoln, who replied that he was "not pledged to the ultimate extinction of slavery; does not hold the black man to be the equal of the white, unqualifiedly as Mr. S. states it; and never did stigmatize their white people as immoral & unchristian." Lincoln's parsing of terms was revealing. It was true that he had not explicitly pledged to put slavery on a path to "ultimate extinction." He had, however, pledged himself to follow what he defined as the Founders' intended course—which was to put slavery on a path to "ultimate extinction." That he felt compelled to reassure white America of his pro-white bona fides was a sign of both the depth of the pro-white feeling in the country he was trying to lead and of his own willingness to accommodate a racist order.

His inaugural address concluded, the oath sworn, Lincoln rode back to the White House with Buchanan. There the fifteenth president took his leave of the sixteenth. "If you are as happy, my dear sir, on entering this house as I am in leaving it and returning home," Buchanan told Lincoln, "you are the happiest man in this country."

Lincoln dined with about seventeen guests. Called away from the table by a delegation from New York, the president underscored his conciliatory midday words with an allusion to a New Testament parable. To the "disaffected portion of our fellow-citizens," Lincoln remarked to the New Yorkers, "I will say ... that there will be more rejoicing over one sheep that is lost, and is found, than over the ninety-and-nine which have gone not astray."

Late on the evening of the inauguration, at eleven P.M., Lincoln and Mary made the short trip from the White House to Judiciary Square for a ball. "The rooms were crowded," it was reported, "with strangers from the north and west." Dressed in a blue gown, boasting a feather in her hair, Mrs. Lincoln danced a quadrille with Stephen Douglas. The president went home about one o'clock in the morning, leaving the First Lady to keep the party going.

Walking into his White House office the next morning, Lincoln was startled by news from Fort Sumter's commanding officer, Robert Anderson. "The first thing that was handed to me after I entered this room, when I came from the inauguration, was the letter from Maj. Anderson saying that their provisions would be exhausted before an expedition could be sent to their relief," Lincoln recalled. Anderson had bread, pork, beans, rice, coffee, and sugar for twenty-six to possibly forty additional days—and then he and his men, under threat from the Confederates, would face starvation. The secession crisis had thus far been largely peaceable. All of that could quickly change in Charleston Harbor. While Lincoln was determined not to appear overly aggressive, he was also intent on discharging his duties—and that included protecting federal soldiers and property.

Sumter was the fulcrum. "Assuming it to be possible to now provision Fort-Sumpter [*sic*]," he asked his cabinet, "under all the circumstances, is it wise to attempt it?" The new president confronted a sequential test to the one he had faced in the winter: Would he remain committed to his vision of a Union in which antislavery values would take precedence over the proslavery agenda of the white South and of its allies in the North?

Two key figures—William Seward and Winfield Scott—argued that the issues at hand were not worth civil war. "I have built up the Republican party," Seward said; "I have brought it to triumph; but its advent to power is accompanied by great difficulties & perils. I must save the party & save the Government in its hands. To do this, war must be averted; the negro question must be dropped; the 'irrepressible conflict' ignored." Under Seward's influence, Scott, who had proven so steadfast in the winter, told Lincoln much the same thing. The president should revive and accept Senator Crittenden's plan, Scott argued, or even accept secession as a permanent fact.

Should Lincoln have shared this view, the end of American slavery would not have come when it did; it was only in the tumult of war that emancipation would be effected.

It was a brutal time. An insomniac Lincoln, Mary recalled, "keeled over with [a] sick headache for the first time in years." Senator Benjamin Wade of Ohio, a stalwart Republican, scorned the Seward-Scott position. "Give up fortress after fortress," Wade told Lincoln, "*and Jeff Davis will have you as prisoner of war in less than thirty days!*" Seward, however, was dogged. "My system is built on this *idea* as a ruling one," he wrote to Lincoln on Monday, April 1, "namely that we must *change the question before the Public from one upon Slavery, or about Slavery*, for a question upon *Union or Disunion*."

That was something Lincoln would not do. The question was the question. He was antislavery and pro-Union, and he would not sacrifice the former for the latter. He made his decision: He wanted Sumter resupplied. Yet before the expedition could be undertaken—cast, as Lincoln put it, as an effort to "send bread to Anderson"—the Confederate forces made their own decision. Passions needed to be kept high if secession was to be sustained and spread. As one hard-liner told Jefferson Davis, in power at Montgomery, "unless you sprinkle blood in the face of the people of Alabama, they will be back in the old Union in less than ten days." From Washington, Confederate commissioners sent word that there were to be no negotiations between the federal government and representatives of the seceded states. "This Government politely declines . . . to recognize our official character or the power we represent," the commissioners wrote to the Confederate capital on Monday, April 8.

The tug, as Lincoln had called it, had come. The seceded white South's sense of grievance and of doom, of declining influence and flourishing self-righteousness, found manifest expression in Charleston Harbor in the hours just before dawn on the morning of Friday, April 12, 1861, when the first shots were fired on Sumter from Confederate batteries. At four o'clock, a sleepless Mary Chesnut, the wife of the secessionist James Chesnut, had heard the bells of St. Michael's Church—bells cast in 1764 and usually pealed in these years by an enslaved man, Washington McLean Gadsden.

Then came the sounds of war. "At half-past four, the heavy booming of a cannon," Mary Chesnut wrote in her diary. "I sprang out of bed. And on my knees—prostrate—I prayed as I never prayed before."

The next day, in company with other women of the city, she heard it said, "God is on our side."

"Why?" Mrs. Chesnut asked.

"Of course He hates the Yankees," was the reply.

On the eve of Fort Sumter, the governor of South Carolina, Francis Pickens, reportedly acknowledged the clash of realities in a private conversation with a U.S. Army officer in Charleston. Pickens told the army man about "the whole plan and secret of the Southern conspiracy," admitting that "the South had never been wronged, and that all their pretenses of grievance in the matter of tariffs, or anything else, were invalid. 'But,' said [Pickens], 'we must carry the people with us; and we allege these things, as all statesmen do many things that they do not believe, because they are the only instruments by which the people can be managed.' He then and there declared that the two sections of the country were so antagonistic in ideas and policies that they could not live together, that it was foreordained that Northern and Southern men must keep apart . . . and that all the pretenses of the South about wrongs suffered were but pretenses, as they very well knew."

As news of the attack reached Washington—it had rained all night in the national capital as Friday became Saturday—the president of the United States pithily but unmistakably made himself clear. "And, in every event," Lincoln wrote on Saturday, April 13, "I shall, to the extent of my ability, repel force by force."

His initial policy to hold the nation together had failed. "The last ray of hope for preserving the Union peaceably expired at the assault upon Fort Sumter," Lincoln remarked. To his friend Orville Browning, the president confided, "Browning, of all the trials I have had since I came here, none begin to compare with those I had between the inauguration and the fall of Fort Sumter. They were so great that could I have anticipated them, I would not have believed it possible to survive them." The rebel South would not be convinced. The Union would not hold. War had come.

Sunday morning, April 14, 1861, was cool and pleasant. The Lincolns dressed and left the White House for services at New York Avenue Presbyterian Church, presided over by the Reverend Phineas Densmore Gurley. "I wish to find a church whose clergyman holds himself aloof from politics," Lincoln had said on arriving in Washington. Gurley fit the bill. "I like Gurley," Lincoln reportedly remarked. "He don't preach politics. I get enough of that through the week. When I go to church, I like to hear the gospel."

Tall, eloquent, and popular, Gurley had been born in Hamilton, New York, in 1816. Educated at Union College and at Princeton Theological Seminary, he was an Old School Presbyterian, a theological conservative who disliked the emotionalism of the revivals of the Second Great Awakening. A student of Charles Hodge's at Princeton, Gurley was a high-minded, scholarly preacher and an articulate proponent of a doctrine of Divine Providence that held the world was charged with theological import, even if the purposes of the Almighty remained mysterious. God's kingdom, Gurley argued, "ruleth over all." Neither random nor meaningless, history instead unfolded in the way ancient Israel had understood it: as a drama with a beginning, a middle (where things were now), and a promised end of judgment and redemption. In a providential world, the task of the believer was to struggle to adhere to God's laws as revealed in scripture, confident that one day all things would be set to rights. Pain and death were terrible, but they were rendered less cataclysmic by a vision of life as divinely ordered. To Gurley, "the awful mysteries of Divine sovereignty were only a dark background on which were revealed more strikingly the light and glory of God's redeeming love."

A subject of intense debate, the doctrine of Divine Providence offered a man like Lincoln a worldview that acknowledged the invisible
while simultaneously investing humankind with the responsibility of
bringing the visible and the tangible into closer accord with an ideal of
justice. "*Now*, if we are Christians," Gurley preached, "our highest desire, our highest . . . aim, our highest endeavor, is to be conformed to
our Redeemer in character, and we draw from the Word of God no
grander idea of duty or happiness than that of reflecting His image."
On his pages for a sermon in this first year of war—possibly for the
Sunday after Sumter—Gurley added a prayer: "In this day of darkness
and rebuke, when war clouds are gathering over us & men's hearts are
failing them for fear, & for looking after those things which are coming
upon the land, may the Lord increase the faith of his people, & enable
them calmly, steadily, & hopefully to put their trust in Him, for Jesus's
sake. Amen."

Gurley would be a source of pastoral and philosophical insight for
Lincoln as the president fought the most terrible of American wars.
Lincoln's experience with Gurley did not amount to a conversion. It
was, rather, more of an immersion in a Presbyterian theology in which
God was an active participant in the affairs of the world. Gurley also
saw the battle for Union as a holy cause, as did the minister's old
teacher, Charles Hodge of Princeton. In January, Hodge had published
an essay in the *Biblical Repertory and Princeton Review*, a widely read Presbyterian journal. "There are occasions when political questions rise into
the sphere of morals and religion; when the rule for political action is
to be sought, not in considerations of state policy, but in the law of
God," Hodge had written. "When the question to be decided turns on
moral principles, when reason, conscience, and the religious sentiment
are to be addressed, it is the privilege and duty of all who have access in
any way to the public ear, to endeavor to allay unholy feeling, and to
bring truth to bear on the minds of their fellow-citizens."

To Hodge the relevant truth was not the destruction of slavery but
the preservation of Union. He accepted the Constitution's provisions
about slavery and argued that the Bible did in fact sanction some form
of human chattel. What Hodge did not accept was secession and disunion. To Hodge—and this was a common view in the white North—
the Union was sacred, as, to some extent, was slavery. Hodge estimated
that this perspective was shared by "nine-tenths of the intelligent
Christian people of this country, north and south, east and west."

A month after Sumter, Gardiner Spring, pastor of the Brick Church in Manhattan, proposed, and a Presbyterian convention ratified, pro-Union resolutions: "In the spirit of that Christian patriotism which the Scriptures enjoin . . . [we] do hereby acknowledge and declare our obligations to promote and perpetuate . . . the integrity of these United States." Just over two weeks later, on Saturday, June 1, the Lincolns reserved a family pew at New York Avenue Presbyterian Church.

Religious language and imagery were ubiquitous as the war opened. Lincoln encountered it at New York Avenue Presbyterian; Americans cast the struggle as a war not only for Mammon but for God. Frederick Douglass abandoned his plans for Haiti in the aftermath of the Confederate attack. He was an American, and he would stand his ground. "Now is the time to change the cry of vengeance long sent up from the . . . toiling bondman into a grateful prayer for the peace and safety of the Government," Douglass said. *"Repent, Break Every Yoke, let the Oppressed Go Free for Herein alone is deliverance and safety!"*

"Now we are to have *war*—yes!" the chief clerk of the Smithsonian Institution, William Jones Rhees, wrote to his wife. "Let it come and God sustain the right. I feel today as if the government ought to punish these rebels & traitors. Why call them brothers? Have they not been arming themselves for months against us, stealing our guns, powder, money, everything—So, they must be whipped . . . We cannot talk of peace and compromise & recognition of independence now—it is *too late.*"

In New York, the lawyer George Templeton Strong was relieved. "The Northern backbone is much stiffened already," he told his diary. "Many who stood up for 'Southern rights' and complained of wrongs done the South now say that, since the South has fired the first gun, they are ready to go all lengths in supporting the government." On Sunday the fourteenth, Strong attended Trinity Church on Wall Street. The rector read a collect, "In Time of War and Tumults." In a defiant flourish, "the 'Amen' of the white-robed choir boys was emphasized by a suggestive trumpet-stop coloring from the organ." Strong closed his diary for Tuesday, April 16, with a proclamation and a prayer in all capital letters: "GOD SAVE THE UNION, AND CONFOUND ITS ENEMIES. AMEN."

Many in the white South thought God had different plans. "A kind

Providence seems to watch over our Confederacy," the Reverend Charles C. Jones, Sr., of Georgia wrote to his son. The "Black Republican party," Jones declared, "is essentially *infidel!*" The secessionists saw themselves not as rebels but as true Americans. To Jefferson Davis, the war was sacred. "We feel," the Confederate president wrote, "that our cause is just and holy."

So it began. On Monday, April 15, Lincoln issued a call for 75,000 militiamen. Federal soldiers could arrive none too soon. "Thank God for this hour!" Lucius E. Chittenden, a Republican from Vermont, wrote as the Seventh New York Regiment marched past the Treasury to the White House. "How they came we know not, nor do we care. It is enough to know that they are here and the Capitol of the Nation is safe!"

Confederates spun conspiracy theories and thrived on rumor. Lincoln was a teetotaler, but that did not stop the slander in the South. "The fact of Lincoln's constant intoxication is confirmed by a gentleman just from Washington," a Memphis newspaper wrote in mid-May. "It appears that he became addicted to the vice in this way: The cares of the place affected his nervous system so much that he could not sleep. His physician administered him large quantities of opium and brandy each evening until stupidity would ensue, and then he would fall into profound slumber. In the morning his prostration would become so great that liquor would be resorted to; and thus, by a frequent repetition of this treatment, he has become so demoralized by the use of liquors as to be perfectly imbecile and thoroughly indifferent to what is passing around him."

John Hay, Lincoln's newly appointed assistant secretary, recalled the martial feeling of the moment. Senator-elect James Lane of Kansas organized a small company of Union volunteers and came to the White House. The light was fading at the end of the afternoon when Lane and his men, bearing "very new, untarnished muskets," drilled in the East Room "under the light of the gorgeous gas chandeliers." The hastily assembled fighting force, Hay thought, was "a blending of masquerade and tragedy, of grim humor and realistic seriousness—a combination of Don Quixote and Daniel Boone altogether impossible to describe."

Lincoln needed all the Don Quixotes and Daniel Boones he could get his hands on. The national capital seemed surrounded by secessionists and enemies of the Union. On Saturday, April 27, confronting newly seceded Virginia and worried about disunionists in Maryland, the president suspended habeas corpus—the constitutional obligation to justify an individual's arrest and detention before a judge—along select military lines. (He also did so soon after in Florida.) According to the Constitution, "The Privilege of the Writ of Habeas Corpus shall not be suspended, unless when in Cases of Rebellion or Invasion the public Safety may require it." The text appeared in Article I, the section delineating the powers of the legislative branch. Since Congress was not in session, Lincoln issued the order as commander in chief.

His critics saw the suspension as tyrannical. He believed it sensible and justified. The arrest and detention of a Maryland planter, John Merryman, was soon the subject of a Taney ruling, in *Ex Parte Merryman*, that the president's order was unconstitutional. The president was unmoved. Throughout the war he would deploy executive power to secure the Union against those who would undermine it. "Mr. Lincoln probably thought it more convenient, to say the least, to have a country left without a constitution, than a constitution without a country," the poet and editor James Russell Lowell wrote in 1864. "We have no doubt we shall save both; for if we take care of the one, the other will take care of itself. . . . We have no sympathy to spare for the pretended anxieties of men who . . . were willing that Jefferson Davis should break all the ten commandments together, and would now impeach Mr. Lincoln for a scratch on the surface of the tables where they are engraved."

The conflict, Lincoln told Congress on Thursday, July 4, 1861, was total, and therefore required a total response. The war "presents to the whole family of man the question whether a constitutional republic, or a democracy—a government of the people, by the same people—can, or cannot, maintain its territorial integrity against its own domestic foes." The apple of gold of which Lincoln had written in the winter (the principles of the Declaration) was more important than the frame of silver (the letter of the Constitution).

A year later, in September 1862, came this presidential proclamation: "all Rebels and Insurgents, their aiders and abettors within the United States, and all persons discouraging volunteer enlistments, resisting militia drafts, or guilty of any disloyal practice, affording aid and comfort to Rebels against the authority of the United States, shall be subject to martial law and liable to trial and punishment by Courts

Martial or Military Commission." Moreover, Lincoln wrote, "the Writ of Habeas Corpus is suspended in respect to all persons arrested, or who are now, or hereafter during the rebellion shall be, imprisoned in any fort, camp, arsenal, military prison, or other place of confinement by any military authority or by the sentence of any Court Martial or Military Commission."

He defended his executive actions on habeas corpus, on calling for troops, on extending enlistment periods, and on ordering a blockade of Southern ports without express congressional approval. "These measures, whether strictly legal or not, were ventured upon under what appeared to be a popular demand and a public necessity; trusting, then as now, that Congress would readily ratify them," Lincoln said. In this he was working within the tradition of President Jefferson, who had argued that the executive had implied powers to protect and extend the country's interests. As president, Jefferson had seen the office as that of a guardian, writing, "it is the case of a guardian, investing the money of his ward in purchasing an important adjacent territory; & saying to him when of age, I did this for your good."

Lincoln defined the war clearly. "This is essentially a People's contest," he said. "On the side of the Union, it is a struggle for maintaining in the world that . . . government whose leading object is to elevate the condition of men—to lift artificial weights from all shoulders—to clear the paths of laudable pursuit for all—to afford all an unfettered start, and a fair chance, in the race of life." The use of the word "unfettered" was unintentionally ironic. The war was not designed to unchain the enslaved. At least not yet.

CHAPTER EIGHTEEN

"A White Man's War"

The battle of Manassas gave the Lincoln Govt. a vital
& mortal stab. We fought and conquered the *elite* of
Yankeedom. . . . May our heavenly Father overthrow
our enemies, & give us peace.

—EDWARD FONTAINE of Mississippi, August 1861

I am fighting to preserve the integrity of the Union & the
power of the Govt—on no other issue. To gain that end we
cannot afford to raise up the negro question—it must be
incidental & subsidiary.

—GENERAL GEORGE B. MCCLELLAN, November 1861

THERE WERE THOSE WHO SENSED that the war would, somehow
and in some way, create a different, freer Union. The *fact* of the
war, a clash of arms Lincoln could have avoided had he compromised on slavery, was itself a sign that things would change. "Slavery
offers itself more vulnerable to our attack than at any point in any century," John Hay noted in his diary in May 1861. "The time is not yet,"
Orville Browning told the president, "but it will come when it will be
necessary to march an army into the South and proclaim freedom to
the slaves." "We cannot think that the war we are entering on can end
without some radical change in the system of African slavery," James
Russell Lowell wrote in the June 1861 *Atlantic Monthly*. Lincoln's antislavery convictions had begotten secession. Secession had begotten
war. Now war was likely to beget a revolutionary new order.

First blood was said to have been shed by a Black man. Born into
slavery in Delaware around 1796, Nicholas "Nick" Biddle volunteered
to accompany soldiers from Pottsville, Pennsylvania, on a march to
Washington. Biddle had escaped to Pennsylvania years before. At sixty-
five, Biddle was said to be "aged 'but full of alacrity.'" On Thursday,

April 18, 1861, a white mob attacked the Pennsylvania troops as they came through Baltimore. The scene was terrible, Benjamin Brown French wrote, "the R.R. track . . . torn up—bridges burnt—the telegraph wires cut." And Biddle was reportedly injured "with a missile hurled by a rioter" that "cut so severely as to expose the bone." The mob also cried "N——r in uniform!"

Biddle's courage was remarkable but not unique. "At the sound of the tocsin at the North, Negro waiter, cook, barber, bootblack, groom, porter and laborer stood ready at the enlisting office," Joseph T. Wilson, a Black man who became a Union soldier, recalled. "Fire must be met with water, darkness with light, and war for the destruction of liberty must be met with war for the destruction of slavery," Frederick Douglass wrote in May 1861. *Let the slaves and free colored people be called into service, and formed into a liberating army.*" Whether to allow Black Americans to fight was one question. Another was whether to announce a plan of emancipation for the enslaved. Early on, Lincoln was against both. "At Washington I found that the mere mention of a Negro made the President nervous, and frightened some others of his cabinet much more," the minister and abolitionist Moncure D. Conway recalled. "We don't want to fight side and side with the n——r," wrote a young soldier from New York. "We think we are a too superior race for that." It was, it was widely said, "a white man's war."

Race was central not only to the cause of the conflict but to its conduct. At Fort Pickens in the early days of the administration, four escaping enslaved persons "came to the fort, entertaining the idea that we were placed here to protect them and grant them their freedom," reported Adam J. Slemmer, commander of the First Artillery. Slemmer rounded them up and transported them to municipal authorities in Pensacola "to be returned to their owners." On the evening of the same day, four additional enslaved people presented themselves at Pickens, only to meet the same fate. In the White House, John Hay thought Slemmer had been "unnecessarily squeamish in imprisoning & returning to their masters the fugitives who came to their gates begging to be employed." Slemmer had made his decision in March; in May, Union general Benjamin Butler chose a different course at Fortress Monroe on the Atlantic.

It was a Thursday night. Three enslaved men—Frank Baker, Shepard

Mallory, and James Townsend, whom Butler described as "field hands belonging to Col. Charles K. Mallory now in command of the secession forces in this district"—arrived at the federal fort at the mouth of the Chesapeake near Norfolk. Interviewing the men, the general learned they were "about to be taken to Carolina for the purpose of aiding the secession forces there." Butler's decision was quick and certain. The men were to be admitted to federal protection as "property that was designed, adapted and about to be used against the United States."

Butler put a key question to Washington. "I am credibly informed that the negroes in this neighborhood are now being employed in the erection of batteries and other works by the rebels which it would be nearly or quite impossible to construct without their labor," he wrote. "Shall they be allowed the use of this property against the United States and we not be allowed its use in aid of the United States?" Lincoln followed Butler's lead. "Your action in respect to the negroes . . . is approved," the War Department wrote to the general, who was instructed to "refrain from surrendering to alleged masters any persons who may come within your lines." Fortress Monroe became known as the "freedom fort." The House of Representatives affirmed Butler and the administration in July, voting 93 to 55 that "it is no part of the duty of the soldiers of the United States to capture and return fugitive slaves." The enslaved people who escaped to Union lines were referred to as "contraband"—a cold term that accepted and perpetuated the notion of people as property. Yet the flight to Union lines and to federal forts was a step toward freedom.

The secessionist South was outraged. "I cannot bring my mind to entertain even the impression that a God of justice and of truth will permit a blinded, fanatical people . . . who set at defiance the right of private property by seizing Negroes, the personal chattels of others . . . to triumph in this unholy war," the mayor of Savannah, Georgia, wrote in June 1861. "The purposes of Mr. Lincoln are now no longer a matter of doubt," Leonidas Polk wrote in an unfinished May 1861 letter to Confederate Secretary of War LeRoy P. Walker. "His line is that of aggression & if possible conquest. . . . What is to be done?" In a letter to Polk, Dr. William A. Shaw wrote: "The Yankee raid of the 19th Century will be the laughing stock of Universal History, the everlasting disgrace of Yankeeism and Northeastern Radicals! To the honor of the South, loyally, she clung to God, the Constitution and the laws, till she saw the wreck of liberty, fraternity, equality and true religion, would bury her with the ruins of the old U.S.!... The new Confederate Nation, under the smiles of The God of The Bible and of The Universe, will soon work out for themselves, by their valor and virtues, a future and a destiny [to] eclips[e] all the ... prosperity of the old U.S., which is now corrupt, effete, and forever decomposed." "Time will prove the South were right in never living under Abraham Lincoln & Black republican rule," the Tennessee farmer Robert H. Cartmell wrote on the last day of August 1861. "Their object is to wipe out state lines & bury state rights."

Calling on Lincoln in the White House shortly after the war began in 1861, Charles Sumner, the bloodied senator from Massachusetts, wanted to be sure the president understood the full implications of the rebellion. "I ... told him ... that under the war power the right had come to him to emancipate the slaves," Sumner recalled. Then and for a long time afterward—a very long time for the enslaved and for their abolitionist allies—Lincoln demurred. "If Mr. Lincoln could only be wakened to the idea ... that God gives him the thunderbolt of slavery with which to crush the rebellion," the abolitionist Wendell Phillips observed in the summer of 1862.

The president never lacked for such advice. A cousin of Mary's recalled that Lincoln was beset by "the importunities, meddlesomeness, impatient censure, and arrogance of preachers, politicians, newspaper writers and cranks who virtually dogged his footsteps, demanding that he should 'free the slaves,' 'arm the slaves,' and 'emancipate the slaves and give them the ballot.'" The abolitionists were certain they knew what Lincoln should do—as were those on the other side of the spectrum of opinion within the Union.

In popular memory, the Civil War is broadly cast as a death-struggle between North and South and abolition and slavery. For Abraham Lincoln and the people of his time, however, reality was much more complicated. He was a minority president; he faced opposition not only in the Confederacy but in the tenuously loyal border states; and the Union itself was far from monolithic. From day to day, week to week, month to month, and year to year, Lincoln faced powerful and numerous opponents in the North.

They were known as Copperheads—after the snake. The term was coined to denote the antiwar Democrats, a virulently anti-Lincoln political force in the Northern and border states. Sometimes called Peace Democrats, they were persistent critics of the president, attacking his wartime measures and lobbying for a negotiated settlement to the war. One sign of the Copperheads' strength: Lincoln drafted, but did not include, a passage in his March 1862 message to Congress that would have offered a *status quo ante* if rebellious states would rejoin the Union. "Should the people of the insurgent districts now reject the councils of treason, revive loyal state governments, and again send Senators and Representatives to Congress, they would at once find themselves at peace, *with no institution changed,** and with their just influence in the councils of the nation, fully re-established." To the president, the opposition in the North was "a fire in the rear."

Copperheads called for "the Union as it was, and the Constitution as it is." A corollary Copperhead goal was said to be the "Negro in his place." The Peace Democrats "did not want the Confederacy to win or the Union to split," the historian Jennifer L. Weber observed. "They just wanted the nation to return to the *status quo ante bellum.*" In judging Lincoln's actions as president of that nation, a democratic republic, we must bear public opinion in mind—not public opinion as we wish it to have been but as what it was. One plausible lesson of the 1860 campaign was that 39.8 percent of the electorate—Lincoln's popular vote total—was theoretically, if not universally, open to antislavery measures. The other 60.2 percent had registered their will by supporting one of the candidates who held a range of proslavery, or at least proslavery-extension, views. Even in the North, then, Lincoln was constrained by significant portions of dissenting opinion (Stephen Douglas had carried the popular vote in New Jersey); the same was true in the upper South and border regions (Douglas had also won Missouri; John Bell had carried Virginia, Kentucky, and Tennessee).

Maneuvering in a universe shaped by forces that included abolitionists and Copperheads in the midst of armed rebellion, the president tried to stay on the conservative side of antislavery in the late autumn and winter of 1861–62. Lincoln drafted plans for gradual, compensated emancipation for Delaware, a border state with a small population of enslaved people, only to see the proposal defeated in the state's legisla-

---

* Italics mine.

ture by a single vote. When he learned that the secretary of war's annual report included the assertion that the Union had the "right and the duty" to arm and deploy Black soldiers, the president ordered the passage stricken. "This," he said, "will never do!"

An important impetus behind Lincoln's decisions: keeping the border states in the Union. Delaware, Kentucky, Maryland, and Missouri had not seceded, but the president was always worried about losing them to the Confederacy. "Lincoln would like to have God on his side," it was said, "but he must have Kentucky." As the president had written to Orville Browning, "Kentucky gone, we cannot hold Missouri, nor, as I think, Maryland. These all against us, and the job on our hands is too large for us." Moderation, therefore, guided Lincoln as the war grew more intense and widespread in the late spring and summer of 1861.

The Baltimore attack on Nick Biddle had been part of the Pratt Street Riot, a violent episode in which pro-secessionists attacked federal troops. In June, Union and Confederate forces engaged on three occasions in Virginia: at Fairfax Courthouse; near Philippi, in what soon became West Virginia; and at the Battle of Big Bethel, not far from Butler's Fortress Monroe. In these early weeks of the war, casualties were minimal. For Lincoln, though, the clash of arms was not abstract but tangible, proximate, and intimate.

Six weeks after the fall of Fort Sumter, the president received word that his young friend Elmer E. Ellsworth, a former law clerk of his in Springfield who was now a Union colonel, had been killed across the Potomac in Alexandria. Virginia had seceded in the third week of May. Alexandria was hostile territory, as was Arlington, whose heights had been seized by federal troops. In early June, at Christ Episcopal Church, the Reverend Doctor Cornelius B. Walker "preached a strong Secession sermon, significantly omitting the prayer for the President of the United States from the regular service," the *New York Tribune* reported. Ellsworth had been removing a Confederate flag from atop the Marshall House inn when the innkeeper, James Jackson, shot him to death. "May God give you that consolation which is beyond all earthly power," Lincoln wrote to Ellsworth's parents.

The capital was a pageant of war. In early July, Lincoln reviewed twenty thousand New York soldiers from a pavilion at the White House. The next afternoon, he did the same with two regiments from

Pennsylvania. The day after that he joined Colonel William Sprague, the governor of Rhode Island, to view an "exhibit by 2d Rhode Island Regiment of James rifled cannon on Monument grounds." Lincoln toured the Washington Navy Yard; raised ceremonial flags; and was serenaded by Colonel Blenker's German Rifles, Eighth N.Y. Volunteers. On Tuesday, July 9, "The President's levee . . . was largely attended," *The New York Herald* wrote. "The military display was brilliant, and the ladies never made a finer appearance."

"We had a grand review today before the President," the Union soldier Robert Shortelle wrote to his mother. "We were on the parade ground from 9 A.M. till 4 o'clock P.M. under a hot sun. . . . When we were marching by the crowd of people . . . to witness our parade, I noticed an elderly couple sitting in a coach with an umbrella to shade them from the sun's rays. I afterwards found out that they were the President and his spouse. She is a somewhat dark complexioned woman, dressed very plain, but she is very pleasant looking, smiling all the time we were passing, but the *Ol[d]* Man looked rather sorrowful. He seemed to be deeply affected."

The poet Walt Whitman lived in Washington, D.C., during the war, leaving an eloquent record of his impressions of the city in years of strife.

Despite the ubiquity of troops and of martial preparations, many lawmakers, and many others throughout the North, did not fully appreciate the threat posed by the rebellious states. A "great and cautious national official" predicted to Walt Whitman that the conflict would be over "in sixty days." The mayor of Brooklyn, in conversation with Whitman aboard a ferry, said he "hoped the Southern fire-eaters would commit some overt act of resistance, as they would then be at once so effectually squelch'd, we would never hear of secession again—but he was afraid they never would have the pluck to really do anything."

Then came Manassas—or, as the North referred to it, Bull Run. The Union army met Confederate forces in combat in northern

A struggling farmer in Kentucky, Indiana, and Illinois, Thomas Lincoln was known to have remarked that "everything that I ever touched either died, got killed, or was lost." He also lived with rumors that he was not in fact Abraham's natural father.

As a stepmother, Sarah Bush Lincoln was a kind of savior, arriving in the Lincolns' household in Spencer County, Indiana, in the winter of 1819–20. She brought order and supported young Abraham's interest in books and in improving himself. As Lincoln recalled, "She proved a good and kind mother" to him.

In his *History of the United States*, which Lincoln read, William Grimshaw reproduced the Declaration of Independence and wrote: "Since the middle of the last century, expanded minds have been, with slow gradations, promoting the decrease of slavery in North America."

Lincoln encountered the English essayist, poet, and politician Joseph Addison in the pages of Lindley Murray's *The English Reader*. "The philosopher, the saint, or the hero, the wise, the good, or the great man," Addison had written, "very often lies hid and concealed in a plebeian, which a proper education might have disinterred, and have brought to light."

Lincoln's Illinois law partner and friend William H. Herndon was an admirer of Theodore Parker, with whom he corresponded. Herndon's extensive postbellum research into Lincoln's early life is invaluable. "I know him," Herndon wrote of Lincoln in the winter of 1860–61, "as well as he does himself."

Bethel A. M. E. Church, the first Colored Methodist Church in Philadelphia, Established in 1787

Born into enslavement in 1760, Richard Allen became a minister and a founder of the African Methodist Episcopal Church. His main congregation, the Bethel AME Church, was located at South Sixth and Lombard streets in Philadelphia; a center of spirituality, culture, and activism for Black Americans, it became known as "Mother Bethel."

Sold into enslavement and brought to Massachusetts in 1761, Phillis Wheatley was a noted poet. Benjamin Rush praised her "singular genius," and Wheatley corresponded with George Washington, whom she praised as a "great chief" in "freedom's cause." In her poem "On Being Brought from Africa to America," she wrote: "Remember, *Christians, Negroes,* black as *Cain,* / May be refin'd and join th' angelic train."

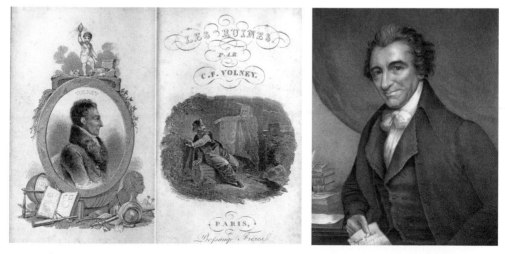

In the New Salem years, Lincoln read Constantin Volney's 1791 *The Ruins, or, Meditation on the Revolutions of Empires,* and Thomas Paine's 1794–95 *The Age of Reason.* Their insistence on individual interpretation of reality rather than on the blind acceptance of tradition intrigued Lincoln. Volney argued for the rule of law to protect the weak from the strong; Paine, against traditional religion. "I believe that religious duties consist in doing justice, loving mercy, and endeavoring to make our fellow-creatures happy," Paine wrote. "I do not believe . . . in the creed of any church I know of."

In the 1846 general election for the Seventh Congressional District, Lincoln faced Peter Cartwright, a popular Methodist preacher. Cartwright rode circuit, it was said, "with Bible and rifle; if a sinner came in drunk and interrupted the sermon Cartwright jumped from the pulpit and personally threw him out." Lincoln won the race by about 13 percentage points.

Under the titular leadership of James Madison and James Monroe, the American Colonization Society promoted the voluntary removal of free Black Americans and the establishment of colonies that would accept them. Then and later, some Black leaders favored different colonization efforts as a means to create a secure nation for Black Americans away from enslavement and subjugation, but the chief support for the decades-long campaign came from white Americans.

Born in 1810 in Lexington, Massachusetts, Theodore Parker graduated from Harvard Divinity School in 1836. Inspired by William Ellery Channing of the Federal Street Church and by Lyman Beecher of the Hanover Street Church, Parker pursued the ministry; John Quincy Adams attended his ordination. Untethered by orthodoxy or by settled opinion, Parker, who influenced Lincoln's thinking, explored the deepest of questions.

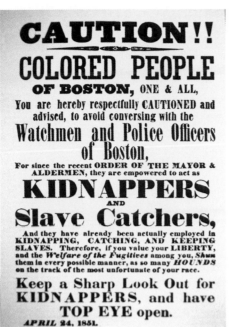

CAUTION!!
COLORED PEOPLE
OF BOSTON, ONE & ALL,
You are hereby respectfully CAUTIONED and
advised, to avoid conversing with the
Watchmen and Police Officers
of Boston,
For since the recent ORDER OF THE MAYOR &
ALDERMEN, they are empowered to act as
KIDNAPPERS
AND
Slave Catchers,
And they have already been actually employed in
KIDNAPPING, CATCHING, AND KEEPING
SLAVES. Therefore, if you value your LIBERTY,
and the Welfare of the Fugitives among you, Shun
them in every possible manner, as so many HOUNDS
on the track of the most unfortunate of your race.
Keep a Sharp Look Out for
KIDNAPPERS, and have
TOP EYE open.
APRIL 24, 1851.

The passage of the Fugitive Slave Act of 1850 roiled the North, infuriating free states by ending due process for escaped enslaved persons, authorizing penalties for people found guilty of aiding those seeking freedom, and creating a financial incentive for the federal commissioners— known more widely as "*Slave Catchers*"—who captured and returned the enslaved to captivity.

"There are men, who, by their sympathetic attractions, carry nations with them, and lead the activity of the human race," Ralph Waldo Emerson said in a lecture on power in Springfield. "All successful men have agreed in one thing, they were *causationists*. . . . A belief in causality, or strict connection between every pulse-beat and the principle of being . . . characterizes all valuable minds."

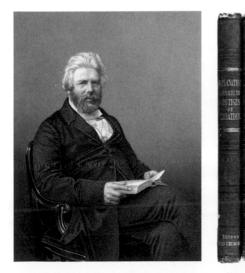

Robert Chambers's 1844 *Vestiges of the Natural History of Creation* "interested [Lincoln] so much," William Herndon recalled, "that he read it through." Published a decade and a half before Darwin's *On the Origin of Species, Vestiges* fascinated popular, scientific, and theological audiences with its argument that the solar system and humankind were products of evolution.

In 1821, an influential white Southern Baptist minister, Basil Manly, Sr., saw slavery as "an evil under which this country has long groaned. . . . [S]lavery seems to be utterly repugnant to the spirit of republican institutions." By 1837, Manly was preaching a different gospel, arguing that slavery was divinely sanctioned and should be defended out of a duty to God.

"The parties in this conflict are not merely abolitionists and slaveholders—they are atheists, socialists, communists . . . on the one side, and friends of order and regulated freedom on the other," the Presbyterian clergyman James Henley Thornwell of South Carolina said in 1850. To Thornwell, slave owners were true Christians and adherents to the "ordinance of God." To defend slavery, then, was to defend Christianity itself.

Born in 1813 in Vermont, Stephen A. Douglas had come to Illinois and, like Lincoln, become a lawyer in the early 1830s and later a state legislator. Called the "Little Giant" because of his five-foot-four height, Douglas had once even been thought of as a candidate for the hand of Mary Todd. He had, a New England journalist noted, "excellent prize fighting qualities."

Bearing what one observer called "the face of a galvanized corpse," Chief Justice Roger B. Taney ruled, in the Dred Scott case, that Black people "are not included, and were not intended to be included, under the word 'citizens' in the Constitution. . . . On the contrary, they were at that time considered as a subordinate and inferior class of beings, who had been subjugated by the dominant race, and, whether emancipated or not, yet remained subject to their authority."

A Democrat from Pennsylvania, James Buchanan won the 1856 election, defeating John C. Frémont, the first presidential nominee of the new Republican party. In his inaugural address, Buchanan argued that his election had shown that "the will of the majority" was in favor of the extension of slavery into the territories.

Under pressure not to certify Lincoln's Electoral College victory, Vice President John C. Breckinridge of Kentucky was "pale and a little nervous," it was recalled, "but firm on his feet and unfaltering in his utterance" as he announced: "I therefore declare Abraham Lincoln duly elected President of the United States for the term of four years from the fourth day of March next."

"We cannot, in our judgment, be either true Christians or real freemen, if we impose on another a chain that we defy all human power to fasten on ourselves," William H. Seward of New York declared in 1850. The Constitution might allow for the evil, Seward added, "But there is a higher law than the Constitution." Defeated by Lincoln for the presidential nomination in 1860, Seward would become secretary of state.

Born in Kentucky in 1808, Jefferson Davis had grown up in Mississippi and graduated from West Point. A lawmaker and Franklin Pierce's secretary of war, Davis was serving in the U.S. Senate in 1860 as the crisis of disunion came. "We want nothing more than a simple declaration that negro slaves are property," Davis said, "and we want the recognition of the obligation of the Federal Government to protect that property like all other."

The vice president of the Confederacy, Alexander H. Stephens of Georgia declared that the rebel nation's "foundations are laid, its corner-stone rests, upon the great truth that the negro is not equal to the white man; that slavery subordination to the superior race is his natural and normal condition."

At the 1860 Democratic convention, Alabama's William Lowndes Yancey spoke for the fractious and defensive slave-owning interest: "Ours is the property invaded; ours are the institutions which are at stake; ours is the peace that is to be destroyed; ours is the property that is to be destroyed; ours is the honor at stake."

Known as "the Grey-Eyed Man of Destiny," William Walker led noted filibusters in the 1850s. Derived from Spanish, French, and Dutch words for "freebooter" and "pirate," the term applied to private citizens who launched military operations to subdue and then control lands outside the United States. In 1856, Walker reinstituted slavery in Nicaragua.

SOUTHERN CHIVALRY — ARGUMENT versus CLUB'S.

On Thursday, May 22, 1856, Representative Preston S. Brooks of South Carolina physically attacked Senator Charles Sumner of Massachusetts on the floor of the Senate. "Every lick went where I intended," Brooks recalled. "I . . . gave him about 30 first rate stripes. . . . I wore my cane out completely but saved the Head which is gold." Brooks was hailed in the white South and vilified in the free North.

President Lincoln with his secretaries John G. Nicolay and John M. Hay. Nicolay and Hay lived in the White House in the Civil War years and co-authored a landmark ten-volume work entitled *Abraham Lincoln: A History*. "There is no man in the country, so wise, so gentle, and so firm," Hay observed of Lincoln in mid-1863. "I believe the hand of God placed him where he is."

The photographer Alexander Gardner took this image of the president with Tad Lincoln during the war. After the loss of Willie in 1862 and the assassination in 1865, Tad cried, "O what shall I do? What *shall* I do? My Brother is dead. My Father is dead. O what shall I do? What will become of me?"

In the White House years, the Lincolns rented a pew at New York Avenue Presbyterian Church. Its pastor, Phineas Gurley, grew close to the president, particularly in the terrible wake of young Willie Lincoln's death. "I like Gurley," Lincoln reportedly remarked. "He don't preach politics. I get enough of that through the week. When I go to church, I like to hear the gospel."

Known as the "Young Napoleon," General George B. McClellan rose to power after the fall of Winfield Scott, the initial Union commander. "I find myself in a new & strange position here—Presdt, Cabinet, Genl Scott & all deferring to me—by some strange operation of magic I seem to have become *the* power of the land," McClellan wrote to his wife in the summer of 1861.

Ulysses S. Grant rose from relative obscurity with a series of Union victories—all too rare at the time—in the West. At Shiloh in April 1862, when the Confederate armies had surprised the Union with resilient fighting, Grant recalled that he "gave up all idea of saving the Union except by complete conquest." Lincoln would come to share Grant's view: There could be no negotiated peace, only unconditional military triumph.

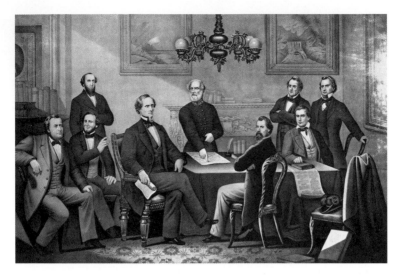

Jefferson Davis with high Confederate officials in Richmond. In the last phase of the war, as the city was about to fall, the Confederate president was fatalistic. "The war came," Davis remarked, "and now it must go on till the last man of this generation falls in his tracks, and his children seize his musket and fight our battle."

"The fiery trial through which we pass," Lincoln wrote in 1862, "will light us down in honor or dishonor to the latest generation." According to demographic estimates, the Civil War claimed perhaps as many as 750,000 lives. "It is rather for us to be here dedicated to the great task remaining before us—that from these honored dead we take increased devotion to that cause for which they gave the last full measure of devotion," the president said at Gettysburg in 1863.

Born in Ulster County, New York, in the late eighteenth century, Sojourner Truth had escaped from slavery and become an advocate for abolition and the rights of women. "I said, 'I appreciate you, for you are the best president who has ever taken the seat,'" Truth recalled of an 1864 White House meeting with Lincoln.

A half sister of Mary Lincoln's, Emilie Todd Helm was married to a Confederate general who was killed in action at Chickamauga; her subsequent visit to the White House fed rumors of the First Lady's Southern sympathies. "I feel that my being here is more or less an embarrassment to all of us," Emilie remarked.

Lincoln kept a portrait of John Bright in the president's office in the White House. An English politician and reformer, Bright defended the Western liberal tradition that prized individual rights over inherited authority. Bright thought Lincoln's administration "an honest endeavor faithfully to do the work of his great office."

The *New York Tribune*'s Horace Greeley was ubiquitous and changeable, variously despondent over the war, impatient for emancipation, and pessimistic about Lincoln's chances for reelection. In the end, however, Greeley thought "Mr. Lincoln. . . . a wiser, abler man when he entered upon his second than when he commenced his first Presidential term."

Lydia Marie Child published an abolitionist work, *An Appeal in Favor of That Class of Americans Called Africans,* in 1833. Three decades later, she observed, "I think we have reason to thank God for Abraham Lincoln."

Sometimes called Peace Democrats, Northern opponents of the war—and of Lincoln—were also known as Copperheads, after the snake. The president thought of hostility within the Union as a "fire in the rear." And Lincoln was thought to be running behind the Democratic ticket for much of 1864.

Andrew Johnson of Tennessee replaced Vice President Hannibal Hamlin of Maine as Lincoln's running mate on the 1864 ticket. "Can't you find a candidate for Vice President in the United States without going down to one of those damned rebel provinces to pick one up?" lamented Thaddeus Stevens of Pennsylvania.

On Saturday, March 4, 1865, Lincoln took the oath of office for a second time. John Wilkes Booth was there, as was Frederick Douglass. House chaplain William Henry Channing noted that "white and colored troops were ranked shoulder to shoulder, and . . . freedmen in their rough plantation garments stood side by side with fashionably attired citizens from the Free States."

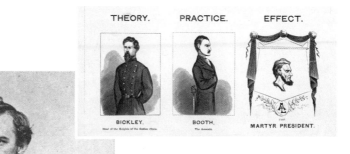

"The South can make no choice," the actor John Wilkes Booth wrote. "It is either extermination or slavery for *themselves* (worse than death) . . . I know *my* choice." His murder of the president was seen as the result of a climate of vicious and violent opposition to Lincoln that included the secretive and proslavery Knights of the Golden Circle.

The services for Lincoln—whose body was borne in this carriage—in the White House and in the Capitol were followed by ceremonies in Baltimore, Harrisburg, Philadelphia, New York, Albany, Buffalo, Cleveland, Columbus, Indianapolis, Michigan City, and Chicago.

Purchased from the Episcopal clergyman Charles Dresser, the Lincolns' residence at Eighth and Jackson in Springfield was the house where they spent most of their tumultuous married life.

Virginia about thirty miles from Washington early on the morning of Sunday, July 21, 1861. It was a great victory for the rebels, who lost about two thousand men compared to twenty-nine hundred federal casualties. "The enemy were completely routed, with tremendous slaughter," a Charleston diarist wrote. In humiliation, Union soldiers retreated to Washington, where weary and wounded men straggled in, accepted food and drink, and then slept, many of them outdoors.

Edward Fontaine of Mississippi was at the battle. "After passing through such a tempest of all the missiles of death, as beat upon us" during the engagement, he wrote to his wife, "I shall dread nothing of its kind hereafter." Like many Confederates, Fontaine thought a quick victory was in sight. "We will whip them again," Fontaine wrote, "& they will then make peace." It shouldn't take much more than a few months, he predicted, writing, "The battle of Manassas gave the Lincoln Govt. a vital & mortal stab. We fought and conquered the *elite* of Yankeedom. . . . May our heavenly Father overthrow our enemies, & give us peace."

The Confederate triumph in July hastened the fall of Winfield Scott as the Union's commanding officer. The old general was replaced by a young one: George B. McClellan. Born into a prominent family in Philadelphia in 1826, McClellan had graduated second in his class at West Point and served under Scott in the Mexican War. Nicknamed "Young Napoleon," McClellan was prone to egotism and became noted for his reluctance to march the armies he had organized into actual battle. "I find myself in a new & strange position here—Presdt, Cabinet, Genl Scott & all deferring to me—by some strange operation of magic I seem to have become *the* power of the land," McClellan wrote to his wife.

McClellan was taking command at a bleak hour. At midnight in New York City on Monday, July 29, 1861, an exhausted Horace Greeley shared his post–Bull Run anxieties in a letter to the president. "On every brow sits sullen, scowling, black despair," Greeley wrote of the aftermath of the defeat in northern Virginia. "This is my seventh sleepless night—yours, too, doubtless— . . . But to business."

The business began with a blunt assertion. "You are not considered a great man, and I am a hopelessly broken one," Greeley told Lincoln. "You are now undergoing a terrible ordeal, and God has thrown the gravest responsibility upon you." The editor posed a question:

Can the Rebels be beaten after all that has occurred, and in view of the actual state of feeling caused by our late awful disaster? If they can—and it is your business to ascertain and decide—write me that such is your judgment, so that I may know and do my duty.

And if they *cannot* be beaten—if our recent disaster is fatal—do not fear to sacrifice yourself to your country. If the Rebels are not to be beaten—if that is your judgment in view of all the light you can get—then every drop of blood henceforth shed in this quarrel will be wantonly, wickedly shed, and the guilt will rest heavily on the soul of every promoter of the crime. . . .

If the Union is irrevocably gone, an Armistice for thirty, sixty, ninety, 120 days—better still, for a year—ought at once to be proposed with a view to a peaceful adjustment. Then Congress should call a National convention to meet at the earliest possible day. . . .

It would be easy to have Mr. Crittenden move any proposition that ought to be adopted. . . .

If it is best for the country and for mankind that we make peace with the Rebels at once and on their own terms, do not shrink even from that.

It was an emotional but not irrational letter. Lincoln apparently did not reply, instead steadying his gaze on what had to be done. As in the Secession Winter and during the Fort Sumter crisis, he might have pursued a quick peace, but the president was committed to rescuing the Union—and to putting as many of his antislavery principles into practice as he believed he could.

Lincoln had an opportunity to work against slavery after Bull Run, when Congress passed, and he signed, the Confiscation Act of 1861. Henceforth Union officers were empowered to view any enslaved person thought to be deployed in the Confederate war effort as the "lawful subject of prize and capture wherever found." "This bill will be considered as giving an anti-slavery character and application to the war," Kentucky's John Crittenden said, not approvingly. "Visibly the question is fast resolving itself into the form, 'Shall American slavery longer exist or not?'" a Kentucky correspondent wrote to a Northern newspaper in December. *"A great many important steps towards this great end have been taken."*

In Missouri, General John Frémont, the 1856 Republican presidential nominee, issued a dramatic proclamation on the second to last day of August 1861, ordering the permanent emancipation of all enslaved people in the state owned by those "who shall take up arms against the United States, or who shall be directly proven to have taken an active part with their enemies in the field." Lincoln was not ready to go that far. Worried that the Missouri declaration of emancipation "will alarm our Southern Union friends, and turn them against us—perhaps ruin our rather fair prospect for Kentucky," he asked Frémont to rescind that element of the proclamation and to abide by the Confiscation Act, which did not address slavery beyond the period of the rebellion.

The president shared his thinking with Orville Browning. "Genl. Frémont's proclamation, as to confiscation of property, and the liberation of slaves, is *purely political,* and not within the range of *military* law, or necessity," Lincoln wrote. "If a commanding General finds a necessity to seize the farm of a private owner, for a pasture, an encampment, or a fortification, he has the right to do so. . . . But to say the farm shall no longer belong to the owner, or his heirs forever . . . is purely political, without the savor of military law about it. And the same is true of slaves. If the General needs them, he can seize them, and use them; but when the need is past, it is not for him to fix their permanent future condition." To the president, the issue was too large to be settled by a single general in a single place.

Lincoln's decision about the Frémont emancipation was reassuring to many white Americans. "Help me to dodge the n——r—we want nothing to do with him," George McClellan wrote to a Democratic friend in New York in November 1861. "I am fighting to preserve the integrity of the Union & the power of the Govt—on no other issue. To gain that end we cannot afford to raise up the negro question—it must be incidental & subsidiary." To his father in Illinois in this season, U. S. Grant wrote, "My inclination is to whip the rebellion into submission, preserving all constitutional rights. If it cannot be whipped in any other way than through a war against slavery, let it come to that legitimately. If it is necessary that slavery should fall that the Republic may continue its existence, let slavery go. But that portion of the press that advocates the beginning of such a war now, are as great enemies to their country as if they were open and avowed secessionists." William Seward believed "the negro question must be dropped."

The Confederates harbored grand hopes. A "decisive blow," Edward Fontaine wrote to his wife in September, could soon "be struck, Lincoln & his cabinet will be fugitives flying towards the Lakes & the ruins of Washington will be ours. I hope that the barbarians will spare the noblest works of American art for the sake of science, history, & all the memories of the past; or rather I pray that the omnipotent may save these ornaments of our Country from the savage race of the Northern barbarians who now hold them polluted, & who are determined to deprive all future generations of them, by giving them to the flames."

In a sermon to the Georgia legislature in Milledgeville in the first November of war, a Baptist minister, Henry Tucker, called on the armies of Heaven to join the Confederates' battle on earth. "Retaliation! To arms! To arms! Let us kill! Let us destroy!" Tucker preached. "Let us by faith, obedience and love, so engage the Lord of Hosts on our side that he will fight for us."

To Tucker, the path to victory for the slave-owning South was the path of righteousness—as defined by the slave-owning South: "My countrymen, before God . . . I do believe that if the people of this Confederacy were to turn with one heart and one mind to the Lord and walk in his ways, he would drive the invader from our territories and restore to us the blessings of peace."

The Confederates were not thinking of surrender. And neither was Lincoln.

CHAPTER NINETEEN

My Boy Is Gone—He Is Actually Gone

I am satisfied that when the Almighty wants me to do or not
to do a particular thing, he finds a way of letting me know it.
—ABRAHAM LINCOLN

THE WINTER OF 1861–62 was a wearying season. The president longed for military victories and was bedeviled by a series of commanders, beginning with an ill McClellan, who he believed failed to deliver. In October 1861, after the Southern victory at Bull Run, Confederate forces further embarrassed the Union at the Battle of Ball's Bluff on the Potomac. Edward D. Baker, the Lincoln friend and Oregon senator who had become a federal officer, was killed, as were 222 other Union troops, some of whom drowned in the river's waters. Only thirty-six Confederates were recorded killed. There were victories in the West—from February to April, 1862, U. S. Grant prevailed in battles at Fort Donelson and at Shiloh in Tennessee—but the defeats in Virginia beginning with Bull Run loomed large. "The people are impatient; Chase has no money, and he tells me he can raise no money; the Gen. of the Army has typhoid fever," Lincoln remarked. "The bottom is out of the tub. What shall I do?" "The President looks grave and absorbed, and a little worse for cares," an observer noted.

Mary Lincoln was one of those cares. Ambitious and hungry for deference, she had returned to the national capital with clear memories of her time there during Lincoln's House term. Mary, it was later noted, was now "clothed with power to reward magnanimously the few who had given her social recognition, and to repay in kind the neglect of others." Washington society had been long dominated by Southern ladies, but Mary's Kentucky pedigree did her little good amid the secession crisis: The First Lady was seen not as a Todd of Lexington but as a Lincoln of Springfield. She went through a number of passing favorites among the ladies of the capital, including, for a time, Mrs. Elizabeth

Crittenden, Mrs. Myra Clark Gaines, and Mrs. Adele Cutts Douglas. As a Republican woman in a Democratic city, Mary was in the odd position of being at once the highest-ranking social figure in Washington and something of a pariah. She felt this tension viscerally, and the resulting uncertainty may have exacerbated a few of her more troubling habits, chiefly her temperamental jags and her penchant for spending money.

Lots of money. To Orville Browning, Lincoln confided that he "was constantly under great apprehension lest his wife should do something which would bring him into disgrace." Mary was fond of shopping for herself and for the White House, which she had found to be threadbare. What funds she could not get from the government—sometimes by padding expense accounts and arranging kickbacks—she borrowed. "You understand, Lizabeth, that Mr. Lincoln has but little idea of the expense of a woman's wardrobe," Mary said to Elizabeth Keckly, her Washington dressmaker and a formerly enslaved woman. "He glances at my rich dresses, and is happy in the belief that the few hundred dollars that I obtain from him supply all my wants. The people scrutinize every article I wear with critical curiosity. The very fact of having grown up in the West, subjects me to more searching observation. . . . He is too honest to make a penny outside of his salary; consequently, I had, and still have, no alternative but to run into debt."

On trips to Philadelphia and to New York, the First Lady overspent the federal budget for the White House as she acquired French wallpaper, expensive drapery, and elegant furnishings. Her partner in the enterprise was William S. Wood, the acting commissioner of public buildings. Mary's connection with Wood provoked rumors of infidelity, and the president and First Lady had at least one pitched fight about him. Afterward, John Nicolay recalled, the Lincolns "scarcely spoke together for several days."

Mary had fueled her husband's ambition for great office. Now that it had been achieved, she wanted to continue to weigh in on public questions, particularly on appointments. "She is said to . . . rule with an iron hand at the White House and has done things that will d—n herself & her husband in the eyes of decent peoples throughout all eternity," Nathan Daniels observed in early 1864. Born in 1836 in New York, Daniels served as a colonel of the Second Regiment of the Louisiana Native Guard, a regiment of Black soldiers, and kept a revealing diary of the capital in the second half of the war.

The First Lady's influence was exaggerated but still real enough to be a source of criticism in the press and of stress at home. "Mrs. Lincoln was dressed in a dark rich silk, elaborately ornamented but still as the fashions go in good taste," Daniels wrote after a New Year's Day reception. "She appeared very amiable and looked her position well. I for one am not disposed to follow the lead of the masses, who think it their special duty to heap all sorts of ridicule and smart sayings upon this lady. . . . [S]he has a good heart . . . and that should at least silence the tongue of slander."

Her own tongue was problematic. Known as "an injudicious talker," Mary once regaled the Union general Carl Schurz "with a flood of gossip about the various members of the cabinet and leading men in Congress who in some way had incurred her displeasure . . . I learned more state secrets in a few hours than I could otherwise in a year."

In quieter hours Mary sometimes read novels, borrowing the mystery *Why Paul Ferroll Killed His Wife* from the Library of Congress. Fond of Charles Sumner, the First Lady came to depend on his company. "Mrs. L. is embarrassed a little," Lincoln once wrote to Sumner. "She would be pleased to have your company again this evening, at the Opera, but she fears she may be taxing you. I have undertaken to clear up the little difficulty. If, for any reason, it will tax you, decline, without any hesitation; but if it will not, consider yourself already invited." And she worried about her husband. "Mother has got a notion into her head that I shall be assassinated, and to please her I take a cane when I go over to the War Department at nights—when I don't forget it," Lincoln said. Benjamin Brown French was appointed commissioner of public buildings, which included supervision of the White House, in early September 1861. "I certainly shall do all in my power to oblige her and make her comfortable," French told his diary after meeting with the First Lady. "She is evidently a smart, intelligent woman, & likes to have her own way pretty much."

That she certainly did. On Saturday, December 13, 1861, the First Lady sent for French to discuss what to do about her overspending on the White House. "The money was . . . expended by Mrs. Lincoln, & she was in much tribulation, the President declaring he would not approve the bills overrunning the $20,000 appropriated," French recalled. Mary tried a bit of subterfuge: "Mrs. L. wanted me to see him & endeavor to persuade him to give his approval to the bills," French said, "but not to let him know that I had seen her!" The commissioner duly went to the president, who was implacable. "He said it would stink in the land to have it said that an appropriation of $20,000 for furnishing the house had been overrun by the President when the poor freezing soldiers could not have blankets, & he *swore* he would never approve the bills for *flub dubs for that damned old house!*"

In February 1862, the First Lady decided to throw a large private party at the White House. The tone and the timing were terrible. Rather than an open reception, which was the common practice, the event was by invitation only in a season shadowed by Union defeats. But Mrs. Lincoln would not be dissuaded. "I can't do anything!" White House secretary John Nicolay lamented. "It will make all sorts of trouble, 'She' is determined to have her own way." To Henry Dawes, "Trifling at the White House in these times seems as inappropriate as jollity at a funeral"; Senator Benjamin Wade of Ohio asked, "Are the President and Mrs. Lincoln aware there is a Civil War?"

Soon darkness fell. Willie Lincoln, who had turned eleven in December, was diagnosed with typhoid fever and died within two weeks. Lincoln had been a vigilant father at the sick-bed, devoting "pretty much all his attention" to Willie and to Tad, who was also ill; further White House entertainments had been called off; and when the end came, on Thursday, February 20, Lincoln told Nicolay, "Well, Nicolay, my boy is gone—he is actually gone," and wept. A grief-stricken Mary Lincoln confined herself to her private quarters. Willie's body lay in repose in the Green Room.

On the day of the funeral, the president, the First Lady, and Robert Lincoln asked for time alone with Willie. "They desired that there should be no spectator of their last sad moments in that house with their dead child & brother," Benjamin Brown French told his diary. In the half hour the small family spent in the Green Room, "there came one of the heaviest storms of rain & wind that has visited this city for years, and the terrible storm without seemed almost in unison with the storm of grief within, for Mrs. Lincoln, I was told, was terribly affected at her loss and almost refused to be comforted."

The Reverend Phineas Gurley presided over the funeral, which was held in the East Room on Monday, February 24, 1862. Much of official Washington was there, including the vice president, the cabinet, McClellan, and the Illinois congressional delegation. "The heart of the Nation sympathizes with its Chief Magistrate," Gurley said in his sermon. Addressing the president and the family, he prayed that "God's grace may be sufficient for them, and that in this hour of sore bereavement and trial, they may have the presence and succor of Him who has said, 'Come unto me all ye that labor and are heavy laden, and I will give you rest.' " There was a lengthy procession—observers thought it "about 1/2 a mile long"—to Oak Hill Cemetery in Georgetown. There Willie would lie in a tomb pending a return to Illinois.

Lincoln liked and trusted Gurley. In the wake of Willie's death, Lincoln was drawn to the biblical drama of life and death, and Gurley proved a comforting interlocutor. A fellow churchgoer of the president's, Alban Jasper Conant, recalled that "ever after" Willie's death, "there was a new quality in [Lincoln's] demeanor—something approaching awe. I sat in the fifth pew behind him every Sunday in Dr. Gurley's church, and I saw him on many occasions, marking the change in him."

Gurley recalled being with the president one evening when Lincoln proposed an early-morning visit the next day. "Doctor, you rise early; so do I," Lincoln said. "Come over tomorrow morning about seven o'clock. We can talk for an hour before breakfast."

Gurley did as he was asked and was stepping through the gate on his

"*Our Willie.*"

Willie Lincoln's death in February 1862
devastated the president and the First Lady.

way after the morning meeting when he ran into a congregant from New York Avenue Presbyterian.

"'Why doctor,' said my friend," Gurley recalled, "'it is not nine o'clock. What are you doing at the Executive Mansion?'

"To this I replied, 'Mr. Lincoln and I have been having a morning chat.'

"'On the war, I suppose?'

"'Far from it,' said I. 'We have been talking about the state of the soul after death. That is a subject of which Mr. Lincoln never tires. I have had a great many conversations with him on the subject. This morning, however, I was a listener, as Mr. Lincoln did all the talking.'"

In this season Mary Lincoln asked the Reverend Francis Vinton of New York's Trinity Church to have a word with her anguished husband. "Your son is *alive,* in Paradise," Vinton told the president. "Do you remember that passage in the Gospels: 'God is not the God of the *dead* but of the living, for *all* live unto him'?"

"Alive!" Lincoln replied. "*Alive!* Surely you mock me."

"No, sir, believe me, it is a most comforting doctrine of the church, founded upon the words of Christ himself. . . . Seek not your son among the dead; he is not there; he lives today in Paradise! . . . Doubt it not."

This kind of deeply personal religious inquiry was new to Lincoln. "He first seemed to think about the subject when our boy Willie died," Mary Lincoln recalled. We cannot know what he truly believed. We cannot even know whether *he* knew what he truly believed. What we do know is that from the time of Willie's death until his own he mused frequently about the will of God and the workings of the world.

In a private note, the president wrote:

The will of God prevails. In great contests each party claims to act in accordance with the will of God. Both *may* be, and one *must* be wrong. God cannot be *for,* and *against* the same thing at the same time. In the present civil war it is quite possible that God's purpose is something different from the purpose of either party— and yet the human instrumentalities, working just as they do, are of the best adaptation to effect His purpose. I am almost ready to say this is probably true—that God wills this contest, and wills that it shall not end yet. By his mere quiet power, on the minds of the now contestants, He could have either *saved* or *destroyed* the

Union without a human contest. Yet the contest began. And having begun He could give the final victory to either side any day. Yet the contest proceeds.

In the summer of 1862, not long after Willie's death, a delegation of Quakers called on the president. One of the visitors, William Barnard, spoke up, "expressing . . . an earnest desire that [Lincoln] might, under divine guidance, be led to free the slaves and thus save the nation from destruction."

The president replied thoughtfully. He was "deeply sensible of his need of Divine assistance," Lincoln told his visitors. "He had sometime thought that perhaps he might be an instrument in God's hands of accomplishing a great work and he certainly was not unwilling to be. Perhaps, however, God's way of accomplishing the end which the memorialists have in view may be different from theirs." At all events, though, "it would be his earnest endeavor, with a firm reliance upon the Divine arm, and seeking light from above, to do his duty in the place to which he had been called."

For Lincoln, the Lord was now an engaged force in history—a God whose will prevailed. The death of his child—the second the Lincolns had lost—had presented the president with a choice. He could collapse in grief and in cynicism, howling against an indifferent universe. Or he could follow Gurley's counsel and see a world informed by providence— that even the horrifying loss of a child was part of a plan devised by an all-powerful and all-loving God. It was the coldest of comfort, but at least it was comfort, and Lincoln appears to have embraced it. One accepted tragedy in the hope that pain was but prelude to light and peace.

Whatever the nature of his internal drama, Lincoln believed that the world was not random and that morality—right and wrong—could never truly and finally be divorced from politics, his chosen life. To Lincoln, people were obligated by conscience, informed by scripture and by experience, to pursue the ideals of love and of generosity—and each person would be accountable for action or inaction to the extent one undertook or impeded this pursuit. The lives of individuals and of nations were thus defined by a moral drama. Lincoln memorably said events had controlled him, but the man who ran for office on an anti-slavery platform, who effected emancipation, who went to Gettysburg, and who delivered the Second Inaugural Address viewed the world not

as mechanistic but as moral. Conscience and character were not incidental to human affairs, but instrumental.

In this Lincoln was moving closer to a vision articulated by, among
others, Frederick Douglass. "The slave power might silence the voice of
Wendell Phillips, or the pen of William Lloyd Garrison," Douglass observed. "They might blot out our anti-slavery organization in order to
give peace to the slaveholder. They might cut out my tongue, and all
our tongues. They might gather all the Anti-Slavery literature, 'Uncle
Tom's Cabin' included, set a match to it, send its flames toward the sky
and scatter its ashes to the four winds of heaven, and yet the slaveholder will be ill at ease; for deep down in his own dark conscience
would come an accusing voice: 'Thou art verily guilty concerning thy
brother.'"

The scriptural allusion was to the betrayal of Joseph by his brothers
in the Book of Genesis: "And they said one to another, We *are* verily
guilty concerning our brother, in that we saw the anguish of his soul,
when he besought us, and we would not hear; therefore is this distress
come upon us." The story is one of accountability, of punishment for
violating standards of right conduct, of pain inflicted for a sin against
another.

And what could be interpreted as a greater sin against another than
human enslavement?

Lincoln attacked slavery where and when he thought he safely could.
On Wednesday, April 16, 1862, he agreed to Congress's immediate
abolition of slavery in the District of Columbia, a subject he had been
thinking about since his days in the House. "Thanks Be to the Almighty," wrote Michael Shiner, who worked in the Washington Navy
Yard, when the news came.

Long an antislavery goal—it had been proposed as early as 1805,
nearly sixty years before—abolition in the District was within the
power of Congress, which, under the Constitution, had authority over
the national capital. The president had his reservations, but he was an
antislavery man, and here was a place he could act. The bill provided
slave owners with compensation of $300 per enslaved person and rec-
ommended that the formerly enslaved voluntarily emigrate from the
United States. *The New York Times* hailed the news as evidence of "the
genius of the age, as well as Christianity. This act of Government is but

the record of a progress in this country in liberal ideas, common to the whole civilized world." All in all, abolition in the District could be defended and explained as a conventional constitutional decision, not as an extra-legal or wartime measure.

The same could not be said for the news from Hilton Head, South Carolina. In May, David Hunter, now the Union commander of the Department of the South, issued an order that "the persons in these three States—Georgia, Florida, and South Carolina—heretofore held as slaves, are therefore declared forever free." Lincoln rescinded the directive and pointed the border states to his plan for gradual, compensated emancipation.

Attentive readers of the president's proclamation revoking Hunter's order would have noted a glint of steel. "I . . . make known," Lincoln wrote, "that whether it be competent for me, as Commander-in-Chief of the Army and Navy, to declare the Slaves of any state or states, free, and whether at any time, in any case, it shall have become a necessity indispensable to the maintenance of the government, to exercise such supposed power, are questions which, under my responsibility, I reserve to myself."

It was a careful, comma-heavy sentence. But its meaning was clear. In the middle of May, 1862, a president of the United States was saying that he believed the war had given him the power to emancipate the enslaved in a stroke. It was a bold assertion of executive power, and the nation was on notice. Lincoln was reserving the right to move forward on emancipation—*at any time*, as the president said, *in any case*.

The war itself was not going well. In the West in the spring of 1862, particularly at Forts Henry and Donelson and at Shiloh, U. S. Grant had won costly Union victories, but the fighting in Virginia was a more complicated story. In May and June 1862, the Confederate general Thomas "Stonewall" Jackson led a successful campaign in the Shenandoah Valley. Hard-won victories as well as discouraging defeats—and there were plenty of both in these first two years of war—brought unhappiness in the North. "Not a spark of genius has he; not an element of leadership; not one particle of heroic enthusiasm," Henry Ward Beecher wrote of Lincoln in the summer of 1862.

Jackson's rout of the Union in the Shenandoah came at the same time as Confederate victories around Richmond, at the Battle of Seven

Pines—the clash that brought Robert E. Lee to command after the wounding of Joseph Johnston. Seven Pines ended around June 1; a month later, Lee's forces defeated McClellan's in the mid-Virginia action known collectively as the Seven Days' Battles. Then came the Second Battle of Bull Run in late August 1862—a repeat of the first, with Union forces falling before the Confederate assault.

Lincoln's troops were being forced to settle in for the longest of sieges. At Shiloh in April 1862, when the Confederate armies had surprised the Union with resilient fighting, Grant recalled that he "gave up all idea of saving the Union except by complete conquest." William Tecumseh Sherman pressed the point: "We are not only fighting hostile armies, but a hostile people, and must make [them] . . . feel the hard hand of war." Unconditional surrender had been a battlefield principle since Fort Donelson in February. In response to a Confederate request for terms during the fighting on the Cumberland River, General Charles F. Smith had said, "I'll make no terms with rebels with arms in their hands—my terms are unconditional and immediate surrender!" To Grant, Smith repeated the point: "No terms to the damned Rebels!"

Grant agreed. "No terms except an immediate and unconditional surrender can be accepted," Grant wrote to the enemy. "Unconditional surrender" was battlefield policy—but for Lincoln, it was not official wartime policy. Though he insisted that the war could end only when the Confederates put down their arms and accepted national authority, the president was vague about the details in 1863 and well into 1864.

What he was less and less vague about was his hope that he might enlist Black men in the armed service of the Union. To do so, the president believed, the nation had to offer a promise of emancipation. Why else, Lincoln wondered, would a Black man fight for a government that enslaved him?

Between March and July 1862, the president made a choice. As he had with abolition in the District of Columbia, he would move against slavery—this time in the seceded states. "I am satisfied that when the Almighty wants me to do or not to do a particular thing, he finds a way of letting me know it," Lincoln once said. "I am confident that it is his design to restore the Union. He will do it in his own good time. We should obey and not oppose his will." Discerning that will was now Lincoln's consuming concern.

Across the Potomac, the Confederacy was unbending. The rebel South "is profoundly impressed with the conviction that . . . all that makes life desirable is involved in a dissolution of her connection with the northern states," Leonidas Polk wrote in the winter of 1861–62. "This is the sentiment of the Southern people. It is my sentiment. *It is my profound conviction* . . . that the interest and happiness of the Southern States is to be found in a total and final Separation. . . . And I beg leave to add that at no time has the determination of the Southern people to free themselves from their connection with the north been more firm and unflinching than at the present moment."

Lincoln understood this—and he, too, was unbending. "I expect to maintain this contest until successful, or till I die, or am conquered, or my term expires, or Congress or the country forsakes me," the president wrote in June.

Part of the contest was to build a nation that could thrive should the Union survive. Lincoln was always focused on opportunity—he believed in a country that made lives like the one he was living possible. "Whatever is calculated to advance the condition of the honest, struggling laboring man, so far as my judgment will enable me to judge of a correct thing, I am for that thing," Lincoln said in 1861. The president's credo: "The prudent, penniless beginner in the world, labors for wages awhile, saves a surplus with which to buy tools or land for himself; then labors on his own account another while, and at length hires another new beginner to help him. This is the just, and generous, and prosperous system, which opens the way to all—gives hope to all, and consequent energy, and progress, and improvement of condition to all."

To him, the federal government that was under such assault should be not weakened in the face of the rebellion, but strengthened. The president approved a federal income tax and signed national banking legislation that brought structure and stability to the financial system. The Homestead Act of 1862 distributed Western land to burgeoning farmers and powered the growth of American agriculture—all while further displacing indigenous peoples from their ancestral lands.

On successive days in July 1862, Lincoln signed legislation designed to provide for what he once called "man's vast future." First, on Tuesday, July 1, the president approved the Pacific Railroad Act, the bill making the transcontinental railroad possible. The next day, Wednesday, July 2, came an act, sponsored by Representative Justin Smith Morrill, a Re-

publican from Vermont, to create land grant institutions of higher education. This legislation, too, exploited Native Americans by taking
nearly eleven million acres in exchange for no, or at best negligible,
compensation.

Several days later, Lincoln traveled to George McClellan's headquarters at Harrison's Landing, Virginia. Robert E. Lee had just defeated
the Union forces in the Seven Days' Battles near Richmond, securing
the Confederate capital. In his meeting with Lincoln, McClellan
handed the president a letter heavily inflected by Democratic politics.
"A declaration of radical views, especially upon slavery," McClellan told
Lincoln, "will rapidly disintegrate our present Armies."

Lincoln returned to Washington and did the opposite. On Thursday, July 17, the president approved the Second Confiscation Act, "an
Act to suppress Insurrection, to punish Treason and Rebellion, to seize
and confiscate the Property of Rebels, and for other Purposes."

A sweeping law, the Second Confiscation Act declared that slaves
owned by "persons . . . engaged in rebellion against the government of
the United States" who came "under the control of the government
of the United States," including at Union lines, "shall be forever free of
their servitude, and not again held as slaves." An emancipatory measure, the act indicated that antislavery public opinion was growing
stronger. The bill authorized Lincoln "to employ as many persons of
African descent as he may deem necessary and proper for the suppression of this rebellion, and for this purpose he may organize and use
them in such manner as he may judge best for the public welfare."

The legislation also gave the president the power "to make provision
for the transportation, colonization, and settlement, in some tropical
country beyond the limits of the United States, of such persons of the
African race, made free by the provisions of this act, as may be willing
to emigrate."

The exigencies of war were reshaping America. The Second Confiscation Act was a landmark achievement. Union victories in Confederate territory now took on a much deeper significance, for the progress
of arms would have the effect of permanently liberating enslaved people owned by those in rebellion.

"You can form no conception at the change of opinion here on the
Negro question," Senator John Sherman of Ohio wrote to his brother,

the Union general William Tecumseh Sherman, in August 1862. "Men of all parties who now appreciate the magnitude of the contest . . . agree that we must seek and make it the interests of the Negroes to help us."

The antebellum world was giving way. "I shall not do *more* than I can, and I shall do *all* I can, to save the government," Lincoln said in the summer of 1862. And saving the government, he had decided, meant emancipation.

In June, the president had sent to the Library of Congress for a book: *A Key to Uncle Tom's Cabin; Presenting the Original Facts and Documents upon Which the Story Is Founded. Together with Corroborative Statements Verifying the Work*. In its pages Harriet Beecher Stowe had included her research material, which taken together offered moving evidence of slavery's human toll. "The great object of the author in writing has been to bring this subject of slavery, as a moral and religious question, before the minds of all those who profess to be followers of Christ, in this country," Stowe wrote in her introduction to the *Key*. Lincoln's great object was to bring that subject before the minds of every American, Christian or no.

CHAPTER TWENTY

I Think the Time Has Come Now

I now determined upon the adoption of the
emancipation policy.

—ABRAHAM LINCOLN, summer 1862

The children of the black man have enriched the soil by
their tears, and sweat, and blood. Sir, we were born here,
and here we choose to remain.

—The abolitionist ROBERT PURVIS, on colonization, August 1862

T
HERE WERE TWO PORTRAITS, and only two portraits, in Lincoln's White House office. One, of Andrew Jackson, defender of the Union, was a holdover from President Buchanan. The other was of a man Lincoln never met and with whom he only indirectly corresponded: the English politician and reformer John Bright, a member of Parliament. Like Lincoln, Bright was an advocate of the Western liberal tradition that prized individual rights over inherited authority. Karl Marx thought Bright "one of the most gifted orators that England has ever produced." "If you could take the opinion of the whole House," his ally and fellow reformer Richard Cobden remarked, Bright "would be pronounced by a large majority to combine more earnestness, courage, honesty and eloquence than any other man." When Bright died, in 1889, William Gladstone told the House of Commons, "He has lived to witness the triumph of almost every great cause—perhaps I might say of every great cause—to which he had especially devoted his heart and mind."

Abolition, democracy, and equality of economic opportunity were among those causes. Born in 1811 in Lancashire, raised in the Quaker faith, Bright was deeply interested in the American experiment. He was connected to important figures across the Atlantic, including Charles Sumner, William Lloyd Garrison, Horace Greeley, and Frederick Douglass, who had been Bright's guest in England. "Everywhere there is an open career," Bright said of the United States; "there is no privileged class; there is complete education extended to all; and every man feels that he is not born to be in penury and in suffering, but that there is no point in the social ladder to which he may not fairly hope to raise himself by his honest efforts." In December 1861, in Rochdale, England, Bright declared a hope that "the whole of that vast continent might become one great confederation of States . . . with freedom everywhere, equality everywhere, law everywhere, peace everywhere." He was as clear-eyed as Lincoln about what the American Civil War was about. "The object of the South is . . . to found a Slave State freed from the influence and opinions of freedom," Bright said. The struggle was about whether "a handful of white men on that continent shall lord it over countless millions of blacks, made black by the very hand that made us white. The object is, [whether] they should have the power to breed negroes, to work negroes, to lash negroes, to chain negroes, to buy and sell negroes, to deny them the commonest ties of family, or to break their hearts by rending them at their pleasure."

Such were the kinds of words Lincoln might think of when, in the course of a long day, his eyes drifted to Bright's portrait. They were words of liberation and of equality, of possibility and of progress. They were words of the sort that had inspired the Lincoln who read Parker and Emerson, Mill and Butler, Jefferson and Kossuth. In the summer of 1862, Lincoln the student would act as Lincoln the president.

The occasion was grim. The infant son of Edwin Stanton, young James, was dead, and the ranking powers of the nation were paying their respects as the child was buried at Oak Hill in Georgetown. Lincoln and Stanton had been spending time in neighboring cottages at the Soldiers' Home, an enclave about three miles from the White House near Silver Spring, Maryland. Founded as a "Military Asylum" about a decade before on land purchased from the banker George Riggs, the Soldiers' Home offered the Lincolns an attractive retreat from the pressures of the White House—and from the rats and bugs that were a feature of life on the Potomac in the warmer months. "The air is swarming with them," John G. Nicolay wrote of the armies of insects; "they are on the ceiling, the walls and the furniture in countless numbers, they are buzzing about the room, and butting their heads against the window panes, they are on my clothes, in my hair, and on the sheet I am writing on." One summer Benjamin Brown French wrote that "the effluvia from dead rats was offensive in all the passages and many of the occupied rooms to both the occupants of, and visitors to, the Presidential mansion."

The Soldiers' Home was also a retreat, or at least a respite, from the enduring grief over Willie. The White House, Mary wrote, was "very beautiful . . . [and] the world still smiles & pays homage, yet the charm is dispelled, everything appears a mockery, [because] the idolized one is not with us."

As secretary of war, Stanton had use of a neighboring cottage; as his son failed, the secretary cancelled a breakfast with Lincoln, writing the president, "If my child is not dying I will be in town as early as possible."

The July 1862 day that brought the funeral of young James Stanton was filled with painful resonance for Lincoln; Willie lay in a tomb at the same hilltop cemetery. The president was riding in a carriage with

Secretary of the Navy Gideon Welles called Lincoln's broaching of emancipation in the summer of 1862 "a new departure for the President."

Seward, Seward's daughter-in-law Anna, and Secretary of the Navy Gideon Welles when, to their surprise, he reportedly broached the subject of emancipation. "It was a new departure for the President, for until this time in all our previous intercourse, whenever the question of emancipation or the mitigation of slavery had been in any way alluded to, he had been prompt and emphatic in denouncing any interference by the general government with the subject," Welles told his diary. "But the reverses before Richmond, and the formidable power and dimensions of the insurrection which extended through all the Slave States . . . impelled the administration to adopt extraordinary measures to preserve the National existence."

Military necessity in the cause of Union was one motive. Conscience in the service of justice was another. The president was doing the right thing for practical reasons—a political being pursuing a course grounded in morality. To skeptics who would see Lincoln's decision as solely utilitarian—as a means to win the war only—the test of his moral commitment to emancipation would come in the future, if and when victory was in hand. What then? Would he pursue the end of slavery even if there were fewer compelling military reasons to do so? That would be the great question of 1864–65.

But now it was 1862–63. He was open about the practical aspect of the move. Emancipation would encourage Black Americans to fight for the Union, for they, Lincoln later noted, "like other people, act upon motives. Why should they do anything for us if we will do nothing for them? If they stake their lives for us, they must be prompted by the strongest motive, even the promise of freedom. And the promise, being made, must be kept." In a meeting of the cabinet on Tuesday, July 22, Lincoln read a draft of an emancipation proclamation. He had composed it over a period of time, reportedly using a brass inkwell on a desk in the quiet of the War Department's Telegraph Office. Throughout the war the president frequented these rooms in the building a short walk from the White House to monitor incoming news and dispatch orders. The army's telegraph superintendent, Major Thomas T. Eckert, said that he recalled Lincoln's work on the proclamation. "The President came to my office every day and invariably sat at my desk," Eckert wrote. "I became much interested . . . with the idea that he was engaged upon something of great importance, but did not know what it was until he had finished the document and then for the first time he told me that he had been writing an order giving freedom to the slaves in the South, for the purpose of hastening the end of the war."

The proposed proclamation's scope was surprising. "Every member of the council was, we may infer, bewildered by the magnitude and boldness of the proposal," Hay and Nicolay recalled. "I now determined upon the adoption of the emancipation policy; and without consultation with, or the knowledge of, the Cabinet, I prepared the original draft of the proclamation," Lincoln recalled. Once he was ready, he called them into session, and the cabinet officers seated themselves around the table in the middle of the president's office, the southern light coming in the windows. Lincoln told them that he "had resolved upon this step, and had not called them together to ask their advice, but to lay the subject-matter of a proclamation before them, suggestions as to which would be in order after they had heard it." As he read his draft, nearby military maps marked with pins to show the disposition of troops told a good part of the story of why, and why now: The Confederate forces were strong in Virginia, and General Lee was soon to come north.

There were a few thoughts. Montgomery Blair, the postmaster general, spoke out against the measure. "Mr. Blair . . . deprecated the policy on the ground that it would cost the Administration the fall elections," Lincoln later noted. The president did not need to be told that. He knew the politics. "Nothing . . . was offered that I had not already fully anticipated and settled in my own mind," Lincoln recalled.

Then Seward weighed in. "Mr. President, I approve of the proclamation, but I question the expediency of its issue at this juncture," the secretary of state said. "The depression of the public mind, consequent upon our repeated reverses, is so great that I fear the effect of so important a step. It may be viewed as the last measure of an exhausted Government, a cry for help; the Government stretching forth its hands to Ethiopia, instead of Ethiopia stretching forth her hands to the Government." The proclamation could thus "be considered our last *shriek* on the retreat . . . I suggest, sir, that you postpone its issue until you can give it to the country supported by military success, instead of issuing it, as would be the case now, upon the greatest disasters of the war."

Lincoln agreed. "The wisdom of the view of the Secretary of State struck me with very great force," the president recalled. "It was an aspect of the case that, in all my thought upon the subject, I had entirely overlooked. The result was that I put the draft of the proclamation aside . . . waiting for victory." And so he would wait.

I n this summertime caesura, with Lee on the march and emancipation seemingly decided but certainly delayed, the president received an unusual delegation at the White House—a group the newspapers referred to as "a Committee of colored men." It was the afternoon of Thursday, August 14, 1862, and the visitors' leader, Edward M. Thomas, said they would gladly "hear what the Executive had to say to them." They took their seats, and Lincoln began. Also present: a reporter. Lincoln wanted what he said to be known, and known widely. His calculus: White Americans who heard that colonization was a live possibility might be more open to emancipation.

The topic of the meeting, according to the president: voluntary colonization of "the people, or a portion of them, of African descent." Congress had appropriated funds for the project, Lincoln said, "thereby making it his duty, as it had for a long time been his inclination, to favor that cause; and why, he asked, should the people of your race be colonized, and where? Why should they leave this country?"

Lincoln had long coupled emancipation with colonization. In mid-July 1862 a congressional report recommended colonization as a necessary condition of emancipation. "Apart from the antipathy which nature has ordained, the presence of a race among us who cannot, and ought not to, be admitted to our social and political privileges, will be a perpetual source of injury and inquietude to both," the committee said.

Many possibilities were discussed and debated. Liberia was one; Hay and Nicolay recalled other conversations about "the Danish island of St. Croix, West Indies; in the Netherland colony of Surinam; in the British colony of Guiana; in British Honduras; in Hayti; . . . in New Granada, and in Ecuador." In October 1861, Lincoln had asked his secretary of the interior, Caleb Smith, about a plan to settle Black Americans in Chiriqui, in Central America. Championed by the Blair family, the Chiriqui Improvement Company was led by an investor named Ambrose W. Thompson, who proposed acquiring and developing the Chiriqui region in present-day Panama as a home for Black Americans.

An element of the American debate about slavery and race for decades, colonization provoked deep skepticism among many white people and Black people. "How much better would be a manly protest against prejudice against color!—and a wise effort to give freemen homes in America!" Treasury Secretary Salmon Chase told his diary. To William Lloyd Garrison, it was clear that "the nation's four million slaves are as much the natives of this country as any of their oppressors."

The colonization proposals underscored a tragic reality. One could—and many white Americans did—oppose slavery while failing to engage the prospective creation of a multiracial democracy. "Lincoln held the strong belief that colonization would accomplish a dual purpose: rid the South of human bondage and rid the country of the colored man," the historian Benjamin Quarles wrote. "Slavery and the race problem would thus vanish simultaneously." The president had made a major statement on the subject not quite eight months after Sumter. In his December 1861 annual message to Congress, Lincoln discussed the disposition of those who fell under the protection of the First Confiscation Act, asking that "such persons, on such acceptance by the general government, be at once deemed free; and that, in any event, steps be taken for colonizing . . . at some place, or places, in a climate congenial to them. It might be well to consider, too, whether the free colored people already in the United States could not, so far as individuals may desire, be included in such colonization."

The words were grave. So was the question. Except in the most advanced quarters of the abolition movement, the free states were far from prepared to welcome a new day of full racial equality. "The *everlasting Negro* is the rock upon which the Ship of State must split," a Providence, Rhode Island, newspaper wrote. "Will the people stand for this much longer? Will they make the Negro their god?" "We can make emancipation acceptable to the whole mass of non-slave-holders at the South by coupling it with the policy of colonization," Representative Francis P. Blair, Jr., told the House. "The very prejudice of race which now makes the non-slaveholders give their aid to hold the slave in bondage will induce them to unite in a policy which will rid them of the presence of negroes."

At the White House on this August afternoon in 1862, the president spoke with equal candor. "You and we are different races," he told his visitors. "We have between us a broader difference than exists between almost any other two races. Whether it is right or wrong I need not discuss, but this physical difference is a great disadvantage to us both, as I think your race suffer very greatly, many of them by living among us, while ours suffer from your presence. In a word we suffer on each side. If this is admitted, it affords a reason at least why we should be separated."

He paused and asked: "You here are freemen I suppose."

"Yes, sir," came the reply.

"Perhaps you have long been free, or all your lives," Lincoln went on. "Your race are suffering, in my judgment, the greatest wrong inflicted on any people. But even when you cease to be slaves, you are yet far removed from being placed on an equality with the white race. . . . Go where you are treated the best, and the ban is still upon you."

Lincoln continued:

I do not propose to discuss this, but to present it as a fact with which we have to deal. I cannot alter it if I would. It is a fact, about which we all think and feel alike, I and you. We look to our condition, owing to the existence of the two races on this continent. I need not recount to you the effects upon white men, growing out of the institution of Slavery. I believe in its general evil effects on the white race. See our present condition—the country engaged in war!—our white men cutting one another's throats, none knowing how far it will extend; and then consider what we know to be the truth. But for your race among us there could not be war, although many men engaged on either side do not care for you one way or the other. Nevertheless, I repeat, without the institution of Slavery and the colored race as a basis, the war could not have an existence. It is better for us both, therefore, to be separated.

He raised Chiriqui. "The place I am thinking about having for a colony is in Central America," Lincoln said. "It is nearer to us than Liberia—not much more than one-fourth as far as Liberia, and within seven days' run by steamers. Unlike Liberia it is on a great line of travel—it is a highway. The country is a very excellent one for any people, and with great natural resources and advantages, and especially because of the similarity of climate with your native land—thus being suited to your physical condition. . . . If I could find twenty-five able-bodied men, with a mixture of women and children, good things in the family relation, I think I could make a successful commencement."

Edward Thomas, the chairman of the delegation, said that "they would hold a consultation and in a short time give an answer."

"Take your full time—no hurry at all," Lincoln said, and the visitors took their leave.

It was thought to have been the first conference ever held between Black leaders and a president of the United States on a matter of policy. While Edward Thomas later wrote to Lincoln that he would take up the cause the president had outlined, many others were furious. "To these colored people without power and without influence the President is direct, undisguised and unhesitating," Frederick Douglass said. "He says to the colored people: I don't like you, you must clear out of the country." "We can find nothing in the religion of our Lord and Master, teaching us that color is the standard by which He judges his creatures," read *An Appeal from the Colored Men of Philadelphia.* "The children of the black man have enriched the soil by their tears, and sweat, and blood," Robert Purvis, a mixed-race abolitionist in Philadelphia, wrote to the government's emigration agent. "Sir, we were born here, and here we choose to remain."

Lincoln met with Ambrose Thompson and others on the Chiriqui project in mid-August and appointed Senator Samuel C. Pomeroy of Kansas as "commissioner of African colonization." On Thursday, September 11, 1862, the president approved the Chiriqui contract, but resistance from the region and charges of corruption against the company scuttled the project.

Another Lincoln effort—a proposed $250,000 federal contract to colonize five thousand Black Americans on Île-à-Vache, off Haiti— went further. An expedition transporting about 450 Black people to the island was disastrous, their stay on Île-à-Vache marred by disease, exposure, and want. The experiment lasted less than a year; the president brought the 368 survivors back to the United States in early 1864. Lincoln remained interested in proposals for colonization, pursuing possibilities in 1863 and into 1864 concerning British Honduras, Guiana, and Surinam. By July 1864, Congress had cut off colonization funding. After the war, Gideon Welles wrote that Lincoln "by no means abandoned his policy of deportation and emancipation, for the two were in his mind indispensably and indissolubly connected. Colonization in fact had precedence with him."

Six days after the August 1862 meeting with the Black leaders, Horace Greeley published an editorial in his *Tribune* chiding Lincoln for failing to be bolder on emancipation. "We complain that the Union cause has suffered, and is now suffering immensely, from mistaken deference to Rebel Slavery," Greeley wrote, continuing:

> We complain that the Confiscation Act which you approved is habitually disregarded by your Generals, and that no word of rebuke for them from you has yet reached the public ear. Frémont's Proclamation and Hunter's Order favoring Emancipation were promptly annulled by you; . . . [W]e complain that you, Mr. President, elected as a Republican, knowing well what an abomination Slavery is, and how emphatically it is the core and essence of this atrocious Rebellion, seem never to interfere with these atrocities, and never give a direction to your Military subordinates . . .
>
> On the face of this wide earth, Mr. President, there is not one disinterested, determined, intelligent champion of the Union cause who does not feel that all attempts to put down the Rebellion and at the same time uphold its inciting cause are preposterous and futile—that the Rebellion, if crushed out tomorrow, would be renewed within a year if Slavery were left in full vigor.

With an eye on public opinion and in the hope that he could soon issue his proclamation, Lincoln replied to Greeley with characteristic care:

> If there be those who would not save the Union, unless they could at the same time *save* slavery, I do not agree with them. If there be those who would not save the Union unless they could at the same time *destroy* slavery, I do not agree with them. My paramount object in this struggle *is* to save the Union, and is *not* either to save or to destroy slavery. If I could save the Union without freeing *any* slave I would do it, and if I could save it by freeing *all* the slaves I would do it; and if I could save it by freeing some and leaving others alone I would also do that. What I do about slavery, and the

colored race, I do because I believe it helps to save the Union; and what I forbear, I forbear because I do *not* believe it would help to save the Union. I shall do *less* whenever I shall believe what I am doing hurts the cause, and I shall do *more* whenever I shall believe doing more will help the cause. I shall try to correct errors when shown to be errors; and I shall adopt new views so fast as they shall appear to be true views.

I have here stated my purpose according to my view of *official* duty; and I intend no modification of my oft-expressed *personal* wish that all men everywhere could be free.

The letter to Greeley has long been deployed to portray Lincoln as at best agnostic on slavery. It should be read, however, with the understanding that the president had already drafted the Emancipation Proclamation, had presented it to the cabinet, and was awaiting the right moment to announce his decision to the country. In that light, Lincoln's emphasis on preserving the Union can be read as a politician's effort to frame a controversial decision in terms that stood the best chance of winning broad public acceptance. Without Union there could be no emancipation, for a victorious Confederacy would enshrine slavery for an indefinite future. Lincoln's stated hierarchy of concerns in the Greeley letter might seem callous but was in fact well calibrated both to secure the nation and to effect emancipation. In presenting himself as a pragmatist, the president was preparing the way to render a decision with the most profound practical *and* moral implications.

Lincoln's struggle to emancipate in a nation that saw and treated Black people as unequal was also evident in an hour-long session he held on Saturday, September 13, with two religious leaders from Chicago, the Reverend William W. Patton and the Reverend John Dempster. He and his guests, who presented him with a "memorial," or petition, for emancipation, were frank, and the exchange offers a window on the forces competing within Lincoln's heart and mind. "The subject presented in the memorial is one upon which I have thought much for weeks past, and I may even say for months," Lincoln said, continuing:

I am approached with the most opposite opinions and advice, and that by religious men, who are equally certain that they represent the Divine will. . . . I hope it will not be irreverent for me to say that if it is probable that God would reveal his will to others, on a point so connected with my duty, it might be supposed he would reveal it directly to me; for, unless I am more deceived in myself than I often am, it is my earnest desire to know the will of Providence in this matter. *And if I can learn what it is I will do it!* These are not, however, the days of miracles, and I suppose it will be granted that I am not to expect a direct revelation. I must study the plain physical facts of the case, ascertain what is possible and learn what appears to be wise and right. The subject is difficult, and good men do not agree.

He was just getting going. "What *good* would a proclamation of emancipation from me do, especially as we are now situated?" Lincoln said. "I do not want to issue a document that the whole world will see must necessarily be inoperative. . . . Would *my word* free the slaves, when I cannot even enforce the Constitution in the rebel States? Is there a single court, or magistrate, or individual that would be influenced by it there?"

The president also reflected the racial prejudices of much of the white North. "And suppose they could be induced by a proclamation of freedom from me to throw themselves upon us, *what should we do with them?* How can we feed and care for such a multitude?"

The Chicago ministers replied with spirit. "We observed . . . that good men indeed differed in their opinions on this subject; nevertheless *the truth was somewhere,* and it was a matter of solemn moment for him to ascertain it."

To the visitors, it was clear that "the Bible denounced oppression as one of the highest of crimes, and threatened Divine judgments against nations that practice it; . . . that the virus of secession is found wherever the virus of slavery extends, and no farther; so that there is the amplest reason for expecting to avert Divine judgments by putting away the sin, and for hoping to remedy the national troubles by striking at their cause."

Lincoln replied:

I admit that slavery is the root of the rebellion, or at least its *sine qua non.* The ambition of politicians may have instigated them to act, but they would have been impotent without slavery as their instrument. I will also concede that emancipation would help us in Europe, and convince them that we are incited by something more than ambition. I grant further that it would help *somewhat* at the North, though not so much, I fear, as you and those you represent imagine. Still, some additional strength would be added in that way to the war. And then unquestionably it would weaken the rebels by drawing off their laborers, which is of great importance. But I am not so sure we could do much with the blacks. If we were to arm them, I fear that in a few weeks the arms would be in the hands of the rebels; and indeed thus far we have not had arms enough to equip our white troops. I will mention another thing, though it meet only your scorn and contempt: There are fifty thousand bayonets in the Union armies from the Border Slave States. It would be a serious matter if, in consequence of a proclamation such as you desire, they should go over to the rebels. I do not think they all would—not so many indeed as a year ago, or as six months ago—not so many to-day as yesterday. Every day increases their Union feeling. . . . Let me say one thing more: I think you should admit that we already have an important principle to rally and unite the people in the fact that constitutional government is at stake. This is a fundamental idea, going down about as deep as anything.

The delegation disagreed. "We answered that, being fresh from the people, we were naturally more hopeful than himself as to the necessity and probable effect of such a proclamation. The value of constitutional government is indeed a grand idea for which to contend; but the people know that *nothing else has put constitutional government in danger but slavery*; that the toleration of that aristocratic and despotic element among our free institutions was the inconsistency that had nearly wrought our ruin and caused free government to appear a failure before the world, and therefore the people demand emancipation to preserve and perpetuate constitutional government."

Hearing an affirmation of his point, Lincoln interjected, "Yes, that is the true ground of our difficulties."

The guests stayed focused on slavery. Emancipation "would rouse the people and rally them to his support beyond anything yet witnessed—appealing alike to conscience, sentiment, and hope. . . . If the leader will but utter a trumpet call the nation will respond with patriotic ardor. No one can tell the power of the right word from the right man to develop the latent fire and enthusiasm of the masses."

"I know it," Lincoln admitted.

"The struggle has gone too far," the delegation said, "and cost too much treasure and blood, to allow of a partial settlement. Let the line be drawn at the same time between freedom and slavery, and between loyalty and treason."

"Do not misunderstand me, because I have mentioned these objections," Lincoln said as the meeting with Patton and Dempster wound down. "They indicate the difficulties that have thus far prevented my action in some such way as you desire. I have not decided against a proclamation of liberty to the slaves, but hold the matter under advisement. And I can assure you that the subject is on my mind, by day and night, more than any other. Whatever shall appear to be God's will I will do." That, as ever, was the question.

An answer came at Antietam. After bloody fighting, the Union turned back Lee's forces in Maryland. "I now consider it safe to say that Gen. McClellan has gained a great victory over the great rebel army in Maryland between Fredericktown and Hagerstown," Lincoln wrote on the afternoon of Monday, September 15, 1862. "He is now pursuing the flying foe." The "general feeling over public affairs," the *Boston Advertiser* wrote, "was decidedly more hopeful than for some time past."

On Monday, September 22, 1862, Lincoln told the cabinet he was issuing the Preliminary Emancipation Proclamation. "I think the time has come now," the president said. "When the rebel army was at Frederick," he had decided that should the Union forces prevail in Maryland, he would go forward.

"I said nothing to anyone; but I made the promise to myself and"—here Salmon Chase noted that Lincoln briefly hesitated—"to my Maker," Lincoln announced. "The Rebel army is now driven out, and I am going to fulfill that promise." According to Gideon Welles, Lincoln "remarked that he had made a vow a covenant—that if God gave us the victory in the approaching battle, he would consider it an indication of Divine will, and that it was his duty to move forward in the cause of emancipation."

Seward's summertime counsel to await a more propitious hour went unmentioned. It seems likely the president was being candid about his talk of God and covenants. The hesitation in his announcement, which suggested a hint of embarrassment about speaking prophetically, was one clue to his sincerity. Had Lincoln not seen the timing of his decision as a matter of conscience he probably would have forgone the talk of the Almighty altogether, for there were sound military reasons to take this step. To speak of his sense of providence rather than framing the decision only in the temporal suggests that he in fact believed emancipation was in accordance with divine will, and he was pledged, as a man and as a president, to act in that light.

"It might be thought strange, he said, but there were times when he felt uncertain how to act, [and] he had in this way submitted the disposal of matters . . . when the way was not clear to his mind what he should do," Welles reported. Lincoln then added: "God had decided this question in favor of the slave."

God—and Abraham Lincoln.

There were important caveats. In the Preliminary Proclamation, Lincoln held out the possibility that the seceded states could return to the Union before year's end and keep slavery intact. The president was also working to advance voluntary colonization so that the freedmen, as they were called, would be encouraged to leave a postwar United States.

Yet Lincoln's contemporaries understood the proclamation meant that the president of the United States was marshalling the power of his office to strike against chattel slavery. To Frederick Douglass the struggle was only now "invested with sanctity." The *Morning Star* in London wrote, "It is indisputably the great fact of the war—the turning point in the history of the American commonwealth—an act only second in courage and probable results to the Declaration of Independence."

The proclamation was dated Monday, September 22, 1862:

That on the first day of January in the year of our Lord one thousand eight hundred and sixty-three, all persons held as slaves within any state, or designated part of a state, the people whereof shall then be in rebellion against the United States, shall be then, thenceforward, and forever free; and the Executive Government of the United States, including the military and naval authority thereof, will recognize and maintain the freedom of such persons, and will do no act or acts to repress such persons, or any of them, in any efforts they may make for their actual freedom.

An approving crowd gathered at the White House to celebrate on Wednesday, September 24. "What I did, I did after very full deliberation, and under a very heavy and solemn sense of responsibility," Lincoln said. "I can only trust in God I have made no mistake." To Vice President Hamlin, Lincoln remarked, "The North responds to the proclamation sufficiently in breath; but breath alone kills no rebels."

CHAPTER TWENTY-ONE

The President Has Done Nobly

This is a great Era! A sublime period in History! The
Proclamation is grand.

—ROBERT C. WATERSTON of the Church Anti-Slavery Society,
on the Emancipation Proclamation

T HE PRESIDENT LOOKED TERRIBLE. Watching Lincoln walk into
services at New York Avenue Presbyterian with Mary on Sunday,
November 30, 1862, the journalist Noah Brooks was struck by
the toll the war and the White House had taken on the president. At
fifty-three, Lincoln was aging rapidly. "His hair is grizzled, his gait more
stooping, his countenance sallow, and there is a sunken, deathly look
about the large, cavernous eyes," Brooks observed.

Nearly everything was working against the president in the fall and
winter of 1862–63, a time of wide public dissatisfaction with Lincoln's
war leadership. In early November the president removed General
McClellan from command. So went the news from the battlefield; the
word from the ballot box was also bad.

The president had suspected that the Republicans would face trouble in the midterm elections of 1862–63, many of which took place
between October 14 and November 4. (Fourteen states voted in that
window; eight others held their elections in 1863.) When the returns
came in, Republicans lost the governorships of New York and New
Jersey as well as their outright majority in the House of Representatives, where the Republican share of seats fell from 59 to 46.2 percent;
only the party's alliance with pro-war Unionist Democrats kept the
staunchly anti-Lincoln Democrats from controlling the chamber.
There were sundry reasons for the congressional defeats, including
high Union casualty rates in competitive districts. And military defeats,
emancipation, the suspension of habeas corpus, and other wartime
measures affecting civil liberties created a national anti-Lincoln, anti-

Republican atmosphere. The elections, David Davis remarked, were "disastrous in the extreme" for Lincoln's party.

The Battle of Fredericksburg, Virginia, was disastrous, too. In the second week of December, Confederates crushed the Union forces there, exacting about thirteen thousand casualties to the South's nearly five thousand. "If there is a worse place than Hell," Lincoln said, "I am in it." As in the Secession Winter, there were calls for peace through compromise and negotiation—calls that were more urgent in light of the death toll and the Confederate victories. Unless the Union could triumph in the field, Lincoln said privately, "the bottom would be out of the whole affair."

For Lincoln to soldier on required him to hold fast to his belief that the moral ends to which he was devoted—the survival of the Republic, the preservation of liberty, and the antislavery cause—were worth the bewildering and exhausting costs of command.

Only news of victory from Tennessee—at Stone's River, near Murfreesboro just south of Nashville—brightened the gloom over New Year's 1862–63. "God bless you, and all with you!" Lincoln wrote to Union general William S. Rosecrans. "Please tender to all, and accept for yourself, the Nation's gratitude for yours, and their, skill, endurance, and dauntless courage." The president, who needed courage of his own, appreciated it in others.

Disturbing reports from Minnesota were also reaching the capital. Elements of the Sioux tribe were massacring white settlers. Encouraged by the removal of federal troops from the West to fight the Confederacy, frustrated by broken treaties, and reduced, as one historian noted, "to a state of near starvation," the Sioux struck. Beyond his service during the brief Black Hawk War, Lincoln had not been deeply engaged in Native American issues. In the 1858 Senate race, when Stephen Douglas had argued that the Declaration did not include "the negro, nor the savage Indians, nor the Fejee Islanders, nor any other barbarous race," Lincoln had pushed back. "I think the authors of that noble instrument intended to include *all* men." As president, Lincoln viewed Native Americans as "simultaneously foreign and respectable," the scholar Christopher W. Anderson wrote. To Lincoln and his era, however, they were a problem to be managed, not a people to be treated justly. Minnesota militia and the U.S. military quelled the revolt; 303 Sioux were convicted of war crimes and sentenced to death. "We cannot hang men by the hundreds," wrote Henry B. Whipple, the Episcopal bishop of Minnesota. Typically inclined to clemency, Lincoln reviewed the records of the tribunal in late 1862 and decided to spare all but thirty-eight. Told in 1864 that a mass execution would have been more politically beneficial, the president said, "I could not afford to hang men for votes."

On Monday, December 1, he sent Congress his annual message—a document known for its deathless peroration:

> Fellow-citizens, *we* cannot escape history. We of this Congress and this administration will be remembered in spite of ourselves. No personal significance, or insignificance, can spare one or another of us. The fiery trial through which we pass will light us down, in honor or dishonor, to the latest generation. We *say* we are for the Union. The world will not forget that we say this. We know how to save the Union. The world knows we do know how to save it. We—even *we here*—hold the power, and bear the responsibility. In *giving* freedom to the *slave*, we *assure* freedom to the *free*—honorable alike in what we give, and what we preserve. We shall nobly save, or meanly lose, the last best hope of earth. Other means may succeed; this could not fail. The way is plain, peaceful, generous, just—a way which, if followed, the world will forever applaud, and God must forever bless.

The poetry of these lines has tended to obscure the substance of the address. In it, Lincoln proposed a constitutional amendment on "compensated emancipation"—the Anglo-American norm at that point—and called for voluntary colonization:

> Every State, wherein slavery now exists, which shall abolish the same therein, at any time, or times, before the first day of January, in the year of our Lord one thousand and nine hundred, shall receive compensation from the United States.... All slaves who shall have enjoyed actual freedom by the chances of the war, at any time before the end of the rebellion, shall be forever free; but all owners of such, who shall not have been disloyal, shall be compensated for them ... [and] Congress may appropriate money,

and otherwise provide, for colonizing free colored persons, with their own consent, at any place or places without the United States.

Unsurprisingly, the message was poorly received in abolitionist circles. "How it makes one's heart bleed for his country to have its chief magistrate proposing measures to be accomplished in 1900 as a remedy for evils and perils which have thrust us . . . into the very jaws of death," Henry Dawes wrote. "Whether the Republic shall live six months or not is the question thundering in our ears and the chief magistrate answers, 'I've got a plan which is going to work well in the next century.'"

Lincoln knew what the abolitionists thought of him. But he was working on his time—which he hoped was also God's time. Once, when a Republican congressman from Massachusetts accused Lincoln of having changed his mind, Lincoln replied, "Yes, I have; and I don't think much of a man who is not wiser today than he was yesterday."

The central question was whether the president would issue the final emancipation proclamation at New Year's. "Christmas is a great institution, especially in time of trouble and disaster and impending ruin," George Templeton Strong told his diary in December 1862. On Saturday, December 27, Strong wrote: "Public affairs unchanged. Will Uncle Abe Lincoln stand firm and issue his promised proclamation on the first of January, 1863? Nobody knows, but I think he will."

He did. The president met several times with the cabinet and spent part of Christmas Eve discussing the proclamation with Charles Sumner. In the final version, Lincoln also authorized the recruitment and the arming of Black men. "I have made up my mind to give the black man every possible encouragement to fight for us," the president reportedly said. "I will do him justice, and I will dismiss any officer who will not carry out my policy. If the people dislike this policy they will say so at the next presidential election—but so long as I am president the government shall deal fairly with this unfortunate race."

On New Year's Day, after a long reception of hand shaking and small talk beginning at eleven in the morning, Lincoln walked up to his office on the second floor of the White House. It was mid-afternoon, and a formal copy of the text was ready to sign. Worn out from the receiving line, Lincoln "could not for a moment, control my arm," the president recalled. "I paused, and a superstitious feeling came over me which made me hesitate." But only for a moment. "I never, in my life, felt more certain that I was doing right, than I do in signing this paper," Lincoln said. "If my name ever goes into history it will be for this act, and my whole soul is in it."

News of the proclamation surged through the country by telegraph. "Men, women, young and old, were up," Frederick Douglass recalled of the scenes in Boston; "hats and bonnets were in the air, and we gave three cheers for Abraham Lincoln." "This is a great Era!" the Church Anti-Slavery Society's Robert C. Waterston said. "A sublime period in History! The Proclamation is grand. The President has done nobly." To Jefferson Davis, the proclamation meant that "several millions of human beings of an inferior race, peaceful and contented laborers in their sphere," were now "doomed to extermination, while at the same time they are encouraged to a general assassination of their masters." Of Lincoln, the *Richmond Enquirer* asked, "What shall we call him? Coward, assassin, savage, murderer . . . ? Or shall we consider them all as embodied in the word 'fiend' and call him Lincoln, The Fiend?"

The president was at peace. "Many of my strongest supporters urged emancipation before I thought it indispensable, and, I may say, before I thought the country ready for it," Lincoln would say in April 1864. "I can now solemnly assert, that I have a clear conscience in regard to my action on this momentous question. I have done what no man could have helped doing, standing in my place." The world was also paying heed. Overseas, the British had long watched the war with concern. It was in London's financial interest to secure sources of cotton, and thus there was much speculation about whether Lord Palmerston's government might recognize the Confederacy. "The North may be assured of one thing," *The London Review* had written in August 1861, "which is, that if the war lasts much longer, and the South continue to win all the battles, the kingdoms and states of Europe—and Great Britain among the number—will be compelled to recognize the Southern Confederation as a *de facto* Government."

The rebel South lived in hope. "There is no doubt that the Southern Confederacy will be recognized by England in ninety days, and that ends the war," the Confederate secretary of state, Judah P. Benjamin, remarked in Richmond in early 1862. It was not a bad bet. After Second Bull Run, Palmerston wrote that "it seems not altogether unlikely that still greater disasters" could befall the Union. In that event, the prime minister wondered, "would it not be time for us to consider whether ... England and France might not address the contending parties and recommend an arrangement on the basis of separation?" The Union victory at Antietam that had reassured Lincoln also changed British thinking. For now there would be no recognition for the Confederacy. London would wait.

The Emancipation Proclamation served the Union well across the Atlantic. Charles Francis Adams, Sr., had gone to London as the American envoy to the Court of St. James's; his son Henry was serving as his secretary. The decision on emancipation, the younger Adams remarked, had "done more for us here than all our former victories and all our diplomacy. It is creating an almost convulsive reaction in our favor all over this country." In the view of one member of Parliament, Lincoln had ended the chances of a London-Richmond alliance forever. "Recognition of the South, by England, whilst it bases itself on Negro slavery, is an impossibility," said Richard Cobden.

To win the war, Lincoln needed to isolate the Confederacy and weaken the infrastructure of the white South; emancipation was a potent weapon on both fronts. Emancipation in 1862–63 was designed to appease abolitionist sentiment and still be acceptable to a Union that had little to no interest in racial egalitarianism. Hence Lincoln's enduring political arguments for gradual, compensated emancipation and for voluntary colonization. The proclamation was a battle *against* slavery gained, not a war *for* full equality won.

"Where have you been, father?" Mary asked Lincoln one day in the White House.

"To the War Department."

"Any news?"

"Yes, plenty of news, but no good news. It is dark, dark everywhere."

Lincoln took up a small Bible and settled down to read. Fifteen minutes later, Elizabeth Keckly, who was in the family library with the president and the First Lady, noticed that "the face of the President seemed more cheerful. . . . The change was so marked that I could not but wonder at it, and wonder led to the desire to know what book of the Bible afforded so much comfort to the reader." He was, she found, engrossed

Elizabeth Keckly, a formerly enslaved woman,
became Mary Lincoln's dressmaker and
confidante in the White House.

in Job, the story of a faithful but unfortunate man whom God tested through tribulation.

It was a fitting biblical parallel for the wartime Lincoln. Beset by constant trial, the president struggled with the most complicated and charged of military matters, political realities, and moral decisions. As Harriet Beecher Stowe remarked, Lincoln was "a plain working man of the people, with no more culture, instruction, or education than any such working man may obtain for himself, called on to conduct the passage of a great people through a crisis involving the destinies of the whole world."

In 1863, no one knew whether the crisis of which Stowe spoke would be resolved to Lincoln's satisfaction. For Lincoln and for the nation, the events of New Year's Day 1863 were part of an unfolding, contingent, and unknowable whole. The Union remained in mortal danger. Most of the enslaved were still in chains. Racial prejudice ruled. The Confederacy stood. And the presidency of Abraham Lincoln was troubled.

Senator John P. Hale of New Hampshire, a Republican, believed the president "had made a great mistake upon the slavery question, and that it would have been better for the cause of the Country, and of emancipation if nothing had been said in regard to the negro since the war commenced." Orville Browning thought the party was "upon the brink of ruin, and could see no hope of an amendment in affairs unless the President would change his policy, and withdraw or greatly modify his proclamation." Defeat in the field in 1863, the largely sympathetic Brooks observed, might lead "popular feeling" to "look to a change in the Presidency, as a hopeful means of a change in the conduct of the war."

The year had begun with renewed speculation about peace. Given the horrifying casualty counts, the impulse for talks between North and South could be seductive, and the seasonal surges in peace sentiment presented Lincoln with a series of little-remembered tests of resolve. It was eminently reasonable for a president engulfed in civil war to entertain negotiations. A good deal of opposition to the administration—the Copperhead interest in particular—wanted to restore the prewar Republic. No politician could have dismissed the occasional overture out of hand, and Lincoln was a politician. By and large, the president remained strong in the face of suggestions for a settled peace—evidence of his commitment to preserve the Union not on any available terms but on *his* terms. With his antislavery platform in 1860 and his moves toward emancipation and enlistment in 1862–63, he had set out on a course that was at once politically driven and inherently moral. It was a course he did not want to abandon, but the pressures and the possibilities of mediation would try him to the end.

In early 1863, Horace Greeley conducted freelance diplomacy with intermediaries and French officials interested in a negotiated settlement to the American war. "In some respects Mr. Greeley is a great man," Lincoln once remarked, "but in many others he is wanting in common sense." The French episode began with the nation's minister to the United States, Henri Mercier, informing Paris that the Democratic gains in the 1862 elections and the troubling military news for the Union had led him to "see conditions developing which I believe most opportune for the emperor's government to prepare some conciliatory act which would aid in reestablishing peace." As Mercier saw it, according to the scholar Warren F. Spencer, "the South had won its independence and that further bloodshed was useless. . . . Mercier felt that, despite separation, French interests required a strong Northern Union to balance the naval and mercantile power of England. He also feared that continued warfare could very well lead to the withdrawal of the western states. To prevent this truncation and to assure a strong Federal Union, he sought peace."

A shadowy figure named William Jewett then entered the story. Born in New York, he had made his life in the West, particularly in Colorado. After a visit to France, Jewett became an advocate for French diplomatic intervention and served as an intermediary, connecting Mercier and Greeley, who in turn lobbied for the French initiative in conversations in Washington. "The French Minister in an interview granted today to William Cornell Jewett," Greeley reported in the *Tribune,* "declared that [it was] the policy of the Emperor of France . . . to see the Union re-established upon a basis of mutual concession." From Lincoln's point of view, of course, the issue was what concessions the white South might make, and the talk of such mediation just after the Emancipation Proclamation only complicated the president's efforts to manage Northern opinion. Though the Greeley-Jewett-Mercier affair fizzled, it did dramatize the desire for peace at an as yet unknown price in influential quarters. With assistance from Seward, *The New York Times*'s Henry Raymond dismissed Greeley's maneuvering. "The war must go on until the Rebellion is conquered," Raymond wrote. "Our people . . . will . . . never consent, under any circumstances, that any foreign Power shall dictate the destiny or decide the fate of this Republic."

Grand sentiments, but politics and racial prejudice fueled peace sentiment. "The war for the Union is . . . a most bloody and costly failure," the Ohio Democratic congressman Clement Vallandigham said in January 1863. "The President confessed it on the 22d of September. . . . War for the Union was abandoned; war for the negro openly begun. . . . Slavery is only the subject, but Abolition the cause of this civil war."

Comments like Vallandigham's showed that the injection of emancipation into a war for the Union had created freedom for many, but fresh political hell for Lincoln. "Last night to have seen Old Abe he looks like a shadow to what he did last year," a Union soldier wrote after encountering the president in the spring of 1863. Rumors of secessionism in the western states were growing in intensity. "These are dark hours," Charles Sumner wrote after a mid-January conference with Lincoln. "The President tells me that he now fears a 'fire in the rear'—meaning the [Democrats], especially at the Northwest—more than our military chances." In early February, in a missive labeled "Strictly Confidential," Governor Oliver P. Morton of Indiana warned Lincoln about the Northwest's potentially disruptive role:

> The Democratic scheme may be briefly stated thus; End the war by any means whatever at the earliest moment. This of course lets the Rebel States go, and acknowledges the Southern Confederacy. They will then propose to the Rebels a re-union and re-construction upon the condition of leaving out the New England States; this they believe the Rebel leaders will accept and so do I. It would withdraw twelve votes from the Senate, and leave the Slave States in a permanent majority in that body, which they would take care to retain by admitting no more Free States into the new Union.

Morton said that Governor Horatio Seymour of New York, a Democrat and a Lincoln critic, and other "leading politicians of New York and Pennsylvania are believed to be in the scheme and hope to be able to Carry their States for it."

Morton was anxious, too, about "secret societies" in the mold of the Knights of the Golden Circle, which he said "are being established in every County and Township in the State of Indiana." Vallandigham, now a former congressman, was a leader of the shadow movement. In a long report to Lincoln, General Rosecrans highlighted the "evident extent and anti-national purposes of this great conspiracy" conducted by "an oath-bound secret society, under various names . . . the objects of which are the overthrow of the existing national Government and the dismemberment of this nation." Vallandigham was the "Supreme Commander of the Northern wing of this society," a society that "claim[s] to have 25,000 members in Missouri, 140,000 in Illinois, 100,000 in Indiana, 80,000 in Ohio 70,000 in Kentucky; and that they are extending through New York, New Jersey, Pennsylvania, Delaware, and Maryland." The numbers were surely exaggerated, but whatever they were, they represented extreme anti-Lincoln sentiment. The clandestine subversives would be an irritant to the president for the whole of the war—and their durability was testimony to the intractable divisions of opinion within the Union.

Lincoln agreed with Governor Morton on the most important means to combat the overt and covert disunionists inside the South and outside it: The "vigorous and successful prosecution of the War, unto the final suppression of the Rebellion." Victory in the field would settle most matters. And so, as commander in chief, Lincoln pressed on.

To succeed, the president needed a larger army. Seeking congressional authority for a military draft, Lincoln heard all the old arguments once more. Vallandigham had denounced the Enrollment Act of 1863 as a means for the "coercion, invasion, and . . . abolition of negro slavery by force." "It is believed by at least one-half of the people of the loyal States that the conscription act is in itself a violation of the supreme constitutional law," Horatio Seymour said. The courts disagreed, but the New York governor was not wrong about the politics of the issue. The draft was seen by Lincoln's opponents as further evidence of the president's alleged contempt for the Constitution.

Championed by Senators Henry Wilson of Massachusetts and Jacob Collamer of Vermont, the conscription law required males from the ages of twenty to forty-five to register for the draft; those who could afford a $300 fee were allowed to buy their way out of service, or pay to send a substitute. The anger in the North over being forced to fight in what was dismissed as a "n——r war" was most manifest among working-class white men, many of whom rioted in New York City over five bloody days in the summer. The violent mob targeted Black people, "dashed with the merriment of fiends on every colored face they saw," Hay and Nicolay recalled, and set fire to the Colored Orphan Asylum at Fifth Avenue and Forty-third Street.

Lincoln had gone to the Capitol for the final hours of the Thirty-seventh Congress and set up headquarters in a private room behind the Senate chamber. The president worked through the night. Hay and Nicolay scampered through the building, armed with legislation for Lincoln to sign; the Congress finished its business just short of noon on Wednesday, March 4, 1863.

Along with the Enrollment Act, a law authorizing the president to suspend habeas corpus as he deemed fit was among the session's bills— further enraging his opponents in the North. "It was with great reluctance that I came to recognize the necessity which demanded" the suspensions beginning in 1861, Lincoln remarked to Henry Wilson. "But when that became plain to my mind, I did not hesitate to do my duty. I have had to do many unpleasant things since the country imposed on me the task of administering the government, and I will continue to do them when they come in the line of my official duty, always with prayerful care, and without stopping to consider what personal result may come to me."

The congressional sanction on habeas corpus gave his critics more fodder to portray the president as "King Lincoln." "Our foes have given absolute control of their purse and sword to the tyrant Lincoln," the governor of South Carolina, Milledge Luke Bonham, declared. "Lincoln is now the President Dictator, and is invested with a power equal to that of Napoleon," wrote the *Mobile Advertiser and Register*.

Religious liberty was one civil right Lincoln left untouched. Amid a blizzard in Washington in mid-January 1863—he could reportedly hear "frozen crystals beat on windows of his office"—the president endorsed the revocation of an order of Grant's expelling Jews from the general's sphere of command. Issued on Wednesday, December 17, 1862, General Order No. 11 had been designed to end the illegal trade in cotton, which Grant and others believed was being carried on by Jewish merchants and traders. The directive provoked fury; a statement from a group of Jewish people in Paducah, Kentucky, denounced Grant's order as an "enormous outrage on all laws and humanity." Lincoln agreed. "The President has no objection to your expelling traitors and Jew peddlers, which, I suppose, was the object of your order," General Henry W. Halleck, then the army's general in chief, wrote to Grant in a letter endorsed by Lincoln, "but, as it in terms proscribed an entire religious class, some of whom are fighting in our ranks, the President deemed it necessary to revoke it." To a visiting delegation of Jewish leaders, Lincoln acknowledged that "to condemn a class is, to say the least, to wrong the good with the bad. I do not like to hear a class or nationality condemned on account of a few sinners."

The ubiquitous Vallandigham soon offered Lincoln a high-profile test case of wartime speech. In General Order No. 38, the commander of the Ohio region, General Ambrose E. Burnside, had directed that "the habit of declaring sympathy for the enemy will not be allowed in this department." As if on cue, Vallandigham walked onto the stage Burnside had erected. In a May 1863 speech at Mount Vernon, Ohio, the former congressman declared that Lincoln's "wicked abolition war" would leave "the people . . . deprived of their liberties and a monarchy established." Arrested in the night, Vallandigham was kept in a military prison and tried for violating General Order No. 38. "I am here in a military bastile [*sic*] for no other offense than my political opinions, and the defense of them, and of the rights of the people, and of your constitutional liberties," Vallandigham wrote from jail.

He was convicted, and Lincoln ordered Vallandigham sent into the Confederacy. The president was unhappy about the prosecution but chose to support Burnside. As Lincoln saw it, "Mr. Vallandigham avows his hostility to the war on the part of the Union; and his arrest was made because he was laboring, with some effect, to prevent the raising of troops, to encourage desertions from the army, and to leave the rebellion without an adequate military force to suppress it." Vallandigham ended up in Canada, which was a wartime home to white Southern sympathizers, agents, and provocateurs. Lincoln's foes made the most of the moment. In New York, Horatio Seymour said that Vallandigham's arrest and trial "is not merely a step toward revolution, it is revolution; it will not only lead to military despotism, it establishes a military despotism."

In April 1863, Lincoln drafted a resolution on slavery for sympathetic elements in Great Britain that grounded the Union cause in an antislavery Christianity. Describing the creation of the Confederacy as the world's first "attempt . . . to construct a new Nation, upon the basis of, and with the primary and fundamental object to maintain, enlarge, and perpetuate human slavery," Lincoln argued that "no such embryo State should ever be recognized by, or admitted into, the family of christian and civilized nations; and that all christian and civilized men everywhere should, by all lawful means, resist to the utmost, such recognition or admission."

Coming from Lincoln's hand, these sentiments tended toward an egalitarianism based on a biblically informed idea of human equality. If Christianity were irreconcilable with slavery, could the faith be deployed to justify only limited equality? It could be, and would be—but the barriers were weakening. It was growing more difficult to read passages like Saint Paul's assertion in the Book of Acts that "God . . . made the world and all things therein. . . . And hath made of one blood all nations of men for to dwell on all the face of the earth" as anything other than an injunction to see one another as free and equal.

U nseasonable late-spring snows and high winds came in mid-April as the president and his family set out on a visit to the front in Virginia. A snowstorm drove the party's steamer, the *Carrie Martin*, into a cove for the night on the Potomac near Indian Head, Maryland. "The thoughtful wife of the President, an able and a noble woman, ought to have the credit of originating the plan of a tour through the Army by the President," Noah Brooks reported, "as she saw what an excellent effect would be given to the troops . . . by coming in contact with their Commander-in-Chief and his family."

A visitor among the wounded in hospitals in and around Washington, the First Lady understood the power of such moments. "It was a touching scene," Brooks wrote, "and one to be long remembered, as the large-hearted and noble President moved softly between the beds, his face shining with sympathy and his voice often low with emotion" in the Army of the Potomac's hospital tents at Falmouth, Virginia. There was, however, an uncomfortable domestic moment that, unfortunately for Lincoln, took place for all to see. Agnes Salm-Salm, the young, alluring, Vermont-born wife of Prince Salm-Salm, a Prussian who was serving in the Union army, kissed the president, enraging Mrs. Lincoln.

The president must have experienced his wife in the way that many of those in his official circle did when the First Lady lost control. "I always felt as if the eyes of a hyena were upon me, & that the animal was ready, if I made a single mismove, to pounce upon me!" Benjamin Brown French recalled. "You and Mary love each other—it is good for her to have you with her—I feel worried about Mary, her nerves have gone to pieces," Lincoln told Emilie Todd Helm. "She cannot hide from me that the strain she has been under has been too much for her mental as well as her physical health,"

Always there was grief over Willie, which never dissipated for either parent. "Think you better put 'Tad's' pistol away," Lincoln telegraphed his wife, who was then in Philadelphia, in June 1863. "I had an ugly dream about him." Death and memories of the dead were everywhere.

About two years after the loss of Willie, the White House stables caught fire, killing the president's horses. It was an emotional moment. Lincoln watched the scene from the East Room windows, and he wept. "Tad explained it was because Willie's pony was there," an observer recalled. The death of the pony was the loss of a last link to the little boy—a blow to the still grieving father.

The Lincolns' sadness led them to imagine that their son occasionally returned to them. "When my noble little Willie was first taken from me, I felt that I had fallen into a deep pit of gloom and despair without a ray of light anywhere," Mary told her half sister Emilie during the war. "If Willie did not come to comfort me I would still be drowned in tears, and while I long inexpressibly to touch him, to hold him in my arms, and still grieve that he has no future in this world that I might watch with a proud mother's heart—he lives, Emilie! He comes to me every night, and stands at the foot of my bed with the same sweet, adorable smile he has always had; he does not always come alone; little Eddie is sometimes with him and twice he has come with our brother Alec, he tells me he loves his Uncle Alec and is with him most of the time."

Lincoln himself kept Willie alive in his mind and in his heart, if less melodramatically. "Did you ever dream of some lost friend and feel that you were having a sweet communion with him, and yet have a consciousness that it was not a reality?" the president asked a friend. "That is the way I dream of my lost boy Willie."

Late May brought more miserable military news, this time from Chancellorsville, Virginia. "My plans are perfect, and when I start to carry them out, may God have mercy on General Lee, for I will have none," the Union general Joseph Hooker had said. Once the fighting began, however, the Confederate forces, though only about half the Union strength, had the better of it. The Union sustained about seventeen thousand casualties to the Rebels' thirteen thousand. Stonewall Jackson was fatally wounded, but the Confederates were covered in glory. "Had a thunderbolt fallen upon the President he could not have been more overwhelmed," Brooks wrote.

Lincoln was despondent. "What will the country say?" he asked aloud. "Oh, what will the country say?" In a story related long afterward, the president was at the lowest of ebbs after Chancellorsville.

"My God, Stanton, our cause is lost!" Lincoln reportedly lamented to the secretary of war. "We are ruined; we are ruined; and such a fearful loss of life! My God! This is more than I can endure." He paused, then went on: "If I am not about early tomorrow, do not send for me, nor allow anyone to disturb me. Defeated again, and so many of our noble countrymen killed! What will the people say?" Stanton was said to have recalled even bleaker words of Lincoln. Allegedly, the president "had fully made up his mind to go immediately to the Potomac River and there end his life, as many a poor creature (but none so half as miserable as he was at that time) had done before him."

Lincoln's despair passed. It had to. There was so much to do. He had a war to win, a Union to save, a reelection campaign to run—and slavery, perhaps, not only to wound, but to kill. As the days of June dwindled, Lincoln telegraphed a Union officer. "Have you any reports," the president inquired, "of the enemy moving into Pennsylvania?"

A NEW BIRTH OF FREEDOM

1863–1864

That All Men Could Be Free

I call the war which the Confederates are waging against the Union a "rebellion," because it is one, and in grave matters it is best to call things by their right names.

—EDWARD EVERETT, oration at Gettysburg, November 1863

I have given the subject of arming the negro my hearty support. This, with the emancipation of the negro, is the heaviest blow yet given the Confederacy.

—ULYSSES S. GRANT, August 1863

A T LONG LAST, on the Fourth of July 1863, amid gloom and death, there were, for the Union, light and life in a pair of victories more than a thousand miles apart: one at Gettysburg, in Pennsylvania, the other at Vicksburg, in Mississippi. In the spring and early summer, Lincoln's friend and ally Ward Lamon recalled, "things" had been "going very slow and the public mind was in very great suspense." For Lincoln, the new Union triumphs were answered prayers. In a conversation with General Daniel E. Sickles, who lost a leg at Gettysburg, Lincoln described the anxious hours as he had waited for the verdict from the hard-fought battle. "In the pinch of your campaign up there . . . oppressed by the gravity of our affairs, I went into my room one day and locked the door and got down on my knees before Almighty God and prayed to him mightily for victory at Gettysburg," the president told the wounded Sickles. "I told him . . . we couldn't stand another Fredericksburg or Chancellorsville. And I then and there made a solemn vow to Almighty God that if he would stand by our boys at Gettysburg, I would stand by him. And he *did,* and I *will.*" In this, Lincoln was echoing his private remarks to the cabinet about emancipation after Antietam—another example of his comfort with discussing the divine amid the temporal.

In this "gigantic Rebellion, at the bottom of which is an effort to overthrow the principle that all men are created equal," the president told a celebratory crowd at the White House, "we have the surrender of a most powerful position and army." And yet his generals failed him again. Lee evaded the Union forces and managed to escape with his army intact—all to fight again another day. "If I had gone up there I could have licked them myself," the president muttered.

So much was in chaos: riots in the North, lethargic commanders, Copperhead opposition. All Lincoln could do was to fight on—to crush the enemy wholly and decisively. To do so he would need the hero of the West to come to the East—U. S. Grant. "I do not remember that you and I ever met personally," the president wrote to Grant in July. "I write this now as a grateful acknowledgment for the almost inestimable service you have done the country." There was much more such service to render.

Gettysburg and Vicksburg dominated the headlines of the summer of 1863, but other, less celebrated battles were also substantively and symbolically significant. In June and July, the performance of Black soldiers at Port Hudson and Milliken's Bend in Louisiana and at Fort Wagner in South Carolina convinced the president of the utility of having Black men under arms. It had taken a long time. "We needed that the vast tide of death should roll by our own doors, and sweep away our fathers and sons, before we could come to our senses and give the black man the one boon he has been asking for so long—permission to fight for our common country," Chaplain George H. Hepworth of the Forty-seventh Massachusetts observed in 1863. A 1792 act of Congress had limited militia service to "white male citizens," but legislation in the summer of 1862 and the Emancipation Proclamation had opened military service to Black men. "When first the rebel cannon shattered the walls of Sumter . . . I predicted that the war . . . would not be fought out entirely by white men," Frederick Douglass wrote in a broadside headlined MEN OF COLOR, TO ARMS! "Slowly and reluctantly that appeal is beginning to be heeded. Stop not now to complain that it was not heeded sooner. . . . Action! action! not criticism, is the plain duty of this hour."

From Richmond, Jefferson Davis and the Confederate Congress ordered that escaped slaves under arms for the Union be reenslaved;

freedmen in federal uniform could be executed. On Thursday, July 30, 1863, Lincoln struck back. "It is the duty of every government to give protection to its citizens, of whatever class, color, or condition, and especially to those who are duly organized as soldiers in the public service," the president wrote in General Order No. 252. "To sell or enslave any captured person, on account of his color, and for no offence against the laws of war, is a relapse into barbarism and a crime against the civilization of the age." The order proved difficult to enforce, and Black soldiers faced particular horrors, including a massacre at Fort Pillow in Tennessee.

A delegation of Black clergy from the American Baptist Missionary Convention came to see the president in mid-August 1863. They wanted access to the Black men under arms, and Lincoln agreed. "The object," he wrote, "is a worthy one."

Important inequities endured. Black soldiers were paid less than white soldiers; despite Lincoln's order of retaliation, in practice they did not have the same protections as white men, often suffering battlefield executions; and they were not allowed to serve as officers or to be promoted and honored in accordance with demonstrated valor. On Monday, August 10, Frederick Douglass, who was actively recruiting Black men for the Union army, called on the president at the White House to discuss these matters.

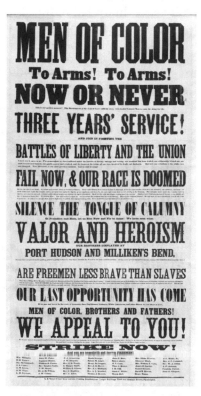

After escaping from slavery in Maryland, Douglass was understandably wary of heading south from his base in Rochester. "For twenty-five years . . . you know that when I got as far South as Philadelphia, I felt that I was rubbing against my prison wall, and could not go any further," he recalled. But this time on he went.

Frederick Douglass's broadside summoned Black American men to join the fight for the Union.

Once in Washington, he and Senator Samuel C. Pomeroy of Kansas went to the White House, making their way through the usual crowds on the staircases and in the anterooms. Douglass was the "only dark spot" among the white faces, he recalled. "I expected to have to wait at least half a day; I had heard of men waiting a week; but in two minutes after I sent in my card, the messenger came out, and respectfully invited 'Mr. Douglass' in."

"Yes, damn it," Douglass heard someone remark, "I knew they would let the n——r through"—a "Peace Democrat, I suppose," Douglass wryly recalled.

Lincoln was seated in a low armchair, papers strewn about the room. As usual, his legs were stretched out—"his feet," Douglass later joked, "in different parts of the room." The president rose to greet his guest. Douglass began to explain who he was, but Lincoln cut him off. "I know who you are, Mr. Douglass; Mr. Seward has told me all about you," he said, extending a hand. "Sit down. I am glad to see you."

As Douglass recalled, "I will tell you how he received me—just as you have seen one gentleman receive another—with a hand and a voice well-balanced between a kind cordiality and a respectful reserve. I tell you I felt big there!"

Douglass did not flinch in the presence of power. "I told [the president] that he had been somewhat slow in proclaiming equal protection to our colored soldiers and prisoners; and he said that the country needed talking up to that point," Douglass recalled. "He knew that the colored man throughout this country was a despised man, a hated man, and that if he at first came out with such a proclamation, all the hatred which is poured on the head of the Negro race would be visited on his administration."

The Black soldiers themselves, Lincoln added, had changed the calculus for the better at Milliken's Bend, Port Hudson, and Fort Wagner. On the question of pay, the president frustratingly counseled patience. Black men under arms remained "a serious offense to popular prejudice," but they "had larger motives for being soldiers than white men" and therefore ought to "be willing to enter the service upon any condition; that the fact that they were not to receive the same pay as white soldiers seemed a necessary concession to smooth the way to their employment at all as soldiers, but that ultimately they would receive the same." Lincoln would endeavor to enforce his retaliation order, though the matter was complicated. And he would sign "any commission to colored soldiers" that Secretary Stanton recommended. "Though I was not entirely satisfied with his views," Douglass concluded, "I was so well satisfied with the man and with the educating tendency of the conflict that I determined to go on with the recruiting." After meeting with the president, Douglass was imbued with "the full belief that the true course to the black man's freedom and citizenship was over the battle-field."

The Union of Lincoln was not perfect, but to Douglass the Union of Lincoln was worth the war. "We are fighting for something incomparably better than the old Union," Douglass said in December 1863. "We are fighting for unity; unity of idea, unity of sentiment, unity of object, unity of institutions, in which there shall be no North, no South, no East, no West, no black, no white, but a solidarity of the nation, making every slave free, and every free man a voter." The words were characteristically eloquent, but to Douglass they were more than words. Listening to him, looking him in the eye, taking his measure, Frederick Douglass decided to trust Abraham Lincoln. On this Douglass was willing to stake the lives of his sons—who were in uniform— and the lives of his people. Out of war, Douglass wagered, would come liberty.

In a public letter to a meeting of Union supporters in Springfield to be held in early September, Lincoln argued for the course that Douglass had tacitly agreed to support. The president knew many white voters were skeptical of emancipation and of the enlistment of Black soldiers. "To be plain, you are dissatisfied with me about the negro," Lincoln wrote. "Quite likely there is a difference of opinion between you and myself upon that subject. I certainly wish that all men could be free, while I suppose you do not." He continued:

> You say you will not fight to free negroes. Some of them seem willing to fight for you; but, no matter. Fight you, then, exclusively to save the Union. I issued the proclamation on purpose to aid you in saving the Union. . . .
>
> Peace does not appear so distant as it did. I hope it will come soon, and come to stay; and so come as to be worth the keeping in all future time. It will then have been proved that, among free men, there can be no successful appeal from the ballot to the bul-

let; and that they who take such appeal are sure to lose their case, and pay the cost. And then, there will be some black men who can remember that, with silent tongue, and clenched teeth, and steady eye, and well-poised bayonet, they have helped mankind on to this great consummation; while, I fear, there will be some white ones, unable to forget that, with malignant heart, and deceitful speech, they have strove to hinder it.

For Lincoln, there could be no peace, and no victory, without emancipation.

In September the president's attention was directed toward the Tennessee Valley, where Union and Confederate forces clashed in and around a cluster of mountains and ridges in eastern Tennessee and northern Georgia a hundred miles north of Atlanta. A titanic September battle at Chickamauga pitting Rosecrans against Confederate general Braxton Bragg cost roughly thirty-five thousand combined casualties—a figure second only to the Battle of Gettysburg. One of the combat deaths: Confederate general Benjamin Hardin Helm, a brother-in-law of Mary's who was close to Lincoln. David Davis found the president "in the greatest grief" on hearing the news.

"'Davis,' said he, 'I feel as David of old did when he was told of the death of Absalom. "Would to God I had died for thee, oh Absalom, my son, my son!"' I saw how grief stricken he was so I closed the door and left him alone."

Mary Lincoln, too, was distressed. Her summer had already been difficult. She had been injured in a carriage accident between the White House and the Soldiers' Home. In August, Mary took Robert and Tad from the Washington heat to the White Mountains of New Hampshire. "All as well as usual, and no particular trouble [in] any way," Lincoln wrote to his wife on August 8. "Tell dear Tad, poor 'Nanny Goat' is lost; . . . The weather continues dry, and excessively warm here. . . . But enough." During these uncomfortably hot weeks, the president took John Hay to the Soldiers' Home, where Hay dozed off one evening as Lincoln read Shakespeare aloud. To Mary, in New York, Lincoln telegraphed: "The air is so clear and cool, and apparently healthy, that I would be glad for you to come. Nothing very particular, but I would be glad [to] see you and Tad."

In reaction to Willie's death, Mary spent time with spiritualists who were part of the Victorian milieu of mediums and psychics who claimed to communicate with the dead. Lincoln attended a few séances as well, most of them led by Nettie Colburn Maynard, who wrote a book on the subject: *Was Abraham Lincoln a Spiritualist? Or, Curious Revelations from the Life of a Trance Medium.* "Mrs Crosby told me the other evening that she attended a spiritual circle not long since in company with Mr Lincoln, the President, and that she then asked him if he believed in Spiritualism," Nathan Daniels told his diary in late 1863. In a typical Lincoln reply, the president said "he dared not investigate the same, as if he did he feared the affairs of state would not receive their share of attention equivalent to assessing the truth of the doctrine and his belief in the same." It is likely that Lincoln would try anything that might assuage his wife's grief and bring some measure of peace to his domestic realm. "Mrs. Lincoln was more enthusiastic regarding the subject than her husband," Nettie Colburn Maynard recalled, "and openly and avowedly professed herself connected with the new religion."

Mary found comfort with spiritualists; Lincoln, at the theater. In early October 1863 the president watched a performance of *Othello* at Grover's Theatre in Washington. He had enjoyed a concert at John Ford's Theatre in 1862, and his patronage of Ford's picked up in the autumn of 1863. He saw *Fanchon, the Cricket* and took in a staging of *The Marble Heart*. The latter starred a celebrated young actor named John Wilkes Booth.

I n October, during the off-year elections in Pennsylvania and Ohio, Lincoln telegraphed Andrew Curtin, the Republican Pennsylvania governor, who was facing a Democratic challenger. "How does it stand," the president wrote, simply and to the point. The election news was good. "My majority cannot vary much from 20,000," Curtin replied. A little later, Lincoln wrote again. "How does it stand now?" The news was still good.

It was arguably even better in Ohio, where the Unionist John Brough defeated Clement Vallandigham for governor in a hundred-thousand-vote landslide. Lincoln was hugely relieved. Democratic victories—the candidates, Gideon Welles observed, were "rebel sympathizers"—would have been a proxy censure of the president. Lincoln had admitted that he had been "nervous" about the verdict—the first major election since the final Emancipation Proclamation went into full effect.

The president's allies were thrilled. In Seward's home of Auburn, New York, "one hundred guns were fired in this city this evening over the Union victories in Pennsylvania and Ohio," *The New York Times* reported. "It is the great vindication of the President," the writer and editor George William Curtis observed, "and the popular verdict upon the policy of the war."

On Wednesday, November 18, the president left the White House for a quick trip aboard a special four-car train from the B&O Railroad. "We started from Washington," John Hay wrote in his diary, "to go to the Consecration of the Soldiers' Cemetery at Gettysburg." Though Tad was ill, and Mary was upset, Lincoln kept his schedule. The president was to give a speech, a brief one, but he knew the occasion was important. He had drafted the remarks in Washington. In the crush of business, amid the unrelenting demands of the present, he had decided to speak not only to the moment, but to the ages.

L incoln left the capital about noon. The invitation had come from the lawyer and future judge David Wills, an agent of Governor Curtin of Pennsylvania. To bury the thirty-five hundred Union combat dead of seventeen states at Gettysburg was a monumental task. Now, in November 1863, the architects of the new national cemetery were ready to dedicate the project. Edward Everett of Massachusetts, a former secretary of state and onetime Harvard president, would deliver the main address.

Seward traveled with Lincoln. Initial plans had called for the presidential party to come in on the day of the dedication itself, but Lincoln did not want to be rushed. "I do not wish to so go that by the slightest accident we fail entirely," he wrote, "and, at the best, the whole to be a mere breathless running the gauntlet."

The president arrived about five in the afternoon and spent the evening at David Wills's house in town, briefly addressing a serenade at ten P.M. by the Fifth New York Artillery. Seward delivered a longer set of remarks in the Gettysburg night. "I thank my God that I believe this strife is going to end in the removal of that evil which ought to have been removed by deliberate councils and peaceful means," Seward said.

Afterward the president went to bed, cheered by news from home. "By inquiry Mrs. Lincoln informed me that your son is better this evening," Edwin Stanton telegraphed the president.

After breakfast the next morning, the president received a few callers, including a correspondent for *The Pittsburgh Commercial*. One visitor asked Lincoln for an anecdote. "The President replied it was a bad time to be joking when they were just going to a funeral," the *Commercial* wrote. Dressed in his usual black suit, Lincoln put the finishing touches on his speech and mounted a "magnificent chestnut charger" for the journey from town to the cemetery. "The procession formed itself in an orphanly sort of way & moved out with very little help from anybody," John Hay wrote. It was a fifteen-minute ride; the president arrived at the platform in the fields of Gettysburg at a quarter past eleven. Quiet prevailed among the guests, and the men in the audience removed their hats as a sign of respect for the president. "A great crowd were present and it was in reality a national congregation," Nathan Daniels told his diary.

At the cemetery, Hay noted that the chaplain of the U.S. House, Thomas H. Stockton, "made a prayer" that the long-winded clergyman apparently "thought . . . was an oration." Everett spoke "as he always does, perfectly," framing the rebellion as an act against God. "To levy war against the United States is the constitutional definition of treason," Everett said, "and that crime is. . . . an imitation on earth of that first foul revolt of 'the Infernal Serpent,' against which the Supreme Majesty of Heaven sent forth the armed myriads of his angels."

At one point during Everett's two-hour address, an observer noted, Lincoln "took out his steel-bowed spectacles, put them on his nose, took two pages of manuscript from his pocket, looked them over and put them back."

Everett finished, and a dirge was sung:

> *Great God in Heaven!*
> *Shall all this sacred blood be shed—*
> *Shall we thus mourn our glorious dead,*
> *Oh, shall the end be wrath and woe,*
> *The knell of Freedom's overthrow—*
> *A Country riven?*

It will not be!
We trust, Oh God! Thy gracious Power
To aid us in our darkest hour.
This be our prayer—"Oh Father! Save
A people's Freedom from its grave—
All praise to Thee!"

Finally, at two P.M., the president rose and spoke:

Four score and seven years ago our fathers brought forth on this continent, a new nation, conceived in Liberty, and dedicated to the proposition that all men are created equal.

Now we are engaged in a great civil war, testing whether that nation, or any nation so conceived and so dedicated, can long endure. We are met on a great battle-field of that war. We have come to dedicate a portion of that field, as a final resting place for those who here gave their lives that that nation might live. It is altogether fitting and proper that we should do this.

But, in a larger sense, we can not dedicate—we can not consecrate—we can not hallow—this ground. The brave men, living and dead, who struggled here, have consecrated it, far above our poor power to add or detract. The world will little note, nor long remember what we say here, but it can never forget what they did here. It is for us the living, rather, to be dedicated here to the unfinished work which they who fought here have thus far so nobly advanced. It is rather for us to be here dedicated to the great task remaining before us—that from these honored dead we take increased devotion to that cause for which they gave the last full measure of devotion—that we here highly resolve that these dead shall not have died in vain—that this nation, under God, shall have a new birth of freedom—and that government of the people, by the people, for the people, shall not perish from the earth.

The speech was so short that John R. Young, who was there to report on it for a Philadelphia newspaper, leaned over to Lincoln afterward to ask "if that was all."

"Yes, for the present," the president replied.

According to Hay, Lincoln "in a firm free way, with more grace than is his wont said his half dozen lines of consecration and the music wailed and we went home through crowded and cheering streets."

The press reaction fell along predictable partisan lines. The Harrisburg *Daily Patriot and Union*, a Democratic paper, was unimpressed: "We pass over the silly remarks of the President; for the credit of the Nation we are willing that the veil of oblivion shall be dropped over them and that they shall no more be repeated or thought of." Republican commentators had different views. "Could the most elaborate and splendid oration be more beautiful, more touching, more inspiring than those thrilling words of the President?" wrote the *Providence Daily Journal*. Everett himself wrote to Lincoln, "I should be glad, if I could flatter myself that I came as near to the central idea of the occasion in two hours, as you did in two minutes." The *Chicago Tribune* was effusive: "The dedicatory remarks by President Lincoln will live among the annals of man." To Benjamin Brown French, "Abraham Lincoln is the idol of the American people at this moment."

The speech distilled decades of Lincoln's thinking. It echoed elements of Theodore Parker, of George Bancroft, of Louis Kossuth, and of the King James Version of the Bible. A cogent case not only for a democracy of white men but for freedom for the enslaved, the Gettysburg Address was a defense of popular government, of emancipation, and of the principle of equality. A nation "under God" could not forever resist the dictates of that God—and Lincoln took the Hebrew Bible and the New Testament to mean that human equality was innate. If this were true, then restrictions or barriers to the recognition of that equality—to granting all the rights to life, liberty, and the pursuit of happiness—were in conflict with conscience.

Lincoln's enemies saw what he was doing. By rooting the American Founding in 1776 rather than in 1787–88, he was giving the Declaration's assertion of equality primacy of place. "We submit that Lincoln did most foully traduce the motives of the men who were slain at Gettysburg," the *Chicago Times* wrote. "They gave their lives to maintain the old government. . . . How dare he, then, standing on their graves, misstate the cause for which they died, and libel the statesmen who founded the government? They were men possessing too much self-respect to declare negroes were their equals, or were entitled to equal privileges."

The Gettysburg Address was an eloquent attempt to frame American politics as not only a mediation of interests but as a moral undertaking. Slave owners portrayed slavery as divinely ordained; Lincoln portrayed individual liberty as God-given. Slave owners invoked the Constitution as a shield for suppression; Lincoln invoked the Declaration of Independence as a higher, older, superseding authority. Slave owners defended an aristocracy of color; Lincoln defended democracy.

He did so by fusing the scripture of old with the scripture of America and interpreting the result by the light of conscience. Theodore Parker had marked the path. As the historian Garry Wills observed, Parker had "kept to his pulpit because he contrasted the *ideal* Jesus with all the provisional expressions of that ideal in biblical texts or church doctrines. Thus Parker drew his all-important theological-political analogy: as Jesus is to the Bible (the ideal to the limited reality), so is the Declaration to the Constitution." As Parker put it:

> By Christianity, I mean that form of religion which consists of piety—the love of God, and morality—the keeping of His laws. That is not the Christianity of the Christian church, nor of any sect. It is the ideal religion which the human race has been groping for. . . . By Democracy, I mean government over all the people, by all the people, and for the sake of all. . . . This is not the democracy of the parties, but it is that ideal government, the reign of righteousness, the kingdom of justice. . . .
>
> Here is the American programme of political principles: All men are endowed by their Creator with certain natural rights. . . . [T]he means to that end, the Constitution itself . . . is a provisional compromise between the ideal political principle of the Declaration, and the actual selfishness of the people North and South.

That "provisional compromise," Lincoln was saying at Gettysburg, must change. "In public life, by the side of the actual state of the world, there exists the ideal state toward which it should tend," the historian George Bancroft had said in a lecture Lincoln knew.* "The subtle and

---

* Born in Massachusetts in 1800, Bancroft, who also served as secretary of the Navy and as a diplomat, was the author of the influential *History of the United States,* published across several

irresistible movement of mind, silently but thoroughly correcting opinion and changing society, brings liberty both to the soul and to the world." Lincoln shared this vision and was doing all he could to impress it on a nation at war. Wary of self-righteousness, the president was nevertheless convinced that what Bancroft had called "the movement of mind" had led the United States to new and different ground—ground on which slavery must give way to liberty. That was what God demanded, and what Abraham Lincoln wanted.

---

decades. The 1854 lecture quoted here was entitled *The Necessity, the Reality, and the Promise of the Progress of the Human Race*.

CHAPTER TWENTY-THREE

Who Shall Be the Next President?

I confess that I do not fully understand and foresee it all. But
I am placed here where I am obliged, to the best of my poor
ability, to deal with it.

—ABRAHAM LINCOLN

We are fighting for independence; and that, or
extermination, we will have.

—JEFFERSON DAVIS

"THE PRESIDENT," John Hay told his diary, was "quite unwell."
Lincoln, who had arrived back in Washington at ten past one
o'clock in the morning after his address in Pennsylvania, had
contracted a mild case of smallpox. On the train ride home, the president was said to have been "suffering from a severe headache and lying
down . . . with his head bathed in cold water." "Now I have something I
can give everybody," the president joked. Under partial quarantine for
several weeks, he worked from his bedroom. Doctors kept visitors and
cabinet members alike away for several days. By mid-December, Lincoln was well enough to attend a performance of Shakespeare's *Henry
IV* in which James Henry Hackett, a noted actor whom Lincoln admired, did a star turn as Falstaff.

War and politics swirled on. "I have rarely seen him more serene &
busy," Hay noted of the president in mid-1863. "He is managing this
war, the draft, foreign relations, and planning a reconstruction of the
Union, all at once. . . . I am growing more and more firmly convinced
that the good of the country absolutely demands that he should be kept
where he is till this thing is over. There is no man in the country, so
wise, so gentle, and so firm. I believe the hand of God placed him where
he is."

Hay's affectionate opinion would be tested by the presidential campaign of 1864. A monumental contest, the election put the issues so far tried by the sword to a vote of the people of the loyal states. A second Lincoln term would vindicate his course and give him the power to move forward; a Democratic president would likely arrest and reverse much if not all of Lincoln's policy, including emancipation. Like the Secession Winter, like Fort Sumter, like the decisions leading to emancipation, like the overtures for peace with the Confederacy, the 1864 election would try Lincoln's convictions. On the verdict of the voters hung the war, the nature of freedom, and the future of the American nation.

"Who shall be the next President? Probably no people but ours would, while convulsed by a civil strife which our sister nations consider fatal, be so stoical as to agitate such a question as the above," Noah Brooks wrote in the early summer of 1863. Count Adam Gurowski, a translator in the State Department, detected "the buzzing of presidential intriguing." In a private conversation with Brooks, the president made his intentions plain. If "the people think that I have managed their case for them well enough to trust me to carry up to the next term," Lincoln said, "I am sure that I shall be glad to take it."

Like many presidents, Lincoln had surveyed the field and found himself to be the best available option. "I confess that I desire to be reelected," he told the Republican abolitionist and Pennsylvania congressman Thaddeus Stevens. "God knows I do not want the labor and responsibility of the office for another four years. But I have the common pride of humanity to wish my past four years Administration endorsed; and besides I honestly believe that I can better serve the nation in its need and peril than any new man could possibly do."

Providence, Lincoln had come to believe, had made him the Lord's instrument—an improbable thing, a mysterious thing, but there it was. "I don't know but that God has created some one man great enough to comprehend the whole of this stupendous crisis and transaction from end to end, and endowed him with sufficient wisdom to manage and direct it," Lincoln remarked to Senator Lot M. Morrill of Maine. "I confess that I do not fully understand and foresee it all. But I am placed here where I am obliged, to the best of my poor ability, to deal with it." It was his duty to save the Union and, in pursuit of that duty, he had taken steps to put his antislavery principles into practice. He would not give up the fight.

After the painful 1862 elections and given the high Union casualties and the Confederates' battlefield successes from 1861 to the middle of 1863, Lincoln had seemed likely to serve a single term, as had every president since Andrew Jackson a quarter of a century before. "As to the politics of Washington, the most striking thing is the absence of personal loyalty to the President," the lawyer, author, and abolitionist Richard Henry Dana, Jr., had written to Charles Francis Adams, Sr., in March 1863. "It does not exist. He has no admirers, no enthusiastic supporters, none to bet on his head. If a Republican convention were to be held to-morrow, he would not get the vote of a State." When Lincoln was in Gettysburg for the cemetery dedication, Thaddeus Stevens had acidly remarked, "Let the dead bury the dead." Recalling the story, the artist Francis Carpenter noted that Stevens's comment had come "when it was thought by some of the leaders of the party that Mr. Lincoln's chances for a re-nomination"—much less a reelection—"were somewhat dubious."

The political class—officeholders and party organizers, activists and agitators, editors and pamphleteers—was polarized. Radical Republicans like Stevens did not think Lincoln had gone far enough, fast enough. Many Democrats, even outside the ranks of the Copperheads, thought he had moved too far, too fast. By virtue of his role and in keeping with his temperament, Lincoln had disappointed hard-liners across the spectrum. Depending on one's perspective, the steps Lincoln took could be thrilling or enraging, transcendent or cataclysmic, brilliant or diabolical. Radical Republicans wanted more, Democrats less. The voters would decide whether Lincoln was striking the right balance.

The very fact of the 1864 election was notable: A nation engulfed by civil war was holding a national election whose results could remove the incumbent commander in chief at an hour of active rebellion. "If we come triumphantly out of this war, with a presidential election in the midst of it," Francis Lieber, the Columbia University professor, observed in the summer, "I shall call it the greatest miracle in all the historic course of events." "I, like you, am called by my vote to determine into whose hands the precious trust shall now be confided," William Seward told an audience in Auburn, New York, in early September. "We might wish to avoid, or at least to postpone that duty, until the present fearful crisis is passed. But it cannot and it ought not to be avoided or adjourned. It is a constitutional trial, and the nation must go through it deliberately and bravely."

It was a credit to the constitutional system that the election went forward—and that President Lincoln was committed to accepting an outcome adverse to his own interests. Democrats portrayed Lincoln as a tyrant, yet there is no evidence that he ever considered the tyrannical act of cancelling or postponing the presidential election. "We cannot have free government without elections," Lincoln said, "and if the rebellion could force us to forgo, or postpone a national election, it might fairly claim to have already conquered and ruined us." After all the sulfurous newspaper columns, all the incendiary pamphlets, and all the sneering speeches, there was only one way to ascertain whether the enfranchised people of the Union approved or disapproved of the president's leadership. "The most reliable indication of public purpose in this country," Lincoln wrote, "is derived through our popular elections."

He was exhausted. There was no end in sight. Interrupted one day at the Soldiers' Home, the president reportedly snapped, "Am I to have no rest? Is there no hour or spot when or where I may escape this constant call?" Francis Carpenter thought the Lincoln of the first half of the year had "the saddest face I ever knew." The president would pace the halls of the White House, "his hands behind him, great black rings under his eyes, his head bent forward upon his breast—altogether such a picture of the effects of sorrow, care, and anxiety as would have melted the hearts of the worst of his adversaries." Carpenter, who was painting a portrait of the president and the cabinet discussing emancipation, was reminded of the prophet Jeremiah, who had "wept over the desolations of the nation." "This war is eating my life out," Lincoln remarked. "I have a strong impression that I shall not live to see the end." Yet he was willing to face the judgment of the people. He *believed* in facing the judgment of the people.

As usual, Lincoln was under pressure from all sides. In the storm and clamor of criticism, he recalled an old story. "A traveller on the frontier found himself out of his reckoning one night in a most inhospitable region," the president said in early March. "A terrific thunderstorm came up, to add to his trouble. He floundered along until his horse at length gave out. The lightning afforded him the only clue to his way, but the peals of thunder were frightful. One bolt, which seemed to crash the earth beneath him, brought him to his knees. By no means a praying man, his petition was short and to the point—'O Lord, if it is all the same to you, give us a little more light and a little less noise!'"

But the noise would not abate. In late 1863, Lincoln had announced a plan for Reconstruction policy. The year before, Charles Sumner had offered a proposal under which the seceded states would revert to territorial status as the price of "treason"; the defeated regions would then fall "under the exclusive jurisdiction of Congress." The more radical interest saw Sumner as its champion. "Chas Sumner is the only orator in the Senate," Nathan Daniels wrote in his diary. "When he speaks, choice pearls fall and ideas are given forth." In a New Year's Day 1864 entry, Daniels, a progressive on many issues, wrote: "I pray for the advancement of [Black] people and the recognition of all their rights as human beings. They are entitled to something else besides their mere personal freedom[—]political social and moral rights are theirs and the day will soon arrive when we shall all be willing to concede such Justice." Daniels had encountered the president one day on the White House lawn in March. Lincoln was wearing a "common gray shawl . . . his tall body swaying to and fro like some huge force in a storm." Daniels thought the image appropriate. "He is a drifter and only acts when forced & by public opinion. . . . The Radicals are for more earnest work and they are thoroughly convinced that Mr Lincoln is not the man to speedily and successfully close this war."

Typically, the president was moderate on postwar plans. In his Proclamation of Amnesty and Reconstruction, issued on Tuesday, December 8, 1863, the president stood by emancipation but would leave the states largely sovereign on questions of the rights of Black Americans once slavery was ended and the Union restored. He would pardon those in rebellion who swore an oath of allegiance to the United States—an oath that included adherence to the Emancipation Proclamation. He would recognize state governments formed after 10 percent of voters (based on the state's total number of votes cast in the 1860 presidential election) pledged fealty under those terms. Finally, the president promised to abide by "any provision . . . in relation to the freed people of such State, which shall recognize and declare their permanent freedom, [and] provide for their education." To reverse his antislavery policies, Lincoln told Congress, "would be not only to relinquish a lever of power, but would also be a cruel and an astounding breach of faith."

An abolition amendment—Representative James M. Ashley of Ohio had introduced one—as well as suffrage and citizenship for Black people went unmentioned. To Wendell Phillips, Lincoln was planning on a postwar world in which "the negro's freedom" would be "a mere sham," a victim of the resurgent power of the "large landed proprietors of the South." Still, as Jesse Fell had once remarked, while Lincoln "don't go forward as *fast* as some of us like, he *never goes backward.*"

A step—not a stride, but a step—came on Sunday, March 13, 1864, when Lincoln signaled support for limited Black suffrage. "I barely suggest for your private consideration, whether some of the colored people may not be let in—as, for instance, the very intelligent, and especially those who have fought gallantly in our ranks," the president wrote to the newly elected governor of Union-occupied Louisiana, Michael Hahn. "They would probably help, in some trying time to come, to keep the jewel of liberty within the family of freedom. But this is only a suggestion, not to the public, but to you alone."

Suffrage for Black Americans was crucial if the United States were to realize an egalitarian future in which the nation was not only free of slavery but was also more genuinely democratic. Yet some in the abolitionist world defended Lincoln's failure to argue explicitly and publicly for the rights of citizenship for Black people. "When was it ever known that liberation from bondage was accompanied by a recognition of political equality?" William Lloyd Garrison asked in 1864. "According to the laws of development and progress, it is not practicable.... Nor, if the freed blacks were admitted to the polls by Presidential fiat, do I see any permanent advantage likely to be secured by it; for . . . as soon as the state was organized and left to manage its own affairs, the white population . . . would unquestionably alter the franchise in accordance with their prejudices, and exclude those summarily brought to the polls."

Radical Republicans who felt the president too timid on such matters maneuvered to push Lincoln off the 1864 ticket. The efforts illustrated how the realities of passionate critics were different from the realities of even the most passionate politicians. "The reformer is careless of numbers, disregards popularity, and deals only with ideas, conscience, and common sense," Wendell Phillips remarked. "He feels, with Copernicus, that as God waited long for an interpreter, so he can wait for his followers. He neither expects nor is overanxious for immediate success. The politician dwells in an everlasting NOW. His motto is 'Success'—his aim, votes. His object is not absolute right, but . . . as much right as the people will sanction. His office is not to instruct public opinion, but to represent it." And many reformers were frustrated with Lincoln's representation of that opinion.

A group approached Vice President Hamlin, who declined the overture to stand against his president. "While he thought that the President had been slow in starting in the right direction, he was moving ahead now, and with the slaves freed, the negroes armed, and McClellan dismissed, events would surely soon favor the Union," Hamlin's grandson recalled.

Then there was Secretary of the Treasury Salmon Chase, who was reportedly "working like a beaver" on a presidential bid. Lincoln thought his Treasury secretary's shadow campaign in "very bad taste" but "had determined to shut his eyes to all these performances," Lincoln told Hay; "that Chase made a good Secretary and that he would like to keep him where he is: if he becomes Presidt., all right. I hope we may never have a worse man. I have all along clearly seen his plan of strengthening himself." Support for the Treasury secretary was weak, and Republicans in Chase's Ohio ended the speculation by endorsing Lincoln's reelection. (Chase resigned from the cabinet in June.)

Hamlin and Chase were out, but the Radical threats to Lincoln's reelection persisted. The abolitionist and Lincoln ally Owen Lovejoy was furious. "Any attempt to divide the [Republican] party at such a time was criminal in the last degree," Lovejoy remarked to Francis Carpenter. "I tell you, Mr. Lincoln is at heart as strong an anti-slavery man as any of them, but he is compelled to *feel* his way. . . . I say to you frankly, that I believe his course to be right. His mind acts slowly, but when he moves, it is *forward*." At a gathering in Cleveland—supported by Wendell Phillips, Frederick Douglass, and Elizabeth Cady Stanton—a few hundred reformers nevertheless nominated John Frémont for the presidency under the banner of a new Radical Democracy party. The Cleveland platform attacked the president Lovejoy had praised, lamenting that "the honor and dignity of the nation have been sacrificed to conciliate the still existing and arrogant slave power."

Others wondered whether General Grant should be enlisted to displace the president. "The question astonishes me," Grant wrote to the head of the Ohio Democratic Central Committee. "I am not a candidate for any office nor for favors from any party." Grant was insistent on the point. "Nothing would induce me to think of being a presidential candidate, particularly so long as there is a possibility of having Mr. Lincoln re-elected," he wrote. Lincoln was relieved. "No man knows, when that Presidential grub gets to gnawing at him, just how deep it will get until he has tried it," the president reportedly remarked, "and I didn't know but what there was one gnawing at Grant."

The toils of office and the complexities of war were stubborn and ubiquitous. Mary's half sister Emilie Todd Helm came to Washington from the South—or, as John Hay put it, from "Secessia." The widow of the Confederate general who had been killed at Chickamauga, "Mrs. Gen. Helm," as Hay referred to her, was a problematic guest. Always the subject of Unionist suspicion, Mary was loyal to her husband's cause, but the presence of Todd kinsmen in the White House fed rumors in wartime Washington. "Mr. Lincoln and my sister met me with the warmest affection, we were all too grief-stricken at first for speech," Mrs. Helm recalled. "I have lost my husband, they have lost their fine little son Willie. Mary and I have lost three brothers in the Confederate service. We could only embrace each other in silence and tears. . . . Our tears gathered silently and fell unheeded as with choking voices we tried to talk of immaterial things."

Her stay in the White House raised uncomfortable questions for Lincoln. In an act of familial kindness, the president had granted Emilie passage through Union lines without requiring an oath of loyalty.* "I feel that my being here is more or less an embarrassment to all of us," Emilie admitted. She had cross words with Senator Ira Harris of New York who disparaged the Confederate forces.

"Well, we have whipped the rebels at Chattanooga," Harris said, "and I hear, madam, that the scoundrels ran like scared rabbits."

---

* The Lincolns would ultimately fall out with Mrs. Helm when she attacked the president for not allowing her to go into Confederate territory to collect cotton.

"It was the example, Senator Harris, that you set them at Bull Run and Manassas," Emilie retorted.

They kept at it. "I have only *one* son and he is fighting for his country," Harris remarked. "And, Madam, if I had twenty sons they should all be fighting the rebels."

"And if I had twenty sons, General Harris, they should all be opposing yours."

Lincoln's thoughts were never far from the grave—his son's, his troops', his own—and from the judgments of eternity. During a sitting for Francis Carpenter in early March, the president mused aloud about Shakespeare. "There is one passage of the play of 'Hamlet' which is very apt to be slurred over by the actor, or omitted altogether, which seems to me the choicest part of the play," Lincoln told Carpenter. "It is the soliloquy of the king, after the murder. It always struck me as one of the finest touches of nature in the world." Reciting the verses from memory, Lincoln assumed the voice of Claudius, who has taken his brother's life, wife, and crown. The king wonders, in anguish, whether he can ever be truly forgiven when he refuses to give up the fruits of his crime. "Help, angels! Make assay!" Claudius cries. "Bow, stubborn knees, and heart with strings of steel, Be soft as sinews of the newborn babe!" There, in a few lines, was an essential human conundrum, one that fascinated Lincoln: the tension in a moral world between dark and light, ambition and rectitude, power and goodness.

On the evening of Friday, March 25, 1864, the president was at work in his study. Carpenter was again with him, and Lincoln looked up from his papers. Young Tad was dispatched for a copy of Shakespeare, from which the president read for a while. He then recalled a poem—"a great favorite"—that he knew by heart: "Mortality," by William Knox, a contemporary of Sir Walter Scott's. The poem is a bleak meditation on the inevitability of death:

> *The hand of the king that the sceptre hath borne,*
> *The brow of the priest that the mitre hath worn,*
> *The eye of the sage, and the heart of the brave,*
> *Are hidden and lost in the depths of the grave.*

Here was the depressive Lincoln, staring into the darkness, contemplating the inherent tragedy of the world, lamenting the limitations of

life. He remembered, too, a line of Oliver Wendell Holmes, Sr.'s, from
the poem "The Last Leaf":

> *The mossy marbles rest*
> *On the lips that he has prest*
> *In their bloom,*
> *And the names he loved to hear*
> *Have been carved for many a year*
> *On the tomb.*

"For pure pathos, in my judgment," Lincoln said, "there is nothing
finer than those six lines in the English language!"

Lincoln soldiered on. In March 1864, empowered by a vote in Congress, he elevated Grant to the rank once held by George Washington: lieutenant general. The unassuming hero arrived in Washington
quietly, accompanied by his son, and registered at Willard's by writing
"U. S. Grant and son, Galena, Ill." The Grants passed the dinner hour
in the hotel's public rooms nearly without notice. The general was finally recognized, and cheered, midway through the meal. Later that
evening Grant walked over to the White House to pay his respects at
the Lincolns' Tuesday reception.

He and the president had never met. The diminutive Grant made
his way through the crowds on the state floor to the tall, angular Lincoln, and the two men clasped hands. "This is General Grant, is it?" the
president said.

"Yes," the general replied—directly and to the point.

Grant shared the president's view that the Union's salvation lay with
total victory on the battlefield. Negotiation seemed futile. The only
concession that might alter the calculus would be on slavery, and Lincoln would give no ground there. All that was left to do was to fight it
out. In elevating Grant and unleashing him, the president was pursuing
a morally informed course through harsh military means.

Grant returned to the field from Washington and opened one of the
bloodiest and most consequential chapters in American history. In the
Wilderness of Virginia under Grant and in Georgia and in South Carolina under William T. Sherman, Union forces engaged the enemy
with relentless ferocity. The casualty counts were vast, progress slow,
reversals common. A moderate compared to the Radicals of his own

party, the Lincoln of 1864 was nevertheless prosecuting an aggressive war not for the antebellum Union but for a new version of the old—one in which slavery could not stand.

As the summer began, Lincoln remained seemingly popular with Northern Republican voters even amid the skepticism from the Radicals. "Providence has decreed your reelection, and no combination of the wicked can prevent it," Simon Cameron of Pennsylvania had told the president. Asked why he was supporting Lincoln, Senator Henry Wilson of Massachusetts, a frequent critic, replied that the president was strong with the people and that, therefore, "the best must be made of it."

The Republican nominating convention in Baltimore in early June made quick work of things. "The State of Illinois," B. C. Cook, the delegation's chairman, said, "again presents to the loyal people of this nation, for President of the United States, Abraham Lincoln—God bless him!" On a motion from Missouri—which had initially cast its 22 votes for General Grant—Lincoln's nomination was declared unanimous.

The Republican platform was a case for modernity. It called for the Confederacy's unconditional surrender in the "Rebellion now raging" and argued that "the Government owes to all men employed in its armies, without regard to distinction of color, the full protection of the laws of war." Looking beyond the war, the party endorsed the "speedy construction" of the transcontinental railroad and a "liberal and just" policy of immigration given that "foreign immigration . . . has added so much to the wealth, development of resources and increase of power to the nation."

As events would prove, the most significant plank of the Baltimore platform was a call to use the Constitution to break the consensus that precluded the federal abolition of slavery where it existed: "*Resolved,* That as slavery was the cause, and now constitutes the strength of this Rebellion," the platform said, "justice and the National safety demand its utter and complete extirpation from the soil of the Republic" by the passage of "such an amendment to the Constitution, to be made by the people in conformity with its provisions, as shall terminate and forever prohibit the existence of Slavery within the limits of the jurisdiction of the United States."

On Monday, December 14, 1863—just after the Gettysburg Address and while Lincoln was still recuperating from smallpox—Representative James M. Ashley of Ohio had proposed the "submission to the several States of a proposition to amend the national Constitution prohibiting slavery, or involuntary servitude, in all of the States and Territories now owned or which may be hereafter acquired by the United States." The war was proving more than a match for the long-standing federal consensus that had protected slavery where it existed. Battle after battle, casualty count after casualty count, military campaign after military campaign, Northerners who had been willing to let the institution stand were impatient and more open to radical measures. "The havoc of war aroused northern passions for vengeance, and emancipation was the perfect instrument of retribution," the historian Michael Vorenberg observed. An abolition amendment was approved by the Senate on Friday, April 8; the House would narrowly fail to muster the necessary two-thirds majority for passage on Wednesday, June 15.

Lincoln had apparently been quietly supportive of the amendment before June, but he had also wanted time to gauge public reaction to the proposal before committing himself. Baltimore gave him the moment he had been looking for. "The unconditional Union men, North and South, perceive [the abolition amendment's] importance, and embrace it," the president wrote in the published acceptance of his renomination. "In the joint names of Liberty and Union, let us labor to give it legal form, and practical effect." The Lincoln who went before the voters in 1864, therefore, was unambiguously linked with, and in favor of, the immediate, uncompensated, and permanent abolition of slavery.

There was one unsettled question: Who was to be vice president? As a wartime measure, the Republicans were calling themselves the National Union Party. As newspaper commentary and the 1862–63 elections had shown, white opinion on emancipation was very much mixed. Looking to the fall of 1864, Republicans believed New England largely safe, which made Hannibal Hamlin of Maine a redundant feature on the ticket. The voters to worry about were in more moderate states where emancipation was less popular. The "general impression, in and out of the Convention," Hay and Nicolay recalled, was that "it would be advisable to select as a candidate for the Vice-Presidency a war Democrat." In Baltimore, Hamlin had his adherents, as did Daniel S. Dickerson of New York, L. H. Rousseau of Kentucky, and Benjamin Butler of Massachusetts. Another name was widely bruited: Andrew Johnson of Tennessee.

The president publicly insisted that the choice was wholly in the hands of the convention—the common political practice in that era. "It was . . . with minds absolutely untrammeled by even any knowledge of the President's wishes that the Convention went about its work of selecting his associate on the ticket," Hay and Nicolay wrote. Lincoln's friend Leonard Swett was plumping for Joseph Holt, the Kentucky lawyer and politician whom Lincoln had appointed judge advocate general of the United States. Given Swett's proximity to the president, the campaign for Holt attracted attention, and Nicolay wrote to Hay for guidance: "Cook [of Illinois] wants to know confidentially whether Swett is all right; whether in urging Holt for Vice-President he reflects the President's wishes; whether the President has any preference, either personal or on the score of policy; or whether he wishes not even to interfere by a confidential intimation."

"Wish not to interfere about V.P.," Lincoln replied. "Convention must judge for itself."

Johnson was a Unionist and a racist. "I have lived among negroes, all my life, and I am for this Government with slavery under the Constitution as it is, if the Government can be saved," he said during the war. "I am for the Government of my fathers with negroes, I am for it without negroes. Before I would see this Government destroyed, I would send every negro back to Africa, disintegrated and blotted out of space." He endorsed emancipation but reiterated, "I am for my Government with or without slavery, but if either the Government or slavery must perish, I say give me the Government and let the negroes go." Thaddeus Stevens asked a reasonable question: "Can't you find a candidate for Vice President in the United States without going down to one of those damned rebel provinces to pick one up?"

Apparently the answer was no. Why did Lincoln go along with the choice of Johnson? The question is somewhat anachronistic. Presidential nominees did not choose the vice presidential nominee until well into the twentieth century. It was the convention's decision to make. Though constitutionally a part of the executive branch, vice presidents in practice were more associated with their role as president of the Senate. That is, if they were associated with anything at all: the post could be a path to obscurity. Their fitness to serve as president was not a great concern. Given the numerous threats of assassination that Lincoln faced, it is both puzzling and troubling that neither he nor the Republican leadership seriously weighed whether a President Johnson would be a good thing or a bad thing for the country.

No one would know how momentous the choice was until later, after Ford's Theatre. Andrew Johnson's nomination to be vice president was a political decision by a party in a political moment to achieve a particular political end: the votes of moderate to conservative Unionists who might be uncomfortable with Lincoln's emancipation policies and with the party's proposed abolition amendment. Beginning in April 1865, a President Hannibal Hamlin, a New England Republican, would have governed very differently than President Johnson, the Tennessee Democrat. That, of course, is historical supposition. The Republicans of the moment in 1864 were focused on neither a President Hamlin nor a President Johnson, but on reelecting President Lincoln.

The certitudes of June were certitudes only in that moment, and the Republican unanimity behind Lincoln was not something the president could rely upon. He well knew that popularity was more fleeting than durable—as the midsummer weeks of 1864 would demonstrate.

First there was a Radical Republican plan of Reconstruction passed in the first days of July. Named for its main sponsors, Senator Wade of Ohio and Representative Henry Davis of Maryland, the bill contemplated a much more revolutionary postwar approach to the Confederate states than Lincoln had proposed the previous December. The bill would have permanently abolished slavery by legislative fiat. Another feature of the legislation was the declaration that the existing state governments in the Confederacy were no longer valid, a legal assertion that ran counter to the president's insistence that the states were not now part of a separate nation but were only in rebellion to the Union. To follow the Wade-Davis course would be to reverse progress made in reconstructing Arkansas and Louisiana, which Lincoln valued.

The president pocket-vetoed the bill. Wade and Davis published an incendiary manifesto attacking Lincoln as too moderate and soft on the rebel South. To some Radical Republicans, the dispute over the Wade-Davis bill underscored their long-standing reservations about Lincoln's moderation.

The Confederate general Jubal Early was soon reminding the Union that the war itself was far from over. Under Early's command, Confederate troops fought their way within "sight of the dome of the Capitol." Early headquartered himself briefly at the Blair country house in Silver Spring. Lincoln was convinced to return to the White House from the Soldiers' Home for fear that Confederate cavalry might capture him. "Old Abe is in great danger from Secesh here as many have threatened his life," Nathan Daniels wrote. The Navy Department quietly arranged for a waterborne escape on the Potomac if the rebels closed in on the president.

The crux came at Fort Stevens, in northwest Washington, where federal troops turned back the invasion. Lincoln observed the battle firsthand and came under enemy fire. "He stood there with a long frock coat and plug hat on, making a very conspicuous figure," one contemporary recalled of the commander in chief. "Get down, you damn fool!" a young officer, perhaps Oliver Wendell Holmes, Jr., of the Twentieth Massachusetts, reputedly snapped at the president.

The war's casualties and apparent military stalemate fed hopes for peace and eroded confidence in the president. "The country was struck with one of those bewilderments which dethrone reason for the moment," Frederick Douglass observed of the summer of 1864. "Everybody was thinking and dreaming of peace, and the impression had gone abroad that the President's antislavery policy was about the only thing which prevented a peaceful settlement with the Rebels . . . men were ready for peace almost at any price."

The impetus for settlement talks came, as before, from Horace Greeley. William Jewett was back on the scene, purportedly in contact with Confederate representatives in Canada. "I venture to remind you that our bleeding, bankrupt, almost dying country also longs for peace," Greeley wrote to Lincoln. For the president, there could be no peace without emancipation, and he did not believe the Confederacy would accede to such terms. But if there were any way to make that state of things absolutely clear, the president was open to it. His reply to Greeley welcomed the opportunity to show that the Union was not the stumbling block to peace. "If you can find any person, anywhere, professing to have any proposition of Jefferson Davis in writing, for peace, embracing the restoration of the Union, and abandonment of slavery, whatever else it embraces, say to him he may come to me with you," Lincoln wrote to Greeley in July.

A rendezvous slated for Niagara Falls offered Lincoln the chance, in his own hand, to lay out his requirements for a cessation of arms. In a note he entrusted to John Hay, who traveled to Niagara to meet with the Confederate representatives, the president wrote:

Executive Mansion,
Washington, July 18, 1864.

TO WHOM IT MAY CONCERN: Any proposition which embraces the restoration of peace, the integrity of the whole Union, and the abandonment of slavery, and which comes by and with an authority that can control the armies now at war against the United States will be received and considered by the Executive government of the United States, and will be met by liberal terms on other substantial and collateral points; and the bearer, or bearers, thereof shall have safe-conduct both ways.

Abraham Lincoln.

With its emphasis on the "abandonment of slavery," this letter of the president's was a political gift to white Southern sympathizers, who characterized it as a "caprice of his imperial will." The president's opponents wanted to agitate Northern and border state Democrats into seeing Lincoln as an intransigent abolitionist. Democratic hard-liners, meanwhile, still hoped insurrection might weaken the president. Lincoln knew the stakes, and he called for five hundred thousand more men in mid July. There was only one way to end war weariness, and that was to win the war.

Grant's campaigns in Virginia were being followed closely from the idyllic Orange Mountain, New Jersey, estate of George McClellan. "They must have had a terrible time down there!" McClellan wrote of the fighting in the Wilderness. "God give them victory!" Democrats had long courted the displaced general for a bid against Lincoln, and "Young Napoleon" was open to avenging his removal by defeating the president who had sacked him. Preserving the Union, the general wrote, was "possible only by a change of Administration & policy," and he was happy to offer himself as that change. McClellan stood on interesting political ground. The general said he wanted Union military victory, but as a War Democrat in a party with powerful Peace Democrats, he was in a precarious position.

As the seventeenth president of the United States, George McClellan would have reversed the Emancipation Proclamation, which he had always opposed, thus removing the incentive for Black Americans to fight in the Union ranks. McClellan's insistence on a return to antebellum "Constitution & laws" suggested that those who had already been freed in the storm of war could be reenslaved. In Richmond, Davis showed no signs of compromise: "We are fighting for independence; and that, or extermination, we will have." But what if, as promised, a McClellan administration restored slavery in a postwar Union? Would the Confederacy still hold out for independence? Why not take a pro-slavery deal from a President McClellan and end the war? The antebellum issues of slavery extension and fugitive slave enforcement, among others, would likely be settled according to the wishes of the seceded South, probably as the price of reunion under McClellan.

"If I am elected," McClellan reportedly said in August, "I will recommend an immediate armistice and a call for a convention of all the states and insist upon exhausting all and every means to secure peace without further bloodshed." In the autumn his tone against the Confederacy toughened, but never beyond this: "The Union is the one condition of peace—we ask no more." McClellan wanted Union with slavery. Lincoln ran on Union without it. The voters had their choice.

So much blood, so much treasure, so much hope—and all that Lincoln had fought for was in the balance. "The great election of next November looks more and more obscure, dubious, and muddled every day," George Templeton Strong told his diary in mid-August. In a summer of Union military setbacks, Radical discontent over Reconstruction, and much white opposition to emancipation, a change in the presidency seemed not only possible but likely. "Mr. Lincoln is already beaten," Horace Greeley wrote in the summer. "He cannot be elected."

The rebel South did not try to hide its hope. "The fact begins to shine out clear . . . that Abraham Lincoln is lost; that he will never be president again," the Confederate *Daily Richmond Examiner* wrote. "The obscene ape of Illinois is about to be deposed from the Washington purple."

Lincoln knew the politics. In these August weeks, he had a decision to make: Should he back away from his insistence, expressed in the Niagara letter, that slavery could in no way be preserved in a postwar Union? At times Lincoln seemed resolute that there could be no peace without the "abandonment of slavery." In early August he said he would "never consent to an armistice, or to peace, on any other terms but the explicit abolition of slavery in all the Southern states." He was, moreover, "determined to prosecute the war with all the means at his command till the rebels were conquered or exterminated, even if it took four years more."

Yet in a draft letter to a Wisconsin War Democrat in mid-August, Lincoln appeared to waver. "If Jefferson Davis wishes, for himself, or for the benefit of his friends at the North, to know what I would do if he were to offer peace and re-union, saying nothing about slavery," Lincoln wrote in the draft, "let him try me."

So much depended on where Lincoln landed. He was weighing the most fundamental of issues—the present and the future of slavery—against his own political fortunes. He was being asked to surrender ground on slavery to secure his own reelection. He was being told he had to do it, or that all would be lost. He was being inundated with pro-compromise opinion from the established political powers of the age.

The temptation to give in was great, and Lincoln was turning things over in his mind when Frederick Douglass returned to the White House on Friday, August 19. "The President was pressed on every hand to modify his letter, '*To whom it may concern,*'" Douglass recalled. "How to meet this pressure he did me the honor to ask my opinion. He showed me a letter written with a view to meet the peace clamor raised against him." The issue was momentous. "Now the question he put to me," Douglass recalled, "was—Shall I send forth this letter [reassuring War Democrats]—To which I answered—Certainly not. It would be given a broader meaning than you intend to convey; it would be taken as a

Henry J. Raymond of The New York Times *also served as chairman of the Republican National Committee.*

complete surrender of your anti-slavery policy, and do you serious damage."

Lincoln, Douglass recalled, "treated me as a man; he did not let me feel for a moment that there was any difference in the color of our skins! The President is a most remarkable man. I am satisfied now that he is doing all that circumstances will permit him to do." Lincoln, too, was impressed with his caller. "Considering the conditions from which Douglass rose," the president remarked, "and the position to which he had attained, he was . . . one of the most meritorious men in America."

Lincoln had still not decided what to do about possibly modifying his Niagara pledge. No less a figure than the chairman of the Republican National Committee, Henry Raymond, was telling the president that the end of slavery as a precondition of peace—the Niagara position—was untenable. "The tide is setting strongly against us," Raymond wrote to the president on the Monday after Douglass's Friday call. Raymond's counsel: Reach out to Richmond without reference to emancipation. "Why would it not be wise . . . *to make distinct proffers of peace to Davis, as the head of the rebel armies, on the sole condition of acknowledging the supremacy of the constitution*—all other questions to be settled in a convention of the people of all the States?"

It was a lonely hour for the president. Radical Republicans were angry over plans for Reconstruction; white Northern Democrats were unhappy about his insistence on emancipation as the price of peace. "One denounces Mr. Lincoln because he didn't abolish Slavery soon enough—another because he assumed to touch it at all," Raymond remarked. The New York *Evening Post* was more optimistic, writing that Lincoln was "popular with the plain people, who believe him honest, . . . with the soldiers, who believe him their friend, and with the religious people, who believe him to have been specially raised up for this crisis." Would that be enough?

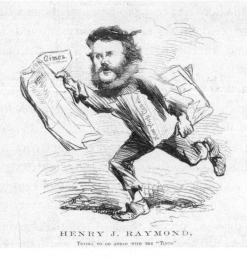

HENRY J. RAYMOND,
TRYING TO GO AHEAD WITH THE "TIMES."

In August 1864, Raymond urged Lincoln to abandon emancipation as a precondition of peace with the Confederacy.

Vanishingly few thought so in the heat of August. In New York City, former mayor George Opdyke wrote letters seeking to replace Lincoln as the Republican nominee. "Everything is darkness and doubt and discouragement," John Nicolay wrote. To Lincoln's friend Leonard Swett, "the prospect of the election looked very blue." Swett had a simple question for the president: Did Lincoln think he would win?

"Well," the president replied, "I don't think I ever heard of any man being elected to an office unless someone was for him."

Lincoln thought everything was over. He was to be defeated, his policies to be repudiated by the people, his vision of America to be lost. "This morning, as for some days past, it seems exceedingly probable that this Administration will not be re-elected," Lincoln wrote in a memorandum dated Tuesday, August 23. "Then it will be my duty to so co-operate with the President elect, as to save the Union between the election and the inauguration; as he will have secured his election on such ground that he cannot possibly save it afterwards." He asked his cabinet to sign the outside of the note without telling them its contents.

As Thurlow Weed observed, Lincoln knew that the "People are wild for Peace. They are told that the President will only listen to terms of Peace on condition Slavery be 'abandoned.'" Weed reported that Raymond believed the hour had come to give up emancipation as a precondition. "Mr Raymond thinks commissioners should be immediately sent, to Richmond, offering to treat for Peace on the basis of Union"— not on the basis of the end of slavery.

Lincoln wanted to be strong. But could he hold the line alone? His party was wavering. There were no cheering reports from the battlefield. He needed Black men in the fighting forces. He believed no man would fight without an incentive—and the incentive in this case was liberty. He had long ago made the moral decision that slavery was wrong and could have no place in a nation truly devoted to the principles of the Declaration of Independence.

The waning days of August 1864 tested that commitment to the ideal of liberty for all. There was a practical reason for the maintenance of the Niagara doctrine (the need for Black soldiers), but Lincoln might have finessed that by renewing a commitment to freeing the fighting men and those who reached Union lines while leaving open the larger question of a total end to slavery. He had said as much to Douglass on August 19. "The thing which alarmed me most was this: The President said he wanted some plan devised by which he could get more of the Slaves within our lines," Douglass recalled. "He thought now was their time—*and that such only of them as succeeded in getting within our line would be free after the war was over.*" In fact Lincoln wanted more than this—and the only way to achieve more was to make emancipation a condition of peace.

He just wasn't sure he could have his way and still win reelection. On Thursday, August 25, 1864, Raymond and other members of the Republicans' national executive committee came to the White House. "Hell is to pay," Nicolay wrote to Hay. "The N.Y. politicians have got a stampede on that is about to swamp everything. Raymond and the National Committee are here today. R. thinks a commission to Richmond is about the only salt to save us. . . . The matter is now undergoing consultation." The moment felt decisive. "I think that today and here is the turning-point in our crisis," Nicolay told Hay. "Our men see giants in the airy and unsubstantial shadows of the opposition, and are about to surrender without a fight." Raymond had made himself plain. Lincoln would have to commit one way or the other.

Overcoming his doubts—or perhaps having worked through them by putting the alternative course on paper in his draft letters and in conversations—the president summoned his strength and made his case to his callers. "If the President can infect R. and his committee with some of his own patience and pluck, we are saved," Nicolay wrote. "If our friends will only rub their eyes and shake themselves, and become convinced that they themselves are not dead we shall win the fight overwhelmingly."

The president would not back down. To send word to Richmond that emancipation was negotiable, Lincoln told Raymond and the party elders, "would be worse than losing the Presidential contest—it would be ignominiously surrendering it in advance." That Abraham Lincoln would not do. As in the Secession Winter, the president insisted on his prescribed policy toward slavery at immense peril—and, unlike in the post-1860 election season, this time he took his staunch stand when he himself was on the ballot. To end slavery, Lincoln risked defeat and banishment to Springfield—the highest of prices for a political man to pay.

But he was ready to pay it. He would rise or fall on emancipation. He thought it was right. There would be no reversal, no concession. "We may be defeated; we may fail, but we will go down with our principles," Lincoln remarked to Senator Henry Wilson in August. "I will not modify, qualify, nor retract my proclamation, nor my letter."

If he returned the Black men who had fought at Port Hudson and elsewhere to slavery, the president said, "I should be damned in time & in eternity for so doing. The world shall know that I will keep my faith to friends & enemies, come what will." In early September, to a group of Black supporters of the Union from Baltimore, Lincoln said that "it has always been a sentiment with me that all mankind should be free. So far as able, within my sphere, I have always acted as I believed to be right and just; and I have done all I could for the good of mankind generally."

I have done all I could. "I claim not to have controlled events, but confess plainly that events have controlled me," Lincoln had written to a Kentucky editor in the spring. This was not quite right. He *had* controlled events—or at least shaped them, which was all a mortal could do. He had done so, in terms of his policy toward slavery, by heeding his conscience—choppily, perhaps hesitantly, but also surely.

While waiting for a carriage at the door of the White House one day in 1864, the president was spotted by "a countryman," Carpenter recalled, "plainly dressed, with his wife and two little boys." The sightseer was shocked to see Lincoln. "There is the President!" the man whispered and approached the tall figure to ask if he might shake the president's hand. Lincoln was gracious, and the father parted with these words: "The Lord is with you, Mr. President—and the people too, sir; and the people too!" Whether the Lord and the people would be mighty enough to defeat McClellan would soon become clear. "Old Abe," Nathan Daniels observed, "must now gather up his skirts and put on steam for a tough race."

CHAPTER TWENTY-FOUR

The Strife of the Election

Thousands of bits of paper are falling into ballot-boxes today,
all over the country. It is a little thing, and can be done very
easily, but mighty consequences may hang on the result.

—PRIVATE WILBUR FISK of the Second Vermont, early November 1864

The only rumor we have heard of Abraham since his reelection is that he has "proclaimed" all the negros free all over
the universe. . . . God only knows what is before us.

—Confederate diarist LUCY VIRGINIA FRENCH, late November 1864

ON SATURDAY, SEPTEMBER 3, 1864, the world turned over
again. "Atlanta is ours," William T. Sherman telegraphed early
that morning, "and fairly won." "Glorious news this morning—
Atlanta taken at last!!!" George Templeton Strong told his diary. "Sherman has had a great battle," Nathan Daniels observed, "and the country
is this morning sending Joyful shouts to heaven for the glorious news."
The fall of the Georgia city came along with news of Union victories in
the Gulf, at Mobile, Alabama (Forts Powell, Gaines, and Morgan were
captured), and Lincoln issued orders of honor and gratitude.

It was a new day. The skeptics of August were now the hawks of
September. "The political skies begin to brighten," Raymond's *New York
Times* wrote. "The clouds that lowered over the Union cause a month
ago are breaking away." Under pressure from the Radicals, Lincoln
agreed to remove the conservative postmaster general Montgomery
Blair from the cabinet to soothe the forces that had nominated John
Frémont as the candidate of the Radical Democracy at Cleveland. Frémont in turn withdrew from the campaign, clarifying the choice before
the voters. Blair "had no doubt he was a peace-offering to Frémont and
his friends," he told Gideon Welles. "They wanted an offering, and he
was the victim whose sacrifice would propitiate them."

A satisfied Frederick Douglass wrote that "all hesitation ought to cease, and every man who wishes well to the slave and to the country should at once rally with all the warmth and earnestness of his nature to the support of Abraham Lincoln and Andrew Johnson." As October went by, Union arms were progressing. In the Shenandoah Valley, General Philip Sheridan defeated Confederate forces in a climactic action at Cedar Creek, Virginia.

The campaign of 1864 did not feature debates or candidate travel. Lincoln and McClellan relied on the publication of the party's platforms, newspaper broadsides, and the organizing work of allies in the states. Lincoln was aware that written remarks of his—or reports of such comments, whether made in public or in private—would be disseminated. The president relied on occasional addresses, delivered at the White House, usually from the steps of the mansion, to make his case.

He spoke of equality and of opportunity, of democracy and prosperity. "We have . . . a free Government, where every man has a right to be equal with every other man," the president told the 164th Ohio Regiment in mid-August. "In this great struggle, this form of Government and every form of human right is endangered if our enemies succeed." A repeated theme: "To the humblest and poorest amongst us are held out the highest privileges and positions. . . . Stand fast to the Union and the old flag."

Lincoln made a specific rhetorical foray into Maryland politics to endorse a new state constitution that included abolition. "I wish all men to be free," the president wrote in October. The constitution was approved shortly thereafter. "I had rather have Maryland upon that issue than have a state twice its size upon the presidential issue," Lincoln remarked; "it cleans up a piece of ground."

Emancipation in the states fed Democratic fears that a second Lincoln term could be even worse for white supremacy than the first, and the president's openness to receiving some Black Americans in the White House, Sojourner Truth among them, was another cause for racist anger. Born into slavery in Ulster County, New York, in the last years of the eighteenth century, Sojourner Truth escaped from bondage and became an influential voice for abolition and for the rights of women. Referring to her as "Aunty," Lincoln spoke to her with respectful candor during a White House meeting. "I said, 'I appreciate you, for you are the best president who has ever taken the seat,'" Truth recalled. "He replied: 'I expect you have reference to my having emancipated the slaves in my proclamation. But,' said he, mentioning the names of several of his predecessors (and among them emphatically that of Washington), 'they were all just as good, and would have done just as I have done if the time had come. If the people over the river [pointing across the Potomac] had behaved themselves, I could not have done what I have; but they did not, which gave me the opportunity to do these things.' I then said, 'I thank God that you were the instrument selected by him and the people to do it.'"

Not all the people, of course, which was evident when the campaign was roiled by a seventy-two-page pamphlet entitled *Miscegenation: The Theory of the Blending of the Races, Applied to the American White Man and Negro*. Purportedly written from an egalitarian viewpoint by unnamed authors, it was a piece of racist propaganda designed to frighten white voters. "All that is needed to make us the finest race on earth is to engraft upon our stock the negro element; the blood of the negro is the most precious because it is the most unlike any other that enters into the composition of our national life," the authors—two Democratic newspapermen—wrote. The pamphlet was mailed to select abolitionists seeking comment. Most of those replying expressed guarded approval for the sentiments about a true equality of the races but doubted the wisdom of advancing such arguments at that time. Democrats in turn seized on the words of endorsement to argue that the Republicans were intent on encouraging interracial intimacy and marriage. The *Miscegenation* attack was part of a virulently anti-Black, anti-Lincoln climate. "Abraham Africanus the First," the president was called in a New York weekly. "He is obscene. . . . He is an animal. . . . Filthy black n——s, greasy, sweaty, and disgusting, now jostle white people and even ladies everywhere, even at the President's levees."

Democratic disinformation included talk that Lincoln might not surrender the White House in the event of a McClellan victory. Another line of speculation had it that a triumphant McClellan could attempt to seize power immediately after the election. To settle things down, Lincoln spoke reassuringly to a visiting crowd of Marylanders in mid-October. "I am struggling to maintain government, not to overthrow it," the president said. "I am struggling especially to prevent others from overthrowing it." If he lost the election, he would remain in office as the Constitution prescribed, until March 4, 1865; work with his successor in the interval "to save the ship"; and then transfer power peaceably on Inauguration Day. "This is due to the people both on principle, and under the constitution," Lincoln said. "Their will, constitutionally expressed, is the ultimate law for all." He closed with a word of tribute for the Union forces, whom he believed steadfast in support of the administration. "Do they not have the hardest of it?" Lincoln asked. "Who should quail while they do not? God bless the soldiers and seamen, with all their brave commanders."

Lincoln's appreciation for the Union men under arms was a running theme of the autumn. "It is said that we have the best Government the world ever knew, and I am glad to meet you, the supporters of that Government," he told the 189th New York Volunteers. "To you who render the hardest work in its support should be given the greatest credit." For Lincoln, soldiers were essential not only on the battlefield but at the ballot box. Hundreds of thousands of Union fighting men, many of whom voted Republican, were hundreds of miles from home. Democrats understood, and they believed they would stand a better chance of defeating Lincoln if they could keep Republican soldiers from voting. Their estimation was correct: The *Detroit Advertiser and Tribune* calculated that Republican votes were lost 3 to 1 when soldiers were unable to vote in the 1862 midterm elections.

Several states adopted absentee voter policies for soldiers away from home. "They are American citizens, [and] they have as much right to [vote] as those citizens who remain at home," General Grant wrote. "Nay, more, for they have sacrificed more for their country." Nevertheless, some states with strong Democratic state governments—including Indiana, Illinois, and New Jersey—refused to authorize absentee voting. In response, the Lincoln administration worked to furlough Union soldiers in Republican-leaning units from these states to return home to vote. Democrats made the journey, too: When Lincoln was told that a pro-McClellan soldier had been detained en route to vote, he said, "Let this man have transportation immediately."

Long ill, Roger Taney died in early October. "Last night Chief Justice Taney went home to his fathers," John Hay told his diary. "Already (before his old clay is cold) they are beginning to canvass vigorously for his successor. Chase men say the place is promised to their *magnifico*." It wasn't, but Lincoln was intrigued by the thought of nominating his firmly abolitionist former Treasury secretary. A Chase court was likely to be open to more progressive measures in a postwar nation, and the president would send Chase's name to the Senate in early December.

As the November election neared, John Bright dispatched a letter to Horace Greeley for publication in his *New York Tribune*. McClellan was the choice of those Englishmen who "have preferred to see a Southern slave empire rather than a restored and free republic," Bright wrote; those who "believe that slavery weakens your power and tarnishes your good name" were for Lincoln. With the perspective offered by an ocean, Bright explained why:

> It is not because they believe Mr. LINCOLN to be wiser or better than all other men on your continent, but they think they have observed in his career a grand simplicity of purpose and a patriotism which knows no change and which does not falter. To some of his countrymen there may appear to have been errors in his course. It would be strange indeed if, in the midst of difficulties so stupendous and so unexpected, any Administration or any ruler should wholly avoid mistakes. To us, looking on from this distance, and unmoved by the passions from which many of your people can hardly be expected to be free . . . we see in it an honest endeavor faithfully to do the work of his great office.

Lincoln found Bright's words comforting—so much so that he clipped the column from the paper and put it in his brown leather wallet. Kind sentiments were hard to come by.

Election Day in the capital was rainy, humid, and long. At the front, in the Shenandoah Valley, Private Wilbur Fisk of the Second Vermont mused, "Thousands of bits of paper are falling into ballot-boxes today, all over the country. It is a little thing, and can be done very easily, but mighty consequences may hang on the result." He continued:

> It is almost a new thing in the history of the world, when such great results as whether this country shall be governed by one principle, or another in almost complete hostility to it, can be de-

cided by such simple means. God hasten the day when *all* questions may be decided in the same way, and then war, with its terrible list of horrors, will be remembered as one of the evils buried forever in the grim Past.

The White House was quiet. "This is election day and a dirty unpleasant rainy day it is, but it is the most momentous epoch in the nation's history," Nathan Daniels told his diary. "This day decides whether we are under Lincoln's election to have a speedy and successful closing of the war and peace and the establishment of the model Democratic Republic, or whether under McClellan's establishment we are to have first an armistice, then a Convention of the states, then Recognition by all Europe of the South, then the haughty demands of Jeff Davis."

Lincoln was reflective. His mind had been ranging through the decades, back to his first arriving in the capital for the Thirtieth Congress nearly seventeen years before. "It is a little singular," he remarked to Hay, "that I, who am not a vindictive man, should have always been before the people for election in canvasses marked for their bitterness—always but once; when I came to Congress it was a quiet time: But always besides that, the contests in which I have been prominent have been marked with great rancor."

He appeared calm; Mary, less so. "I don't know how I would bear up under defeat," she said. "I could have gone down on my knees to ask votes for him and again and again he said: 'Mary, I am afraid you will be punished for this overweening anxiety. If I am to be re-elected it will be all right; if not, you must bear the disappointment.'"

At seven P.M., Lincoln and Hay splashed through the mud on the White House lawn to reach the Telegraph Office at the War Department. They passed a soaked sentry in a rubber cloak; a collection of "idle orderlies" inside; and climbed the stairs. Initial word was encouraging—perhaps, Lincoln thought, too encouraging. "As the President entered," Hay recalled, "they handed him a dispatch from [Pennsylvania politician and editor John W.] Forney claiming ten thousand Union majority in Philadelphia."

"Forney is a little excitable," the president remarked.

But positive numbers kept coming in. Lincoln and his intimates paused at midnight for fried oysters and coffee; the president made sure to keep Mary up to date. "She is more anxious than I," he remarked. A muddied and bedraggled Thomas Eckert arrived; he reported that he had fallen in the street—which, as Hay wryly noted, reminded Lincoln of a story.

"For such an awkward fellow, I am pretty sure-footed," the president said. "It used to take a pretty dexterous man to throw me. I remember, the evening of the day in 1858, that decided the contest for the Senate between Mr. Douglas and myself, was something like this, dark, rainy & gloomy. I had been reading the returns, and had ascertained that we had lost the Legislature and started to go home. The path had been worn hog-backed & was slippering. My foot slipped from under me, knocking the other one out of the way, but I recovered myself & lit square: and I said to myself, *'It's a slip and not a fall.'*"

There would be no slip, much less a fall, tonight. "Abraham Lincoln has been elected by an overwhelming majority," the Washington *Evening Star* reported the next day. Lincoln told Noah Brooks that he "was grateful that the verdict of the people was likely to be so full, clear, and unmistakable that there could be no dispute."

The president won with 55 percent of the popular vote; McClellan polled 45 percent while carrying New Jersey, Kentucky, and Delaware. Absentee legislation had helped. In the dozen states that changed their absentee policies in 1864 and kept independent records of military voting, Lincoln received 78 percent of the soldier absentee ballots in comparison to the 53 percent share of the vote that he received from the general population of those same states. The men in uniform had stood with their commander in chief.

On the evening of the election, Ward Hill Lamon, Lincoln's on-again, off-again bodyguard, stationed himself outside Lincoln's bedroom. "He took a glass of whiskey," Hay recalled, "and then refusing my offer of a bed went out & rolling himself up in his cloak lay down at the President's door; passing the night in that attitude of touching and dumb fidelity with a small arsenal of pistols & bowie knives around him. In the morning he went away leaving my blankets at my door, before I or the President were awake."

That the nation had passed through the crisis of the election was a battle won. "Judging by the recent canvass and its result, the purpose of the people, within the loyal States, to maintain the integrity of the Union, was never more firm, nor more nearly unanimous, than now," Lincoln wrote. "The extraordinary calmness and good order with which the millions of voters met and mingled at the polls, give strong assurance of this." "That our national democratic experiment, principle, and machinery could triumphantly sustain such a shock, and that the Constitution could weather it, like a ship in a storm, and come out of it as sound and whole as before," Walt Whitman observed, "is by far the most signal proof yet of the stability of that experiment—Democracy—and of those principles and that Constitution." General Grant, John Hay recalled, was "deeply impressed with . . . the late Presidential election. The point which impressed him most powerfully was that which I regarded as the critical one—the pivotal centre of our history—the quiet and orderly character of the whole affair. No bloodshed or riot. . . . It proves our worthiness of free institutions, and our capability of preserving them without running into anarchy or despotism." To Nathan Daniels, "The inevitable destiny of events & the spirit of Progress must carry us safely through this terrible crisis."

The administration would survive. So would emancipation. "God be praised that our country has been again saved," Daniels wrote on hearing the news of Lincoln's reelection. At the White House on Thursday, November 10, Lincoln said, "It has long been a grave question whether any government, not *too* strong for the liberties of its people, can be strong *enough* to maintain its own existence, in great emergencies." He had taken care to draft the remarks he was making. "I know what you are thinking about," Lincoln remarked to Noah Brooks, who saw him at work. "You think it mighty queer that an old stump-speaker like myself should not be able to address a crowd like this outside without a written speech. But you must remember I am, in a certain way, talking to the country, and I have to be mighty careful." To the audience, the president said:

> The strife of the election is but human-nature practically applied to the facts of the case. What has occurred in this case, must ever recur in similar cases. Human-nature will not change. In any future great national trial, compared with the men of this, we shall have as weak, and as strong; as silly and as wise; as bad and good. Let us, therefore, study the incidents of this, as philosophy to learn wisdom from, and none of them as wrongs to be revenged.
>
> But the election, along with its incidental, and undesirable

A self-taught reader of philosophy and of political economy, of the King James Bible and of Shakespeare, Abraham Lincoln believed in the capacity of politics to shed light in a world given to darkness. And he longed to play his part in the arena. "Every man is said to have peculiar ambition," Lincoln remarked when first offering himself to voters, in Illinois, at the age of 23. "Whether it be true or not, I can say for one that I have no other so great as that of being truly esteemed by my fellow men, by rendering myself worthy of their esteem."

An artist's speculative portrait of Nancy Hanks Lincoln, Abraham's mother. A Lincoln neighbor recalled that she was "Loose," observing that "not only was Nancy Hanks an illegitimate child herself but that Nancy was not what she ought to have been."

A daughter of a prominent Lexington, Kentucky, family, Mary Todd met Lincoln in Springfield while visiting her sister Elizabeth Todd Edwards. "In her bearing she was proud, but handsome and vivacious," William Herndon recalled of Mary. "She not only had a quick intellect but an intuitive judgment of men and their motives."

The Lincolns were indulgent parents. Just as Lincoln wanted never to replicate Thomas Lincoln's household, Mary was trying to redeem the unhappiness of her stepmother's reign in Lexington. This image depicts, left to right, Tad, Robert, and Willie.

Lincoln admired Joseph Butler's book *Analogy of Religion,* first published in 1736. A bishop in the Church of England, Butler argued that conscience could ameliorate avarice and appetite. Without it there would be only perpetual war. Butler argued, too, that a theocentric universe encouraged moral action in light of the possibility of reward or punishment after death.

Born into enslavement in Delaware in 1746, Absalom Jones purchased his freedom in 1784. With Richard Allen, Jones created the Free African Society. Allen would go on to found the AME church while Jones became a clergyman in the Episcopal Church.

Frederick Douglass alternately called Lincoln "emphatically, the black man's President" and "preeminently the white man's President"; what remained constant was Douglass's regard for the sixteenth president's ultimate decisions on emancipation.

On New Year's Day 1831, William Lloyd Garrison published the first edition of *The Liberator*. He long argued the Constitution was "a covenant with death, and an agreement with hell"; and his belief that the Union was fatally flawed led him to eschew electoral politics.

Frederick Douglass, the Reverend Henry Highland Garnet, and Bishop
Richard Allen were included in this lithograph commemorating leading
Black figures.

Lincoln's politics were like those of Henry Clay's, and Lincoln's assent to the Whig Party platform put him in the political mainstream in the age of Jackson. Lincoln was, as he recalled in 1859, "always a Whig in politics." From the Whig perspective, the Constitution's powers could be interpreted beyond the plain text of the document.

"[L]et me not be understood as admitting, even by implication, that the existing relations between the races in the slaveholding States is an evil:—far otherwise; I hold it to be a good—a positive good," John C. Calhoun of South Carolina told the Senate in 1837.

"He was tall, thin, and ungainly in his movements, and sprawled rather than sat on a chair or sofa," a contemporary recalled of Senator Charles Sumner of Massachusetts. "Nothing saved his face from ugliness but his white gleaming teeth and his expression of bright intelligence and entire amiability."

135,000 SETS, 270,000 VOLUMES SOLD.

UNCLE TOM'S CABIN

FOR SALE HERE.

AN EDITION FOR THE MILLION, COMPLETE IN 1 Vol., PRICE 37 1-2 CENTS.
"   "   IN GERMAN, IN 1 Vol., PRICE 50 CENTS.
"   "   IN 2 Vols., CLOTH, 6 PLATES, PRICE $1.50.
SUPERB ILLUSTRATED EDITION, IN 1 Vol., WITH 153 ENGRAVINGS,
PRICES FROM $2.50 TO $5.00.

The Greatest Book of the Age.

Beginning in June 1851, Harriet Beecher Stowe's *Uncle Tom's Cabin or Life Among the Lowly* had been serialized in Washington's *National Era* and was published as a stand-alone novel in March 1852. A decade later, Lincoln received Stowe in the White House. "Is this the little woman who made this great war?" he reputedly asked.

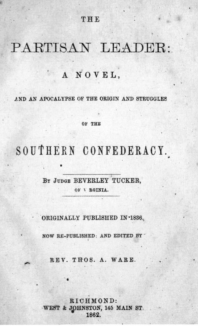

THE

PARTISAN LEADER:

A NOVEL,

AND AN APOCALYPSE OF THE ORIGIN AND STRUGGLES

OF THE

SOUTHERN CONFEDERACY.

By Judge BEVERLEY TUCKER,
OF VIRGINIA.

ORIGINALLY PUBLISHED IN 1836,

NOW RE-PUBLISHED: AND EDITED BY

REV. THOS. A. WARE.

RICHMOND:
WEST & JOHNSTON, 145 MAIN ST.
1862.

Written by the Virginian Nathaniel Beverley Tucker, *The Partisan Leader: A Tale of the Future,* published in 1836, imaginatively invented a Southern confederacy. "If we will not *have* slaves, we must *be* slaves," Tucker remarked. Tucker's book appeared three years before the abolitionist *American Slavery As It Is: Testimony of a Thousand Witnesses.*

Militant and driven by religiously rooted fervor, John Brown led violent attacks in "Bleeding Kansas" and at Harpers Ferry. Captured and executed, Brown was a symbol of the widening chasm in American life. After Harpers Ferry, Lincoln said: "We have a means provided for the expression of our belief in regard to Slavery—it is through the ballot box—the peaceful method provided by the Constitution."

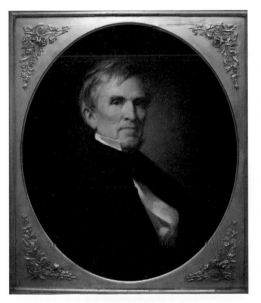

Senator John J. Crittenden of Kentucky had been in public service since 1809, the year Lincoln was born. In 1860–61, to avert war, Crittenden sought a compromise, the central feature of which was extending the Missouri Compromise line west—which would also have allowed slavery in territory "hereafter acquired." Petitions calling for passage poured into Washington; Crittenden estimated that a quarter of a million people had gone on record in favor of a deal.

Jefferson Davis was sworn in as president of the Confederate States of America at the Alabama state capitol in Montgomery on Monday, February 18, 1861; Alexander Stephens served as vice president. The breakaway polity had nearly been christened "the Republic of Washington." "Our cause," Davis declared, "is just and holy."

Jeff. Davis, Pres.

A Secession Envelope

Alexr H. Stephens. VicePres.

On Monday, September 22, 1862, Lincoln told the cabinet he was issuing the Preliminary Emancipation Proclamation. To Frederick Douglass the struggle was only now "invested with sanctity." The *Morning Star* in London wrote, "It is indisputably the great fact of the war—the turning point in the history of the American commonwealth—an act only second in courage and probable results to the Declaration of Independence."

A depiction of "Watch Night," the hours spent by Black Americans as they awaited the issuance of the Final Emancipation Proclamation on New Year's Day 1863. News of the proclamation surged through the country by telegraph. "Men, women, young and old, were up," recalled Frederick Douglass, who was in Boston. "Hats and bonnets were in the air, and we gave three cheers for Abraham Lincoln."

When Frederick Douglass first called on Lincoln in the White House, the president cut him off when he began to explain who he was. "I know who you are, Mr. Douglass," Lincoln said. "I am glad to see you." As Douglass recalled, "I will tell you how he received me—just as you have seen one gentleman receive another—with a hand and a voice well-balanced between a kind cordiality and a respectful reserve. I tell you I felt big there!"

In 1852, the abolitionist Martin R. Delany had published *The Condition, Elevation, Emigration, and Destiny of the Colored People of the United States, Politically Considered,* an effort to build support for an all-Black nation. During the Civil War, Delany promoted the enlistment of Black men into the Union armed forces and was commissioned a major in the U.S. Army.

"The great election of next November looks more and more obscure, dubious, and muddled every day," George Templeton Strong told his diary in mid-August 1864. In a summer of Union military setbacks, Radical discontent over Reconstruction, and much white opposition to emancipation, a change in the presidency seemed not only possible but likely. "Mr. Lincoln is already beaten," Horace Greeley wrote in these months. "He cannot be elected."

George P. A. Healy's rendering of the March 1865 conference aboard the *River Queen* at City Point, Virginia, with William Tecumseh Sherman, Ulysses S. Grant, President Lincoln, and Rear Admiral David D. Porter. During his visit to the front, Lincoln would venture out on horseback, consulting a map marked with troop positions, to watch the burial of the dead, inspect captured Confederate prisoners, and bring some of the wounded back to City Point on his train.

"The South lies prostrate—their foot is on us—there is no help," the young Columbia, South Carolina, diarist Emma LeConte wrote on hearing news of Lee's surrender to Grant. After Lincoln's assassination, she observed: "It may be abstractly wrong to be so jubilant, but I just can't help it. . . . Could there have been a fitter death for such a man?"

After shooting the president and fleeing Ford's Theatre, John Wilkes Booth reached Richard H. Garrett's farm near Port Royal, Virginia. The manhunt ended on Wednesday, April 26, when Union cavalry trapped Booth in a burning barn; the assassin was shot to death by Sergeant Boston Corbett.

IN MEMORY OF ABRAHAM LINCOLN.
THE REWARD OF THE JUST.

Shot on Good Friday, commemorated from pulpits on Easter Sunday, Lincoln quickly became a figure of religious significance. At the president's funeral service in the East Room, Phineas Gurley preached: "Though our beloved President is slain, our beloved country is saved. And so we sing of mercy as well as of judgment. . . . When the *sun* has risen, full-orbed and glorious, and a happy reunited people are rejoicing in its light—alas! Alas! It will shine upon his grave."

strife, has done good too. It has demonstrated that a people's government can sustain a national election, in the midst of a great civil war. Until now it has not been known to the world that this was a possibility. . . .

But the rebellion continues; and now that the election is over, may not all, having a common interest, re-unite in a common effort, to save our common country?

Lincoln went back to work, relieved and cheered. "Being only mortal, after all, I should have been a little mortified if I had been beaten in the canvass before the people," Lincoln said. The morning after the election, an assistant secretary in the White House, E. D. Neill, came upon the president in his office. Lincoln took off his glasses and "chatted familiarly" with his clerk, Nicolay recalled. Neill was impressed to note that Lincoln was diligently reviewing the case of a private who had been court-martialed. "Mr. Neill concluded that a man who could go back to his office and resolutely take up the dull routine drudgery of his post with such equanimity, on the morning after a triumphant reelection to the Presidency . . . must be a man full of the elements of greatness, and one who would not lose his self-possession on any probable emergency."

Now that it was over, Lincoln explained what he had been thinking in August, when there had been so much pressure to weaken on emancipation. In a meeting after the election, he reminded the cabinet of the paper he had asked them to sign. On it, Lincoln said, he had "resolved, in case of the election of General McClellan . . . that I would see him and talk matters over with him. I would say, 'General, the election has demonstrated that you are stronger, have more influence with the American people than I. Now let us together, you with your influence and I with all the executive power of the Government, try to save the country. You raise as many troops as you possibly can for this final trial, and I will devote all my energies to assisting and finishing the war.'"

"And the General would answer you 'Yes, Yes;'" Seward said, "and the next day when you saw him again and pressed these views upon him, he would say, 'Yes, Yes;' & so on forever, and would have done nothing at all."

"At least," Lincoln replied, "I should have done my duty and have stood clear before my own conscience."

There it was again: *conscience*. Lincoln believed he was acting according to motives higher than the merely political. "The purposes of the Almighty are perfect, and must prevail, though we erring mortals may fail to accurately perceive them in advance," Lincoln had written to the Quaker Eliza P. Gurney in September. "Meanwhile we must work earnestly in the best light He gives us."

There had been "rain, & clouds, & murky skies, and mud, & general discomfort," the Tennessean Lucy Virginia French wrote after the election in November. "I suppose it is prophetic of the second term of 'Abraham,' assisted by the Tailor of Tennessee.... The only rumor we have heard of Abraham since his re-election is that he has 'proclaimed' all the negros free all over the universe.... God only knows what is before us."

Lincoln knew many white Americans felt this way. He was not so arrogant or so certain that he believed himself or the Union cause infallible. As he had said to Eliza Gurney, all he could do was judge "by the best light He gives us," and hope for the best. "Of course I may err in judgment, but my present position in reference to the rebellion is the result of my best judgment, and according to that best judgment, it is the only position upon which any Executive can or could save the Union," Lincoln had written in September. "Any different policy in regard to the colored man, deprives us of his help, and this is more than we can bear.... Nor is it possible for any Administration to retain the service of these people with the express or implied understanding that upon the first convenient occasion, they are to be re-enslaved. It *can* not be; and it *ought* not to be." That he fought for the *ought* is testament to his moral sensibility.

Lincoln was in a curious humor once the election was done. "It was just after my election in 1860, when the news had been coming in thick and fast all day, and there had been a great 'Hurrah, boys!' so that I was well tired out, and went home to rest, throwing myself down on a lounge in my chamber," he recalled after his reelection. "Opposite where I lay was a bureau, with a swinging-glass upon it, and, looking in that glass, I saw myself reflected, nearly at full length; but my face, I noticed, had *two* separate and distinct images.... I was a little bothered, perhaps startled, and got up and looked in the glass, but the illusion vanished. On lying down again I saw it a second time—plainer, if possible, than before; and then I noticed that one of the faces was a little paler, say five shades, than the other. I got up and the thing melted away."

He could not shake the sensation of worry about the episode. On his telling Mary about it, she, too, fretted. "She thought it was 'a sign' that I was to be elected to a second term of office, and that the paleness of one of the faces was an omen that I should not see life through the last term."

In the world of the tactile, Lincoln quickly followed up on the proposed abolitionist Thirteenth Amendment. "In a great national crisis, like ours, unanimity of action among those seeking a common end is very desirable—almost indispensable," the president told the Congress in December 1864. "And yet no approach to such unanimity is attainable, unless some deference shall be paid to the will of the majority, simply because it is the will of the majority. In this case the common end is the maintenance of the Union; and, among the means to secure that end, such will, through the election, is most clearly declared in favor of such constitutional amendment."

Lincoln left no doubt that slavery in America must—and, on his watch, would—die. "I repeat the declaration made a year ago, that 'while I remain in my present position I shall not attempt to retract or modify the emancipation proclamation, nor shall I return to slavery any person who is free by the terms of that proclamation, or by any of the Acts of Congress,'" the president said after the election. "If the people should, by whatever mode or means, make it an Executive duty to re-enslave such persons, another, and not I, must be their instrument to perform it."

In the fourth year of war, two hundred forty-five years after the arrival of the enslaved at Jamestown, eighty-eight years after the Declaration of Independence, and seventy-six years after the ratification of the Constitution, an American president insisted that a core moral commitment to liberty must survive the vicissitudes of politics, the prejudices of race, and the contests of interest. This is not to separate Lincoln's moral vision from his political sensibilities—an impossibility—but to underscore that he was acting not only for the moment, not only for dominion in the arena, but for all time. His achievement is remarkable not because he was otherworldly, or saintly, or savior-like, but because he was what he was—an imperfect man seeking to bring a more perfect Union into being.

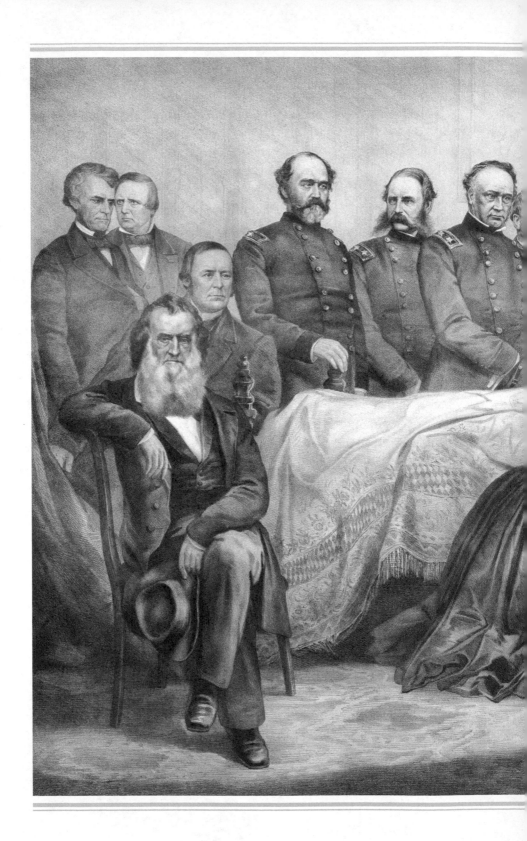

HIS ILLIMITABLE WORK

1864 to the End

This Great Moral Victory

Liberty has been won. The battle for Equality is still pending.
—CHARLES SUMNER, 1865

Whatever may have been the views of your people before the
war, they must be convinced now that slavery is doomed.
—ABRAHAM LINCOLN, to Alexander Stephens at Hampton Roads,
Virginia, February 1865

HIS AWARENESS that he governed best when he thought not
only of pragmatism but of providence was by now acute. "I
should be the veriest shallow and self-conceited blockhead
upon the footstool if, in my discharge of the duties which are put upon
me in this place, I should hope to get along without the wisdom which
comes from God and not from men," Lincoln told Noah Brooks after
the 1864 election. To Francis Carpenter, the painter who had depicted
Lincoln reading the Emancipation Proclamation to the cabinet, the
president said, "Yes, as affairs have turned, it is the central act of my
administration and the great event of the nineteenth century." In a
wartime meeting with a Tennessee woman whose husband, whom she
described as a "religious man," was a Union prisoner, Lincoln remarked: "You say your husband is a religious man; tell him when you
meet him, that I say I am not much of a judge of religion, but that, in
my opinion, the religion that sets men to rebel and fight against their
government, because, as they think, that government does not sufficiently help *some* men to eat their bread on the sweat of *other* men's
faces, is not the sort of religion upon which people can get to heaven!"

Long an extreme on the wide spectrum of American politics, abolitionists believed the 1864 election a turning point. A constitutional
amendment, Wendell Phillips had said during the campaign, would put

"*things* beyond *men* in all time to come." James Ashley had spoken of emancipation as a necessary condition for American survival. "Man's capacity for self-government is on trial before the world," he said, "and we must conquer or the verdict will be against democratic government and in favor of privilege and despotism everywhere. The conspirators and rebels are attempting the destruction of our democratic government, because democracy . . . is opposed to privilege and slavery."

The tide of the time was running in favor of abolition. "We can never have an entire peace in this country as long as the institution of slavery remains," said Representative James S. Rollins of Missouri, himself a slave owner. "We may as well unsheathe the sword and cut the Gordian knot!" "I would rather stand solitary, with my name recorded for this amendment, than to have all the honors which could be heaped upon me by any party in opposition to this proposition," said Representative John Kasson, a Republican from Iowa. "In my judgment, the fate of slavery is sealed," said William S. Holman, Democrat of Indiana, who opposed the amendment. "It dies by the rebellious hand of its votaries. . . . Its fate is determined by the war; by the measures of the war; by the results of the war."

Lincoln and his men lobbied for the requisite two-thirds majority in the House. It was the right thing to do, and the president believed its success, with border state votes, would at last show the Confederacy that war was done. "The passage of this amendment will clinch the whole subject," Lincoln said; "it will bring the war, I have no doubt, rapidly to a close." Federal appointments, legislative favors, even bribes were rumored to be on offer. "Money will certainly do it, if patriotism fails," one of Seward's agents said. "The greatest measure of the nineteenth century," Thaddeus Stevens remarked, "was passed by corruption, aided and abetted by the purest man in America"—Lincoln himself. God might be omnipotent, but in this case He needed a bit of help. And Lincoln provided it.

At four o'clock on the afternoon of Tuesday, January 31, 1865, the House approved the Thirteenth Amendment, 119 to 56, with eight members not voting. Lincoln delivered brief but heartfelt remarks at the White House. The amendment, he was reported to have said, "is a King's cure for all the evils. It winds the whole thing up. . . . He could not but congratulate all present, himself, [and] the country and the whole world upon this great moral victory."

At the last moment, the amendment's passage had been threatened by reports that Jefferson Davis had dispatched envoys to Washington to treat for peace. The prospect of negotiations could have defeated or delayed action on the grounds that talks with the Confederacy should not be encumbered by the Union's pursuit of abolition. Realizing the danger, Lincoln had issued the most calibrated of denials. "So far as I know," the president wrote, "there are no peace commissioners in the city, or likely to be in it." The statement was true if not complete: the conversations, led by Seward, were to take place not in Washington but at Hampton Roads, Virginia. Francis Preston Blair, Sr., was somewhat responsible for the initiative. Blair's idea: End the fighting between the two sections and unite in a common expedition against French operations in Mexico—deploying the Monroe Doctrine in order to focus the energies of North and South on repelling a threat from an encroaching European power.

Lincoln gave Blair permission to go to Richmond. Davis expressed interest in the Mexican proposal, but the American president was not fully invested in the possibility. Nevertheless, after Blair and Davis spoke, Lincoln sent word to Davis that he was "ready to receive any agent whom he, or any influential person now resisting the national authority, may informally send to me, with the view of securing peace to the people of our one common country."

Led by Alexander Stephens, the Confederate representatives rendezvoused with Seward at Hampton Roads. The secretary of state had arrived at Fortress Monroe late on the evening of Wednesday, February 1, aboard the steamer *River Queen,* but an initial conversation the next morning appeared futile. Seward prepared to return to Washington when a surprising telegram arrived from Lincoln. "Induced by a despatch of Gen. Grant, I join you at Fort-Monroe so soon as I can come."

Grant had written to Edwin Stanton that he thought Stephens and his compatriots were "sincere" in their mission. "I fear now their going back without any expression from any one in authority will have a bad influence," Grant wrote. Lincoln took his commanding general's advice. "Say to the gentlemen I will meet them personally at Fortress Monroe as soon as I can get there," Lincoln telegraphed. The president took up headquarters aboard the *River Queen.* Tired from his journey, he would receive the Confederate commissioners after a good night's sleep.

The three-hour meeting began on the morning of Friday, February 3. As the session unfolded, Stephens recalled, a Black man working as a steward "came in occasionally to see if anything was wanted, and to bring in water, cigars, and other refreshments." Lincoln and Stephens reminisced briefly, recalling the Zachary Taylor campaign of 1848 and retelling anecdotes about John Quincy Adams. Lincoln, Stephens recalled, "seemed to be in a splendid humor, and was in excellent spirits." Here was Lincoln in something of a familiar element. Though in a saloon on a steamer, rather than in a courtroom or on a debate platform in Illinois, the president was face-to-face with an audience gathered, ostensibly, to hear opposing points of view and ideally render a verdict based on facts and mutual interest. To make a case in such a venue came naturally to Lincoln.

As he had said many times, peace had to be founded on the restoration of the Union, and the restoration of the Union began with "those who were resisting the laws of the Union to cease that resistance." Stephens tried a different tack, pursuing the Francis Preston Blair thought about a joint campaign against the French in Mexico.

The president cut his old colleague off. "Lincoln appeared to have become impatient and interrupted with the remark that there was but one ground on which propositions could be made or received, and that was the restoration of the national authority over all places in the states," a Confederate diarist wrote. Stephens tried once more, offering "historical instances of nations at war laying aside their quarrel to take up other matters of mutual interest to both." Lincoln was uninterested.

What he was interested in was reiterating his conditions for peace. Surrender would be followed by the restoration of the Southern states' "practical relations to the Union," including representation in Congress. "As to all questions involving rights of property, the courts could determine them," Lincoln said, and he and the Congress "would no doubt be liberal in making restitution of confiscated property, or by indemnity, after the passions that had been excited by the war." At one point Seward even suggested that the Southern states could block the Thirteenth Amendment's passage if they returned in time to vote against ratification.

The Confederates complained that they were being forced into a humiliating position. Seward noted, however, that to yield to "the execution of the laws under the Constitution of the United States, with all its guarantees of and securities for personal and political rights" was hardly punitive. The delegation from Richmond was unmoved. "This ends the peace *fiasco*," the Confederate official Robert G. H. Kean wrote. Briefed on Hampton Roads, Jefferson Davis dismissed Lincoln, whom he called "His Majesty Abraham the First," as an "insolent enemy" to whom the Confederacy would never submit.

The Lincoln of the *River Queen* was resolute on the Union and was devoted to ultimate emancipation. He was seeking reunion without heavy sanction, democracy without guaranteed universal suffrage. And he was, even now, struggling to find a way to make abolition more palatable to white America.

On his return to Washington, Lincoln drafted a message proposing a $400 million compensation plan for slave owners in the seceded states. The money would be paid on two conditions. Half of the sum would be forthcoming if "all resistance to the National authority shall be abandoned and cease, on or before the first day of April." The rest would be distributed "only upon the amendment of the National Constitution recently proposed by Congress becoming valid law, on or before the first day of July." The president was offering the white South a bribe (or, more kindly, an incentive) to lay down their arms and to embrace, with compensation, abolition under the terms of the Thirteenth Amendment.

The cabinet unanimously opposed the president. "It did not meet with favor, [and] was dropped," Gideon Welles told his diary. "The earnest desire of the President to conciliate and effect peace was manifest, but there may be such a thing as so overdoing as to cause a distrust or adverse feeling"—particularly in the Republican-controlled Congress. According to Secretary of the Interior John P. Usher, Lincoln was "somewhat surprised" at the opposition. "How long will the war last?" the president asked the cabinet. When no one replied, he said: "A hundred days. We are spending now in carrying on the war three millions a day, which will amount to all this money, besides all the lives." Greeted by silence, Lincoln gave up. "But you are all opposed to me, and I will not send the message."

It was a busy weekend for the returning president. On Friday night, February 10, he and Grant went to Ford's Theatre. "The audience welcomed the distinguished visitors with the most vociferous cheering, the orchestra struck up 'Hail to the Chief,' and for some moments the performance on the stage was altogether suspended," *The Evening Star* reported. "The President and General Grant remained until the close of the programme," which featured two plays: *Everybody's Friend* and *Love in Livery*. The next afternoon, Lincoln and the First Lady hosted a reception at the White House; one reporter believed it "in many respects the finest of the season." Mrs. Lincoln was resplendent in "a rich lilac colored dress trimmed with black velvet and narrow ribbon, the skirt being set with white satin and velvet formed in the shape of diamonds; a head-dress of point lace and feathers: necklace of pearls, breastpin, white kid gloves and fan."

On Sunday, February 12, 1865, Henry Highland Garnet delivered a sermon in the chamber of the House of Representatives.

Post–Hampton Roads, Lincoln was also in correspondence with Alexander Stephens about prisoner exchanges. Stephens's voice—the voice that had declared slavery and white supremacy to be the cornerstones of the Confederate nation—represented one part of America. Not long after Lincoln returned to Washington another, distinctly different voice was heard. At noon on Sunday, February 12, 1865—it was Lincoln's fifty-sixth birthday—the Reverend Henry Highland Garnet, who had escaped slavery in Maryland and now served as pastor of Washington's Fifteenth Street Presbyterian Church, became the first Black man to speak in the chamber of the House of Representatives. William Slade, Lincoln's White House usher, was an elder of Garnet's church, and Dr. Joseph P. Thompson, pastor of the Broadway Tabernacle Church in New York and a leading abolitionist, recalled that the invitation, which Lincoln reportedly approved, "told the whole story" of America's transformation during the war. Never before had the powers of the nation gathered to hear what Thompson described as "words of plain and stinging truth from the lips of a slave-born negro."

Garnet's sermon came about at the instigation of the Reverend William Henry Channing, a nephew of William Ellery Channing, the New

England minister who had influenced Theodore Parker. A Unitarian like his uncle, the younger Channing was chosen chaplain of the House of Representatives for the Thirty-eighth Congress, which sat from December 1863 to March 1865. He was elected, Channing was told, because he "best represent[ed] the antislavery policy of the Republican Party in Washington."

As chaplain, Channing had pledged that "a woman's voice should give utterance to the conscience of the mothers, wives, sisters, and daughters of the heroes who were risking life and all they held dearest in behalf of the liberties and equal laws of the Republic," and he subsequently invited the Quaker Rachel Howland to preach. Now, after the Thirteenth Amendment, the overture to Garnet fulfilled a second promise of Channing's: "That a colored minister should stand on the speaker's platform, and by that practical illustration, demonstrate that one central principle of the War for Freedom and Union was to prove that 'in Christ' all disciples are alike free, and that all God's children, black and white, are peers in the Father's House."

The audience for Garnet's sermon in the House was racially mixed. As one listener put it, "white and colored" were "all mingled and seemingly comfortable." The Fifteenth Street Presbyterian choir sang "All Hail the Power of Jesus' Name" and "Arise, My Soul, Shake Off Thy Fears"; then the pastor rose to speak in the chamber that had voted only a dozen days before to abolish the system of human bondage into which he had been born.

"Great God!" Garnet preached. "I would as soon attempt to enslave Gabriel or Michael as to enslave a man made in the image of God, and for whom Christ died." He cited Plato, Socrates, Moses, Cyrus, Augustine, Constantine, Ignatius, Polycarp, Maximus, Washington, Jefferson, Patrick Henry, Pope Leo X, and Lafayette—all witnesses to the evils of slavery. "It is often asked when and where will the demands of the reformers of this and coming ages end?" Garnet said. "It is a fair question, and I will answer. When all unjust and heavy burdens shall be removed from every man in the land." Like Lincoln, Garnet saw abolition as essential to democracy. "Upon the total and complete destruction of this accursed sin" of slavery, Garnet preached, "depends the safety and perpetuity of our Republic and its excellent institutions." Work remained to be done: "If slavery has been destroyed merely from *necessity*," Garnet said, "let every class be enfranchised at the dictation of *justice*."

In the course of the sermon the *Weekly Anglo-African* thought "dazzling," Garnet turned to the country's guilt for the sin of slavery and what God would require to expiate it. "We have paid some of the fearful installments, but there are other heavy obligations to be met," Garnet said. "The great day of the nation's judgment has come, and who shall be able to stand?"

Garnet's themes: sin and atonement; race and reconciliation; the will of God and the tragic fact of human failing. In twenty days, the president would offer his own thoughts on these questions, standing not far from the House, on the steps of the East Front for his second inauguration.

As Garnet had preached, and as Lincoln understood, abolition was only the beginning of the work facing the nation. "Liberty has been won," Charles Sumner said. "The battle for Equality is still pending." In January, General Sherman had issued Special Field Order No. 15, which, with Lincoln's approval, assigned four hundred thousand confiscated acres of coastline in South Carolina, Georgia, and Florida— including the Sea Islands—to freed Black people. Sherman added Union mules to the arrangements.

In Syracuse, New York, in the first week of October 1864, Frederick Douglass and others had organized a national Black rights convention. "We want the elective franchise in all the states," the convention declared. "We believe that the highest welfare of this great country will be found . . . by establishing one law for the white and colored people alike."

Lincoln knew that a central postwar concern was how "to keep the rebellious populations from overwhelming and outvoting the loyal minority." One solution: Black suffrage, and Louisiana was long a test case on the issue. "Nearly all the free persons of color read and write," said the former Union captain Arnold Bertonneau, a free Black man and leader in New Orleans. "The free people have always been on the side of law and good order, always peaceful and self-sustaining, always loyal." Excluded from the ballot box as the state was being reconstructed, Bertonneau and the Black newspaper publisher Jean Baptiste Roudanez went to Washington to lobby the president for the franchise. "We are men; treat us as such," read a petition that Bertonneau and Roudanez presented to Lincoln. "The right to vote must be secured," Bertonneau publicly argued; "the doors of our public schools must be opened, that our children, side by side, may study from the same books, and . . . learn the great truth that God 'created of one blood all nations of men to dwell on all the face of the earth'; so will caste, founded on prejudice against color, disappear."

Moved, Lincoln had made his private suggestion to Governor Hahn about extending suffrage to some Black people. For the moment, however, the president was unwilling to declare himself in favor of the ballot for Black people—a failure Charles Sumner obliquely criticized when he denounced the proposed Louisiana constitution, which required congressional approval and which did not include Black suffrage, as the product of "criminal conjunction with the spirit of caste."

Sumner prevailed in the Senate, and the Louisiana constitution was defeated. Frederick Douglass thanked the senator profusely. "The friends of freedom all over the country have looked to you and confided in you, of all men in the United States Senate, during all this terrible war," Douglass told Sumner. "They will look to you all the more now that peace dawns, and the final settlement of our national troubles is at hand. God grant you strength equal to your day and your duties, is my prayer and that of millions!"

Sumner articulated a broad and inclusive view of the future. "I insist that the rebel states shall not come back except on the footing of the Declaration of Independence, with all persons equal before the law, and government founded on the consent of the governed," he wrote to John Bright in March, continuing:

> In other words, there shall be no discrimination on account of color. If all whites vote, then must all blacks. . . . It is sometimes said "What! Let the freedman, yesterday a slave, vote?" I am inclined to think that there is more harm in refusing than in conceding the franchise. It is said that they are as intelligent as the Irish just arrived; but the question has become immensely practical in this respect: Without their votes we cannot establish stable governments in the Rebel States. Their votes are as necessary as their muskets; of this I am satisfied. Without them, the old enemy will reappear, and under the forms of law take possession of the governments, choose magistrates and officers, and in alliance with the Northern Democracy, put us all in peril again, [and] postpone

the day of tranquility. . . . To my mind, the nation is now bound by self-interest—ay, self-defense—to be thoroughly just. The Declaration of Independence has pledges which have never been redeemed. We must redeem them, at least as regards the rebel states which have fallen under our jurisdiction. Mr. Lincoln is slow in accepting truths. I have reminded him that if he would say the word we might settle this question promptly and rightly. He hesitates.

Lincoln approved important bills on Friday, March 3, the day before his second inauguration. One declared that the wife and children "of any person" who had served in the military "shall . . . be forever free." Another authorized the creation of "a bureau of refugees, freedmen, and abandoned lands," to be popularly known as the Freedmen's Bureau. The legislation passed, Nathan Daniels remarked, "after many trials and much tribulation of spirit."

Led by General Oliver O. Howard, who had lost his right arm in combat and received the Medal of Honor, the bureau gave the federal government hitherto unusual power to shape the lives of individual people. "The Freedmen's Bureau was the most extraordinary and far-reaching institution of social uplift that America has ever attempted," W.E.B. Du Bois observed in 1935. "It was a government guardianship for the relief and guidance of white and black labor from a feudal agrarianism to modern farming and industry." In Oliver Howard's opinion, "scarcely any subject that has to be legislated upon in civil society failed, at one time or another, to demand the action of this singular Bureau."

Under Howard, the Freedmen's Bureau that was brought into being with Lincoln's signature was to feed the hungry, clothe the impoverished, provide health care, establish schools, negotiate fair wages, and offer rudimentary judicial protections. It was not everything, but it was something—something tangible, the beginning of a kind of reparation for the system of slavery that Lincoln had decided could not stand.

Observers sensed that a moral rudder was guiding the president's statecraft. "The great shifter, the great political shuffler, Abraham Lincoln, some day or other will turn up a radical," the translator Adam Gurowski observed. William Lloyd Garrison told the president that he, for one, was certain of ultimate victory: "I am sure you will consent to no compromise that will leave a slave in his fetters." Nothing about the work ahead would be simple. "This country was formed for the *white,* not for the black man," a Southern sympathizer remarked during the war; "and looking upon *African Slavery* from the same stand-point held by the noble framers of our constitution, I for one, have ever considered *it* one of the greatest blessings (both for themselves and us) that God has ever bestowed upon a favored nation."

So said John Wilkes Booth.

CHAPTER TWENTY-SIX

The Almighty Has His Own Purposes

Men are not flattered by being shown that there has been a
difference of purpose between the Almighty and them. To
deny it, however, in this case, is to deny that there is a God
governing the world.

—ABRAHAM LINCOLN, 1865

T HE FRIDAY EVENING BEFORE the second inauguration was wet,
foggy, and chaotic. As night fell on March 3, 1865, there were
"driving mists and black skies, rendering it an unpleasant job for
new arrivals to pick their way through the muddy streets of a strange
city in discouraging quest of lodgings," *The Evening Star* reported. Firemen bearing torches created a "silvery haze" in the night; the Capitol,
too, seemed a warm and inviting beacon in the gloom. The Stars and
Stripes flying above the houses of Congress was illuminated "in radiant
relief."

Partly because the Capitol offered shelter from the elements, the
final hours of the congressional session turned the House into "almost
a Pandemonium," Nathan Daniels wrote. "The Rules were in abeyance
and the ladies permitted to come upon the floor." The House was exciting; the Senate, less so. "Within the Capitol curious crowds vibrated
between the two Houses," *The Evening Star* wrote, "now interesting
themselves with the bustle, confusion and noisy whirl of the House
proceedings, and anon taking a sedative by listening to the tranquil debate of the Senate upon the question whether the Smithsonian trust
fund interest should or not be paid in gold; and if so, what about the
Indian annuities."

After a brief but pitched storm struck early on Saturday morning,
spectators—Black and white—climbed Capitol Hill for Lincoln's second inauguration. The atmosphere was celebratory. But the racially
mixed crowd would have to wait. There was business to conduct in-

doors first: the swearing-in of the new vice president, Andrew Johnson, in the Senate chamber.

Governor Johnson was fresh from Tennessee, where he had addressed a state convention that abolished slavery but opposed Black suffrage. "You took me by the hand when a poor and friendless boy, and led me to honor, and by God's blessing, in the close of my little political career, I shall try to be your friend still and protect your interests," Johnson had said in Nashville on Thursday, January 12, 1865. He was not feeling well as he left for Washington. A long night of drinking on the evening before the inauguration did not help matters. On the morning of the ceremony, Johnson arrived at the Capitol and met with Hannibal Hamlin. To steady himself, the incoming vice president asked the incumbent for a favor. "Mr. Hamlin, I am not well, and need a stimulant," Johnson said. "Have you any whiskey?" He then drank three glasses, straight.

It was not the best of choices. Hamlin had hoped that Johnson, "a hard drinker," would be able to "stand the liquor he had taken," but events soon proved the gentleman from Maine wrong. After Johnson walked into the chamber "arm in arm" with Hamlin—one suspects the gesture of intimacy was as much practical as symbolic—the Tennessean, "in a state of manifest intoxication," delivered a disastrous speech. "Johnson," Hamlin murmured, "stop!" "In vain did Hamlin nudge [Johnson] from behind, audibly reminding him that the hour for the inauguration ceremony had passed," Noah Brooks reported, but Johnson "kept on, though the President of the United States sat before him patiently waiting for his tirade to be over." Johnson finally took the oath of office, adding, at various points, "I can say that with perfect propriety." Wielding the Bible, Johnson called out, "I kiss this Book in the face of my nation of the United States." "All this is in wretched bad taste," Attorney General James Speed remarked. "The man is certainly deranged."

He was surely drunk. Johnson, it had been said, "enjoyed the meanest whiskey hot from the still, . . . stuff which would vomit a gentleman." Lincoln shrugged off the scene. "I have known Andy Johnson for many years," he said to Treasury secretary Hugh McCulloch afterward. "He made a bad slip the other day, but you need not be scared; Andy ain't a drunkard." Still, the New York *World* referred to the new vice president as a "drunken boor," and *The Times* of London said his "behav-

ior was that of an illiterate, vulgar, and drunken rowdy." Said Senator
Zachariah Chandler, "the Vice President Elect was too drunk to perform his duties & disgraced himself. . . . I was never so mortified in my
life, had I been able to find a hole I would have dropped through it out
of sight."

Blessedly, attention shifted quickly from the confines of the Senate
chamber to the East Front. Given the recent rain, no one had been sure
that they would be able to hold the presidential ceremony outdoors,
but things were clear enough at midday. As he had in 1861, Lincoln
looked across a mass of faces and could see his old congressional quarters to his right. Standing near the president, William Henry Channing
noted that "white and colored troops were ranked shoulder to shoulder, and . . . freedmen in their rough plantation garments stood side by
side with fashionably attired citizens from the Free States" as Lincoln
"spoke the sublimely simple, touchingly humble, yet prophetically
hopeful words of his second inaugural—words never to be forgotten so
long as English is a living tongue."

In his address, Lincoln squarely named slavery as the cause of the
conflict. "To strengthen, perpetuate, and extend [slavery] was the object for which the insurgents would rend the Union, even by war," the
president said. "It may seem strange that any men should dare to ask a
just God's assistance in wringing their bread from the sweat of other
men's faces; but let us judge not that we be not judged." Here Lincoln
had moved from Genesis to the Gospels. In raising the question of
judgment, he was quoting the words of Jesus in Matthew: "Judge not,
that ye be not judged. . . . And why beholdest thou the mote that is in
thy brother's eye, but considerest not the beam that is in thine own
eye?" In this charge against hypocrisy, Jesus calls on his listeners to heed
him and shares, in the same chapter, this parable:

> Therefore whosoever heareth these sayings of mine, and doeth
> them, I will liken him unto a wise man, which built his house
> upon a rock: And the rain descended, and the floods came, and
> the winds blew, and beat upon that house; and it fell not: for it was
> founded upon a rock. And every one that heareth these sayings of
> mine, and doeth them not, shall be likened unto a foolish man,
> which built his house upon the sand: And the rain descended, and
> the floods came, and the winds blew, and beat upon that house;
> and it fell: and great was the fall of it.

The American house had nearly fallen. Lincoln's implication was that it had teetered because the slave interest had not taken to heart the gospel of doing unto others as you would have them do unto you. From this sin the Civil War had arisen. Still, the president was not in a condemnatory spirit. Lincoln did not assume himself or his allies to be morally superior. He had tried to build his house, and the house of the Union, upon a rock, but that did not mean that he took any pleasure in watching the collapse of his neighbor's house, which had been built on sand.

He was not yet done with marshaling the Bible. Lincoln quoted Jesus again—"'Woe unto the world because of offences! For it must needs be that offences come; but woe to that man by whom the offence cometh'"—continuing: "If we shall suppose that American Slavery is one of those offences which, in the providence of God, must needs come, but which, having continued through His appointed time, He now wills to remove, and that He gives to both North and South, this terrible war, as the woe due to those by whom the offence came, shall we discern therein any departure from those divine attributes which the believers in a Living God always ascribe to Him?"

The "Woe unto the world" quotation also came from Matthew. In the chapter, Jesus is speaking of the kingdom of heaven—a place where hierarchy is not determined by birth or race. "At the same time came the disciples unto Jesus, saying, Who is the greatest in the kingdom of heaven? And Jesus called a little child unto him, and set him in the midst of them, And said, Verily I say unto you, Except ye be converted, and become as little children, ye shall not enter into the kingdom of heaven. Whosoever therefore shall humble himself as this little child, the same is greatest in the kingdom of heaven." Such was the role of virtue, but Jesus knew the inevitability of sin and the persistence of human ambition. Here, then, Jesus made the remark about the "woe" of "offences," and went on: "Wherefore if thy hand or thy foot offend thee, cut them off, and cast them from thee: it is better for thee to enter into life halt or maimed, rather than having two hands or two feet to be cast into everlasting fire." The lesson was hyperbolic, but the point was clear. The faithful were called to remove the means by which sin was perpetuated. And slavery was one such means. By implication, to hold another in bondage was the gravest of "offences." As Jesus said, "But whoso shall offend one of these little ones which believe in me, it were better for him that a millstone were hanged about his neck, and *that* he were drowned in the depth of the sea."

"Fondly do we hope—fervently do we pray—that this mighty scourge of war may speedily pass away," Lincoln went on. "Scourge" was a crucial word. Gurley had spoken of the "direst scourge" of civil war after Sumter, and the term has been thought to have evoked images of punishing the enslaved. There is another possibility. For many, "this mighty scourge of war" could have brought to mind the Roman torture of the Christian Messiah before the crucifixion. In Mark and in Matthew, the pain of Golgotha is foreseen: "And they shall mock him, and shall scourge him, and shall spit upon him, and shall kill him: and the third day he shall rise again." In John, the prophecy is fulfilled: "Then Pilate therefore took Jesus, and scourged him. And the soldiers platted a crown of thorns, and put it on his head, and they put on him a purple robe, And said, Hail, King of the Jews! And they smote him with their hands." By connecting the war with the suffering of the Passion, Lincoln was speaking in terms that suggested the Christian drama of victory through defeat, and life through death, was playing out anew. The darkness of Good Friday was but a gateway—a miserable and bloody gateway, but a gateway nonetheless—to the light of Easter, and of resurrection. Jesus had risen again. Now America might, too.

But only after the expiation of the sin of slavery—an expiation Lincoln said could require "every drop of blood drawn with the lash . . . be paid by another drawn with the sword." And if this were so, "as was said three thousand years ago, so still it must be said, 'the judgments of the Lord, are true and righteous altogether.'"

The "judgments of the Lord" quotation was from the Nineteenth Psalm, the totality of which speaks to the centrality of the Lord's injunctions:

The heavens declare the glory of God; and the firmament sheweth his handywork. . . .

The law of the LORD *is* perfect, converting the soul: the testimony of the LORD *is* sure, making wise the simple.

The statutes of the LORD *are* right, rejoicing the heart: the commandment of the LORD *is* pure, enlightening the eyes.

The fear of the LORD *is* clean, enduring for ever: the judgments of the LORD *are* true *and* righteous altogether.

More to be desired *are they* than gold, yea, than much fine gold: sweeter also than honey and the honeycomb.

Moreover by them is thy servant warned: *and* in keeping of them *there is* great reward. . . .

Keep back thy servant also from presumptuous *sins*; let them not have dominion over me: then shall I be upright, and I shall be innocent from the great transgression.

Let the words of my mouth, and the meditation of my heart, be acceptable in thy sight, O LORD, my strength, and my redeemer.

Note the objects of the Psalmist's praise: "the law of the Lord," "the statutes of the Lord," "the fear of the Lord." "Fear" in the Hebrew sense of the word is not only negative, as one might fear danger or loss. It is better understood as an acknowledgment and appreciation of love and majesty. To Lincoln, the sum of the law was love of neighbor and of God (likely in that order); he had little to no interest in the niceties of· more specific biblical rules. The "judgments of the Lord" which are "true and righteous altogether" were not only sanctions and retributions, though there were surely—as evidenced in the Civil War—such judgments. In the Hebrew Bible, "judgment" encompassed the rule of God in its entirety: punishment *and* reward, bounty *and* burden, pain *and* mercy. The word also connoted "justice" and could be translated, in different contexts, as "take up" or "defend." As Isaiah wrote, "Learn to do well; seek judgment, relieve the oppressed, judge the fatherless, plead for the widow." To "judge the fatherless," for example, was to *care for* the orphaned—an element of the broader idea of "judgment" as it would have been understood to readers and hearers of Hebrew.

The judgments of which Lincoln was speaking, then, were manifestations of providence—of God's rule over the world. The president was summoning the nation to see itself as a player in a divinely charged—and ultimately merciful and just—creation. Such was certainly the intent of the Psalmist, who had gone on to say that the "judgments of the Lord" were "more to be desired . . . than gold, yea, than much fine gold: sweeter also than honey and the honeycomb. Moreover by them is thy servant warned: *and* in keeping of them *there is* great reward."

This was the essence of Lincoln's vision: God had revealed Himself in the history of Israel, given commandments, made promises. The business of humankind was to live in history, obey those command-

ments, and one day avail itself of those promises. Faith was rewarded—
sometimes. The kind and the generous were rewarded—sometimes.
The upright and the loving were rewarded—sometimes. Why not all
the time? We did not know. All we could know was that our duty lay in
seeking to do right as we understood it and hope for the best. It was not
the neatest or most satisfactory of explanations, but it had the virtue of
being rooted in experience.

The reaction to the speech at the Capitol had been muted. A number of the Black people in the crowd were moved and enthusiastic,
but all in all the speech was too dense, too complex, to provoke a spontaneous emotional response. The audience realized they were hearing
something more than a conventional address. Many appear to have listened with care. "They seemed to hang on his words as though they
were meat and drink," an observer recalled. "And when he concluded
the last paragraph, beginning, 'With malice toward none, with charity
for all,' which fell like a benediction from heaven, the shout of the people seemed to rise to the very sky."

The concluding cheer was the exception, not the rule. "The whole
proceeding was wonderfully quiet, earnest, and solemn," Douglass recalled, noting a "leaden stillness about the crowd." The quiet did not
surprise Lincoln. "I expect the [Second Inaugural] to wear as well as—
perhaps better than—anything I have produced; but I believe it is not
immediately popular," he wrote to Thurlow Weed. "Men are not flattered by being shown that there has been a difference of purpose between the Almighty and them. To deny it, however, in this case, is to
deny that there is a God governing the world."

Lincoln had been preaching, and his message was neither wholly sectarian nor wholly secular. *The National Intelligencer* offered a useful caution, warning that "the written laws which men enact for their
government" should not be "construed according to the consciences
and religious theories of those temporarily entrusted with their protection and execution." Fair enough—but Lincoln's point was that the
government of a people required attention to, and the elevation of, the
motives of that people. To appeal solely to material self-interest or to
the appetite for power risked plunging the nation into the state of nature of which he had read long ago in Volney's *Ruins*. Lincoln knew that
theocracy was no more the answer than slavocracy was, for both were
about dominion rather than deliberation.

Observers sensed the power of Lincoln's framing of the American story in a moral context. "That rail-splitting lawyer is one of the wonders of the day," Charles Francis Adams, Jr., wrote to his father in London. "Once at Gettysburg and now again on a greater occasion he has shown a capacity for rising to the demands of the hour. . . . This inaugural strikes me in its grand simplicity and directness as being for all time the historical keynote of this war"—and, Lincoln might have added, of this world. "I am taken captive by so striking an utterance as this," William Gladstone remarked. "I see in it the effect of sharp trial when rightly borne to raise men to a higher level of thought and feeling." "The leading characteristic of the address is its devout recognition of the moral and religious elements involved in the contest, in words which the people of the United States, as a Christian nation, will welcome from their Chief Magistrate and approve," the *Chicago Tribune* wrote. "The Inaugural was short, humane, and satisfactory," Nathan Daniels wrote. "Humanity stamped the document throughout."

"Four years ago," the Janesville, Wisconsin, *Daily Gazette* observed, "Traitors lurked beneath the shadow of the capitol, and infested every department of the government. The Chief Magistrate of the nation had been compelled to seek the Federal city in disguise. . . . The dagger of the assassin was whetted to strike down the man whom the people had chosen to rule over them. It was doubtful whether he would be allowed to take the oath of office. What has transpired since then is a matter of history, and every child is familiar with the events that have been written in blood. We have passed through many a dark hour since then, and there were times when the overthrow of Republican institutions seemed to be not improbable. But He who holds the destinies of nations in the hollow of his hand, has permitted us to see the bow of promise hanging once more resplendent overhead."

Yet others—including many Republican and, naturally, white Southern voices—thought Lincoln had missed the mark. "He makes no boasts of what he has done, or promises of what he will do," Henry Raymond's *New York Times* wrote. "All he does is simply to advert to the cause of the war; . . . and to drop an earnest exhortation that all will now stand by the right and strive for a peace that will be just and lasting." "With a soul loaded down with the guilt of wholesale murder, robbery, and arson," the Petersburg, Virginia, *Daily Express* wrote of the speech, Lincoln had committed "the greatest and blackest catalogue of offenses against God, his country, humanity, that one man on the American continent could present for the world's abhorrence." *The Spirit of Democracy* newspaper in Woodsfield, Ohio, was contemptuous. "Don't fail to read the Inaugural Addresses of President Lincoln and Vice President Johnson," the paper wrote. "They are a disgrace to our nation. The pretended sanctity of the one is not a whit better than the drunken maudlin of the other."

The New York Herald dismissed the address as "a little speech of 'glittering generalities' used only to fill in the program." The "glittering generalities" criticism evoked an older debate over whether the Declaration of Independence was lovely but empty language—a debate in which Lincoln had taken part some years before. To call Jefferson's words "glittering generalities," Lincoln had argued in 1859, had the "object and effect" of "supplanting the principles of free government, and restoring those of classification, caste, and legitimacy." The same could be said of Lincoln's Second Inaugural Address—to sneer at his sentiments was to sneer at the possibilities of democracy.

The president took Mrs. Lincoln on a drive in the afternoon, stopping in at Willard's for Mary to call on a friend. The president met with the Perseverance Fire Company of Philadelphia at four P.M.; the doors of the White House opened to the public at eight. As the Marine Band played, thousands of well-wishers descended on the president, who had stationed himself in the East Room.

Frederick Douglass was among those who arrived to pay respects. "The usual reception was given at the executive mansion, and though no colored persons had ever ventured to present themselves on such occasions, it seemed, now that freedom had become the law of the republic, and colored men were on the battle-field mingling their blood with that of white men . . . that it was not too great an assumption for a colored man to offer his congratulations to the President with those of other citizens," Douglass recalled.

Mrs. Louise Dorsey, the wife of a prominent Black businessman in Philadelphia, agreed to accompany Douglass. They "joined in the grand procession of citizens from all parts of the country," he recalled. "I had for some time looked upon myself as a man, but now in this multitude of the élite of the land, I felt myself a man among men."

This newfound sense of belonging was soon disrupted. Two policemen at the White House door "took me rudely by the arm and ordered me to stand back, for their directions were to admit no persons of my color," Douglass recalled. "I told the officers I was quite sure there must be some mistake, for no such order could have emanated from President Lincoln; and that if he knew I was at the door he would desire my admission." Seeing that he and Mrs. Dorsey were "obstructing the doorway, and were not easily pushed aside," the guards said they would take the visitors in. But the sudden grace was an act of subterfuge: The plan was to lead Douglass and Mrs. Dorsey in one door and through another exit. "We halted so soon as we saw the trick," Douglass recalled.

"You have deceived me," Douglass said to the officers. "I shall not go out of this building till I see President Lincoln."

Fortunately, at that point a man who recognized Douglass came by. Douglass asked him a favor: "Be so kind as to say to Mr. Lincoln that Frederick Douglass is detained by officers at the door." On hearing that Douglass was trying to appeal directly to the president, the guards wavered and at last gave way. Douglass and Mrs. Dorsey were soon shown into the East Room. Lincoln towered above the others—like "a mountain pine," Douglass recalled.

"Here comes my friend Douglass," the president said. "I am glad to see you."

Douglass's contrasting experiences at the White House said much about race in America. The near-denial of entry spoke to the old order; Lincoln's respect for Douglass hinted at the hope of a new one. "It came out that the officers at the White House had received no orders from Mr. Lincoln, or from anyone else," Douglass recalled. "They were simply complying with an old custom, the outgrowth of slavery, as dogs will sometimes rub their necks, long after their collars are removed, thinking they are still there." He continued:

I have found in my experience that the way to break down an unreasonable custom, is to contradict it in practice. To be sure in pursuing this course I have had to contend not merely with the white race, but with the black. The one has condemned me for my presumption in daring to associate with it, and the other for pushing myself where it takes for granted I am not wanted. I am pained to think that the latter objection springs largely from a consciousness of inferiority, for as colors alone can have nothing against each other, and the conditions of human association are founded upon character rather than color, and character depends upon mind and morals, there can be nothing blameworthy in people thus equal meeting each other on the plane of civil or social rights.

The next morning, a Sunday, the Lincolns returned to the Capitol for church services in the House of Representatives. The Methodist bishop Matthew Simpson of Philadelphia, a devoted Union man, was scheduled to preach at eleven o'clock. In his diary, Simpson recorded the bare facts of the morning: "Preached in Capitol House of Representatives to an immense throng—text: 'If I Be Lifted Up.'" The morning was "pleasant and cheerful," the newspapers reported, and the capital's leading lights gathered in the chamber for services. Guests included the president and the First Lady, Chief Justice Salmon P. Chase, Speaker of the House Schuyler Colfax, Secretary of State William Seward, and Secretary of War Edwin Stanton. The chamber's furnishings had been designed by Thomas U. Walter, the Architect of the Capitol; the members' desks and chairs were in Renaissance revival, a Victorian fashion. The fronts of the desks bore a carved globe with the word "America." The tops of the chairs were decorated with a shield of stars and stripes set between oak and laurel branches. Flags hung behind the Speaker's chair, and there was a single fresco: *Cornwallis Sues for Cessation of Hostilities Under the Flag of Truce.*

The president entered the chamber bearing, as he often did, a walking stick and took his seat in front of the speaker's rostrum. Music was played, and then Bishop Simpson began to preach. His was a message of unity, of mercy, and of love. A good preacher, he knew how to connect the particular with the universal. The day before, during the inauguration, the sun had come out, brightening the moment Lincoln rose to address the nation. The bishop recalled just this detail in his sermon. "He spoke of the power of Christ to diminish war and promote peace," an observer recalled, "and . . . added: 'I am not much of a believer in signs and omens; but when, yesterday, just as the old Administration expired and the new one began, the rifted clouds let God's sunshine flow, I could not but regard it as an augury of returning peace, and that the war would soon close, and the new Administration would be one of peace.'"

The mention of peace startled the crowd, which was so accustomed to war. "Instantly, as if by electricity, the audience were stirred," an observer recalled; "they cheered earnestly; many rose to their feet; hats were thrown up; men embraced each other, and wept and shouted." Seated in his chair, absorbing the words and the moment, the president of the United States began to rap his walking stick on the floor of the House chamber. So much had happened; so much, he knew, was still to come. On this Sunday morning, in the heart of an embattled and frail democracy, Abraham Lincoln was briefly overcome. And he wept.

The Methodist bishop Matthew Simpson noted that the sun had emerged during the second inauguration—"an augury," he said, "of returning peace."

That evening, Nathan Daniels brought two spiritualist friends to see the First Lady in the Green Room on the first floor of the White House. The president was "engaged in his own Apartments," and Mary was with Tad and her cousin General John Blair Smith Todd. One of Daniels's friends "described little Willie Lincoln, said that she saw him around his mother, and that he had a beautiful vase of flowers for her," Daniels told his diary. She "described the vase, which Mrs Lincoln recognized as one her son had in his room at the time of his death."

The last ceremonial inaugural event was a ball to be held on Monday night, March 6, at the Patent Office building, an elegant space lately a makeshift hospital for the Union wounded.* "I have been up to look at the dance and supper-rooms, for the inauguration ball, at the Patent office; and I could not help thinking, what a different scene they presented to my view a while since, fill'd with a crowded mass of the worst wounded of the war, brought in from second Bull Run, Antietam, and

---

* The Patent Office of the Civil War era is now home to the Smithsonian's Museum of American Art and the National Portrait Gallery.

Fredericksburgh," Walt Whitman wrote. "To-night, beautiful women, perfumes, the violins' sweetness, the polka and the waltz; then the amputation, the blue face, the groan, the glassy eye of the dying, the clotted rag, the odor of wounds and blood, and many a mother's son amid strangers, passing away untended there." Blue and gold sofas and chairs were brought in for the president and his party; the large marble-floored halls were festooned with American flags.

The president asked Charles Sumner to come along. "Unless you send me word to the contrary," Lincoln wrote to the senator, "I shall this evening call with my carriage at your house, to take you with me to the Inauguration Ball." The president and Sumner were at odds over Reconstruction. Lincoln, who wanted to use military powers as commander in chief and a generosity of spirit to run Reconstruction, held that "we shall sooner have the fowl by hatching eggs than by smashing it"; Sumner, who favored congressional control and a firm hand against the white South, disagreed. "The eggs of crocodiles can produce only crocodiles," the senator remarked, "and it is not easy to see how eggs laid by military power can be hatched into an American state."

Yet they were friendly, and Mary wanted the senator there, and so all was arranged. The president's party arrived about ten thirty in the evening. "Mrs. Lincoln . . . wore a white silk skirt and bodice, an elaborately-worked white lace dress over the silk skirt," the Washington *Evening Star* reported. "The President was dressed in black, with white kid gloves." Lincoln put on a cheerful face, but shrewd reporters saw something else. "Mr. Lincoln was evidently trying to throw off care for the time; but with rather ill success, and looked very old," *The New York Times* wrote; "yet he seemed pleased and gratified, as he was greeted by the people." Mrs. Lincoln made a favorable impression. "She looked exceedingly well with her soft, white complexion," the *Times* said, "and her toilet was faultless." After an hour and a half, Lincoln was shown into the "supper-room."

Oysters, duck, beef, veal, and dozens of sweets filled the 250-foot buffet table—and the hungry crowd swarmed it. "The floor of the supper room," *The Evening Star* wrote, "was soon sticky, pasty and oily with wasted confections, mashed cake, and debris of fowl and meat." The president made his exit, returning to the White House through the darkened streets. It had been a long few days.

The 1865 inaugural ball, Walt Whitman observed, was held in a hall that had only recently been "fill'd with a crowded mass of the worst wounded of the war."

Perhaps weakened by the strain of the close of the congressional session, the inauguration, the endless White House reception that day, the inaugural ball, and another four-hour afternoon entertainment hosted by the First Lady on Saturday, March 11, the president became ill. "Mr. Lincoln is reported quite sick to-day, and has denied to himself all visitors," *The New York Herald* reported. The cabinet met with him in his bedroom on Tuesday, March 14.

Something new was on Lincoln's mind—a desperate bid by the Confederacy to enlist the enslaved in the white Southern army. "At the time of the second inauguration the rebellion was apparently vigorous, defiant, and formidable, but in reality weak, dejected, and desperate," Frederick Douglass recalled. "It had reached that verge of madness when it had called upon the negro for help to fight against the freedom which he so longed to find, for the bondage he would escape—against Lincoln the emancipator [and] for Davis the enslaver." From his vantage point, Robert E. Lee saw no other path to victory. The enlistment and arming of Black men as soldiers was "not only expedient but necessary," the Confederate commander wrote. But at a steep price: "Those who are employed should be freed," Lee wrote. "It would be neither just nor wise . . . to require them to serve as slaves."

The debate in Richmond fascinated Lincoln. In his life, he told an Indiana regiment on Friday, March 17, he had "heard many arguments—or strings of words meant to pass for arguments—intended to show that the negro ought to be a slave." If the enslaved were now to "really fight to keep himself a slave, it will be a far better argument why [he] should remain a slave than I have ever before heard. We have to reach the bottom of the insurgent resources; and that they employ, or seriously think of employing, the slaves as soldiers, gives us glimpses of the bottom."

He wanted to see the bottom for himself. Near the Virginia front, Grant had headquartered himself next to the James and Appomattox rivers at City Point, about twenty miles from Richmond. "Can you not visit City Point for a day or two?" the general wrote to Lincoln. "Had already thought of going immediately after the next rain," the president replied. "Will go sooner if any reason for it." He chartered the *River Queen,* familiar to him from the Hampton Roads conference. As Lincoln prepared to slip away from Washington, he met with Sumner, who was bearing a letter he had received from the Duchess of Argyll, Elizabeth Georgiana Campbell, an aristocratic abolitionist. "We feel great confidence in the President," she wrote, adding that she had liked an article on Lincoln in *Macmillan's Magazine.*

Written by the Englishman Goldwin Smith, the piece the duchess mentioned had noted the presidential characteristics evident at Gettysburg and in Lincoln's second inaugural address:

> If he suffers himself to be guided by events, it is not because he loses sight of principles, much less because he is drifting, but because he deliberately recognizes in events the manifestation of moral forces, which he is bound to consider, and the behests of Providence, which he is bound to obey. He neither floats at random between the different sections of his party, nor does he aban-

don himself to the impulse of any one of them, whether it be that of the extreme Abolitionists or that of the mere Politicians; but he treats them all as elements of the Union party, which it is his task to hold together, and conduct as a combined army to victory.

At one o'clock on the afternoon of Thursday, March 23, Lincoln quietly left Washington by water from the Sixth Street wharf, bound for a visit with his actual army—one on the cusp of ultimate success, the capture of the enemy capital.

It was not a pleasant trip. What Edwin Stanton called a "furious gale" came up not long after the *River Queen* got under way. Apparently affected by contaminated drinking water, Lincoln suffered from an upset stomach severe enough to require a new supply. Traveling with Mary and Tad, the president arrived at City Point about eight hours after leaving the capital. Early the next morning, Robert Lincoln came aboard. Though the president was still unwell—he ate little—he walked to Grant's headquarters with Robert and Rear Admiral David Porter and took a military train to Petersburg, the scene of an attempted, but repulsed, Confederate thrust near Fort Stedman. "Robert just now tells me there was a little rumpus up the line this morning," Lincoln had telegraphed Stanton, "ending about where it began."

On horseback, consulting a map marked with troop positions, Lincoln toured parts of Petersburg, watched the burial of the dead, inspected captured Confederate prisoners, and brought some of the wounded back to City Point on his train. What had long been largely remote was now immediate: The action Lincoln had for years monitored from the White House and the small Telegraph Office was fully evident in the March sunlight.

Back at Grant's headquarters, the president took a seat at a campfire. "The smoke curled about his head during certain shiftings of the wind," an officer recalled, "and he brushed it away from time to time by waving his right hand in front of his face." Still a bit ill, Lincoln chose not to dine with Grant and returned to the *River Queen* for the evening. In all, the president would spend sixteen days in Virginia, awaiting the anticipated fall of Richmond. From afar—he was visiting Rome—George McClellan sensed what was coming. "We are in daily expectation of hearing something decisive . . . —the last meagre accounts we have look very much as if Secesh were pretty nearly on his last legs—tho' war is a very uncertain game," McClellan wrote to Samuel L. M. Barlow.

The interval was nerve-racking. In Grant's tent at City Point, Lincoln noticed three kittens, "little wanderers" who had lost their mother. Moved by their "mewing," he picked them up to comfort them. "Poor little creatures, don't cry; you'll be taken good care of," Lincoln said. To an officer, the president added, "Colonel, I hope you will see that these poor little motherless waifs are given plenty of milk and treated kindly."

"I will see, Mr. President," the colonel replied, "that they are taken in charge by the cook of our mess, and are well cared for."

The Union officer Horace Porter was struck by the scene. "It was a curious sight at an army headquarters, upon the eve of a great military crisis in the nation's history, to see the hand which had affixed the signature to the Emancipation Proclamation, and had signed the commissions of all the heroic men who served in the cause of the Union . . . tenderly caressing three stray kittens," Porter recalled.

It was not only curious—it was revealing. In the midst of carnage, fresh from battlefields strewn with the corpses of those he had ordered into battle, Lincoln was seeking some kind of affirmation of life, some evidence of innocence, some sense of kindliness amid cruelty. The orphaned kittens were a small thing, but they were *there,* and his focus on their welfare was a passing human moment in a vast drama. He could not control much. But he could control this.

His wife was another matter. Her jealousy of other women persisted. Believing (wrongly, as it turned out) that Lincoln had met with the young wife of General Charles Griffin during the City Point visit, she snapped at an officer, "Do you know that I never allow the President to see any woman alone?" At another point, the president was reviewing the troops with Major General Edward O. C. Ord, who commanded the Army of the James. Mrs. Ord was a well-known beauty—"a handsome woman," it has been reported, "and a skilled equestrienne." She had accompanied Lincoln during the review when Mary was delayed by bad roads. Enraged and suffering from the beginnings of a migraine attributed to her banging her head on the roof of the carriage en route, the First Lady unleashed her anger in front of all assembled.

The president "bore it as Christ might have done with an expression of pain and sadness that cut one to the heart, but with supreme calmness and dignity," an observer recalled. "He called her 'mother,' with his old-time plainness; he pleaded with his eyes and tones . . . till she turned on him like a tigress; and then he walked away, hiding that noble, ugly face that we might not catch the full expression of its misery." The First Lady retreated to the *River Queen* and then returned to Washington. The tension between husband and wife did not last long; they were in warm touch by telegraph between City Point and the White House.

As the days passed, the Union forces closed in on Richmond. "The battle now rages furiously," Grant wrote to Lincoln. On Saturday, April 1, at Grant's request, the war correspondent Sylvanus Cadwallader brought Lincoln several Confederate flags captured at the Battle of Five Forks. "Here is something material—something I can see, feel, and understand," the president said as he unfurled them. "This means victory. This *is* victory."

CHAPTER TWENTY-SEVEN

Old Abe Will Come Out All Right

Slavery they admit to be defunct.

—Assistant Secretary of War Charles Dana, in a report of a
presidential meeting with defeated Confederate officials, April 1865

Don't kneel to me. That is not right. You must kneel to God
only and thank him for the liberty you will hereafter enjoy.

—Abraham Lincoln, to newly liberated Black residents of Richmond,
Virginia, April 1865

H E WAS RIGHT. The end was near. Sunday, April 2, was "bright
and beautiful" in Richmond, the Confederate John B. Jones
told his diary. "No sound disturbed the stillness of the Sabbath morn, save the subdued murmur of the river, and the cheerful
music of the church bells," remembered Sallie Brock, the daughter of a
hotelkeeper. At Grace and Ninth streets, Jefferson Davis was attending
services at St. Paul's Episcopal Church. The collect for the day asked
God "mercifully to look upon thy people; that by thy great goodness
they may be governed and preserved evermore, both of body and soul."
The choir sang a hymn of Charles Wesley's:

> Hide me, O my Saviour, hide,
> Till the storm of life is past;
> Safe into the haven guide;
> O receive my soul at last!

The storm, Davis knew, was not past, but raging: "The war came," he
said, "and now it must go on till the last man of this generation falls in
his tracks, and his children seize his musket and fight our battle." Davis
gave his wife a Colt pistol—he had asked General Josiah Gorgas, the
Confederate chief of ordnance, for fifty cartridges for it—so she could
defend herself in case of Union capture.

At about noon on this Sunday, as the congregation in St. Paul's were kneeling, the Reverend Charles Minnigerode noticed the church's sexton walking up the aisle to Davis's pew. "It was Sunday, like that of the first Manassas," Minnigerode recalled, "and the air seemed full of something like a foreboding of good or bad." The messenger—"a large, pompous, swaggering kind of fellow"—handed the Confederate president a note. The message was from John C. Breckinridge, the former vice president of the United States who now served as the Confederacy's secretary of war: "General Lee telegraphs, that he can hold his position no longer. Come to the office immediately." Davis quietly slipped out of the church. "There was no confusion at all, for it was a common occurrence for persons to be called out of church during the war," a congregant recalled, "and no one knew there was anything unusual the matter."

The service ended as usual, and the congregants walked out into a changed world. The Confederate capital was falling. It was time to evacuate. "The direful tidings spread with the swiftness of electricity," Sallie Brock recalled. By late afternoon, there was a swarm to load wagons for the flight from the city. Banks were opened and emptied of deposits. Prison guards left their posts. By order of the City Council, tavernkeepers poured barrels of liquor into the streets. "In the gutters ran a stream of whiskey," Brock wrote, "and its fumes filled and impregnated the air."

Dallas Tucker, a child of a secessionist family who had lost a son in combat, recalled the day in detail. He had been at St. Paul's and watched as the Union forces struck the Confederate colors over the Virginia capitol, replacing them with the Stars and Stripes. "I remembered my dead soldier brother, what we had suffered for what we deemed right, and my young heart was filled with bitter hate," Tucker wrote.

The rebel South had believed it was fighting God's battles on earth. Two years earlier, the Reverend Dr. Joseph Stiles, a Presbyterian and Confederate chaplain, had argued that God would never allow that which had now come to pass: a Union victory. Should the North "bring up the very gates of hell in all their strength to compose the center of her grand army," Stiles had preached, still the Lord would rescue the Confederacy.

As Lincoln had told the nation, the rebels read the same Bible and prayed to the same God. Yet, in the eyes of the religious, the Lord had found the cause of the Confederacy wanting. To the president, this result was explicable in light of the moral good that the Union was about liberation and mercy and love. To the diehard rebels, there had to be another explanation. Why was the affliction of conquest being visited upon them if God, as they believed, was on their side?

To John Blair Dabney, a Virginia lawyer who had become an Episcopal clergyman, defeat was a signal of the Apocalypse—a precursor to the end of history itself. "The signs of the times clearly indicate important changes in the constitution of human society, and the face of the world," Dabney preached on Sunday, March 26, 1865. "The elements of discord are at work, and the explosion cannot be much longer delayed. . . . It behooves us to be prepared for this awful event: for we know not at what moment it may come. Then we shall see our blessed Lord 'coming in the clouds of heaven with power and great glory' to judge the world."

That the defeat of a cause designed to perpetuate the enslavement of others could not be the triumph of the right but a harbinger of Armageddon illustrates the depth of the white South's ambitions, self-regard, and self-certitude. Such delusions about its own virtue would fuel the rise of the Lost Cause in the postwar world. Where Lincoln had seen the pain of the war as a national Good Friday leading to an Easter of emancipation and of union, the rebels chose to view their loss as a sustained Passion—a theological worldview that precluded their conversion from enslavers to fellow citizens.

"It is certain now that Richmond is in our hands, and I think I will go there to-morrow," Lincoln wrote to Stanton at five o'clock on Monday, April 3. "I will take care of myself." In New York, George Templeton Strong wrote, "Petersburg and Richmond! *Gloria in excelsis Deo.*" Elizabeth Keckly was in her shop with Mrs. Ann Eliza Harlan when they spotted artillery marching by outside, "on its way to fire a salute"; on learning why, Keckly and the Iowa senator's wife clasped hands and "rejoiced together."

On Tuesday, April 4, the president of the United States entered the fallen capital of the rebellion. As Lincoln walked the streets of the city, he was hailed as a liberator, particularly by the city's Black population, which was said to be "wild with enthusiasm." "Why, Doctor," Lincoln told Phineas Gurley, "I walked alone on the street, and anyone could have shot me from a second story window." Thomas Morris Chester of *The Philadelphia Press* watched the president carefully. "As soon as he landed the news sped, as if upon the wings of lightning, that 'Old Abe,' for it was treason in this city to give him a more respectful address, had come," Chester wrote. A Black man, Chester had composed an earlier dispatch from the chair of the Speaker of the Confederate Congress. "Some of the negroes," he wrote, "feeling themselves free to act like men, shouted that the President had arrived." One woman cried out, "Thank you, dear Jesus, for this! Thank you, Jesus!" A few were so moved that they knelt at Lincoln's feet. "Don't kneel to me," the president said. "That is not right. You must kneel to God only, and thank him for the liberty you will hereafter enjoy."

Thomas Morris Chester filed dispatches from captured Richmond for The Philadelphia Press.

Lincoln inspected the house the Davises had occupied. "This must have been President Davis's chair," Lincoln remarked as he briefly sat at his defeated foe's desk. "The hated, despised, ridiculed, the brute, the beast, the baboon of the Yankee nation, as the Richmond editors have named him, is here, in the house from which Jeff. Davis fled in haste and terror on Sunday last!" wrote the *Boston Daily Journal*'s Charles Carleton Coffin. A huge company cheered the American president as he proceeded to the capitol building.

The hour was rich in promise. "I know that I am free, for I have seen Father Abraham and felt him," an elderly Black woman remarked. Chester noticed something else, too. "Nothing can exceed the courtesy and politeness which the whites everywhere manifest to the negroes," he wrote. "Not even the familiarity peculiar to Americans is indulged in, calling the blacks by their first or Christian names, but even masters are addressing their slaves as 'Mr. Johnson,' 'Mrs. Brown,' and 'Miss Smith.'"

In his dispatch for the *Boston Daily Journal,* Charles Coffin noted "the enthusiastic bearing of the people—the blacks and poor whites who have suffered untold horrors during the war . . . the shouting, dancing, the thanksgivings to God, the mention of the name of Jesus—as if President Lincoln were next to the son of God in their affections."

Coffin described "men in heart and soul—free men henceforth and forever, their bonds cut asunder in an hour—men from whose limbs the chains fell yesterday morning, men who through many weary years have prayed for deliverance—who have asked sometimes if God were dead—who, when their children were taken from them and sent to the swamps of South Carolina and the cane brakes of Louisiana, cried to God for help and cried in vain, who told their sorrows to Jesus and asked for help, but had no helper." There were, Coffin concluded, "thousands of men in Richmond to-night who would lay down their lives for President Lincoln—their great deliverer—their best friend on earth."

Mrs. Lincoln rejoined her husband on Thursday, April 6. As Mary noted, "even our stately dignified Mr Sumner acknowledged himself transformed into a lad of sixteen. We had a gay time I assure you, & Richmond we visited as a matter of course, & 'the banquet halls' of Jeff Davis looked sad and deserted. Each & every place will be repeopled with our own glorious & loyal people & the traitors meet the doom which a just Heaven ever awards the transgressor." Lincoln warned his wife not to speak of retribution. Richmond, she had remarked, "is filled with our enemies."

"Enemies!" Lincoln replied. "We must never speak of that"—an affirmation of the views he had expressed in his second inaugural address.

Elizabeth Keckly was one of the party. Touring Richmond, the formerly enslaved dressmaker walked through the abandoned Confederate legislative chambers and sat in the chairs of Jefferson Davis and of Alexander Stephens. The floors were littered with papers. Keckly picked one up at random. It was a resolution banning freed people from entering the state of Virginia.

The president met with John A. Campbell, a former associate justice of the U.S. Supreme Court who had resigned when the war broke out and had served as assistant secretary of war in Davis's cabinet. To Campbell, Lincoln underscored again that any surrender would have to be total and that there would be no alteration of the administration's emancipation measures. Charles Dana, a Union assistant secretary of war, telegraphed a report of the conversation to Stanton. A six-word sentence in the midst of the message contained multitudes: "Slavery," Dana wrote, "they admit to be defunct."

On Friday, April 7, Lincoln telegraphed Grant, who was in the field. "Gen. Sheridan says 'If the thing is pressed I think that Lee will surrender,'" the president said. "Let the *thing* be pressed." On Sunday, April 9—Palm Sunday—General Lee wrote to Grant to request a meeting. "I ask a suspension of hostilities pending the discussion of the Terms of surrender of this army," Lee said. A rendezvous was set for that afternoon at Wilmer McLean's house in the Virginia town known as Appomattox Court House.

Lincoln had left City Point at eleven P.M. on Saturday to return to Washington. He was aboard the *River Queen* for much of Sunday, including during the surrender in McLean's parlor. Lee was in resplendent dress uniform; Grant in simple soldier's garb, with muddied boots. Grant mentioned that the two men had met once before, during the Mexican War, but when Lee failed to remember the moment, the Union chief passed over that awkwardness with grace.

The articles of surrender fulfilled the policy articulated first at Fort Donelson and lately reaffirmed at Hampton Roads and in Richmond: The Confederate capitulation had to be total and unconditional. There had been fears in the Union that Lee would carry on the fight. "It is desirable that Lee should be captured," Gideon Welles told his diary after the fall of Richmond. "He, more than anyone else, has the confidence of the Rebels, and can, if he escapes . . . rally for a time a brigand force in the interior." Lee, however, saw that the war was lost. "There is nothing left for me to do but to go and see General Grant," he had told his officers, "and I would rather die a thousand deaths." In Columbia, South Carolina, a young diarist, Emma LeConte, wrote, "The South lies prostrate—their foot is on us—there is no help."

Before leaving City Point, the president called on a band to play "La Marseillaise" and "Dixie." "That tune is now Federal property," he said of "Dixie"; "it belongs to us, and, at any rate, it is good to show the rebels that with us they will be free to hear it again." In transit, Lincoln read aloud. Among his selections were passages from Shakespeare's *Macbeth*. He mused on Macbeth's soliloquy after the murder of Duncan—verses that touched on ambition, the pain of difficult decisions, and the inescapability of tragedy. The *River Queen* arrived in Washington at about six P.M.

When word of Lee's surrender reached Louisiana, the Confederate diarist Sarah Morgan observed, "Peace! Blessed Peace! Was the cry. I whispered 'Never! Let a great earthquake swallow us up first! Let us leave our land and emigrate to any desert spot of the earth, rather than to return to the Union, even as it Was!' "

In Washington, the news of Appomattox was announced with the roar of cannon at dawn on Monday, April 10. Big gun after big gun after big gun was fired, five hundred in all. Lincoln, who was breakfasting with Noah Brooks in the White House, could hear them clearly. Windows in houses on Lafayette Square cracked amid the cacophony. "The streets, horribly muddy, were all alive with people," Brooks wrote, "cheering and singing, carrying flags and saluting everybody, hungering and thirsting for speeches." "The very day after his return from Richmond," Stanton recalled of the president, "I passed with him some of the happiest moments of my life; our hearts beat with exultation at the victories." Clerks gathered in the Treasury Department and sang the Doxology:

> *Praise God, from whom all blessings flow;*
> *Praise Him, all creatures here below;*
> *Praise Him above, ye heavenly host;*
> *Praise Father, Son, and Holy Ghost. Amen.*

A celebratory crowd marched from the Washington Navy Yard to the White House. "The bands played, the howitzers belched forth their thunder, and the people cheered," *The National Intelligencer* reported. A delighted Tad waved a captured Confederate flag from a window.

At last the president showed himself. He was, Brooks noted, "radiant with happiness . . . and bowed and smiled his thanks." Brooks thought the scene "of the wildest confusion; men fairly yelled with delight, tossed up their hats and screamed like mad. Seen from the windows, the surface of the crowd looked like an agitated sea of hats, faces and men's arms."

Far from being triumphant or even especially eloquent in victory, Lincoln spoke only briefly. Seeing the musicians close to hand, he said, "I have always thought 'Dixie' one of the best tunes I have ever heard. Our adversaries over the way attempted to appropriate it, but I insisted yesterday that we fairly captured it." He went on: "I presented the question to the Attorney General, and he gave it as his legal opinion that it is our lawful prize." Amid laughter and applause, the president added, "I now request the band to favor me with its performance." They complied, and followed the Confederate anthem with a rendition of "Yankee Doodle"—a musical moment of attempted unity.

By calling for "Dixie"—he had now done so twice—the president gave popular expression to his instincts for Reconstruction. He wanted the new Louisiana government admitted, and he favored allowing the Confederate legislature in Virginia to meet again in order to end the war officially. Sumner, among other Radical Republicans, opposed this moderate course. Such moves, Sumner believed, would lead to "confusion and uncertainty in the future—with hot controversy." In a letter to John Bright, Sumner predicted trouble if Reconstruction failed to go far enough. "A practical difficulty is this; can Emancipation be carried out without using the lands of the slave-masters," Sumner wrote. "The great plantations, which have been so many nurseries of the rebellion, must be broken up, & the freedmen must share the pieces."

Typically, the president was feeling his way through the twilight. He believed that a uniform and inflexible approach to Reconstruction would be impracticable, and he was not interested in widespread retribution. "Whatever aspect the question may now wear to the great mass of the people, they have an implicit and trustful faith in Lincoln, which is almost unreasonable and unreasoning," Brooks observed; "he has so often proved himself wiser than his critics and advisers that many truly wise men say that they have done with contending against his better judgment, while 'the simple people' say, 'Oh, well, Old Abe will come out all right—he always does, you know.'"

The night was noisy. On Tuesday, April 11, the Washington darkness was rent with celebratory guns still firing occasionally from the

Washington Navy Yard; the murmur and cheers of crowds; the playing of brass bands; the *pop-pop-pop* of fireworks. In the White House, Lincoln prepared his remarks for the evening. Elizabeth Keckly was there too. She had asked the First Lady if she might attend. "Certainly, Lizabeth; if you take any interest in political speeches, come and listen." Tad again entertained the crowd with a captured Confederate banner. Noah Brooks held a candle close to Lincoln so that the president could make out the words on the pages; Tad picked up the sheets as they dropped to the floor in the course of the speech. "I stood a short distance from Mr. Lincoln," Keckly recalled, "and as the light . . . fell full upon him, making him stand out boldly in the darkness, a sudden thought struck me, and I whispered . . . 'What an easy matter would it be to kill the President, as he stands there! He could be shot down from the crowd, and no one would be able to tell who fired the shot.'"

Reconstruction was Lincoln's central theme. "It is fraught with great difficulty. . . . We simply must begin with, and mold from, disorganized and discordant elements. Nor is it a small additional embarrassment that we, the loyal people, differ among ourselves as to the mode, manner, and means of reconstruction." The vote, education, the work of the Freedmen's Bureau, and citizenship were to be debated throughout the country. In the late spring of 1865, the *New York Tribune* offered a platform for progress; in his landmark book *Black Reconstruction in America,* W.E.B. Du Bois summarized the *Tribune's* list this way:

1. Everyone must realize that the blacks will not emigrate but stay in America.

2. The blacks may not be spared, for their labor makes land valuable, and the land may not be spared.

3. Fair pay for fair work is a sine qua non.

4. Education for freedmen.

5. With education comes self-elevation, and the desire to deny him the vote will disappear.

6. However, white men who are ignorant and vicious, vote. Suffrage for blacks regardless of this ignorance.

7. Fidelity to the political creed of the nation to secure the happiness of all.

Such were the aspirations, but realizing them would be difficult. "Wherever I go—the street, the shop, the house, the hotel, or the steamboat—I hear the people talk in such a way as to indicate that they are yet unable to conceive of the Negro as possessing any rights at all," Carl Schurz reported from the South after Appomattox. "Men who are honorable in their dealings with their white neighbors, will cheat a Negro without feeling a single twinge of their honor. To kill a Negro, they do not deem murder; to debauch a Negro woman, they do not think fornication; to take the property away from a Negro, they do not consider robbery. The people boast that when they get freedmen's affairs in their own hands, to use their own expression, 'the n——s will catch hell.'"

The work was hard but essential. "In respectful earnestness I must say that if at the end of all the blood that has been shed and the treasure expended, the unfortunate Negro is to be left in the hands of his infuriated and disappointed former owners to legislate and fix his *status*, God help him, for his cup of bitterness will overflow indeed," one observer wrote.

The New York Times framed the issue of Reconstruction well. "The real concern here is whether the Southern States, if restored at once to their full State rights, would not abuse them by an oppression of the black race," the *Times* wrote. "This race has rendered an assistance to the government in the time of danger that entitles them to its benign care. The government cannot, without the worst dishonor, permit the bondage of the black man to be continued in any form. It is bound by every moral principle, as well as every prudential consideration, not to remit him to the tender mercies of any enemy."

Lincoln understood, and the reconstruction of Louisiana, already under way, was a first step. "The amount of constituency, so to speak, on which the new Louisiana government rests, would be more satisfactory to all, if it contained fifty, thirty, or even twenty thousand, instead of only about twelve thousand, as it does," the president said at the White House. "It is also unsatisfactory to some that the elective franchise is not given to the colored man. I would myself prefer that it were now conferred on the very intelligent, and on those who serve our cause as soldiers."

"It was just like Abraham Lincoln" to begin with limited Black suffrage, Frederick Douglass recalled. "He never shocked prejudices unnecessarily. Having learned statesmanship while splitting rails, he always used the thin edge of the wedge first—and the fact that he used it at all meant that he would if need be, use the thick as well as the thin." The president said:

Some twelve thousand voters in the heretofore slave-state of Louisiana have sworn allegiance to the Union, assumed to be the rightful political power of the State, held elections, organized a State government, adopted a free-state constitution, giving the benefit of public schools equally to black and white, and empowering the Legislature to confer the elective franchise upon the colored man. Their Legislature has already voted to ratify the constitutional amendment recently passed by Congress, abolishing slavery throughout the nation. These twelve thousand persons are thus fully committed to the Union, and to perpetual freedom in the state—committed to the very things, and nearly all the things the nation wants—and they ask the nation's recognition, and its assistance to make good their committal. Now, if we reject, and spurn them, we do our utmost to disorganize and disperse them. . . . To the blacks we say "This cup of liberty which these, your old masters, hold to your lips, we will dash from you, and leave you to the chances of gathering the spilled and scattered contents in some vague and undefined when, where, and how." If this course, discouraging and paralyzing both white and black, has any tendency to bring Louisiana into proper practical relations with the Union, I have, so far, been unable to perceive it. If, on the contrary, we recognize, and sustain the new government of Louisiana the converse of all this is made true. We encourage the hearts, and nerve the arms of the twelve thousand to adhere to their work, and argue for it, and proselyte for it, and fight for it, and feed it, and grow it, and ripen it to a complete success. The colored man too, in seeing all united for him, is inspired with vigilance, and energy, and daring, to the same end. Grant that he desires the elective franchise, will he not attain it sooner by saving the already advanced steps toward it, than by running backward over them?

As with wartime emancipation and the Thirteenth Amendment, Lincoln was traveling a path toward human rights rather than limitations based on caste. "There can be no doubt that Abraham Lincoln never would have accepted the Black Codes," W.E.B. Du Bois argued. "I think we have reason to thank God for Abraham Lincoln," wrote Lydia Maria Child, who as early as 1833 had published an abolitionist book, *An Appeal in Favor of That Class of Americans Called Africans*. "With all his deficiencies, it must be admitted that he has grown continuously; and considering how slavery had weakened and perverted the moral sense of the whole country, it was great good luck to have the people elect a man who was *willing* to grow." To Horace Greeley, "Mr. Lincoln . . . was a wiser, abler man when he entered upon his second than when he commenced his first Presidential term."

John Wilkes Booth had been on the White House grounds on the evening of Lincoln's remarks. The actor had urged a companion, the fellow Confederate sympathizer Lewis Powell, to fire on the president then and there. Powell refused, but Booth reached a new resolve as he listened to Lincoln in the night.

"That," Booth said, "is the last speech he will ever make."

CHAPTER TWENTY-EIGHT

Lincoln Was Slain; America Was Meant

Hurrah! Old Abe Lincoln has been assassinated!

—EMMA LECONTE of Columbia, South Carolina, Friday, April 21, 1865

No one dare speak a word against the President. If anyone does not have their house dressed in mourning they are called traitors.

—PHEEBE CLARK of Washington, D.C., Saturday, April 22, 1865

T HE PRESIDENT HAD LONG BEEN far too sanguine about threats on his life. "Oh, assassination of public officers is not an American crime," Lincoln had said in the summer of 1863. In March 1864, agents of the Confederacy were reportedly planning to assassinate or abduct him. And in August a sniper tried to take advantage of Lincoln's fondness for the Soldiers' Home by ambushing the president as he rode out to his retreat. "Soon after I was nominated at Chicago, I began to receive letters threatening my life," Lincoln said. "The first one or two made me a little uncomfortable, but I came at length to look for a regular installment of this kind of correspondence in every week's mail, and up to inauguration day I was in constant receipt of such letters. It is no uncommon thing to receive them now; but they have ceased to give any apprehension. . . . There is nothing like getting *used* to things!" To Noah Brooks, he remarked, "I long ago made up my mind that if anybody wants to kill me, he will do it. If I wore a shirt of mail, and kept myself surrounded by a body-guard, it would be all the same. There are a thousand ways of getting at a man if it is desirable that he should be killed."

The opposition press had openly discussed violence against the president. In the fevered atmosphere of secession and of war, the rebels and their Northern sympathizers, convinced of the full righteousness of their cause, saw Lincoln as a legitimate target. "Assassination in the abstract is a horrid crime," *The Richmond Dispatch* had written, "but to slay a tyrant is no more assassination than war is murder." After Lincoln's reelection, a Selma, Alabama, lawyer publicly sought funds to decapitate the federal government. "If the citizens of the Southern Confederacy will furnish me with the cash, or good securities for the sum of one million dollars, I will cause the lives of Abraham Lincoln, William H. Seward, and Andrew Johnson to be taken by the 1st of March next," the lawyer wrote. "This will give us peace, and satisfy the world that cruel tyrants cannot live in a 'land of liberty.' If this is not accomplished, nothing will be claimed beyond the sum of fifty thousand dollars, in advance, which is supposed to be necessary to reach and slaughter the three villains."

If one were fighting God's battles, then anything—including slavery and murder—was justified. Reason, proportion, and a respect for the rule of law—democracy's threshold features—were casualties once public life ceased to be about the peaceful mediation of differences. To Lincoln, the nation had to be guided by conscience but also by the conviction that no one could be totally certain that they were acting with divine sanction.

Not so with the white South that went to war in 1861. Slaveholding and secession had put the rebellion outside the protocols of politics and beyond the ethos of reason, law, and faith that Lincoln championed. Words had consequences. So, obviously, did actions—and the slave-owning interest's words and actions propelled the conspiracy that brought John Wilkes Booth to the president's box during John T. Ford's production of *Our American Cousin*.

G ood Friday 1865 fell on April 14—the fourth anniversary of Fort Sumter. "This day four long years ago!—the joy—the excitement— how well I remember it," South Carolina's Emma LeConte wrote in her diary. "For weeks we had been in fever of excitement. On the day the news came of the Fall of Sumter . . . [t]he bell commenced to ring. At the first tap we knew the joyful tidings had come. . . . We women ran trembling to the verandah—to the front gate, eagerly asking the news of passers-by. The whole town was in a joyful tumult. . . . What changes—what a lifetime we have lived in the four years past!"

This Friday began pleasantly for Lincoln—vastly more pleasantly than April 14, 1861, had—with the arrival, from Virginia, of Robert

Todd Lincoln, who was home for Easter and breakfasted with his father. The president had been ill the night before with a headache troubling enough that he had asked General Grant to take his place as a companion for the First Lady at a celebration of the Union victory. "Mr. Lincoln is indisposed with quite a severe headache," Mary had written to Grant, "yet would be very much pleased to see you at the house, this evening about 8 o'clock, & I want you to drive around with us to see the illumination!" Mary had been visibly annoyed by the adulation accorded the general on the outing; she had been so unpleasant that Grant declined an invitation to join the Lincolns at the theater on Friday night. Mrs. Grant, too, had no interest in spending more time with the irascible First Lady, and so the general decided that they were going to "visit our children . . . this will be a good excuse."

The president had a busy morning. He met with Representative Schuyler Colfax, who was bound for the West, as well as a number of other congressmen. Lincoln took a ride with General Grant and paid a quick visit to the War Department. Grant had just begged off for the theater that night; Edwin Stanton urged the president to take "a competent guard" along, prompting Lincoln to ask Thomas Eckert, whom he liked, to join the party.

"Stanton," the president asked, "do you know that Eckert can break a poker over his arm?"

"No," Stanton replied, "why do you ask such a question?"

"Well, Stanton, I have seen Eckert break five pokers, one after another, over his arm, and I am thinking he would be the kind of man to go with me this evening." As it turned out, the Lincolns were to take Clara Harris, a daughter of Senator Ira Harris, and her fiancé, Major Henry Rathbone. At ten o'clock that morning, after his stop at the War Department, the president received a call from the governor of Maryland and one of the state's senators.

About the same time, at Sixth and Pennsylvania, John Wilkes Booth was entering the dining room of the National Hotel, where he boarded, for a late breakfast. A handsome child of a theatrical dynasty, Booth, now twenty-six, was fond of brandy, attractive women, white supremacy, and the Confederate States of America. He had, a contemporary recalled, "large lustrous eyes, and a graceful form, features regular as a statue, and a rich voice that lingered in the ears of those who heard him."

Born in 1838 in Maryland, Booth was a son of Junius Brutus Booth, Sr., and the elder Booth's longtime mistress, Mary Ann Holmes. Booth Sr. and Holmes married in 1851 after Booth, who had emigrated from England to the United States thirty years before, was divorced from the wife he had left behind. A gifted athlete and a good shot, John Wilkes Booth became, along with two of his brothers, a noted actor. Accompanying Virginia militiamen in 1859, Booth was present at the execution of John Brown after Harpers Ferry. "I was proud of my little share in the transaction, for I deemed it my duty, and that I was helping our common country to perform an act of justice," Booth wrote in 1864. "But what was a crime in poor JOHN BROWN is now considered (by themselves) as the greatest and only virtue of the whole Republican party. Strange transmigration! *Vice* to become a *virtue*, simply because *more* indulge in it."

Booth's racial and political obsessions were not extraordinary. His views were widely shared within Confederate and Copperhead circles—circles that prized slavery and white supremacy over the Union. "I thought then, *as now*, that the Abolitionists *were the only traitors* in the land, and that the entire party deserved the same fate of poor old BROWN," Booth wrote. "The South can make no choice. It is either extermination or slavery for *themselves* (worse than death). . . . I know *my* choice." In August 1864, inflamed by the war and by Confederate rhetoric, Booth set out to kidnap Lincoln, spirit the president south to Richmond, and exchange him for Confederate prisoners of war. "I love *justice* more than I do a country that disowns it. . . . My love (as things stand to-day) is for the South alone." He recruited with charm and hospitality, inviting possible co-conspirators to his rooms at the National Hotel for milk punch and cigars. The kidnapping plot went nowhere, and as the Union advanced through the winter and into the spring of 1865, Booth's thoughts turned to assassination. He had attended the second inauguration in March and stood not far from Lincoln. "What an excellent chance I had to kill the President on inauguration day," Booth remarked, with regret. "For six months we had worked to capture" Lincoln, Booth wrote in a pocket diary entry dated from April 13 to 14, 1865. "But our cause being almost lost, something decisive & great must be done."

SATAN TEMPTING BOOTH TO THE MURDER OF THE PRESIDENT.

Handsome, athletic, and charming, John Wilkes Booth was entranced by white supremacy and the Confederate cause.

After breakfasting on Friday, April 14, Booth stopped off in the hotel's barbershop and made his way to Ford's Theatre. As he walked along Tenth Street, he cut an elegant figure. "He was faultlessly dressed in a suit of dark clothes and wore a tall silk hat," a contemporary recalled. "He had on a pair of kid gloves of a subdued color, a light overcoat was slung over his arm, and he carried a cane." On seeing Booth come into view, Harry Ford, one of the theater's owners, said, "Here comes the handsomest man in the United States."

"What's on tonight?" Booth asked Ford.

"*Our American Cousin,* and we are going to have a big night," Ford replied. "The President and General Grant are going to occupy the President's box, and"—in an attempt at an amusing allusion to Booth's politics—"General Lee is going to have the adjoining one."

Booth appears to have missed the joke. "I hope they are not going to do like the Romans—parade their prisoners before the public to humiliate them," he said.

Ford waved the point away. He had been "jesting" about Lee. But it was true that the president was coming.

Booth took his leave. He walked from Tenth Street to Pennsylvania Avenue, where he encountered John F. Coyle, an editor of the *National Intelligencer* newspaper; the two men were friends. Stopping in a restaurant, Booth had a few questions.

"Suppose Lincoln was killed, what would be the result?" he asked.

"Johnson would succeed," Coyle replied.

"But if he was killed?"

"Then Seward."

"But suppose he was killed, then what?"

"Then anarchy or whatever the Constitution provides," Coyle said. "But what nonsense: they don't make Brutuses nowadays."

"No—no, they do not," Booth said.

At the White House, the cabinet was in session. The meeting ran from eleven to two o'clock. Grant sat in on the gathering, which was taken up by issues of Reconstruction—which, Lincoln told his colleagues, was "the great question now before us, and we must soon begin to act." He had had a dream—a dream that had come before "nearly every great and important event of the war," Welles reported. "He said it related to the water—that he seemed to be in some singular, indescribable vessel, and that he was moving with great rapidity [towards an indefinite shore]. That he had this dream preceding Sumter, Bull Run, Antietam, Gettysburg, Stone River, Vicksburg, Wilmington &c."

Clemency for the Confederates, suffrage for Black Americans, investments to rebuild the South and give the formerly enslaved education and justice—all these things lay ahead. Thus far Lincoln had been more intent on reunion than on Reconstruction—on bringing the rebel states back on terms less likely to force genuinely egalitarian and democratic reform than the plans being offered by Charles Sumner and others. The president did not know precisely what he could and should do, but he knew this: He had never abandoned his fundamental antislavery commitment, and now the Union was saved. He had done right as he understood the right. The price had been staggering, but here he stood, with a nation preserved, slavery destroyed, and his conscience clear. The arc of Theodore Parker's moral universe had been bent toward justice. It had not brought about the Kingdom of God, nor a new age of milk and honey, but the America of 1865 was fuller, freer, and fairer than the America of 1861. That was not everything. But neither was it a small thing.

Booth, meanwhile, had hired a horse. During the afternoon he was seen inspecting the alley behind Ford's Theatre. He called at Kirkwood House, where Andrew Johnson was boarding, but Johnson was out. On Pennsylvania Avenue at Thirteenth and Fourteenth streets, Booth came across John Matthews, a fellow actor. As they chatted, a collection of defeated Confederate officers passed by. "Johnny, have you seen Lee's officers just brought in?" Matthews asked.

"Yes, Johnny, I have," Booth said. "Great God! I have no longer a country!"

Noticing Booth's "paleness, nervousness and agitation," Matthews asked, "John, how nervous you are! What is the matter?"

"Oh, it is nothing," Booth replied. "Johnny, I have a little favor to ask of you, will you grant it? . . . I may leave town tonight and I have a letter here which I desire to publish in the *National Intelligencer;* please see to it for me unless I see you before ten o'clock to-morrow; in that case I will see to it myself." The letter, which Matthews later destroyed, reportedly concluded this way: "Many will blame me for what I am about to do, but posterity, I am sure, will justify me."

In the course of the day Booth and his co-conspirators prepared to execute their plans. To avenge the war, the government was to be decapitated. Lincoln was to be shot at the theater. Johnson was to be killed at his lodgings, and Seward assassinated in his house.

The Lincolns spent part of the afternoon on a drive to the Washington Navy Yard. Two days before, on Wednesday, the president had written Mary a "playfully & tenderly worded" note "notifying, the hour, of the day, he would ride with me," the First Lady recalled. Friday was the day. "We must be more cheerful," the president remarked to his wife. "Between the war & the loss of our darling Willie—we have both been very miserable."

At dusk, Booth left his key with the clerk at the National. "Are you going to Ford's Theatre tonight?" Booth asked him.

"No," the clerk said.

"You ought to go; there is to be some splendid acting there tonight."

At eight thirty P.M., the Lincolns arrived at Ford's. The play—a British farce starring Laura Keene—was under way, but in deference to the president the actors paused as the audience cheered Lincoln and the house band played "Hail to the Chief." The Lincolns entered the box on the second tier, one decorated with flags and a portrait of George Washington. The president took his seat—a special rocking chair—with Mary to his right.

The play resumed. In the second scene of the third act, Booth made his way to the president's box. Once there,

The actress Laura Keene was starring in John T. Ford's production of Our American Cousin *on the evening of Friday, April 14, 1865.*

he peered through a small hole he had made in the door separating a small anteroom from the president's seats. Bearing a .44-caliber single-shot pistol designed by the Philadelphia gunsmith Henry Deringer, Booth opened the door, stepped toward the president, and shot Lincoln in the left side of the head. The pistol produced a puff of smoke. Major Rathbone swiveled his head to the left and saw the assassin standing behind Lincoln's chair. Rising quickly, Rathbone hurled himself at Booth, who dropped his gun on the carpeted floor, produced a knife, and slashed Rathbone in the arm. "The knife went from the elbow nearly to the shoulder inside—cutting an artery, nerves & veins," Clara Harris recalled. Thus gaining a brief advantage, Booth leaped from the box to the stage, a distance of about ten feet. His spur caught in the flags on the box, and he injured his leg as he hit the boards. "Sic semper tyrannis!" cried Booth from the stage. Still wielding his knife, he fled the theater through the wings.

There was a strange calm in the house for a moment. William M. Springer later told John Nicolay that he had been "sitting six or eight rows back from the stage. That when Booth jumped or fell from the

In the second scene of the third act, armed with a .44-caliber pistol, Booth shot Lincoln in the left side of the head. "My husband's blood," cried Mary, "my dear husband's blood!"

stage-box there was perfect silence and quiet...until Booth raised himself from his fall and flourishing his knife in his hand walked deliberately and unmolested diagonally across the stage. About the moment he disappeared behind the wings there was a shriek from Mrs Lincoln in the box, which seemed to break the spell of stupefaction which had fallen upon the house."

"My husband's blood, my dear husband's blood!" the First Lady screamed.

As Springer told it, "Thereupon the audience rose almost *en masse* and several persons sprang forward and climbed upon the stage, himself being one of the first of these. He called for a doctor in the audience and several coming forward he assisted one of them to climb up into the President's box." Those who reached Lincoln, the Associated Press reported that night, found that "some of the brain was oozing out."

It was about a quarter past ten, and Abraham Lincoln was dying.

As Booth escaped the theater, Lewis Powell (also known as Lewis Payne) presented himself at the Sewards' door, claiming to be bearing medicine for the secretary of state, who was recuperating from a carriage accident. Armed with a pistol and a knife, Powell wounded Seward's son Frederick and a nurse before falling upon Seward himself and kniving the secretary's face. The planned attack on Andrew Johnson did not come off; his would-be assassin, George Atzerodt, had spent the evening drinking and failed to strike at Kirkwood House. The coup to destroy the government by taking out the president, the vice president, and the secretary of state had failed—but only barely.

"In jumping broke my leg," Booth wrote in his diary as he hid in the Virginia countryside. "I passed all his pickets, rode sixty miles that night, with the bones of my leg tearing the flesh at every jump. I can never repent it, though we hated to kill: Our country owed all her troubles to [Lincoln], and God simply made me the instrument of his punishment. The country is not what it *was*. This forced union is not what I *have* loved. I care not what *becomes* of me. I have no desire to out-live my country."

Lincoln was carried from his second-floor box down the stairs to the lobby and across Tenth Street to a red brick Federal-style boardinghouse owned by William Petersen, a German-born tailor, and his wife, Anna. There, in a tiny nine-by-fifteen-foot bedroom, the president was attended by surgeons through the watches of the night. At first Lincoln swallowed a tablespoon of diluted brandy, but soon he could not manage even that.

Nothing could be done. The bullet would have entered Lincoln's head at a speed of about 400 feet per second, or 273 miles per hour. The head wound was mortal. Sometimes twitching, he breathed and he bled as his body shut down.

On hearing the news of the shooting, most of the cabinet came to the Petersen house through the darkened streets, as did Robert Lincoln, John Hay, Senator Sumner, and Chief Justice Chase. The president, Gideon Welles observed, "lay extended diagonally across the bed which was not long enough for him"—a perennial problem for Lincoln, whose feet had dangled off so many beds on the Illinois circuit as he would read into the night. Welles was surprised by the apparent strength of the president's bare arms; they were "of a size which one would scarce have expected from his spare appearance." Lincoln's breathing lifted the sheet that had been laid over him. "His features were calm and striking," Welles recalled. "I had never seen him to better advantage than for the first hour, perhaps, that I was there. After that his right eye began to swell and became discolored."

The inconsolable Mrs. Lincoln was taken into the Petersens' parlor. She often rose, attended to the president, and came back again. At one point the First Lady fainted at the bedside and had to be carried out "insensible." In the night the attorney general, James Speed, prepared a letter for Johnson "informing him of the event, and that the government devolved upon him." Benjamin Brown French ordered the Capitol Building closed: The extent of the conspiracy was still unclear. Sumner and Robert Lincoln, who was "crying audibly," kept watch near the head of the bed.

Phineas Gurley arrived as Lincoln faded. The minister divided his time between Mrs. Lincoln in the parlor—he would walk with her on her visits to her husband's bedside—and Robert and the dying president in the back room. Toward seven o'clock in the morning, about ninety minutes after sunrise, a quiet fell in the house. "For the last half hour before the death, the utmost stillness had prevailed in the room," a diarist, Horatio Nelson Taft, recalled; "not a *word*, not a *whisper* was heard."

In the end, there was only Gurley's voice. "Let us pray," he said, and those gathered "all knelt down upon our knees around his dying bed, while he offered a most solemn and impressive prayer," one surgeon recalled. "After which, we arose to witness the struggles between life and death."

The battle was done at twenty-two minutes after seven o'clock on the morning of Saturday, April 15, 1865. His head on a bloodied pillow, Abraham Lincoln was dead. "He is gone," one of the surgeons said.

Edwin Stanton broke the silence. "Doctor," the secretary of war asked Gurley, "will you say anything?"

"I will speak to God," Gurley replied.

"Do it just now."

His hands lifted, Gurley prayed to "Our Father and our God," commending the president's soul to the Almighty. James Tanner, a War Department clerk who had lost his legs at Second Bull Run, tried to capture the precise words, but in his haste he broke his pencil in pulling it from his pocket. Edwin Stanton sobbed, his head down in Lincoln's bedclothes. Speaking in "subdued and tremulous tones," Gurley con-

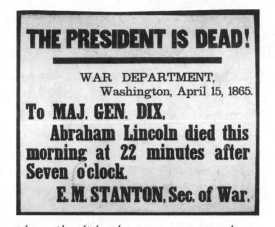

THE PRESIDENT IS DEAD!

WAR DEPARTMENT,
Washington, April 15, 1865.

To MAJ. GEN. DIX,
Abraham Lincoln died this morning at 22 minutes after Seven o'clock.
E. M. STANTON, Sec. of War.

The president died at about 7:22 A.M. on Saturday,
April 15. Vice President Johnson was sworn in later
that morning at Kirkwood House.

cluded: "Thy will be done, Amen." At this, Stanton, his face pained, his voice cracking, said, "Now he belongs to the ages." Lincoln had moved from the temporal to the eternal.

Gurley walked to the parlor and broke the news to Mrs. Lincoln.

"The President is dead," he told her.

"O—*why* did you not let me know?" she cried. "*Why* did you not *tell* me?"

"Your friends thought it not *best*," Gurley replied. "You must be resigned to the will of God. You must be calm and trust in God and in your friends."

Gurley accompanied the First Lady home to the White House, where a distraught and fearful Tad was waiting. They met him on the portico; the city's church bells had been tolling for the president. "Where is my *Pa*?" the boy asked. "Where *is* my Pa?" The youngest living Lincoln had "heard that his Pa had been shot but evidently expected him when his mother came," Horatio Nelson Taft recalled. "He was very much excited and alarmed but had not thought that his Pa *could be dead*." It fell to Gurley to tell him.

"Taddy," the minister said, "your Pa is dead."

In the house where a father had mourned a son's loss, now a son mourned a father. "O what shall I do?" Tad screamed. "What *shall* I do? My Brother is dead. My Father is dead. O what shall I do? What will become of me? O what *shall* I do? O mother *you* will not die will you? O don't *you* die, *Ma*. You *won't* die, will you, Mother? If *you* die I shall be all alone. O *don't* die, Ma."

Gurley had not yet wept. Now he did. "Dr. Gurley said that up to that time *he* himself had not shed a tear, but he could not witness *Tad's* grief unmoved, and the tears flowed freely," the diarist Horatio Nelson Taft recalled. The minister did what he could and took his leave, arriving at his own home about ten o'clock in the morning. "I felt as though I had been engaged all night in a terrible Battle," Gurley noted, "and had but just strength enough left to drag myself off the field." The next day was Easter. He had a new sermon to prepare.

Saturday was rainy and dark in Washington. "I went after breakfast to the Executive Mansion," Welles told his diary. "There was a cheerless cold rain and everything seemed gloomy. On the avenue in front of the White House were several hundred colored people, mostly women and children, weeping and wailing their loss. This crowd did not appear to diminish through the whole of that cold, wet day; they seemed not to know what to be their fate since their great benefactor was dead, and their hopeless grief affected me more than anything else, though strong and brave men wept when I met them."

At ten o'clock in the morning, in his rooms at Kirkwood House, Andrew Johnson was sworn in as president by Chief Justice Chase. "I shall ask and rely upon you and others in carrying the government through its present perils," the new president told the cabinet.

Those loyal to the Union saw the assassination as a sequential battle in the rebellion. "This blow was aimed at the life of the Government and of the nation," Henry Ward Beecher said. "Lincoln was slain; America was meant. . . . It was because he stood in the place of government, representing government, and a government that represented right and liberty, that he was singled out." "The deed of horror and infamy . . . is nothing more than the expression in action, of what secession politicians and journalists have been for years expressing in words," a California newspaper wrote. "Wilkes Booth has simply carried out what the Copperhead journalists who have denounced the President as a 'tyrant,' a 'despot,' a 'usurper,' hinted at, and virtually recommended. His weapon was the pistol, theirs the pen; and though he surpassed them in ferocity, they equaled him in guilt." Pheebe Clark, the wife of a

Union soldier serving in the Seventeenth Connecticut Infantry Regiment, captured the spirit of the capital in these dark days. "The city is dressed in mourning from one end to the other on account of the murder of the President," Clark wrote to her sister from Washington on Monday, April 17. "Any man here [who] says they are glad he is dead are shot right down. There was a soldier shot for saying he ought to have been killed a year ago."

The climate had been conducive to the crime. "It is you Republicans who set up at the head of the nation a hideous clown . . . who became a shameless tyrant," a Copperhead wrote, "a tyrant justly felled by an avenging hand, and who now rots in his tomb while his poisonous soul is consumed by the eternal flames of hell." "This morning when I went down to breakfast at seven, Brother read the announcement of the assassination of Lincoln," Sarah Morgan of Louisiana wrote. "'Vengeance is mine; I will repay, saith the Lord.' This is murder! God have mercy on those who did it!" In South Carolina, Emma LeConte was even more explicit. "Hurrah! Old Abe Lincoln has been assassinated!" she told her diary. "It may be abstractly wrong to be so jubilant, but I just can't help it. After all the heaviness and gloom . . . this blow to our enemies comes like a gleam of light. We have suffered till we feel savage. . . . Could there have been a fitter death for such a man?" A Texas newspaper editor wrote that some would consider the assassination "wicked" while others might think it "righteous retribution which descends direct from the hand of God upon the destroyer of human liberty, and the oppressor of a free people."

The news was refracted through the nation's religious prism. Some went to church on Easter Sunday 1865 and heard Lincoln portrayed as a martyr and messiah. Others, especially in the white South, interpreted the assassination as divine retribution for defeating the Confederacy and for freeing the enslaved. "Lincoln was not a martyr for, as much as we may object to and condemn assassination, he committed a monstrous crime in making war upon us," a soldier in the Savannah, Georgia, Volunteer Guards said, "and his tragic death was no more than just punishment for the crime." "It is certainly a matter of congratulation that Lincoln is dead," *The Texas Republican* wrote, "because the world is happily rid of a monster that disgraced the form of humanity." In South Carolina, Emma LeConte looked ahead. "Andy Johnson will succeed him—the rail-splitter will be succeeded by the drunken ass," she told her diary. "Such are the successors of Washington and Jefferson—such are to rule the South."

The view was starkly different from Union pulpits. "Rest, oh weary heart!" Henry Ward Beecher cried in Brooklyn. "An Easter Sunday unlike any I have seen," George Templeton Strong wrote. Buildings in Manhattan were shrouded with black bunting. Trinity Church, at Broadway and Wall Street, was filled; the Episcopal congregation was uncharacteristically emotional. "The whole service was a new experience for me," Strong wrote. "Men and women . . . were sobbing and crying bitterly all around. My own eyes kept filling, and the corners of my mouth would twitch now and then in spite of all I could do."

In Washington, Lincoln's empty pew at New York Avenue Presbyterian Church was draped in black. The rest of the sanctuary was filled beyond capacity. Hundreds of worshippers could not make their way inside. "This is such a Sabbath as our nation never saw before," Gurley told the Easter flock. "But while we mourn we must not murmur, while we weep we must not complain."

In the Second Inaugural Address, Lincoln had speculated that the war was a purifying punishment for slavery—and that " 'the judgments of the Lord are true and righteous altogether,' " even when those judgments are also incomprehensible. At the president's funeral service in the East Room, Gurley preached along similar lines, arguing that the assassination could not be separated from the same providential order: "It is His prerogative to bring light out of darkness and good out of evil. . . . Let us not be faithless, but believing."

Gurley was in character, asserting, as he had at the time of Willie's death, that the horror of the hour was part of a creation and of a plan that was fundamentally good. "As we stand here today, mourners around this coffin and around the lifeless remains of our beloved Chief Magistrate, we recognize and we adore the sovereignty of God," Gurley preached. Therein lay a complexity of faith and of life: One could *recognize* that sovereignty without being willing to *adore* it. That had been Lincoln's decision.

"Though our beloved President is slain, our beloved country is saved," Gurley said. "And so we sing of mercy as well as of judgment. . . . When the *sun* has risen, full-orbed and glorious, and a happy reunited people are rejoicing in its light—alas! Alas! It will shine upon his grave."

The president was taken from the White House to the Capitol to lie in state. "It was a splendid sight," the Washington resident Pheebe Clark wrote. "The procession was nearly 3 hours in passing. I never saw so many people together before in my life." After viewing the president's open casket in the Capitol, Mrs. Clark wrote, "He looks just as I had an idea he did. . . . I think the whole city is in mourning. The men wear crape on the left arm. Some have crape bows on their coats. No one dare speak a word against the President. If anyone does not have their house dressed in mourning they are called traitors."

The manhunt for John Wilkes Booth ended on Wednesday, April 26, when federal troops tracked him to the Confederate Richard H. Garrett's Caroline County farm near Port Royal, Virginia. "Here is a wounded Confederate soldier that we want you to take care of for a day or so," a Booth associate had said to Garrett on Monday, April 24. "Will you do it?" Garrett agreed, but soon Union cavalry arrived. Trapped in a burning barn, Booth was struck in the neck by a .44-caliber bullet fired by Sergeant Boston Corbett. By July, four of Booth's fellow conspirators would be arrested, tried, executed, and buried.

Among Booth's last words as he lay dying at Garrett's farm was a final, bleak affirmation of allegiance to the failed experiment of the Confederate States of America: "Tell my mother—tell my mother that I did it for my country—that I die for my country."

Lincoln's journey home to Springfield was complicated, emotional, and long—the sixteenth president's funeral solemnities were the most involved in American history. Mary Lincoln was not in public view. Remaining in the White House until late May, she was beginning a wretched widowhood. There were moments of grace: the former First Lady gave Frederick Douglass, Henry Highland Garnet, and William Slade three of the late president's walking sticks as mementos. But as time went on, she grew ever more erratic—spending money, seeking favors, demanding attentions from merchants, Congress, the press, and politicians—and ultimately provoked her son Robert Todd Lincoln to have her briefly committed to a mental institution in Batavia, Illinois. Observers believed her instability had been exacerbated by the assassination. "I went up and bade her good-by, and felt really very sad, although she has given me a world of trouble," Benjamin Brown French told his diary when the former First Lady left Washington in May 1865. "I think the sudden and awful death of the President somewhat unhinged her mind, for at times she has exhibited all the symptoms of madness."

The services for Lincoln in the White House and in the Capitol were followed by ceremonies in Baltimore, Harrisburg, Philadelphia, New York, Albany, Buffalo, Cleveland, Columbus, Indianapolis, Michigan City, and Chicago as the president's remains, with those of Willie, whose coffin had been removed from its temporary home in a mausoleum at Oak Hill Cemetery in Georgetown, traveled back to the Illinois capital by train.

The world was watching. Emotions were high. Everyone, it seemed, had a view and wanted to express it. "Though a stranger to you I cannot remain silent when so terrible a calamity has fallen upon you & your Country & most personally express my *deep & heartfelt* sympathy with you under the shocking circumstances of your present dreadful misfortunes," Queen Victoria, still mourning her Prince Albert, wrote to Mary Lincoln. "*No* one can better appreciate than *I* can, who am myself *utterly broken-hearted* by the loss of my own beloved Husband, who was the *Light* of my Life—my Stay—*my All*—what your sufferings must be." In New York, at Cooper Union, Frederick Douglass said: "The colored people, from first to last, and through all, whether through good or through evil report, fully believed in Abraham Lincoln. Even though he sometimes smote them, and wounded them severely, yet they firmly trusted in him: This was however, no blind trust unsupported by reason: They early caught a glimpse of the man, and from the evidence of their senses, they believed in him." "What do the Copperheads say . . . ?" Pheebe Clark asked her sister on Monday, May 1. "If they say here they are glad the President is dead they shoot them like dogs."

Far from the train route, far from the public tears, far from the formal eulogies, grief was less visible but no less real. On St. Helena Island, midway between Charleston and Savannah, the abolitionist Laura Matilda Towne, a Pennsylvania Unitarian, had founded the first school for freed Black Americans.

"It was a frightful blow at first," Towne wrote after the assassination. "The people have refused to believe he was dead. Last Sunday the Black minister of Frogmore said that if they knew the President were dead they would mourn for him, but they could not think that was the truth, and they would wait and see."

A freed Black man who came to Towne's school for clothing was distracted. She wondered why. "Oh," the man said, "I have lost a friend. I don't care much now about anything."

"What friend?" she asked.

"They call him Sam," the man said of Lincoln; "Uncle Sam, the best friend ever I had." Another freed person asked Towne "if it were true that the 'Government was dead.'" And yet another said, "Lincoln died for we, Christ died for we, and me believe him the same man."

EPILOGUE

I See Now the Wisdom of His Course

"DEAD, *DEAD*, DEAD, he yet speaketh!" Henry Ward Beecher cried in a sermon on the second Sunday after Ford's Theatre. "Disenthralled of flesh . . . he begins his illimitable work." "Is it not true that this is the leading lesson of Lincoln's life—that true . . . greatness, the greatness that will survive the corrosion and abrasion of time, change and progress, must rest upon character?" the newspaperman John L. Scripps wrote to William Herndon in the wake of the assassination. Lincoln's character, Scripps said, had "given him his fame—have made him for all time to come the great American Man— the grand central figure in American (perhaps the World's) History." George McClellan was generous in his sentiments. "How strange it is that the military death of the rebellion should have been followed with such tragic quickness by the atrocious murder of Mr Lincoln!" the general wrote. "Would for our country's sake that a better man had succeeded him. I fear that the destinies of the nation are not safe in the hands of the person whom fate & party folly have elevated to the head of the Government."

After the briefest period of hope, that head of government, Andrew Johnson, proved disastrous. Self-involved, reactionary, and racist, the Tennessean set about undoing the verdict of the war and the implications of President Lincoln's views of American life and governance. Nominated on the 1864 ticket because of momentary political considerations rooted in his being a white Southerner and a Unionist, Johnson showed himself to be more white Southerner than Unionist. We do not know how Lincoln would have handled Reconstruction—he was an improviser—and as even many white Southerners saw, Lincoln's views of Reconstruction were based more on conciliation than on confrontation or on sanction. Yet the evidence of 1860–1865 shows him to have been evolving politically and consistently devoted to the moral work of expanding, not constricting, human liberty and human rights. It is also clear that initiatives considered or undertaken on Lincoln's watch unraveled under Johnson. Prospects for the redistribution of land in the South, for suffrage for the formerly enslaved, and for an effective Freedmen's Bureau faded after Ford's Theatre.

"White men alone must manage the South," Johnson said in 1865; in 1867, the president argued that Black people were incapable of self-government. "No independent government of any form has ever been successful in their hands," Johnson wrote in his annual message. "On the contrary, wherever they have been left to their own devices they have shown a constant tendency to relapse into barbarism."

The war was supposed to be over, and the Union was supposed to have won, but the white South found strength in defeat. The white Southern minister Benjamin Morgan Palmer had hinted at a future in which the Confederate war aims were pursued by other means. "Can a cause be lost when it has passed through such a baptism as ours?" Palmer asked. "Principles never die, and if they seem to perish it is only to experience a resurrection in the future."

Edward Alfred Pollard was a motive force behind that resurrection. A Virginia-born editor who had served as clerk to the House Judiciary Committee before the war, Pollard published a book, *The Lost Cause: A New Southern History of the War of the Confederates*, in 1866 and followed it with a second work, *The Lost Cause Regained*, in 1868. Slavery was lost, but white supremacy could endure, Pollard argued, if the white South held fast to its commitment to a racial hierarchy. To survive military defeat, the old Confederacy would pursue the subjugation of Black people even in the face of emancipation and, after the passage of the Fourteenth Amendment, of citizenship and equal protection under the Constitution. A powerful federal establishment, Pollard wrote, was "odious, and especially in the present instance, with the stripe of Negro government in it." He quoted Jefferson Davis: "The principle for which we contended is bound to reassert itself, though it may be at another time and in another form." That principle: white supremacy. Pollard summoned his readers to renewed struggle. "The 'Lost Cause' needs no war to regain it," he wrote. "We have taken up new hopes, new arms, new methods."

The rise of the Ku Klux Klan in the South was the most vivid example of white intransigence. "If," W.E.B. Du Bois wrote in 1935, "the Reconstruction of the Southern states, from slavery to free labor, and from aristocracy to industrial democracy, had been conceived as a major national program of America, whose accomplishment at any price was well worth the effort, we should be living today in a different world." Instead came a world of segregation.

In 1876–77, the period during which federal troops were withdrawn from the statehouses of South Carolina and Louisiana, leaving the white South fully to its own devices, Frederick Douglass spoke at the dedication of the Freedmen's Memorial Monument in Washington. Sober, candid, and moving, Douglass gave posterity a Lincoln in full. "It must be admitted, truth compels me to admit, even here in the presence of the monument we have erected to his memory, Abraham Lincoln was not, in the fullest sense of the word, either our man or our model," Douglass said. "In his interests, in his associations, in his habits of thought, and in his prejudices, he was a white man." Yet in "a broad survey, in the light of the stern logic of great events," Douglass said, "we came to the conclusion that the hour and the man of our redemption had somehow met in the person of Abraham Lincoln."

In these postbellum decades, discriminatory Jim Crow laws came to dominate the South, and the North was home to both de jure and de facto segregation. In 1896, in *Plessy v. Ferguson,* the Supreme Court upheld the racist principle of "separate but equal"; lynchings went on unabated, unprosecuted, and too little noted. "The whole South—every state in the South—had got into the hands of the very men who held us as slaves," said a formerly enslaved person. "The cry is delusive that slavery is dead," George Bancroft had remarked in a eulogy for Lincoln. The formerly enslaved person and the historian-statesman were both right. White Americans remained firmly in control.

The Lincoln legend grew as the shadows of segregation lengthened. His virtues were noted, as well as his vices—virtues and vices that were also evident in the American populace, for they were the virtues and vices common to the mass of humankind. "Abraham Lincoln was perhaps the greatest figure of the nineteenth century," W.E.B. Du Bois wrote in 1922. "I love him not because he was perfect but because he was not and yet triumphed. The world is full of illegitimate children, The world is full of folk whose taste was educated in the gutter. The world is full of people born hating and despising their fellows. To these I love to say: See this man. He was one of you and yet he became Abraham Lincoln."

In his 1963 *Letter from a Birmingham Jail,* composed during his incarceration for nonviolently protesting segregation in Alabama, Martin Luther King, Jr., included Lincoln in the company of Jesus, of Amos, and of Paul. King had been called an extremist—a label he had at first resisted but now embraced. "Was not Jesus an extremist for love?" King asked. He then quoted the "extremist" Amos—"Let justice roll down like waters and righteousness like an ever flowing stream," and the "extremist" Paul: "I bear in my body the marks of the Lord Jesus" before citing the "extremist" Lincoln's words as their own kind of scripture: "This nation cannot survive half slave and half free."

King stood on the steps of the Lincoln Memorial on Wednesday, August 28, 1963, to address the March on Washington for Jobs and Freedom. The imagery linked past and present with an eye on the future—a future rooted in the Emancipation Proclamation, which had come, King said, "as a joyous daybreak to end the long night of their captivity." And on the stormy Memphis night of Wednesday, April 3, 1968, King thought of Lincoln. During a rhetorical flight in a sermon at Mason Temple, King imagined a kind of time travel. Where would he go, he asked, if God gave him the chance to take flight through the great ages of humankind? King mused about visiting the Greece of Plato, Socrates, and Aristotle, the Wittenberg of Martin Luther—and the America of Abraham Lincoln.

King would be shot to death outside Room 306 of the Lorraine Motel at sunset the next day. In Atlanta, he was eulogized by Benjamin E. Mays, the longtime president of Morehouse College. "Each man must respond to the call of God in his lifetime," Mays said. "Abraham, leaving his country in the obedience to God's call; Moses leading a rebellious people to the Promised Land; Jesus dying on a cross; Galileo on his knees recanting; Lincoln dying of an assassin's bullet. . . . Martin Luther King Jr. dying fighting for justice for garbage collectors—none of these men were ahead of their time. With them the time was always ripe to do that which was right and that which needed to be done."

Lincoln kept America's democratic project alive. He did not do so alone. Innumerable ordinary people made sacrifices, even unto death, to preserve the Union against the designs of the rebel South. But Lincoln was essential, and his ultimate vision of the nation—that the country should be free of slavery—was informed by a moral understanding. To him, America ought to seek to practice the principles of the Declaration of Independence as fully as possible, for the alternatives were so much worse.

The progressives' verdicts on Lincoln were striking. "But what was A. Lincoln to the colored people or they to him?" Frederick Douglass had asked in 1865. "As compared with the long line of his predecessors, many of whom were merely the facile and servile instruments of the slave power, Abraham Lincoln, while unsurpassed in his devotion to the welfare of the white race, was also in a sense hitherto without example, emphatically, the black man's President: the first to show any respect for their rights as men." "There is no mistake about it in regard to Mr. Lincoln's desire to do all that he can see it right and possible for him to do to uproot slavery, and give fair play to the emancipated," William Lloyd Garrison observed. "To those who have struggled so long for the total abolition of slavery, and whose desires for the speedy realization of all their aims and aspirations have naturally been of the most ardent character, Mr. Lincoln has seemed exceedingly slow in all his emancipatory measures. For this he has been severely chided. . . . Yet what long strides he has taken in the right direction, and never a backward step!" The suffragist and abolitionist Elizabeth Cady Stanton, who had opposed the president in the 1864 presidential race, came to regret it. "I see now the wisdom of his course, leading public opinion slowly but surely up to the final blow for freedom," Stanton said. "My conscience pricks me now when I recall how I worked and prayed in 1864 for the defeat of Lincoln's re-election."

Abraham Lincoln did not bring about heaven on earth. Yet he defended the possibilities of democracy and the pursuit of justice at an hour in which the means of amendment, adjustment, and reform were under assault. What if the constitutional order had failed and the Union had been permanently divided? What would have come next? A durable oligarchical white Southern slave empire, surely strengthened and possibly expanded, would have emerged from the war; and, as Lincoln saw, the viability of popular self-government would have been in ruins.

In life, Lincoln's motives were moral as well as political—a reminder that our finest presidents are those committed to bringing a flawed nation closer to the light, a mission that requires an understanding that politics divorced from conscience is fatal to the American experiment in liberty under law. In years of peril he pointed the country toward a future that was superior to the past and to the present; in years of strife he held steady. Lincoln's life shows us that progress can be made by fallible and fallen presidents and peoples—which, in a fallible and fallen world, should give us hope.

The sun set in Washington at 6:44 P.M. on Friday, April 14, 1865, and the president, as was his habit, was having coffee after supper. As he prepared to depart for Ford's Theatre, Lincoln carried his china cup to his southerly-facing suite and set it on one of the two windowsills in his bedroom. He was wearing a black Brooks Brothers suit, a gift for his second inauguration. Leaving in his carriage for the theater, Lincoln donned a hat that bore a mourning ribbon he had first affixed to it after Willie's death three years before.

In his pocket the president carried a leather wallet in which he kept a collection of newspaper clippings. There was John Bright's letter to Horace Greeley, a comparison of the 1864 party platforms, accounts of emancipation in Missouri, and General Sherman's orders to his troops. One article included an excerpt from the *Liverpool Daily Post*: "Absolute truth, stern resolution, clear insight, solemn faithfulness, courage that cannot be daunted, hopefulness that cannot be dashed—these are qualities that go a long way to make up a hero. And it would not be easy to dispute Mr. Lincoln's claim to all these."

Truth, resolution, insight, faithfulness, courage, hopefulness: Such was Lincoln at his best. Half a century later, a monument to the man who left his coffee in the window would rise outside that room, down the South Lawn toward the Potomac and a bit to the west. There, in gleaming marble, facing the obelisk honoring the first president, rests a Greek temple to the sixteenth. The statue of Lincoln sits behind mighty pillars. His words at Gettysburg and in the Second Inaugural are etched in stone, for all time. If we look closely, though, we see a human face—a weathered Lincoln who gazes out not grandly but whose eyes are inclined slightly downward, looking less into the far distance than at all who come to him.

In that tumultuous spring of 1865, the mortal Lincoln would never return to claim his china cup in the bedroom window, nor would he peruse anew the clippings in his wallet. The world moved on, turning over again and again and again, for worse and for better. Now the immortal Lincoln sits not far from the room, and from the house, in which he proved that right does make might. There, in the heart of the capital, on the National Mall, Abraham Lincoln remains, at once elevated and proximate, historic and humble, a source of strength for the struggle that seems to have no end.

SOURCE NOTES

Selected Abbreviations Used

Burlingame, AL: Michael Burlingame, *Abraham Lincoln: A Life* (Baltimore, Md., 2008), 2 vols.

CW: Roy Basler et al., eds., *Collected Works of Abraham Lincoln* (New Brunswick, N.J., 1953), 8 vols.

Hay and Nicolay, AL: John M. Hay and John G. Nicolay, *Abraham Lincoln: A History* (New York, 1890), 10 vols.

HAPE: Gil Troy, Arthur M. Schlesinger, Jr., and Fred L. Israel, eds., *History of American Presidential Elections, 1789 to 2008* (New York, 2012)

Holzer, ed., TLA: Harold Holzer, ed., *The Lincoln Anthology: Great Writers on His Life and Legacy from 1860 to Now* (New York, 2009)

JALA: *Journal of the Abraham Lincoln Association*

KJV: King James Version of the Holy Bible

LDBD: Earl S. Miers et al., eds., *Lincoln Day by Day: A Chronology 1809–1865*

LOC: Library of Congress, Washington, D.C.

NYT: *The New York Times*

RWAL: Don E. Fehrenbacher and Virginia Fehrenbacher, eds., *Recollected Words of Abraham Lincoln* (Stanford, Calif., 1996)

Epigraphs

ix "I DO NOT DESPAIR" Frederick Douglass, "The Meaning of July Fourth for the Negro," speech at Rochester, New York, July 5, 1852, in Philip S. Foner, ed., *The Life and Writings of Frederick Douglass* (New York, 1950), 2:203.

ix "I DO NOT PRETEND" Francis Power Cobbe, ed., *The Collected Works of Theodore Parker: Containing His Theological, Polemical, and Critical Writings, Sermons, Speeches, and Addresses and Literary Miscellanies,* vol. 2, *Sermons and Prayers* (London, 1863), 48.

ix "MORAL COWARDICE IS SOMETHING" Michael Burlingame, ed., *Lincoln Observed: Civil War Dispatches of Noah Brooks* (Baltimore, Md., 1998), 205.

Prologue: A Big, Inconsistent, Brave Man

xvii THE STORM HAD COME Washington *Evening Star*, March 4, 1865. On the weather and the conditions of the city for the second inauguration, see also *The New York Herald*, March 6, 1865; Edward Achorn, *Every Drop of Blood: The Momentous Second Inauguration of Abraham Lincoln* (New York, 2020), 150–65; Noah Brooks, *Abraham Lincoln and the Downfall of American Slavery* (New York, 1895), 412–15; Burlingame, ed., *Lincoln Observed,* 165; James B. Conroy, *Lincoln's White House: The People's House in Wartime* (Lanham, Md., 2017), 232–33; Philip Van Doren Stern, *An End to Valor: The Last Days of the Civil War* (Boston, 1958), 1–3; Ronald C. White, Jr., *Lincoln's Greatest Speech: The Sec-*

ond Inaugural (New York, 2002), 29–32; Michelle Krowl, "Here Comes the Sun: Seeing Omens in the Weather at Abraham Lincoln's Second Inauguration," LOC, March 4, 2015, https://blogs.loc.gov/loc/2015/03/here-comes-the-sun-seeing -omens-in-the-weather-at-abraham-lincolns-second-inauguration/.

xvii AT DAWN ON SATURDAY *Astronomical and Meteorological Observations Made at the United States Naval Observatory During the Year 1865* (Washington, D.C., 1867), 517 (footnote).

xvii A FOOT COULD SINK *The New York Herald*, March 5, 1865.

xvii WAS PACKED WITH 1,008 GUESTS *The Daily National Republican*, March 7, 1865.

xvii "THE OTHER HOTELS" Ibid.

xvii "THE CROWD IN THE CITY" Nathan W. Daniels Diary and Scrapbook, March 5, 1865, LOC.

xvii BOSWELL'S FANCY STORE Washington *Evening Star*, March 6, 1865.

xvii THE RETAILERS BURNS & WILSON *The National Republican*, March 4, 1865.

xvii AN INTIMATE OF PRESIDENT LINCOLN'S See, for instance, Burlingame, ed., *Lincoln Observed*, 1–12. Wayne C. Temple, *Lincoln's Confidant: The Life of Noah Brooks* (Urbana, Ill., 2019), is comprehensive.

xvii "DARK AND DISMAL" Brooks, *Abraham Lincoln and the Downfall of American Slavery*, 412.

xvii WEATHER IMPROVED SLIGHTLY Ibid.; White, *Lincoln's Greatest Speech*, 31.

xvii COMPLETED IN THE WAR YEARS White, *Lincoln's Greatest Speech*, 34–35; RWAL, 147; "Constructing a National Symbol," United States Senate, https://www.senate.gov /artandhistory/history/minute/ConstructingaNationalSymbol.htm.

xvii WORKERS, MANY OF THEM ENSLAVED William C. Allen, "History of Slave Laborers in the Construction of the United States Capitol," Report of the Architect of the Capitol, June 1, 2005, https://emancipation.dc.gov/sites/default/files/dc/sites /emancipation/publication/attachments/History_of_Slave_Laborers_in_the _Construction_of_the_US_Capitol.pdf.

xviii "IT SEEMED A STRANGE CONTRADICTION" "Constructing a National Symbol"; "Glimpses of War: Our Washington Correspondence," NYT, April 24, 1861.

xviii "IF PEOPLE SEE" "Glimpses of War," NYT, April 24, 1861.

xviii HUNDREDS OF THOUSANDS Drew Gilpin Faust, *This Republic of Suffering: Death and the American Civil War* (New York, 2008), xi–xvii; Gary W. Gallagher, *The Union War* (Cambridge, Mass., 2011), 164–65; J. David Hacker, "A Census-Based Count of the Civil War Dead," *Civil War History* 57, no. 4 (December 2011): 307–48.

xviii "WE ARE NOW ON THE BRINK" RWAL, 67.

xix "THE ADDRESS WILL" White, *Lincoln's Greatest Speech*, 22–23.

xix HAD HAD THE SPEECH PRINTED Ibid., 41–42.

xix WITH HIS SPECTACLES Alexander Gardner, *Abraham Lincoln Delivering His Second Inaugural Address as President of the United States, Washington, D.C.* [March 4, 1865] Photograph. https://www.loc.gov/item/2009633604/. See also White, *Lincoln's Greatest Speech*, 40.

xix A SMALL TABLE White, *Lincoln's Greatest Speech*, 41; "Table Used During President Abraham Lincoln's Second Inaugural," https://www.masshist.org/database/viewer .php?item_id=1788&pid=36.

xix A GLASS OF WATER White, *Lincoln's Greatest Speech*, 40.

xix "SOUNDED MORE LIKE" David W. Blight, *Frederick Douglass: Prophet of Freedom* (New York, 2018), 458.

xix "THE CONSCIENCE OF THE NATION" Foner, ed., *Life and Writings of Frederick Douglass*, 2:192.

xix "OUR ENTERPRISE IS" Richard J. Hofstadter, *The American Political Tradition and the Men Who Made It* (New York, 1989), 185–86.

xix "BROUGHT TO A LIVING" CW, 6:535.

xix LINCOLN'S OWN FAITH On Lincoln's faith and the broader religious story of his lifetime, see, for instance, Sydney E. Ahlstrom, *A Religious History of the American People* (New Haven, Conn., 1972), especially 385–509, 648–729; William E. Barton, *The Soul of Abraham Lincoln* (New York, 1920); Samuel W. Calhoun and Lucas E. Morel, "Abraham Lincoln's Religion: The Case for His Ultimate Belief in a Personal, Sovereign God," *JALA* 33, no. 1 (2012): 38–74; Lucas E. Morel, *Lincoln's Sacred Effort: Defining Religion's Role in American Self-Government* (Lanham, Md., 2000); Richard Carwardine, *Lincoln: A Life of Purpose and Power* (New York, 2007); Richard Carwardine, "Lincoln's Religion," in Eric Foner, ed., *Our Lincoln: New Perspectives on Lincoln and His World* (New York, 2008), 223–48; Richard Carwardine, "'Simply a Theist': Herndon on Lincoln's Religion," *JALA* 35, no. 2 (2014): 18–36; Thomas L. Carson, *Lincoln's Ethics* (New York, 2015); Andrew Delbanco, "Lincoln's Sacramental Language," in Foner, ed., *Our Lincoln*, 199–222; Allen C. Guelzo, *Abraham Lincoln: Redeemer President* (Grand Rapids, Mich., 1999); Allen C. Guelzo, "Abraham Lincoln and the Doctrine of Necessity," *JALA* 18 (1997): 57–81; Nicholas Guyatt, *Providence and the Invention of the United States, 1607–1876* (Cambridge, UK, 2007); Nathan O. Hatch, *The Democratization of American Christianity* (New Haven, Conn., 1989); William H. Herndon and Jesse W. Weik, *Herndon's Life of Lincoln* (New York, 1983), xxx, xlvi–vi, 354–60, 432; H. L. Mencken, "From Prejudices: Third Series," in Holzer, ed., *TLA*, 441–44; William Lee Miller, *Lincoln's Virtues: An Ethical Biography* (New York, 2002); William Lee Miller, *President Lincoln: The Duty of a Statesman* (New York, 2008); Hans J. Morgenthau and David Hein, *Essays on Lincoln's Faith and Politics*, ed. Kenneth W. Thompson (Lanham, Md., 1983); Mark A. Noll, *The Civil War as a Theological Crisis* (Chapel Hill, N.C., 2006); George C. Rable, *God's Almost Chosen Peoples: A Religious History of the American Civil War* (Chapel Hill, N.C., 2010); David S. Reynolds, *Abe: Abraham Lincoln in His Times* (New York, 2020), 37–40; Harry S. Stout, *Upon the Altar of the Nation: A Moral History of the American Civil War* (New York, 2006); Elton Trueblood, *Abraham Lincoln: Theologian of American Anguish* (New York, 1973); White, *Lincoln's Greatest Speech,* especially 132–43; Douglas L. Wilson, *Honor's Voice: The Transformation of Abraham Lincoln* (New York, 1999); Stewart Winger, *Lincoln, Religion, and Romantic Cultural Politics* (DeKalb, Ill., 2003); William J. Wolf, *The Almost Chosen People: A Study of the Religion of Abraham Lincoln* (Garden City, N.Y., 1959). "His confidence in the people had its roots in religious reality and its presupposition in God," William J. Wolf wrote. "It was not the secular theory that the will of the people constituted right. That is the principle of mobocracy. *Vox populi, vox dei* meant for Lincoln that, if not thwarted by man's rebellion, God so guided the consciences of men in history that the people's verdict was properly their response to His guidance." Wolf, *Almost Chosen People,* 116.

xix "MY GREAT RESPONSIBILITY" CW, 5:146. As William Herndon wrote: "Conscience . . . is that faculty which induces in us a love of the just. Its real office is justice; right and equity are its correlatives. As a court, it is in session continuously; it decides all acts at all times. Mr. Lincoln had a deep, broad, living conscience. . . . His conscience ruled his heart; he was always just before he was generous. It cannot be said of any mortal that he was always absolutely just. Neither was Lincoln always just; but his general life was." Herndon and Weik, *Herndon's Life of Lincoln,* 481.

xix RAISED IN AN ANTISLAVERY BAPTIST ETHOS See chapter 1.

xix "EVERY KNEE SHOULD BOW" Philippians 2:10–11, KJV.

xx TO DO JUSTICE Micah 6:8, KJV.

xx   "IN THE MATERIAL WORLD" "Speech of Theodore Parker at the Grand Mass Anti-Slavery Celebration of Independence Day at Abington, Mass., July 5, 1852," *The Liberator*, July 30, 1852.

xx   "I MAY ADVANCE SLOWLY" Benjamin Quarles, *Lincoln and the Negro* (New York, 1962), 123.

xx   PHINEAS D. GURLEY See, for instance, John A. O'Brien, "Seeking God's Will: President Lincoln and Rev. Dr. Gurley," *JALA* 39 (Summer 2018): 29–54; David R. Barbee, "President Lincoln and Doctor Gurley," *Abraham Lincoln Quarterly* 5 (March 1948): 3–24; Dewey D. Wallace, Jr., Wilson Golden, and Edith Holmes Snyder, eds., *Capital Witness: A History of the New York Avenue Presbyterian Church in Washington, DC* (Franklin, Tenn., 2011); Phineas Densmore Gurley Papers, Presbyterian Historical Society, Philadelphia, Pennsylvania.

xx   "GOD'S WAYS," HE SAID O'Brien, "Seeking God's Will," 42.

xx   "WHAT WE NEED" Ibid.

xx   "I HAVE OFTEN WISHED" CW, 6:536.

xx   "LOOK AT THE FACTS" Samuel A. Eliot, ed., *The Works of Theodore Parker: Sermons of Religion* (Boston, 1908), 64. On Parker in general, see, for instance, Paul E. Teed, *A Revolutionary Conscience: Theodore Parker and Antebellum America* (Lanham, Md., 2012); Dean Grodzins, *American Heretic: Theodore Parker and Transcendentalism* (Chapel Hill, N.C., 2002); John W. Chadwick, *Theodore Parker: Preacher and Reformer* (Boston, 1901); Henry S. Commager, *Theodore Parker* (Boston, 1936); Octavius B. Frothingham, *Theodore Parker: A Biography* (Boston, 1874); Arthur I. Ladu, "The Political Ideas of Theodore Parker," *Studies in Philology* 38, no. 1 (1941): 106–23.

xxi "THIS STRUGGLE MAY BE" Frederick Douglass, "If There Is No Struggle, There Is No Progress," 1857, https://www.blackpast.org/african-american-history/1857-frederick-douglass-if-there-no-struggle-there-no-progress/.

xxi HIS "ANCIENT FAITH" CW, 2:266. See also James Oakes, *The Crooked Path to Abolition: Abraham Lincoln and the Antislavery Constitution* (New York, 2021), 108.

xxi WAS FOUNDED ON THIS INJUNCTION Wolf, *Almost Chosen People*, 126. Henry C. Deming, a Connecticut politician and Union officer, recalled Lincoln's saying that he "had never united himself to any church because he found difficulty in giving his assent, without mental reservation, to the long, complicated statements of Christian doctrine which characterize their articles of belief and confessions of faith. When any church [he continued] will inscribe over its altar, as its sole qualification for membership, the Savior's condensed statement of the substance of both law and gospel, 'Thou shalt love the Lord thy God with all thy heart, and with all thy soul, and with all thy mind, and thy neighbor as thyself,' that church will I join with all my heart and all my soul." RWAL, 137. "The honesty of Mr. Lincoln appeared to spring from religious convictions; and it was his habit, when conversing of things which most intimately concerned himself, to say that, however he might be misapprehended by men who did not appear to know him, he was glad to know that no thought or intent of his escaped the observation of that Judge by whose final decree he expected to stand or fall in this world and the next," Noah Brooks wrote. "It seemed as though this was his surest refuge at times when he was most misunderstood or misrepresented." Brooks, "Personal Recollections of Abraham Lincoln," in Holzer, ed., *TLA*, 171–72.

xxi "AS I WOULD NOT BE A *SLAVE*" CW, 2:532.

xxi THE PRESIDENT HAD QUIETLY ARRIVED Burlingame, ed., *Lincoln Observed*, 167.

xxi THE PRESIDENT SLEPT IN A ROOM "Inventory of the President's House," May 26, 1865, Records of the Former Commissioners of Public Buildings and Grounds,

National Archives, Washington, D.C.; "Second Floor of the White House. Modified by Jo-Ann Parks; original drawing by Fred D. Owen, Library of Congress," in Conroy, *Lincoln's White House*; "Second Floor Plan in Lincoln's Time" in illustrations following 394 in vol. 1 of William Seale, *The President's House: A History* (Washington, D.C., 1986). See also Burlingame, ed., *Lincoln Observed*, 79–88. For details and documents about the Lincoln White House, I am grateful to Stewart McLaurin, president of the White House Historical Association, and to Dr. Matthew Costello, Senior Historian at the David M. Rubenstein National Center for White House History.

xxi TWO LARGE WINDOWS Communication to author, National Center for White House History and Office of the White House Curator.

xxi FROM THIS VANTAGE POINT Kristi Finefield, "The Washington Monument: A Long Journey to the Top," *Picture This: Library of Congress Prints and Photos,* September 19, 2019, https://blogs.loc.gov/picturethis/2019/09/the-washington-monument-a-long-journey-to-the-top/; *Frank Leslie's Illustrated Newspaper*, February 1, 1862.

xxii EARLY IN THE REBELLION William O. Stoddard, *Inside Lincoln's White House in War Times* (New York, 1890), 11.

xxii "DARK MAHOGANY DOORS" Burlingame, ed., *Lincoln Observed*, 83–84.

xxii THE PLUMBING WAS IMPRESSIVELY MODERN Conroy, *Lincoln's White House,* 37; Seale, *President's House,* 1:90, 316–17.

xxii A "DEGRADATION" Conroy, *Lincoln's White House*, 36–37. I am grateful to James Conroy for his assistance on these details.

xxii SHE SOON RENOVATED See, for instance, Conroy, *Lincoln's White House,* 91–93; Burlingame, *AL*, 2:280–81.

xxii THIS *"DAMNED OLD HOUSE"* Benjamin Brown French, *Witness to the Young Republic: A Yankee's Journal, 1828–1870,* ed. Donald B. Cole and John J. McDonough (Hanover, N.H., 1989), 382.

xxii "PERENNIALLY OVERRUN" Ronald D. Rietveld, "The Lincoln White House Community," *JALA* 20 (Summer 1999): 21.

xxii "FARM HOURS" Stoddard, *Inside Lincoln's White House,* 12.

xxii LIKED TO RISE EARLY Ibid.

xxii HIS WHITE HOUSE USHER AND VALET Jonathan W. White, *A House Built by Slaves: African American Visitors to the White House* (Lanham, Md., 2022), xviii, 174, 209. See also Natalie Sweet, "A Representative 'of Our People': The Agency of William Slade, Leader in the African American Community and Usher to Abraham Lincoln," *JALA* 34 (Summer 2013): 21–41.

xxii PRESIDENT WOULD DRESS The details about Lincoln's clothes and personal effects are drawn from the author's inspection of the collections of the Smithsonian Institution's National Museum of American History. I am grateful to Harry R. Rubenstein, the longtime chair of the museum's Division of Politics and Reform, for his steadfast and generous counsel. See also Harry R. Rubenstein, *Abraham Lincoln: An Extraordinary Life* (Washington, D.C., 2008), a volume about the museum's Lincoln collections published on the occasion of the bicentennial of the sixteenth president's birth. For Lincoln's daily routine in the presidential years, see John Hay to William H. Herndon, September 5, 1866, in Douglas L. Wilson and Rodney O. Davis, eds., *Herndon's Informants: Letters, Interviews, and Statements about Abraham Lincoln* (Urbana and Chicago, 1998), 330–32.

xxii THERE WOULD BE A BREAKFAST Burlingame, *AL*, 2:252–56, details Lincoln's daily routine in the White House, as does Rietveld, "Lincoln White House Community," 28–39.

xxii   THE WORN STONES Stoddard, *Inside Lincoln's White House,* 3.

xxii   HE LOVED APPLES This list is drawn from Wilson and Davis, eds., *Herndon's Informants,* 466, and Rietveld, "Lincoln White House Community," 17–48; Michael Burlingame and John R. Turner Ettlinger, eds., *Inside Lincoln's White House: The Complete Civil War Diary of John Hay* (Carbondale and Edwardsville, Ill., 1997), 246; David Homer Bates, *Lincoln in the Telegraph Office* (Lincoln, Neb., 1995), 212–13; "The White House Grounds & Entrance: Pets," http://www.mrlincolnswhite house.org/the-white-house/the-white-house-grounds-entrance/white-house -grounds-entrance-pets/.

xxii   OF SHAKESPEARE, AND OF ROBERT BURNS *RWAL,* 502. "They are my two favorite authors, and I must manage to see their birthplaces someday, if I can contrive to cross the Atlantic," Lincoln said. Ibid.

xxiii   "EVERY MAN IS SAID" *CW,* 1:8–9. See also John Dos Passos, "Lincoln and His Almost Chosen People," in Holzer, ed., *TLA,* 719.

xxiii   "I HAVE BEEN TOO FAMILIAR" *CW,* 1:9.

xxiii   WHEN HE FAILED TO WIN Hofstadter, *American Political Tradition,* 127. "With all his quiet passion Lincoln had sought to rise in life, to make something of himself through his own honest efforts," Hofstadter wrote. Ibid.

xxiii   "THAT MAN WHO THINKS" Ibid.

xxiii   "YOUR DISTRICT DID NOT" F. B. Carpenter, *The Inner Life of Abraham Lincoln: Six Months at the White House* (New York, 1868), 53.

xxiii   "IT WAS IN THE WORLD OF POLITICS" Hofstadter, *American Political Tradition,* 124.

xxiii   MRS. LINCOLN LEFT THE WHITE HOUSE *Lincoln's Greatest Speech,* 32–33.

xxiii   WAS CHEERED BY Burlingame, ed., *Lincoln Observed,* 167.

xxiii   THE THRONGS INCLUDED White, *Lincoln's Greatest Speech,* 32.

xxiv   "THOUSANDS OF COLORED FOLK" "Abraham Lincoln's Second Inauguration," http://www.abrahamlincolnonline.org/lincoln/education/inaugural2.htm.

xxiv   "ABOUT THE HOMELIEST" Nathaniel Hawthorne, "From Chiefly About War-Matters by a Peaceable Man," in Holzer, ed., *TLA,* 33.

xxiv   "DRESSED IN A RUSTY" Ibid., 34.

xxiv   A PHOTOGRAPH TAKEN Richard S. Lowry, *The Photographer and the President: Abraham Lincoln, Alexander Gardner, and the Images That Made a Presidency* (New York, 2015), 140–58. This image is best known as the "cracked plate" photograph of Lincoln; it is now in the National Portrait Gallery in Washington. https://www.si.edu /exhibitions/cracked-plate-photograph-lincoln%3Aevent-exhib-5760.

xxiv   "WHY, I CAN'T" *RWAL,* 78.

xxiv   "PEOPLE SEEMED DELIGHTED" Brooks, "Personal Recollections of Abraham Lincoln," in Holzer, ed., *TLA,* 165.

xxiv   WHEN A FRIEND ADDRESSED LINCOLN Ibid.

xxiv   MUSING ABOUT AN ACQUAINTANCE Ibid., 167.

xxiv   SPOTTING FREDERICK DOUGLASS Blight, *Frederick Douglass,* 458.

xxiv   THE PRESIDENT POINTED HIM OUT Ibid.; Frederick Douglass, *Autobiographies,* ed. Henry Louis Gates, Jr. (New York, 1994), 802.

xxiv   ADDLED FROM AN INFUSION Hans L. Trefousse, *Andrew Johnson: A Biography* (New York, 1989), 188–91.

xxiv   "BITTER CONTEMPT" Douglass, *Autobiographies,* 802.

xxiv   DOUGLASS TURNED TO Ibid.

xxv   "CLEAR, RESONANT" Brooks, *Abraham Lincoln and the Downfall of American Slavery,* 413.

xxv   "WHY DO WE SUFFER" *RWAL,* 113.

xxv   "FELLOW COUNTRYMEN" *CW,* 8:332. On the Second Inaugural Address, see, for instance, Achorn, *Every Drop of Blood;* Edwin Black, "The Ultimate Voice of Lincoln," *Rhetoric and Public Affairs* (Spring 2000): 49–57; James P. Byrd, *A Holy Baptism of Fire and Blood: The Bible and the American Civil War* (New York, 2021), 254–59; Glen E. Thurow, *Abraham Lincoln and American Political Religion* (Albany, N.Y., 1976), 88–108; Andrew C. Hansen, "Dimensions of Agency in Lincoln's 'Second Inaugural,'" *Philosophy and Rhetoric* 37, no. 3 (2004): 223–54; White, *Lincoln's Greatest Speech;* Burlingame, *AL,* 2:765–72; Carwardine, *Lincoln: A Life of Purpose and Power,* 244–48; David Herbert Donald, *Lincoln* (New York, 1995), 565–68; Doris Kearns Goodwin, *Team of Rivals: The Political Genius of Abraham Lincoln* (New York, 2005), 697–701; Hay and Nicolay, *AL: A History,* 10:132–47; Mark A. Noll, *America's God: From Jonathan Edwards to Abraham Lincoln* (New York, 2002), 426–37.

xxv A BRIEF ON SECESSION AND UNION For the First Inaugural Address, see *CW,* 4:262–71.

xxv "BOTH PARTIES DEPRECATED WAR" Ibid., 8:332.

xxv "ONE EIGHTH OF THE WHOLE POPULATION" Ibid.

xxv "BOTH READ THE SAME BIBLE" Ibid., 333.

xxvi "IT MAY SEEM STRANGE" Ibid.

xxvi "IN THE SWEAT OF THY FACE" Genesis 3:19, KJV.

xxvi "JUDGE NOT, THAT YE BE NOT JUDGED" Matthew 7:1, KJV. Lincoln was always careful to avoid self-righteousness. "Browning," he remarked to his friend Orville Browning, "suppose God is against us in our view on the subject of slavery in this country and our method of dealing with it." *RWAL,* 62.

xxvi "THE PRAYERS OF BOTH" *CW,* 8:333.

xxvi "YET," LINCOLN SAID Ibid.

xxvi "THESE SOLEMN WORDS" Douglass, *Autobiographies,* 802.

xxvii "THE AUTHOR OF OUR BEING" *RWAL,* 2.

xxvii "WITH MALICE TOWARD NONE" *CW,* 8:333.

xxvii TURNED TO CHIEF JUSTICE SALMON P. CHASE Achorn, *Every Drop of Blood,* 238. "The men in the crowd respectfully removed their hats," Achorn wrote. Ibid.

xxvii THE SUN CAME THROUGH *RWAL,* 56.

xxvii "IT MADE MY HEART" Brooks, *Abraham Lincoln and the Downfall of American Slavery,* 413.

xxvii "WAS JUST SUPERSTITIOUS ENOUGH" *RWAL,* 56.

xxvii RECORDED THE MOMENT IN HIS DIARY Michael Shiner Diary, Michael Shiner Papers, LOC. See also Krowl, "Here Comes the Sun," LOC.

xxvii THE CHIEF JUSTICE NOTED White, *Lincoln's Greatest Speech,* 181; Achorn, *Every Drop of Blood,* 238–39.

xxvii "NONE SHALL BE WEARY" Isaiah 5:27–28, KJV.

xxvii THE PRESIDENT WOULD ASK Douglass, *Autobiographies,* 802–5; details the Douglass visit to the White House on the day of Lincoln's second inauguration.

xxvii "HALF *SLAVE* AND HALF *FREE*" *CW,* 2:461.

xxviii THE MARSHALING OF POWER IN A DEMOCRACY See, for instance, Sean Wilentz, *The Rise of American Democracy: Jefferson to Lincoln* (New York, 2005); Eddie S. Glaude, Jr., *Democracy in Black: How Race Still Enslaves the American Soul* (New York, 2016); Michael J. Sandel, *Democracy's Discontent: America in Search of a Public Philosophy* (Cambridge, Mass., 1996); Michael J. Sandel, *Public Philosophy: Essays on Morality in Politics* (Cambridge, Mass., 2005).

xxviii THE DURABILITY OF RACISM Theodore W. Allen, *The Invention of the White Race: The Origin of Racial Oppression in America* (New York, 1997); Adam H. Domby, *The False Cause: Fraud, Fabrication, and White Supremacy in Confederate Memory* (Charlottesville, Va., 2020); Mike Hill, ed., *Whiteness: A Critical Reader* (New York, 1995); William Sumner Jenkins, *Pro-Slavery Thought in the Old South* (Chapel Hill, N.C., 1935); Nell Irvin Painter, *The History of White People* (New York, 2010); Winthrop D. Jordan, *White over Black: American Attitudes toward the Negro, 1550–1812* (Chapel Hill, N.C., 1968); Donald Yacovone, *Teaching White Supremacy: America's Democratic Ordeal and the Forging of Our National Identity* (New York, 2022). One of the first instances of the use of the phrase came in 1824, when an Englishman, T. S. Winn, published *Emancipation; Or, Practical Advice to British Slave-Holders: With Suggestions for the General Improvement of West India Affairs,* in which Winn spoke of "order and obedience under White supremacy." "White Supremacy," Oxford English Dictionary. See also Ben Zimmer, " 'Supremacist': A Proxy for Racism Since Its Early Days," *The Wall Street Journal,* October 1, 2020, https://www.wsj.com/articles/supremacist-a-proxy-for-racism-since-its-early-days-11601589261.

xxviii THE CAPACITY OF CONSCIENCE Derived from the Greek, "conscience" comes from the elements *scientia,* or "knowledge," and *con,* meaning "with." Conscience, then, is about acting upon the knowledge one possesses. Alberto Giubilini, "Conscience," *The Stanford Encyclopedia of Philosophy* (Spring 2021 edition), ed. Edward N. Zalta, https://plato.stanford.edu/archives/spr2021/entries/conscience/. On the politics of conscience in America, see, for instance, H. Richard Niebuhr, *Christ and Culture* (New York, 1951); H. Richard Niebuhr, *The Kingdom of God in America* (New York, 1937); Reinhold Niebuhr, *Faith and History: A Comparison of Christian and Modern Views of History* (New York, 1949); Noll, *America's God;* Mark A. Noll, *One Nation under God? Christian Faith and Political Action in America* (New York, 1988); Michael J. Sandel, *Justice: What's the Right Thing to Do?* (New York, 2009); Michael J. Sandel, ed., *Justice: A Reader* (New York, 2007); Michael Tomasello, *A Natural History of Human Morality* (Cambridge, Mass., 2016).

xxviii THIS IS WHY HIS STORY I am particularly indebted to the following biographical works, all of which have informed my own: Isaac N. Arnold, *The Life of Abraham Lincoln* (Chicago, 1885); Sidney Blumenthal, *A Self-Made Man, 1809–1849,* vol. 1 of *The Political Life of Abraham Lincoln* (New York, 2016); Sidney Blumenthal, *Wrestling with His Angel, 1849–1856,* vol. 2 of *The Political Life of Abraham Lincoln* (New York, 2017); Sidney Blumenthal, *All the Powers of Earth, 1856–1863,* vol. 3 of *The Political Life of Abraham Lincoln* (New York, 2019); Burlingame, *AL,* both in print and the unedited manuscript version posted online; Michael Burlingame, *The Inner World of Abraham Lincoln* (Urbana and Chicago, 1994); Donald, *Lincoln;* Goodwin, *Team of Rivals;* Reynolds, *Abe;* Ronald C. White, Jr., *A. Lincoln: A Biography* (New York, 2009); Hay and Nicolay, *AL: A History;* David Von Drehle, *Rise to Greatness: Abraham Lincoln and America's Most Perilous Year* (New York, 2012); and John Locke Scripps, *The First Published Life of Abraham Lincoln* (Detroit, 1900). On Lincoln, slavery, race, and religion, central books for me include Edward E. Baptist, *The Half Has Never Been Told: Slavery and the Making of American Capitalism* (New York, 2014); Michael Burlingame, *The Black Man's President: Abraham Lincoln, African Americans, and the Pursuit of Racial Equality* (New York, 2021); Byrd, *Holy Baptism of Fire and Blood;* David B. Chesebrough, *"God Ordained This War": Sermons on the Sectional Crisis, 1830–1865* (Columbia, S.C., 1991); Eric Foner, *The Fiery Trial: Abraham Lincoln and American Slavery* (New York, 2010); Henry Louis Gates, Jr., *The Black Church: This Is Our Story, This Is Our Song* (New York, 2021); Henry Louis Gates, Jr., ed., *Lincoln on Race and Slavery* (Princeton, N.J., 2009); Eddie S. Glaude, Jr., *Exodus! Religion, Race, and Nation in Early Nineteenth-Century Black America* (Chicago, 2000); Paul Goodman, *Of One Blood: Abolitionism and the Origins of Racial Equality* (Berkeley, Calif., 1998); Daniel Walker Howe, *What Hath God Wrought: The Transformation of America, 1815–1848* (New

York, 2007); Nikole Hannah-Jones, Caitlin Roper, Ilena Silverman, and Jake Silverstein, eds., *The 1619 Project: A New Origin Story* (New York, 2021); Vincent Harding, *There Is a River: The Black Struggle for Freedom in America* (New York, 1981); C. Eric Lincoln and Lawrence H. Mamiya, *The Black Church in the African American Experience* (Durham, N.C., 1990); Noll, *America's God*; James Oakes, *Freedom National: The Destruction of Slavery in the United States* (New York, 2012); Albert J. Raboteau, *Canaan Land: A Religious History of African Americans* (New York, 2001); Albert J. Raboteau, *Slave Religion: The "Invisible Institution" in the Antebellum South* (New York, 2004); Manisha Sinha, *The Slave's Cause: A History of Abolition* (New Haven, Conn., 2016); and Cornel West and Eddie S. Glaude, Jr., eds., *African American Religious Thought: An Anthology* (Louisville, Ky., 2003). On the Civil War in general, see Adam Goodheart, *1861: The Civil War Awakening* (New York, 2011); James M. McPherson, *Battle Cry of Freedom: The Civil War Era* (New York, 1988); Allan Nevins, *Ordeal of the Union* (New York, 1947); Allan Nevins, *The Emergence of Lincoln* (New York, 1950); Allan Nevins, *The War for the Union* (New York, 1959, 1960, 1971); and Elizabeth R. Varon, *Armies of Deliverance: A New History of the Civil War* (New York, 2019).

xxviii THE WORLD'S LAST, BEST HOPE CW, 5:537.

xxviii "DOMESTIC SLAVERY IS" Abel P. Upshur, "Domestic Slavery," *Southern Literary Messenger* 5 (October 1839): 677.

xxviii WHITE SOUTHERNERS DREAMED See, for instance, Robert E. May, *The Southern Dream of a Caribbean Empire, 1854–1861* (Gainesville, Fla., 1973).

xxviii "A GREAT DESTINY" *The Southern Standard* (Charleston, S.C.), 1853, reprinted in *The Daily Constitutionalist and Republic* (Augusta, Ga.), July 21, 1853; Henry Charles Carey, *The North and the South* (New York, 1854), 19–20.

xxviii "CORNER-STONE" Alexander H. Stephens, "Cornerstone Speech," March 21, 1861, https://www.battlefields.org/learn/primary-sources/cornerstone-speech.

xxviii "THAT SLAVERY IS SANCTIONED" David B. Chesebrough, "The Civil War and the Use of Sermons as Historical Documents," *OAH Magazine of History* 8, no. 1 (1993): 26.

xxix "AS A PEOPLE" Savannah, Georgia, *Daily Morning News*, April 23, 1863.

xxix A FORMATIVE FORCE See, for instance, Ruth Benedict, *Race: Science and Politics* (New York, 1940); Ruth Benedict, *Race and Racism* (London, 1942); Francisco Bethencourt, *Racisms: From the Crusades to the Twentieth Century* (Princeton, N.J., 2013); Miriam Eliav-Feldon, Benjamin Isaac, and Joseph Ziegler, eds., *The Origins of Racism in the West* (Cambridge, UK, 2009); William McKee Evans, *Open Wound: The Long View of Race in America* (Urbana, Ill., 2009); George M. Fredrickson, *Racism: A Short History* (Princeton, N.J., 2002); George M. Fredrickson, *The Arrogance of Race: Historical Perspectives on Slavery, Racism, and Social Inequality* (Hanover, N.H., 1988); George M. Fredrickson, *The Black Image in the White Mind: The Debate on Afro-American Character and Destiny, 1817–1914* (New York, 1971); Ivan Hannaford, *Race: The History of an Idea in the West* (Baltimore, Md., 1996); Ibram X. Kendi, *Stamped from the Beginning: The Definitive History of Racist Ideas in America* (New York, 2016); Philip A. Klinkner with Rogers M. Smith, *The Unsteady March: The Rise and Decline of Racial Equality in America* (Chicago, 1999); Tommy Lee Lott, *The Invention of Race: Black Culture and the Politics of Representation* (Malden, Mass., 1999); M. Mead, T. Dobzhansky, E. Tobach, Robert E. Light, eds., *The Concept of Race* (New York, 1968); John Rex and David Mason, eds., *Theories of Race and Ethnic Relations* (New York, 1986); Ronald T. Takaki, *A Different Mirror: A History of Multicultural America* (Boston, 1993); Gary Taylor, *Buying Whiteness: Race, Culture, and Identity from Columbus to Hip Hop* (New York, 2005); Alden T. Vaughan, *Roots of American Racism: Essays on the Colonial Experience* (New York, 1995);

Joseph R. Washington, *Anti-Blackness in English Religion, 1500–1800* (New York, 1984). George M. Fredrickson wrote that racism could be understood as the "assigning of fixed or permanent differences among human descent groups and using this attribution of difference to justify their differential treatment," and it "exists when one ethnic group or historical collectivity dominates, excludes, or seeks to eliminate another on the basis of differences that it believes are hereditary and unalterable." Fredrickson, *Racism,* 156, 170.

xxix JOHN H. VAN EVRIE "John Evrie and Scientific Racism," https://collections.count way.harvard.edu/onview/exhibits/show/this-abominable-traffic/john-van-evrie. On Van Evrie in general, see Fredrickson, *Black Image in the White Mind,* 62–63, 92–96; Michael E. Woods, "Popularizing Proslavery: John Van Evrie and the Mass Marketing of Proslavery Ideology," *Journal of the Civil War Era,* May 26, 2020, https://www.journalofthecivilwarera.org/2020/05/popularizing-proslavery-john-van-evrie-and-the-mass-marketing-of-proslavery-ideology/.

xxix "ALL THE ARGUMENTS" James Warley Miles, *The Relation Between the Races at the South* (Charleston, S.C., 1861), 15.

xxix "THE IDEA OF THE EQUALITY OF RACE" *The New Orleans Bee,* March 16, 1861.

xxix "WE DO NOT SAY" Lewis L. Gould, *Grand Old Party: A History of the Republicans* (New York, 2003), 19.

xxix "THE NATURAL EQUALITY" *Congressional Globe,* 36th Congress, 1st Session (Washington, D.C., 1860), 1685. In another example, Abigail Adams wrote this after watching a performance of *Othello* in 1785: "My whole soul shuddered when ever I saw the sooty Moor touch the fair Desdemona." John Quincy Adams had similar views of Shakespeare's play, writing, "Who can sympathize with the love of Desdemona? The daughter of a Venetian nobleman, born and educated to a splendid and lofty station in the community—she falls in love and makes a runaway match with a Blackamoor. . . . The great moral lesson of the Tragedy of Othello, is that black and white blood cannot be intermingled in marriage without a gross outrage upon the laws of nature, and that in such violations nature will vindicate her laws." See William Jerry MacLean, "Othello Scorned: The Racial Thought of John Quincy Adams," *Journal of the Early Republic* 4, no. 2 (Summer 1984): 147–49.

xxix SENATOR LYMAN TRUMBULL Burlingame, *Black Man's President,* 206.

xxix "I WANT TO HAVE NOTHING TO DO" Ibid.; see also "Speech of Lyman Trumbull in Chicago, 7 August 1858," *The National Era,* September 2, 1858.

xxix IN THIS ATMOSPHERE In an 1848 speech, Henry Clay asked where in "this entire nation . . . does the black man . . . enjoy an equality with his white neighbor in social and political rights? In none: nowhere. . . . In no city, town, or hamlet throughout the entire land is he regarded on an equal footing with us." Robert V. Remini, *Henry Clay: Statesman for the Union* (New York, 1992), 696–97. Data are hard to come by on such matters, but the historian Sean Wilentz estimates that 100,000 to 150,000 people belonged to abolition societies around 1850. Author communication with Sean Wilentz. Abolitionists were, therefore, a decided minority; the number of white Americans who favored equal rights for Black people even smaller still. In the middle of the nineteenth century, civil rights for Black people in free states were few and far between. In the 1860 election—a good referendum on antislavery sentiment—60 to 70 percent of voters in New England supported antislavery candidates, and just over 50 percent did so in the lower North. Ibid.

xxix LINCOLN DEFENDED BLACK AMERICANS Mary Frances Berry, "Lincoln and Civil Rights for Blacks," *Papers of the Abraham Lincoln Association* 2 (1980): 46–57; Mary

Frances Berry, *Military Necessity and Civil Rights Policy: Black Citizenship and the Constitution, 1861–1868* (Port Washington, N.Y., 1977); Oakes, *Crooked Path to Abolition*, 108–12; George Kateb, *Lincoln's Political Thought* (Cambridge, Mass., 2015); Mark E. Steiner, *Lincoln and Citizenship* (Carbondale, Ill., 2021). On the Declaration and the perennial struggles of interpretation and application, see Danielle Allen, *Our Declaration: A Reading of the Declaration of Independence in Defense of Equality* (New York, 2014); David Armitage, *The Declaration of Independence: A Global History* (Cambridge, Mass., 2008); Pauline Maier, *American Scripture: How America Declared Its Independence from Britain* (New York, 1997).

xxx "ULTIMATE EXTINCTION" See, for instance, CW, 2:461.

xxx THE PREPONDERANCE OF HIS WORDS See, for instance, Manisha Sinha, "Did He Die an Abolitionist? The Evolution of Abraham Lincoln's Antislavery," *American Political Thought* 4, no. 3 (2015): 439–54; Burlingame, *Black Man's President*; Oakes, *Crooked Path to Abolition*; Foner, *Fiery Trial*. On Lincoln and egalitarianism, Oakes wrote: "Some Republicans—Owen Lovejoy, Thaddeus Stevens, Charles Sumner—were thoroughgoing racial egalitarians, more so than Lincoln. Others were unabashed racists in a way that Lincoln never was. But the most salient feature of the racial ideology of the Republican Party was its insistence that, when it came to the natural rights of life, liberty, and property, or the privileges and immunities of citizenship, whites and Blacks were fundamentally equal. It is sometimes said that Lincoln's commitment to emancipation was held in check by his racial prejudice, but the evidence suggests something like the opposite. As his immersion in antislavery politics deepened and his commitment to antislavery constitutionalism intensified, it became harder for Lincoln to distinguish his opposition to slavery from his baseline commitment to fundamental equality for whites and Blacks." Oakes, *Crooked Path to Abolition*, 107. True, but, as Oakes adds, "Yet if Lincoln endorsed all the equality the Constitution demanded, beyond that his commitment to equal justice for Blacks and whites faltered. Just as the Constitution placed limits on what the federal government could do about slavery in the states where it was legal, so did it leave states free to deny Blacks the right to vote, to marry white people, to serve on juries." Ibid. Illinois was one such state and, in the late 1850s, "Lincoln, though relatively untouched by racial prejudice, was nevertheless surrounded by it, and he was not above pandering to that prejudice on occasion. . . . Not until the end of his life did he begin to contemplate the possibility of a multiracial democracy." Ibid., 107–8. Lincoln's contemporary Donn Piatt wrote: "Descended from the poor whites of a slave State, through many generations, he inherited the contempt, if not the hatred, held by that class for the negro. A self-made man, with scarcely a winter's schooling from books, his strong nature was built on what he inherited, and he could no more feel a sympathy for that wretched race than he could for the horse he worked or the hog he killed." Allen Thorndike Rice, ed., *Reminiscences of Abraham Lincoln by Distinguished Men of His Time* (New York, 1888), 481–82.

xxx "VIEWED FROM THE GENUINE ABOLITION GROUND" Frederick Douglass, "Oration in Memory of Abraham Lincoln" in Holzer, ed., *TLA*, 230. On Douglass and Lincoln, see also, for instance, Blight, *Frederick Douglass*; Burlingame, *Black Man's President*; James Oakes, *The Radical and the Republican: Frederick Douglass, Abraham Lincoln, and the Triumph of Antislavery Politics* (New York, 2007); John Stauffer, *Giants: The Parallel Lives of Frederick Douglass and Abraham Lincoln* (New York, 2008); Manisha Sinha, "Allies for Emancipation? Lincoln and Black Abolitionists," in Foner, ed., *Our Lincoln*, 167–96.

xxx   "Abraham Lincoln was" W.E.B. Du Bois, "From *The Crisis*: Abraham Lincoln," in Holzer, ed., *TLA*, 435.

xxx   "Lincoln must be seen" Lerone Bennett, Jr., "Was Abe Lincoln a White Supremacist?" in Holzer, ed., *TLA*, 752. Bennett's essay was first published in *Ebony* in February 1968; he elaborated on his arguments in his *Forced into Glory* in 2000. On Lincoln's status in the first decades of the twenty-first century, see, for instance, John Blake, "Did Black Lives Matter to Abraham Lincoln? It's Complicated," CNN, March 14, 2021, https://www.cnn.com/2021/03/14/us/abraham-lincoln-racism-blake/index.html; Hannah-Jones et al., eds., *The 1619 Project*, especially 8–36; Peter S. Field, "Our Shrinking Lincoln: The Sixteenth President and the 'Meaning of America,'" *Australasian Journal of American Studies* 40, no. 1 (2021): 33–48; Allen C. Guelzo, "How Abe Lincoln Lost the Black Vote: Lincoln and Emancipation in the African American Mind," *JALA* 25, no. 1 (2004): 1–22; Chandra Manning, "The Shifting Terrain of Attitudes Toward Abraham Lincoln and Emancipation," *JALA* 34, no. 1 (2013): 18–39.

xxx   "sloughed off" Burlingame and Ettlinger, eds., *Inside Lincoln's White House*, 217. On colonization, see, for instance, Burlingame, *Black Man's President*, 57–108; Douglas R. Egerton, "Its Origin Is Not a Little Curious: A New Look at the American Colonization Society," *Journal of the Early Republic* 4 (1985): 468–72; Eric Foner, "Lincoln and Colonization," in Foner, ed., *Our Lincoln*, 135–66; Nicholas Guyatt, "'An Impossible Idea?': The Curious Career of Internal Colonization," *Journal of the Civil War Era* 4, no. 2 (2014): 234–63; P. J. Staudenraus, *The African Colonization Movement, 1816–1865* (New York, 1961); Beverly C. Tomek and Matthew J. Hetrick, eds., *New Directions in the Study of African American Recolonization* (Gainesville, Fla., 2017); Phillip W. Magness and Sebastian N. Page, *Colonization After Emancipation: Lincoln and the Movement for Black Resettlement* (Columbia, Mo., 2011); Phillip W. Magness, "Benjamin Butler's Colonization Testimony Reevaluated," *JALA* 29 (Summer 2009): 1–27; Eric Burin, *Slavery and the Peculiar Solution: A History of the American Colonization Society* (Gainesville, Fla., 2005); Phillip S. Paludan, "Lincoln and Colonization: Policy or Propaganda?" *JALA* 25 (Winter 2004): 23–37; Kate Masur, "The African American Delegation to Abraham Lincoln: A Reappraisal," *Civil War History* 56 (June 2010): 117–44.

xxxi   his decision on wartime emancipation See, for instance, John Hope Franklin, *The Emancipation Proclamation* (New York, 1965); Allen C. Guelzo, *Lincoln's Emancipation Proclamation: The End of Slavery in America* (New York, 2004); Allen C. Guelzo, *Redeeming the Great Emancipator* (Cambridge, Mass., 2016); Harold Holzer, Edna Greene Medford, and Frank J. Williams, *The Emancipation Proclamation: Three Views* (Baton Rouge, La., 2006); Harold Holzer, *Emancipating Lincoln: The Proclamation in Text, Context, and Memory* (Cambridge, Mass., 2012); Forrest G. Wood, *Black Scare: The Racist Response to Emancipation and Reconstruction* (Berkeley, Calif., 1968).

xxxi   "it had got" Burlingame, *AL*, 2:333.

xxxi   that anti-Black prejudice made On Lincoln's "racial pessimism," see, for instance, James Oakes, *The Scorpion's Sting: Antislavery and the Coming of the Civil War* (New York, 2014), 83–84; Oakes, *Crooked Path to Abolition*, 107–33; Don E. Fehrenbacher, "Only His Stepchildren: Lincoln and the Negro," *Civil War History* 20 (1974): 304–5.

xxxi   "you may have" CW, 3:313. "Slavery is not a matter of little importance," Lincoln also said. "[I]t overshadows every other question in which we are interested." Ibid., 84. See also, for instance, Ira Berlin, *Many Thousands Gone: The First Two Centuries of Slavery in America* (Cambridge, Mass., 1998); Stanley Elkins, *Slavery: A Problem in American Institutional and Intellectual Life* (Chicago, 1959); Peter Garnsey, *Ideas of Slavery from Aristotle to Augustine* (New York, 1996); Sinha, *Slave's Cause*.

xxxi HE JUGGLED POLITICAL REALITY See, for instance, Foner, *Fiery Trial*, 65–72. On Lincoln and racial equality, see also Oakes, *Scorpion's Sting*, 77–103.

xxxi PROPELLED BY ANTISLAVERY PRINCIPLES See, for instance, Oakes, *Crooked Path to Abolition*; Oakes, *Scorpion's Sting*; Oakes, *Freedom National*; James Oakes, "Natural Rights, Citizenship Rights, States' Rights, and Black Rights: Another Look at Lincoln and Race," in Foner, ed., *Our Lincoln*, 109–34; Graham Peck, "Abraham Lincoln and the Triumph of an Antislavery Nationalism," *JALA* 28, no. 2 (2007): 1–27; William M. Weicek, *The Sources of Antislavery Constitutionalism in America, 1760–1848* (Ithaca, N.Y., 1977); Sean Wilentz, *No Property in Man: Slavery and Antislavery at the Nation's Founding* (Cambridge, Mass., 2018), 206–62; David Brion Davis, review of *Antislavery or Abolition?* by Gerald Sorin, *Reviews in American History* 1, no. 1 (1973): 95–99.

xxxi HE WAS ATTACKED FOR DEFENDING See, for instance, William Lloyd Garrison, *No Compromise with Slavery: An Address Delivered in the Broadway Tabernacle, New York, February 14, 1854* (New York, 1854), 34. "With the South, the preservation of Slavery is paramount to all other considerations," William Lloyd Garrison said in 1854. "With the North, the preservation of the Union is placed above all other things— above honor, justice, freedom, integrity of soul, the Decalogue and the Golden Rule—the Infinite God himself. All these she is ready to discard for the Union. Her devotion to it is the latest and the most terrible form of idolatry." Ibid. See also Wendell Phillips, *Can Abolitionists Vote or Take Office Under the United States Constitution?* (New York, 1845). On Garrison in general, see, for instance, Henry Mayer, *All on Fire: William Lloyd Garrison and the Abolition of Slavery* (New York, 1998). On abolition, see Sinha, *Slave's Cause*; Stanley Harrold, *Lincoln and the Abolitionists* (Carbondale, Ill., 2018).

xxxii "GLORIOUS LIBERTY DOCUMENT" Foner, ed., *Life and Writings of Frederick Douglass*, 2:202.

xxxii "PREFER THE UNION" Burlingame, *AL*, 2:403.

xxxii AFTER CONGRESSIONAL PASSAGE See, for instance, Harold Holzer and Sara Vaughn Gabbard, eds., *Lincoln and Freedom: Slavery, Emancipation, and the Thirteenth Amendment* (Carbondale, Ill., 2007); Michael Vorenberg, *Final Freedom: The Civil War, the Abolition of Slavery, and the Thirteenth Amendment* (Cambridge, UK, 2001).

xxxii THE HISTORICAL WAR OVER LINCOLN AND RACE See, for instance, Christopher W. Anderson, "Native Americans and the Origin of Abraham Lincoln's Views on Race," *JALA* 37, no. 1 (2016): 11–29; Lerone Bennett, Jr., *Forced into Glory: Abraham Lincoln's White Dream* (Chicago, 2000); Burlingame, *Black Man's President*; Orville Vernon Burton, Jerald Podair, and Jennifer L. Weber, eds., *The Struggle for Equality: Essays on Sectional Conflict, the Civil War, and the Long Reconstruction* (Charlottesville, Va., 2011); Carson, *Lincoln's Ethics*; John Milton Cooper and Thomas J. Knock, eds., *Jefferson, Lincoln, and Wilson: The America Dilemma of Race and Democracy* (Charlottesville, Va., 2010); LaWanda Cox, *Lincoln and Black Freedom: A Study in Presidential Leadership* (Columbia, S.C., 1994); Brian Danoff, "Lincoln and the 'Necessity' of Tolerating Slavery before the Civil War," *Review of Politics* 77, no. 1 (2015): 47–71; Brian R. Dirck, *Abraham Lincoln and White America* (Lawrence, Kans., 2012); Brian R. Dirck, ed., *Lincoln Emancipated: The President and the Politics of Race* (DeKalb, Ill., 2007); Paul D. Escott, *"What Shall We Do with the Negro?": Lincoln, White Racism, and Civil War America* (Charlottesville, Va., 2009); Paul D. Escott, *Lincoln's Dilemma: Blair, Sumner, and the Republican Struggle over Racism and Equality in the Civil War Era* (Charlottesville, Va.,

2014); Eric Foner, "The Education of Abraham Lincoln," *NYT*, February 10, 2012; John Hope Franklin, "The Use and Misuse of the Lincoln Legacy," *Papers of the Abraham Lincoln Association* 7 (1985): 30–42; George M. Fredrickson, *Big Enough to Be Inconsistent: Abraham Lincoln Confronts Slavery and Race* (Cambridge, Mass., 2008); George M. Fredrickson, "A Man but Not a Brother: Abraham Lincoln and Racial Equality," *Journal of Southern History* 41, no. 1 (1975): 39–58; J. Blaine Hudson, "Abraham Lincoln: An African American Perspective," *Register of the Kentucky Historical Society* 106 (Summer/Autumn 2008): 513–35; Philip A. Klinkner and Rogers M. Smith, *The Unsteady March: The Rise and Decline of Racial Equality in America* (Chicago, 1999); Kate Masur, *Until Justice Be Done: America's First Civil Rights Movement, from the Revolution to Reconstruction* (New York, 2021); James M. McPherson, "Lincoln the Devil," *NYT*, August 27, 2000; Quarles, *Lincoln and the Negro*; John Stauffer, *The Black Hearts of Men: Radical Abolitionists and the Transformation of Race* (Cambridge, Mass., 2002); Richard Striner, *Father Abraham: Lincoln's Relentless Struggle to End Slavery* (Oxford, 2007); Arthur Zilversmit, "Lincoln and the Problem of Race: A Decade of Interpretations," *Papers of the Abraham Lincoln Association* 2, no. 1 (1980): 22–45. "It is not true, as is sometimes asserted, that there are no degrees of racism—that one is either a racist or one is not," Fredrickson argued. "There is actually a spectrum of attitudes that might legitimately be labeled 'racist,' ranging from genocidal hatred of 'the other' to mere conformity to the practices of a racially stratified society. Although political necessity forced him to endorse those practices publicly, Lincoln's personal attitudes, to the extent that we can determine them, were much closer to racism as conformity than to racism as pathology." Fredrickson, *Big Enough to Be Inconsistent*, 84.

xxxii   "I HAVE ONLY TO SAY" CW, 2:501. "There is no reason in the world why the negro is not entitled to all the rights enumerated in the Declaration of Independence—the right of life, liberty and the pursuit of happiness. I hold that he is as much entitled to these as the white man." Ibid., 3:249.

xxxii   "I WILL SAY THEN" Ibid., 3:145–46.

xxxiii   "RIGHT TO EAT" Ibid., 402.

xxxiii   HE WAS AN ARCHITECT See, for instance, Gabor S. Boritt, *Lincoln and the Economics of the American Dream* (Memphis, Tenn., 1978); Harold Holzer and Norton Garfinkle, *A Just and Generous Nation: Abraham Lincoln and the Fight for American Opportunity* (New York, 2015); Daniel Walker Howe, *The Political Culture of the American Whigs* (Chicago, 1979).

xxxiii   "I WANT EVERY MAN" Holzer and Garfinkle, *Just and Generous Nation*, 50. This was, Holzer and Garfinkle observed, the "most direct synthesis of his economic beliefs." Ibid.

xxxiii   "I AM OPPOSED" Herndon and Weik, *Herndon's Life of Lincoln*, 495. See also Hofstadter, *American Political Tradition*, 130.

xxxiii   "EVERY MAN MAY" Dos Passos, "Lincoln and His Almost Chosen People," 719.

xxxiii   "COMPOSITE IDEA" Garry Wills, *Lincoln at Gettysburg: The Words That Remade America* (New York, 1992), 107.

xxxiv   CONSCIENCE IN AMERICA See, for instance, Byrd, *Holy Baptism of Fire and Blood*; Glaude, *Exodus!*; Hatch, *Democratization of American Christianity*; Noll, *America's God*.

xxxiv   "I DO NOT KNOW" Alexis de Tocqueville, *Democracy in America*, ed. Harvey C. Mansfield and Delba Winthrop (Chicago, 2000), 280. See also James M. Sloat, "The Subtle Significance of Sincere Belief: Tocqueville's Account of Religious Belief and Democratic Stability," *Journal of Church and State* 42, no. 4 (2000): 759–79.

xxxiv   "WHATEVER MAY BE CONCEDED" "Transcript of President George Washington's

Farewell Address (1796)," https://www.ourdocuments.gov/doc.php?flash=false &doc=15&page=transcript. See also John Avlon, *Washington's Farewell: The Founding Father's Warning to Future Generations* (New York, 2017).

xxxv THE CLOSEST PARALLEL See, for instance, Nicholas Draper, *The Price of Emancipation: Slave-Ownership, Compensation, and British Society at the End of Slavery* (Cambridge, UK, 2010); Christopher L. Brown, "Empire without Slaves: British Concepts of Emancipation in the Age of the American Revolution," *William and Mary Quarterly* 56, no. 2 (1999): 273–306; Joseph T. Murphy, "The British Example: West Indian Emancipation, the Freedom Principle, and the Rise of Antislavery Politics in the United States, 1833–1843," *Journal of the Civil War Era* 8, no. 4 (2018): 621–46.

xxxv IT IS ESTIMATED See, for instance, Natasha L. Henry, "Slavery Abolition Act, United Kingdom [1833]," *Encyclopedia Britannica,* July 25, 2021, https://www.britannica.com /topic/Slavery-Abolition-Act; "Freedom of Information Act 2000: Slavery Abolition Act 1833," https://assets.publishing.service.gov.uk/government/uploads/system /uploads/attachment_data/file/680456/FOI2018-00186_-_Slavery_Abolition _Act_1833_-_pdf_for_disclosure_log__003_.pdf.

xxxv "THEY TELL ME" "Mother of a Black Northern Soldier to the President, July 31, 1863," Freedman and Southern Society Project, http://www.freedmen.umd.edu /hjohnsn.htm.

xxxv "THE FAILURE TO RECOGNIZE" Franklin, "Use and Misuse," 36. "As the experiment had not been made, the large majority of Americans of Lincoln's day believed that the two races could not dwell together on the basis of social and political equality," Carter G. Woodson, the historian and a founder of the Association for the Study of Negro Life and History, wrote. "A militant minority of the descendants of those Americans do not believe it now." Yet, Woodson argued, Lincoln "gradually grew unto the full stature of democracy." Carter G. Woodson, *The Negro in Our History* (Washington, D.C., 1941), 381. Frederick Douglass viewed emancipation as but the first of many steps. Events, he remarked of Lincoln, "may be relied on to carry him forward in the same direction." Berry, "Lincoln and Civil Rights for Blacks," 55; see also David W. Blight, *Frederick Douglass' Civil War: Keeping Faith in Jubilee* (Baton Rouge, La., 1991), 108.

xxxv "MR. LINCOLN WAS ESSENTIALLY" Horace Greeley, *Recollections of a Busy Life* (New York, 1869), 409.

xxxv "I AM NOT ONE" Carpenter, *Inner Life of Abraham Lincoln*, vi.

xxxvi "DETERMINED HIM IN WHAT" Burlingame, ed., *Lincoln Observed*, 211.

xxxvi "THE HON ABRAHAM LINCOLN" Michael Shiner Diary, LOC.

xxxvi "MORAL COWARDICE IS SOMETHING" Burlingame, ed., *Lincoln Observed*, 205.

Chapter One: My Mind and Memory

5 "'THE SHORT AND SIMPLE ANNALS'" Wilson and Davis, eds., *Herndon's Informants,* 57.

5 "EQUAL RIGHTS FOR ALL MEN" Francis Marion Van Natter, *Lincoln's Boyhood: A Chronicle of His Indiana Years* (Washington, D.C., 1963), 134.

5 THE ROADS WERE ROUGH Herndon and Weik, *Herndon's Life of Lincoln,* 2–3.

5 IN ABOUT HIS FORTIETH YEAR Ibid.

5 NINETEEN-MILE TRIP https://www.distance-cities.com/distance-springfield-il-to -petersburg-il.

5 THE COURTHOUSE IN PETERSBURG For a history of Menard County, see T. G. Onstot, *Pioneers of Menard and Mason Counties: Made Up of Personal Reminiscences of an Early Life in Menard County, Which We Gathered in a Salem Life from 1830 to 1840, and a Petersburg*

Life from 1840 to 1850; Including Personal Reminiscences of Abraham Lincoln and Peter Cart-wright (Forest City and Peoria, Ill., 1902). Of the Petersburg courthouse, Onstot wrote: "The old settlers of Menard will recollect the legal battles that were fought under its roof. There were Abraham Lincoln, John T. Stewart, Ben. Edwards, E. D. Baker, Murray McConnell, Stephen A. Douglas, and a number of other intellectual giants who attended court in those early days—men who had won their spurs in many a legal encounter.... Court would open up Monday afternoon, after the lawyers would get in from Springfield, and would be ready to adjourn by Friday." Ibid., 176.

5 HIS LAW PARTNER WILLIAM HERNDON On the Herndon-Lincoln relationship, see, for instance, David Herbert Donald, *Lincoln's Herndon* (New York, 1948); David Herbert Donald, *"We Are Lincoln Men": Abraham Lincoln and His Friends* (New York, 2003), 65–100; William H. Herndon, *Herndon on Lincoln: Letters,* ed. Douglas L. Wilson and Rodney O. Davis (Urbana, Chicago, and Springfield, Ill., 2016).

5 "WAS ONE IN WHICH" Herndon and Weik, *Herndon's Life of Lincoln,* 2.

5 "HE SAID" Ibid., 2–3. On the issue of Nancy Hanks Lincoln's birth, see, for instance, Donald, *Lincoln,* 603; William E. Barton, *The Paternity of Lincoln* (New York, 1920); Burlingame, *AL,* 1:12; Louis A. Warren, *Lincoln's Parentage and Childhood* (New York, 1926). "There used to be much controversy about the legitimacy of Nancy Hanks," Donald observed in 1995. "The argument has now died down, and most—but not all—scholars believe she was illegitimate." Donald, *Lincoln,* 603.

5 "HIS THEORY" Herndon and Weik, *Herndon's Life of Lincoln,* 3.

5 THE BUGGY BUMPED Ibid.

5 "THE REVELATION—PAINFUL AS IT WAS" Ibid.

6 "BURYING HIMSELF IN THOUGHT" Ibid.

6 ASIDE FROM THE DATE Ibid., 1.

6 TO A CORRESPONDENT WHO ASKED CW, 3:511.

6 FOREBEARS WHOM HE KNEW See, for instance, Lincoln's autobiographical sketches at CW, 3:511–12; 4:60–67. He had, wrote a campaign biographer, William Dean Howells, "the stubborn notion that because the Lincolns had always been people of excellent sense, he, a Lincoln, might become a person of distinction." Burlingame, *AL,* 1:2.

6 THE ROOTS OF HIS AMBITION Burlingame, *Inner World,* 236–67; Burlingame, *AL,* 1:3; Donald, *Lincoln,* 20; Blumenthal, *Self-Made Man,* 23. Donald wrote: "Like other gifted young men, he wondered how he could be the offspring of his ordinary and limited parents. Some in Lincoln's generation fancied themselves the sons of the dauphin, who allegedly fled to America during the French Revolution. Lincoln imagined a noble Virginia ancestor." Donald, *Lincoln,* 20. Burlingame observed: "Lincoln's description of his aristocratic grandsire represents a variation of the 'family romance' phenomenon, which causes some children to speculate that they are actually the offspring of more distinguished parents than the ones who raised them. Most people outgrow these fantasies, but some adults—including exceptional people or men with very distant fathers—tend to maintain an unusually strong sense of family romance throughout life. Lincoln fits this category on both counts, for he was truly exceptional and had a distant relationship with his father." Burlingame, *AL,* 1:3. Blumenthal wrote: "Lincoln's story as he told it contained the themes of a classic fairy tale, an Old World tale of a pauper who is really a prince, a romance substituting for squalor. The poor boy is unrecognized as the natural-born offspring of aristocracy, possessing not only nobility of lineage but also of mind." Blumenthal, *Self-Made Man,* 23.

6 THE FAMILY'S NEW WORLD SAGA Burlingame, AL, 1:1–2; Donald, Lincoln, 20–21; White, A. Lincoln, 8–13; Ida M. Tarbell, In the Footsteps of the Lincolns (New York, 1924), 1–65; Blumenthal, Self-Made Man, 21–22; Waldo Lincoln, History of the Lincoln Family: An Account of the Descendants of Samuel Lincoln of Hingham, Massachusetts, 1637–1920 (Worcester, Mass., 1923), 1–525, covers the family from the seventeenth to the mid-nineteenth centuries.

6 PURITAN DISSENTERS IN ENGLAND White, A. Lincoln, 8–9; Tarbell, In the Footsteps, 3–4.

6 PROSPERING IN BUSINESS Donald, Lincoln, 20; White, A. Lincoln, 9.

6 HELPING TO BUILD Donald, Lincoln, 20; White, A. Lincoln, 9; Tarbell, In the Footsteps, 14.

6 SAMUEL AND HIS WIFE Lincoln, History of the Lincoln Family, 6–9; Tarbell, In the Footsteps, 9.

6 ONE OF THEIR GRANDCHILDREN Donald, Lincoln, 20–21; Tarbell, In the Footsteps, 32–38.

6 HANNAH SALTAR Lincoln, History of the Lincoln Family, 45. There are competing spellings of Hannah Lincoln's maiden name. See ibid.; Donald, Lincoln, 21; White, A. Lincoln, 9–10.

6 A WELL-CONNECTED DAUGHTER Donald, Lincoln, 20–21; White, A. Lincoln, 9–10.

7 HANNAH LINCOLN GAVE BIRTH Burlingame, AL, 1:1–2; Tarbell, In the Footsteps, 42–52.

7 THEIR SON ABRAHAM Burlingame, AL, 1:2; Tarbell, In the Footsteps, 53–63.

7 IN 1774, HE FOUGHT Burlingame, AL, 1:2; see also Glenn F. Williams, Dunmore's War: The Last Conflict of America's Colonial Era (Yardley, Penn., 2017).

7 LINCOLN WAS PART Burlingame, AL, 1:2; Louis A. Warren, "Abraham Lincoln, Senior, Grandfather of the President," Filson Club History Quarterly, July 1931. See also Eric Sterner, "The Siege of Fort Laurens, 1778–1779," Journal of the American Revolution, December 17, 2019, https://allthingsliberty.com/2019/12/the-siege-of-fort-laurens-1778-1779/#google_vignette.

7 FOLLOWING FAMILIAL PATTERN Burlingame, AL, 1:2. See also Tarbell, In the Footsteps, 57–65.

7 IN 1786, AN INDIAN ATTACKED Burlingame, AL, 1:2; Herndon and Weik, Herndon's Life of Lincoln, 10–11; Wilson and Davis, eds., Herndon's Informants, 36, 95–96; CW, 3:511.

7 "NOT IN BATTLE" CW, 3:511.

7 "JUMPED OVER THE FENCE" Wilson and Davis, eds., Herndon's Informants, 36.

7 OF ABOUT 160 PACES Ibid., 95.

7 "DREW HIS 'BEED'" Ibid., 36.

7 THE ASSAILANT WAS DISCOVERED Ibid., 36, 95–96.

7 "THE STORY OF HIS DEATH" CW, 2:217.

7 THOMAS LINCOLN'S LIFE On Thomas Lincoln, see, for instance, Burlingame, AL, 1:3–11; Donald, Lincoln, 21–33; White, A. Lincoln, 13–41.

7 "OWING TO MY FATHER BEING LEFT" CW, 1:456.

7 "THE REASON WHY" Burlingame, AL, 1:3.

8 "THESE LINCOLNS" Wilson and Davis, eds., Herndon's Informants, 65.

8 "THOMAS . . . BY THE EARLY DEATH" Herndon and Weik, Herndon's Life of Lincoln, 6.

8 "AN UNEDUCATED MAN" Wilson and Davis, eds., Herndon's Informants, 67.

8 THOMAS WAS HIRED OUT Herndon and Weik, Herndon's Life of Lincoln, 6.

8 "HE WAS, WE ARE TOLD" Ibid., 12.

8 IN A CEREMONY White, A. Lincoln, 14.

8   WHOM A GRAND JURY ONCE CHARGED Burlingame, *AL*, 1:12. See also Donald, *Lincoln*, 20.

8   "A HALFWAY PROSTITUTE" Burlingame, *AL*, 1:13.

8   "MY MOTHER'S MOTHER" Ibid., 13.

8   RUMORS THAT HE WAS NOT THE SON Herndon and Weik, *Herndon's Life of Lincoln*, 7–8.

8   "THAT NANCY HANKS WAS OF LOW CHARACTER" Wilson and Davis, eds., *Herndon's Informants*, 82.

8   ONE STORY IN LOCAL CIRCLES Ibid. This was one of several speculating that Thomas Lincoln was not Abraham Lincoln's biological father.

8   "OF ILLEGITIMATE BIRTH" Du Bois, "From *The Crisis:* Abraham Lincoln," in Holzer, ed., *TLA*, 435.

9   "SHE WAS A WOMAN" Ibid., 86.

9   ENLOW INSISTED IT WAS TRUE Ibid., 82, 87.

9   "ABE ENLOW WAS AS LOW" Ibid., 82.

9   "WERE PECULIAR" Herndon and Weik, *Herndon's Life of Lincoln*, 14.

9   A LINCOLN NEIGHBOR RECALLED Burlingame, *AL*, 1:12.

9   "REPUTATION OF MRS. LINCOLN" Ibid.

9   HERNDON WAS CONVINCED Ibid.

9   "THE HANKSES WERE" Wilson and Davis, eds., *Herndon's Informants*, 83.

9   "WAS ABOVE THE ORDINARY" Herndon and Weik, *Herndon's Life of Lincoln*, 14.

9   RAISED BY RELATIVES Burlingame, *AL*, 1:12.

9   "RUDE & ROUGH" Ibid., 14.

9   "HE OFTEN BECAME" Ibid., 5.

10 "EVERYTHING THAT I EVER" Ibid., 6.

10 THOMAS'S BROTHER MORDECAI Ibid.

10 "THE LINCOLN HORRORS" Ibid.

10 ANOTHER RELATIVE WAS COMMITTED Ibid.

10 (SIXTEEN BY EIGHTEEN FEET) Donald, *Lincoln*, 22; White, *A. Lincoln*, 16.

10 "WHY, SCRIPPS" Herndon and Weik, *Herndon's Life of Lincoln*, 1–2.

10 HE REMEMBERED THE COLD Burlingame, *AL*, 1:16.

10 "TO ALL HUMAN APPEARANCE" Wilson and Davis, eds., *Herndon's Informants*, 67.

10 "BY THE NAME" William Grimshaw, *History of the United States, from Their First Settlement as Colonies, to the Cession of Florida* (Philadelphia, 1826), 208.

10 THOMAS LINCOLN MOVED THE FAMILY White, *A. Lincoln*, 16.

10 "MY EARLIEST RECOLLECTION" CW, 4:69–70. On Lincoln and Kentucky, see, for instance, John David Smith, "'Gentlemen, I Too, Am a Kentuckian': Abraham Lincoln, the Lincoln Bicentennial, and Lincoln's Kentucky in Recent Scholarship." *Register of the Kentucky Historical Society* 106, no. 3/4 (2008): 433–70.

10 THE FAMILY'S FARM THERE CW, 4:61.

10 "THE 30 ACRE FARM" Wilson and Davis, eds., *Herndon's Informants*, 38.

10 SOLDIERS RETURNING HOME Ibid., 36.

10 A YOUNGER BROTHER White, *A. Lincoln*, 18.

11 "A.B.C. SCHOOLS" CW, 4:61; Donald, *Lincoln*, 23; White, *A. Lincoln*, 19–20.

11 "TAUGHT ABE . . . WITH A BUZZARD'S QUILLEN" Wilson and Davis, eds., *Herndon's Informants*, 37.

11 LINCOLN LOVED THE EXPERIENCE Scripps, *First Published Life*, 16.

11 "I REMEMBER WHEN" Louis Austin Warren, *The Slavery Atmosphere of Lincoln's Youth* (Fort Wayne, Ind., 1933), no page numbers.

11 "ONE SUCH SCENE" Ibid.

11 "I SAW IT ALL" *RWAL*, 61.

11 TO HAVE BEEN BROADLY ANTISLAVERY On the roots of Lincoln's antislavery commitment, see, for instance, Burlingame, *Inner World*, 20–56; Warren, *Slavery Atmosphere*.

11 AFRICAN SLAVERY EXISTED David Brion Davis, *The Problem of Slavery in Western Culture*
(New York, 1966), 8.

11 HAD COME TO ENGLISH NORTH AMERICA Ibid.; Kendi, *Stamped from the Beginning*,
37–38.

11 OVER THE THREE-HUNDRED-ODD-YEAR COURSE Steven Mintz, "Historical Context: Facts About the Slave Trade and Slavery," Gilder Lehrman Institute of
American History, https://www.gilderlehrman.org/history-resources/teaching
-resource/historical-context-facts-about-slave-trade-and-slavery.

11 THE POPULATION OF ENSLAVED PEOPLE Baptist, *Half Has Never Been Told*, xxiii.

11 "FROM THE HOUR" Davis, *Problem of Slavery in Western Culture*, 70.

12 BASED MORE ON CONQUEST See, for instance, Ibid., 29–121; Kendi, *Stamped from the
Beginning*, 17–18.

12 THE SUMERIAN TERM Davis, *Problem of Slavery in Western Culture*, 47.

12 FOR NEARLY A MILLENNIUM AND A HALF Fredrickson, *Racism*, 11–13, 51–59. "What
makes Western racism so autonomous and conspicuous in world history has been
that it developed in a context that presumed human equality of some kind," Fredrickson wrote. "First came the doctrine that the Crucifixion offered grace to all
willing to receive it and made all Christian believers equal before God. Later came
the more revolutionary concept that all 'men' are born free and equal and entitled
to equal rights in society and government.... If equality is the norm in the spiritual or temporal realms (or in both at the same time), and there are groups of
people within the society who are so despised or disparaged that the upholders of
the norms feel compelled to make them exceptions to the promise or realization
of equality, they can be denied the prospect of equal status only if they allegedly
possess some extraordinary deficiency that makes them less than fully human. It is
uniquely in the West that we find the dialectical interaction between a premise of
equality and an intense prejudice toward certain groups that would seem to be a
precondition for the full flowering of racism as an ideology or worldview." Ibid.,
11–12.

12 BY THE SIXTEENTH CENTURY Fredrickson, *Racism*, 51–95; Kendi, *Stamped from the Beginning*, 3–11, 55–56, 79–119.

12 GEOPOLITICS ALSO PLAYED A KEY ROLE Klein, *Atlantic Slave Trade*, 22.

12 "SLUGGISH, LAZY ... [C]RAFTY" Kendi, *Stamped from the Beginning*, 82.

12 SOME WRITERS WENT SO FAR See, for instance, Jenkins, *Pro-Slavery Thought*, 242–84;
Kendi, *Stamped from the Beginning*, 84–86.

12 OTHER WORKS THAT CONTRIBUTED See, for instance, Jamelle Bouie, "The Enlightenment's Dark Side," *Slate*, June 5, 2018.

12 "THE ETHNOLOGIST" Jenkins, *Pro-Slavery Thought*, 239.

13 SPREAD OF PSEUDO-SCIENTIFIC RACIST THEORIES For details on Nott, Morton, and
Agassiz, see, for instance, "Josiah Clark Nott," Penn and Slavery Project, University of Pennsylvania, http://pennandslaveryproject.org/exhibits/show/medschool
/southerndoctors/josiahnott; "Samuel George Morton," http://pennandslavery
project.org/exhibits/show/medschool/southerndoctors/samuelmorton; "Louis
Agassiz," Department of Earth and Planetary Scientists, Harvard University,
https://eps.harvard.edu/louis-agassiz. See also Paul D. Escott, *The Worst Passions of
Human Nature: White Supremacy in the Civil War North* (Charlottesville, Va., 2020), 2;
"Germantown Quaker Petition Against Slavery," National Park Service, https://
www.nps.gov/articles/quakerpetition.htm.

13 FIGURES SUCH AS ANTHONY BENEZET Edward Raymond Turner, "The First Abolition Society in the United States," *Pennsylvania Magazine of History and Biography* 36,
no. 1 (1912): 92–109.

13 "THE COLOUR OF A MAN" Mason I. Lowance, ed., *Against Slavery: An Abolitionist Reader*
(New York, 2000), 21–22.

14 THE AFRICAN-BORN PHILLIS WHEATLEY See, for instance, Vincent Carretta, *Phillis
Wheatley: Biography of a Genius in Bondage* (Athens, Ga., 2011); Phillis Wheatley, *Complete Writings,* ed. Vincent Carretta (New York, 2001); Thomas J. Steele, "The Figure of Columbia: Phillis Wheatley Plus George Washington," *New England Quarterly*
54, no. 2 (June 1981): 264–66; Vincent Carretta, ed., *Unchained Voices: An Anthology
of Black Authors in the English-Speaking World of the Eighteenth Century* (Lexington, Ky.,
2004), 59–71.

14 "SINGULAR GENIUS" Wheatley, *Complete Writings,* xv.

14 WHEATLEY CORRESPONDED WITH GEORGE WASHINGTON George Washington to
Phillis Wheatley, February 28, 1776, https://founders.archives.gov/documents
/Washington/03-03-02-0281; Ron Chernow, *Washington: A Life* (New York, 2010),
219–21.

14 THE FIRST FORMAL ABOLITION ORGANIZATION Turner, "First Abolition Society." See
also www.paabolition.org.

14 IN MASSACHUSETTS, ELIZABETH FREEMAN Kerri Lee Alexander, "Elizabeth Freeman," National Women's History Museum, www.womenshistory.org/education
-resources/biographies/elizabeth-freeman. See also Transcript of Case No. 1, *Brom
& Bett v. John Ashley Esq.,* Book 4A, 55, Inferior Court of Common Pleas, Berkshire
County, Great Barrington, Mass., 1781, Berkshire County Courthouse.

14 "ALL MEN ARE BORN FREE" "Massachusetts Constitution," https://malegislature.gov
/laws/constitution.

14 BETWEEN 1777 AND 1817 I am grateful to Sean Wilentz for his guidance on these
points. See also Leon F. Litwack, *North of Slavery: The Negro in the Free States, 1790–1860*
(Chicago, 1965), 3; "United States and Anti-Slavery Timeline," http://www
.americanabolitionists.com/us-abolition-and-anti-slavery-timeline.html.

14 THE NORTHWEST ORDINANCE See, for instance, "Northwest Ordinance (1787),"
National Archives, https://www.archives.gov/milestone-documents/northwest
-ordinance.

14 UNDER ITS PROVISIONS "The Northwest Ordinance of 1787," https://history.house
.gov/Historical-Highlights/1700s/Northwest-Ordinance-1787/.

14 "NEITHER SLAVERY NOR" "Northwest Ordinance (1787)," National Archives.

14 "GENERAL EMANCIPATION OF SLAVES" Jenkins, *Pro-Slavery Thought,* 51. In the First
Congress of the new federal government, in 1790, Representative William
Smith of South Carolina argued against petitions for emancipation. "When we
entered into this confederation, we did it from political, not from moral motives," Smith said, "and I do not think my constituents want to learn morals
from the petitioners; I do not believe they want improvement in their moral
system, [and] if they do, they can get it at home." Ibid., 51. Representative Peter
Early of Georgia told the Congress in 1806, "A large majority of the people in
the Southern States do not consider slavery as a crime. They do not believe it
immoral to hold human flesh in bondage." Ibid., 55. In 1798, the Methodist
bishop Francis Asbury observed: "I am brought to conclude that slavery will
exist in Virginia perhaps for ages; there is not a sufficient sense of religion nor of
liberty to destroy it." Ibid., 54.

14 IN 1792, THE CONVENTION Ibid., 54.

15 INSTEAD THE KENTUCKY DELEGATES Ibid.; see also Michael J. Herrick, "Kentucky and Slavery: The Constitutional Convention of 1792," master's thesis, Dalhousie University, Halifax, Nova Scotia, November 2010. For the text of the article, see "Text of Kentucky Constitutions of 1792, 1799 and 1850," Frankfort, Ky., Legislative Research Commission, 1965, 7.

15 THE 1800 CENSUS "Hardin County (KY) Slaves, Free Blacks, and Free Mulattoes, 1850–1870," *Notable Kentucky African Americans Database,* https://nkaa.uky.edu/nkaa /items/show/2360.

15 BY 1811, TWO YEARS AFTER Warren, *Slavery Atmosphere*; Brian Dirck, "Lincoln's Kentucky Childhood and Race," *Register of the Kentucky Historical Society* 106, no. 3/4 (2008): 307–32; Marion B. Lucas, *A History of Blacks in Kentucky: From Slavery to Segregation, 1760–1891* (Lexington, Ky., 2003); R. Gerald McMurtry, "The Lincoln Migration from Kentucky to Indiana," *Indiana Magazine of History* 33 (December 1937): 385–421.

15 AN "AVERAGE OF AT LEAST" Warren, *Slavery Atmosphere*.

15 THOUGH THERE WERE SLAVE OWNERS Ibid.

15 "DAILY EXPERIENCE" Burlingame, *AL,* 1:21.

15 IN THE AUTUMN OF 1816 CW, 4:61–62; Wilson and Davis, eds., *Herndon's Informants,* 39.

15 LITTLE PIGEON CREEK White, *A. Lincoln,* 24–25.

15 HAD "WISELY RESOLVED" Scripps, *First Published Life,* 16.

15 "IT IS SAID" Wilson and Davis, eds., *Herndon's Informants,* 36.

16 "CHIEFLY ON ACCOUNT" CW, 4:61–62.

16 "PARTLY ON ACCOUNT" Ibid.

16 AS WELL AS ECONOMIC Burlingame, *AL,* 1:21; Donald, *Lincoln,* 24. On white views of labor and slavery, see also Eric Foner, *Free Soil, Free Labor, Free Men: The Ideology of the Republican Party Before the Civil War* (New York, 1995), especially 40–72.

16 "BEING CONSCIOUS TO MYSELF" Warren, *Slavery Atmosphere;* "Calendar of Bond and Power of Attorney Book No. 1, Jefferson County, Kentucky, 1783–1798," in *Early Kentucky Settlers: The Records of Jefferson County, Kentucky, from the Filson Club History Quarterly* (Baltimore, 1988), 408. See also J. Blaine Hudson, "References to Slavery in the Public Records of Early Louisville and Jefferson County, 1780–1812," *Filson Club History Quarterly* 73, no. 4 (October 1999): 325–54. "There was no community in America, west of the Allegheny mountains, where a more bitter and consistent controversy had been waged over the slavery question, during the first forty years of the nation's existence, than within the small area comprising a radius of fifteen miles from the home site where the birth of Abraham Lincoln took place, and within which area the three Lincoln homes were located," Warren wrote. Warren, *Slavery Atmosphere.*

16 IN 1796, A BAPTIST CHURCH Warren, *Slavery Atmosphere*. On Baptists and slavery in the area and in the age of Lincoln's youth, see, for instance, Monica Najar, " 'Meddling with Emancipation': Baptists, Authority, and the Rift over Slavery in the Upper South," *Journal of the Early Republic* 25, no. 2 (2005): 157–86; Louis A. Warren, *Lincoln's Youth: Indiana Years Seven to Twenty-one, 1816–1830* (New York, 1959), 112–24; Van Natter, *Lincoln's Boyhood,* 64–143; Typed Transcript, Minute Book / Little Pigeon Creek Baptist Church, Spencer County, Indiana, June 8, 1816–February 28, 1840, S.B.C. 1958, Southern Baptist Theological Library and Archives, Nashville, Tennessee (the original Minute Book is now in the Abraham Lincoln Presidential Library and Museum in Springfield, Illinois); Louis A. Warren, "The Grave of David Elkin," *Indiana Magazine of History* 22, no. 2 (June 1926):

203–4; Louis A. Warren, ed., "Reverend David Elkin," *Lincoln Lore* 69 (August 4, 1930), Bulletin of the Lincoln Historical Research Foundation, Fort Wayne, Indiana; Louis A. Warren, ed., "William Downs," *Lincoln Lore* 74 (September 8, 1930), Bulletin of the Lincoln Historical Research Foundation, Fort Wayne, Indiana; Louis A. Warren, ed., "Hidden Lincoln Treasures: Note to Parson Elkin," *Lincoln Lore* 516 (February 27, 1939), Bulletin of the Lincoln Historical Research Foundation, Fort Wayne, Indiana; Louis A. Warren, ed., "Sources of Traditional Quotations: Religion," *Lincoln Lore* 552 (November 6, 1939), Bulletin of the Lincoln Historical Research Foundation, Fort Wayne, Indiana; Louis A. Warren, ed., "Lincoln's Religious Heritage," *Lincoln Lore* 606 (November 18, 1940), Bulletin of the Lincoln Historical Research Foundation, Fort Wayne, Indiana; Louis A. Warren, ed., "Thayer's Pioneer Boy: Letter to Parson Elkin," *Lincoln Lore* 689 (June 22, 1942), Bulletin of the Lincoln Historical Research Foundation, Fort Wayne, Indiana.

16   "CAN WE, AS A CHURCH" Warren, *Slavery Atmosphere.*

16   "EMANCIPATION CHURCH" Ibid. More generally, see also W. Harrison Daniel, "Virginia Baptists and the Negro in the Early Republic," *Virginia Magazine of History and Biography* 80, no. 1 (1972): 60–69; John Lee Eighmy, "The Baptists and Slavery: An Examination of the Origins and Benefits of Segregation," *Social Science Quarterly* 49, no. 3 (1968): 666–73; James D. Essig, *The Bonds of Wickedness: American Evangelicals Against Slavery, 1770–1808* (Philadelphia, 1982); John Patrick Daly, *When Slavery Was Called Freedom: Evangelicalism, Proslavery, and the Causes of the Civil War* (Lexington, Ky., 2002); Hatch, *Democratization of American Christianity*, 102–13; J. Brent Morris, "'We Are Verily Guilty Concerning Our Brother': The Abolitionist Transformation of Planter William Henry Brisbane," *South Carolina Historical Magazine* 111 (2010): 118–50.

16   "TOM AND NANCY AND SALLY BUSH" Burlingame, *Inner World,* 21.

16   THOMAS LINCOLN BELONGED White, *A. Lincoln,* 17. On Lincoln's early exposure to religion see, for instance, ibid., 17–18; Guelzo, *Abraham Lincoln: Redeemer President* 36–38, 474; Wolf, *Almost Chosen People,* 34–42; Barton, *Soul of Abraham Lincoln,* 33–50; Blumenthal, *Self-Made Man,* 24–25; John F. Cady, "The Religious Environment of Lincoln's Youth," *Indiana Magazine of History* 37 (March–December 1941): 16–30; Richard J. Carwardine, *Evangelicals and Politics in Antebellum America* (New Haven, Conn., 1993), 46–47; Reynolds, *Abe,* 37–40. For details on the faith of the elder Lincolns, see William Dudley Nowlin, *Kentucky Baptist History, 1770–1922* (Louisville, 1922), 71–77; John H. Spencer, *A History of Kentucky Baptists: From 1769 to 1885* (Cincinnati, 1886), 1:33–38, and 2:21, 32, 47, 113, 125, 196, 204; Warren, *Slavery Atmosphere*; White, *A. Lincoln,* 17–18; Wolf, *Almost Chosen People,* 34–38. It is often reported that the elder Lincolns were "hard-shell" Baptists, meaning that they belonged to a group of believers that was self-consciously standoffish about most political and temporal matters. If the elect had been chosen by God, then all was decided. There was little need to look outward and worry about applying the gospel to the world. Carwardine, *Evangelicals and Politics in Antebellum America,* 126–27; Guelzo, *Abraham Lincoln: Redeemer President* 36–38. William D. Nowlin, a historian of Kentucky Baptists, offered convincing evidence, however, that the elder Lincolns were not "hard-shell" but were simply Baptists. Nowlin, *Kentucky Baptist History,* 190–93.

16   LICKING-LOCUST ASSOCIATION Nowlin, *Kentucky Baptist History,* 190–93.

16   "EMANCIPATION ASSOCIATION" Ibid.

16   ACCORDING TO A CLERGYMAN "A Log Meeting House and a Deerskin Record Book," *Lincoln Lore* 767 (December 20, 1943).

17   "NATURALLY ANTISLAVERY" CW, 7:281; Blumenthal, *Self-Made Man,* 27–28. "Thus

the figures of moral authority of the tiny rural community where Lincoln experienced his earliest formative shaping were antislavery," Blumenthal wrote. Ibid.

17 RELIGIOUS ANTISLAVERY CONVICTIONS Bertram Wyatt-Brown, "American Abolitionism and Religion," Divining America, TeacherServe, National Humanities Center; Sinha, *Slave's Cause*, 12—14.

17 ESSENTIAL TO THE LONG WAR Sinha, *Slave's Cause*, is comprehensive on the history of abolition, which Sinha calls "a radical, interracial movement, one which addressed the entrenched problems of exploitation and disenfranchisement in a liberal democracy and anticipated debates over race, labor, and empire." Ibid., 1.

17 ABSALOM JONES, RICHARD ALLEN Ibid., 130—59; Howe, *What Hath God Wrought*, 182—85.

17 THERE WERE ALLIANCES Sinha, *Slave's Cause*, 136.

17 IN THE LATTER DECADES Wyatt-Brown, "American Abolitionism and Religion."

17 THE METHODIST JOHN WESLEY See, for instance, John Wesley, *Thoughts upon Slavery*, https://docsouth.unc.edu/church/wesley/wesley.html.

17 THE ABOLITIONIST MOTTO Wyatt-Brown, "American Abolitionism and Religion." See also "Am I not a man and a brother," LOC, https://www.loc.gov/pictures /item/2008661312/.

18 FIRST GREAT AWAKENING Hatch, *Democratization of Christianity*, 102—3; Stephen J. Stein, "George Whitefield on Slavery: Some New Evidence," *Church History* 42, no. 2 (1973): 243—56.

18 PUBLISHED A SERMON Peter J. Morden, "British Baptists and Slavery," https://bwa -baptist-heritage.org/wp-content/uploads/2016/07/British-Baptists-and -Slavery.pdf.

18 OF WHICH KENTUCKY WAS STILL A PART "Statehood of Kentucky," *Journal of Applied Research in Economic Development*, http://journal.c2er.org/history/vol-1-part-1 -chapter-4-statehood-creating-a-state-policy-system-h-kentuckys-drive-to -statehood/.

18 "SLAVERY IS A VIOLENT" Daniel, "Virginia Baptists," 66.

18 DAVID BARROW Diane Perrine Coon, "Emancipationists in Northern Kentucky," *Encyclopedia of Northern Kentucky*, http://www.historybyperrine.com/emancipationists -northern-kentucky/; David Brion Davis, *The Problem of Slavery in the Age of Revolution, 1770—1823* (Ithaca, N.Y., 1975), 201; Keith Harper, "'A Strange Kind of Christian': David Barrow and Involuntary, Unmerited, Perpetual, Absolute, Hereditary Slavery, Examined; on the Principles of Nature, Reason, Justice, Policy, and Scripture," *Ohio Valley History* 15, no. 3 (2015): 68—77; Lowell H. Harrison and James C. Klotter, *A New History of Kentucky* (Lexington, Ky., 1997), 175; Miles Mark Fisher, "Friends of Humanity: A Quaker Anti-Slavery Influence," *Church History* 4, no. 3 (1935): 187—202; Walter B. Posey, "The Baptists and Slavery in the Lower Mississippi Valley," *Journal of Negro History* 41, no. 2 (1956): 117—30.

18 HEAVILY INFLUENCED BY THOMAS CLARKSON Coon, "Emancipationists in Northern Kentucky."

18 PUBLISHING HIS OWN Ibid.

18 "ABE WOULD GO OUT" Wilson and Davis, eds., *Herndon's Informants*, 110.

18 SUCH SERMONS WERE PREACHED Warren, *Slavery Atmosphere*; Burlingame, *AL*, 1:19—20.

18 WILLIAM DOWNS Warren, ed., "William Downs."

19 "ONE OF THE MOST BRILLIANT" Warren, *Slavery Atmosphere*.

19 "DISORDERLY" Burlingame, *AL*, ch. 1, 69—70, Unedited Manuscript Chapters, Knox College, https://www.knox.edu/documents/LincolnStudies/Burlingame Vol1Chap1.pdf.

19 DOWNS HAD BEEN INFLUENCED BY Warren, ed., "William Downs."

19 "FANATICAL ON THE SUBJECT" Spencer, *History of Kentucky Baptists*, 1:163.

19 "FIRST WENT" Louis A. Warren, ed., "Reverend David Elkin," *Lincoln Lore* 69 (August 4, 1930), Bulletin of the Lincoln Historical Research Foundation, Fort Wayne, Indiana; Burlingame, *AL*, 1:20. The original interview notes, cited by Burlingame, can be found in Interview with Fields Elkin, Elizabethtown, Kentucky, June 21, 1922, conducted by Louis A. Warren, copy, Lincoln files, "David Elkins" folder, Lincoln Museum, Lincoln Memorial University, Harrogate, Tennessee. See also Louis A. Warren, *Lincoln's Parentage and Childhood: A History of the Kentucky Lincolns* (New York, 1926), 246.

19 BORN ABOUT 1779 Warren, ed., "Reverend David Elkin."

19 REPORTEDLY GREW UP Ibid.

19 "A MAN OF EXTRAORDINARY" Spencer, *History of Kentucky Baptists*, 1:336.

19 ELKIN'S VOICE, IT WAS SAID Van Natter, *Lincoln's Boyhood*, 66.

19 "THOSE MINISTERS" Morgan Scott, *History of the Separate Baptist Church with a Narrative of Other Denominations* (Indianapolis, 1901), 184.

19 ADAM SHOEMAKER, KNOWN AS Van Natter, *Lincoln's Boyhood*, 134.

20 "EXPOSED THE HORRORS" Ibid.

20 "EQUAL RIGHTS FOR ALL" Ibid.

20 THREE OTHER MINISTERS IN INDIANA Blumenthal, *Self-Made Man*, 27–28.

20 "AS A POLITICAL EVIL" Najar, "'Meddling with Emancipation,'" 181.

20 "A VIOLATION OF" Ibid., 182. See also Charles Tarrants, "Carter Tarrant (1765–1816): Baptist and Emancipationist," *Register of the Kentucky Historical Society* 88, no. 2 (1990): 121–47.

20 WOULD BE RELATIVELY SHORT-LIVED See, for instance, Daly, *When Slavery Was Called Freedom*, 30–56.

20 THERE WAS SOMETHING Guelzo, *Abraham Lincoln: Redeemer President*, 38–39. As Guelzo observed: "[O]n no other point did Abraham Lincoln come closer to an outright repudiation of his father than on religion. . . . Lincoln showed no flicker of interest in joining his father's church." Ibid., 36–38.

20 THE BAPTIST EXPRESSION OF PREDESTINATION Ibid., 36–39; Carwardine, *Evangelicals and Politics in Antebellum America*, 126–27.

21 "WOULD HEAR SERMONS" Wilson and Davis, eds., *Herndon's Informants*, 107.

21 "WHEN THEY WERE GONE" Ibid., 109. Abraham was never especially musical. "Lincoln sometimes attempted to sing but always failed," Dennis Hanks recalled. Ibid., 42.

21 "PROBABLY IT IS" Wolf, *Almost Chosen People*, 51.

21 "IF I EVER" Herndon and Weik, *Herndon's Life of Lincoln*, 64.

Chapter Two: Abe Was Hungry for Books

22 "HE WAS A CONSTANT" Wilson and Davis, eds., *Herndon's Informants*, 41.

22 "THE PROGRESS OF TRUTH" Grimshaw, *History*, 300–301.

22 SHE WAS WEAVING Wilson and Davis, eds., *Herndon's Informants*, 37.

22 "WOULD SAY TO HIMSELF" Ibid., 42.

22 "IT WAS A WILD REGION" Herndon and Weik, *Herndon's Life of Lincoln*, 21–22. "Indiana [was] a wilderness and wholly a timbered Country," Dennis Hanks recalled. "We all hunted pretty much all the time, Especially so when we got tired of work—which was very often, I will assure you." Wilson and Davis, eds., *Herndon's Informants*, 39.

23 "WHEN MY FATHER" CW, 1:386; Donald, *Lincoln*, 25.

23   GOOD COMPANY IN THE LIMITED WORLDS On Thomas Lincoln in general, see, for instance, Blumenthal, *Self-Made Man*, 29–31. "Thomas Lincoln . . . could beat his son telling a story—cracking a joke—Mr Thomas Lincoln was a good, clean, social, truthful & honest man," Dennis Hanks recalled. "He never thought that gold was God." Wilson and Davis, eds., *Herndon's Informants*, 37.

23   HE BUILT A FLATBOAT Wilson and Davis, eds., *Herndon's Informants*, 38.

23   SHE READ TO HIM Ibid., 37.

23   "AT THIS PLACE" CW, 4:62.

23   HIS MOTHER HAD LOADED Wilson and Davis, eds., *Herndon's Informants*, 39.

23   NANCY HANKS LINCOLN DIED Burlingame, *AL*, 1:25–27.

23   "MILK SICKNESS" Ibid., 25; Blumenthal, *Self-Made Man*, 26; Donald, *Lincoln*, 26; White, *A. Lincoln*, 27–28.

23   KNOWN AT FIRST AS Walter J. Daly, "The 'Slows': The Torment of Milk Sickness on the Midwest Frontier," *Indiana Magazine of History* 102, no. 1 (2006): 31–34.

23   "A WHITISH COAT" Herndon and Weik, *Herndon's Life of Lincoln*, 25–26.

24   DEATH, THE DOCTOR REPORTED Ibid., 26. See also White, *A. Lincoln*, 27.

24   "STRUGGLED ON" Wilson and Davis, eds., *Herndon's Informants*, 40.

24   THE DISEASE KILLED HER Donald, *Lincoln*, 26; Burlingame, *AL*, 1:25

24   "THERE WAS NO PHYSICIAN" Wilson and Davis, eds., *Herndon's Informants*, 40.

24   "HERE IN THIS RUDE HOUSE" Ibid.

24   SHE WAS BURIED Donald, *Lincoln*, 26; White, *A. Lincoln*, 27.

24   IT TOOK SEVERAL MONTHS Burlingame, *AL*, 1:25; Herndon and Weik, *Herndon's Life of Lincoln*, 27; Barton, *Soul of Abraham Lincoln*, 34.

24   THE GRAVE REMAINED UNMARKED Wilson and Davis, eds., *Herndon's Informants*, 80.

24   IN THE LAST WINTER Ibid.

24   ABE SO RESENTED Burlingame, *Inner World*, 37–42; Blumenthal, *Self-Made Man*, 30–31; Guelzo, *Abraham Lincoln: Redeemer President,* 121. Of the son's being forcibly hired out, Guelzo wrote: "This slavery was what he experienced as a young man under his father, and he came to associate it with subsistence farming, and the Jeffersonian ideology that glorified it, with a backwards-looking mentality that conveniently froze wealthy landholders in places of power while offering the placebo of subsidy and protection (especially in the form of cheap land) to bungling yeomen in order to pacify their disgruntlements." Guelzo, *Abraham Lincoln: Redeemer President,* 121.

24   "I USED TO BE A SLAVE" Ibid., 121.

24   "I HAVE SEEN HIS FATHER" White, *A. Lincoln*, 29.

24   "THOS. LINCOLN NEVER SHOWED" Ibid., 30.

25   "THE ELDER LINCOLN" Herndon and Weik, *Herndon's Life of Lincoln*, 24.

25   "SOMETIMES ABE WAS A LITTLE RUDE" Wilson and Davis, eds., *Herndon's Informants*, 39.

25   "HE WAS AMBITIOUS" Ibid., 42.

25   "HE ALWAYS APPEARED" Herndon and Weik, *Herndon's Life of Lincoln*, 32.

25   LINCOLN WAS A FIGURE Ibid. "Elements of leadership in him," Herndon wrote, "seem to have manifested themselves already." Ibid.

25   HE HAD SOME HELP Wilson and Davis, eds., *Herndon's Informants*, 84–85. On Sarah Bush Johnston Lincoln and the brief courtship with Thomas Lincoln, see, for instance, Herndon and Weik, *Herndon's Life of Lincoln*, 27–31; Burlingame, *AL*, 1:27–29; Donald, *Lincoln*, 27–28; White, *A. Lincoln*, 28–30.

26   THOMAS OFFERED HIS SUIT Burlingame, *AL*, 1:27.

26   "WELL, MISS JOHNSTON" Wilson and Davis, eds., *Herndon's Informants*, 85.

26   "TOMMY, I KNOW YOU" Ibid.

26 "ASKED HER" Ibid.

26 A KIND OF SAVIOR Herndon and Weik, *Herndon's Life of Lincoln*, 27–30.

26 "THIS [WAS] A NEW ERA" Wilson and Davis, eds., *Herndon's Informants*, 82.

26 "SHE PROVED A GOOD" White, *A. Lincoln*, 28.

26 "WILD—RAGGED & DIRTY" Wilson and Davis, eds., *Herndon's Informants*, 41. For Sarah Bush Johnston Lincoln's recollections of her arrival in the Lincoln household, see ibid., 106–7.

26 "IN [MY] TENTH YEAR" CW, 4:62.

26 THOMAS LINCOLN'S SECOND WIFE Herndon and Weik, *Herndon's Life of Lincoln*, 28–29; Burlingame, *AL*, 1:27–28.

26 AS DID THREE STEPSIBLINGS Herndon and Weik, *Herndon's Life of Lincoln*, 28.

26 "THOS LINCOLN NOW HURRIED" Wilson and Davis, eds., *Herndon's Informants*, 41.

26 "WORKED FOR ME" Herndon and Weik, *Herndon's Life of Lincoln*, 38.

27 "I INDUCED MY HUSBAND" Ibid., 33.

27 "A SLENDER WELL BEHAVED" Wilson and Davis, eds., *Herndon's Informants*, 82.

27 "THERE WERE SOME SCHOOLS" White, *A. Lincoln*, 31; CW, 3:511.

27 "NO SMALL PART" Reynolds, *Abe*, 51.

27 "ABE WAS NOT ENERGETIC" White, *A. Lincoln*, 30.

27 HE ABSORBED STANDARDS Ibid., 31.

27 THE BIBLE, AESOP's *Fables* Reynolds, *Abe*, 54–55; Blumenthal, *Self-Made Man*, 28–29; Wilson and Davis, eds., *Herndon's Informants*, 41; White, *A. Lincoln*, 31–34; Herndon and Weik, *Herndon's Life of Lincoln*, 36; Burlingame, *AL*, 1:36.

27 "ABE WAS A GOOD BOY" Wilson and Davis, eds., *Herndon's Informants*, 106–7.

27 THE PSALMS White, *A. Lincoln*, 32. See also Lindley Murray, *The English Reader: or, Pieces in Prose and Poetry, Selected from the Best Writers Designed to Assist Young Persons to Read with Propriety and Effect; to Improve Their Language and Sentiments; and to Inculcate Some of the Most Important Principles of Piety and Virtue* (New York, 1826), 70.

27 THE HYMNS OF ISAAC WATTS Wilson and Davis, eds., *Herndon's Informants*, 109.

27 HIS TIME IN A CLASSROOM CW, 4:62.

27 "WHAT [I HAVE] IN THE WAY" Ibid.

28 "I AM WRITING MR L's LIFE" Wilson and Davis, eds., *Herndon's Informants*, xiii–xiv.

28 "THE BEST SCHOOLBOOK" See, for instance, Charles Monaghan, "The Murrays of Murray Hill: A New York Quaker Family Before, During and After the Revolution," *Quaker History* 87, no. 1 (1998): 35–56. On Lincoln's literary pursuits over his lifetime, see Robert Bray, "What Abraham Lincoln Read: An Evaluative and Annotated List," *JALA* 28, no. 2 (2007): 28–81; and Robert Bray, *Reading with Lincoln* (Carbondale, Ill., 2010).

28 AN ANTHOLOGY PUBLISHED IN 1799 Murray, *The English Reader*.

28 "TO ASSIST YOUNG PERSONS" Ibid.

28 "NOTHING IS SO INCONSISTENT" Ibid., 20–21.

28 "IN JUDGING OF OTHERS" Ibid., 21.

28 "WE SHOULD CHERISH" Ibid., 26.

28 "IN SEASONS OF DISTRESS" Ibid., 28.

29 A PENNSYLVANIA QUAKER Charlotte Fell Smith, "Murray, Lindley" in Sidney Lee, ed., *Dictionary of National Biography, 1885–1900* (London, 1894). See also Bryan A. Garner, "Remembering Lindley Murray," *ABA Journal*, October 1, 2013, https://www.abajournal.com/magazine/article/remembering_lindley_murray_an_inspirational_lawyer-grammarian.

29 OF HUGH BLAIR "Significant Scots: Hugh Blair," https://www.electricscotland.com/history/other/blair_hugh.htm. On the Scottish Enlightenment in general, see, for instance, Alexander Broadie, ed., *The Scottish Enlightenment: An Anthology* (Edin-

burgh, 1998); James Buchan, *Crowded with Genius: Edinburgh's Moment of the Mind* (New York, 2004); Arthur Herman, *How the Scots Invented the Modern World: The True Story of How Western Europe's Poorest Nation Created Our World and Everything in It* (New York, 2002).

29 "I CONSIDER A HUMAN SOUL" Murray, *English Reader*, 40.

29 THE STORY IS TOLD Wilson and Davis, eds., *Herndon's Informants*, 85.

29 HE WAS STRONG Burlingame, *AL*, 1:61–62; Donald, *Lincoln*, 40–41.

29 "HE COULD THROW" Wilson and Davis, eds., *Herndon's Informants*, 6–7.

30 "BY WHATEVER MEANS" Murray, *English Reader*, 101–2.

30 "WE FIND MAN PLACED" Ibid., 58.

30 THE WISE MAN, ADDISON OBSERVED Ibid., 107–8.

30 TOOK A PROGRESSIVE VIEW Grimshaw, *History*, 300. See also Blumenthal, *Self-Made Man*, 37.

30 "A NEW ERA" Grimshaw, *History*, 120.

30 HE QUOTED Ibid., 120–24.

31 "SINCE THE MIDDLE" Ibid., 300–301.

31 "THE LITTLE ADVANCE" CW, 3:511.

31 "I WAS RAISED" Ibid., 511–12.

31 WHEN HE JOINED HIS FAMILY Burlingame, *AL*, 1:48.

31 LINCOLN'S SISTER SARAH Herndon and Weik, *Herndon's Life of Lincoln*, 42–44.

31 HE WAS A FERRYMAN Ibid., 43–44.

31 "LINGER AND TRADE" CW, 4:62.

31 ON A SECOND TRIP Foner, *Fiery Trial*, 10.

32 WHAT IS CERTAIN Ibid.

32 "THE FACES WITH EVERY SHADE" Ibid.

32 FOR THE JOURNEY Herndon and Weik, *Herndon's Life of Lincoln*, 57–58; CW, 4:63.

32 "BUT I COULD NOT ENDURE" Herndon and Weik, *Herndon's Life of Lincoln*, 58.

32 THE FAMILY SETTLED CW, 4:63.

32 "HERE THEY BUILT" Ibid.

32 HE SOON MOVED Ibid., 3:512. On Lincoln's New Salem years, see, for instance, Blumenthal, *Self-Made Man*, 53–72.

32 THE OWNER WAS DENTON OFFUTT Herndon and Weik, *Herndon's Life of Lincoln*, 61.

32 "A WILD, HARUM-SCARUM" Wilson and Davis, eds., *Herndon's Informants*, 73.

32 SLEEPING FOR A TIME White, *A. Lincoln*, 47–48.

32 "MR. L WAS VERY FOND" Wilson and Davis, eds., *Herndon's Informants*, 73.

32 A FABLED WRESTLING MATCH White, *A. Lincoln*, 46–47.

33 "SCARCELY HAVE YOU DESCENDED" Tocqueville, *Democracy in America,* 232.

33 DRAWN TO THE DRAMA OF TRIALS Herndon and Weik, *Herndon's Life of Lincoln*, 50–51.

33 IN BOONVILLE, INDIANA Ibid.

33 YEARS LATER, THE LAWYER CALLED Ibid.

33 "IF I COULD, AS I THEN THOUGHT" Ibid., 51.

33 HIS FIRST POLITICAL SPEECH Ibid., 60–61; Burlingame, *AL*, 1:50; White, *A. Lincoln*, 41.

Chapter Three: I Am Humble Abraham Lincoln

34 "THERE WAS NOTHING" Wilson and Davis, eds., *Herndon's Informants*, 90.

34 "THE CONTINUED THOUGHT" Burlingame, *AL*, 1:101. The friend was Mentor Graham.

34 IN THE PAGES OF White, *A. Lincoln*, 49. On Lincoln's first campaign, see, for in-

stance, ibid., 48–50, 52–53; Burlingame, *AL*, 1:71–75; Donald, *Lincoln*, 41–43, 46; Paul Simon, *Lincoln's Preparation for Greatness: The Illinois Legislative Years* (Urbana and Chicago, 1971), 3–14.

34   "RAPIDLY MADE ACQUAINTANCES" CW, 4:64.

34   WHO ENCOURAGED HIS AMBITIONS Ibid.; Wilson and Davis, eds., *Herndon's Informants*, 6.

34   LINCOLN'S PUBLISHED STATEMENT White, *A. Lincoln*, 49–50.

34   "THE MOST IMPORTANT SUBJECT" CW, 1:8.

34   THOMAS LINCOLN IS THOUGHT Hofstadter, *American Political Tradition*, 128.

34   "HOW FAR I SHALL" CW, 1:8–9.

35   WORD OF A FRONTIER WAR Burlingame, *AL*, 1:67–71; Blumenthal, *Self-Made Man*, 57–60; White, *A. Lincoln*, 50; Howe, *What Hath God Wrought*, 419. See also, for instance, Francis Paul Prucha, *The Great Father: The United States Government and the American Indians* (Lincoln, Neb., 1984), 253–57; Ellen M. Whitney, ed., *Black Hawk War, 1831–1832* (Springfield, Ill., 1970–78).

35   "BY A UNANIMOUS VOTE" Wilson and Davis, eds., *Herndon's Informants*, 6.

35   TO A NEIGHBOR Burlingame, *AL*, 1:67.

35   MEMBERS OF THE FOURTH ILLINOIS Ibid.

35   "GENEROUS RUFFIANS" Herndon and Weik, *Herndon's Life of Lincoln*, 78.

35   LINCOLN'S FIRST ORDER Ibid.

35   "A SUCCESS WHICH GAVE ME" CW, 3:512.

35   HE LATER JOKED Ibid., 1:509–10.

35   ON TUESDAY, MAY 15 White, *A. Lincoln*, 51.

35   AT STILLMAN'S RUN Burlingame, *AL*, 1:68.

35   "ALL SCALPED" Ibid., 67–68.

35   RIDING UP A SMALL HILL Herndon and Weik, *Herndon's Life of Lincoln*, 83. See also Burlingame, *AL*, 1:67–68.

35   "WERE HORRIBLY MANGLED" Wilson and Davis, eds., *Herndon's Informants*, 371.

35   LINCOLN REMEMBERED THE SCENE Herndon and Weik, *Herndon's Life of Lincoln*, 83. "The red light of the morning sun was streaming upon them," he recalled, "as they lay heads toward us on the ground." Ibid. For other recollections of violence during the Black Hawk War, see Wilson and Davis, eds., *Herndon's Informants*, 371–72, and Burlingame, *AL*, 1:68.

35   "ONE MAN HAD" Herndon and Weik, *Herndon's Life of Lincoln*, 83.

35   AN AGED INDIAN MAN Burlingame, *AL*, 1:69–70; Wilson and Davis, eds., *Herndon's Informants*, 18–19; 372.

36   DISCHARGED FROM MILITIA DUTY White, *A. Lincoln*, 52.

36   "FELLOW CITIZENS, I PRESUME" Ibid.

36   "ALWAYS A WHIG" CW, 3:512. See also Burlingame, *AL*, 1:71–73. On Lincoln and Clay, see, for instance, Blumenthal, *Self-Made Man*, 70–72.

36   THE ORIGINS OF THE WHIG PARTY For this summary, I am indebted to, among others, Michael F. Holt, *The Rise and Fall of the American Whig Party: Jacksonian Politics and the Onset of the Civil War* (New York, 1999); Howe, *What Hath God Wrought*; Wilentz, *Rise of American Democracy*; Remini, *Henry Clay*.

36   BECAME SECRETARY OF STATE See, for instance, Jon Meacham, *American Lion: Andrew Jackson in the White House* (New York, 2008), 44–45, 388; Remini, *Henry Clay*, 270; Wilentz, *Rise of American Democracy*, 255.

36   "CORRUPT BARGAIN" Holt, *Rise and Fall*, 7, 15, 40.

37   "THE STATES HAVING NO SLAVES" Howe, *What Hath God Wrought*, 221.

37   "'THE COMMONWEALTH' IS" Burlingame, *AL*, 1:71.

38   IN THE WORDS OF THE MOTTO William Ernest Smith, *The Francis Preston Blair Family in Politics* (New York, 1933), 1:71.

38   AS AN ASPIRING WHIG Burlingame, *AL*, 1:72; CW, 2:221. See also Daniel Walker Howe, "Why Abraham Lincoln Was a Whig," *JALA* 16 (1995): 27–38.

38   "IF ELECTED, I SHALL" White, *A. Lincoln*, 52.

38   HE WAS DEFEATED Ibid. "Lincoln came in eighth in a field of thirteen candidates [four seats were on offer] with 657 votes. He was not too disheartened, however, for in the precinct that included New Salem, he received 277 of the 300 votes." Ibid.

38   "THE ONLY TIME" CW, 4:64.

38   A MITIGATING FACTOR Ibid.

38   "WHEN I HAVE BEEN" Burlingame, *AL*, 1:74. See also Wilson and Davis, eds., *Herndon's Informants*, 7.

38   A FRIEND RECALLED Burlingame, *AL*, 1:75.

38   "[I] WAS NOW WITHOUT" CW, 4:64–65.

38   DENTON OFFUTT'S STORE White, *A. Lincoln*, 55.

38   "ESPECIALLY AS [I] HAD" CW, 4:65.

38   HE BRIEFLY OPENED Ibid.

38   "OF COURSE" Ibid.

38   "WINKED OUT" Ibid.

38   "[I] STUDIED" Ibid.

39   THE END OF A CRISIS On nullification, see, for instance, Richard E. Ellis, *The Union at Risk: Jacksonian Democracy, States' Rights, and the Nullification Crisis* (New York, 1987); William W. Freehling, *Prelude to Civil War: The Nullification Controversy in South Carolina, 1816–1836* (New York, 1966) and *Secessionists at Bay, 1776–1854* (New York, 1990), the first volume of his multivolume work *Road to Disunion*; and Freehling's edited volume *The Nullification Era: A Documentary Record* (New York, 1967); Howe, *What Hath God Wrought*, 395–410; Wilentz, *Rise of American Democracy*, 374–92; Merrill D. Peterson, *Olive Branch and Sword: The Compromise of 1833* (Baton Rouge, La., 1982).

39   "THE TARIFF WAS ONLY" John Spencer Bassett, ed., *Correspondence of Andrew Jackson* (Washington, D.C., 1926–35), 5:72.

39   SIX DAYS LATER Donald, *Lincoln*, 50. See also Burlingame, *AL*, 1:77; Meacham, *American Lion*, 247.

39   "TOO INSIGNIFICANT TO MAKE" CW, 4:65.

39   THE COUNTY SURVEYOR Ibid.

39   "ACCEPTED, PROCURED" Ibid.

39   "THIS PROCURED BREAD" Ibid.

39   BECAME A DEVOTEE White, *A. Lincoln*, 53–54.

39   "IT MAY BE LAID DOWN" Samuel Kirkham, *English Grammar in Familiar Lectures* (New York, 1823), 219.

39   "REMEMBER THAT" Ibid., 15.

39   VORACIOUSLY CURIOUS White, *A. Lincoln*, 54–55; Blumenthal, *Self-Made Man*, 64–67.

39   CONSTANTIN VOLNEY'S C. F. Volney, *The Ruins, or, Meditation on the Revolutions of Empires* (New York, 1890).

39   *The Age of Reason* Thomas Paine, *Collected Writings*, ed. Eric Foner (New York, 1995), 665–830. See also Harvey J. Kaye, *Thomas Paine and the Promise of America* (New York, 2005), 81–84.

39   HOBBES'S WAR Mitchell Cohen and Nicole Fermon, *Princeton Readings in Political Thought: Essential Texts Since Plato* (Princeton, N.J., 1996), 208. Hobbes described the "natural condition of mankind" thusly: "Hereby it is manifest, that during the time men live without a common power to keep them all in awe, they are in that condi-

tion which is called war; and such a war, as is of every man, against every man." Ibid., 207–8.

39   "What one seizes" Volney, *Ruins*, 26–27.

40   "The Americans combine" Howe, *What Hath God Wrought*, 307.

40   "I believe in" Kaye, *Thomas Paine and the Promise of America*, 83; Paine, *Collected Writings*, 666.

40   God had created Kaye, *Thomas Paine and the Promise of America*, 81–83.

40   These points moved Herndon and Weik, *Herndon's Life of Lincoln*, 355–60.

40   "passed from hand to hand" Ibid., 355.

40   "prepared an extended essay" Ibid.

40   "read and freely discussed" Ibid.

40   Then Samuel Hill intervened Ibid.

40   "snatched the manuscript" Ibid.

40   "The book went up" Ibid.

41   "In my intercourse" Ibid., 356–57.

41   "Where wast thou" Job 38:4, KJV.

41   "O the depth" Romans 11:33, KJV.

41   "When I do good" Herndon and Weik, *Herndon's Life of Lincoln*, 354–55.

41   surveying paid for his daily bread CW, 4:65.

41   In 1834, two years after Ibid.

41   "by the highest vote" Ibid.

41   Monday, August 4 The Lincoln Log: A Daily Chronology of the Life of Abraham Lincoln, August 4, 1834, http://thelincolnlog.org/Results.aspx?type=basicSearch &terms=August+4%2c+1834&r=LINlYXJjaC5hc3B4.

41   three subsequent elections CW, 4:65.

42   He borrowed $200 Herndon and Weik, *Herndon's Life of Lincoln,* 104.

42   "reveled" Burlingame, *AL,* 1:88.

42   freshman's low profile Burlingame, *AL,* 1:92–97, details Lincoln's first legislative session. See also Blumenthal, *Self-Made Man,* 73–93; and Simon, *Lincoln's Preparation for Greatness,* 19–33.

42   "the dullest, dreariest" Burlingame, *AL,* 1:93. See also Edmund Flagg, "Disappointment at Vandalia," *Journal of the Illinois State Historical Society* 41, no. 3 (September 1948): 312–14.

42   "Lincoln had seen" Burlingame, *AL,* 1:94.

42   "The society of Vandalia" Herndon and Weik, *Herndon's Life of Lincoln*, 131.

42   "Men of capital" Ibid., 130–31.

42   ten-week session Burlingame, *AL,* 1:95.

42   Illinois–Michigan canal Ibid., 96.

42   "Lincoln improved rapidly" Burlingame, *AL,* 1:97; Simon, *Lincoln's Preparation for Greatness,* 32.

42   suggested that Lincoln Burlingame, *AL,* 1:89. For Lincoln's early interest in the law, see ibid., 86–92.

42   borrowed books Wilson and Davis, eds., *Herndon's Informants,* 81.

42   from David Turnham Herndon and Weik, *Herndon's Life of Lincoln*, 40.

42   from Stuart Ibid., 91–92.

42   "studied with nobody" CW, 4:65.

42   "When the Legislature" Ibid.

42   "Work, work, work" Ibid., 121.

42   He was licensed Ibid., 65.

43   the perfect girl For the Ann Rutledge story, see Herndon and Weik, *Herndon's*

Life of Lincoln, 105–15; Burlingame, *AL*, 1:98–101; Burlingame, *Inner World*, 135–36; Blumenthal, *Self-Made Man*, 76–79; Donald, *Lincoln*, 55–58; White, *A. Lincoln*, 99–101; John Evangelist Walsh, *The Shadows Rise: Abraham Lincoln and the Ann Rutledge Legend* (Urbana and Chicago, 1993); Jean H. Baker, *Mary Todd Lincoln: A Biography* (New York, 1987), 267–69; Jean H. Baker, "Mary and Abraham: A Marriage" in Sean Wilentz, ed., *Best American History Essays on Lincoln* (New York, 2009), 109.

43 WITH WHOM LINCOLN Herndon and Weik, *Herndon's Life of Lincoln*, 106.

43 "BEAUTIFUL AND VERY AMIABLE" Wilson and Davis, eds., *Herndon's Informants*, 80.

43 PROMINENT SOUTH CAROLINA FAMILY Herndon and Weik, *Herndon's Life of Lincoln*, 106.

43 "LIKE OTHER SOUTHERN PEOPLE" Ibid.

43 THERE WERE NINE CHILDREN Ibid.

43 "WINNING WAYS" Ibid.

43 "SHE WAS AMIABLE" Ibid., 107.

43 "MISS RUTLEDGE" Ibid.

43 "MISS RUTLEDGE WAS A GENTLE" Ibid., 111.

43 KNOWN AS JOHN MCNEIL, A SUITOR Ibid., 107.

43 "HE WENT TO WORK" Ibid.

44 SAMUEL HILL HAD TRIED Ibid., 108.

44 VILLAGERS SPECULATED Ibid.

44 MCNEIL TOLD HER Ibid.

44 "I LEFT BEHIND ME" Ibid.

44 "FEAR THAT IF" Ibid., 108–9.

44 THE YOUNG LADY SAID Ibid., 109.

44 MCNAMAR TOOK ILL Ibid.

44 "HER FRIENDS ENCOURAGED" Ibid.

44 BY THE TIME MCNAMAR Ibid., 110.

45 "GROWING LESS ARDENT" Ibid.

45 "MR. LINCOLN WAS NOT" Ibid., 111.

45 WOULD LINCOLN WAIT Ibid.

45 "THE SLOW-MOVING MAILS" Ibid., 111–12.

45 "IN A HALF-HEARTED WAY" Ibid., 112.

46 THOUGH HE COULD NEVER MATCH Ibid.

46 "AS SOON AS HIS STUDIES" Ibid.

46 ANN WAS STRICKEN Ibid.

46 AN ANXIOUS LINCOLN KEPT WATCH Ibid.

46 THE ATTENDING DOCTOR ADVISED Ibid.

46 "KEPT INQUIRING FOR LINCOLN" Ibid.

46 "I HAVE HEARD MOTHER SAY" Ibid.

46 "VAIN MAN, THY FOND PURSUITS" Ibid.; "Vain Man, Thy Fond Pursuits Forbear," https://hymnary.org/text/vain_man_thy_fond_pursuits_forbear.

46 "THE LAST THING" Herndon and Weik, *Herndon's Life of Lincoln*, 112.

46 LINCOLN WENT FROM HER HOUSE Ibid., 113.

47 TUESDAY, AUGUST 25, 1835 Ibid., 112.

46 "LINCOLN TOOK IT" Wilson and Davis, eds., *Herndon's Informants*, 80.

46 ANN WAS BURIED Herndon and Weik, *Herndon's Life of Lincoln*, 112.

46 "I CANNOT ENDURE" Walsh, *Shadows Rise*, 16.

47 "SHE WAS CONTRACTED" Murray, *English Reader*, 106.

47 "HAD TO LOCK HIM UP" Burlingame, *AL*, 1:100.

47 LINCOLN TOOK REFUGE Ibid.

47 "THE EFFECT UPON" Herndon and Weik, *Herndon's Life of Lincoln*, 113.

47 "HE HAD FITS" Ibid.

47 "FROM THE SUDDEN SHOCK" Burlingame, *AL*, 1:100.

47 LINCOLN'S DEPRESSION WAS PROFOUND Ibid., 100–101. On Lincoln and depression, see, for instance, Joshua Wolf Shenk, *Lincoln's Melancholy: How Depression Challenged a President and Fueled His Greatness* (New York, 2005).

47 "I [RAN] OFF THE TRACK" Wilson and Davis, eds., *Herndon's Informants*, 440; Burlingame, *AL*, 1:101.

47 HE LOST WEIGHT Burlingame, *AL*, 1:101. According to Burlingame, Lincoln "grew emaciated." Ibid.

47 HE "WAS STUDIOUS" Ibid.

47 "LONG AFTER ANN DIED" Ibid., 100.

48 THERE WAS THE LAW Herndon and Weik, *Herndon's Life of Lincoln*, 132.

48 A SPECIAL SESSION Ibid., 132–33; Burlingame, *AL*, 1:101–3; Simon, *Lincoln's Preparation for Greatness*, 34–41.

48 DEMOCRATS REGISTERED THEIR SUPPORT Herndon and Weik, *Herndon's Life of Lincoln*, 132–33; Blumenthal, *Self-Made Man*, 80–88; Simon, *Lincoln's Preparation for Greatness*, 34–35, 43–44. See also Joel H. Silbey, "Election of 1836," in *HAPE*, 1:252–74.

48 "MANY VOTERS" *CW*, 1:48.

48 "AGREED. HERE'S MINE!" Ibid.

48 "I GO FOR ALL" Ibid. See also Herndon and Weik, *Herndon's Life of Lincoln*, 133–34; Burlingame, *AL*, 1:104–5.

48 "IF ELECTED, I SHALL" *CW*, 1:48.

48 "YOUR REPRESENTATIVE" Edmund Burke, Speech to the Electors of Bristol, https://press-pubs.uchicago.edu/founders/documents/v1ch13s7.html.

49 OF SIGNIFICANT ISSUES Herndon and Weik, *Herndon's Life of Lincoln*, 134.

49 IN THE 1836 CONTEST *Herndon's Life of Lincoln*, 135–36; *CW*, 1:48–49.

49 "NO ONE HAS NEEDED" *CW*, 1:49.

49 HAD NOTHING TO SAY Herndon and Weik, *Herndon's Life of Lincoln*, 136.

49 "AT ONE FELL STROKE" *CW*, 1:49–50. For Lincoln's skill on the stump, see also Herndon and Weik, *Herndon's Life of Lincoln*, 136–38.

Chapter Four: Founded on Injustice and Bad Policy

51 "AMERICA IS MORE" Peter P. Hinks, ed., *David Walker's Appeal to the Coloured Citizens of the World* (University Park, Pa., 2000), 67.

51 "A PEOPLE, OWNING SLAVES" *Speeches Delivered in the Convention, of the State of South-Carolina, Held in Columbia, in March, 1833* (Charleston, S.C., 1833), 25; Freehling, *Prelude to Civil War*, 297.

51 IN THE CLOSING DAYS Hay and Nicolay, *AL: A History*, 1:149–50; Simon, *Lincoln's Preparation for Greatness*, 131–34.

51 THE KENTUCKY-BORN GOVERNOR Elizabeth Duncan Putnam, "Governor Joseph Duncan of Illinois," *Tennessee Historical Magazine* 7, no. 4 (January 1922): 243–51.

51 ILLINOIS WAS PUTATIVELY A FREE STATE Simon, *Lincoln's Preparation for Greatness*, 121–45; Merton Lynn Dillon, "The Antislavery Movement in Illinois, 1824–1835," *Journal of the Illinois State Historical Society (1908–1984)* 47, no. 2 (Summer 1954): 149–66; Harrold, *Lincoln and the Abolitionists*, 13–14. For a recounting of the "exclusion of blacks from the franchise" in Illinois, as well as other discriminatory laws, see Burlingame, *AL*, 1:103–4. "Between 1819 and 1846, the General Assembly outlawed interracial marriage and cohabitation, forbade blacks to testify in court

against whites, and denied them the right to attend public schools," Burlingame wrote. "In 1848, by a margin of 60,585 to 15,903 (79% to 21%), the Illinois electorate adopted a new constitution banning black suffrage; it voted separately on an article prohibiting black immigration, which passed 50,261 to 21,297 (70% to 30%). With that, Illinois became the only Free State forbidding blacks to settle within its borders. (Oregon and Indiana soon followed its lead.)" Ibid.

51 "SHOULD PERMIT" Simon, *Lincoln's Preparation for Greatness*, 126.

51 A TERRITORIAL GOVERNOR "Edwards, Ninian, 1775–1833," https://bioguide.congress .gov/search/bio/E000078.

51 LIKE OTHER ILLINOIS GOVERNORS Simon, *Lincoln's Preparation for Greatness*, 121.

51 IN AN ADVERTISEMENT Ibid., 121–22. At the constitutional convention to bring about statehood, it was said that "slaves held by the members of the convention were more numerous than the delegates themselves." Ibid., 125.

52 "NAY, THE BLISSFUL PERIOD" Jeremiah Gloucester, *An Oration, Delivered on January 1, 1823, in Bethel Church, on the Abolition of the Slave Trade* (Philadelphia, 1823), 15.

52 STRUGGLE OVER SLAVERY See, for instance, Jenkins, *Pro-Slavery Thought*, 65–71; Freehling, *Road to Disunion*, 1:144–57; Wilentz, *Rise of American Democracy*, 222–53.

52 THE MASSACHUSETTS GENERAL COLORED ASSOCIATION Goodman, *Of One Blood*, 26.

52 THE NEXT YEAR BROUGHT THE FOUNDING Ibid., 27–28.

52 ONE OF THE PAPER'S AGENTS Ibid., 28.

52 "THE MOST DEGRADED" Meacham, *American Lion*, 46–47.

52 "I AM IN EARNEST" William Lloyd Garrison, "To the Public," *The Liberator,* January 1, 1831.

52 ABOLITIONIST AMERICAN ANTI-SLAVERY SOCIETY For the rise of abolitionist sentiment and activism, see, for instance, Foner, *Fiery Trial*, 19–24, and, more generally, Goodman, *Of One Blood;* Masur, *Until Justice Be Done;* C. Peter Ripley, ed., *The Black Abolitionist Papers* (Chapel Hill, N.C., 1985–1992), 1–5.

52 "CONVINCE ALL" "Constitution of the American Anti-Slavery Society," December 4, 1833, https://chnm.gmu.edu/courses/omalley/nclc/slavery/aas.html.

52 MORE GENERAL ANTISLAVERY SENTIMENT See, for instance, Wilentz, *No Property in Man*, especially 1–57; Oakes, *Crooked Path to Abolition*, especially xxi–98.

53 NUMEROUS COMPROMISES See, for instance, Paul Finkelman, *Slavery and the Founders: Race and Liberty in the Age of Jefferson* (Armonk, N.Y., 2014), 3–46.

53 TO ABOLISH THE ATLANTIC SLAVE TRADE Wilentz, *No Property in Man,* 3.

53 PREVENTED THE DOCUMENT Ibid., 3–5.

53 "THE CONSTITUTION OF THE UNITED STATES" Tyrone Tillery, "The Inevitability of the Douglass-Garrison Conflict," *Phylon* 37, no. 2 (1976): 137–49, quotation on 144. See also *The North Star,* March 16, 1848.

53 "FEDERAL CONSENSUS" Crofts, *Lincoln and the Politics of Slavery*, 25–29; Oakes, *Freedom National*, 2–8. Oakes observed: "For seventy-five years hardly anybody—North or South, proslavery or antislavery—doubted that the Constitution put slavery in the states beyond the reach of federal power." Ibid., 3. William Lloyd Garrison and other radical abolitionists shared this view. "Each State, in which Slavery exists, has, by the Constitution of the United States, the exclusive right to *legislate* in regard to its abolition in said State," Garrison wrote in the 1833 "Declaration of Sentiments" of the American Anti-Slavery Society. Oakes, *Freedom National,* 3–4.

54 THAT "CONGRESS HAVE" Maeve Glass, "Slavery's Constitution: Rethinking the Federal Consensus," *Fordham Law Review* 89, no. 5 (April 2021): 1816. "The morality or wisdom of Slavery," Oliver Ellsworth of Connecticut said, "are considerations be-

longing to the States themselves." Oakes, *Freedom National*, 3. A. Christopher Bryant, "Stopping Time: The Pro-Slavery and 'Irrevocable' Thirteenth Amendment," *Harvard Journal of Law and Public Policy* 26, no. 2 (Spring 2003): 501–49, is also illuminating.

54 THE "FEDERAL GOVERNMENT" Bryant, "Stopping Time," 525.

54 "THERE IS NO MAN" Ibid.

54 THUS THE FOCUS Crofts, *Lincoln and the Politics of Slavery*, 52–55.

54 "SCORPION'S STING" Oakes, *Scorpion's Sting*, especially 22–50.

54 "CORDON OF FREEDOM" Ibid., 13–14.

54 "CIRCLE OF FIRE" Ibid., 25.

54 THE ENERGIZED MOVEMENT Foner, *Fiery Trial*, 20.

54 IN 1830, IT IS ESTIMATED Chambers, "The Election of 1840," in *HAPE*, 1:311–12. "It is felt that men are henceforth to be held together by new ties, and separated by new barriers," John Stuart Mill wrote, "for the ancient bonds will no longer unite, nor the ancient boundaries confine." James A. Secord, *Victorian Sensation: The Extraordinary Publication, Reception, and Secret Authorship of* Vestiges of the Natural History of Creation (Chicago, 255), 2.

55 "ANY ATTEMPT" Elizabeth Duncan Putnam, "Governor Joseph Duncan of Illinois," *Tennessee Historical Magazine* 7, no. 4 (January 1922): 250.

55 SEVERAL STATES Simon, *Lincoln's Preparation for Greatness*, 131.

55 THE GOVERNOR REFERRED Hay and Nicolay, *AL: A History*, 1:149–50.

55 THE LAWMAKERS PASSED Burlingame, *AL*, 1:122; Foner, *Fiery Trial*, 24–25; Blumenthal, *Self-Made Man*, 155–57; Simon, *Lincoln's Preparation for Greatness*, 132.

55 THE VOTE IN THE HOUSE Burlingame, *AL*, 1:122; Foner, *Fiery Trial*, 25; Simon, *Lincoln's Preparation for Greatness*, 133.

55 BEFORE THE MID-1830S "There must doubtless be an unhappy influence on the manners of our people produced by the existence of slavery among us," Thomas Jefferson had written in 1781. "The whole commerce between master and slave is a perpetual exercise of the most boisterous passions, the most unremitting despotism on the one part, and degrading submissions on the other." Adrienne Koch and William Peden, eds., *The Life and Selected Writings of Thomas Jefferson* (New York, 1998), 257. Even earlier, in 1762, James Otis of Massachusetts wrote, "Kings were (and plantation Governors should be) made for the good of the people, and not the people for them. No government has a right to make hobby horses, asses, and slaves of the subject, nature having made sufficient of the two former, for all the lawful purposes of man, from the harmless peasant in the field, to the most refined politician in the cabinet; but none of the last, which infallibly proves they are unnecessary." James Otis, *A Vindication of the Conduct of the House of Representatives of the Province of the Massachusetts-Bay* (Boston, 1762), 18–19. See also Jenkins, *Pro-Slavery Thought*, 23–24.

56 "WE CONSIDER THE VOLUNTARY" Hinton Rowan Helper, *The Impending Crisis of the South: How to Meet It* (New York, 1857), 260–61; *Minutes of the General Assembly of the Presbyterian Church in the United States of America: 1789–1820* (New York, 1820), 692; Jenkins, *Pro-Slavery Thought*, 93. A decade later, in 1828, William Drayton of South Carolina said, "Slavery, in the abstract, I condemn and abhor.... However ameliorated by compassion—however corrected by religion—still slavery is a bitter draught, and the chalice which contains the nauseous potion, is, perhaps, more frequently pressed by the lips of the master than of the slave." Freehling, *Prelude to Civil War*, 76–77.

56 "TO SUM UP ALL" Jenkins, *Pro-Slavery Thought*, 27.

56 "[L]ET ME NOT" Ibid., 80. See also John C. Calhoun, *Speech on the Reception of Abolition Petitions* (Washington, D.C., 1837), 5.

56 *"SLAVERY IS NOT"* Jenkins, *Pro-Slavery Thought*, 76–77.

56 THE CASE OF BASIL MANLY, SR. See, for instance, A. James Fuller, *Chaplain to the Confederacy: Basil Manly and Baptist Life in the Old South* (Baton Rouge, La., 2000); The Southern Baptist Theological Seminary, *Report on Slavery and Racism in the History of the Southern Baptist Theological Seminary*, December 2018, especially 13–15.

56 "AN EVIL UNDER WHICH" Fuller, *Chaplain to the Confederacy*, 33–34.

56 PREACHING A DIFFERENT GOSPEL Ibid., 213–15; *Report on Slavery and Racism*, 13.

58 REBELLIONS FROM SOUTH CAROLINA Freehling, *Prelude to Civil War*, 49–86; Richard Wade, "The Vesey Plot: A Reconsideration," *Journal of Southern History* 30 (May 1964): 143–60; Henry I. Tragle, ed., *The Southampton Slave Revolt of 1831: A Compilation of Source Material* (Amherst, Mass., 1971). "The year 1822 . . . I shall never forget," a white South Carolinian wrote. "I then had an opportunity of seeing something of the fruits of Abolitionists." Freehling, *Prelude to Civil War*, 60.

58 FROM 1829 TO 1837 *Historical Statistics of the United States, Earliest Times to the Present*, 2:385.

58 FROM 1830 TO 1835 Ibid., 390.

58 "A PEOPLE, OWNING SLAVES" *Speeches Delivered in the Convention, of the State of South-Carolina, Held in Columbia, in March, 1833* (Charleston, S.C., 1833), 25; Freehling, *Prelude to Civil War*, 297. South Carolina was largely isolated in the battle over the tariff, but radicals insisted the truth would slowly dawn on their fellow slave-owning states. "Do they not know," a Charleston pamphleteer wrote, "that after the Tariff comes the question of *Emancipation!*" John McCardell, *The Idea of a Southern Nation: Southern Nationalists and Southern Nationalism, 1830–1860* (New York, 1979), 57. John Calhoun made the same argument: "The truth can no longer be disguised, that the peculiar domestic institutions of the Southern States, and the consequent direction which that and her soil and climate have given to her industry, has placed them in regard to taxation and appropriation in opposite relation to the majority of the Union." Freehling, *Prelude to Civil War*, 257. And there was the abolitionists' campaign to flood the country with antislavery tracts in the mid-1830s. "Anti-Slavery Abolition Societies," the Congregationalist minister, educator, and American Colonization Society agent Rufus W. Bailey argued, were deluging the South with "officious and importunate and unwelcome instructions. The most unhappy and disastrous is the political aspect they have given to the question." Rufus W. Bailey, *The Issue, Presented in a Series of Letters on Slavery* (New York, 1837), 25; Larry E. Tise, *Proslavery: A History of the Defense of Slavery in America, 1701–1840* (Athens, Ga., 2004), 325–27.

58 "PLAUSIBLE DREAM" Tise, *Proslavery*, 319–20.

58 "DECIDES THAT GOD" Noll, *Civil War as a Theological Crisis,* 88; CW, 3:204. Proslavery theology depended on what the *Richmond Enquirer,* writing in 1820, described this way: "That if one or more decisions of the written word of God, sanction the rectitude of any human acquisitions, for instance, the acquisition of a servant by inheritance or purchase, whoever believes that the written word of God is *verity itself,* must consequently believe in the absolute rectitude of slave-holding." Larry R. Morrison, "The Religious Defense of American Slavery Before 1830," *Journal of Religious Thought* 37, no. 2 (1980/1981): 16–29, quotation on 17, http://www.kingscollege.net/gbrodie/The%20religious%20justification%20of%20slavery%20before%201830.pdf.

59 SECOND GREAT AWAKENING See, for instance, Ahlstrom, *Religious History of the American People,* 387–454; Hatch, *Democratization of American Christianity,* 3–16; Howe, *What Hath God Wrought,* 186–202.

59 THE CURSE OF HAM See, for instance, Stephen R. Haynes, *Noah's Curse: The Biblical Justification of American Slavery* (New York, 2007).

59 A DRUNKEN NOAH Genesis 9:21–27, KJV.

59 "THE PROPHECY OF NOAH" Morrison, "Religious Defense," 18. See also Frederick Dalcho, *Practical Considerations Founded on the Scriptures, Relative to the Slave Population of South Carolina by a South Carolinian* (Charleston, S.C., 1823), 10–11; Jenkins, *Pro-Slavery Thought*, 72.

60 "BOTH THY BONDMEN" Leviticus 25:44–46, KJV.

60 THE NEW TESTAMENT "Union to Disunion," Mississippi State University, http://projects.leadr.msu.edu/uniontodisunion/exhibits/show/scripture-passages/new-testament. "If domestic slavery had been deemed by Jesus Christ the atrocious crime which it is now represented to be," an American writer wondered in 1819, "could it have been passed over without censure? . . . [S]hould we not have been told, not that the rich man, but that the slave-holders, could not enter the kingdom of heaven?" Morrison, "Religious Defense," 23. A few years later the Reverend Richard Furman, a South Carolina Baptist, said: "Had the holding of slaves been a moral evil, it cannot be supposed, that the inspired Apostles, who feared not the faces of men, and were ready to lay down their lives in the cause of their God, would have tolerated it, for a moment, in the Christian Church." James A. Rogers, *Richard Furman: Life and Legacy* (Macon, Ga., 1985), 278–79; Jenkins, *Pro-Slavery Thought*, 72.

Antislavery voices within different denominations rested their case on the commandments to love one's neighbor—a commandment found in the same book, Leviticus, as the "bondmen" and "bondmaids" section—and to see all God's children as equal in value and worthy of respect and dignity. If, as Paul said in his epistles, "all are one in Christ Jesus," then there could be no distinctions of condition. "Are *you* yet stumbling blocks in the way of the Lord. . . . Do you know the love of God as it is in Christ, and still not abhor slavery with your whole heart?" an abolitionist in Massachusetts asked in 1843. Allen Carden, "Religious Schism as a Prelude to the American Civil War: Methodists, Baptists, and Slavery," *Andrews University Seminary Studies* 24, no. 1 (Spring 1986), 18. "But the church of this country is not only indifferent to the wrongs of the slave, it actually takes sides with the oppressors," Frederick Douglass remarked. "It has made itself the bulwark of American slavery, and the shield of American slave-hunters. Many of its most eloquent Divines, who stand as the very lights of the church, have shamelessly given the sanction of religion and the Bible to the whole slave system. They have taught that man may, properly, be a slave; that the relation of master and slave is ordained of God; that to send back an escaped bondman to his master is clearly the duty of all the followers of the Lord Jesus Christ; and this horrible blasphemy is palmed off upon the world for Christianity. For my part, I would say, welcome infidelity! welcome atheism! welcome anything! in preference to the gospel, *as preached by those Divines!*" Foner, ed., *Life and Writings of Frederick Douglass*, 2:197.

60 SUCH PROSLAVERY THINKING See, for instance, Carden, "Religious Schism"; Richard J. Carwardine, "Lincoln, Evangelical Religion, and American Political Culture in the Era of the Civil War," *JALA* 18, no. 1 (Winter 1997): 27–55; David Donald, "The Proslavery Argument Reconsidered," *Journal of Southern History* 37, no. 1 (Feb. 1971): 3–18; Keith Harper, " 'And All the Baptists in Kentucky Took the Name United Baptists': The Union of the Separate and Regular Baptists of Kentucky," *Register of the Kentucky Historical Society* 110, no. 1 (Winter 2012): 3–31; April Holm, "As the Churches Go, So Goes the Nation? Evangelical Schism and American

Fears on the Eve of the Civil War," *Journal of the Civil War Era*, May 14, 2019; Glen Jeansonne, "Southern Baptist Attitudes Toward Slavery, 1845–1861," *Georgia Historical Quarterly* 55, no. 4 (Winter 1971): 510–22; Irving Stoddard Kull, "Presbyterian Attitudes Toward Slavery," *American Society of Church History* 7, no. 2 (June 1938), 101–14; David Paul Nord, *The Evangelical Origins of Mass Media in America, 1815–1835,* Journalism Monographs No. 88, Association for Education in Journalism and Mass Communication; Spencer, *History of Kentucky Baptists*; John Michael Wiley, "The Baptists' Parallel Revolution," paper for Adams State University, Alamosa, Colorado, 2014.

60 "DIVISION OF OUR CHURCH" Carden, "Religious Schism," 22.

60 ON FRIDAY, MARCH 3 CW, 1:74–76. See also Burlingame, *AL*, 1:122–27; Foner, *Fiery Trial*, 24–26; Miller, *Lincoln's Virtues*, 116–29.

60 WHO WAS LEAVING Burlingame, *AL*, 1:122.

61 "THEY BELIEVE THAT" CW, 1:75.

61 NO EVIDENT POLITICAL GAIN See, for instance, Burlingame, *AL*, 1:122–27. "To proclaim that 'slavery is founded on both injustice and bad policy' was a remarkably bold gesture for 1837, where antislavery views enjoyed little popularity in central Illinois—or elsewhere in the nation for that matter," Burlingame wrote, adding: "The boldness of the Lincoln-Stone protest is notable but uncharacteristic of Lincoln in his twenties and thirties. When in March 1837 he moved to Springfield from the dying hamlet of New Salem, he was essentially a clever partisan whose promise of future statesmanship would long remain unfulfilled." Ibid., 122, 127. "There was no sympathy with nor even toleration for any public expression of hostility to slavery," Hay and Nicolay wrote. "He had many years of growth and development before him. There was a long distance to be traveled between the guarded utterances of this protest and the heroic audacity which launched the proclamation of emancipation. But the young man who dared declare, in the prosperous beginning of his political life, in the midst of a community imbued with slave-State superstitions, that 'he believed the institution of slavery was founded both on injustice and bad policy,'—attacking thus its moral and material supports, while at the same time recognizing all the constitutional guarantees which protected it,—had in him the making of a statesman and, if need be, a martyr." Hay and Nicolay, *AL: A History*, 1:149–52.

61 "I AM NATURALLY ANTI-SLAVERY" CW, 7:281.

61 AS A CHILD Simon, *Lincoln's Preparation for Greatness*, 127–29; Louis A. Warren, "Lincoln's Baptist Background," *Lincoln Lore* 1042 (March 28, 1949), Bulletin of the Lincoln National Life Foundation, Fort Wayne, Indiana.

61 AS A YOUTH Simon, *Lincoln's Preparation for Greatness*, 129; Warren, "Lincoln's Baptist Background"; Tarbell, *In the Footsteps*, 109–10.

61 "SLAVERY RAN THE IRON" Herndon and Weik, *Herndon's Life of Lincoln*, 63.

61 "ONE MORNING IN . . . THE CITY" Ibid., 64.

61 "THE SLAVERY QUESTION" Burlingame, *AL*, 1:124–25.

62 "ALL AMERICA ACKNOWLEDGES" Remini, *Henry Clay*, 27.

62 "THE SOONER WE ATTEMPT" Ibid.

62 "ALWAYS LOVED" Wilson and Davis, eds., *Herndon's Informants*, 229.

62 "THE BEAU IDEAL" Burlingame, *AL*, 1:123.

62 "HENRY CLAY WAS" Wilson and Davis, eds., *Herndon's Informants*, 8.

62 "HE EVER WAS, ON PRINCIPLE" CW, 2:130. Lincoln was familiar with Clay's 1827 address to the American Colonization Society. In it, Clay had cast slavery as immoral, unreasonable, and out of sync with the ideals of the nation. "If they would

repress all tendencies towards liberty, and ultimate emancipation, they must. . . . blow out the moral lights around us, and extinguish that greatest torch of all which America presents to a benighted world," he had said. "They must penetrate the human soul, and eradicate the light of reason, and the love of liberty." Ibid., 131. Lincoln quoted this passage in his 1852 eulogy. Ibid.

62   THE AMERICAN COLONIZATION SOCIETY See, for instance, Nicholas Guyatt, "The American Colonization Society: 200 Years of the 'Colonizing Trick,'" *Black Perspectives,* African American Intellectual History Society, December 22, 2016, https://www.aaihs.org/the-american-colonization-society-200-years-of-the -colonizing-trick/; Bernice Finney, "The American Colonization Society," *Negro History Bulletin* 12, no. 5 (February 1949): 116–18; Henry Noble Sherwood, "The Formation of the American Colonization Society," *Journal of Negro History* 2, no. 3 (July 1917), 209–28.

62   SOME BLACK LEADERS FAVORED Guyatt, "The American Colonization Society."

62   CAPTAIN PAUL CUFFE Ibid.; Sinha, *The Slave's Cause,* 161–63.

62   THERE WERE WHITE SOUTHERNERS Guyatt, "The American Colonization Society."

62   AS A PROSLAVERY DEVICE Goodman, *Of One Blood,* 54–64.

63   IN PUBLICLY DECLARING Given the ambient realities of the hour, however, Lincoln was a force—if a halting one—for a more expansive understanding of the principles of equality and of justice. "Abstractly, and from the standpoint of conscience, he abhorred slavery," Herndon wrote of Lincoln during his legislative years. "But born in Kentucky, and surrounded as he was by slave-holding influences, absorbing their prejudices and following in their line of thought, it is not strange . . . that he should fail to estimate properly the righteous indignation and unrestrained zeal of a Yankee Abolitionist." Herndon and Weik, *Herndon's Life of Lincoln,* 143.

63   "LINCOLN WAS TALKING" Burlingame, *AL,* 1:124.

63   NEWLY ADMITTED TO THE BAR Ibid., 131.

63   LINCOLN MOVED FROM NEW SALEM Ibid., 127.

63   THE COUNTY SEAT Herndon and Weik, *Herndon's Life of Lincoln,* 145.

63   HE HAD FOUGHT TO LOCATE Burlingame, *AL,* 1:114–18; Simon, *Lincoln's Preparation for Greatness,* 76–105.

63   "THE OWNER OF REAL ESTATE" Baker, *Mary Todd Lincoln,* 76.

63   "RATHER A DULL BUSINESS" Burlingame, *AL,* 1:129–30.

63   HE LIKED AN OLD JOKE Ibid., 129.

63   "IT IS MY PRIVATE OPINION" *LDBD, 1809–1848,* 193.

63   "THE TONE OF HIS VOICE" Herndon and Weik, *Herndon's Life of Lincoln,* 148.

64   "HE WAS THE MOST UNCOUTH" Ibid., 145.

64   "HE HAD RIDDEN" Ibid., 148–49.

64   "NO MAN EVER HAD" Hofstadter, *American Political Tradition,* 129.

64   "ACCOUNTS OF OUTRAGES" CW, 1:109. See, for instance, "Riot in New York," *The Daily Picayune,* February 23, 1837; Blumenthal, *Self-Made Man,* 165–82.

65   "THE PRICE OF FLOUR" "Riot in New York," *The Daily Picayune.*

65   "THESE LAWLESS, HIGH-HANDED MEASURES" Ibid.

65   AN INCIDENT IN WHICH *The Daily Picayune,* April 21, 1837.

65   "THIS OUTRAGE ALONE" Ibid.

65   AN ABOLITIONIST EDITOR Burlingame, *AL,* 1:141–42; Foner, *Fiery Trial,* 23–24; Harrold, *Lincoln and the Abolitionists,* 15; "The Alton Murder," *The Liberator,* December 8, 1837; "The Riot and Murder at Alton," *Alton Observer,* December 28, 1837.

65   LOVEJOY HAD ALREADY Foner, *Fiery Trial,* 22–23.

65   THE FIRST MARTYR *Vermont Telegraph,* November 29, 1837.

65 "INFATUATED EDITOR" Quoted in *Vermont Telegraph,* November 29, 1837.

65 "AT LENGTH FALLEN" *The Liberator,* December 8, 1837.

65 FRANCIS L. MCINTOSH *Daily Missouri Republican,* April 30, 1836; *Nashville Centennial Whig,* May 11, 1836; "Horrible Tragedy," *Raleigh Register,* May 24, 1836; Burlingame, *AL,* 1:142.

65 "WAS SEIZED IN THE STREET" *CW,* 1:110.

65 "NEGROES, SUSPECTED OF" Ibid., 109–10.

66 IN A PRESCIENT ADDRESS Ibid., 108–15.

66 "MOBOCRATIC SPIRIT" Ibid., 111.

66 "WE FIND OURSELVES" Ibid., 108–12.

66 "WILD AND FURIOUS PASSIONS" Ibid., 109.

66 "AT WHAT POINT" Ibid.

67 "*THE CAPABILITY*" Ibid., 113.

67 "TOWERING GENIUS DISDAINS" Ibid., 113–14.

67 "*WERE* THE PILLARS" Ibid., 115.

67 "LOVED PRINCIPLES AND SUCH LIKE" Wilson and Davis, eds., *Herndon's Informants,* 64–65.

67 BEGINNING IN 1836 William Lee Miller, *Arguing About Slavery: John Quincy Adams and the Great Battle in the United States Congress* (New York, 1998), 139–49.

67 "GAG" RESOLUTION Ibid., 144. Pinckney's resolution read: "All petitions, memorials, resolutions, propositions, or papers, relating in any way, or to any extent whatsoever, to the subject of slavery or the abolition of slavery, shall, without either being printed or referred, be laid on the table and . . . no further action whatever shall be had thereon." Ibid.

67 BY THE EARLY 1840s Miller, *Arguing About Slavery,* 370–73.

68 PRESIDENT JACKSON HAD PROPOSED Ibid., 97–103.

68 "WHEN *MAIL-ROBBING* IS" *Third Annual Report of the American Anti-Slavery Society,* New York, May 10, 1836, 45–46. See also Sinha, *Slave's Cause,* 651–53, 656–58, 671, 675.

68 "LINCOLN AS EARLY AS 1830" Burlingame, *AL,* 1:166.

68 THE 1840 RACE William Nisbet Chambers, "The Election of 1840," in *HAPE,* 1:278–322; Holt, *Rise and Fall,* 89–121; Robert Gray Gunderson, *The Log Cabin Campaign* (Lexington, Ky., 1957).

68 A VETERAN OF THE INDIAN WARS Chambers, "Election of 1840," 295–304.

68 "THE PEOPLE—THE BONE AND SINEW" Burlingame, *AL,* 1:148. Though he had come from a well-off slaveholding family (his father had signed the Declaration of Independence) and been educated at Hampden-Sydney College, Harrison was presented to the nation as a tribune of republican simplicity, a Whig man for the age of Jackson. Chambers, "Election of 1840," 1:296. The Democratic opposition inadvertently helped Harrison, who was running with John Tyler of Virginia, when it claimed that "upon the condition of his receiving a pension of $2,000 and a barrel of cider, General Harrison would no doubt consent to withdraw his pretensions, and spend his days in a log cabin on the banks of the Ohio." Ibid., 284. The offending editorial, in the Baltimore *Republican,* gave the Whigs what they wanted: A powerful and pithy message that a vote for Harrison was a vote for "Log Cabin and Hard Cider." Ibid. Another popular Whig line of attack came in a widely circulated speech by Charles Ogle of Pennsylvania entitled "The Regal Splendor of the Presidential Palace" that portrayed the president—"Martin Van Ruin," he was called after the Panic of 1837, who was in truth "a *democratic peacock*"—as an elitist who spent too much on furnishings. Ibid., 285, 306, 313; Holt, *Rise and Fall,* 107. Van Buren's vice presidential running mate, Richard Mentor Johnson of Ken-

tucky, was also a target. Johnson had had an "enslaved wife," Julia Chinn, a common-law marriage that led opponents to denounce him for "openly and shamefully liv[ing] in adultery with a buxom young *negro wench*." Chambers, "Election of 1840," 304. See also Ronald G. Shafer, "He Became the Nation's Ninth Vice President. She Was His Enslaved Wife," *The Washington Post,* February 7, 2021, https://www.washingtonpost.com/history/2021/02/07/julia-chinn-slave-wife -vice-president/.

69   "The whole country is" Chambers, "Election of 1840," 281.

69   A Harrison supporter Burlingame, *AL,* 1:148–61.

69   "characterized by" CW, 1:157–58.

69   Within three weeks Ibid., 159–79.

69   The lawyer Josiah Lamborn Burlingame, *AL,* 1:152.

69   "every state" CW, 1:178.

69   "Address *that* argument" Ibid.

69   "Let none falter" Ibid., 179.

69   Lincoln fed racial fears Burlingame, *AL,* 1:154. "Negrophobia loomed large in the campaign," Burlingame wrote. "The few extant examples of Lincoln's speeches show that he indulged in the same race-baiting that he had so freely employed four years earlier." Ibid.

69   In 1821, in New York Ibid., 1:154–55.

69   first in 1836 Ibid., 108–9.

70   to launch the Liberty Party See, for instance, Reinhard O. Johnson, *The Liberty Party, 1840–1848: Antislavery Third-Party Politics in the United States* (Baton Rouge, La., 2009).

70   Birney polled .031 percent "1840 General Presidential Results," https://uselection atlas.org/RESULTS/national.php?year=1840.

70   Harrison and Tyler defeated Holt, *Rise and Fall,* 112.

70   The Whigs won Chambers, "Election of 1840," 278.

70   Lincoln was reelected Burlingame, *AL,* 1:161.

70   In the December session Herndon and Weik, *Herndon's Life of Lincoln,* 161–62; Burlingame, *AL,* 1:162.

70   The sergeant at arms despaired Burlingame, *AL,* 1:162.

70   "My God!" Ibid.

70   By the end of 1840 Herndon and Weik, *Herndon's Life of Lincoln,* 160; Burlingame, *AL,* 1:166–67.

70   "He was ambitious" Wilson and Davis, eds., *Herndon's Informants,* 42.

Chapter Five: She Had the Fire, Will, and Ambition

71   "Mary, I agree with you" Eugenia Jones Hunt, "My Personal Recollections of Abraham and Mary Todd Lincoln," *The Abraham Lincoln Quarterly* 3, no. 5 (March 1945): 236–37.

71   "She loved show and power" Herndon and Weik, *Herndon's Life of Lincoln,* 166–67.

71   Standing six feet four, he was Ibid., 34–35.

71   "His habits, like himself" Ibid., 411.

72   In 1836, Mary S. Owens Ibid., 116. See also Burlingame, *AL,* 1:168–73.

72   She was recalled Herndon and Weik, *Herndon's Life of Lincoln,* 117. This is Mary Owens's description of herself to Herndon. Ibid.

72   child of a prosperous family Ibid., 116–17.

72   "They talked the matter" Wilson and Davis, eds., *Herndon's Informants,* 81.

72 HE STARTED AND DISCARDED CW, 1:78.

72 "I AM OFTEN THINKING" Ibid.

72 "I THOUGHT MR. LINCOLN" Herndon and Weik, *Herndon's Life of Lincoln*, 119; Wilson and Davis, eds., *Herndon's Informants*, 256.

72 ON AN OUTING Burlingame, *AL*, 1:170; Herndon and Weik, *Herndon's Life of Lincoln*, 120–21.

72 AT ANOTHER POINT Herndon and Weik, *Herndon's Life of Lincoln*, 121.

72 "THE OTHER GENTLEMEN" Ibid.

73 "WRITE BACK AS SOON AS" CW, 1:55.

73 HE COULD BE CHARMING He once wrote Mrs. Orville Browning, "We, the under-signed, respectfully represent to your *Honoress*, that we are in great need of your society in this town of Springfield; and therefore humbly pray that your *Honoress* will repair, forthwith, to the Seat of Government, bringing in your train all ladies in general, who may be at your command; and all Mr. Browning's sisters in par-ticular." Ibid., 156.

73 "I WANT IN ALL CASES" Ibid., 94.

73 "WE NEVER HAD" Herndon and Weik, *Herndon's Life of Lincoln*, 121.

73 "TELL YOUR SISTER" Ibid.

73 "CHARACTERISTIC OF THE MAN!" Ibid.

73 AN ACIDIC LETTER CW, 1:117–19.

73 "I KNEW SHE WAS" Ibid., 118.

73 "COULD NOT FOR MY LIFE" Ibid.

73 "MY VANITY WAS" Ibid., 119.

74 "THE SOBER TRUTH" Herndon and Weik, *Herndon's Life of Lincoln*, 163.

74 THE TODD CLAN On Mary Lincoln, the Todd family, and the Lincoln marriage, see, for instance, Baker, *Mary Todd Lincoln*; Baker, "Mary and Abraham"; Stephen Berry, *House of Abraham: Lincoln and the Todds, a Family Divided by War* (New York, 2007); Bur-lingame, *AL*, 1:173–212; Burlingame, *Inner World*, 268–355; Burlingame, *An American Marriage: The Untold Story of Abraham Lincoln and Mary Todd* (New York, 2021); Blu-menthal, *Self-Made Man*, 212–34, 269–76; Daniel Mark Epstein, *The Lincolns: Portrait of a Marriage* (New York, 2008); Jason Emerson, *Mary Lincoln for the Ages* (Carbon-dale, Ill., 2019); Jason Emerson, *The Madness of Mary Lincoln* (Carbondale, Ill., 2007); Katherine Helm, *The True Story of Mary, Wife of Lincoln: Containing the Recollections of Mary Lincoln's Sister Emilie (Mrs. Ben Hardin Helm), Extracts from Her War-Time Diary, Nu-merous Letters and Other Documents Now First Published* (New York, 1928); Ruth Painter Randall, *Mary Lincoln: Biography of a Marriage* (Boston, 1953); Justin G. Turner and Linda Levitt Turner, *Mary Todd Lincoln: Her Life and Letters* (New York, 1972); Donald, *Lincoln*, 84–87; White, *A. Lincoln*, 105–17; Frank J. Williams and Michael Burk-himer, eds., *The Mary Lincoln Enigma: Historians on America's Most Controversial First Lady* (Carbondale and Edwardsville, Ill., 2012).

In several works, Burlingame argues the marriage was an unrelieved misery for Lincoln; Jean Baker has taken a more moderate course. "I believe that her histori-cal reputation suffered—and still suffers—from criticism because she was consid-ered an 'unruly woman,' that is, she was ahead of her time in both her inherited interest in politics and her intention to establish her presence in American culture as First Lady," Baker wrote. "She embraced the role of 'Republican Queen,' deco-rating the White House with sumptuous taste and inappropriate expense during the Civil War. She wanted to shine in the social life of politics, rather than in the recommended style of her predecessors who stayed upstairs, properly invisible in the private family quarters of the president's house." Baker, *Mary Todd Lincoln*, xiii.

Burlingame's view: "Lincoln is justly known as a man of sorrows, largely because of the soul-crushing responsibilities he shouldered as president during the nation's bloodiest war. But it is impossible to understand the depth of that sorrow without realizing just how woe-filled his marriage truly was." Burlingame, *American Marriage,* vii.

Blumenthal wrote: "In important ways it was an unusual relationship. His interest in her opinions was part of her attraction to him. Respectable women were not supposed to have any interest in politics and certainly not to speak about it. Yet he was remarkably egalitarian for the standards of the time. He accepted her speaking on subjects that other men would actively disapprove of any woman voicing. . . . For all the difficulties she caused him, plaguing him with her fits to the end, their devotion to each other was apparent." Blumenthal, *Self-Made Man,* 273–75.

74 A CHILD OF THE FAMILY Baker, *Mary Todd Lincoln,* 48; Blumenthal, *Self-Made Man,* 212–15.

74 IN THE EDWARDSES' HILLTOP HOUSE Baker, *Mary Todd Lincoln,* 77; Turner and Turner, *Mary Todd Lincoln: Her Life and Letters,* 10.

74 ANDREW PORTER Baker, *Mary Todd Lincoln,* 15–17; "Andrew Porter," http://www.famousamericans.net/andrewporter/.

74 HER GRANDFATHERS, LEVI TODD AND ROBERT PARKER Baker, *Mary Todd Lincoln,* 4.

74 THEY HAD BOTH FOUGHT Ibid., 6.

74 "I AM COUNTY LT" Ibid.

74 THE TWO MEN OWNED SLAVES Ibid., 6–9.

74 "A RISING BEAUTY" Ibid., 11.

74 EDUCATED AT TRANSYLVANIA UNIVERSITY Ibid., 12–13.

74 BECOME CLERK Ibid., 32.

74 THE COUPLE HAD SEVEN CHILDREN Ibid., 17–23.

74 INITIALLY NAMED MARY ANN Ibid., 4.

74 AT THE AGE OF THIRTY-ONE Ibid., 20–22.

75 HE SET HIS SIGHTS . . . Ibid., 25–26.

75 FRANKFORT, KENTUCKY, FAMILY Ibid.

75 "AS YOUR FEELINGS IN THIS MATTER" Ibid., 25.

75 THE WEDDING TOOK PLACE Ibid., 28.

75 THEN ABOUT TO MARK Ibid.

75 HER UPBRINGING, SHE WOULD RECALL Ibid.

75 NO FEWER THAN NINE CHILDREN Ibid., 30.

75 "I WISH I COULD" Ibid., xxi.

75 ONE REPRIEVE Ibid., 37.

75 MARY WOLLSTONECRAFT'S *A VINDICATION* Ibid., 36.

75 "FAR IN ADVANCE" Ibid., 40.

75 "CLEAR BLUE EYES" Ibid., 51.

75 "IN HER BEARING" Herndon and Weik, *Herndon's Life of Lincoln,* 165–66.

76 A LOVE OF POLITICS Baker, *Mary Todd Lincoln,* 59–61.

76 MARY COULD BOAST Herndon and Weik, *Herndon's Life of Lincoln,* 164.

76 IN THE AUTUMN OF 1837 Baker, *Mary Todd Lincoln,* 78–79.

76 "WE EXPECT A VERY" Ibid., 84.

76 SHE JOINED LINCOLN Ibid., 86.

76 "QUITE A POLITICIAN" Ibid., 85–86.

76 "LINCOLN WENT INTO" Wilson and Davis, eds., *Herndon's Informants,* 474.

76 "I HAVE OFTEN HAPPENED" Herndon and Weik, *Herndon's Life of Lincoln,* 166–67.

77 "THE POINT OF ENGAGEMENT" Ibid., 167.

77 "THE COTERIE" Turner and Turner, *Mary Todd Lincoln: Her Life and Letters*, 10.

77 LINCOLN APPEARS ALSO Baker, "Mary and Abraham: A Marriage" in Wilentz, ed., *Best American History Essays on Lincoln*, 109–10; Burlingame, *AL*, 1:181–82.

77 VISITING SPRINGFIELD IN 1840 Burlingame, *AL*, 1:181.

77 "FELL DESPERATELY IN LOVE" Ibid., 182.

77 "NEVER MENTIONED" Ibid.

77 WITH WHOM LINCOLN HAD BOARDED Ibid., 187.

77 "MR. LINCOLN DID PROPOSE" Ibid.; Wilson and Davis, eds., *Herndon's Informants*, 664; Herndon and Weik, *Herndon's Life of Lincoln*, 182–83.

77 "HIS PECULIAR MANNER" Burlingame, *AL*, 1:187.

77 "MISS TODD IS FLOURISHING" Baker, *Mary Todd Lincoln*, 90.

77 "DASHING AND HANDSOME" Herndon and Weik, *Herndon's Life of Lincoln*, 167.

78 "SHE LOVED DOUGLAS" Ibid.

78 EDWIN B. WEBB Baker, *Mary Todd Lincoln*, 85.

78 HIS FRIENDS CALLED HIM "BAT" "Webb, Edwin B.," Papers of Abraham Lincoln Digital Library, https://papersofabrahamlincoln.org/persons/WE04514.

78 "PRINCIPAL LION" Baker, *Mary Todd Lincoln*, 85.

78 ON FRIDAY, JANUARY 1, 1841 Ibid., 90.

78 "THAT FATAL FIRST" Herndon and Weik, *Herndon's Life of Lincoln*, 176; CW, 1:282.

78 "I HAD IT FROM GOOD AUTHORITY" Baker, *Mary Todd Lincoln*, 90.

78 "WHEN I TOLD MARY" Herndon and Weik, *Herndon's Life of Lincoln*, 168–69.

78 "GO," SHE IS SAID Baker, *Mary Todd Lincoln*, 90.

78 "WHAT ELSE DID" Herndon and Weik, *Herndon's Life of Lincoln*, 169.

78 "WORLD HAD IT" Burlingame, *AL*, 1:182.

79 "SHE WOULD HOLD" Ibid.

79 "RESTLESS, GLOOMY, MISERABLE" Herndon and Weik, *Herndon's Life of Lincoln*, 170.

79 "THE DOCTORS SAY" Burlingame, *AL*, 1:182.

79 "IN HIS CONFLICTS" Ibid.

79 "KNIVES AND RAZORS" Herndon and Weik, *Herndon's Life of Lincoln*, 170.

79 "REDUCED, AND EMACIATED IN APPEARANCE" Baker, *Mary Todd Lincoln*, 91.

79 HE MISSED A NUMBER Ibid., 90–91; Herndon and Weik, *Herndon's Life of Lincoln*, 171.

79 "I AM NOW THE MOST" CW, 1:229; Herndon and Weik, *Herndon's Life of Lincoln*, 170.

79 JOSHUA SPEED INVITED HIM Herndon and Weik, *Herndon's Life of Lincoln*, 171–72.

79 LINCOLN READ THE BIBLE Ibid., 172.

79 "HE WAS MUCH DEPRESSED" Ibid.

79 JOSHUA SPEED'S BROTHER Ibid.

80 "HE READ MY BOOKS" Ibid.

80 IN THE SECOND PRESBYTERIAN CHURCH CW, 1:271–79. See also Susan Zaeske, "Hearing the Silences in Lincoln's Temperance Address: Whig Masculinity as an Ethic of Rhetorical Civility," *Rhetoric and Public Affairs* 13, no. 3 (2010): 389–419.

80 "WHEN THE DRAM-SELLER" CW, 1:272–73.

80 "WHEN THE CONDUCT OF MEN" Ibid., 273.

80 "IF YOU WOULD WIN" Ibid., 273–79.

81 "WHATEVER [GOD] DESIGNS" Ibid., 289.

81 THE QUOTATION IS Exodus 14:13, KJV.

81 "DEEMS ME UNWORTHY" Baker, *Mary Todd Lincoln*, 91.

81 IT WAS ELIZA FRANCIS Ibid., 93–94; Herndon and Weik, *Herndon's Life of Lincoln*, 178–80.

81 THOUGH THEY ARRIVED SEPARATELY Herndon and Weik, *Herndon's Life of Lincoln*, 179.

81 "BE FRIENDS AGAIN" Ibid.

81   SO QUIET AND SO QUICK Ibid., 180.

81   "I ASKED MARY" Ibid.

81   "LINCOLN HAD POOR JUDGMENT" Burlingame, *AL*, 1:175.

81   "I WANT TO DANCE" Ibid.

81   SHE WOULD COMPLAIN FOR YEARS Ibid.; see also Baker, *Mary Todd Lincoln*, 133.

81   FAILED TO USE THE PROPER KNIFE Burlingame, *AL*, 1:175.

81   GREETED CALLERS AT THE DOOR Ibid.

81   HIS CLOTHES WERE TATTERED Ibid.

81   SOCKS FAILED TO MATCH Baker, *Mary Todd Lincoln*, 133.

81   "WHY DON'T YOU DRESS UP" Ibid.

81   "HOW MUCH I WISH" Ibid., 142.

82   IN THE FIRST DAYS OF NOVEMBER Burlingame, *American Marriage*, 33.

82   WHO HAD BEGUN TO CALL Baker, *Mary Todd Lincoln*, 99.

82   "I NOW SUGGEST" Hunt, "My Personal Recollections," 236–37.

82   MARY WAS DELIGHTED Ibid.

82   "MARY, I AGREE WITH YOU" Ibid.

82   "A HURLY-BURLY DAY" Ibid.

82   THE EPISCOPAL RECTOR Herndon and Weik, *Herndon's Life of Lincoln*, 180–81.

82   "DANCED UNTIL MIDNIGHT" Hunt, "My Personal Recollections," 236–37.

82   "A GOOD MAN" Baker, *Mary Todd Lincoln*, 85.

83   "A POLICY MATCH" Wilson and Davis, eds., *Herndon's Informants*, 64.

83   "HIS WIFE MADE HIM" Ibid., 63. This is not to say, however, that the marriage was wholly one of mutual calculation. "I love him not," Mary wrote of another suitor, "and my hand will never be given where my heart is not." Baker, *Mary Todd Lincoln*, 85.

83   "LINCOLN'S MARRIED LIFE" Burlingame, *Inner World*, 268.

83   MARY PHYSICALLY STRUCK Wilson and Davis, eds., *Herndon's Informants*, 467.

83   "VERY VIOLENT TEMPER" Burlingame, *Inner World*, 270.

83   "AS MAD AS" Ibid., 271.

83   "MRS. LINCOLN OFTEN GAVE" Ibid.

83   THAT MARY SUFFERED FROM MENTAL ILLNESS Burlingame, *American Marriage*, 11–18; James A. Brussel, "Mary Todd Lincoln: A Psychiatric Study," *Psychiatric Quarterly* 15, supp. 1 (January 1941): 7–26; James S. Brust, "A Psychiatrist Looks at Mary Lincoln," in Williams and Burkhimer, eds., *The Mary Lincoln Enigma*, 237–58; Emerson, *Madness of Mary Lincoln*; Jason Emerson, *Mary Lincoln's Insanity Case: A Documentary History* (Urbana, Ill., 2015); Mark E. Neely, Jr., and R. Gerald McMurtry, *The Insanity File: The Case of Mary Todd Lincoln* (Carbondale, Ill., 1986); John G. Sotos, "'What an Affliction': Mary Todd Lincoln's Fatal Pernicious Anemia," *Perspectives in Biology and Medicine* 58 (Autumn 2015): 419–43.

83   THERE WERE OTHER INSTANCES Brust, "A Psychiatrist Looks," 249.

83   "ONE OF MARY'S BROTHERS" Ibid. See also Burlingame, *AL*, 1:179–81; Burlingame, *American Marriage*, 15–17.

83   "I CANNOT GOVERN" Burlingame, *American Marriage*, 17.

83   "IF MARY LINCOLN" Ibid.

83   "MARY TODD MADE" Ibid., x.

84   ON ONCE SEEING HIS WIFE Baker, *Mary Todd Lincoln*, 196.

84   THEIR FIRST CHILD WAS BORN Burlingame, *American Marriage*, 40–46.

84   ON THE NORTH SIDE "Globe Tavern—Robert Lincoln's Birthplace," *Lincoln Lore* 940 (April 21, 1947), Bulletin of the Lincoln National Life Foundation, Fort Wayne, Indiana.

84 FOR $4 A WEEK Ibid.
84 IN THE *SANGAMO JOURNAL* Ibid.
85 THE SAME QUARTERS CW, 1:325.
85 GENERAL WILLIAM F. THORNTON "Thornton, William F.," https://papersofabraham
    lincoln.org/persons/TH05781.
85 HOSTED A LARGE PARTY *LDBD, 1809–1848*, 201–2; "Globe Tavern—Robert Lincoln's
    Birthplace," *Lincoln Lore*.
85 "NOW IF YOU SHOULD HEAR" CW, 1:307.
85 "IT WOULD ASTONISH" Ibid., 1:320.
85 "I MUST CONFESS" Burlingame *AL*, 1:395; Burlingame, *Inner World*, 28.
85 "THERE WAS … THE STRANGEST" CW, 1:320.
86 "DESPERATELY HOMESICK" *LDBD, 1809–1848*, 205.
86 "A MATTER OF" CW, 1:305.
86 MARY GAVE BIRTH *LDBD, 1809–1848*, 210; Baker, *Mary Todd Lincoln*, 102–3.
86 THE SON SHE NAMED ROBERT Baker, *Mary Todd Lincoln*, 102.
86 "YOUNG BOB LINCOLN" "Globe Tavern—Robert Lincoln's Birthplace," *Lincoln Lore*.
86 SOON THE LINCOLNS MOVED Ibid.
86 IN A HOUSE PURCHASED *LDBD, 1809–1848*, 229.
86 A SECOND SON CW, 1:391.
86 "HE TALKS VERY PLAINLY" CW, 1:391.
86 WHIG CAMPAIGNER *LDBD, 1809–1848*, 217.
86 IN A POLITICAL CIRCULAR CW, 1:315.
86 DISMISSED AS "HIS ACCIDENCY" Charles Sellers, "Election of 1844," in *HAPE*, 1:324.
86 THE ELECTION WAS FOUGHT Remini, *Henry Clay*, 611–67. Denouncing the admis-
    sion of "the rogues and renegades of Texas" to the Union—which would enhance
    the slaveholding power—an abolitionist newspaper in Cincinnati, the *Philanthro-
    pist*, asked: "Are the people of the free States prepared to see all their political
    power and influence unjustly wrested from them? To see the protection of their
    interests, their rights, their liberties, taken out of their own hands, and given to
    those who have never exhibited any particular affection for them?" *Philanthropist*,
    September 8, 1837.
87 "*POLK, SLAVERY, AND TEXAS*" Sellers, "Election of 1844," 362. Clay initially opposed
    bringing Texas into the Union, then muddled the issue; Polk favored annexation.
    Lincoln believed, as he reportedly put it at a May 1844 meeting at the State House,
    that "annexation at this time upon the terms agreed upon by John Tyler was alto-
    gether inexpedient." CW, 1:337. The Whig nominee, however, straddled the Texas
    issue, alienating both North and South. To support annexing Texas would infuri-
    ate antislavery voters. To oppose it would enrage slaveholders and anti-
    abolitionists. Clay wobbled. "Personally, I could have no objection to the
    annexation of Texas," he wrote, "but I certainly would be unwilling to see the ex-
    isting Union dissolved or seriously jeopardized for the sake of acquiring Texas."
    Remini, *Henry Clay*, 659. No one was happy. "Mr Clay's letter has caused much
    depression, & some consternation, among his friends," the New York politician
    Edward Curtis told Daniel Webster, "& great exultation among his enemies." Ibid.
    He attempted to clarify things, but failed. "In the contingency of my election … if
    the affair of acquiring Texas should become a subject of consideration, I should be
    governed by the state of fact, and the state of public opinion existing at the time I
    might be called upon to act," Clay wrote in the summer of 1844. "Above all, I
    should be governed by the paramount duty of preserving the Union entire." Sell-
    ers, "Election of 1844," 326.

There were lessons to be learned from the campaign, though, and Lincoln was determined to mine the experience. "If the whig abolitionists of New York had voted with us last fall, Mr. Clay would now be president, whig principles in the ascendent, and Texas not annexed; whereas by the division, all . . . was lost," Lincoln wrote in the fall of 1845. He deprecated anti-Clay voters as overly purist. To him, the anti-Clay view was: "'We are not to do *evil* that *good* may come.' This general proposition is doubtless correct; but did it apply? . . . By the *fruit* the tree is to be known. An *evil* tree can not bring forth *good* fruit. If the fruit of electing Mr. Clay would have been to prevent the extension of slavery, could the act of electing [him] have been *evil*?" CW, 1:347.

As he had in his Washington's birthday address to the temperance society, Lincoln was articulating a realistic view of politics. At the Second Presbyterian Church in 1842, he had made the case for speaking *to*—not *at*—those whom one wished to persuade. Here, three years and a presidential election defeat later, he argued that the perfect should not the enemy of the good.

87 BELIEVING THE CLAY PLATFORM CW, 1:338–40.
87 "LINCOLN IS A LONG-LEGGED" *LDBD, 1809–1848*, 222–23.
87 "OLD SANGAMON . . ." Ibid., 232.
87 FAILURE TO REASSURE CW, 1:347.
87 "THE NIGHT WAS ONE" *LDBD, 1809–1848*, 243.
87 ELIZABETH AND NINIAN W. EDWARDS FOLLOWED ON Ibid.
87 "SHE WAS AN EXTREMELY AMBITIOUS" Wilson and Davis, eds., *Herndon's Informants*, 443.
87 "WHO HAS THE BEST" Ibid., 444.

Chapter Six: From the Very Depths of Society

91 "HE WILL FIND" *LDBD, 1809–1848*, 295.
91 "IT IS LIKE THE PLAGUE" Tarbell, *In the Footsteps*, 284.
91 LINCOLN PREPARED TO SEEK On Lincoln and congressional politics in the Seventh District see, for instance, Burlingame, *AL*, 1:213–56; Blumenthal, *Self-Made Man*, 322–46; Donald, *Lincoln*, 111–15; White, *A. Lincoln*, 119–24, 131–37; Donald W. Riddle, *Congressman Abraham Lincoln* (Urbana, Ill., 1957), 4–6; Paul Findley, *A. Lincoln: The Crucible of Congress, The Years Which Forged His Greatness* (New York, 1979), 22–68. See also Donald W. Riddle, *Lincoln Runs for Congress* (New Brunswick, NJ, 1948); Kenneth Winkle, *The Young Eagle: The Rise of Abraham Lincoln* (Dallas, 2001).
91 "I WOULD REJOICE" CW, 1:354.
91 "A TALL MAN" "The Politicians: John J. Hardin (1610–1847)," http://www.mr lincolnandfriends.org/the-politicians/john-hardin/.
91 "HARDIN IS A MAN" CW, 1:354. On the Lincoln-Hardin tension generally, see Burlingame, *AL*, 1:231–35.
91 A LONG-STANDING ARRANGEMENT Riddle, *Congressman Abraham Lincoln*, 4–6.
91 "WHEN THIS [STATE] SUPREME COURT" CW, 1:354.
92 "MORGAN & SCOTT ARE BEYOND" Ibid.
92 HARDIN WITHDREW FROM THE RACE *LDBD, 1809–1848*, 268; Burlingame, *AL*, 1:235.
92 LINCOLN WAS OFFICIALLY NOMINATED *LDBD, 1809–1848*, 272.
92 "MR. LINCOLN, WE ALL KNOW" Ibid.
92 BORN IN VIRGINIA "The Preachers: Peter Cartwright (1785–1872)," http://www .mrlincolnandfriends.org/the-preachers/peter-cartwright/. See also Burlingame, *AL*, 1:235–40; Donald, *Lincoln*, 114; White, *A. Lincoln*, 134; Robert Bray, *Peter Cart-*

wright, Legendary Frontier Preacher (Urbana, Ill., 2005). Lincoln and Cartwright knew each other well. The politician and Lincoln friend William Butler recalled a conversation between the two men that had taken place a decade and a half earlier. "Lincoln at this time was not prepossessing—he was awkward and very shabbily dressed, and Cartwright being already then a presiding elder in the Methodist Church, and dressed as became his station," Butler recalled. The talk turned to politics. "Cartwright laid down his doctrines in a way which undoubtedly seemed to Lincoln a little too dogmatical," Butler said. "A discussion soon arose between him and Cartwright, and my first special attention was attracted to Lincoln by the way in which he met the great preacher in his arguments, and the extensive acquaintance he showed with the politics of the state—in fact he quite beat him in the argument." Michael Burlingame, ed., *An Oral History of Abraham Lincoln: John G. Nicolay's Interviews and Essays* (Carbondale, Ill., 1996), 20.

92   "WITH BIBLE AND RIFLE" Carl Sandburg, *Abraham Lincoln* (New York, 1925), 2:335–36. Cartwright opposed slavery in a limited way. To him, the best path forward was to "ameliorate the condition of slaves, and Christianize them, and finally secure their freedom [without] meddl[ing] politically with slavery." Connie L. Lester, "Peter Cartwright," *Tennessee Encyclopedia*, https://tennesseeencyclopedia.net/entries/peter -cartwright/.

92   THE STORY IS TOLD Tarbell, *In the Footsteps*, 270.

92   IN AN OFT-REPEATED TALE Ibid., 270–71.

92   CARTWRIGHT USED THE MEANS CW, 1:383–84; Herndon and Weik, *Herndon's Life of Lincoln*, 218–19.

92   "MR. LINCOLN HAD NO FAITH" Herndon and Weik, *Herndon's Life of Lincoln*, 359–60.

92   "SLYLY SOW[ING] THE SEED" CW, 1:383.

93   "WHISPERING THE CHARGE" Ibid.

93   "A STRONG METHODIST" Wilson and Davis, eds., *Herndon's Informants*, 432.

93   "I HAVE OFTEN HEARD" Ibid. See also Ibid., 762.

93   "FELLOW CITIZENS" CW, 1:382.

93   "AN OPEN SCOFFER" Ibid. "I do not think I could myself, be brought to support a man for office, whom I knew to be an open enemy of, and scoffer at, religion," Lincoln wrote. "Leaving the higher matter of eternal consequences, between him and his Maker, I still do not think any man has the right thus to insult the feelings, and injure the morals, of the community in which he may live." Ibid.

93   ELIHU WALCOTT, A NOMINEE Riddle, *Congressman Abraham Lincoln*, 6.

93   "THE LIBERTY PARTY" *The Influence of the Slave Power, with Other Anti-Slavery Pamphlets* (Westport, Conn., 1970), 1–3.

93   LINCOLN WON THE ELECTION LDBD, *1809–1848*, 275; Blumenthal, *Self-Made Man*, 331; "Seventh Congressional District Election Returns (1846)," https://www.ilsos.gov /departments/archives/online_exhibits/100_documents/1846-seventh-congress -election-more.html. Walcott polled 249 votes to Lincoln's 6,430 and Cartwright's 4,829. "Seventh Congressional District Election Returns (1846)."

93   "BEING ELECTED TO CONGRESS" CW, 1:391.

94   MEXICAN-AMERICAN WAR For the background, course, and implications of the Mexican-American War, see, for instance, Michael Beschloss, *Presidents of War: The Epic Story, from 1807 to Modern Times* (New York, 2018), 96–156; Blumenthal, *Self-Made Man*, 325–26; Freehling, *Road to Disunion*, 1:353–462; Howe, *What Hath God Wrought*, 658–836; Wilentz, *Rise of American Democracy*, 581–86; Foner, *Fiery Trial*, 51–54; Robert W. Merry, *A Country of Vast Designs: James K. Polk, the Mexican War, and the Conquest of the American Continent* (New York, 2009).

94　"If the Union" Beschloss, *Presidents of War*, 101.

94　Lincoln opposed the acquisition CW, 1:348. "I hold it to be a paramount duty of us in the free states . . . and perhaps to liberty itself (paradox though it may seem) to let the slavery of the other states alone," Lincoln wrote in October 1845, "while, on the other hand, I hold it to be equally clear, that we should never knowingly lend ourselves directly or indirectly, to prevent that slavery from dying a natural death—to find new places for it to live in, when it can no longer exist in the old." Ibid.

94　He and his party Freehling, *Road to Disunion*, 1:447–49.

94　Eager for the extensive Beschloss, *Presidents of War*, 107–15; Freehling, *Road to Disunion*, 1:456; Arthur Schlesinger, Jr., *War and the American Presidency* (New York, 2004), 76–78; Wilentz, *Rise of American Democracy*, 583.

94　Armed conflict and a declaration Beschloss, *Presidents of War*, 97–100; Howe, *What Hath God Wrought*, 738–43.

94　"Hostilities may now" Beschloss, *Presidents of War*, 99.

94　By late 1847 Ibid., 151–53; Freehling, *Road to Disunion*, 1:459; Wilentz, *Rise of American Democracy*, 613.

94　"Our nation seems" *The North Star*, January 21, 1848.

94　River and Harbor Convention Burlingame, *AL*, 1:420; Donald, *Lincoln*, 115; White, *A. Lincoln*, 136–37.

95　"Not a single line" Tarbell, *In the Footsteps*, 274.

95　Horace Greeley and Thurlow Weed Ibid., 274–75.

95　"Tall, angular, and awkward" LDBD, *1809–1848*, 290–91.

95　Greeley approvingly called him Ibid., 291.

95　"We expect much" Tarbell, *In the Footsteps*, 277.

95　Three and a half months later LDBD, *1809–1848*, 294; CW, 1:406–7.

95　"to be especially careful" CW, 1:407.

95　left Springfield for Washington LDBD, *1809–1848*, 295; Baker, *Mary Todd Lincoln*, 136–37; Burlingame, *AL*, 1:253–54; Donald, *Lincoln*, 118; White, *A. Lincoln*, 139; Turner and Turner, *Mary Todd Lincoln: Her Life and Letters*, 35. See also William H. Townsend, *Lincoln in His Wife's Hometown* (Indianapolis, 1929).

95　congressman's wife and family Baker, *Mary Todd Lincoln*, 136–37.

95　"She wishes to loom largely" Ibid., 136.

95　"Mr. Lincoln, the member of Congress" LDBD, *1809–1848*, 295.

96　The Lincolns stopped Findley, *A. Lincoln: The Crucible of Congress*, 62–63; Burlingame, *AL*, 1:255–56.

96　"Mary came in first" Findley, *A. Lincoln: The Crucible of Congress*, 63.

96　To the nearly eleven-year-old Emilie Ibid.

96　"Mr. Lincoln followed" Ibid.

96　Lincoln noticed Ibid.

96　"So this is" Ibid.

96　"His voice and smile" Ibid.

96　Lincoln browsed through Findley, *A. Lincoln: The Crucible of Congress*, 68; Burlingame, *AL*, 1:255.

96　"So live, that" William Cullen Bryant, "Thanatopis," Poetry Foundation, https://www.poetryfoundation.org/poems/50465/thanatopsis.

96　a speech of Henry Clay's "The Great Speech of the Hon. Henry Clay on the War with Mexico," *The New York Herald*, November 15, 1847; "Mr. Clay's Great Speech," *Louisville Daily Courier*, November 13, 1847; "Mr. Clay's Speech," *The (Louisville) Examiner*, November 20, 1847; "Speech of Mr. Clay," *Richmond Enquirer*, November 26,

1847; Remini, *Henry Clay*, 691–95; Burlingame, *AL*, 1:256; Blumenthal, *Self-Made Man*, 342–46; White, *A. Lincoln*, 140–42.

97   AT ELEVEN O'CLOCK *The New York Herald*, November 15, 1847.

97   WAS A VICE PRESIDENT *The* (Louisville) *Examiner*, November 20, 1847.

97   "IT HAD RAINED" *The New York Herald*, November 15, 1847.

97   "THE DAY IS DARK" Henry Clay, "Market Speech," November 13, 1847, http://henry clay.org/wp-content/uploads/2016/02/Market-Speech.pdf.

97   TWO-AND-A-HALF-HOUR SPEECH *The New York Herald*, November 15, 1847.

97   "I HAVE EVER REGARDED" Remini, *Henry Clay*, 693. "If slavery is not wrong," Lincoln would later say, "nothing is wrong." *CW*, 7:281. The remark comes from an April 4, 1864, letter to Albert G. Hodges.

97   "IT MAY BE ARGUED" Clay, "Market Speech."

97   THE LINCOLNS REACHED Washington *LDBD, 1809–1848*, 295–96; Blumenthal, *Self-Made Man*, 347–50.

97   "THE NIGHT WAS CLOUDY" Alexander Mackay, *The Western World; Or, Travels in the United States in 1846–47* (London, 1850), 1:164. To Mackay, Washington when Congress was out of session was "like a body without animation, a social *cadavere*, a moral Dead Sea." Only the coming of lawmakers in early December each year shook the city from its "state of torpidity." Ibid., 180.

97   "I HAVE SEEN IT" Ibid., 173.

97   AT BROWN'S INDIAN QUEEN HOTEL *LDBD, 1809–1848*, 296; Burlingame, *AL*, 1:259; Donald, *Lincoln*, 119–20; White, *A. Lincoln*, 142; "Brown's Indian Queen Hotel, Washington City," https://www.loc.gov/item/93506552/.

97   THE SPRIGG HOUSE Burlingame, *AL*, 1:259–60; Blumenthal, *Self-Made Man*, 364–79; Donald, *Lincoln*, 119–20; White, *A. Lincoln*, 142–43.

97   DUFF GREEN WAS Burlingame, *AL*, 1:273. See also Findley, *A. Lincoln: The Crucible of Congress*, 85.

97   "I WILL TELL YOU" Burlingame, *AL*, 1:259; Baker, *Mary Todd Lincoln*, 137.

98   A NUMBER OF ANTISLAVERY MEN Samuel C. Busey, *Personal Reminiscences and Recollections of Membership in the Medical Society of the District of Columbia and Residence in the City of Washington, D.C.* (Washington, D.C., 1859), 25–28; Burlingame, *AL*, 1:259–60; Blumenthal, *Self-Made Man*, 364–68; Foner, *Fiery Trial*, 55–56; Donald, *Lincoln*, 120–21; White, *A. Lincoln*, 148.

98   "ABOLITION HOUSE" "Ann Sprigg," http://bytesofhistory.com/Collections/UGRR /Sprigg_Ann/Sprigg_Ann-Biography.html.

98   PART OF THE UNDERGROUND RAILROAD Ibid.; Blumenthal, *Self-Made Man*, 369; Reynolds, *Abe*, 298.

98   THE INFORMAL NETWORK See, for instance, Eric Foner, *Gateway to Freedom: The Hidden History of the Underground Railroad* (New York, 2015).

98   BREAKFAST WAS SERVED Findley, *A. Lincoln: The Crucible of Congress*, 95.

98   AFTERWARD LINCOLN WOULD Ibid., 95–100.

98   THERE WERE PEDESTALS Mackay, *Western World*, 1:174. The Columbus statue had "an aboriginal native of the new world, a female figure, crouching beside him in mingled fear and admiration." Ibid.

98   REPRESENTATIONS OF PEACE AND WAR Ibid.

98   GRAND PAINTINGS OF JOHN TRUMBULL https://www.aoc.gov/explore-capitol-campus /art/john-trumbull.

98   TO THE LEFT OF THE ROTUNDA Mackay, *Western World*, 1:174.

98   LINCOLN'S DESK, NO. 191 I am grateful to Matthew Wasniewski for a tour of, and conversation about, the Capitol in Congressman Lincoln's time. See also White,

A. Lincoln, 143–44, 148–49. "As a lowly freshman," Burlingame wrote, "Lincoln occupied an undesirable seat at the back of the House chamber in what was known as the 'Cherokee Strip' on the Whig side of the aisle." Burlingame, *AL,* 1:263.

98   A STATUE OF CLIO Author observation.

98   TWENTY-TWO PILLARS ENCIRCLED Ibid.

98   THEY HAD BEEN QUARRIED Office of the Historian, U.S. House of Representatives. See also Allen, "History of Slave Laborers in the Construction of the United States Capitol," 17.

98   NEAR POINT OF ROCKS, MARYLAND Charles F. Withington, "Building Stones of Our Nation's Capital," United States Department of the Interior Geological Survey (USGS: INF-74-35), https://pubs.usgs.gov/gip/70039206/report.pdf.

98   THERE WAS A VISITORS' GALLERY Mackay, *Western World,* 1:175.

98   "THE CONFUSION AND NOISE" Findley, *A. Lincoln: The Crucible of Congress,* 97.

98   LINCOLN WAS UNINTIMIDATED For contemporary reaction to Lincoln in Congress, see Burlingame, *AL,* 1:260–61.

98   "SELF-MADE" Jim Cullen, *The American Dream: A Short History of an Idea That Shaped a Nation* (New York, 2003), 69.

98   "THE POLITICAL ARENA IS" Mackay, *Western World,* 1:200.

99   POLK HAD ACCUSED MEXICO *LDBD, 1809–1848,* 296.

99   A FORTY-FIVE-MINUTE SPEECH CW, 1:448. On Lincoln and his critique of the Mexican War, see also Blumenthal, *Self-Made Man,* 360–64; Riddle, *Congressman Abraham Lincoln,* 56–69; Donald, *Lincoln,* 122–26; White, *A. Lincoln,* 149–53.

99   "ANY PEOPLE ANYWHERE" CW, 1:438.

99   "WHETHER THE PARTICULAR SPOT" White, *A. Lincoln,* 150; Donald, *Lincoln,* 123.

99   HIS RESOLUTIONS WERE DISMISSED White, *A. Lincoln,* 150; Donald, *Lincoln,* 123–25; Riddle, *Congressman Abraham Lincoln,* 59–69.

99   "THIS VOTE HAS NOTHING" CW, 1:447.

99   "ALLOW THE PRESIDENT" CW, 1:451.

99   "LET HIM ANSWER" CW, 1:439.

99   GEORGE WASHINGTON'S MEMORY On Lincoln and the Founders, see, for instance, Richard Brookhiser, *Founders' Son: A Life of Abraham Lincoln* (New York, 2014); Ronald L. Hatzenbuehler, *Jefferson, Lincoln, and the Unfinished Work of the Nation* (Carbondale, Ill., 2016); Foner, *Fiery Trial,* 70–72.

100   "THEIR *ALL* WAS STAKED UPON" CW, 1:113.

100   "WASHINGTON IS THE MIGHTIEST" *Ibid.,* 279.

100   "IRON MEN" Ibid., 2:499.

100   ON MONDAY, FEBRUARY 21 *LDBD, 1809–1848,* 304; Riddle, *Congressman Abraham Lincoln,* 75; Blumenthal, *Self-Made Man,* 372.

100   OF THE TWELFTH DISTRICT William J. Cooper, *The Lost Founding Father: John Quincy Adams and the Transformation of American Politics* (New York, 2017), 276.

100   "WAS OBSERVED TO BE" *LDBD, 1809–1848,* 304.

100   THE SON OF See, for instance, Leonard L. Richards, *The Life and Times of Congressman John Quincy Adams* (New York, 1986); Cooper, *Lost Founding Father;* Louisa Thomas, *Louisa: The Extraordinary Life of Mrs. Adams* (New York, 2016); Robert V. Remini, *John Quincy Adams* (New York, 2002).

100   ADAMS HAD WATCHED Richards, *Life and Times,* 4.

100   HE HAD TRAVELED Ibid., 3–4.

100   "THE SUN OF MY POLITICAL LIFE" Cooper, *Lost Founding Father,* 258.

100   WON ELECTION TO THE HOUSE Richards, *Life and Times,* 3–7. "There are some very

silly plans going on here," his wife, Louisa Catherine Adams, wrote their son John of the possible race, "and God only knows in what they will end, but I fear not at all to my taste." She was done with politics; her husband was decidedly not. The former president declined to take his wife's advice, sought election to the House of Representatives, was elected in 1830, and took his seat in December 1831. Ibid., 6.

100 "Slave and Abolition whirligig" Ibid., 113.
100 Southerners attacked him Ibid., 4.
101 "Old Man Eloquent" Ibid.
101 reached to his right Ibid., 202; Cooper, *Lost Founding Father*, 434.
101 "Mr. Adams is dying" Richards, *Life and Times*, 202.
101 Adams was carried Ibid.
101 "This is the end" Ibid.; Cooper, *Lost Founding Father*, 434.
101 at seven thirty *LDBD, 1809–1848*, 304.
101 Lincoln was appointed Ibid.; Riddle, *Congressman Abraham Lincoln*, 75.
101 The old man's desk *LDBD, 1809–1848*, 304.
101 read from the Book of Job Cooper, *Lost Founding Father*, 437; Job 11:17, KJV.
101 "a splendid pageant" Cooper, *Lost Founding Father*, 438.
101 This "black question" Tarbell, *In the Footsteps*, 284. According to Burlingame, "As Massachusetts Senator Henry Wilson recalled, 'the subject of slavery in the abstract was a topic of frequent discussion in the XXXth Congress. Its sinfulness, its wrongs, its deleterious influences, its power over the government and the people, were perhaps more fully discussed in that than in any previous Congress.' In fact, slavery was by far the most frequently discussed topic in that Congress." Burlingame, *AL*, 1:284.

Chapter Seven: We Have Got to Deal with This Slavery Question

102 "The true rule" CW, 1:484.
102 "He has a very tall" *LDBD, 1809–1848*, 319.
102 Entering the Senate balcony Mackay, *Western World*, 1:175–76.
102 "The ceiling of the chamber" Ibid., 176.
102 "so well pleased" Wilson and Davis, eds., *Herndon's Informants*, 700.
102 Lincoln voted in favor Foner, *Fiery Trial*, 51–52.
102 Wilmot Proviso See, for instance, Wilentz, *Rise of American Democracy*, 596–601, 623–28; Eric Foner, "The Wilmot Proviso Revisited," *Journal of American History* 56, no. 2 (1969): 262–79; Chaplain Morrison, *Democratic Politics and Sectionalism* (Chapel Hill, N.C., 1967); Arthur Schlesinger, *The Age of Jackson* (Boston, 1945); Charles G. Sellers, *The Market Revolution: Jacksonian America, 1815–1846* (Oxford, 1991).
103 "I think I may venture" Foner, *Fiery Trial*, 52. As Foner pointed out, this 1854 comment was something of an exaggeration. Ibid.
103 John C. Calhoun's arguments "Sir, we are accused of fanaticism in the North," the antislavery Representative Jacob Brinkerhoff of Ohio said. "But there is a fanaticism which . . . overtops all others. There are men who yield to the doctrines of the Satanic philosophy of the school of Fort Hill. Yes, slavery a good: and, as such, is to be extended and perpetuated!" *Congressional Globe,* 29th Congress, 2nd Session, 378.
103 "a good—a positive good" Calhoun, *Speech on the Reception of Abolition Petitions*, 8.
103 "The Wilmot Proviso" Busey, *Personal Reminiscences*, 26.
103 John Dickey, for instance Ibid.; Burlingame, *AL*, 1:260.

103 "MAY HAVE BEEN" Blumenthal, *Self-Made Man*, 368.

104 LINCOLN STOOD WITH ABOLITIONISTS *LDBD, 1809–1848,* 297; Riddle, *Congressman Abraham Lincoln*, 162.

104 HE VOTED THE SAME PRINCIPLE Riddle, *Congressman Abraham Lincoln*, 162–63. Lincoln's antislavery sympathies had been evident since his protest in the legislature a dozen years before.

104 NOT ENTIRELY CONSISTENT Riddle, *Congressman Abraham Lincoln*, 162–80; Findley, *A. Lincoln: The Crucible of Congress*, 122–43; Burlingame, *AL*, 1:284–94. Riddle wrote: "It is difficult to make a correct estimate of Lincoln's Congressional career with reference to the slavery question.... [H]e was consistent in the matter of antislavery petitions, and he was almost consistent in voting against tabling resolutions or motions whose purpose was the shutting off of debate on slavery.... A[n] ... accurate estimate ... is that Lincoln maintained the principle that there should be no extension of slavery into the areas where it did not then exist. But his votes show he had no clear conception how this was to be accomplished." Riddle, *Congressman Abraham Lincoln*, 178.

104 HE DID OPPOSE Riddle, *Congressman Abraham Lincoln*, 163. The resolution "directed the committees to which the antislavery petitions had been referred to report a bill," Donald W. Riddle, a historian of Lincoln's congressional term, wrote. Tuck "moved to suspend the rules in order to get the resolution before the House. On the motion there was a clear-cut division between the proslavery and the antislavery men. All abolitionists and antislavery men voted to suspend the rules. Southern members, Whigs and Democrats alike, and a few Northern Whigs voted against the suspension, thus blocking consideration of the resolution. Lincoln was one of the majority voting against consent to introduce the resolution." Ibid.

104 THE EVILS OF SLAVE CATCHING Blumenthal, *Self-Made Man*, 370–72; Burlingame, *AL*, 1:286.

104 HENRY WILSON Blumenthal, *Self-Made Man*, 370–71; Findley, *A. Lincoln: The Crucible of Congress*, 130; *LDBD, 1809–1848*, 300.

104 THREE MEN REPORTEDLY Harrold, *Lincoln and the Abolitionists*, 24; *Congressional Globe,* 30th Congress, 1st Session, 179–81.

104 WHILE LINCOLN SAID NOTHING Riddle, *Congressman Abraham Lincoln*, 164.

104 JOSHUA GIDDINGS WENT TO THE HOUSE FLOOR Findley, *A. Lincoln: The Crucible of Congress*, 131.

104 "THE PROPRIETY OF REPEALING" Ibid. See also *Congressional Globe,* 30th Congress, 1st Session, 179–81.

104 "THE SPEAKER WAS MUCH TROUBLED" *Richmond Enquirer*, January 18, 1848.

104 THOUGH HE TOOK NO PART Findley, *A. Lincoln: The Crucible of Congress*, 131–32. See also Riddle, *Congressman Abraham Lincoln*, 164.

104 GIDDINGS ORGANIZED "Ann Sprigg," http://bytesofhistory.com/Collections/UGRR/Sprigg_Ann/Sprigg_Ann-Biography.html.

104 THE PROSLAVERY GAG RULE "The House 'Gag Rule,'" https://history.house.gov/Historical-Highlights/1800-1850/The-Houseof-Representatives-instituted-the-"gag-rule"/.

105 THE *PEARL* AFFAIR ROILED Don E. Fehrenbacher, *The Slaveholding Republic: Its Significance in American Law and Politics* (New York, 1979), 50–53; Blumenthal, *Self-Made Man*, 375–83.

105 "HISTORY WILL RECORD" Fehrenbacher, *Slaveholding Republic*, 52.

105 THE DEBATE OPENED Findley, *A. Lincoln: The Crucible of Congress*, 133.

105 THE STORM CONTINUED Ibid., 133–34.

105 THE GIDDINGS-PALFREY ARGUMENTS Ibid.

105 LINCOLN VOTED WITH Ibid., 136.

105 LINCOLN CAST AN ANTISLAVERY VOTE Riddle, *Congressman Abraham Lincoln*, 165–66.

105 THE MEASURE WAS DEFEATED Ibid., 165.

105 DECLINED TO SUPPORT CALLS Harrold, *Lincoln and the Abolitionists*, 25; Burlingame, *AL*, 1:287–88.

105 "A MODERATE . . . MAN" Harrold, *Lincoln and the Abolitionists*, 24; Burlingame, *AL*, 1:288; Foner, *Fiery Trial*, 57.

105 1848 PRESIDENTIAL RACE Blumenthal, *Self-Made Man*, 382–91; Holt, *Rise and Fall*, 284–382; Burlingame, *AL*, 1:273–84; Holman Hamilton, "Election of 1848," in *HAPE*, 1:373–404; Donald, *Lincoln*, 126–33; White, *A. Lincoln*, 155–56; Riddle, *Congressman Abraham Lincoln*, 99–142. Polk had committed to serving only a single term, and the Whigs were coalescing around Zachary Taylor of Louisiana, a hero of the Mexican War known as "Old Rough and Ready." Henry Clay's day had passed; the presidency was not his destiny. Wilentz, *Rise of American Democracy*, 616–17.
By early February 1848 Lincoln had declared himself in favor of Taylor. The calculus was purely political, for Taylor was hardly an inspired choice in terms of philosophy or of experience. As "the lone Whig representative from a heavily Democratic state," the historian Michael F. Holt observed, Lincoln "believed that only an apparently nonpartisan hero like Taylor could help Illinois Whigs attract the Democratic votes they needed to win additional congressional seats in August and perhaps even carry the state in the presidential contest itself." Holt, *Rise and Fall*, 286–88; *LDBD, 1809–1848*, 302. Though he appeared to support the Wilmot Proviso, Taylor was a slave owner, a compromise candidate who might give the troubled Whigs—who had not elected a president since Harrison, eight years before—the White House and buoy down-ballot aspirants. Holt, *Rise and Fall*, 286. In the Taylor campaign Lincoln also got to know Alexander H. Stephens of Georgia. Stephens, Lincoln wrote, was "a little, slim, pale-faced consumptive man"; still, in those days, the two men agreed in their criticism of Polk's Mexican War, which led Lincoln to say that Stephens had "just concluded the very best speech, of an hour's length, I ever heard. My old, withered, dry eyes, are full of tears yet." Burlingame, *AL*, 1:274–75; *CW*, 1:448. See also *CW*, 1:501–16; Donald, *Lincoln*, 129–30; White, *A. Lincoln*, 157–59.
Lewis Cass, the general and U.S. senator from Michigan who had served as Jackson's secretary of war, won the 1848 Democratic nomination for president in Baltimore. Hamilton, "Election of 1848," 380. An advocate of popular sovereignty—the proposal that slavery be decided by the people of new territories—Cass divided the Democrats as antislavery Northerners, led in part by Martin Van Buren, broke off to form a Free Soil Party.

105 THE NEW ANTISLAVERY FREE SOIL PARTY Blumenthal, *Self-Made Man*, 393–99; Burlingame, *AL*, 1:280–84; Donald, *Lincoln*, 127; White, *A. Lincoln*, 157. See also Jonathan H. Earle, *Jacksonian Antislavery and the Politics of Free Soil, 1824–1854* (Chapel Hill, N.C., 2004); Wilentz, *Rise of American Democracy*, 615; Foner, *Free Soil, Free Labor, Free Men*, 93; *Boston Whig*, June 20, 1848; "Free Soil Party Platform, 1848," https://www.presidency.ucsb.edu/documents/free-soil-party-platform-1848

105 IN NEW ENGLAND TO CAMPAIGN Burlingame, *AL*, 1:280–83; *LDBD, 1809–1848*, 319–21; Donald, *Lincoln*, 131–32; White, *A. Lincoln*, 158–60.

105 "HE HAS A VERY TALL" *LDBD, 1809–1848*, 319; James Schouler, "Abraham Lincoln at Tremont Temple in 1848," *Proceedings of the Massachusetts Historical Society* 42 (October 1908–June 1909): 73.

106 HE WAS MOVING Burlingame, *AL*, 1:305–6.

106 "I had been chosen" Ibid., 306.

106 After a memorable dinner *LDBD, 1809–1848*, 319–20.

106 "remarked upon" Burlingame, *AL*, 1:306.

106 In Boston Schouler, "Abraham Lincoln at Tremont Temple," 70–87; *LDBD, 1809–1848*, 320; White, *A. Lincoln*, 160; Blumenthal, *Self-Made Man*, 400–404.

106 Faneuil Hall was unavailable Schouler, "Abraham Lincoln at Tremont Temple," 74.

106 Seward's speech "The Old Bay State Arousing! Great Meeting in Boston—Ex-Governor Seward's Speech," *St. Johnsbury Caledonian*, September 30, 1848; "Speech of Gov. Seward at Boston," *Buffalo Commercial Advertiser*, September 26, 1848.

106 Born in 1801 Blumenthal, *Self-Made Man*, 405–19; Walter Stahr, *Seward: Lincoln's Indispensable Man* (New York, 2012); John M. Taylor, *William Henry Seward: Lincoln's Right Hand* (New York, 1991); Stephen G. Yanoff, *Turbulent Times: The Remarkable Life of William H. Seward* (Bloomington, Indiana, 2017); Goodwin, *Team of Rivals*, 11–16. See also William Henry Seward, "Speech to the United States Senate," March 11, 1850, http://nationalhumanitiescenter.org/pds/triumphnationalism/america1850/text3/seward.pdf.

106 "believed in the force" *Buffalo Commercial Advertiser*, September 26, 1848.

106 "It was to be done" Ibid.

106 "I have been thinking" *LDBD, 1809–1848*, 321; Tarbell, *In the Footsteps*, 287; White, *A. Lincoln*, 160; *RWAL*, 398. See also Stahr, *Seward*, 110–11, where Stahr casts doubt the veracity of a related and oft-repeated report that Lincoln and Seward spent an evening together in the same lodgings on this occasion in Massachusetts. That the two did not share a room, however, does not preclude the possibility that Lincoln made remarks along these lines during their time in one another's company around the Tremont event.

106 In the spring of 1848 Burlingame, *AL*, 1:262; Baker, *Mary Todd Lincoln*, 141; Epstein, *Lincolns*, 135; Donald, *Lincoln*, 130–31; White, *A. Lincoln*, 154. Turner and Turner observed: "One suspects that her life in Washington was something of a disappointment: no one made the slightest fuss over the wife of a freshman congressman, and no boardinghouse could contain for long the likes of Bobby and Eddy Lincoln, who, with their father busier than ever before, were constantly at their mother's skirts. She would miss her husband acutely, but she could look forward to a long, leisurely visit with the relatives and friends she had left behind seven years before." Turner and Turner, *Mary Todd Lincoln: Her Life and Letters*, 35.

106 "Lincoln & his wife" Wilson and Davis, eds., *Herndon's Informants*, 453.

107 by telling jokes Burlingame, *AL*, 1:261.

107 "In this troublesome world" *CW*, 1:465.

107 "I went yesterday" Ibid.

107 "All the house" Ibid.

107 "Lincoln's wife was" Wilson and Davis, eds., *Herndon's Informants*, 465.

107 "And you are" *CW*, 1:466.

107 "Even E[ddy]'s eyes" Turner and Turner, *Mary Todd Lincoln: Her Life and Letters*, 38.

107 Writing to him Epstein, *Lincolns*, 138–39.

107 "Bobby" had found Turner and Turner, *Mary Todd Lincoln: Her Life and Letters*, 37.

108 "*tenderness* broke forth" Ibid.

108 No fan of cats Ibid.

108 Eddy's resulting cries Ibid.

108 "Tis unusual for her" Ibid.

108 HE WROTE TO HER FROM HIS DESK CW, 1:477.

108 WORN OUT FROM HIS JOURNEY Ibid.

108 "I WAS SO TIRED" Ibid.

108 "THE LEADING MATTER" Ibid.

108 SEXUAL ALLUSIONS WERE NOT Baker, *Mary Todd Lincoln*, 141–42; Epstein, *Lincolns*, 140–43.

108 "THE MUSIC IN" CW, 1:495.

108 A PAIR OF PRESUMED PROSTITUTES Ibid., 495–96.

109 "*PATTY WEBB'S* SCHOOL" Turner and Turner, *Mary Todd Lincoln: Her Life and Letters*, 38.

109 MARY AND THE BOYS *LDBD, 1809–1848*, 316.

109 ON THE SLAVERY QUESTION Burlingame, *AL*, 1:284–94; Blumenthal, *Self-Made Man*, 424–35; Foner, *Fiery Trial*, 57–59; Donald, *Lincoln*, 133–37; White, *A. Lincoln*, 161–63.

109 "THIS DISTRICT IS" Fehrenbacher, *Slaveholding Republic*, 52–53.

109 "MR. DICKEY . . ." Burlingame, *AL*, 1:290.

109 LINCOLN ROSE TO OFFER Ibid., 288–90; CW, 2:20–22.

109 "AN ACT TO ABOLISH" CW, 2:20.

109 CURRENTLY IN THE DISTRICT Ibid., 21.

109 "FORTHWITH AND FOREVER FREE" Ibid. All children born of enslaved mothers in the District after January 1, 1850, "shall be free" but would be "reasonably supported and educated by the respective owners of their mothers or by their heirs or representatives, and shall owe reasonable service, as apprentices, to such owners" until a to-be-resolved age. Ibid.

109 "PUBLIC BUSINESS" Ibid.

109 "REQUIRED TO PROVIDE" Ibid.

109 TO RATIFY OR REJECT Ibid.

109 SHOULD A MAJORITY APPROVE Ibid., 22.

109 "AUTHORIZED TO SAY" Ibid.

110 "WHO ARE THEY?" Burlingame, *AL*, 1:289.

110 SAID NOTHING IN REPLY Ibid.

110 HE HAD CALLED ON Burlingame, *AL*, 1:289. See also CW, 2:22.

110 PURISTS WERE UNIMPRESSED Burlingame, *AL*, 1:289–90; Foner, *Fiery Trial*, 57–59.

110 "NO CREDIT TO ANY MAN" Foner, *Fiery Trial*, 58.

110 "THE SLAVE-HOUND OF ILLINOIS" Ibid.; Burlingame, *AL*, 1:292; *The Liberator*, June 22, 1860.

110 COMPROMISE AND COMPENSATION Burlingame, *AL*, 1:290–91.

110 "OUR WHOLE MESS" Ibid., 290.

110 "HE IS A STRONG" Ibid., 292.

110 "MY MIND HAS BEEN" Howard, "Biographical Notes," May 1860, Abraham Lincoln Papers, LOC.

110 ACCORDING TO WHIG CUSTOM As noted above, see Riddle, *Congressman Abraham Lincoln*, 4–6.

110 WHO WON 47.3 PERCENT Hamilton, "Election of 1848," 402–3.

111 GENERAL LAND OFFICE Burlingame, *AL*, 1:296–310. On Lincoln and patronage, see also Blumenthal, *Self-Made Man*, 435–46; Donald, *Lincoln*, 139–41; White, *A. Lincoln*, 163–65.

111 "IN THESE DAYS" CW, 2:25.

111 "NOW CANNOT YOU" Ibid., 50.

111 "ALMOST SWEATING BLOOD" Ibid., 49.

111 "I AM IN THE CENTER" Ibid., 54.

111   "When we went" *LDBD, 1849–1860*, 9.

111   Lincoln was admitted Ibid.

111   setting off for Springfield Ibid., 10.

111   new Taylor administration offered Burlingame, *AL*, 1:307; Blumenthal, *Self-Made Man*, 442; Donald, *Lincoln*, 140–41; White, *A. Lincoln*, 165.

111   the territorial governorship Burlingame, *Oral History*, 15.

111   Stuart was in favor Ibid.

111   "Mr. Lincoln finally" Ibid. On Mary's opposition, see also Burlingame, *AL*, 1:307; Turner and Turner, *Mary Todd Lincoln: Her Life and Letters*, 39–40.

111   "with greater earnestness" CW, 4:67.

112   "The true rule" Ibid., 1:484.

Chapter Eight: The Conscience of the Nation Must Be Roused

113   right is of no sex *The North Star*, "Frederick Douglass Newspapers, 1847 to 1874," LOC, https://www.loc.gov/collections/frederick-douglass-newspapers/about-this-collection/.

113   "The spirit of our age" "Kossuth Before Ohio Legislature," *Ohio Archaeological and Historical Publications* 12, no. 2 (April 1903): 114.

113   "power to excite" CW, 2:10–11.

113   A paraphrase of Psalm 90 Isaac Watts, *The Psalms of David Imitated in the Language of the New Testament* (London, 1719), 229–30.

114   "With *me*, the race of ambition" CW, 2:382–83.

114   Lincoln considered the works See, for instance, Brookhiser, *Founders' Son*, especially 151–70; Herndon and Weik, *Herndon's Life of Lincoln*, 248, 257–59; Kateb, *Lincoln's Political Thought*, especially 1–105; Foner, *Fiery Trial*, 60–131; and Hatzenbuehler, *Jefferson, Lincoln, and the Unfinished Work of the Nation*.

114   On learning he had lost *LDBD, 1849–1860*, 16. William Herndon, who was to spend much of the decade with Lincoln in the practice of law, recalled, "Political defeat had wrought a marked effect on him. It went below the skin and made a changed man of him." Herndon and Weik, *Herndon's Life of Lincoln*, 248.

114   in small inns and taverns Ibid.

114   read by candlelight Ibid.

114   Lincoln's companions Ibid.

114   "Notes for a Law Lecture" CW, 2:81.

114   Lincoln practiced law On Lincoln's legal career, see, for instance, Burlingame, *AL*, 1:310–57; Blumenthal, *Wrestling with His Angel*, 134–49; Donald, *Lincoln*, 142–61; White, *A. Lincoln*, 167–85; Mark E. Steiner, *An Honest Calling: The Law Practice of Abraham Lincoln* (DeKalb, Ill., 2006), is comprehensive; see also John J. Duff, *A. Lincoln, Prairie Lawyer* (New York, 1960).

114   "an educational process" Steiner, *An Honest Calling*, 15.

115   In 1847, Lincoln unsuccessfully represented Ibid., 103–36.

115   On another occasion Ibid., 127, 225.

115   The Hungarian patriot and reformer See, for instance, *Authentic Life of His Excellency Louis Kossuth, Governor of Hungary* (London, 1851); Louise L. Stevenson, *Lincoln in the Atlantic World* (New York, 2015); Blumenthal, *Wrestling with His Angel*, 154–65.

115   Lincoln, moved as so many were *LDBD, 1849–1860*, 20; 67; see also CW, 2:115–16.

115   "The spirit of our age" "Kossuth Before Ohio Legislature," *Ohio Archaeological and Historical Publications* 12, no. 2 (April 1903): 114. From the perspective of Hungary, a nation struggling to overcome autocracy, Kossuth invested the American experiment with overarching significance. "With self-government is freedom, and with

freedom is justice and patriotism," he told a congressional dinner at the National Hotel in Washington in January 1852. "The lesson you give to humanity will not be lost." *Washington Republic*, January 8, 1852; *Louisville Daily Courier*, January 14, 1852.

115 THE OLD WORLD REVOLUTIONS OF 1848 Howe, *What Hath God Wrought*, 792–836.

115 AUTHORED RESOLUTIONS CW, 2:115–16.

116 "SUCH COMPLETE SATISFACTION" M. L. Weems, *The Life of George Washington* (Philadelphia, 1808), 81.

116 "THE WORLD'S BEST HOPE" Thomas Jefferson, "First Inaugural Address," March 4, 1801, https://avalon.law.yale.edu/19th_century/jefinau1.asp.

116 WHO HAD DIED Remini, *Henry Clay*, 781.

116 "FEELING, AS HE DID" CW, 2:126.

116 DELIVERED IN SPRINGFIELD *LDBD, 1849–1860*, 78.

116 "WITH OTHER MEN" CW, 2:125.

116 "THE PRESIDENCY, EVEN TO" Ibid., 89.

116 "I REPAIR, THEN" Jefferson, "First Inaugural Address."

116 "BOLD AND DOUBTFUL" Thomas Jefferson to Roger C. Weightman, June 24, 1826, https://founders.archives.gov/documents/Jefferson/98-01-02-6179.

117 "THE PRINCIPLES OF JEFFERSON" CW, 3:375.

117 "ALL HONOR TO JEFFERSON" Ibid., 376.

117 "I HAVE NEVER HAD A FEELING" Ibid., 4:240.

117 "NO MAN . . . CAN BE" John Milton, *Complete Poems and Major Prose*, ed. Merritt Y. Hughes (New York, 1957), 754.

117 "TO UNDERSTAND POLITICAL POWER" John Locke, *Two Treatises of Government and a Letter Concerning Toleration*, ed. Ian Shapiro (New Haven, Conn., 2003), 101.

117 "THE LIBERTY OF" Algernon Sidney, *Discourses Concerning Government*, ed. Thomas G. West (Indianapolis, 1996), 510.

117 "ALL MEN ARE BORN" *The Papers of George Mason, 1725–1792*, vol. 1, *1749–1778*, ed. Robert A. Rutland (Chapel Hill, N.C., 1970), 282–86.

118 THE INSTITUTION OF SLAVERY For the contrasting views of slavery and the Constitution, see, for instance, Finkelman, *Slavery and the Founders*; and Oakes, *Crooked Path to Abolition*.

118 LINCOLN ARGUED, HOWEVER Kateb, *Lincoln's Political Thought*, 77–80.

118 "A STANDARD MAXIM" CW, 2:406.

118 LINCOLN DID NOT FOLLOW See, for instance, Kateb, *Lincoln's Political Thought*, 53–104; Burlingame, *Black Man's President*, especially 193–232; Fredrickson, *Arrogance of Race*, 54–72; Foner, *Fiery Trial*, 70–72; Kendi, *Stamped from the Beginning*, 203–34; Oakes, *Crooked Path to Abolition*, 112–20.

118 THE FOUNDERS, HE SAID CW, 2:406.

119 RIGHT IS OF NO SEX *The North Star*, "Frederick Douglass Newspapers, 1847 to 1874," LOC, https://www.loc.gov/collections/frederick-douglass-newspapers/about-this-collection/.

119 EDITED BY FREDERICK DOUGLASS On Douglass, see, for instance, Blight, *Frederick Douglass*.

119 "THIS, TO YOU" Foner, ed., *Life and Writings of Frederick Douglass*, 2:182.

119 "THE SUNLIGHT THAT" Ibid., 189.

119 "THE FEELING OF" Ibid., 192.

120 "THERE ARE FORCES" Ibid., 203.

120 "NATIONS DO NOT NOW" Ibid.

120 LITTLE EDDY LINCOLN Baker, *Mary Todd Lincoln*, 125; Epstein, *Lincolns*, 159–60; Burlingame, *AL*, 1:359–60; White, *A. Lincoln*, 179–81.

120 "HE WAS SICK" CW, 2:77.

120 LIKELY OF PULMONARY TUBERCULOSIS Baker, *Mary Todd Lincoln,* 125.

120 THE COLD MORNING Epstein, *Lincolns,* 160.

120 "LAY PROSTRATED, STUNNED" Ibid.

121 "I GRIEVE TO SAY" Baker, *Mary Todd Lincoln,* 128.

121 "EAT, MARY, FOR WE" Ibid., 126.

121 BURIAL IN HUTCHINSON'S CEMETERY Ibid.; *LDBD, 1849–1860,* 65.

121 LIKELY IN LOT 490 Ibid.

121 PRESIDED OVER BY Baker, *Mary Todd Lincoln,* 126; Epstein, *Lincolns,* 160.

121 "CAME INTO THE ROOM" Epstein, *Lincolns,* 160.

121 THE FUNERAL TOOK PLACE Ibid.; Baker, *Mary Todd Lincoln,* 126.

121 A POEM ENTITLED "LITTLE EDDIE" Samuel P. Wheeler, "Solving a Lincoln Literary Mystery: 'Little Eddie,'" *JALA* 33, no. 2 (Summer 2012): 34–46.

121 "WE MISS HIM" CW, 2:77.

121 TEN AND A HALF MONTHS AFTER *LDBD, 1849–1860,* 45; CW, 1:304.

121 THE SON'S ALIENATION CW, 2:96–97.

121 "BECAUSE IT APPEARED" Ibid., 96.

121 "YOU ALREADY KNOW" Ibid., 96–97.

122 "AS UNPOETICAL AS" Ibid., 1:378.

122 "I SINCERELY HOPE" Ibid., 2:96–97.

122 THOMAS LINCOLN DIED "Thomas Lincoln," https://www.nps.gov/abli/learn/history culture/thomas-lincoln.htm. See also Burlingame, AL, 1:360.

122 HAD GIVEN LINCOLN A COPY Carwardine, *Lincoln: A Life of Purpose and Power,* 36–37; Burlingame, AL, 1:359; White, *A. Lincoln,* 181.

122 LATER CLAIMED, UNCONVINCINGLY Herndon and Weik, *Herndon's Life of Lincoln,* xxx–xxxi.

123 "MR LINCOLN," JAMES MATHENY SAID Wilson and Davis, eds., *Herndon's Informants,* 432.

123 "MR LINCOLN BELIEVED IN GOD" Ibid., 441.

123 "IT IS TRUE" CW, 1:382. See also Guelzo, "Abraham Lincoln and the Doctrine of Necessity," 64–66.

123 "WHAT IS" . . . HEARD HER HUSBAND SAY Carwardine, *Lincoln: A Life of Purpose and Power,* 39.

123 "THE WILL TO" Ibid., 43.

123 "THE FATALIST AND ACTIVIST" Ibid, 44. As noted, Guelzo is also crucial on these questions.

123 "ALL THINGS WERE FIXED" Guelzo, "Abraham Lincoln and the Doctrine of Necessity."

123 "THAT THE ALMIGHTY" RWAL, 105.

123 THE COMMON TERM See, for instance, C. Clifton Black, "American Scriptures," *Theology Today* 67, no. 2 (July 2010): 127–68; Grant R. Brodrecht, *Our Country: Northern Evangelicals and the Union During the Civil War Era* (New York, 2018); Charles D. Cashdollar, "The Social Implications of the Doctrine of Divine Providence: A Nineteenth-Century Debate in American Theology," *Harvard Theological Review* 71, no. 3/4 (July–October 1978): 265–84; G. Clark Chapman, Jr., "Lincoln, Bonhoeffer, and Providence: A Quest for Meaning in Wartime," *Union Seminary Quarterly Review* 55, no. 3/4 (2001): 129–49; Allen C. Guelzo, "The Prudence of Abraham Lincoln," *First Things: A Monthly Journal of Religion and Public Life,* no. 159 (January 2006): 11–13; Guyatt, *Providence and the Invention of the United States;* Robert Hastings Nichols, "Lincoln's Leadership in War," *Christianity and Crisis* 2, no. 1 (February 9, 1942): 2–5; Noll, *America's God;* Noll, *Civil War as a Theological Crisis;* Meir Y. So-

loveichik, "The Theologian of the American Idea," *Commentary* 114, no. 5 (December 2017): 13–14; White, *Lincoln's Greatest Speech*, 136–40.

123 "IN THE MOST" Guelzo, "Abraham Lincoln and the Doctrine of Necessity," 79.

Chapter Nine: To Understand the Moral Universe

125 "WE KNOW THAT WE ARE RIGHT" Cobbe, ed., *Collected Works of Theodore Parker,* vol. 5, *Discourses on Slavery* (London, 1863), 132.

125 "WE WERE THUNDERSTRUCK" CW, 2:282.

125 "VINDICATE THE WAYS" Alexander Pope, "An Essay on Man," https://www.poetry foundation.org/poems/44899/an-essay-on-man-epistle-i.

125 A SPRINGFIELD ACQUAINTANCE Herndon and Weik, *Herndon's Life of Lincoln*, 353–54.

125 ROBERT CHAMBERS'S 1844 VESTIGES Secord, *Victorian Sensation,* is comprehensive.

125 PRINCE ALBERT READ Ibid., 168–69.

125 ALFRED, LORD TENNYSON IMMEDIATELY Ibid., 9.

125 CHAMBERS'S WORK GAVE Ibid., 1. "As readable as a romance, based on the latest findings of science, *Vestiges* was an evolutionary epic that ranged from the formation of the solar system to reflections on the destiny of the human race," Secord wrote. "In a hugely ambitious synthesis, it combined astronomy, geology, physiology, psychology, anthropology, and theology in a general theory of creation. It suggested that the planets had originated in a blazing Fire-mist, that life could be created in the laboratory, that humans had evolved from apes." Ibid.

125 LINCOLN WAS INTRIGUED Herndon and Weik, *Herndon's Life of Lincoln,* 354. "The treatise interested him greatly," Herndon recalled, "and he was deeply impressed with the notion of the so-called 'universal law'—evolution." Ibid.

126 "THE SEA OF FAITH" Matthew Arnold, "Dover Beach," https://www.poetryfounda tion.org/poems/43588/dover-beach.

126 AMONG THE FIGURES Bray, "What Abraham Lincoln Read" especially 39, 64, 68, 78; Allen C. Guelzo, "The Unlikely Intellectual Biography of Abraham Lincoln," *Transactions of the Charles S. Peirce Society* 40, no. 1 (2004): 83–106; Allen C. Guelzo, "Lincoln, Cobden, and Bright: The Braid of Liberalism in the Nineteenth Century's Transatlantic World," *American Political Thought* 4, no. 3 (2015): 391–411. See also Herndon and Weik, *Herndon's Life of Lincoln*, 352–54.

126 WROTE SEARCHINGLY ABOUT HUMAN NATURE Guelzo, "Lincoln, Cobden, and Bright."

127 BUTLER'S *ANALOGY OF RELIGION* Burlingame, ed., *Lincoln Observed,* 219. See also Joseph Butler, *The Analogy of Religion, Natural and Revealed, to the Constitution and Course of Nature* (Cincinnati, 1862); Christopher Cunliffe, ed., *Joseph Butler's Moral and Religious Thought: Tercentenary Essays* (Oxford, 1992).

127 "IT IS NOT BECAUSE" John Stuart Mill, *On Liberty,* https://www.econlib.org/library /Mill/mlLbty.html.

127 HE THOUGHT PROSLAVERY THEOLOGY Carwardine, *Lincoln: A Life of Purpose and Power*, 246; CW, 8:155.

127 "HIS RELIGIOUS VIEWS WERE" Herndon and Weik, *Herndon's Life of Lincoln*, 358–59.

127 THEODORE PARKER WAS BORN Teed, *Revolutionary Conscience,* 1; Grodzins, *American Heretic,* 1–2. Teed observed: "Along with most of his contemporaries in antebellum America, [Parker] believed deeply in the importance of religion, morality, economic liberalism, and the republican tradition. But unlike others of his generation, he believed passionately that the concrete reality shaped by these values had somehow become an end in itself, rather than just the beginning of a fairer, more

just society. Whether in theology or in social relations, the progress of America required constant self-criticism, a persistent measuring of the gap between the ideal and the actual. For him, the witness of conscience and ideals of the American Revolutionary tradition became the standards by which to judge that gap." Teed, *Revolutionary Conscience*, xvii.

127   As a child, Parker had heard Teed, *Revolutionary Conscience*, 5. As Parker recalled, "I drew my first breath in a poor little town where the farmers and mechanics first unsheathed that Revolutionary sword," and he was always proud of his grandfather Captain John Parker's leadership in the April 1775 battle on the green that lived on in American memory. Ibid., 1–3. "I learned to read out of his Bible," Parker said, and "with a musket that he captured from the foe I learned that 're-bellion to tyrants is obedience to God.'" Ibid., 2. See also Grodzins, *American Heretic*, 6–8.

127   "Some men call it" Grodzins, *American Heretic*, 7.

127   Inspired by William Ellery Channing Teed, *Revolutionary Conscience*, 9–11; Grodzins, *American Heretic*, 12.

127   He married a daughter Teed, *Revolutionary Conscience*, 12–13; Grodzins, *American Heretic*, 36–39.

128   After divinity school Teed, *Revolutionary Conscience*, 27.

128   In *A Discourse on the Transient* Theodore Parker, *A Discourse on the Transient and Permanent in Christianity: Preached at the Ordination of Mr. Charles C. Shackford in the Hawes Place Church in Boston, May 19, 1841* (Boston, 1841).

128   "The Bible or the New Testament" Teed, *Revolutionary Conscience*, 36.

128   God, in other words Grodzins, *American Heretic*, 144–45.

128   Parker's views were shaped Ibid., 113–15.

128   "These laws refuse" Ralph Waldo Emerson, "Divinity School Address," July 15, 1838, https://emersoncentral.com/texts/nature-addresses-lectures/addresses /divinity-school-address/.

128   "So beautiful, so just" Grodzins, *American Heretic*, 115; Teed, *Revolutionary Conscience*, 39.

128   "There are some things" Chesbrough, *"God Ordained This War,"* 36.

129   "moral universe" Cobbe, ed., *Collected Works of Theodore Parker*, vol. 2, *Sermons and Prayers*, 48.

129   "solitary, poor, nasty" Cohen and Fermon, *Princeton Readings in Political Thought*, 208.

129   Attracted to works Teed, *Revolutionary Conscience*, 151–58, 206–11.

129   "In respect to" Ibid., 153. "If anything, his use of racial explanations for America's political and cultural crisis had become more frequent and more offensive in the late 1850s," Teed wrote. Ibid., 206.

129   In January 1858 Ibid.

129   Parker was in correspondence Herndon and Weik, *Herndon's Life of Lincoln*, xvii.

129   "There must be unity of action" Cobbe, ed., *Collected Works of Theodore Parker*, vol. 5, *Discourses on Slavery*, 104–5.

129   "There is what I call" Ibid., 105–6.

130   "To speak in the pulpit" Ethan J. Kytle, *Romantic Reformers and the Antislavery Struggle in the Civil War Era* (New York, 2014), 89–90.

130   The issues For the Compromise of 1850, see, for instance, Freehling, *Road to Disunion*, 1:487–535; Blumenthal, *Wrestling with His Angel*, 52–104; Foner, *Fiery Trial*, 59, 87, 159; Holt, *Rise and Fall*, 459–552; Wilentz, *Rise of American Democracy*, 637–45, 649, 652–53, 658–67; Fergus M. Bordewich, *America's Great Debate: Henry Clay, Stephen A. Douglas, and the Compromise That Preserved the Union* (New York, 2012).

130 "I HAVE WITNESSED" Charles M. Wiltse, *John C. Calhoun: Sectionalist* (Indianapolis, 1951), 457.

130 "IT IS A GREAT MISTAKE" David M. Potter, *The Impending Crisis, 1848–1861* (New York, 1976), 100–101. See also Wiltse, *John C. Calhoun: Sectionalist*, 458–69. Too ill to speak himself, Calhoun had written his speech, which was read aloud by James M. Mason of Virginia. Ibid., 458–60.

130 "THE NATURE OF THE DISEASE" Wiltse, *John C. Calhoun: Sectionalist*, 467.

131 THE QUESTION NOW Ibid., 464–65.

131 "A GOOD—A POSITIVE GOOD" Calhoun, *Speech on the Reception of Abolition Petitions*, 6. Robert Toombs of Georgia, seeking the speakership of the House in 1849, had said, "I do not hesitate to avow before this House and the Country, and in the presence of the living God, that if, by your legislation, you seek to drive us from the territories of California and New Mexico, purchased by the common blood and treasure of the whole people, and to abolish slavery in this District, thereby attempting to fix a national degradation upon half the states of this Confederacy, *I am for disunion*." Potter, *Impending Crisis*, 94.

131 "WE CANNOT, IN OUR JUDGMENT" Bordewich, *America's Great Debate*, 179.

131 THE CONSTITUTION MIGHT ALLOW Ibid. Of the fate that would await the threatened "new Republic of the South," Seward said Southerners would one day ask, "What is all this for? What intolerable wrong, what unfraternal injustice, have rendered these calamities unavoidable? What gain will this unnatural revolution bring to us? The answer will be: 'All this is done to secure the institution of African slavery.'" *The National Era*, March 21, 1850, 48.

131 "GIVE US A FANATICAL" Bordewich, *America's Great Debate*, 181.

131 "WHETHER THE INSTITUTION OF SLAVERY" *Congressional Globe*, 31st Congress, 1st Session, Appendix, 383–84. To buttress attacks against religiously motivated abolitionists, Professor Moses Stuart, of the Andover Theological Seminary, published a pamphlet, *Conscience and the Constitution*, repeating the biblical defenses of slavery. Moses Stuart, *Conscience and the Constitution: With Remarks on the Recent Speech of the Hon. Daniel Webster in the Senate of the United States on the Subject of Slavery* (Boston, 1850).

131 "IF THE BIBLE DEFENDS SLAVERY" Cobbe, ed., *Collected Works of Theodore Parker*, vol. 5, *Discourses on Slavery*, 122.

131 "THE AMERICAN IDEA" Ibid., 131–32.

132 THE COMPROMISE OF 1850 "Compromise of 1850: Primary Documents in American History," LOC, https://guides.loc.gov/compromise-1850.

132 A STRENGTHENED FUGITIVE SLAVE ACT See, for instance, Wilentz, *Rise of American Democracy*, 645–53.

132 ENDING DUE PROCESS Foner, *Fiery Trial*, 68.

132 KNOWN MORE WIDELY S. M. Africanus, "The Fugitive Slave Law" (Hartford, Conn., 1850), https://memory.loc.gov/ammem/aaohtml/exhibit/aopart3b.html.

132 WELCOMED A NEW CHILD *LDBD, 1849–1860*, 96.

132 MARY LINCOLN STILL MISSED WASHINGTON Willis Steell, "Mrs. Abraham Lincoln and Her Friends," *Munsey's Magazine*, February 1909, 617.

132 "WIFE IS A WOMAN" Howard, "Biographical Notes," Abraham Lincoln Papers, LOC.

132 "HE WAS STILL" Hay and Nicolay, *AL: A History*, 1:372.

132 ON TUESDAY, JANUARY 11 *LDBD, 1849–1860*, 91; Blumenthal, *Wrestling with His Angel*, 473–75.

132 "THERE ARE MEN" Ralph Waldo Emerson, "Power," https://emersoncentral.com/texts/the-conduct-of-life/power/.

132   "ALL SUCCESSFUL MEN" Ibid.

133   STOWE'S *UNCLE TOM'S CABIN* See, for instance, Potter, *Impending Crisis,* 140; Wilentz, *Rise of American Democracy,* 655–58.

133   "NEVER SINCE BOOKS" Frank Luther Mott, *Golden Multitudes: The Story of Best Sellers in the United States* (New York, 1947), 114.

133   AFTER A TRIP TO ITALY Ibid., 118. Known as "this Iliad of the Blacks," the book conveyed great emotional force. Ibid., 114, 119. "It may plausibly be argued that Mrs. Stowe's characters were impossible and her Negroes were blackface stereotypes, that her plot was sentimental, her dialect absurd, her literary technique crude, and her overall picture of the conditions of slavery distorted," the scholar David M. Potter observed. "But without any of the vituperation in which the abolitionists were so fluent, and with a sincere though unappreciated effort to avoid blaming the South, she made vivid the plight of the slave as a human being held in bondage." Potter, *Impending Crisis,* 140.

133   ANOTHER, LESSER-KNOWN NOVEL Nathaniel Beverley Tucker, *The Partisan Leader: A Tale of the Future,* introduction by C. Hugh Holman (Chapel Hill, N.C., 1971).

133   "IF WE WILL NOT" Tucker, *Partisan Leader,* xi–xii. Of a main character, Tucker wrote: "Bred up in the school of State rights, and thoroughly imbued with its doctrines, he had . . . been accustomed to look, with a jealous eye, on the progressive usurpations of the Federal Government. In the hope of arresting these, he had exerted more than his usual activity in aiding to put down the younger Adams, and to elevate his successor. Though no candidate for the spoils of victory, no man rejoiced more sincerely in the result of that contest; and, until the emanation of the proclamation of December, 1832, he had given his hearty approbation, and steady, though quiet, support to the administration of Andrew Jackson." Ibid., 37.

The National Intelligencer understood the significance of Tucker's book. "No one who has been familiar with the topics and tone of the discussions in the South for the last two years but will at once recognize in this fiction—a fiction not at all more strange than the reality—the projected shadow of what has already come to pass," the newspaper wrote in 1851. "From that day to this these defeated 'partisans' have spared no pains to make their story come true, by diffusing doubts and discontents into the quiet homes as well as the political circles of the South, with a view to bring about a revolution, which, had their ambition succeeded, would, in its consequences, have desolated those homes, broken up those abodes of peace and happiness, and devastated the country with the flames of a fierce, unsparing, and unrelenting civil war." Ibid., "Explanatory Introduction," no page number.

133   THE SAME YEAR AS *AMERICAN SLAVERY AS IT IS* Theodore Weld, *American Slavery as It Is: Testimony of a Thousand Witnesses* (New York, 1839).

133   LITERATURE INSPIRED Ripley, ed., *Black Abolitionist Papers,* 4:403, is a useful summary.

133   THERE WERE NOVELS Ibid.

133   IN THE TRADITION OF PHILLIS WHEATLEY See, for instance, Carretta, ed., *Unchained Voices,* 59–62; Lowance, ed., *Against Slavery,* 25–28.

133   IN A LETTER . . . HARRIET A. JACOBS Ripley, ed., *Black Abolitionist Papers,* 4:164–69.

133   "BRUTAL PASSION" Ibid., 166.

133   "BORE TOO STRONG" Ibid.

133   "AND SUCH" Ibid., 167.

134   "HAS NOT TOLD" Ibid.

134   "IS THIS THE LITTLE WOMAN" Harriet Beecher Stowe, "Abraham Lincoln," in Holzer, ed., *TLA,* 84.

134   THE NEBRASKA TERRITORY *Nebraska Trailblazer,* Nebraska Historical Society, https://history.nebraska.gov/sites/history.nebraska.gov/files/doc/ntb6.pdf.

134 To organize the territory On the debates over the Kansas-Nebraska Act, see, for instance, Freehling, *Road to Disunion*, 1:536–65; Blumenthal, *Wrestling with His Angel*, 272–323; Potter, *Impending Crisis*, 145–76; Wilentz, *Rise of American Democracy*, 671–77; Hay and Nicolay, *AL: A History*, 1:330–64; Foner, *Fiery Trial*, 63–72.

134 to lay plans Wilentz, *Rise of American Democracy*, 671–73.

134 through popular sovereignty See, for instance, Richard Bourke and Quentin Skinner, eds., *Popular Sovereignty in Historical Perspective* (Cambridge, UK, 2016); Christopher Childers, *The Failure of Popular Sovereignty: Slavery, Manifest Destiny, and the Radicalization of Southern Politics* (Lawrence, Kans., 2012); Nicole Etcheson, "'A Living, Creeping Lie': Abraham Lincoln on Popular Sovereignty," *JALA* 29, no. 2 (2008): 1–25. On Douglas's problematic relationship with the idea, see Blumenthal, *Wrestling with His Angel*, 95–96.

134 He had tried Wilentz, *Rise of American Democracy*, 672.

134 "raise a hell of a storm" Ibid., 672.

134 "slave power" See, for instance, Russel B. Nye, "The Slave Power Conspiracy: 1830–1860," *Science and Society* 10, no. 3 (1946): 262–74. In 1836, James Henry Hammond connected the positive-good thesis of slavery with a sense of white Southern exceptionalism in a tone of white Southern resentment. "Slavery is said to be an evil; that it impoverishes the people, and destroys their morals," Hammond said. "If it be an evil, it is one to us alone, and we are contented with it—why should others interfere? But it is no evil. On the contrary, I believe it to be the greatest of all the great blessings which a kind Providence has bestowed upon our glorious region." *Selections from the Letters and Speeches of the Hon. James H. Hammond, of South Carolina* (New York, 1866), 34. See also Jenkins, *Pro-Slavery Thought*, 79–80.

134 "The great danger" Max Farrand, ed., *The Records of the Federal Convention of 1787* (New Haven, 1911), 1:476. On the role of slavery in the Constitutional Convention, see also Finkelman, *Slavery and the Founders*, 3–46; Jenkins, *Pro-Slavery Thought*, 149–99; Ralph Ketcham, *James Madison: A Biography* (Charlottesville, Va., 1990), 224–25; Wilentz, *No Property in Man*, 58–114.

135 white Southern nationalism See, for instance, McCardell, *Idea of a Southern Nation*.

135 the House had voted Wilentz, *Rise of American Democracy*, 671–72.

135 Then Douglas called for Ibid., 672; Hay and Nicolay, *AL: A History*, 1:344–51.

135 But Douglas's bill Wilentz, *Rise of American Democracy*, 672.

135 a fiery response Ibid., 672–74; Hay and Nicolay, *AL: A History*, 1:360–62.

136 "We arraign this bill" *Congressional Globe*, 33rd Congress, 1st Session, 281–82.

136 Tuesday, May 30, 1854 *LDBD, 1849–1860*, 123. To Douglas, the new states were a gateway to a glorious Western future. Freehling, *Road to Disunion*, 1:546. To William Seward, popular sovereignty signaled nothing but strife ahead. "Come on then, Gentlemen of the Slave States, since there is no escaping your challenge, I accept it in behalf of the cause of freedom," Seward said on Thursday, May 25, 1854. "We will engage in competition for the virgin soil of Kansas, and God give the victory to the side which is stronger in numbers as it is in right." Potter, *Impending Crisis*, 199.

136 "took us by surprise" CW, 2:282.

136 "aroused" Ibid., 4:67.

Chapter Ten: If All Earthly Power Were Given Me

137 "If the negro is a *man*" CW, 2:266.

137 "I have always hated" Lewis E. Lehrman, *Lincoln at Peoria: The Turning Point* (Mechanicsburg, Pa., 2008), 259.

137 GARRISON HAD LONG ARGUED Paul Finkelman, "Garrison's Constitution: The Covenant with Death and How It Was Made," *Prologue Magazine* 32, no. 4 (Winter 2000), https://www.archives.gov/publications/prologue/2000/winter/garrisons -constitution-1.html.

137 ON THE FOURTH OF JULY Ibid.; Mayer, *All on Fire*, 443–45; "'A Covenant with Death and an Agreement with Hell,'" Massachusetts Historical Society, https://www .masshist.org/object-of-the-month/objects/a-covenant-with-death-and-an -agreement-with-hell-2005-07-01.

137 THAT INCLUDED SPEECHES Mayer, *All on Fire*, 443–44.

137 "THE LAW WILL NEVER" Ibid., 444. "With his gift for aphorism," Mayer observed, "Thoreau distilled a dozen years of Garrisonian criticism into a single sentence." Ibid.

137 "THE SOURCE AND PARENT" Ibid., 445.

137 "SO PERISH ALL" Ibid.

137 "AND LET ALL THE PEOPLE" Ibid.

137 "WOULD YET EXECUTE" "'A Covenant with Death and an Agreement with Hell.'"

138 "SECESSION FROM THE PRESENT" Phillips, *Can Abolitionists Vote or Take Office Under the United States Constitution?*, 3.

138 HE AMENDED GARRISON'S CRY Tillery, "Inevitability of the Douglass-Garrison Conflict," 144–45.

138 THE VOLUNTARY REMOVAL Lincoln linked this opinion with the biblical imagery of the exodus of the people of Israel from Egypt. "Pharaoh's country was cursed with plagues, and his hosts were drowned in the Red Sea for striving to retain a captive people who had already served them more than four hundred years," Lincoln said in 1852. "May like disasters never befall us! If as the friends of colonization hope, the present and coming generations of our countrymen shall by any means, succeed in freeing our land from the dangerous presence of slavery; and, at the same time, in restoring a captive people to their long-lost father-land, with bright prospects for the future; and this too, so gradually, that neither races nor individuals shall have suffered by the change, it will indeed be a glorious consummation." CW, 2:132.

138 MONDAY, JULY 10, 1854 H. Edward Richardson, *Cassius Marcellus Clay: Firebrand of Freedom* (Lexington, Ky., 1976), 73–74.

138 "WHITTLING STICKS, AS HE" Ibid., 74.

138 "STRIKE AT THE MONSTER AGGRESSOR" Ibid., 73.

138 ALL HIS LIFE Ibid., 71.

138 BEFORE THE 1913 RATIFICATION "Electing Senators," Senate Historical Office, https://www.senate.gov/general/Features/ElectingSenators_AHistorical Perspective.htm; Matthew Pinsker, "Senator Abraham Lincoln," *JALA* 14, no. 2 (Summer 1993): 1–21.

139 "IT WAS A PECULIARITY" Hay and Nicolay, *AL: A History*, 1:378.

139 BORN IN 1813 See, for instance, "Stephen A. Douglas," https://www.senate.gov /senators/FeaturedBios/Featured_Bio_Douglas_Stephen.htm; "Stephen Douglas," https://ohiohistorycentral.org/w/Stephen_Douglas; Robert W. Johannsen, *Stephen A. Douglas* (Urbana and Chicago, 1997), is comprehensive.

139 "EXCELLENT PRIZE FIGHTING QUALITIES" Johannsen, *Stephen A. Douglas*, 4.

139 "NO MAN OF HIS TIME" Douglas R. Egerton, *Year of Meteors: Stephen Douglas, Abraham Lincoln, and the Election That Brought on the Civil War* (New York, 2010), 7.

139 "SLOWLY, MEASUREDLY, DISTINCTLY" Sandburg, *Abraham Lincoln*, 2:10.

139 "HAD BEEN NOSING" "The Library and Abraham Lincoln," Illinois State Library

Heritage Project, https://www.ilsos.gov/departments/library/heritage_project/home/chapters/the-early-years-1840-to-1850/the-library-and-abraham-lincoln/; Brookhiser, *Founders' Son*, 151–52.

139   "The famous Georgia Pen" CW, 2:237–38.

140   "were proclaiming ourselves" Ibid., 242.

140   "covered with oak" Lehrman, *Lincoln at Peoria*, 52.

140   Senator Douglas had entered Peoria Lehrman, *Lincoln at Peoria*, 53. Peoria's grandees "seemed to assume that the Judge was the great man of the age—the greatest man of any age in the past, and greater than any man that may flourish in any age in the future." Ibid.

140   Lincoln arrived alone Ibid.; Wilson and Davis, eds., *Herndon's Informants*, 199.

140   checked in to room 84 Wilson and Davis, eds., *Herndon's Informants*, 161.

140   Peoria House hotel Lehrman, *Lincoln at Peoria*, 53. The next morning, "Mr. Douglas went immediately to Mr. L's room," Abner Y. Ellis recalled, "shook hands with him . . . & observed to him, 'I am very sorry that you have come as I well know your business." Davis and Wilson, eds., *Herndon's Informants*, 162.

140   at two o'clock CW, 2:247; Lehrman, *Lincoln at Peoria*, 53–55.

140   Douglas spoke first Wilson and Davis, eds., *Herndon's Informants*, 199–200. "Mr. L said it was the poorest speech that Douglas ever made," Abner Y. Ellis recalled. Ibid., 162. Another observer said, "I listened with much interest to his speech in defense of the repeal of the Missouri Compromise, but was not altogether satisfied with it." Lehrman, *Lincoln at Peoria*, 55.

141   "I do not propose" CW, 2:248–83.

141   Yet everything would have changed Ibid., 249–50; "Northwest Ordinance," LOC, https://www.loc.gov/rr/program//bib/ourdocs/northwest.html.

141   "*declared* indifference" CW, 2:255.

141   "I can not but" Ibid.

141   "I have no" Ibid.

142   "If all earthly power" Ibid., 255–56.

142   "When the white man" Ibid., 266.

142   "Let us re-adopt" Ibid., 276. In an echo of Theodore Parker's address in Boston from 1850, Lincoln added that freedom and slavery "cannot stand together. They are as opposite as God and mammon; and whoever holds to the one, must despise the other." Ibid., 275.

142   Lands owned and worked For a discussion of these issues, see, for instance, Holzer and Garfinkle, *Just and Generous Nation*, 33–44; Lehrman, *Lincoln at Peoria*, 141–42.

143   "The whole nation" CW, 2:268. See also Holzer and Garfinkle, *Just and Generous Nation*, 35–38.

143   "I confess I hate" CW, 2:320.

143   "I do not question" Harold Holzer, ed., *Lincoln as I Knew Him: Gossip, Tributes, and Revelations from His Best Friends and Worst Enemies* (Chapel Hill, N.C., 1999), 138.

143   Lincoln lost the campaign CW, 2:304–6. See also Hay and Nicolay, *AL: A History*, 1:383–84. In the balloting in Springfield on Tuesday, November 7, 1854, Lincoln (he was the 162nd voter of the day to appear at his precinct) was elected to the state house of representatives, an office he soon resigned in hopes of winning the legislature's election to a seat in the United States Senate. *LDBD, 1849–1860*, 131; Hay and Nicolay, *AL: A History*, 1:383–84. The politics of the moment in Illinois were complicated. "There was scarcely a member of Congress from Illinois—indeed, scarcely a prominent man in the State of any party—who did not conceive the flattering dream that he himself might become the lucky medium of compromise and har-

mony," Hay and Nicolay recalled. Filling two small notebooks with careful nota-
tions about each lawmaker, Lincoln also wrote allies—and possible allies—to press
his cause. *CW*, 2:296–98. "It has come round that a [W]hig may, by possibility, be
elected to the U.S. Senate; and I want the chance of being the man," he wrote
Thomas J. Henderson, an anti-Nebraska state representative. "You are a member
of the Legislature, and have a vote to give. Think it over, and see whether you can
do better than to go for me." Ibid., 288. After great back-and-forth, Lyman Trumbull, not Lincoln, was elected to the Senate—with Lincoln throwing his support to
Trumbull at the last minute to prevent the election of a Douglas ally. Ibid., 304–6.

143 "I REGRET MY DEFEAT" *CW*, 2:306.

143 FREE SOILERS, WHIGS, ANTI-NEBRASKA DEMOCRATS See, for instance, Gould, *Grand
Old Party*, 14–15; Blumenthal, *Wrestling with His Angel*, 380–82, 443–72; Heather
Cox Richardson, *To Make Men Free: A History of the Republican Party* (New York, 2014).
On the fall of the Whigs, see, for instance, Holt, *Rise and Fall*, 838–985; Wilentz,
Rise of American Democracy, 662–66, 792.

143 IN JACKSON, MICHIGAN Gould, *Grand Old Party*, 14.

143 "THAT IN VIEW" Ibid.

144 "FORCED UPON US" *Wisconsin Daily State Journal*, July 14, 1854.

144 "MADE SO PLAIN" *CW*, 2:222.

144 IN A LETTER Ibid., 320–23.

144 JOSHUA SPEED, A SLAVEHOLDER "Joshua Speed," Kentucky Government, Farming-
ton Historic Site, https://www.nps.gov/abli/learn/education/upload/JoshuaSpeed2
.pdf. See also Foner, *Fiery Trial*, 177.

144 "YOU MAY REMEMBER" *CW*, 2:320.

144 IN REACTION TO RISING Roy F. Nichols and Philip S. Klein, "Election of 1856" in
HAPE, 1:446–47.

144 "AMERICANS MUST RULE" Ibid., 451.

144 THE MOVEMENT HAD GAINED FORCE See, for instance, Wilentz, *Rise of American Democracy*, 679–96; Blumenthal, *Wrestling with His Angel*, 324–32; Hay and Nicolay, *AL:
A History*, 1:358; Michael F. Holt, *The Political Crisis of the 1850s* (New York, 1978),
156–81; Holt, *Rise and Fall*, 805; Howe, *What Hath God Wrought*, 822–27.

144 TWO SOCIETIES Wilentz, *Rise of American Democracy*, 681–82.

145 "AT THE BOTTOM" Gould, *Grand Old Party*, 6.

145 A KEY TEXT Holt, *Rise and Fall*, 847; Bruce Levine, "Conservatism, Nativism, and
Slavery: Thomas R. Whitney and the Origins of the Know-Nothing Party," *Journal
of American History* 88, no. 2 (September 2001): 455–88.

145 LINCOLN DISLIKED NATIVISM Burlingame, *AL*, 1:407–15; Blumenthal, *Wrestling with
His Angel*, 390–91; Donald, *Lincoln*, 169–70; White, *A. Lincoln*, 192–94.

145 "ON MY WAY DOWN" *CW*, 2:284–85.

145 "I AM NOT" Ibid., 323.

145 "INDEED I DO NOT" Ibid., 316.

145 LINCOLN URGED REPUBLICANS Burlingame, *AL*, 1:411–15.

145 "I HAVE NO OBJECTION" *CW*, 2:316. See also *LDBD, 1849–1860*, 150.

145 "GREAT MASS OF MANKIND" *CW*, 2:281–82.

146 "IS, TO-DAY, THE BEST HOPE" Ibid., 391.

Chapter Eleven: The Hateful Embrace of Slavery

147 "IT WOULD NOT" David Herbert Donald, *Charles Sumner and the Coming of the Civil War*
(New York, 1960), 249.

147 "JUDGE TANEY CAN DO" Frederick Douglass, "The Dred Scott Decision," https://
rbscp.lib.rochester.edu/4399.

147 "I CLEARLY SEE" CW, 2:548.

147 IN MIDSUMMER 1855 Ibid., 317–19. Lincoln's vision of the future was dark. "When
we were the political slaves of King George, and wanted to be free, we called the
maxim that 'all men are created equal' a self evident truth; but now when we have
grown fat, and have lost all dread of being slaves ourselves, we have become so
greedy to be *masters* that we call the same maxim 'a self-evident lie,'" he told Robertson. "The fourth of July has not quite dwindled away; it is still a great day—*for
burning fire-crackers!!!*" Ibid., 318.

148 "WHETHER BY THE ANNEXATION" Augustus Adams to Abraham Lincoln, December
17, 1854, Abraham Lincoln Papers, LOC; May, *Southern Dream*, xiii; Blumenthal,
Wrestling with His Angel, 347–53. Observers tied Cuba in particular to the possibility
of an independent, sustainable Southern confederacy. May, *Southern Dream*, 37. May
wrote: The "Kansas-Nebraska Act encouraged southerners in their desire to expand slavery; and the more antislavery interests railed, the more determined
southern expansionists became." Ibid.

148 PRESIDENT PIERCE HAD TRIED May, *Southern Dream*, 67–76.

148 PRESIDENT JAMES BUCHANAN REVIVED Ibid., 163–89.

148 "WE ANTICIPATE NO TERMINUS" Jenkins, *Pro-Slavery Thought*, 147; William H. Holcombe, *The Alternative: A Separate Nationality, or the Africanization of the South* (New Orleans, 1860), 7.

148 "WE ARE LOOKING" Henry Cleveland, ed., *Alexander Stephens in Public and Private*
(Philadelphia, 1886), 645. In a sermon at St. Peter's Church in Charleston, the
Reverend W. O. Prentiss said, "The Lone Star of our Empire attracts our political
needle to the tropics; there with the Africans we will expand." Jenkins, *Pro-Slavery
Thought*, 147.

148 "THE ONLY POSSIBLE WAY" James Redpath, *Echoes of Harpers Ferry* (Boston, 1860),
476.

148 ONE MEANS OF CONQUEST See, for instance, Robert E. May, *Manifest Destiny's Underworld: Filibustering in Antebellum America* (Chapel Hill, N.C., 2002); May, *Southern
Dream*; David C. Keehn, *Knights of the Golden Circle: Secret Empire, Southern Secession, Civil
War* (Baton Rouge, La., 2013); Charles H. Brown, *Agents of Manifest Destiny: The Lives
and Times of the Filibusters* (Chapel Hill, N.C., 1980).

148 DERIVED FROM SPANISH, FRENCH, AND DUTCH WORDS Brown, *Agents of Manifest Destiny*, 17–18; May, *Manifest Destiny's Underworld*, 3–4.

148 SOME FILIBUSTERING EXPEDITIONS See, for instance, May, *Southern Dream*, 90–91;
134. On Monday, August 11, 1851, a band of filibusters led by the Caracas-born
Narciso López, a veteran of the Spanish army, attacked Cuba. López had long plot-
ted to liberate the island from Spanish control and bring it under U.S.—specifically
white Southern—influence, a cause that intrigued and even thrilled the slave-
owning interest. May, *Southern Dream*, 25–29. "I look to the acquisition of Cuba as
of great importance to the South," John Tyler, Jr., son of the former president, had
written the month before. McCardell, *Idea of the Southern Nation*, 248. López's invasion came to naught; much to the outrage of some American observers, López was
executed. May, *Southern Dream*, 28–29. "American blood has been shed," the New
Orleans *Courier* wrote. "It cries aloud for vengeance . . . blood for blood! Our
brethren must be avenged! Cuba must be seized." John Hope Franklin, *The Militant
South, 1800–1861* (Cambridge, Mass., 1970), 109.

148 JOHN A. QUITMAN OF MISSISSIPPI May, *Southern Dream*, 46–67. See also Robert E.

May, *John A. Quitman: Old South Crusader* (Baton Rouge, La., 1985); Brown, *Agents of Manifest Destiny*, 252–57. A newspaper described Quitman this way in an August 1855 report on a speech he delivered to a friendly audience: "His tall, erect form—his simple dress—the firm lips which more than once trembled with earnest emotions beneath the white moustache—his calm, reflective eye, sometimes flashing with momentary passion, and again assuming its naturally amiable expression—all recalled associations to many men present on the occasion, of other and more exciting scenes, where in the hottest charge that voice, now somewhat enfeebled, was heard above the confusion of battle." His general topic was "the Slavery Question, as viewed from the elevation of States Rights." "General Quitman's Speech," August 18, 1855, Lovell Family Collection, P71, Box 4, Folder 123, William R. Laurie University Archives and Special Collections, University of the South, Sewanee, Tennessee.

149   "As a Southern[er]" "General Quitman's Speech," August 18, 1855, Lovell Family Collection, Sewanee, Tennessee.

149   Cuba was also affixed C. A. Bridges, "The Knights of the Golden Circle: A Filibustering Fantasy," *Southwestern Historical Quarterly* 44, no. 3 (1941): 287–302; Ollinger Crenshaw, "The Knights of the Golden Circle: The Career of George Bickley," *American Historical Review* 47, no. 1 (1941): 23–50; Randolph B. "Mike" Campbell, "Knights of the Golden Circle," *Texas State Historical Association Handbook of Texas*, https://archive.ph/L5xpk.

149   Led by a proslavery Southerner May, *Southern Dream*, 149–50; Keehn, *Knights of the Golden Circle*, 6–16. "With this addition to either our *system*, the Union, or to a Southern Confederacy, we should possess every element of national wealth and power," Bickley said. "We shall have in our own hands the Cotton, Tobacco, Sugar, Coffee, Rice, Corn and Tea lands of the continent, and the world's great storehouse of mineral wealth." May, *Southern Dream*, 150. On the racial imperialism and religious claims of the white Southern nationalists, see, for instance, Samuel Davies Baldwin, *Dominion; or, the Unity and Trinity of the Human Race; With the Divine Political Constitution of the World, and the Divine Rights of Shem, Ham and Japeth* (Nashville, 1858), 448–49; Jenkins, *Pro-Slavery Thought*, 253–54. "As for the continents, the location of American Japheth [a reference to Genesis 10] is the natural seat for the capital of dominion," Baldwin, a Methodist clergyman, wrote. "Shem and Ham, by transgression, having forfeited all right to any share in the supreme government of the world, its entire functions devolve upon Japheth, just as the dominion of the world passed from Adam, by transgression, to Christ, the second Adam." Baldwin, *Dominion*, 447–49.

149   adventurers such as William Walker May, *Southern Dream*, 77–135. See also William Walker, *The War in Nicaragua* (New York, 1860); Blumenthal, *Wrestling with His Angel*, 349–53; Brown, *Agents of Manifest Destiny*, 174–408.

149   "Grey-Eyed Man of Destiny" May, *Southern Dream*, 77.

149   a restless young man Ibid., 78–83.

150   Walker reinstituted slavery May, *Southern Dream*, 106. "The decree . . . made [Americans in Nicaragua] the champions of the Southern States of the Union in the conflict truly styled 'irrepressible,' between free and slave labor," Walker wrote in a memoir. Walker, *War in Nicaragua*, 263.

150   "If we look" Ibid., 271.

150   "men of the South" Ibid., 274.

150   "the inhabitants" William Harper, *Memoir on Slavery, Read Before the Society for the Advancement of Learning of South Carolina* (Charleston, S.C., 1838), 3.

150 "BUT THE FIRST . . . STEP" Gould, *Grand Old Party*, 12. "I could travel from Boston to Chicago by the light of my own effigy," Stephen Douglas recalled. "All along the Western Reserve of Ohio I could find my effigy upon every tree we passed." Johannsen, *Stephen A. Douglas*, 451.

150 "WE WILL BE COMPELLED" Wilentz, *Rise of American Democracy*, 678.

150 "YOU SAY IF" CW, 2:322. "The slave-breeders and slave-traders are a small, odious and detested class, among you," Lincoln added, "and yet in politics, they dictate the course of all of you, and are as completely your masters, as you are the masters of your own negroes." Ibid.

150 IN LAWRENCE . . . "BORDER RUFFIANS" Potter, *Impending Crisis*, 207–9; "The Sack of Lawrence, 1856," http://www.eyewitnesstohistory.com/lawrencesack.htm.

150 "BREATHING LOUD-MOUTHED THREATS" Donald, *Charles Sumner and the Coming of the Civil War*, 234.

151 "LIT UP THE EVENING SKY" "The Sack of Lawrence, 1856."

151 SUMNER . . . HAD RISEN TO SPEAK Blumenthal, *All the Powers of Earth*, 105–55; Donald, *Charles Sumner and the Coming of the Civil War*, 236–37; Potter, *Impending Crisis*, 209–10.

151 BORN IN BOSTON Donald, *Charles Sumner and the Coming of the Civil War*, 2.

151 RAISED IN A HOUSE Ibid., 4.

151 "GAWKY SUMNER" Ibid., 5.

151 "HE WAS TALL" Ibid., 28–29.

151 SUMNER'S DEVOTION TO ABOLITION See, for instance, ibid., 142. "I have been a mark for abuse," Sumner once remarked. "I have been attacked bitterly; but I have consoled myself by what J. Q. Adams said to me . . . "No man is abused whose influence is not felt.'" Ibid.

151 WITH A LARGE AUDIENCE Ibid., 237.

151 "IT IS THE RAPE" Ibid.

151 SUMNER EVISCERATED He told Douglas that "against him is God." Potter, *Impending Crisis*, 210. Butler, Sumner said, was a "Don Quixote who had chosen a mistress to whom he has made his vows, and who . . . though polluted in the sight of the world is chaste in his sight—I mean the harlot, slavery." Ibid. Of Butler's state, Sumner said: "Were the whole history of South Carolina blotted out of existence, from its very beginning down to the day of the last election of the Senator to his present seat on this floor, civilization might lose—I do not say how little, but surely less than it has already gained by the example of Kansas, in its valiant struggle against oppression." Donald, *Charles Sumner and the Coming of the Civil War*, 239–40.

151 LABIAL PARALYSIS Donald, *Charles Sumner and the Coming of the Civil War*, 239.

151 "DUTY TO RELIEVE" Ibid., 243.

151 "I . . . SPECULATED SOMEWHAT" Ibid., 243–44.

151 A GOLD-HEADED CANE Ibid., 244.

151 BROOKS WALKED INTO THE SENATE Ibid., 245.

151 "MR. SUMNER" Ibid., 246.

151 THE CONGRESSMAN DID NOT FINISH Ibid.

151 "EVERY LICK WENT" Ibid.

151 "I . . . GAVE HIM" Ibid., 247.

152 SOAKED IN BLOOD Ibid., 248–49.

152 VILIFIED IN THE NORTH Ibid., 249–60.

152 "IT WOULD NOT TAKE" Ibid., 249. "I do not see how a barbarous community and a civilized community can constitute one state," Ralph Waldo Emerson observed. "I think we must get rid of slavery, or we must get rid of freedom." Ibid., 260.

152 MILITANT ABOLITIONIST JOHN BROWN Potter, *Impending Crisis*, 211–12; Blumenthal, *All the Powers of Earth*, 157–71.

152 JOHN BROWN LED ASSAULTS Potter, *Impending Crisis*, 211–12.

152 THE BODIES OF THE VICTIMS Ibid., 212.

152 SEVERAL HAD DIED Ibid.

152 "BLEEDING KANSAS" Ibid., 214.

152 LINCOLN WAS CHOSEN *LDBD, 1849–1860*, 170.

152 "THE EVILS TO BE APPREHENDED" Ibid., 171.

152 "HE IS ABOUT SIX FEET HIGH" Ibid., 173.

152 EVIDENCE OF LINCOLN'S PROMINENCE Ibid., 171–72; Burlingame, *AL*, 1:422–24; Blumenthal, *All the Powers of Earth*, 225–35.

152 PHILADELPHIA'S MUSICAL FUND HALL Nichols and Klein, "Election of 1856," 438. "You are here today," party chairman Edwin D. Morgan told the delegates, "to give a direction to a movement which is to decide whether the people of the United States are to be hereafter and forever chained to the present national policy of the extension of slavery." Ibid., 440.

153 WILLIAM L. DAYTON OF NEW JERSEY Ibid., 439. William B. Archer of Illinois—described as "a grey-haired old gent, slightly bent with age"—put Lincoln forward for the vice presidency. On the floor, Lincoln was nominated by Representative John Allison of Pennsylvania, who called him a "prince of good fellows"; Archer then rose. He had known Lincoln, he told the assembly, "for 30 years. He had lived in Illinois 40 years. He had gone there when Illinois was a Territory, and had lived there until it had grown to be a populous and flourishing State. During thirty years of that time, he had known Abraham Lincoln, and he knew him well. He was born in gallant Kentucky, and was now in the prime of life . . . and enjoying remarkable good health. And, besides, the speaker knew him to be as pure a patriot as ever lived." Lincoln, moreover, would deliver what was needed: votes. Archer "would give the Convention to understand, that with [Lincoln] on the ticket . . . Illinois was safe with him."

A voice from the Ohio delegation rang out.

"Will he fight?" the man cried.

"Yes," Archer emphatically replied. Burlingame, *AL*, 1:422–23.

A former U.S. House colleague of Lincoln's, John Van Dyke of New Jersey, also weighed in. "I knew Abraham Lincoln in Congress well, and for months I sat by his side," Van Dyke told the convention on Thursday, June 19. "I knew him all through, and knew him to be a first-rate man in every respect." CW, 2:346.

Lincoln was grateful to Van Dyke. "Allow me to thank you for your kind notice of me in the Philadelphia Convention," Lincoln wrote to his old colleague in late June. "When you meet Judge Dayton present my respects, and tell him I think him a far better man than I for the position he is in, and that I shall support both him and Colonel Frémont most cordially." Ibid. Privately, though, Lincoln believed that Supreme Court Justice John McLean of Ohio, who had run second to Frémont for the presidential nomination, would have been the stronger candidate. *LDBD, 1849–1860*, 172; Nichols and Klein, "Election of 1856," 439. Appointed to the Court by Andrew Jackson, McLean had said in May 1856 that he planned to support Dred Scott's plea, adding, "I never doubted that Congress had this power [to prohibit slavery in a territory], and I could never have expressed doubt on the subject." CW, 2:342–43. "It would have been easier for us, I think, had we got McLean," Lincoln wrote Lyman Trumbull after the Republican convention. *LDBD, 1849–1860*, 172.

153 Lincoln was in Urbana *LDBD, 1849–1860,* 172.

153 With good humor Ibid.

153 At Cincinnati's Smith and Nixon's Hall Nichols and Klein, "Election of 1856," 438–39. On the 1856 campaign generally, see Blumenthal, *All the Powers of Earth,* 205–65.

153 "Black Republicans" Nichols and Klein, "Election of 1856," 440.

153 "All this talk" CW, 2:355.

153 In notes he wrote out Ibid., 349–53. "It is constantly objected to Frémont & Dayton, that they are supported by a *sectional* party who, by their *sectionalism,* endanger the National Union," Lincoln wrote in 1856. "The thing which gives most color to the charge of Sectionalism, made against those who oppose the spread of slavery into free territory, is the fact that *they* can get no votes in the slave-states, while their opponents get all, or nearly so, in the slave-states, and also, a large number in the free States. To state it in another way, the Extensionists can get votes all over the Nation, while the Restrictionists can get them only in the free states. This being the fact, *why* is it so? . . . It is because, in that question, the people of the South have an immediate palpable and immensely great pecuniary interest; while, with the people of the North, it is merely an abstract question of moral right, with only *slight,* and *remote* pecuniary interest added. . . . Moral principle is all, or nearly all, that unites us of the North," Lincoln privately observed. "Pity 'tis, it is so, but this is a looser bond, than pecuniary interest." Ibid.

153 "Have we no interest" Ibid., 363–64. He added: "We stand at once the wonder and admiration of the whole world, and we must enquire what it is that has given us so much prosperity, and we shall understand that to give up that one thing, would be to give up all future prosperity. This cause is that every man can make himself." Ibid., 364.

153 "They insist that" Ibid.

154 "great high-priest" Ibid., 366–67.

154 "the depot master" Ibid., 368.

154 November brought bad news https://uselectionatlas.org/RESULTS/national .php?f=0&year=1856. See also Burlingame, *AL,* 1:433–35.

154 "Extremes beget extremes" Franklin Pierce, Fourth Annual Message, December 2, 1856, https://www.presidency.ucsb.edu/documents/fourth-annual-message-7.

154 "Our government rests" CW, 2:385.

154 "Can we not" Ibid.

154 "delightful and magnificent" *LDBD, 1849–1860,* 189–90.

154 "Within the last" Ibid., 190.

155 "the will of the majority" James Buchanan, "Inaugural Address," March 4, 1857, https://www.presidency.ucsb.edu/documents/inaugural-address-33.

155 the case of Dred Scott Wilentz, *Rise of American Democracy,* 708–15; Blumenthal, *All the Powers of Earth,* 267–306; Hay and Nicolay, *AL: A History,* 2:58–80; Walter Ehrlich, *They Have No Rights: Dred Scott's Struggle for Freedom* (Westport, Conn., 1979); Walter Ehrlich, "Was the Dred Scott Case Valid," *Journal of American History* 55, no. 2 (September 1968): 256–65; Don E. Fehrenbacher, *The Dred Scott Case: Its Significance in American Law and Politics* (New York, 1979); Gossie Harold Hudson, "Black Americans vs. Citizenship: The Dred Scott Decision," *Negro History Bulletin* 46, no. 1 (1983): 26–28; Missouri Digital Heritage: Dred Scott: 150th Anniversary Commemoration, Office of the Missouri Secretary of State, https://www.sos.mo.gov /archives/resources/dredscott.asp. On Taney, see, for instance, Bernard Christian Steiner, *Life of Roger Brooke Taney: Chief Justice of the United States Supreme Court* (Balti-

more, 1922); Samuel Tyler, *Memoir of Roger Brooke Taney, LLD, Chief Justice of the Supreme Court of the United States* (Baltimore, 1872).

155   "ONCE FREE, ALWAYS FREE" Missouri State Archives, https://www.sos.mo.gov /archives/resources/africanamerican/scott/scott.

155   IN A MAJOR VICTORY Wilentz, *Rise of American Democracy*, 710.

155   IN THE STATE COURT'S MAJORITY OPINION Missouri State Archives, https://www .sos.mo.gov/archives/resources/africanamerican/scott/scott.

155   "DARK AND FELL SPIRIT" Davis, *Problem of Slavery in the Age of Revolution*, 519.

155   SEVEN WERE DEMOCRATS Hay and Nicolay, *AL: A History*, 2:69.

155   ANNOUNCED IN MARCH 1857 Dred Scott, Plaintiff in Error, v. John F. A. Sandford [*sic*], https://www.law.cornell.edu/supremecourt/text/60/393.

156   "ARE NOT INCLUDED" Ibid.

156   "HAD FOR MORE THAN A CENTURY" Ibid.

156   THE SEVEN JUSTICES WERE DEPLOYING See, for instance, Wilentz, *Rise of American Democracy*, 706–15, and Hay and Nicolay, *AL: A History*, 2:70–71. One of the justices voting with the chief justice, James M. Wayne of Georgia, a Jackson appointee, acknowledged this, writing, "The case involves private rights of value, and constitutional principles of the highest importance, about which there had become such a difference of opinion that the peace and harmony of the country required the settlement of them by judicial decision." Ibid.

156   "YOU WILL READILY ASK ME" Frederick Douglass, "The Dred Scott Decision," https://rbscp.lib.rochester.edu/4399.

156   LINCOLN FOUND THE RULING CW, 2:401.

156   "CHIEF JUSTICE TANEY" Ibid., 403.

157   IN AT LEAST FIVE OF THE THIRTEEN Ibid. "These colored persons were not only included in the body of 'the people of the United States,' by whom the Constitution was ordained and established," Curtis had noted in words Lincoln approvingly cited, "but in at least five of the States they had the power to act, and, doubtless, did act, by their suffrages, upon the question of its adoption." Ibid.

157   NEW JERSEY AND NORTH CAROLINA Ibid., 403–4.

157   STATE LEGISLATURES HAD MADE Ibid.

157   "ALL THE POWERS" Ibid., 404.

157   "IT IS NOT RESISTANCE" Ibid., 401. To Lincoln, the struggle was larger than the Supreme Court, though the Supreme Court had just made the struggle all the harder. "We think its decisions on Constitutional questions, when fully settled, should control, not only the particular cases decided, but the general policy of the country, subject to be disturbed only by amendments of the Constitution as provided in that instrument itself. More than this would be revolution." Ibid.

157   HE WAS ALREADY IN CONFERENCE *LDBD, 1849–1860*, 192.

157   "THE VICISSITUDES OF" Herndon and Weik, *Herndon's Life of Lincoln*, 304.

157   "THE SUCCESSOR OF" *LDBD, 1849–1860*, 194.

157   "I CLAIM" CW, 2:548.

157   "STRENGTH OF LARGE FEE" *LDBD, 1849–1860*, 201.

157   "THE SUMMER HAS SO STRANGELY" Ibid., 198.

158   "I OFTEN LAUGH" Ibid., 201.

158   BACK AT HOME CW, 2:404–5. Lincoln thought he might finally have Douglas where he wanted him. The Democrat James Shields had lost in a Senate race, and William A. Richardson, another Democrat, had been defeated by a Republican for governor in 1856—victories Lincoln attributed to the "untimely agitation, and its gross breach of national faith" produced by the "blaze" Douglas had ignited

with the repeal of the Missouri Compromise. "He has seen his chief aids in his own State, Shields and Richardson, politically speaking, successively tried, convicted, and executed, for an offense not their own, but his," Lincoln remarked in Springfield in June 1857. "And now he sees his own case, standing next on the docket for trial." Ibid.

158 THE STORY IS TOLD Tarbell, *In the Footsteps*, 328.

Chapter Twelve: By White Men for the Benefit of White Men

159 "Now, I DO NOT BELIEVE" CW, 3:10.

159 "I HAVE AN ABIDING FAITH" Ibid., 346.

159 "ON STRAY ENVELOPES" Herndon and Weik, *Herndon's Life of Lincoln*, 324. The year 1858 had begun oddly in the politics of Illinois. The great proponent of popular sovereignty, Douglas, fell out with President Buchanan and many Democrats when they attempted to force an illegitimate proslavery constitution for Kansas through the Congress. Hay and Nicolay, *AL: A History*, 2:90–134. From Springfield, Lincoln watched warily as Douglas appeared to be moving closer to the antislavery ground—a move that intrigued Republicans such as the editor Horace Greeley, who was open to receiving Douglas into the fold if Douglas would permanently turn on Buchanan. Herndon and Weik, *Herndon's Life of Lincoln*, 319–23; Hay and Nicolay, *AL: A History*, 139–43. "I think Greeley is not doing me right," a dejected Lincoln remarked to Herndon in their law office in early 1858. "His conduct, I believe, savors a little of injustice. I am a true Republican and have been tried already in the hottest part of the anti-slavery fight, and yet I find him taking up Douglas, a veritable dodger,—once a tool of the South, now its enemy,—and pushing him to the front. He forgets that when he does that he pulls me down at the same time." Herndon and Weik, *Herndon's Life of Lincoln*, 319–20. Herndon then proposed to travel east to reassure the antislavery forces that Lincoln was their man in Illinois. "Lincoln's greatest fear was that Douglas might be taken up by the Republicans," Herndon recalled. "Senator Seward, when I met him in Washington, assured me there was no danger of it, insisting that the Republicans nor anyone else could place any reliance on a man so slippery as Douglas." Ibid., 320–23. After a period of political pain for Lincoln, it became clear that Douglas would not be leaving the Democratic fold. "I think our prospects gradually, and steadily, grow better; though we are not yet clear out of the woods by a great deal," Lincoln observed in May 1858. "When I once begin making political speeches I shall have no respite till November." *LDBD, 1849–1860*, 216; CW, 2:446–47.

159 LINCOLN READ THE SPEECH *LDBD, 1849–1860*, 218; Herndon and Weik, *Herndon's Life of Lincoln*, 325–26.

159 "EVERY KINGDOM" Matthew 12:25, KJV.

159 "IT IS TRUE" Herndon and Weik, *Herndon's Life of Lincoln*, 325.

159 "THAT EXPRESSION" Ibid.

159 ILLINOIS REPUBLICAN CONVENTION *LDBD, 1849–1860*, 218; Burlingame, *AL*, 1:457–66.

160 AT EIGHT O'CLOCK Hay and Nicolay, *AL: A History*, 2:136.

160 "IF WE COULD FIRST" CW, 2:461. See also Burlingame, *AL*, 1:458–66; Blumenthal, *All the Powers of Earth*, 347–62; Foner, *Fiery Trial*, 99–103; Don E. Fehrenbacher, "The Origins and Purpose of Lincoln's 'House-Divided' Speech," *Mississippi Valley Historical Review* 46, no. 4 (1960): 615–43; Michael William Pfau, "The House That Abe Built: The 'House Divided' Speech and Republican Party Politics," *Rhetoric*

and Public Affairs 2, no. 4 (1999): 625–51; David Zarefsky, "Lincoln and the House Divided: Launching a National Political Career," *Rhetoric and Public Affairs* 13, no. 3 (2010): 421–53.

160 "WELL AND WISELY SAID" Foner, *Fiery Trial*, 111.

160 "I HAVE ALWAYS HATED" CW, 2:492.

160 "LET US DISCARD" Ibid., 501. "These words, with which Lincoln ended his speech," the historian Eric Foner noted, "constituted the most forthright affirmation of equality of Lincoln's entire career." Foner, *Fiery Trial*, 104.

160 "DO YOU DESIRE" CW, 3:9.

161 LINCOLN'S "N——ISM HAS" Burlingame, *AL*, 1:421.

161 "ALL ABOUT 'FREEDOM'" *LDBD, 1849–1860*, 175–76; CW, 2:359.

161 "I BELIEVE THIS GOVERNMENT" CW, 3:9. See also Burlingame, *AL*, 1:521.

161 REMEMBERING THAT HE HAD CW, 3:55–56. Douglas repeated the story in a later debate. Ibid., 105. See also Roy Morris, Jr., *The Long Pursuit: Abraham Lincoln's Thirty-Year Struggle with Stephen Douglas for the Heart and Soul of America* (Washington, D.C., and New York, 2008), 110.

161 "[T]HOSE OF YOU" CW, 3:56.

161 "THERE IS A NATURAL DISGUST" Ibid., 2:405. Sex and race were common topics—the popular term in white society was "amalgamation." "This very Dred Scott case affords a strong test as to which party most favors amalgamation, the Republicans or the dear Union-saving Democracy," Lincoln had said in 1857, alluding to Scott's two daughters. "Could we have had our way, the chances of these black girls, ever mixing their blood with that of white people, would have been diminished. . . . But Judge Douglas is delighted to have them decided to be slaves, and not human enough to have a hearing . . . and thus left subject to the forced concubinage of their masters, and liable to become the mothers of mulattoes in spite of themselves—the very state of case that produces nine tenths of all the mulattoes—all the mixing of blood in the nation." Stop the spread of slavery, Lincoln added, colonize the formerly enslaved, and there would be an end of it. "If white and black people never get together in Kansas, they will never mix blood in Kansas," Lincoln said. "That is at least one self-evident truth." Ibid., 408–9.

161 "SENATOR DOUGLAS IS" Ibid., 2:506.

161 "THE FAME AND PRESTIGE" Hay and Nicolay, *AL: A History*, 2:145.

161 LINCOLN CHALLENGED DOUGLAS CW, 2:522.

161 "WILL IT BE AGREEABLE" Ibid.

162 DOUGLAS ACCEPTED Ibid., 531–32; Hay and Nicolay, *AL: A History*, 2:145.

162 THE INCUMBENT WOULD Hay and Nicolay, *AL: A History*, 2:145; CW, 2:531–32. "Although by the terms as you propose, you take *four* openings and closes to my *three*," Lincoln told Douglas, "I accede, and thus close the arrangement." Ibid. As Hay and Nicolay saw it, the two brought different skills to the stage. "In the whole field of American politics no man has equaled Douglas in the expedients and strategy of debate," they wrote. "He was tireless, ubiquitous, unseizable. It would have been as easy to hold a globule of mercury under the finger's tip as to fasten him to a point he desired to evade. . . . He delighted in enlarging an opponent's assertion to a forced inference ridiculous in form and monstrous in dimensions. In spirit he was alert, combative, aggressive; in manner, patronizing and arrogant by turns." Hay and Nicolay, *AL: A History*, 147. For his part, Lincoln's "principal weapon was direct, unswerving logic. . . . [H]e pursued lines of concise reasoning to maxims of constitutional law and political morals." Ibid.

On the differences between Douglas and Lincoln, the historian David M. Potter wrote: "Douglas did not believe that slavery really mattered very much, because he did not believe that Negroes had enough human affinity with him to make it necessary for him to concern himself with them. Lincoln, on the contrary, believed that slavery mattered, because he recognized a human affinity with blacks which made their plight a necessary matter of concern to him. This does not mean that his position was logically consistent or that he was free of prejudice. In fact . . . philosophically and abstractly he believed in the humanity of blacks and the equality of humans; concretely and culturally he accepted the prevailing practices of Negro subordination. In a very real sense his position was ambiguous. But even an ambiguous position was vastly different from that of Douglas." Potter, *Impending Crisis*, 354.

162 "In this and like communities" CW, 3:27. See also David Zarefsky, "'Public Sentiment Is Everything': Lincoln's View of Political Persuasion," *JALA* 15, no. 2 (1994): 23–40.

162 "tendency to dehumanize" CW, 3:304.

162 Lincoln's challenge On the 1858 debates and campaign, see, for instance, Blumenthal, *All the Powers of Earth*, 363–442; Hay and Nicolay, *AL: A History*, 2:158–64; Burlingame, *AL*, 1:486–557; Donald, *Lincoln*, 196–229; White, *A. Lincoln*, 257–89.

162 "in God's own good time" CW, 3:181.

162 "ultimate extinction" Ibid.

162 Douglas and Lincoln met *LDBD, 1849–1860*, 225.

162 "We were both comparatively" CW, 3:5–6.

163 "He came up again" Ibid., 6.

163 "Now, I do not believe" Ibid., 10. Illinois, Douglas continued, had "provided that the negro shall not be a slave, and we have also provided that he shall not be a citizen, but protect him in his civil rights, in his life, his person and his property, only depriving him of all political rights whatsoever, and refusing to put him on an equality with the white man." The crowd called out: "Good." Ibid.

163 "Why should Illinois" Ibid., 11–12.

163 He leaned forward Herndon and Weik, *Herndon's Life of Lincoln*, 331–33.

163 Lincoln's voice, at the beginning Ibid.

163 His hands behind Ibid., 331.

163 "throwing it with vim" Ibid., 332.

163 As Lincoln settled Ibid., 333.

163 At his most animated Ibid., 332–33.

164 "I have no purpose" CW, 3:16, 145.

164 use of the N-word Burlingame, *Black Man's President*, 208–28.

164 Lincoln's own views As noted above, see, for instance, Bennett, *Forced into Glory*; Franklin, "The Use and Misuse of the Lincoln Legacy," 30–42; Fredrickson, *Big Enough to Be Inconsistent*, 81–84; Gates, ed., *Lincoln on Race & Slavery*, xix–lxviii.

164 respectful dealings Burlingame, *Black Man's President*, 1–24.

165 would welcome Black callers White, *House Built by Slaves*, is comprehensive.

165 he was pessimistic Oakes, *Scorpion's Sting*, 83–84.

165 Martin Delany See, for instance, Eleanor Stanford, "Martin R. Delany (1812–1885)," *Encyclopedia Virginia*, Virginia Humanities (December 22, 2021), https://encyclopediavirginia.org/entries/delany-martin-r-1812–1885/, and Dorothy Sterling, *The Making of an Afro-American: Martin Robison Delany 1812–1885* (New York, 1996).

165 "no reason in the world" CW, 3:16.

165 Interrupted by "Loud cheers" Ibid.

165 "I hold that" Ibid. Of the Founding, with the coming abolition of the slave trade,

Lincoln said, "The public mind *did* rest in the belief that it was in the course of ultimate extinction. But lately, I think—and in this I charge nothing on the Judge's motives—lately, I think, that he, and those acting with him, have placed that institution on a new basis, which looks to the *perpetuity and nationalization of slavery.*" Ibid., 17–18. To nationalize slavery, Lincoln later added on the campaign trail, meant to "Africanize this continent." Ibid., 38. Lincoln characterized the Douglas view this way: "[I]f you can make more money by flogging n——s than by flogging oxen, there is no moral consideration which should interfere to prevent your doing so." Ibid., 2:545.

165   "Douglas and I" CW, 3:37.

165   professed a willingness See, for instance, ibid., 39–43.

165   "If, by all these means" Ibid., 2:552–53.

166   "If A. can prove" Ibid., 222–23.

166   "I know there are" CW, 3:93.

167   "It is far easier" Burlingame, *AL*, 1:384; "The White Man's Party," *Chicago Tribune*, May 30, 1857.

167   "that white men may find a home" CW, 3:312. Lincoln could frame his antislavery views to appeal to white self-interest. "Why this fuss about n——s?" Lincoln asked in Carlinville in late August. His answer was direct: Should slavery expand, "every white laborer will have occasion to regret when he is elbowed from his plow or his anvil by slave n——s. . . . The compromises of the constitution we must all stand by, but where is the justness of extending the institution to compete with white labor and thus to degrade it? Is it not rather our duty to make labor more respectable by preventing all black competition, especially in the territories?" Ibid., 77–79.

167   "Now, when . . . you have" Ibid., 95. Lincoln continued: "What constitutes the bulwark of our own liberty and independence? It is not our frowning battlements, our bristling sea coasts, the guns of our war steamers, or the strength of our gallant and disciplined army. . . . Our reliance is in the *love of liberty* which God has planted in our bosoms. . . . Destroy this spirit, and you have planted the seeds of despotism around your own doors. Familiarize yourselves with the chains of bondage, and you are preparing your own limbs to wear them." Ibid.

167   "Our opinion is" Ibid., 126–27.

167   Lincoln interjected Ibid., 127.

167   "I have said that" Ibid., 2:409.

168   "It will be ever hard" Ibid., 409–10.

168   even some Black Americans Sinha, *Slave's Cause*, 574–80.

168   He followed this up Ibid., 576.

168   weighed the question Ibid., 576–78. Sinha wrote: "On the eve of the Civil War, antislavery colonizationists and black emigrationists joined forces to promote emigration to Africa. . . . Emigrationist sentiment became increasingly popular among black abolitionists. . . . The idea of black nationhood never completely died out among African Americans." Ibid., 576–80.

168   At Charleston, Illinois CW, 3:145–201; Burlingame, *AL*, 1:516–26. "Lincoln had been warned that Negrophobia was intense in Coles County," Burlingame wrote. Burlingame, *AL*, 1:517.

168   "While I was at the hotel" CW, 3:145–46.

168   "I will say" Ibid.

169   "I say upon this occasion" Ibid., 146.

169   ruling racism of the era See, for instance, ibid., 39–43; Burlingame, *AL*, 1:511–26.

169 WOULD NOT FAVOR BLACK CITIZENSHIP CW, 3:179.

169 "NOW MY OPINION" Ibid.

169 STATES WERE THE CONTROLLING AUTHORITIES On Lincoln's limited view of the federal government's role in such matters at this time, see Oakes, *Crooked Path to Abolition*, 112–28. Oakes noted that Lincoln's view of federalism "helps explain a curious disjunction between the fact of Lincoln's racial attitudes and the significance of them." Ibid., 125.

169 "I DO NOT UNDERSTAND" CW, 3:146.

169 "I DO NOT PROPOSE" Ibid.

169 LINCOLN GREETED A CROWD Ibid., 203.

170 TUESDAY, NOVEMBER 2, 1858 Hay and Nicolay, *AL: A History*, 2:164–65; Burlingame, *AL*, 1:545–57.

170 THOUGH THE REPUBLICANS Hay and Nicolay, *AL: A History*, 2:164–65.

170 "I AM GLAD" CW, 3:339–40.

170 "I WRITE MERELY" Ibid., 346.

170 "ANOTHER 'BLOW-UP' " Ibid., 341–42.

170 "WELL, THE ELECTION IS" Ibid., 340.

Chapter Thirteen: Let Us Dare to Do Our Duty

175 "THE QUESTION RECURS" CW, 3:547–48.

175 "IS IT NOT TIME" Reuben Davis, "The Duty of Parties: Speech of Hon. Reuben Davis, of Mississippi, in the House of Representatives, December 8, 1859: On the Reconciliation of Parties and the Organization of the House" (Washington, D.C., 1859), 6.

175 "CLOUDY, FOGGY" LDBD, *1849–1860*, 242.

175 "IT IS A LAW" Hay and Nicolay, *AL: A History*, 2:173.

176 "STAND BY YOUR PRINCIPLES" CW, 3:370.

176 "IF YOU ARE" Turner and Turner, *Mary Todd Lincoln: Her Life and Letters*, 53.

176 LINCOLN WAS HOME LDBD, *1849–1860*, 244.

176 A MAN WITH NATIONAL AMBITIONS On the national scene, Lincoln advised Salmon Chase that an Ohio Republican platform call for "a repeal of the atrocious Fugitive Slave Law" was poor politics. "This is already damaging us here," Lincoln wrote Chase. "I have no doubt that if that plank be even *introduced* into the next Republican National convention, it will explode it. Once introduced, its supporters and its opponents will quarrel irreconcilably." CW, 3:384. The plain text of the Constitution, Lincoln explained, affirmed the federal government's right to force the return of escaped slaves. Ibid.

Lincoln's calculus was cold-eyed. Ohio and New Hampshire were causing trouble with attacks on the Fugitive Slave Law; nativism was roiling Massachusetts; Kansas was insistent on popular sovereignty. Ibid., 390–91. "In these things there is explosive matter enough to blow up half a dozen national conventions, if it gets into them; and what gets very rife outside of conventions is very likely to find its way into them," Lincoln wrote to Representative Schuyler Colfax of Indiana in the summer. "In a word, in every locality we should look beyond our noses," Ibid., 391.

Still, he was not yet ready to make his presidential ambitions explicit and public. In the spring of 1859, as he juggled law, family, and politics, Lincoln opened a letter from the Rock Island, Illinois, editor Thomas J. Pickett, who had written to ask Lincoln's leave to suggest a presidential nomination in 1860. Pickett's plan: a coordinated press announcement to put Lincoln's name forward. On Saturday,

April 16, 1859, Lincoln demurred, writing, "I must, in candor, say I do not think myself fit for the Presidency. I certainly am flattered, and gratified, that some partial friends think of me in that connection; but I really think it best for our cause that no concerted effort, such as you suggest, should be made." Ibid., 377.

176   "WE MUST HOLD" Ibid., 435–36.

176   HE PUBLISHED Ibid., 372–74.

176   CULTIVATED JOURNALISTS Ibid., 385. He kept up his contacts in the press, renewing his subscription to the Republican Chicago *Press and Tribune* with a note that said, "I suppose I shall take the Press & Tribune so long as it, and I both live." Ibid. When he could not accept invitations to out-of-state gatherings, he took care to handle his correspondents with care and grace. Regretting a Jefferson's birthday festival in Boston, Lincoln wrote an eloquent letter designed to appropriate Jefferson, thought to be the founder of the original Democratic Party, for his own. "The [Democrats] of to-day hold the *liberty* of one man to be absolutely nothing, when in conflict with another man's right of *property*," Lincoln wrote the Bostonians in April 1859, "Republicans, on the contrary, are for *both* the *man* and the *dollar*; but in cases of conflict, the man *before* the dollar. . . . [I]t is now no child's play to save the principles of Jefferson from total overthrow in this nation." Ibid., 374–76.

In September 1859, he and Mary and one of the boys traveled to Ohio, where Lincoln was to speak in advance of state elections there. In Columbus on the afternoon of Friday, September 16, standing on the east terrace of the state capitol, he reprised his 1858 themes. *LDBD, 1849–1860*, 261; Hay and Nicolay, *AL: A History*, 2:183–89. The "chief and real purpose of the Republican party is eminently conservative," Lincoln said. "It proposes nothing save and except to restore this government to its original tone in regard to this element of slavery, and there to maintain it, looking for no further change, in reference to it, than that which the original framers of the government themselves expected and looked forward to." *CW*, 3:404. He spoke, too, in Dayton and in Cincinnati, affirming his faith in the broad American system. *LDBD, 1849–1860*, 261. See also Gary Ecelbarger, "Before Cooper Union: Abraham Lincoln's 1859 Cincinnati Speech and Its Impact on His Nomination," *JALA* 30, no. 1 (2009): 1–17.

The Republicans of Ohio asked Lincoln for permission to publish the debates with Douglas and Lincoln's speeches at Columbus and Cincinnati. "We regard them as luminous and triumphant expositions of the doctrines of the Republican party, successfully vindicated from the aspersions of its foes, and calculated to make a document of great practical service to the Republican party in the approaching Presidential contest." Hay and Nicolay, *AL: A History*, 2:188. A shrewd decision, for the book sold well, going into a third edition. Ibid., 189. "The enterprise," Hay and Nicolay recalled, "proved a success beyond the most sanguine expectations." Ibid., 188. Lincoln was pleased and used his one hundred "gratis" copies to give to friends and to curious correspondents. *CW*, 3:516.

He followed his Ohio success with a tour of Wisconsin. He and Mary had spent the night at the Tremont House in Chicago between legs of the journey before leaving town to speak at Milwaukee, Beloit, and Janesville. His theme included an expansion on the pro-white case for containing slavery. *LDBD, 1849–1860*, 262. "The world is agreed that *labor* is the source from which human wants are mainly supplied," Lincoln said in Milwaukee. "There is no dispute upon this point. From this point, however, men immediately diverge." *CW*, 3:477. There were those who "assume that whoever is once a *hired* laborer, is fatally fixed in that condition for life; and thence again that his condition is as bad as, or worse than that of a slave. This is the *'mud-sill'* theory." Ibid., 478. The other theory was that of "Free Labor," which Lincoln described this way: "Southern men declare that their slaves are better off than hired laborers amongst us. How little they *know*, whereof they *speak*! There is no permanent class of hired laborers amongst us. Twenty-five years ago, I was a hired laborer. The hired laborer of yesterday, labors on his own account to-day; and will hire others to labor for him to-morrow. Advancement—improvement in condition—is the order of things in a society of equals. . . . Free labor has the inspiration of hope; pure slavery has no hope." Ibid., 462.

It had been the most effective of political tours. "The old familiar face of A. Lincoln is again amongst us," the Clinton, Illinois, *Central Transcript* reported in early October, "and we cannot help noticing the peculiarly friendly expression with which he greets everybody, and everybody greets him. He comes back to us after electrifying Ohio, with all his blushing honors thick upon him; yet the poorest and plainest amongst our people, fears not to approach, and never fails to receive a hearty welcome from him." *LDBD, 1849–1860,* 262.

On Tuesday, November 1, 1859, to a correspondent who had asked him to lobby for Simon Cameron of Pennsylvania for president, Lincoln said, "For my single self, I have enlisted for the permanent success of the Republican cause; and for this object, I shall labor faithfully in the ranks, unless, as I think not probable, the judgment of the party shall assign me a different position." CW, 3:491; *LDBD, 1849–1860,* 264. Now that autumn had come, the reluctance of April was gone.

176 "You are like" Hay and Nicolay, *AL: A History,* 2:176–77.

176 "You have made" Ibid., 177.

176 "Send Abraham Lincoln" Ibid.

176 To defeat the Democrats CW, 3:388.

176 "Last of all" Jenkins, *Pro-Slavery Thought,* 240; Benjamin M. Palmer, *The South: Her Peril, and Her Duty* (New Orleans, 1860), 10.

176 "the mind and heart" Letter from Gen. Leonidas Polk to Bishop Stephen Elliott, August 20, 1856, Box 9, Folder 40, Polk Papers, William R. Laurie University Archives and Special Collections, University of the South, Sewanee, Tennessee.

177 "There ought to be enough" Ibid.

177 where John Brown On Harpers Ferry and its implications, see, for instance, Blumenthal, *All the Powers of Earth,* 464–513. On Brown generally, see David S. Reynolds, *John Brown, Abolitionist: The Man Who Killed Slavery, Sparked the Civil War, and Seeded Civil Rights* (New York, 2005); Tony Horwitz, *Midnight Rising: John Brown and the Raid That Sparked the Civil War* (New York, 2011); H. W. Brands, *The Zealot and the Emancipator: John Brown, Abraham Lincoln, and the Struggle for American Freedom* (New York, 2020).

177 "I expect nothing" Hay and Nicolay, *AL: A History,* 2:199.

177 "And Samson said" Judges 16:30, KJV.

178 Late on the night Hay and Nicolay, *AL: A History,* 2:204–9.

178 A brief assault Ibid., 208.

178 One marine was killed Ibid.

178 Half of Brown's force "John Brown's Raid," Harpers Ferry National Historical Park, National Park Service, https://www.nps.gov/articles/john-browns-raid.htm.

178 Of the rest, seven Ibid.

178 Brown was quickly tried At trial, Brown delivered a widely circulated final statement. "This Court acknowledges too, as I suppose, the validity of the LAW OF GOD," Brown said. "I saw a book kissed [in court], which I suppose to be the BIBLE, or at least the NEW TESTAMENT, which teaches me that, 'All things what-

soever I would that men should do to me, I should do even so to them.' It teaches me further, to 'Remember them that are in bonds, as bound with them.' . . . Now, if it is deemed necessary that I should forfeit my life, for the furtherance of the ends of justice, and MINGLE MY BLOOD . . . with the blood of millions in this Slave country, whose rights are disregarded by wicked, cruel, and unjust enactments—I say; LET IT BE DONE." "John Brown's Final Speech, 1859," https://www .gilderlehrman.org/sites/default/files/inline-pdfs/05508.051_FPS.pdf.

178 "SOME EIGHTEEN HUNDRED" Hay and Nicolay, *AL: A History*, 2:211.

178 "WE MUST SEPARATE" *Richmond Enquirer*, November 15, 1859.

178 THREE DEMOCRATIC MEMBERS Hay and Nicolay, *AL: A History*, 2:210.

178 "IS IT NOT TIME" Davis, "The Duty of Parties," 6.

178 "WAS A VIOLATION" CW, 3:496. Lincoln's remarks were reported in a Kansas newspaper. Ibid.

179 HE FRAMED THE QUESTION Ibid., 501. "You claim that you are conservative; and we are not," he said to proslavery listeners in Kansas in December. "We deny it. What is conservatism? Preserving the old against the new. And yet you are conservative in struggling for the new, and we are destructive in trying to maintain the old. Possibly you mean you are conservative in trying to maintain the existing institution of slavery. Very well; we are not trying to destroy it. The peace of society, and the structure of our government both require that we should let it alone, and we insist on letting it alone." Ibid.

179 "YOUR OWN STATEMENT" Ibid., 502.

179 "SO, IF CONSTITUTIONALLY" Ibid. The hint of violence was in tune with the temper of the time. In 1859–60, the governor of South Carolina, William Henry Gist, wrote one of his state's congressmen, William Porcher Miles, an alarming letter. "I am prepared to wade in blood rather than submit to *inequality* and degradation; yet if a bloodless revolution can be effected, of course it would be preferable," the governor said. "If, however, you upon consultation decide to make the issue of force in Washington, write or telegraph me, and I will have a regiment in or near Washington in the shortest possible time." Potter, *Impending Crisis*, 389–90. In Congress, Senator James Henry Hammond, a senior colleague of Miles's, observed, "The only persons who do not have a revolver and a knife are those who have two revolvers." Eric H. Walther, *The Shattering of the Union: America in the 1850s* (Wilmington, Del., 2004), 143. Representative Laurence Keitt of South Carolina also lent his voice to the cause. "African slavery is the corner-stone of the industrial, social and political fabric of the South; and whatever wars against it, wars against her very existence," Keitt said in January 1860. Manisha Sinha, *The Counterrevolution of Slavery: Politics and Ideology in Antebellum South Carolina* (Chapel Hill, N.C., 2000), 226.

179 LINCOLN'S WORDS CAME See, for instance, Michael K. Curtis, "The 1859 Crisis over Hinton Helper's Book, the Impending Crisis: Free Speech, Slavery, and Some Light on the Meaning of the First Section of the Fourteenth Amendment," *Chicago-Kent Law Review* 68, no. 3 (June 1993): 1113–77; Blumenthal, *All the Powers of Earth*, 500–505.

179 MISCHARACTERIZING HELPER'S ARGUMENT Curtis, "1859 Crisis."

179 EVEN CALLED IT Ibid.

179 "THE INDISPOSITION OF THE REST" RALPH E. Morrow, "The Proslavery Argument Revisited," *Mississippi Valley Historical Review* 48, no. 1 (1961): 80.

180 "THE PARTIES IN THIS CONFLICT" Chesebrough, *"God Ordained This War,"* 177–78.

180 EARLY IN THE YEAR Davis and Wilson, eds., *Herndon's Informants*, 247.

180 "We all expressed" Ibid.

180 Lincoln returned the next day Ibid.

180 introduced resolutions "Jefferson Davis' Resolutions on the Relations of the States," February 2, 1860, Papers of Jefferson Davis, https://jeffersondavis.rice.edu/archives/documents/jefferson-davis-resolutions-relations-states. See also Hay and Nicolay, *AL: A History*, 2:229–30.

181 Born in Kentucky William C. Davis, *Jefferson Davis: The Man and His Hour* (New York, 1991), 5–7.

181 Tall and angular On Lincoln and Davis, see, for instance, Brian R. Dirck, *Lincoln and Davis: Imagining America, 1809–1865* (Lawrence, Kans., 2001).

181 Davis was well educated Davis, *Jefferson Davis*, 13–38.

181 owned about a hundred William J. Cooper, Jr., ed., *Jefferson Davis: The Essential Writings* (New York, 2003), xviii. Cooper reports that Davis owned 113 enslaved people in 1860. Ibid.

181 Davis served "Davis, Jefferson (1808–1889)," https://history.house.gov/People/Detail/11970.

181 Lincoln left Springfield *LDBD, 1849–1860*, 273.

181 a scheduled lecture Hay and Nicolay, *AL: A History*, 2: 216–17; CW, 3:519. On the Cooper Union address, see also Harold Holzer, *Lincoln at Cooper Union: The Speech That Made Abraham Lincoln President* (New York, 2005); Burlingame, *AL*, 1:582–94; Blumenthal, *All the Powers of Earth*, 525–38; Donald, *Lincoln*, 237–41; White, *A. Lincoln*, 309–14.

181 "Subject, not known" *LDBD, 1849–1860*, 273.

181 the venue was shifted Hay and Nicolay, *AL: A History*, 2:217.

181 the Cooper Union Edwin G. Burrows and Mike Wallace, *Gotham: A History of New York City to 1898* (New York, 1999), 781–82.

181 "No former effort" Herndon and Weik, *Herndon's Life of Lincoln*, 368.

181 Lincoln had received Ibid., 367.

181 "advice and that" Ibid.

181 In the state library Ibid., 367–68.

181 which he owned Ibid., 368. Herndon received the volumes from Lincoln as a gift after the 1860 election. Ibid.

181 Lincoln polished the text *LDBD, 1849–1860*, 273.

181 The Cooper audience Hay and Nicolay, *AL: A History*, 2:217.

181 "The collar" Herndon and Weik, *Herndon's Life of Lincoln*, 369.

182 Lincoln fretted Ibid.

182 the crowd might note Ibid.

182 a lawyerly address See, for instance, ibid., 368.

182 *"This is all"* CW, 3:535.

182 "I do not mean" Ibid., 534–35.

182 "You will grant" Ibid., 535–36.

183 "rule or ruin" Ibid., 543.

183 "A few words" Ibid., 547.

183 "The question recurs" Ibid., 547–48.

183 "all declarations that" Ibid.

183 "Most of them" Ibid., 548.

183 "Their thinking it" Ibid., 549–50.

183 "Wrong as we" Ibid., 550.

184 "Since the days" Hay and Nicolay, *AL: A History*, 2:217, 224.

184 Lincoln spoke the next day *LDBD, 1849–1860*, 274.

184 Over the next two weeks Ibid., 274–76.

184 "I have been" CW, 3:555.

184 "The speech at" Ibid. In New Hampshire, he spoke with "great apparent candor and wonderful interest," the *Manchester Mirror* reported. "For the first half hour his opponents would agree with every word he uttered; and from that point he would lead them off little by little until it seemed as if he had got them all into his fold. He is far from prepossessing in personal appearance, and his voice is disagreeable; and yet he wins your attention from the start." Herndon and Weik, *Herndon's Life of Lincoln*, 368–69.

Back in New York on Sunday, March 11, 1860, Lincoln visited Brooklyn's Plymouth Church, where Beecher preached, and Edwin H. Chapin's Universalist Church of the Divine Paternity on Broadway. *LDBD, 1849–1860*, 275–76. Influenced by Theodore Parker, Chapin once said, "The more we learn of nature, the more clearly is revealed to us this fact—that we know less than we thought we did . . . as science, as nature, opens upon us, we find mystery after mystery, and the demand upon the human soul is for faith, faith in high, yea, in spiritual realities." "Edwin Hubbell Chapin," https://exhibits.tufts.edu/spotlight/john-brown-tufts/about/edwin-hubbell-chapin.

184 Lincoln left New York *LDBD, 1849–1860*, 276.

184 "Mr. Lincoln has" Ibid.

184 the Republican National Convention See, for instance, Michael F. Holt, *The Election of 1860: "A Campaign Fraught with Consequences"* (Lawrence, Kans., 2017), 88–133.

184 "The taste is in my mouth" CW, 4:45.

184 "We hazard nothing" Holt, *Election of 1860*, 97.

185 "I cannot enter" CW, 4:32. He continued: "I say, in the main, the use of money is wrong; but for certain objects, in a political contest, the use of some, is both right, and indispensable." Lincoln would, therefore, be willing to "furnish one hundred dollars to bear the expenses of the trip" to Chicago should the writer become a delegate to the convention. Ibid.

185 "I could not raise" Ibid., 33.

185 William Seward of New York Holt, *Election of 1860*, 89–91.

185 "My name is new" CW, 4:33–34. A letter to the Cincinnati lawyer and Republican delegate Richard M. Corwine captures Lincoln's thinking and tone about "the 'lay of the land' " as the Chicago convention was about to begin. "First then, I think the Illinois delegation will be unanimous for me at the start; and no other delegation will," Lincoln noted on Wednesday, May 2. "A few individuals in other delegations would like to go for me at the start, but may be restrained by their colleagues. . . . Everywhere, except in Illinois, and possibly Indiana, one or another is preferred to me, but there is no positive objection. This is the ground as it now appears." Ibid., 47–48.

185 "give no offense" Ibid., 49.

185 "make no contracts" Ibid., 50.

185 Lincoln emerged as the nominee *LDBD, 1849–1860*, 280; Blumenthal, *All the Powers of Earth*, 563–97; Burlingame, *AL*, 1:601–26; Holt, *Election of 1860*, 111; "From Chicago: The Republican Ticket for 1860," *NYT*, May 19, 1860.

185 Word of his victory *LDBD, 1849–1860*, 280; "From Chicago: The Republican Ticket," *NYT*.

185 After the second ballot *New-York Daily Tribune*, May 25, 1860.

185 A messenger scurried Ibid.

185 "There's a little woman" Ibid.

185 "How gratified . . . Mary" Elizabeth Todd Edwards to Julia Baker, May 20, 1860, Elizabeth Todd Edwards Papers, 1860–1861, LOC.

186 After an evening rally *LDBD, 1849–1860,* 280; CW, 4:50–51.

186 "To-night the City" *NYT,* May 19, 1860. For national reaction to the nomination, see "Opinions of the Press," Ibid. "The nomination for the Presidency does not appear to us to be a strong one," *The Alabama Beacon* observed. "That it will cause much dissatisfaction among Seward's friends, we think quite certain. Lincoln's political opinions are as objectionable as those held by Seward—whilst he possesses neither the ability nor the reputation of his vanquished rival." *The Alabama Beacon,* May 25, 1860.

186 In remarks to the throng CW, 4:50.

186 "We will give" Ibid.

186 A delegation from Chicago Ibid., 51. When Lincoln officially accepted the nomination, by letter dated Wednesday, May 23, he used religious language in the manner of George Washington: "Imploring the assistance of Divine Providence . . . I am most happy to co-operate for the practical success of the principles declared by the convention." Ibid., 52. In a separate note to Ashmun, Lincoln wryly wrote, "The answer, I hope, is sufficiently brief to do no harm." Ibid., 53.

186 During the pleasantries *New-York Daily Tribune,* May 25, 1860.

186 "I was afraid" Ibid.

186 "the sky blazing" Ibid.

186 "Holding myself the" CW, 4:53.

186 "I shall, in the canvass" Ibid., 54.

186 "May the Almighty" Ibid., 51–52.

187 "a third-rate, slang-whanging lawyer" *New-York Daily Tribune,* May 25, 1860. The quotation was from *The Binghamton Democrat.*

Chapter Fourteen: God Help Me, God Help Me

188 "Lincoln is President-elect" French, *Witness to the Young Republic,* 335.

188 "If there is sufficient" Hay and Nicolay, *AL: A History,* 2:313–14.

188 "The triumph of the principles" James H. Thornwell, *Hear the South! The State of the Country: An Article Republished from the Southern Presbyterian Review* (New York, 1861), 22.

188 At noon on *Official Proceedings of the Democratic National Convention, Held in 1860 at Charleston and Baltimore* (Washington, D.C., 1860), 1. On the convention and its sequel at Baltimore, see, for instance, Potter, *Impending Crisis,* 407–41; Holt, *Election of 1860,* 50–66.

188 Within minutes *Official Proceedings,* 3–9.

188 Charleston in the late spring Freehling, *Road to Disunion,* 2:291–92; Holt, *Election of 1860,* 51.

189 William Lowndes Yancey of Alabama See, for instance, Eric H. Walther, *William Lowndes Yancey and the Coming of the Civil War* (Chapel Hill, N.C., 2006). In 1858, Yancey had written a widely disseminated letter about disunion. "The remedy of the South," he had said, would come "if we could as our fathers did—organize 'committees of safety' all over the Cotton States." With such resistance, "we shall fire the Southern heart, instruct the Southern mind, give courage to each other, and at the proper moment . . . precipitate the Cotton States into a revolution." Yancey's views had not shifted in the intervening two years. Hay and Nicolay, *AL: A History,* 2:301.

189 "Ours is the property" *Louisville Daily Courier,* May 11, 1860.

189 A MAJORITY REPORT Hay and Nicolay, AL: A History, 2:233. The report added that "it is the duty of the Federal Government to protect, when necessary, the rights of persons and property on the high seas, in the Territories, or wherever else its constitutional authority extends." Ibid. Far from being open to accepting the Lincolnian idea of containment, influential elements in the white South thrilled to the defense and growth of slavery, world without end. "I want Cuba . . . I want Tamaulipas, Potosi, and one or two other Mexican States; and I want them all for the same reason—for the planting and spreading of slavery," Senator Albert G. Brown of Mississippi declared. McPherson, Battle Cry of Freedom, 106.

189 "WE SHALL GO" Official Proceedings, 78. See also William Lowndes Yancey, April 28, 1860, https://www.bartleby.com/268/9/19.html.

189 "WE WANT NOTHING" Hay and Nicolay, AL: A History, 2:248.

189 A MINORITY REPORT Ibid., 234–35. Senator George E. Pugh of Ohio swore that the party would not ally itself with an uncompromisingly proslavery platform—it was popular sovereignty, or it was nothing. "Gentlemen of the South," Pugh said, "you mistake us—we will not do it." Ibid., 238. Yancey, in turn, attacked his Northern colleagues as weak, vacillating, and untrue. "Anti-slavery sentiment is dominant at the North; the slavery sentiment is dominant at the South," Yancey told the delegates from the North. "Finding the overwhelming preponderance of power in that anti-slavery sentiment, believing it to be the common will of your people, you hesitated; you trembled at its march." Official Proceedings, 71. See also Yancey, April 27, 1860, https://www.bartleby.com/268/9/19.html.

189 NORTHERN DEMOCRATS WERE STRONG Etling Morison, "Election of 1860" in HAPE, 1:480–81; Holt, Election of 1860, 115–33.

189 ALABAMA, FLORIDA, MISSISSIPPI Morison, "Election of 1860," 481.

189 "PERHAPS EVEN NOW" Hay and Nicolay, AL: A History, 2:242.

189 "HIGH GLEE" French, Witness to the Young Republic, 321.

189 BORN IN NEW HAMPSHIRE Ibid., xv–xvi.

189 AT A THREE-HOUR PARTY MEETING Ibid., 321.

190 "ALL ARE THE WORK" "An Act for the Gradual Abolition of Slavery (1780)," https://www.ushistory.org/presidentshouse/history/gradual.php.

190 "IT IS STRONG" French, Witness to the Young Republic, 321–22.

190 THE REGULAR DEMOCRATS Hay and Nicolay, AL: A History, 2:251; Holt, Election of 1860, 115–33.

190 YANCEY-LED FORCES Hay and Nicolay, AL: A History, 2:251. On Breckinridge, see William C. Davis, Breckinridge: Statesman, Soldier, Symbol (Baton Rouge, La., 1974).

190 YET A FOURTH Hay and Nicolay, AL: A History, 2:252–54; Morison, "Election of 1860," 481–82. On Bell and the Constitutional Union Party, see Holt, Election of 1860, 66–87. On the 1860 campaign generally, see Blumenthal, All the Powers of Earth, 599–628; Burlingame, AL, 1:627–83.

190 NO FIRE-EATER Holt, Election of 1860, 126–33.

190 IT WAS SPECULATED Ibid., 128–30; Davis, Breckinridge, 224–27.

190 "BRECKINRIDGE MAY NOT" Morison, "Election of 1860," 468.

190 SPOKE IN THE SENATE Donald, Charles Sumner and the Coming of the Civil War, 294–95.

190 "BARBAROUS IN ORIGIN" "Charles Sumner on the Barbarism of Slavery. The Social Tendencies of the Institution Argued. Bitter Reply of a South Carolina Senator," NYT, June 5, 1860.

190 "IT IS PRONOUNCED" Ibid.

190 DISTRIBUTED WIDELY Donald, Charles Sumner and the Coming of the Civil War, 301.

190 HE SENT LINCOLN A COPY CW, 4:76.

191   "I HAVE NOT YET" Ibid.

191   "I CANNOT POSSIBLY BE ENLIGHTENED" Edward Fontaine to Charles Sumner, August 25, 1860, MS 227, Box 1, Folder 1, Edward Fontaine Collection, William R. Laurie University Archives and Special Collections, University of the South, Sewanee, Tennessee.

191   "YOUR SPEECH IS" Ibid. Fontaine asserted his certitude about the future. "I have too much confidence in the intelligence, & fidelity of our Slaves to fear that you can ever excite them to rebellion," he wrote. "But if you succeed in hurling the North against the South, & plunging our glorious confederacy into the abyss of 'warring Chaos,' I have no idea that you will be found amid 'the elemental strife.'" Fontaine taunted Sumner's personal courage. "No civil or foreign battle-field," Fontaine wrote, "will ever be illumined by the flashing of your sword." Ibid.

191   "I TRUST THAT" Elizabeth Todd Edwards to Edward Edwards, August 26, 1860, Elizabeth Todd Edwards Papers, 1860–1861, LOC.

191   VISIT TO HIS NATIVE STATE CW, 4:69–70.

191   REFERRED TO LINCOLN John Bell of Tennessee, 1860, Library Broadside Collection, ID no. 33948, Tennessee Virtual Archives.

191   "LINCOLN BEARS HIS" LDBD, 1849–1860, 283.

192   "TELL HIM MY" CW, 4:83. To an ally in Indiana, Lincoln wrote, "If my *record* would *hurt* any, there is no hope that it will be over-looked; so that if friends can *help* any with it, they may as well do so." Ibid., 82–83.

192   "THE PROSPECT OF" Ibid., 84.

192   "WE KNOW NOT" Ibid., 82.

192   THE PHRASE WAS AN ALLUSION Proverbs 27:1, KJV.

192   "OUR BOY, IN HIS TENTH YEAR" CW, 4:82.

192   "OUR ELDEST BOY" Ibid.

192   "IN YOUR TEMPORARY FAILURE" Ibid., 87.

192   A TERRIBLE STORM Ibid., 90.

192   "I HESITATE TO" Ibid.

193   A CORRESPONDENT FOR LDBD, 1849–1860, 287; "Hon. Abraham Lincoln at Home: All About His and His," *The New York Herald*, August 13, 1860. See also Kenneth Scott, "Lincoln's Home in 1860," *Journal of the Illinois State Historical Society (1908–1984)* 46, no. 1 (1953): 7–12.

193   "THE LADIES WERE" *The New York Herald*, August 13, 1860.

193   LINCOLN SPOKE OF SLAVERY Ibid.

193   "IT WAS A PLAIN, COMFORTABLE" Rice, ed., *Reminiscences*, 479. On Piatt, see Peter Bridges, *Donn Piatt: Gadfly of the Gilded Age* (Kent, Ohio, 2012).

194   "HIS BODY SEEMED" Rice, ed., *Reminiscences*, 479–80.

194   "MRS. L. DECLARES" CW, 4:122–23.

194   "THIS GOOD LADY" Rice, ed., *Reminiscences*, 481.

194   ARRIVING BY CARRIAGE CW, 4:91–92. "Immense is the only word that describes today's demonstration," the Cincinnati *Gazette* reported. "The enthusiasm was beyond all bounds. . . . I never saw so dense and large a crowd." Ibid., 92.

194   "EVIDENCE THAT FOUR YEARS" Ibid., 91.

194   MAJOR DAVID HUNTER Ibid., 132; "The Generals and the Admirals: David Hunter (1802–1886)," http://www.mrlincolnswhitehouse.org/residents-visitors/the-generals-and-admirals/generals-admirals-david-hunter-1802-1886/.

194   "A NUMBER OF YOUNG MEN" CW, 4:132. That was not all. "I have another letter from a writer unknown to me, saying the officers of the Army at Fort Kearney [in Nebraska], have determined, in case of Republican success, at the approaching Presi-

dential election, to take themselves, and the arms at that point, South, for the purpose of resistance to the government," Lincoln wrote Hunter on Friday, October 26. Ibid.

194 SLAVE-OWNING FARMER Robert H. Cartmell (1828–1915) Papers, 1849–1915, ID no. 34266, Microfilm no. 1076, Tennessee Virtual Archives.

194 "WE ARE HOVERING" Robert H. Cartmell Diaries, October 1860.

194 "I PRESUME . . ." Elizabeth Todd Edwards to Julia Baker, November 1, 1860, Elizabeth Todd Edwards Papers, LOC.

195 ELECTION DAY See Holzer, *Lincoln: President-Elect*, 11–45, for a detailed account of Lincoln's movements. See also Burlingame, *AL*, 1:676–83.

195 "COOL . . . CLEAR AND . . . FINE" *The Pantagraph*, November 7, 1860. See also Harold Holzer, "Election Day 1860," *Smithsonian*, November 2008.

195 IN THE EVENING Baker, *Mary Todd Lincoln*, 161–62.

195 121 SOUTH FIFTH STREET *Proceedings of the Constitution Convention of the State of Illinois Convened Jan. 6, 1920*, vol. 1 (Springfield, Ill., 1920), 230.

195 ROUGHLY EIGHT BLOCKS Author tour of Springfield, Illinois.

195 "MARY! MARY!" Baker, *Mary Todd Lincoln*, 162.

195 THE VOTE REFLECTED See Holt, *Election of 1860*, 167–95. See also "1860," The American Presidency Project, https://www.presidency.ucsb.edu/statistics/elections/1860.

195 "LINCOLN IS PRESIDENT-ELECT" French, *Witness to the Young Republic*, 335.

195 "FOR FIFTY YEARS" Egerton, *Year of Meteors*, 209.

196 "HIS PERSON, COUNTENANCE" John Adams, *The Works of John Adams, Second President of the U.S. with a Life of the Author, Notes, and Illustrations, by His Grandson Charles Francis Adams* (Boston, 1851), 6:255–56.

196 "I AM A LITTLE GIRL" CW, 4:129–30.

196 "AS TO THE WHISKERS" Ibid., 129.

196 SOON APPEARED IN PUBLIC Donald, *Lincoln*, 258.

196 HE CONSTRUCTED HIS CABINET Goodwin, *Team of Rivals*, 279–319; Burlingame, *AL*, 1:719–59.

196 THE POWERFUL BLAIR FAMILY See, for instance, Escott, *Lincoln's Dilemma*; Elbert B. Smith, *Francis Preston Blair* (New York, 1980); Smith, *Francis Preston Blair Family*.

196 ANTISLAVERY BUT NOT EGALITARIAN Escott, *Lincoln's Dilemma*, x.

196 "I FEEL A GREAT RESPONSIBILITY" Burlingame, *AL*, 1:683.

197 "WELL, BOYS" Ibid., 679.

197 LINCOLN WAS HANGED *LDBD, 1849–1860*, 296.

197 "IF THERE IS" Hay and Nicolay, *AL: A History*, 2:313–14. A correspondent of Leonidas Polk's referred to the strife as "the great American struggle," adding that "the present contest between the north and south" offered "some of the greatest and most wonderful events known to history which time has yet enacted." J. N. Harvell to Leonidas Polk, Box 10, Folder 18, Polk Papers, Sewanee, Tennessee.

197 SOUTH CAROLINA'S TWO UNITED STATES SENATORS Hay and Nicolay, *AL: A History*, 2:334.

197 THE STATE CALLED FOR Chronology of Major Events Leading to Secession, American Historical Association, https://www.historians.org/teaching-and-learning/teaching-resources-for-historians/sixteen-months-to-sumter/chronology. In the South Carolina secession convention, Robert Rhett argued that antislavery sentiment had made Union impossible. "Time and the progress of things, have totally altered the relations between the Northern and Southern States, since the Union was established," Rhett said. "That identity of feelings, interests and institutions,

which once existed, is gone. They are now divided, between agricultural—and manufacturing, and commercial States; between slaveholding, and non-slaveholding States. Their institutions and industrial pursuits, have made them, totally different people. That Equality in the Government between the two sections of the Union which once existed, no longer exists." *The Address of the People of South Carolina, Assembled in Convention, to the People of the Slaveholding States of the United States* (Charleston, S.C., 1860), 11–12.

197 LINCOLN WAS DISCOVERED *LDBD, 1849–1860*, 297.

197 STEEL-TIPPED PEN Meacham, *American Lion*, 227.

197 "FORMS A *GOVERNMENT*" Ibid., 228–29.

197 "THE MAD PROJECT OF DISUNION" Jackson, Proclamation to the People of South Carolina, December 10, 1832. https://avalon.law.yale.edu/19th_century/jack01 .asp.

197 "MY OWN IMPRESSION" *LDBD, 1849–1860*, 297.

197 "I AM TOLD" Ibid., 296. Lincoln consistently underestimated the secession threat. Burlingame, *AL*, 1:691–94. He told Thurlow Weed that he believed the South would not break away in the end, and Representative Elihu B. Washburne of Illinois described Lincoln as being "in fine spirits and excellent health, and quite undisturbed by the blustering of the disunionists and traitors." Ibid., 692. Herndon thought Lincoln "apprehended no such grave danger to the Union as the mass of people supposed would result from the Southern threats, and said he could not in his heart believe that the South designed the overthrow of the Government." Ibid.; Herndon and Welk, *Herndon's Life of Lincoln,* 382.

197 "WON'T GIVE UP" Rice, ed., *Reminiscences,* 481. There were white Southern voices counseling patience. "If Lincoln should be elected he may be the best President we could have, & we must wait until he *does* something for us to complain of before we begin" to secede, Eliza Barrington Bayard wrote from Rome, Georgia, on November 3, 1860. "One party has as good a right as another to elect a president." Eliza Barrington Bayard to daughter, November 3, 1860, Harding-Timberlake Collection, MS220, William R. Laurie University Archives and Special Collections, University of the South, Sewanee, Tennessee. In November, Alexander Stephens argued that Lincoln's election did not itself justify secession. The South, Stephens said, should follow the Constitution, accept the result of the campaign, and only act if Lincoln himself overtly struck a blow at slavery. "If all our hopes are to be blasted, if the Republic is to go down, let us be found to the last moment standing on the deck with the Constitution of the United States waving over our heads," Stephens told his fellow Georgians in Milledgeville, then the state capital. "We went into the election with this people. The result was different from what we wished; but the election has been constitutionally held. . . . [I]t is said Mr. Lincoln's policy and principles are against the Constitution, and that if he carries them out it will be destructive of our rights. Let us not anticipate a threatened evil. If he violates the Constitution then will come our time to act." "Secession as Painted by a Seceder, Extracts from a Speech of Hon. A. H. Stephens, Delivered Nov. 14, 1860," *NYT,* April 21, 1861.

"I certainly am in no temper, and have no purpose, to embitter the feelings of the South; but whether I am inclined to such a course as would, in fact, embitter their feelings, you can . . . judge by my published speeches," Lincoln had written to a curious correspondent in mid-October 1860. CW, 4:128.

197 THE LINCOLNS LEFT *LDBD, 1849–1860*, 298.

198 "OLD ABE LOOKS" CW, 4:144.

198   MET HANNIBAL HAMLIN *LDBD, 1849–1860,* 298.

198   EBENEZER PECK'S MANSION Ibid.

198   AT DINNER ONE EVENING Rice, ed., *Reminiscences,* 484.

198   "WELL, WE WON'T" Ibid.

198   "OUR FATHERS MADE" *Address of Hon. W. L. Harris, Commissioner from the State of Missis-sippi, Delivered Before the General Assembly of the State of Georgia, on Monday, Dec. 17th, 1860* (Milledgeville, Ga., 1860), 4–5. See also Albert L. Brophy, *University, Court, and Slave: Proslavery Academic Thought and Southern Jurisprudence* (New York, 2016), 289.

198   "THE DEATH-KNELL OF SLAVERY" Thornwell, *Hear the South! The State of the Country,* 22. "The election of Lincoln . . . is nothing more nor less than a proposition to the South to consent to a Government, fundamentally different upon the question of slavery, from that which our fathers established." Ibid., 9.
      "The institution of slavery is so indissolubly interwoven with the whole frame-work of society in a large portion of our State," James Holcombe, a law professor at the University of Virginia, said in 1861, "and constitutes so immense an element of material wealth and political power to the whole Commonwealth that its sub-version through the operation of any unfriendly policy on the part of the Federal Government . . . would, of necessity, dry up the very fountains of the public strength, change the whole frame of our civilization and inflict a mortal wound upon our liberties." Brophy, *University, Court, and Slave,* 276. And a mortal wound on their wealth. "The slaves of the South, at a moderate estimate, are worth a thou-sand millions of dollars," Lincoln had noted in 1856. "Let it be permanently settled that this property may extend to new territory, without restraint, and it greatly *enhances,* perhaps quite *doubles,* its value at once. This immense, palpable pecuniary interest, on the question of extending slavery, unites the Southern people, as one man. But it can not be demonstrated that the *North* will gain a dollar by restricting it." CW, 2:352.
      Jefferson Davis placed the current crisis in the context of decades of white Southern fear. "Even at this session, after forty years of debate, you have asked us what was the matter," Davis said as he prepared to depart the United States Sen-ate. "Your platform on which you elected your candidate, denies us equality. Your votes refuse to recognize our domestic institutions which pre-existed the forma-tion of the Union, our property which was guarded by the Constitution. You re-fuse us that equality without which we should be degraded if we remained in the Union." *Congressional Globe,* 36th Congress, 2nd Session (Washington, D.C., 1861), 311. See also Michael A. Morrison, *Slavery and the American West: The Eclipse of Manifest Destiny and the Coming of the Civil War* (Chapel Hill, N.C., 1997), 255.

Chapter Fifteen: He Has a *Will of His Own*

199   "TOO MANY OF US" From the *Albany Evening Journal,* "No More Compromises—No Backing Down," *NYT,* December 18, 1860.

199   "IT IS DEMANDED" Burlingame, *AL,* 1:697; William Salter, *The Life of James W. Grimes: Governor of Iowa, 1854–58* (New York, 1876), 134.

199   ARNOLD PEW Massey Hamilton Shepherd, Jr., *History of St. James' Church Chicago, A.D. 1834–1934* (privately printed, 1934), 43.

199   "WAS VERY ATTENTIVE" Ibid. The recollection was from Mrs. Albert Erskine, Sr., who added, "My childish fear was that she might turn around and show some in-dignation, but she never knew how honored that tassel had been." Ibid.

199   BORN IN 1797 "Notable Visitors: Thurlow Weed (1797–1882)," *Mr. Lincoln's White House,* http://www.mrlincolnswhitehouse.org/residents-visitors/notable-visitors

/notable-visitors-thurlow-weed-1797-1882/. "Mr. Lincoln and Mr. Weed, to use our rough phrase, naturally 'took to each other' from the very day they met," Lincoln adviser Leonard Swett recalled. "Often, when knotty questions arose, Mr. Lincoln would send for him for consultation, or, stating a case, ask him to arrange or suggest a way in which what he wanted to be done could be done mostly easily." Ibid.

199 WEED RAISED THE POSSIBILITY *Albany Evening Journal*, November 24, 1860. "He urged concession, not surrender, not 'backing down,'" Weed's grandson wrote, "but that reason and moderation should not be utterly abandoned; that a great people should not be plunged into the most inhuman war of modern times to suit the caprices of Jefferson Davis and Wendell Phillips." Thurlow Weed Barnes, *Memoir of Thurlow Weed* (Boston, 1884), 2:303–7.

200 "LEADING MEN" David M. Potter, *Lincoln and His Party in the Secession Crisis* (New Haven, Conn., 1962), 68.

200 "TOO MANY OF US" From the *Albany Evening Journal*, "No More Compromises"—"No Backing Down," *NYT*, December 18, 1860. See also Barnes, *Memoir of Thurlow Weed*, 2:307. Republican criticism of Weed's words was so ferocious that *The New-York Times* published a defense of its ally in Albany. "The *Evening Journal* has incurred a good deal of censure from an influential section of the Republican Party, for its offers of concession," the *Times* wrote in early December. "That was to have been expected, simply because the mass of the party do not realize, as thoroughly as the veteran Editor . . . , the absolute necessity of such concessions, to the safety of the country and the success of the Republican Administration. As we have more than once remarked, the people in the interior do not believe that there is danger of disunion. . . . Naturally enough, therefore, they resent the suggestion that they are to make sacrifices or concessions . . . for the sake of averting an imaginary danger. . . . The relative wisdom of their course turns on the question whether the danger is imaginary." Potter, *Lincoln and His Party in the Secession Crisis*, 73–74; *NYT*, December 7, 1860.

200 A COMPROMISE IN THE WINTER OF 1860–61 On the compromise efforts in the winter of 1860–61, see also Burlingame, *AL*, 1:684–718; Henry Adams, *The Great Secession Winter of 1860–61 and Other Essays*, ed. George Hochfield (New York, 1958), 3–31; Dean A. Arnold, "The Ultimatum of Virginia Unionists: 'Security for Slavery or Disunion,'" *Journal of Negro History* 48 (1963): 115–29; Frederic Bancroft, "The Final Efforts at Compromise, 1860–61," *Political Science Quarterly* 6, no. 3 (1891): 401–23; William J. Cooper, Jr., *We Have the War Upon Us: The Onset of the Civil War, November 1860–April 1861* (New York, 2012); Charles Desmond Hart, "Why Lincoln Said 'No': Congressional Attitudes on Slavery Expansion, 1860–1861," *Social Science Quarterly* 49, no. 3 (1968): 732–41; Harold Holzer, *Lincoln President-Elect: Abraham Lincoln and the Great Secession Winter, 1860–61* (New York, 2008); Clinton Everett Knox, "The Possibilities of Compromise in the Senate Committee of Thirteen and the Responsibility for Failure," *Journal of Negro History* 17, no. 4 (1932): 437–65; Potter, *Lincoln and His Party in the Secession Crisis*; Kenneth M. Stampp, *And the War Came: The North and the Secession Crisis, 1860–1861* (Baton Rouge, La., 1970), especially 123–58; Frank Towers, "Another Look at Inevitability: The Upper South and the Limits of Compromise in the Secession Crisis," *Tennessee Historical Quarterly* 70, no. 2 (2011): 108–25. "To a great majority of the people the hopes and chances of a successful compromise seemed still cheering and propitious," Hay and Nicolay recalled of the Secession Winter of 1860–61. "Some sort of compromise of the nature of that of 1850 was the prevailing preoccupation in politics." Hay and Nicolay, *AL: A History*, 2:428–29.

200   RHETORIC, SEWARD TOLD Cooper, *We Have the War Upon Us*, 211. On Seward and compromise, see also, for instance, Stampp, *And the War Came*, 123–58; Stahr, *Seward*, 216–18, 228–33; Yanoff, *Turbulent Times*, 245–46. David Potter observed that Seward "was an enigma, and, in all likelihood, will remain one. His close association with Weed creates a strong presumption that he was not hostile to the revival of the Missouri line. Moreover, his customary, and rather cryptic optimism, suggested that he willingly anticipated a compromise. It was reported at the time, and for thirty years following, that Seward had assured various people that he would accept the Crittenden plan." Potter, *Lincoln and His Party in the Secession Crisis*, 182–83. See also ibid., 81–87.

201   "IF SOUTHERN MEMBERS" Barnes, *Memoir of Thurlow Weed*, 2:308.

201   TWO THOUSAND MERCHANTS Potter, *Lincoln and His Party in the Secession Crisis*, 121–22; "The Crisis in New-York," *NYT*, December 17, 1860.

201   "URGE THE SOUTH" "The Crisis in New-York," *NYT*, December 17, 1860. Petitions, lobbying, and a dinner at Willard's Hotel in Washington for Republican lawmakers followed. Potter, *Lincoln and His Party in the Secession Crisis*, 125–26. At Willard's, leading businessmen argued for ignoring the Republican platform of 1860, saying, "Shall we . . . stand upon a platform made some time ago in view of facts which then existed, and which have ceased to exist now; or shall we be willing to . . . yield some fair concession, without any sacrifice of principle?" Ibid., 126.

201   "THE MERCANTILE WORLD" Potter, *Lincoln and His Party in the Secession Crisis*, 127.

201   A FAMILIAR FIGURE On Crittenden, see Albert Dennis Kirwan, *John J. Crittenden: The Struggle for the Union* (Westport, Conn., 1974); Damon R. Eubank, *In the Shadow of the Patriarch: The John J. Crittenden Family in War and Peace* (Macon, Ga., 2009); "John J. Crittenden," https://www.tulane.edu/~sumter/Crittenden.html; "Notable Visitors: John J. Crittenden (1787–1863)," http://www.mrlincolnswhitehouse.org /residents-visitors/notable-visitors/notable-visitors-john-j-crittenden-1787 -1863/.

202   CRITTENDEN WAS SEEKING TO AVERT WAR Kirwan, *John J. Crittenden*, 375–76. "Political affairs here look most gloomy," Crittenden wrote in early December, "they are *mixed* up with darkness." Ibid., 366.

202   A SWEEPING SET *Congressional Globe*, 36th Congress, 2nd Session, December 18–19, 1860, 112–14. See also Potter, *Lincoln and His Party in the Secession Crisis*, 101–11; Cooper, *We Have the War Upon Us*, 102–4; Freehling, *Road to Disunion*, 2:470–75, 495–97, 514; Holzer, *Lincoln President-Elect*, 163–65; Wilentz, *Rise of American Democracy*, 780–82; Knox, "Possibilities of Compromise," 437–65.

To Crittenden the measures were fair prices to pay to avoid war. "You can give increased stability to this Union," he said, "you can give it an existence, a glorious existence, for great and glorious centuries to come, by now setting it upon a permanent basis, recognizing what the South considers as its rights." *Congressional Globe*, December 19, 1860.

Crittenden put numbers to the white Southern fears about diminishing influence. Since the Founding era, the acquisitions of Florida, Louisiana, Oregon, Texas, and those made from Mexico—including California—"have been so divided and so disposed of that the North has now two millions, two hundred thousand square miles of territory, and the South has less than one million," Crittenden said. "The present exasperation; the present feeling of disunion, is the result of a long-continued controversy on the subject of slavery and of territory. . . . I will say, though, that all the wrong is never on one side, or all the right on the other. Right and wrong, in this world, and in all such controversies, are mingled together." Ibid.

Was Crittenden correct? Was slavery as the 1860s began a matter of traditional political mediation, or an issue of such compelling moral significance that the usual protocols were no longer commensurate to the hour? On this question everything turned. Should Lincoln accept a deal of some kind that perpetuated slavery, opening not only the existing American West but perhaps future acquisitions in Latin America, the slave interest would not only survive but thrive into an indefinite future.

In the Senate, Crittenden turned to the Southern lawmakers. "As to the rest of this body, the gentlemen from the South, I would say to them, can you ask more than this? Are you bent on revolution, bent on disunion? God forbid it. I cannot believe that such madness possesses the American people. . . . Once disunited, we are no longer great." Ibid.

202 PETITIONS CALLING FOR Kirwan, *John J. Crittenden*, 403, 416.

202 "THERE CAN BE" Potter, *Lincoln and His Party in the Secession Crisis*, 199.

202 HORACE GREELEY AGREED Ibid.

202 "IT IS DEMANDED" Burlingame, *AL*, 1:697; Salter, *Life of James W. Grimes*, 134.

202 "MEANS THE DISMEMBERMENT" *Congressional Globe*, 36th Congress, 2nd Session (Washington, D.C., 1861), Appendix, 132. See also Hart, "Why Lincoln Said 'No,'" 732, 739.

202 "YOUR UNHOLY CRUSADE" *Congressional Globe*, 36th Congress, 2nd Session (Washington, D.C., 1861), 631. To Representative Francis Kellogg of Michigan, "a compromise implies concessions on both sides; and what do the South yield to us in consideration of a compliance with their demands? A shadow for a substance; an imaginary title to the mountains in the moon for the promised possession of the provinces of Mexico. . . . The South would at once commence an agitation for the conquest of Mexico and Central America; and the persistent and united efforts of her statesmen, encouraged by their continual victories over northern sentiments and opinions, would finally prevail; and nothing but the force of natural laws, or the judgments of Heaven, could save us from centuries of subjection to the power of slavery." Ibid., Appendix, 271. See also Hart, "Why Lincoln Said 'No,'" 732, 739. Though mostly Republican, these sentiments were not entirely partisan. "The Crittenden proposition asks too much," Representative John Haskin, a Democrat of New York, said. *Congressional Globe*, 36th Congress, 2nd Session (Washington, D.C., 1861), Appendix, 268. See also Hart, "Why Lincoln Said 'No,'" 732, 739.

202 IN THE HOUSE Cooper, *We Have the War Upon Us*, 52. The House vote to create the committee was 145–38.

202 THE SENATE DID THE SAME Ibid., 65–66.

202 "THERE MUST BE" Letter from President James Buchanan, December 22, 1860, ID no. nash109, Tennessee Virtual Archives.

203 SOUTH CAROLINA WAS HURTLING Jon L. Wakelyn, "Secession," South Carolina Encyclopedia, https://www.scencyclopedia.org/sce/entries/secession/.

203 BUT OTHER SLAVEHOLDING STATES Cooper, *We Have the War Upon Us*, 165–70; Potter, *Lincoln and His Party in the Secession Crisis*, 45–57, 280–314.

203 THE PRO-COMPROMISE Barnes, *Memoir of Thurlow Weed*, 2:312.

203 REACHED SPRINGFIELD *LDBD, 1849–1860*, 302; Weed, *Autobiography*, 603–14; Barnes, *Memoir of Thurlow Weed*, 2:293–95; Burlingame, *AL*, 1:712; Potter, *Lincoln and His Party in the Secession Crisis*, 164–70.

203 "LINCOLN WAS SIX FEET" Barnes, *Memoir of Thurlow Weed*, 2:294–95.

203 LINCOLN READ WEED'S EDITORIAL Weed, *Autobiography*, 604; Burlingame, *AL*, 1:712.

203 "THE PREVALENT SENTIMENT" From the *Albany Evening Journal*, "No More Compromises—No Backing Down," *NYT*, December 18, 1860.

203 THAT THE NORTH WOULD FIGHT Weed, *Autobiography*, 603–4.

203 "THIS IS A HEAVY BROADSIDE" Ibid., 604.

203 "WHAT CALAMITY MIGHT NOT" *Congressional Globe*, 36th Congress, 2nd Session, 651. See also Hart, "Why Lincoln Said 'No,'" 732, 738.

204 "THE MOST WE CAN DO" CW, 4:159.

204 "LET THERE BE NO" Ibid., 149–50.

204 SEWARD REPORTEDLY ALLOWED Kirwan, *John J. Crittenden*, 379–80.

204 "THURLOW WEED WAS" CW, 4:158.

204 LINCOLN'S SUGGESTED LANGUAGE Ibid., 156–57.

204 "WHILE THERE WERE" Weed, *Autobiography*, 605; Burlingame, *AL*, 1:712.

204 "IS A NEW AND NOVEL" From the *Albany Evening Journal*, "No More Compromises— No Backing Down," *NYT*, December 18, 1860. Anti-compromise Republicans feared the Weed mission, and told Lincoln so. "The rumor having got abroad that you have been visited by a well known politician of New York who has a good deal to do with the stock market and who took with him a plan of compromise manufactured in Wall Street," William Cullen Bryant wrote Lincoln, "it has occurred to me that you might like to be assured of the manner in which those Republicans who have no connections with Wall Street regard a compromise on the slavery question. . . . The restoration of the Missouri Compromise would disband the Republican party." CW, 4:164; Cooper, *We Have the War Upon Us*, 60–63. For Seward's work in this period, see also CW, 4:157. Lincoln's reply was careful. "The 'well-known politician' to whom I understand you to allude did write me, but [did] not press upon me any such compromise as you seem to suppose, or, in fact any compromise at all." CW, 4:163. The lawyerly phrase here is likely "[did] not press" a compromise "upon me"—which is not the same thing as not *raising* different compromises.

205 PRESIDENT BUCHANAN SENT Cooper, *We Have the War Upon Us*, 107–8; Potter, *Impending Crisis*, 557; Potter, *Lincoln and His Party in the Secession Crisis*, 145–46; "Interview of Duff Green with Mr. Lincoln on the Crisis," *The New York Herald*, January 8, 1861.

205 A KEY ISSUE CW, 4:162.

205 "HE BELIEVED THAT" Burlingame, *AL*, 1:713.

205 "I DECLARE THAT" CW, 4:162. The letter was sent to Lyman Trumbull. "Gen. Duff Green is out here endeavoring to draw a letter out of me," Lincoln wrote Trumbull on December 28. "I have written one, which herewith I enclose to you, and which I believe could not be used to our disadvantage. Still, if, on consultation with our discreet friends, you conclude that it may do us harm, do not deliver it." CW, 4:163. Trumbull did apparently deliver it, or some version of it, but the message from Lincoln failed to impress Green or, presumably, Buchanan. "I regret your unwillingness to recommend an amendment to the constitution which will arrest the progress of secession," Green wrote to Lincoln on January 7, 1861. CW, 4:163.

205 "WE RECOMMEND TO" Ibid., 163.

206 IN JANUARY, SOUTH CAROLINA WOULD Chronology of Major Events Leading to Secession, American Historical Association, https://www.historians.org/teaching -and-learning/teaching-resources-for-historians/sixteen-months-to-sumter /chronology.

206 "WE KNOW WHAT" Hay and Nicolay, *AL: A History*, 2:409.

206 "I AM OF THE OPINION" Diary of William Luther Bigelow Lawrence of Nashville, December 25, 1860, Lawrence Family Papers, 1780–1944, IV-K-1, Box 2, Folder 2, Tennessee Virtual Archives.

206 "FOR THE NORTH TO UNDERTAKE" Letter of John S. Brien, December 31, 1860,

Buell-Brien Papers, 1805–1943, ID no. 34093, Microfilm no. 1288, Tennessee Virtual Archives.

206 "Our new government" For the "Corner-Stone Speech," see Cleveland, ed., *Alexander Stephens in Public and Private*, 717–29.

207 The two had known each other Burlingame, *AL*, 1:274–75.

207 "Do the people" CW, 4:160.

207 "When men come" Stephens replied Ibid., 160–61.

207 This last phrase Proverbs 25:11, KJV.

207 "Without the *Constitution*" CW, 4:168–69.

208 "We have just carried" Ibid., 172.

208 "I know him" Wilson and Davis, eds., *Herndon on Lincoln: Letters*, 15.

208 "Prevent, as far as" CW, 4:151. He reiterated the theme again and again. "I will be inflexible on the territorial question," Lincoln wrote Weed on Monday, December 17. "My opinion is that no state can, in any way lawfully, get out of the Union, without the consent of the others; and that it is the duty of the President, and other government functionaries to run the machine as it is." Ibid., 154. The next day, Lincoln saw a troubled future in the event of compromise, including an emboldened white South launching filibusters in Latin America and a Taney-led Supreme Court codifying, and perhaps going beyond, *Dred Scott.* "I am sorry any republican inclines to dally with Pop. Sov. of any sort," Lincoln wrote. "It acknowledges that slavery has equal rights with liberty, and surrenders all we have contended for. Once fastened on us as a settled policy, filibustering for all South of us, and making slave states of it, follows in spite of us, with an early Supreme court decision, holding our free-state constitutions to be unconstitutional." Ibid., 155.

209 "By no act" RWAL, 436.

209 Lincoln's ultimate refusal Potter, *Lincoln and His Party in the Secession Crisis*, 184–86. Lincoln cared deeply about discouraging the slave owners' interest in adding new slave territory to the country. "I am for no compromise which *assists* or *permits* the extension of the institution on soil owned by the nation," Lincoln told Seward in February. He feared, he added, a "high-road to a slave empire." CW, 4:183.

209 "The Thirty-Three committee" Potter, *Lincoln and His Party in the Secession Crisis*, 130–31.

209 "Mr. Weed, . . . who" Ibid., 178.

209 What changed between Ibid., 185–87. As Potter wrote: "The Republican solidarity in rejecting compromise in mid-January marked a complete reversal of the tendency of mid-December, when conciliatory measures seemed to be steadily gaining Republican adherents, and when the prospect of a split in the party had caused grave anxiety to Republican leaders. Yet the crisis was no less ominous, and the pressure from conciliationist groups had not abated. The change in temper, therefore, resulted from no amelioration in crisis conditions, but from new forces at work within the party. These forces may have been multiple, but certainly none was more potent than the intervention of Lincoln." Ibid., 185–86.

209 by a vote of 25 to 23 Ibid., 184–85.

209 Compromise overtures continued Cooper, *We Have the War Upon Us*, 184–86. "You must let us know your terms, for we do not want to part with you," Senator Jacob Collamer of Vermont reportedly said to a colleague from North Carolina. Potter, *Lincoln and His Party in the Secession Crisis*, 182.

209 There was a bid Cooper, *We Have the War Upon Us*, 184.

209 Virginia, which was still Potter, *Lincoln and His Party in the Secession Crisis*, 307–10.

209 sponsored resolutions designed Ibid., 290–303; Cooper, *We Have the War Upon*

Us, 98–100. As Henry Adams put it, Republicans who opposed the Crittenden Compromise "now found themselves in the position of refusing on the one hand to accept the demands of the South, and, on the other, to make any offer of their own." The New Mexico proposal could be that offer, and the debate over it would consume valuable time while reassuring the border states that the Republicans of the North were not totally inflexible. Potter, *Lincoln and His Party in the Secession Crisis*, 291.

209 THE MANEUVER WORKED Potter, *Lincoln and His Party in the Secession Crisis*, 301–3.

210 "AS TO FUGITIVE SLAVES" CW, 4:183.

210 UNDER THE CHAIRMANSHIP Cooper, *We Have the War Upon Us*, 175–84; Potter, *Lincoln and His Party in the Secession Crisis*, 307–14; Robert Gray Gunderson, *Old Gentlemen's Convention: The Washington Peace Conference of 1861* (Madison, Wis., 1961).

210 "ADJUST THE PRESENT" Potter, *Lincoln and His Party in the Secession Crisis*, 307.

210 "THE POLITICAL HORIZON" CW, 4:160.

Chapter Sixteen: *To Take the Capitol by Violence*

211 "TREASON IS ALL AROUND YOU" "Report of the Select Committee on Alleged Hostile Organization Against the Government Within the District of Columbia," February 14, 1861, Report No. 79, 36th Congress, 2nd Session, 57.

211 "MR. LINCOLN ENTERED THE CAPITAL" Blight, *Frederick Douglass*, 336.

211 WASHINGTON WAS RIVEN On the talk of plots against Lincoln and the Constitutional transfer of power, see, for instance, CW, 4:175, 177; Gunderson, *Old Gentlemen's Convention*, 6–9; Holzer, *Lincoln President-Elect*, 322–23; Potter, *Lincoln and His Party in the Secession Crisis*, 253–57; "Report of the Select Committee on Alleged Hostile Organization Against the Government Within the District of Columbia," February 14, 1861, Report No. 79, 36th Congress, 2nd Session, 1–178; Henry L. Dawes, "Washington the Winter Before the War," *The Atlantic Monthly* 72, no. 430 (August 1893), 160–67; H. L. Dawes, "Two Vice-Presidents: John C. Breckinridge and Hannibal Hamlin," *Century Magazine*, 1895, 564; *Congressional Globe* 36th Congress 463–67; Fred Nicklason, "The Secession Winter and the Committee of Five," *Pennsylvania History: A Journal of Mid-Atlantic Studies* 38, no. 4 (October 1971): 373–88; Ted Widmer, *Lincoln on the Verge: Thirteen Days to Washington* (New York, 2020), especially 58–61. Holzer and Widmer's accounts of the period between the election of 1860 and the inauguration are indispensable.

211 "THE TERROR HERE" Gunderson, *Old Gentlemen's Convention*, 7.

211 HENRY WISE, THE FORMER GOVERNOR Potter, *Lincoln and His Party in the Secession Crisis*, 254.

211 "TO POISON HORSES" Kirwan, *John J. Crittenden*, 407.

211 DESTROY THE CAPITOL "Report of the Select Committee on Alleged Hostile Organization Against the Government Within the District of Columbia," 28.

211 HANG LOYAL MEMBERS Ibid., 28, 75.

211 ANOTHER RUMOR HAD Ibid., 53–54, 74–75.

211 "TREASON" Ibid., 57.

211 NEWSPAPERS REPORTED Potter, *Lincoln and His Party in the Secession Crisis*, 253; *The New York Herald*, February 2, 1861.

211 "TO TAKE THE CAPITOL BY VIOLENCE" *The New York Herald*, February 2, 1861.

212 "A WIDESPREAD AND POWERFUL CONSPIRACY" Gunderson, *Old Gentlemen's Convention*, 7.

212 "NOT . . . PROBABLE" Ibid.

212 "OUR FRIENDS ARE HOPEFUL" Cameron to Lincoln, January 2, 1861, Abraham Lincoln Papers, LOC.

212 WILLIAM SEWARD REPORTED CW, 4:170.

212 "I AM NOT GIVING YOU" Ibid.

212 A COMMITTEE OF FIVE "Report of the Select Committee on Alleged Hostile Organization Against the Government Within the District of Columbia"; Dawes, "Washington the Winter Before the War," 160–67; Nicklason, "Secession Winter and the Committee of Five," 373–88.

212 "A CONSPIRACY HAD BEEN" Dawes, "Washington the Winter Before the War," 162.

212 THE COMMITTEE HAD A SECRET SOURCE Ibid., 162–63.

212 AT NIGHT, STANTON WOULD SLIP Ibid., 163. See also Albert E. H. Johnson, "Reminiscences of the Hon. Edwin M. Stanton, Secretary of War," *Records of the Columbia Historical Society, Washington, D.C.* 13 (1910): 69–97.

212 DELIBERATIONS THAT SOMETIMES Hay and Nicolay, *AL: A History*, 2:312–27. See also Donald V. Weatherman, "James Buchanan on Slavery and Secession," *Presidential Studies Quarterly* 15, no. 4 (1985): 796–805.

212 "MR. COBB BELIEVES" Hay and Nicolay, *AL: A History*, 2:318.

212 ATTEMPTED TO MOVE ARMS Dawes, "Washington the Winter Before the War," 163.

212 AUTHORIZED THE SALE Hay and Nicolay, *AL: A History*, 2:321–22. The guns were not the kind the purchasers had asked for, but South Carolina's agent, Thomas F. Drayton, advised taking what was on offer. "Better do this . . . than be without arms at a crisis like the present," Drayton wrote to the governor of South Carolina. Ibid., 322. "The Cabinet may break up at any moment . . . and a new Secretary of War might stop the muskets going South, if not already on their way when he comes into office." Ibid., 324.

212 SURRENDERED THE NAVY YARD Dawes, "Washington the Winter Before the War," 163.

212 TO THE GOVERNOR OF FLORIDA AND TO ALABAMA MILITIA Nicklason, "Secession Winter and the Committee of Five," 376.

212 THE HOUSE CENSURED TOUCEY Ibid., 376–78; Dawes, "Washington the Winter Before the War," 164.

213 THE COMMITTEE ALSO RECEIVED Dawes, "Washington the Winter Before the War," 160–62.

213 "FINE HOUSE" Ibid., 160.

213 "HE WAS A VERY YOUNG MAN" Ibid., 161.

213 "EXTENDING THEIR EMPIRE" C. Vann Woodward, *The Burden of Southern History* (Baton Rouge, La., 1968), 195.

213 "WE SHALL HAVE" "The Future of Our Confederation," *De Bow's Review*, July 1861, 41.

213 "YOU CANNOT BE IGNORANT" Dawes, "Washington the Winter Before the War," 161–62.

213 "IT WAS SO SIMPLE" Ibid., 162.

213 "HE WENT ON" Ibid.

214 "IT SEEMS TO ME" CW, 4:170. "If the two Houses refuse to meet at all, or meet without a quorum of each, where shall we be?" Lincoln asked. "I do not think that this counting is constitutionally essential to the election; but how are we to proceed in absence of it?" Ibid. See, for instance, Potter, *Lincoln and His Party in the Secession Crisis*, 256; L. E. Chittenden, *Recollections of President Lincoln and His Administration* (New York, 1891), 36–39, 40–46; Kirwan, *John J. Crittenden*, 407.

214 "IT IS, OR IS SAID TO BE" Potter, *Lincoln and His Party in the Secession Crisis*, 256.

214 "I HAVE SEEN GENL. SCOTT" Cameron to Lincoln, January 3, 1861, Abraham Lincoln Papers, LOC.

214 DEPLOYING FEDERAL TROOPS Gunderson, *Old Gentlemen's Convention*, 7–8; Holzer, *Lincoln President-Elect*, 322.

214 "WHO ATTEMPTED BY FORCE" Holzer, *Lincoln President-Elect*, 322.

214 MUCH CAME DOWN Widmer, *Lincoln on the Verge*, 190–94, details what Widmer called "The Count." See also Widmer, "The Capitol Takeover That Wasn't," *NYT*, January 8, 2021.

214 "THE CERTIFICATES OF" Dawes, "Washington the Winter Before the War," 164. See also Dawes, "Two Vice-Presidents," 464.

215 "THE EASE WITH WHICH DESPERADOES" Dawes, "Washington the Winter Before the War," 164.

215 A HUNDRED PLAINCLOTHES POLICE Dawes, "Two Vice-Presidents," 464.

215 "PREPARED FOR ANY EMERGENCY" Dawes, "Washington the Winter Before the War," 164.

215 "FILLED TO OVERFLOWING" "Joint Session to Count 1860 Electoral College Votes, February 13, 1861," https://history.house.gov/Historical-Highlights/1851 -1900/1861_02_13_Joint_Session_Electoral_Votes/.

215 "WITH ROMAN FIDELITY" Dawes, "Two Vice-Presidents," 464. See also Widmer, *Lincoln on the Verge*, 192–93; Holzer, *Lincoln President-Elect*, 323.

215 AS A KENTUCKIAN Case of John C. Breckinridge (1861), https://www.senate.gov /about/powers-procedures/expulsion/038Breckinridge_expulsion.htm.

215 "I WOULD PREFER" Ibid.

218 "PALE AND A LITTLE NERVOUS" Dawes, *"Two Vice-Presidents,"* 464.

218 "I THEREFORE DECLARE" Ibid.

218 "UNQUESTIONABLY IT WAS" Holzer, *Lincoln President-Elect*, 322–23.

218 "THIS WAS THE CRITICAL DAY" Widmer, "The Capitol Takeover That Wasn't."

218 "THE OLD WARRIOR IS ROUSED" Cameron to Lincoln, January 3, 1861, Abraham Lincoln Papers, LOC; Gunderson, *Old Gentlemen's Convention*, 8.

218 THE PRESIDENT-ELECT DISPATCHED Herndon and Weik, *Herndon's Life of Lincoln*, 398–99.

218 "GRIZZLY AND WRINKLED" Ibid.

218 SCOTT'S HANDS TREMBLED Ibid., 399. "It was evident that the message from Lincoln had wrought up the old veteran's feelings," Mather recalled. Scott spoke "in great agitation." Ibid.

218 "SAY TO [LINCOLN]" Herndon and Weik, *Herndon's Life of Lincoln*, 398–99.

218 THE CONFEDERATE STATES OF AMERICA CAME INTO BEING Davis, *Jefferson Davis*, 301–4; Jefferson Davis, *The Rise and Fall of the Confederate Government* (New York, 1990), 1:197–98; George C. Rable, *The Confederate Republic: A Revolution Against Politics* (Chapel Hill, N.C., 1994), 43–63.

218 THE BREAKAWAY POLITY Ibid., 46.

218 "WHO SHOULD BE PRESIDENT" Davis, *Rise and Fall*, 1:205.

219 LINCOLN EMBARKED ON HIS JOURNEY CW, 4:190–91; Burlingame, *AL*, 2:1–39; Holzer, *Lincoln President-Elect*, 295–396; Stampp, *And the War Came*, 189–97. Widmer, *Lincoln on the Verge*, is comprehensive. Lincoln saw the trip as a unifying exercise. "I am not vain enough to believe that you are here from any wish to see me as an individual, but because I am, for the time being, the representative of the American people," he told well-wishers at Rochester, New York, on February 18. CW, 4:222.

219 "I DON'T WANT" RWAL, 6.

219 "AN ERRAND OF" CW, 4:191.

219 "PLEASE ARRANGE NO" Ibid., 187.

219 THE GREAT WESTERN DEPOT Widmer, *Lincoln on the Verge*, 115.

219 "FOR MORE THAN" CW, 4:190–91.

220 HE HAD SPENT A DAY Ibid., 181; *LDBD, 1861–1865*, 8.

220 "I CANNOT BUT" CW, 4:204.

220 "WE MEAN TO" Ibid., 198–99.

220 "DURING THE WINTER" Ibid., 200–201.

220 "I WILL SUFFER" Ibid., 175–76. He added that "whatever I might think of the merit of the various propositions before Congress, I should regard any concession in the face of menace the destruction of the government itself. . . . But this thing will hereafter be as it is now, in the hands of the people; and if they desire to call a Convention to remove any grievances complained of, or to give new guarantees for the permanence of vested rights, it is not mine to oppose." Ibid. The allusion—most likely to the Peace Conference in Washington—was timely and politically wise given the president-elect's eagerness to delay or, at best, prevent Virginia's secession.

221 "I REPEAT IT" Ibid., 211.

221 "'SOME THREE MONTHS'" Ibid., 219.

221 LINCOLN EXTENDED A HAND Ibid., 228. He insisted that partisanship need not lead to secession. "Almost all men in this country, and in any country where freedom of thought is tolerated, attach themselves to political parties," Lincoln remarked in Albany, New York, on February 18. "It is but ordinary charity to attribute this to the fact that in so attaching himself to the party which his judgment prefers, the citizen believes he thereby promotes the best interests of the whole country; and when an election is passed, it is altogether befitting a free people, that until the next election, they should be as one people." Ibid., 225.

221 "QUITE HOARSE" Ibid., 218.

221 "I HAVE LOST" Ibid.

221 "THE MAN DOES NOT LIVE" Ibid., 236–37.

222 AT INDEPENDENCE HALL Ibid., 240–41.

222 "I AM EXCEEDINGLY ANXIOUS" Ibid., 236.

222 RUMORS OF A PLAN See, for instance, Hay and Nicolay, *AL: A History*, 3:302–16; Holzer, *Lincoln: President-Elect*, 377–420; Michael J. Kline, *The Baltimore Plot: The First Conspiracy to Assassinate Abraham Lincoln* (Yardley, Pa., 2008).

222 "IT WAS MADE" Hay and Nicolay, *AL: A History*, 3:305.

223 "MR. LINCOLN ENTERED" Blight, *Frederick Douglass*, 336.

223 HAD VETOED STAYING CW, 4:217.

223 GENERAL SCOTT WAS STILL MONITORING French, *Witness to the Young Republic*, 343–44.

223 "THEORY OF WHAT" Ibid., 343.

223 "I TOLD HIM" Ibid.

223 HE VISITED THE HOUSE Holzer, *Lincoln: President-Elect*, 421–22.

223 TO GREET CHIEF JUSTICE TANEY Ibid., 422.

223 SENATOR CRITTENDEN CALLED Ibid., 423–24.

223 AS DID PRESIDENT BUCHANAN Hay and Nicolay, *AL: A History*, 3:317–18.

223 THE PEACE CONVENTION ISSUED Holzer, *Lincoln: President-Elect*, 427–28.

223 "NO FUTURE TERRITORY" Ibid., 428.

223 CRITTENDEN EMBRACED THE AMENDMENT Ibid., 427–28; Cooper, *We Have the War Upon Us*, 208–9.

223 ANOTHER VERSION Cooper, *We Have the War Upon Us*, 206–7. Bryant, "Stopping Time," is invaluable on the Corwin amendment.

223 "NO AMENDMENT SHALL" https://www.gilderlehrman.org/history-resources/spot light-primary-source/proposed-thirteenth-amendment-prevent-secession -1861.

224   WHO SAID HE HAD NO OBJECTION CW, 4:270. Alluding to the Corwin amendment in his Inaugural Address, Lincoln said: "I understand a proposed amendment to the Constitution—which amendment, however, I have not seen—has passed Congress, to the effect that the federal government shall never interfere with the domestic institutions of the States, including that of persons held to service. To avoid misconstruction of what I have said, I depart from my purpose not to speak of particular amendments so far as to say that, holding such a provision to now be implied constitutional law, I have no objection to its being made express, and irrevocable." Ibid.

224   SUPPORT FOR THE PROPOSED THIRTEENTH AMENDMENT Hay and Nicolay, *AL: A History*, 3:234–36.

224   "WILL HE COMPROMISE?" Frederick Douglass, "The New President," in Brooks D. Simpson, Stephen W. Sears, and Aaron Sheehan-Dean, eds., *The Civil War: The First Year Told by Those Who Lived It* (New York, 2011), 209.

224   DESPITE THE LANGUAGE Bryant, "Stopping Time," 532.

225   LINCOLN COULD HAVE SOUGHT Resisting compromise, Burlingame wrote, "was one of Lincoln's most fateful decisions, for the Kentucky senator's scheme, though fraught with many practical problems and silent on the constitutionality of secession and the right of a legally-elected president to govern, represented the best hope of placating the Upper South and thus of possibly averting war, though it was a forlorn hope at best, given Southern intransigence." Burlingame, *AL*, 1:715. In his analysis of the crisis, Potter observed: "The party which drafted the Chicago Platform and achieved the election of Lincoln was, in fact, an unstable minority coalition of true anti-slavery radicals and of opportunist groups which were essentially moderate. Promptly after its victory, this imperfect coalition was subjected to enormous pressure, not only by the threat of secession, but by the entreaties of the Border Unionists, by the united force of the Northern conservative majority, and by the demands of the masters of finance. At the same time, public reaction moved toward compromise, and vast numbers of Republicans who had cast ballots for Lincoln and free territory in November, signed petitions for Crittenden and territorial compromise in the month following. Under this impact, the Republican Congressmen, never oblivious to the tenor of opinion, began to temper their zeal. . . . This movement remained subterranean, but gained momentum and adherents until it was strong enough to induce half of the Republican members of the Committee of Thirty-three to declare themselves in favor of 'constitutional remedies' and 'specific guarantees' for the South." Potter, *Lincoln and His Party in the Secession Crisis*, 132.

225   "I THINK WHEN" RWAL, 7.

226   "THERE IS NEITHER JEW NOR GREEK" Galatians 3:38, KJV.

226   "I MAY NOT BE" Burlingame, ed., *An Oral History of Abraham Lincoln*, 87.

227   A VOICE IN THE CROWD CW, 4:208.

227   "MY FRIEND," LINCOLN REPLIED Ibid.

Chapter Seventeen: The Momentous Issue of Civil War

231   "WHY SHOULD THERE NOT" *CW*, 4:270.

231   "NOW WE ARE TO HAVE" William Jones Rhees to Laura Rhees, April 16, 1861, William Jones Rhees, Chief Clerk of the Smithsonian Institution, Correspondence, 1856–1876, LOC.

231   AT ABOUT TEN PAST NOON French, *Witness to the Young Republic*, 348. "Mr. Buchanan[,]

being detained at the Capitol to approve Bills, did not arrive until that time. See also *LDBD, 1861–1865*, 24.

231 "CLOUDY AND RAW" *LDBD, 1861–1865*, 24.

231 BRIGHT AND WARM Ibid.

231 THE TWO MEN RODE Hay and Nicolay, *AL: A History*, 3:324.

231 DOUBLE FILES OF CAVALRYMEN Ibid.

231 SHARPSHOOTERS WERE STATIONED Ibid.

231 HATLESS AND ADJUSTING HIS EYEGLASSES Holzer, *Lincoln President-Elect*, 452–53.

231 HIS INAUGURAL ADDRESS IN HAND See, for instance, Burlingame, *AL*, 2:58–68; Donald, *Lincoln*, 282–84; Goodwin, *Team of Rivals*, 326–29; White, *A. Lincoln*, 388–94; Holzer, *Lincoln President-Elect*, 452–75 (Holzer includes an annotated version of the First Inaugural as an Epilogue); Kenneth M. Stampp, "Lincoln and the Strategy of Defense in the Crisis of 1861," *Journal of Southern History* 11, no. 3 (1945): 297–323.

231 FEDERAL ARTILLERY WAS DEPLOYED Hay and Nicolay, *AL: A History*, 3:324–25.

231 "APPREHENSION SEEMS TO" CW, 4:262–63.

232 A "DINGY, DUSTY" Herndon and Weik, *Herndon's Life of Lincoln*, 386. See also Meacham, *American Lion*, 355, 445–46.

232 HE HAD ASKED Meacham, *American Lion*, 355.

232 LINCOLN WANTED Clay's Ibid.

232 "LIBERTY AND UNION" The Webster Hayne Debates, https://teachingamerican history.org/document/the-webster-hayne-debates/.

232 HAD THE DRAFT TYPESET Donald, *Lincoln*, 270.

232 "I HAVE THE DOCUMENT" CW, 4:184.

232 "SLIGHTLY PALE AND NERVOUS" Herndon and Weik, *Herndon's Life of Lincoln*, 399.

233 "RELIGION OF HATE" Arnold, "Ultimatum of Virginia Unionists," 120.

233 MEASURES RESTRICTING SLAVERY Ibid., 121.

233 "I DO BUT QUOTE" CW, 4:263.

233 SEWARD HAD RECOMMENDED Hay and Nicolay, *AL: A History*, 3:343.

233 "WE ARE NOT ENEMIES" CW, 4:271.

233 IN HIS CLEAR HAND Hay and Nicolay, *AL: A History*, 3:336–37 (image between pages).

233 THE BRILLIANT FINAL PHRASE David Blankenhorn, "Better Angels in Our Past," *The American Interest*, July 4, 2019. https://www.the-american-interest.com/2019/07/04 /better-angels-in-our-past/. See also https://myshakespeare.me/note/better -angels/.

233 "PLAINLY, THE CENTRAL IDEA" CW, 4:268-70.

234 "THE FACE OF" Sandburg, *The War Years*, 1:122.

234 "OLD ABE DELIVERED" Ibid., 122–23.

234 THURLOW WEED ENCOUNTERED Ibid., 123.

234 "LITTLE BETTER THAN" Stauffer, *Giants*, 217.

234 "AN EXCELLENT SLAVE HOUND" Blight, *Frederick Douglass*, 336–37; Stauffer, *Giants*, 217.

234 IMMIGRATING TO HAITI Stauffer, *Giants*, 215–16; Blight, *Frederick Douglass*, 337–40.

234 "THE UNITED STATES IS" Blight, *Frederick Douglass*, 338.

234 A MISSISSIPPI STATE LEGISLATOR CW, 4:156.

234 "WOULD REGARD DEATH" Ibid., 156.

234 "NOT PLEDGED" Ibid.

235 LINCOLN RODE BACK *LDBD, 1861–1865*, 25.

235 "IF YOU ARE" Sandburg, *The War Years*, 1:137–38.

235 LINCOLN DINED WITH *LDBD, 1861–1865*, 25–26; CW, 4:271.

235 CALLED AWAY FROM CW, 4:272.

235 "DISAFFECTED PORTION" Ibid. The next day, to visitors from Pennsylvania, the president repeated the point using similarly biblical imagery. "We should bear . . . in mind, and act in such a way as to say nothing insulting or irritating. I would inculcate this idea, so that we may not, like Pharisees, set ourselves up to be better than other people." Ibid., 274.

235 LATE ON THE EVENING *LDBD, 1861–1865,* 26.

235 "THE ROOMS WERE CROWDED" Sandburg, *The War Years,* 1:139.

235 DRESSED IN A BLUE GOWN Ibid., 140.

235 MRS. LINCOLN DANCED *LDBD, 1861–1865,* 26.

235 THE PRESIDENT WENT HOME Ibid.

235 LINCOLN WAS STARTLED Hay and Nicolay, *AL: A History,* 3:376–77.

235 "THE FIRST THING" *LDBD, 1861–1865,* 26.

235 ANDERSON HAD BREAD Hay and Nicolay, *AL: A History,* 3:377. General Scott made further inquiries, informing the president that Anderson "has hard bread, flour & rice for about 26 days, & salt meat . . . for about 48. . . . how long he could hold out . . . cannot be answered with absolute accuracy." CW, 4:279.

235 IN CHARLESTON HARBOR See, for instance, Hay and Nicolay, *AL: A History,* 3:375–95; Charles W. Ramsdell, "Lincoln and Fort Sumter," *Journal of Southern History* 3, no. 3 (1937): 259–88. More generally, see also Herman Belz, "Lincoln's Construction of the Executive Power in the Secession Crisis," *JALA* 27, no. 1 (2006): 13–38. Lincoln was trying to avoid bloodshed. He ordered that Fort Pickens, at Pensacola, Florida, be secured against secessionists. He was even willing, if things came to it, to surrender Sumter so long as Pickens remained in the federal fold. Potter, *Lincoln and His Party in the Secession Crisis,* 358–63. "Starvation was not yet upon the garrison" at Sumter, Lincoln later recalled, "and ere it would be reached, Fort Pickens might be reinforced. This last would be a clear indication of policy and would better enable the country to accept the evacuation of Fort Sumter as a military necessity." Ibid., 358–59. See also CW, 4:424.

235 SUMTER WAS THE FULCRUM See, for instance, Burlingame, *AL,* 2:98–130; Cooper, *We Have the War Upon Us,* 210–68; Daniel W. Crofts, "Secession Winter: William Henry Seward and the Decision for War," *New York History* 65, no. 3 (1984): 229–56; Donald, *Lincoln,* 286–94; Stampp, *And the War Came,* 263–98; White, *A. Lincoln,* 398–407.

235 "ASSUMING IT TO BE" CW, 4:284.

236 "I HAVE BUILT UP" Burlingame, *AL,* 2:99.

236 UNDER SEWARD'S INFLUENCE Ibid.

236 THE PRESIDENT SHOULD REVIVE Ibid. There are conflicting accounts of whether Lincoln was willing to abandon Sumter in exchange for Virginia's remaining in the Union. See ibid., 119–23. "A state for a fort is no bad business," the president is said to have remarked at one point. Cooper, *We Have the War Upon Us,* 201.

236 AN INSOMNIAC LINCOLN Burlingame, *AL,* 2:108.

236 "KEELED OVER" Ibid., 108–9; Cooper, *We Have the War Upon Us,* 257.

236 "GIVE UP FORTRESS" Burlingame, *AL,* 2:109.

236 "MY SYSTEM IS BUILT" William H. Seward to Abraham Lincoln, April 1, 1861, Abraham Lincoln Papers, Series 1, General Correspondence, 1833 to 1916, LOC.

236 HE WANTED SUMTER RESUPPLIED Hay and Nicolay, *AL: A History,* 4:34.

236 "SEND BREAD" Ibid., 44.

236 "UNLESS YOU SPRINKLE" Ibid., 45.

237 "THIS GOVERNMENT POLITELY DECLINES" Ibid., 37.

237 IN CHARLESTON HARBOR See, for instance, Freehling, *Road to Disunion*, 2:521–24.

237 AT FOUR O'CLOCK Mary Chesnut, "Diary, April 7–15, 1861" in Simpson, Sears, and Sheehan-Dean, eds., *Civil War: The First Year*, 256–59.

237 BELLS CAST IN 1764 "Clocks & Bells: The Bell Tower of St. Michael's Church," St. Michael's Church, Charleston, South Carolina, https://stmichaelschurch.net /clock-bells/.

237 USUALLY PEALED IN THESE YEARS Ibid.

237 "AT HALF-PAST FOUR" Chesnut, "Diary, April 7–15, 1861," 256–59.

237 ON THE EVE OF FORT SUMTER Beecher, "Sermon Preached in Brooklyn," in Holzer, ed., *TLA*, 131.

237 IT HAD RAINED ALL NIGHT Robert K. Krick, *Civil War Weather in Virginia* (Tuscaloosa, Ala., 2007), 22.

237 "AND, IN EVERY EVENT" CW, 4.330.

238 HIS INITIAL POLICY See, for instance, Potter, *Lincoln and His Party in the Secession Crisis*, 315–75.

238 "THE LAST RAY" CW, 5:49.

238 "BROWNING, OF ALL THE" *LDBD, 1861–1865*, 51.

238 COOL AND PLEASANT Krick, *Civil War Weather in Virginia*, 23; Don Lipman, "April 1861: The War Between the States Begins—What Was the Weather Like?" *The Washington Post*, April 11, 2011.

238 SERVICES AT NEW YORK AVENUE *LDBD, 1861–1865*, 35.

238 "I WISH TO FIND" Guelzo, *Abraham Lincoln: Redeemer President*, 321; Burlingame, *AL*, 2:2731, unedited ms.; *The Washington Post*, March 13, 1893.

238 "I LIKE GURLEY" O'Brien, "Seeking God's Will," 44.

238 TALL, ELOQUENT, AND POPULAR See, for instance, Guide to the Phineas Densmore Gurley Papers, Presbyterian Historical Society, Philadelphia; Barbee, "President Lincoln and Doctor Gurley," *Abraham Lincoln Quarterly*, March 1948; Edgar DeWitt Jones, *Lincoln and the Preachers* (New York, 1948), 34–41; O'Brien, "Seeking God's Will"; White, *Lincoln's Greatest Speech*, 132–40.

238 A STUDENT OF CHARLES HODGE'S O'Brien, "Seeking God's Will," 32; White, *Lincoln's Greatest Speech*, 133, 137–39.

238 A DOCTRINE OF DIVINE PROVIDENCE As noted above, see, for instance, Black, "American Scriptures"; Brodrecht, *Our Country*; Cashdollar, "Social Implications"; Chapman, "Lincoln, Bonhoeffer, and Providence"; Guelzo, "Prudence of Abraham Lincoln"; Guyatt, *Providence and the Invention of the United States*; Nichols, "Lincoln's Leadership in War"; Noll, *America's God*; Noll, *Civil War as a Theological Crisis*; Soloveichik, "Theologian of the American Idea"; White, *Lincoln's Greatest Speech*, 136–40.

238 "RULETH OVER ALL" Phineas D. Gurley, "Faith in God," White House Funeral Sermon for President Lincoln, *NYT*, April 20, 1865.

238 "THE AWFUL MYSTERIES" O'Brien, "Seeking God's Will," 33.

239 "NOW, IF WE ARE CHRISTIANS" Gurley, "The Believer Satisfied," undated, Gurley Sermons, RG 329, Series 4: Sermons, 1862–1865, n.d., Box 1, Folder 10, Presbyterian Historical Society, Philadelphia.

239 "IN THIS DAY" Gurley, "Though he slay me, yet will I trust in him," undated, Gurley Sermons, RG 329, Box 1, Folder 9, Presbyterian Historical Society, Philadelphia.

239 CHARLES HODGE OF PRINCETON See, for instance, Richard Reifsnyder, "Charles Hodge: A Conservative Theologian Finds His Way to Emancipation," August 17, 2018, Presbyterian Historical Society, Philadelphia, https://www.history.pcusa

.org/blog/2018/04/charles-hodge-conservative-theologian-finds-his-way
-emancipation#_edn12; Paul G. Gutjahr, *Charles Hodge: Guardian of Orthodoxy* (New
York, 2011); W. Andrew Hoffecker, *Charles Hodge: The Pride of Princeton* (Phillipsburg,
N.J., 2011); James H. Moorhead, *Princeton Seminary in American Religion and Culture*
(Grand Rapids, Mich., 2012); Noll, *America's God*, 316–19, 413–20, 433–35; John W.
Stewart and James H. Moorhead, eds., *Charles Hodge Revisited: A Critical Appraisal of
His Life and Work* (Grand Rapids, Mich., 2002).

239   "THERE ARE OCCASIONS" Charles Hodge, "The State of the Country," *Biblical Repertory and Princeton Review* (January 1861), 1.

239   "NINE-TENTHS OF THE" Ibid., 14.

240   A MONTH AFTER SUMTER "Historic Documents in American Presbyterian History: The Gardiner Spring Resolutions," https://www.pcahistory.org/documents
/gardinerspring.html.

240   THE LINCOLNS RESERVED *LDBD, 1861–1865*, 45; *Pew Rents Ledger Book* (1860–1870),
1:84, New York Avenue Presbyterian Church Archives, Washington, D.C.

240   FREDERICK DOUGLASS ABANDONED Blight, *Frederick Douglass*, 339.

240   "NOW IS THE TIME" Ibid., 340–41.

240   "NOW WE ARE" William Jones Rhees to Laura Rhees, April 16, 1861, William Jones
Rhees Correspondence, 1856–1876, LOC.

240   "THE NORTHERN BACKBONE" George Templeton Strong, "Diary, April 13–16," in
Simpson, Sears, and Sheehan-Dean, eds., *Civil War: The First Year*, 270.

240   THE RECTOR READ A COLLECT Ibid., 271.

240   "THE 'AMEN' OF" Ibid.

240   STRONG CLOSED HIS DIARY Ibid., 274.

240   "A KIND PROVIDENCE" Charles C. Jones Sr. to Charles C. Jones Jr., April 20, 1861,
in Simpson, Sears, and Sheehan-Davis, eds., *Civil War: The First Year*, 294–95.

241   "WE FEEL" Jefferson Davis, "Message to the Confederate Congress," in Simpson,
Sears, and Sheehan-Dean, eds., *Civil War: The First Year,* 332.

241   LINCOLN ISSUED A CALL CW, 4:331–32.

241   "THANK GOD" Thursday, April 25, 1861, *Invisible Siege: The Journal of Lucius E. Chittenden, April 15, 1861–July 14, 1861* (San Diego, 1969), 14.

241   "THE FACT OF" "Lanky Lincoln—Washington, May 17, 1861," Civil War Collection:
Confederate and Federal MF 824, Confederate Collection, Box 20, Folder 3,
Scrapbooks—Couch, Mary E. Reel 8 Mf. Ac. No. 824, Tennessee State Archives.

241   JOHN HAY . . . RECALLED Hay and Nicolay, *AL: A History*, 4:106–7.

242   THE PRESIDENT SUSPENDED CW, 4:347; Burlingame, *AL*, 2:151–53; James A. Due-
holm, "Lincoln's Suspension of the Writ of Habeas Corpus: An Historical and
Constitutional Analysis," *JALA* 29, no. 2 (Summer 2008): 47–66. See also Noah
Feldman, *The Broken Constitution: Lincoln, Slavery, and the Refounding of America* (New
York, 2021).

242   ARREST AND DETENTION Burlingame, *AL*, 2:151; Dueholm, "Lincoln's Suspension of
the Writ of Habeas Corpus."

242   "MR. LINCOLN PROBABLY THOUGHT" James Russell Lowell, "The President's Policy,"
in Holzer, ed., *TLA*, 80–81.

242   "PRESENTS TO THE WHOLE FAMILY" CW, 4:426.

242   "ALL REBELS AND INSURGENTS" Ibid., 5:436–37.

243   HE DEFENDED HIS EXECUTIVE ACTIONS Burlingame, *AL*, 2:151–54.

243   "THESE MEASURES, WHETHER" CW, 4:429.

243   "IT IS THE CASE OF A GUARDIAN" Thomas Jefferson to John Breckinridge, August 12,
1803, https://founders.archives.gov/documents/Jefferson/01-41-02-0139.

243   "THIS IS ESSENTIALLY" CW, 4:438.

Chapter Eighteen: "A White Man's War"

244 "THE BATTLE OF MANASSAS" Edward Fontaine to his wife, August 3, 1861, Box 1, Folder 2, Edward Fontaine Collection, Sewanee, Tennessee.

244 "*I* AM FIGHTING" George B. McClellan to Samuel L. M. Barlow, November 8, 1861, in Simpson, Sears, and Sheehan-Dean, eds., *Civil War: The First Year*, 588.

244 "SLAVERY OFFERS ITSELF" Burlingame and Ettlinger, eds., *Inside Lincoln's White House*, 22.

244 "THE TIME IS NOT YET" Foner, *Fiery Trial*, 163.

244 "WE CANNOT THINK" James Russell Lowell, "The Pickens-and-Stealin's Rebellion," in Simpson, Sears, and Sheehan-Dean, eds., *Civil War: The First Year*, 425.

244 BORN INTO SLAVERY Benjamin Quarles, *The Negro in the Civil War* (New York, 1989), 24–25.

244 THURSDAY, APRIL 18, 1861 Ibid., 25.

245 THE SCENE WAS TERRIBLE French, *Witness to the Young Republic*, 351.

245 "WITH A MISSILE" Quarles, *The Negro in the Civil War*, 25. Fifteen years later, when Biddle died, the following words were inscribed on his tombstone: "His was the proud distinction of shedding the first blood in the late war for the Union, being wounded while marching through Baltimore with the first volunteers from Schuylkill County 18 April 1861." Ibid., 26.

245 THE MOB ALSO CRIED Ibid., 25.

245 "AT THE SOUND" Ibid., 24.

245 "FIRE MUST BE MET" Frederick Douglass, "How to End the War," in Simpson, Sears, and Sheehan-Dean, eds., *Civil War: The First Year*, 333–34.

245 "AT WASHINGTON I FOUND" Quarles, *The Negro in the Civil War*, 30.

245 "WE DON'T WANT" Ibid., 31.

245 "A WHITE MAN'S WAR" Foner, *Fiery Trial*, 165.

245 AT FORT PICKENS Ibid., 166.

245 "CAME TO THE FORT" *The War of the Rebellion: A Compilation of the Official Records of the Union and Confederate Armies*, Series I, vol. 1, chapter 4, "Operations in Florida" (Washington, D.C., 1880), 362.

245 SLEMMER ROUNDED THEM UP Ibid.

245 FOUR ADDITIONAL ENSLAVED PEOPLE Ibid.

245 "UNNECESSARILY SQUEAMISH" Burlingame and Ettlinger, eds., *Inside Lincoln's White House*, 22.

245 IT WAS A THURSDAY NIGHT Major General Benjamin Butler to Lieutenant Winfield Scott, May 25, 1861, *War of the Rebellion*, Series 2, vol. 1., "Military Treatment of Captured and Fugitive Slaves" (Washington, D.C., 1894), 752. See also Fehrenbacher, *Slaveholding Republic*, 313; McPherson, *Negro's Civil War*, 28; Goodheart, *1861*, 297–347.

245 FRANK BAKER, SHEPARD MALLORY, AND JAMES TOWNSEND Goodheart, *1861*, 317–18.

246 "FIELD HANDS BELONGING TO" Butler to Scott, May 25, 1861, *War of the Rebellion*, 752.

246 "PROPERTY THAT WAS DESIGNED" Ibid.

246 "I AM CREDIBLY INFORMED" Ibid.

246 LINCOLN FOLLOWED BUTLER'S LEAD Foner, *Fiery Trial*, 170–71.

246 "YOUR ACTION IN RESPECT" Simon Cameron to Major General Benjamin Butler, May 30, 1861, *War of the Rebellion*, 754–55.

246 "FREEDOM FORT" Foner, *Fiery Trial*, 170.

246 THE HOUSE OF REPRESENTATIVES AFFIRMED Frank Moore, ed., *The Rebellion Record: A Diary of American Events with Documents, Narratives, Illustrative Incidents, Poetry Etc.* (New York, 1867), 10:22.

246   "CONTRABAND" Foner, *Fiery Trial*, 170–71; Fehrenbacher, *Slaveholding Republic*, 313; Goodheart, *1861*, 329–30.

246   "I CANNOT BRING" Charles C. Jones Jr. to Charles C. Jones Sr. and Mary Jones, June 10, 1861, in Simpson, Sears, and Sheehan-Dean, eds., *Civil War: The First Year*, 404–5.

246   "THE PURPOSES OF MR. LINCOLN" Leonidas Polk to Hon. L. P. Walker, May 27, 1861, Box 10, Folder 42, Polk Papers, Sewanee, Tennessee.

246   IN A LETTER TO POLK Dr. William A. Shaw to Polk, August 9, 1861, Box 10, Folder 63, Polk Papers, Sewanee, Tennessee.

247   "TIME WILL PROVE" Robert H. Cartmell Diaries, October 1860, Robert H. Cartmell (1828–1915) Papers, 1849–1915, ID no. 34266, Microfilm no. 1076, Tennessee Virtual Archives.

247   "I . . . TOLD HIM" Escott, *Lincoln's Dilemma*, 99.

247   "IF MR. LINCOLN COULD ONLY" Holzer, *Emancipating Lincoln*, 59.

247   "THE IMPORTUNITIES" Quarles, *Lincoln and the Negro*, 85–86. After he was subjected to an abolitionist sermon in the White House from a visiting Quaker, Lincoln said, "I have neither time nor disposition to enter into discussion . . . and end this occasion by suggesting for [your] consideration the question whether, if it be true that the Lord has appointed me to do the work [you have] indicated, [is it] not probable that He would have communicated knowledge of the fact to me as well as to [you]?" Rice, ed., *Reminiscences*, 285.

247   KNOWN AS COPPERHEADS See, for instance, Jennifer L. Weber, *Copperheads: The Rise and Fall of Lincoln's Opponents in the North* (New York, 2006); McPherson, *Battle Cry of Freedom*, 493–94.

248   ONE SIGN OF THE COPPERHEADS' STRENGTH Fredrickson, *Big Enough to Be Inconsistent*, 96–97.

248   "A FIRE IN THE REAR" Weber, *Copperheads*, 12.

248   "THE UNION AS IT WAS" Ibid., 67.

248   "NEGRO IN HIS PLACE" Burlingame, *AL*, 2:2428, unedited ms.

248   "DID NOT WANT" Weber, *Copperheads*, 7.

248   LINCOLN DRAFTED PLANS Escott, *Lincoln's Dilemma*, 110–11.

248   ONLY TO SEE Ibid., 113. In March 1862 Lincoln asked Congress "to cooperate with any state which may adopt gradual abolishment of slavery, giving to such state pecuniary aid, to be used by each such states . . . to compensate for the inconveniences public and private, produced by such change of system." Fredrickson, *Big Enough to Be Inconsistent*, 95; *LDBD, 1861–1865*, 98; *CW*, 5:144–46. Gradual, compensated emancipation on a state-by-state basis, Lincoln believed, would isolate the rebellion by building a figurative wall between the border and the Confederate states. *CW*, 5:144–46.

249   WHEN HE LEARNED Quarles, *Lincoln and the Negro*, 72.

249   "THIS . . . WILL NEVER DO" Escott, *Lincoln's Dilemma*, 115.

249   "LINCOLN WOULD LIKE" Quarles, *Lincoln and the Negro*, 84.

249   "KENTUCKY GONE, WE" *CW*, 4:531–32.

249   PRATT STREET RIOT The Pratt Street Riot, https://www.nps.gov/fomc/learn/historyculture/the-pratt-street-riot.htm

249   UNION AND CONFEDERATE FORCES Civil War Timeline, https://www.nps.gov/gett/learn/historyculture/civil-war-timeline.htm.

249   HAD BEEN KILLED Hay and Nicolay, *AL: A History*, 4:313–14; Owen Edwards, "The Death of Colonel Ellsworth," *Smithsonian*, April 2011.

249   VIRGINIA HAD SECEDED Nelson Lankford, "Virginia Convention of 1861," *Encyclopedia Virginia,* https://encyclopediavirginia.org/entries/virginia-convention-of-1861.

249 "PREACHED A STRONG" *LDBD, 1861–1865*, 47.

249 ELLSWORTH HAD BEEN REMOVING Edwards, "Death of Colonel Ellsworth."

249 "MAY GOD GIVE YOU" CW, 4:385–86.

249 THE CAPITAL WAS A PAGEANT All details here drawn from *LDBD, 1861–1865*, 52–53.

250 "THE PRESIDENT'S LEVEE" Ibid., 53.

250 "WE HAD A GRAND REVIEW" Robert Shortelle to his mother, September 12, 1861, Robert Shortelle Family Papers, 1851–1866, LOC.

250 "GREAT AND CAUTIOUS" Walt Whitman, "From *Specimen Days*," in Simpson, Sears, and Sheehan-Dean, eds., *Civil War: The First Year*, 500.

250 THE MAYOR OF BROOKLYN Ibid.

250 THEN CAME MANASSAS McPherson, *Battle Cry of Freedom*, 335–50; Burlingame, *AL*, 2:176–89.

251 IT WAS A GREAT VICTORY https://www.battlefields.org/learn/civil-war/battles/bull-run.

251 "THE ENEMY WERE" Emma Holmes, "Diary, July 22–23, 1861," in Simpson, Sears, and Sheehan-Dean, eds., *Civil War: The First Year*, 495.

251 UNION SOLDIERS RETREATED Ibid., 502. In Richmond, Mary Chesnut wrote, "I feel somewhat easy in mind" after the victory at Manassas. "But they will try again. It is not all over. We will have a death struggle." Ibid., 518–19.

251 "AFTER PASSING THROUGH" Edward Fontaine to his wife, July 25, 1861, Box 1, Folder 2, Edward Fontaine Collection, Sewanee, Tennessee.

251 "WE WILL WHIP THEM" Ibid.

251 "THE BATTLE OF MANASSAS" Edward Fontaine to his wife, August 3, 1861, ibid.

251 BORN INTO A PROMINENT FAMILY On McClellan, see, for instance, McPherson, *Battle Cry of Freedom*, 358–65; Stephen W. Sears, *George B. McClellan: The Young Napoleon* (New York, 1988).

251 "YOUNG NAPOLEON" Sears, *George B. McClellan*, xi.

251 "I FIND MYSELF" George B. McClellan to Mary Ellen McClellan, July 27, 1861, in Simpson, Sears, and Sheehan-Dean, eds., *Civil War: The First Year*, 524.

251 AT MIDNIGHT IN NEW YORK CITY Ibid., 531–32.

251 "YOU ARE NOT CONSIDERED" Ibid., 531.

252 "CAN THE REBELS" Ibid., 531–32.

252 CONFISCATION ACT OF 1861 Foner, *Fiery Trial*, 174–75; "The First Confiscation Act," August 6, 1861, Freedmen and Southern Society Project, University of Maryland, http://www.freedmen.umd.edu/conact1.htm.

252 "LAWFUL SUBJECT" "Confiscation Act, August 6, 1861," in Simpson, Sears, and Sheehan-Dean, eds., *Civil War: The First Year*, 538–39.

252 "THIS BILL WILL BE CONSIDERED" Foner, *Fiery Trial*, 175.

252 "VISIBLY THE QUESTION" "The Abolition of Slavery—Letter from Lincoln Camp in Kentucky to Yankee Paper," December 7, 1861, Civil War Collection: Confederate and Federal MF 824, Confederate Collection, Box 20, Folder 3, Scrapbooks—Couch, Mary E. Reel 8 Mf. Ac. No. 824, Tennessee State Archives.

253 A DRAMATIC PROCLAMATION John C. Frémont, "Proclamation," in Simpson, Sears, and Sheehan-Dean, eds., *Civil War: The First Year*, 562. See also Steve Inskeep, *Imperfect Union: How Jessie and John Frémont Mapped the West, Invented Celebrity, and Helped Cause the Civil War* (New York, 2020), 345–46; Foner, *Fiery Trial*, 176–80; Burlingame, *AL*, 2:202–12. See also Pamela Herr and Mary Lee Spence, eds., *The Letters of Jessie Benton Frémont* (Urbana, Ill., 1993), 266.

253 "WILL ALARM OUR SOUTHERN UNION FRIENDS" CW, 4:506; Abraham Lincoln to John C. Frémont, September 2, 1861, in Simpson, Sears, and Sheehan-Dean, eds., *Civil War: The First Year*, 563.

253 "Genl. Frémont's proclamation" CW, 4:531; Abraham Lincoln to Orville L. Browning, September 22, 1861, in Simpson, Sears, and Sheehan-Dean, eds., *Civil War: The First Year*, 568. Matters of property "must be settled according to laws made by law-makers, and not by military proclamations," Lincoln told Browning. Ibid., 568–69.

253 "Help me to dodge" George B. McClellan to Samuel L.M. Barlow, November 8, 1861, in Simpson, Sears, and Sheehan-Dean, eds., *Civil War: The First Year*, 588.

253 "My inclination is" Ibid., 639–40.

254 "the negro question" Escott, *Lincoln's Dilemma*, 95.

254 "decisive blow" Edward Fontaine to his wife, September 5, 1861, Edward Fontaine Collection, MS227 B1F2, Sewanee, Tennessee.

254 "Retaliation! To arms!" Henry Tucker, "God in the War," November 15, 1861, in Simpson, Sears, and Sheehan-Dean, eds., *Civil War: The First Year*, 607.

254 "Let us by faith" Ibid., 619.

254 "My countrymen, before God" Ibid.

Chapter Nineteen: My Boy Is Gone—He Is Actually Gone

255 "I am satisfied" *RWAL*, 105–6.

255 In October 1861 James A. Morgan, "The Battle of Ball's Bluff," Essential Civil War Curriculum," https://www.essentialcivilwarcurriculum.com/the-battle-of-balls-bluff.html.

255 as were 222 other Union troops Ibid.

255 Only thirty-six Confederates Ibid.

255 victories in the West Kendall D. Gott, "Fort Henry-Fort Donelson Campaign," https://www.essentialcivilwarcurriculum.com/fort-henry-fort-donelson-campaign.html.

255 at Shiloh in Tennessee Timothy B. Smith, "The Battle of Shiloh," https://www.essentialcivilwarcurriculum.com/the-battle-of-shiloh.html.

255 "The people are" *LDBD, 1861–1865*, 89.

255 "The President looks" Ibid., 85.

255 "clothed with power" Willis Steell, "Mrs. Abraham Lincoln and Her Friends," *Munsey's Magazine* 40, no. 5 (February 1909), 617.

255 Washington society had been Ibid., 617–18. See also Baker, *Mary Todd Lincoln*, 178–81.

255 She went through Steell, "Mrs. Abraham Lincoln," 618–21.

256 "was constantly under" Burlingame, *AL*, 2:263.

256 Mary was fond Baker, *Mary Todd Lincoln*, 181–96.

256 What funds she could not get Burlingame, *AL*, 2:273–84; Burlingame, *American Marriage*, 150–61.

256 "You understand, Lizabeth" Burlingame, *AL*, 2:701.

256 On trips to Philadelphia Baker, *Mary Todd Lincoln*, 184–85.

256 Her partner in the enterprise Ibid., 184.

256 provoked rumors of infidelity Ibid., 184–85.

256 "scarcely spoke together" Ibid., 184.

256 Mary had fueled Burlingame, *AL*, 2:263–84.

256 "She is said" Nathan W. Daniels Diary, January 31, 1864, LOC.

256 Born in 1836 https://www.loc.gov/collections/nathan-w-daniels-diary-and-scrapbook/articles-and-essays/timeline/.

257 The First Lady's influence was exaggerated Burlingame, *American Marriage*,

147–48. "In fact, her voice counted for little except in relatively minor cases," Burlingame observed. Ibid., 147.

257 "Mrs. Lincoln was dressed" Nathan W. Daniels Diary, January 1, 1864, LOC.
257 Her own tongue was problematic Burlingame, *American Marriage*, 203–4.
257 "an injudicious talker" Ibid., 203.
257 "with a flood" Ibid.
257 borrowing the mystery *LDBD, 1861–1865*, 163.
257 "Mrs. L. is" CW, 6:185.
257 "Mother has got" *RWAL*, 44–45.
257 "I certainly shall do" French, *Witness to the Young Republic*, 375.
257 the First Lady sent Ibid., 382.
257 "The money was" Ibid.
257 "Mrs. L. wanted me" Ibid.
258 "He said it would stink" Ibid.
258 a large private party Burlingame, *American Marriage*, 209–12.
258 "I can't do anything" Ibid., 209–10.
258 "Trifling at the White House" Ibid., 210.
258 "Are the President" Ibid., 211.
258 Soon darkness fell *LDBD, 1861–1865*, 93–96; Burlingame, AL, 2:297–302; Donald, *Lincoln*, 336–38; Goodwin, *Team of Rivals*, 415–23; White, *A. Lincoln*, 475–78.
258 "Well, Nicolay" Burlingame, AL, 2:298.
258 A grief-stricken Mary Lincoln Burlingame, *American Marriage*, 212–17.
258 Willie's body Baker, *Mary Todd Lincoln*, 210; French, *Witness to the Young Republic*, 389.
258 the president . . . asked French, *Witness to the Young Republic*, 389.
258 "They desired that" Ibid.
258 In the half hour Ibid.
258 Much of official Washington Ibid. There was also "a large attendance of persons in official positions, and citizens," French reported. Ibid.
258 "The heart of the Nation" Funeral Sermon by Dr. Gurley on February 24, 1862. http://www.abrahamlincolnonline.org/lincoln/education/williedeath.htm.
259 There was a lengthy procession French, *Witness to the Young Republic*, 389.
259 There Willie would lie The tomb belonged to William Carroll, clerk of the United States Supreme Court. "The Death of Willie Lincoln," http://www.abraham lincolnonline.org/lincoln/education/williedeath.htm.
259 "ever after" Willie's death Ibid.
259 Gurley recalled being Gurley, "Mourns for His Dead Boy (no. 10)," in *Phineas D. Gurley Collection of Notes* (1861, Oct. 2–1865, May 9), Lincoln Manuscripts, Lilly Library Archives, Indiana University, Bloomington, Indiana; Ervin S. Chapman, *Latest Light on Abraham Lincoln, and War-Time Memories* (New York, 1917), 499–500.
259 "Doctor, you rise early" Gurley, "Mourns for His Dead Boy no. 10)."
259 Gurley did as he Ibid.
260 "'Why doctor'" Ibid.
260 In this season Wolf, *Almost Chosen People*, 123.
260 "Alive!" Carpenter, *Inner Life of Abraham Lincoln*, 118–19.
260 "He first deemed" Herndon and Weik, *Herndon's Life of Lincoln*, 359–60. "Religion up to this time had been an intellectual interest," Ida Tarbell observed, "From this time on he was seen often with the Bible in his hand, and he is known to have prayed frequently. His personal relation to God occupied his mind much." To a nurse who offered him her prayers when Willie had died, Lincoln thanked her and replied, "I will try to go to God with my sorrows." Wolf, *Almost Chosen People*, 122–23.

260   "The will of God" CW, 5:403–4. On this passage, see, for instance, Guelzo, *Abraham Lincoln: Redeemer President,* 325–29; Ronald C. White, Jr., *Lincoln in Private: What His Most Personal Reflections Tell Us About Our Greatest President* (New York, 2021), 149–60.

261   A delegation of Quakers CW, 5:278–79; *LDBD, 1861–1865,* 122.

262   "The slave power might silence" Quarles, *Lincoln and the Negro,* 50.

262   "And they said one to another" Genesis 42:21, KJV.

262   Congress's immediate abolition "End of Slavery in the District of Columbia," *NYT,* April 17, 1862; Fredrickson, *Big Enough to Be Inconsistent,* 94; Damani Davis, "Slavery and Emancipation in the Nation's Capital," *Prologue Magazine* 42, no. 1 (Spring 2010), https://www.archives.gov/publications/prologue/2010/spring/dcslavery.html.

262   "Thanks Be to the Almighty" Michael Shiner Diary, LOC.

262   Long an antislavery goal Oakes, *Crooked Path to Abolition,* 60–72.

262   The president had his reservations Ibid., 94–95. "I am a little uneasy about the abolishment of slavery in this District. . . . I would like the bill to have the three main features—gradual—compensation—and vote of the people," Lincoln remarked. *CW,* 5:169.

262   The bill provided Davis, "Slavery and Emancipation in the Nation's Capital," *Prologue Magazine.* See also "An Act of April 16, 1862 [For the Release of Certain Persons Held to Service or Labor in the District of Columbia]," National Archives, https://catalog.archives.gov/id/299814. In his message announcing that he had signed the bill into law, Lincoln said that he had "never doubted the constitutional authority of congress to abolish slavery in this District; and I have ever desired to see the national capital freed from the institution in some satisfactory way." As he signed the bill, Lincoln noted: "I am gratified that the two principles of compensation, and colonization, are both recognized, and practically applied in the act." *CW,* 5:192.

262   "the genius of the age" *NYT,* April 17, 1862.

263   David Hunter Quarles, *Lincoln and the Negro,* 72–73; *CW,* 5:222–24; *LDBD, 1861–1865,* 113.

263   Lincoln rescinded the directive CW, 5:222–23.

263   "I . . . make known" Ibid.; Burlingame, *AL,* 2:347–50; Foner, *Fiery Trial,* 207.

263   In May and June *LDBD, 1861–1865,* 114.

263   "Not a spark" Nevins, *War for the Union,* 2:301. See also *LDBD, 1861–1865,* 151.

263   Jackson's rout Jonathan A. Noyalas, "'Like a Wind from the Mountains': Stonewall Jackson's 1862 Valley Campaign," https://www.essentialcivilwarcurriculum.com/like-a-wind-from-the-mountains-stonewall-jacksons-1862-valley-campaign.html.

263   Battle of Seven Pines Peter Luebke, "Battle of Seven Pines," *Encyclopedia Virginia,* https://encyclopediavirginia.org/entries/seven-pines-battle-of.

264   Seven Days' Battles Brian K. Burton, "The Seven Days Battles," https://www.essentialcivilwarcurriculum.com/the-seven-days-battles.html.

264   Second Battle of Bull Run Michael Burns, "The Second Battle of Bull Run," https://www.essentialcivilwarcurriculum.com/the-second-battle-of-bull-run.html.

264   At Shiloh in April 1862 McPherson, "The Strategy of Unconditional Surrender" in Wilentz, ed., *Best American History Essays on Lincoln,* 216–17.

264   "gave up all idea" Ibid., 216.

264   "We are not only" Ibid., 217.

264 UNCONDITIONAL SURRENDER HAD BEEN "Peace and Unconditional Surrender: Lincoln & Churchill," https://lincolnandchurchill.org/peace-unconditional -surrender/.

264 "I AM SATISFIED" RWAL, 105–6.

265 "IS PROFOUNDLY IMPRESSED" Leonidas Polk to Colonel Buford, February 23, 1862, Box 11, Folder 5, Polk Papers, Sewanee, Tennessee.

265 "I EXPECT TO MAINTAIN" CW, 5:291–92.

265 "WHATEVER IS CALCULATED" Holzer and Garfinkle, Just and Generous Nation, 3. As they observed: "Lincoln was the first president to use the federal government as an agent to support Americans in their effort to achieve and sustain a middle-class life. Even as the Civil War commenced, Lincoln supported a program of direct government action to support his vision of America's middle-class society." Ibid., 4.

265 "THE PRUDENT, PENNILESS BEGINNER" Holzer and Garfinkle, Just and Generous Nation, 6.

265 SHOULD BE NOT WEAKENED . . . See, for instance, ibid., 75–90; Leonard P. Curry, Blueprint for Modern America: Nonmilitary Legislation of the First Civil War Congress (Nashville, 1968).

265 APPROVED A FEDERAL INCOME TAX Holzer and Garfinkel, Just and Generous Nation, 78. See also Sheldon D. Pollack, "The First National Income Tax, 1861–1872) The Tax Lawyer 67, no. 2 (2014): 311–30. See also Roger Lowenstein, Ways and Means: Lincoln and His Cabinet and the Financing of the Civil War (New York, 2022).

265 SIGNED NATIONAL BANKING LEGISLATION Holzer and Garfinkel, Just and Generous Nation, 77–78.

265 HOMESTEAD ACT OF 1862 Ibid., 78; Lee Ann Potter and Wynell Schamel, "The Homestead Act of 1862," Social Education 61, no. 6 (October 1997): 359–64.

265 FURTHER DISPLACING INDIGENOUS PEOPLES See, for instance, "Native Americans and the Homestead Act," National Park Service," https://www.nps.gov/home /learn/historyculture/native-americans-and-the-homestead-act.htm.

265 "MAN'S VAST FUTURE" CW, 6:410.

265 PACIFIC RAILROAD ACT Ibid., 5:314–15; Holzer and Garfinkel, Just and Generous Nation, 78.

265 AN ACT, SPONSORED BY LDBD, 1861–1865, 125. See also Holzer and Garfinkel, Just and Generous Nation, 78.

266 EXPLOITED NATIVE AMERICANS See, for instance, Robert Lee and Tristan Ahtone, "Land-Grab Universities," High Country News, March 30, 2020, https://www.hcn .org/issues/52.4/indigenous-affairs-education-land-grab-universities. "Unquestionably, the history of land-grant universities intersects with that of Native Americans and the taking of their lands," the Association of Public and Land-Grant Universities said in a written statement to High Country News in 2020. "While we cannot change the past, land-grant universities have and will continue to be focused on building a better future for everyone." Ibid.

266 "A DECLARATION OF RADICAL VIEWS" Sears, George B. McClellan, 227–28.

266 SECOND CONFISCATION ACT LDBD, 1861–1865, 128. See also Paul Finkelman, "The Revolutionary Summer of 1862: How Congress Abolished Slavery and Created a Modern America, Prologue Magazine 49, no. 4 (Winter 2017–18), https://www .archives.gov/publications/prologue/2017/winter/summer-of-1862.

266 "AN ACT TO SUPPRESS" The Second Confiscation Act, July 17, 1862, http://www .freedmen.umd.edu/conact2.htm.

266 A SWEEPING LAW Foner, Fiery Trial, 215–16.

266   "PERSONS" The Second Confiscation Act, July 17, 1862, http://www.freedmen.umd
       .edu/conact2.htm.

266   "TO EMPLOY AS MANY" Ibid.

266   "TO MAKE PROVISION" Ibid.

266   UNION VICTORIES IN CONFEDERATE TERRITORY Foner, *Fiery Trial*; McPherson, *Battle
       Cry of Freedom*, 500–501.

266   "YOU CAN FORM" Quarles, *The Negro in the Civil War*, 158.

267   "I SHALL NOT DO MORE" CW, 5:344–46.

267   THE PRESIDENT HAD SENT *LDBD, 1861–1865*, 121.

267   "THE GREAT OBJECT" Stowe, *A Key to Uncle Tom's Cabin* (New York, 1968), iii–iv.

Chapter Twenty: I Think the Time Has Come Now

268   "I NOW DETERMINED" Hay and Nicolay, *AL: A History*, 6:128–29.

268   "THE CHILDREN OF THE BLACK MAN" Quarles, *The Negro in the Civil War*, 157.

268   THERE WERE TWO PORTRAITS Burlingame, *AL*, 2:250; Conroy, *Lincoln's White House*, 94.

268   ONE, OF ANDREW JACKSON Conroy, *Lincoln's White House*, 94. See also Sandburg, *The
       War Years*, 1:139.

268   ENGLISH POLITICIAN AND REFORMER See, for instance, Herman Ausubel, *John Bright,
       Victorian Reformer* (New York, 1966); Bill Cash, *John Bright: Statesman, Orator, Agitator*
       (London, 2012); Guelzo, "Lincoln, Cobden, and Bright"; G. M. Trevelyan, *The Life
       of John Bright* (Boston, 1913).

268   "ONE OF THE MOST GIFTED" Cash, *John Bright*, xxv.

268   "IF YOU COULD TAKE" Ibid., xxiv.

268   "HE HAS LIVED" Ibid., xvii.

268   BORN IN 1811 Ibid., 5–6.

268   HE WAS CONNECTED Ibid., 145–47.

269   "EVERYWHERE THERE IS" Guelzo, "Lincoln, Cobden, and Bright," 399.

269   "THE WHOLE OF THAT" Cash, *John Bright*, 152–53.

269   "THE OBJECT OF THE SOUTH" John Bright, *Speeches of John Bright, M.P.* (Boston, 1865),
       26–27.

269   "A HANDFUL OF WHITE MEN" Ibid., 111.

269   THE OCCASION WAS GRIM *LDBD, 1861–1865*, 128.

269   SOLDIERS' HOME Burlingame, *AL*, 2:251; Matthew Pinsker, *Lincoln's Sanctuary: Abra-
       ham Lincoln and the Soldiers' Home* (New York, 2003), is comprehensive.

269   "MILITARY ASYLUM" Pinsker, *Lincoln's Sanctuary*, 2–4.

269   "THE AIR IS SWARMING" Burlingame, *AL*, 2:251.

270   "THE EFFLUVIA FROM DEAD RATS" Ibid.

270   "VERY BEAUTIFUL" Pinsker, *Lincoln's Sanctuary*, 22.

270   USE OF A NEIGHBORING COTTAGE Ibid., 32–33.

270   "IF MY CHILD" Ibid., 33.

271   REPORTEDLY BROACHED . . . EMANCIPATION On the Emancipation Proclamation, see
       Burlingame, *AL*, 2:360–473; Oakes, *Freedom National*, 301–92; Holzer, *Emancipating
       Lincoln*; Guelzo, *Lincoln's Emancipation Proclamation*.

271   "IT WAS A NEW DEPARTURE" William E. Gienapp and Erica L. Gienapp, eds., *The Civil
       War Diary of Gideon Welles: Lincoln's Secretary of the Navy* (Urbana, Ill., 2014), 3–4.
       Welles added: "The slaves, if not armed and disciplined, were in the service of
       those who were, not only as field laborers and producers, but thousands of them
       were in attendance upon the armies in the field, employed as waiters & teamsters,
       and the fortifications and [e]ntrenchments were constructed by them." Ibid., 4.

271 "LIKE OTHER PEOPLE" Hay and Nicolay, *AL: A History*, 6:432.

271 IN A MEETING OF THE CABINET Ibid., 123–30; Burlingame, *AL*, 2:362–64.

271 HE HAD COMPOSED IT David Homer Bates, *Lincoln in the Telegraph Office: Recollections of the United States Military Telegraph Corps During the Civil War* (Lincoln, Neb., 1995), 138–53.

271 BRASS INKWELL Rubenstein, *Abraham Lincoln: An Extraordinary Life*, 54.

271 FREQUENTED THESE ROOMS Bates, *Lincoln in the Telegraph Office*, is comprehensive.

271 THE ARMY'S TELEGRAPH SUPERINTENDENT "Notable Visitors: Thomas T. Eckert (1825–1920)," http://www.mrlincolnswhitehouse.org/residents-visitors/notable -visitors/notable-visitors-thomas-t-eckert-1825-1910/.

271 "THE PRESIDENT CAME" Bates, *Lincoln in the Telegraph Office*, 138–41; Rubenstein, *Abraham Lincoln: An Extraordinary Life*, 54.

272 "EVERY MEMBER OF THE COUNCIL" Hay and Nicolay, *AL: A History*, 6:127.

272 "I NOW DETERMINED" Ibid., 128–29.

272 MILITARY MAPS Stoddard, *Inside Lincoln's White House*, 13. For a description of the president's office, see Arnold, *Life of Abraham Lincoln*, 452, as well as Conroy, *Lincoln's White House*, 94–96.

272 THERE WERE A FEW THOUGHTS Hay and Nicolay, *AL: A History*, 6:129–30.

272 "MR. BLAIR . . . DEPRECATED" Ibid.

272 SEWARD WEIGHED IN Ibid., 130.

272 "MR. PRESIDENT, I APPROVE" Ibid.

272 "BE CONSIDERED" Ibid.

272 "THE WISDOM OF THE VIEW" Ibid.

273 IT WAS THE AFTERNOON OF THURSDAY, AUGUST 14 CW, 5:370–75; Burlingame, *AL*, 2:383–89; Oakes, *Freedom National*, 308–13.

273 EDWARD M. THOMAS Burlingame, *AL*, 2:389.

273 ALSO PRESENT Harold Holzer, *Lincoln and the Power of the Press: The War for Public Opinion* (New York, 2014), 396–98.

273 "THE PEOPLE, OR A PORTION OF THEM" CW, 5:371.

273 CONGRESS HAD APPROPRIATED Ibid.

273 LINCOLN HAD LONG COUPLED EMANCIPATION See, for instance, Burlingame, *AL*, 2:383–96; Michael Vorenberg, "Abraham Lincoln and the Politics of Black Colonization," *JALA* 14, no. 2 (Summer 1993), 22–45; Escott, *Lincoln's Dilemma*, 114–15; Hay and Nicolay, *AL: A History*, 6:354–67.

273 "APART FROM THE ANTIPATHY" Report of the Select Committee on Emancipation and Colonization, House Reports no. 148, 37th Congress, 2nd Session, July 16, 1862, 13. See also Burlingame, *AL*, 2:385.

273 LIBERIA WAS ONE Burlingame, *AL*, 2:387.

273 "THE DANISH ISLAND" Hay and Nicolay, *AL: A History*, 6:357.

273 IN OCTOBER 1861 CW, 4:561; Vorenberg, "Abraham Lincoln and the Politics of Black Colonization," 28–29. See also Escott, *Lincoln's Dilemma*, 99–101, 111–15.

273 LED BY AN INVESTOR Escott, *Lincoln's Dilemma*, 100. See also Paul J. Scheips, "Gabriel Lafond and Ambrose W. Thompson: Neglected Isthmian Promoters," *Hispanic American Historical Review* 36, no. 2 (May 1956): 211–28.

273 "HOW MUCH BETTER" Rick Beard, "Lincoln's Panama Plan," *NYT* August 16, 2012; Burlingame, *AL*, 2:391.

274 "THE NATION'S FOUR MILLION" Beard, "Lincoln's Panama Plan."

274 "LINCOLN HELD THE STRONG BELIEF" Quarles, *Lincoln and the Negro*, 108.

274 "SUCH PERSONS, ON SUCH" CW, 5:48.

274 "THE *EVERLASTING NEGRO*" Quarles, *Lincoln and the Negro*, 64.

274 "We can make emancipation" Vorenberg, "Abraham Lincoln and the Politics of Black Colonization," 29.

274 "You and we are different races" CW, 5:371–72.

275 "I do not propose" Ibid., 372.

275 "The place I am thinking" Ibid., 373–75.

275 "they would hold" Ibid., 375.

276 "Take your full time" Ibid.

276 first conference ever held Quarles, *Lincoln and the Negro*, 115. "Ever the experimenter and always the problem solver, Lincoln likely saw colonization as one of many avenues to approach an anguishing difficulty that had no simple resolution," the scholars Phillip W. Magness and Sebastian N. Page wrote. "Retrospection correctly deems this program a folly, but to his contemporaries racial politics were a complex and uncharted course. Nor was he alone in this thinking; black abolitionists such as [John Willis] Menard and [Henry Highland] Garnet saw a possible escape from the United States' racial problems in a colony abroad. To these free black leaders, and perhaps even to Lincoln, colonization presented a voluntary alternative to a future in the United States where the country's commitment to civil rights was anything but certain.... Although this is not to try to rescue Lincoln as a racial progressive—as abolitionists argued, dangling the prospect of colonization justified others' prejudice and helped moderates duck questions of the future shape of America—a distinction may be drawn between personal disdain for African Americans and the kind of pessimistic social outlook which had in fact long been the intellectual mainstay of much of the colonizationist movement." Magness and Page, *Colonization After Emancipation*, 124.

276 Thomas later wrote Burlingame, *AL*, 2:389.

276 "To these colored people" Blight, *Frederick Douglass*, 374.

276 "We can find nothing" Quarles, *Lincoln and the Negro*, 117.

276 "The children of the black man" Quarles, *The Negro in the Civil War*, 157.

276 Lincoln met with *LDBD, 1861–1865*, 134–35.

276 the president approved *LDBD, 1861–1865*, 138; CW, 5:414; Fredrickson, *Big Enough to Be Inconsistent*, 105–6.

276 resistance from the region Burlingame, *AL*, 2:391–95; Escott, *Lincoln's Dilemma*, 141; Hay and Nicolay, *AL: A History*, 6:358–59.

276 proposed $250,000 federal contract Burlingame, *AL*, 2:395; Vorenberg, "Abraham Lincoln and the Politics of Black Colonization," 38–44.

276 expedition transporting about 450 Burlingame, *AL*, 2:395–96; Hay and Nicolay, *AL: A History*, 6:359–67.

276 The experiment lasted Burlingame, *AL*, 2:396; Hay and Nicolay, *AL: A History*, 6:363–67.

276 Lincoln remained interested Magness and Page, *Colonization After Emancipation*, especially 10, 118–28; Escott, *Lincoln's Dilemma*, 189–90.

276 cut off colonization funding Vorenberg, "Abraham Lincoln and the Politics of Black Colonization," 41–42.

276 "by no means" Magness and Page, *Colonization After Emancipation*, 108.

277 "We complain that" Horace Greeley, "The Prayer of Twenty Millions," 1862, https://staush.files.wordpress.com/2012/09/lincolngreeley.pdf.

277 "If there be those" CW, 5:388–89.

278 The letter to Greeley Burlingame, *AL*, 2:403–6; Holzer, *Lincoln and the Power of the Press*, 398–408. As Burlingame observed, "Lincoln's letter has been misunderstood by those who view it as a definitive statement of his innermost feelings about the aims of the war. Some deplored its insensitivity to the moral significance

of emancipation. In fact, the document was a political utterance designed to smooth the way for the proclamation which he intended to issue as soon as the Union army won a victory. He knew full well that millions of Northerners as well as Border State residents would object to transforming the war into an abolitionist crusade. They were willing to fight to preserve the Union but not to free the slaves. As president, Lincoln had to make the mighty act of emancipation palatable to them. By assuring Conservatives that emancipation was simply a means to preserve the Union, Lincoln hoped to minimize the white backlash that he knew was bound to come." Burlingame, *AL*, 2:403.

278   IN AN HOUR-LONG SESSION CW, 5:419–25.
281   AN ANSWER CAME AT ANTIETAM McPherson, *Battle Cry of Freedom*, 538–45.
281   "I NOW CONSIDER" CW, 5:425–26.
281   "GENERAL FEELING" *LDBD, 1861–1865*, 135.
281   LINCOLN TOLD THE CABINET Burlingame, *AL*, 2:407–9.
281   "I THINK THE TIME HAS COME" Ibid., 407.
281   "WHEN THE REBEL ARMY" Ibid., 407–8; White, *A. Lincoln*, 516–17.
281   "I SAID NOTHING" Burlingame, *AL*, 2:408.
281   LINCOLN BRIEFLY HESITATED Ibid.
282   "REMARKED THAT HE HAD" Gienapp and Gienapp, eds., *Civil War Diary of Gideon Welles*, 54; White, *A. Lincoln*, 517.
282   "IT MIGHT BE THOUGHT STRANGE" Gienapp and Gienapp, eds., *Civil War Diary of Gideon Welles*, 54.
282   "GOD HAD DECIDED" Ibid.
282   ADVANCE VOLUNTARY COLONIZATION Ibid., 59–61; Fredrickson, *Big Enough to Be Inconsistent*, 107.
282   STRUGGLE WAS ONLY NOW Quarles, *Lincoln and the Negro*, 131.
282   "IT IS INDISPUTABLY" Nevins, *War for the Union*, 2:270.
282   THE PROCLAMATION WAS DATED CW, 5:433–36.
283   AN APPROVING CROWD *LDBD, 1861–1865*, 141.
283   "WHAT I DID" CW, 5:438.
283   "THE NORTH RESPONDS" *LDBD, 1861–1865*, 142.

Chapter Twenty-one: The President Has Done Nobly

284   "THIS IS A GREAT ERA" Harrold, *Lincoln and the Abolitionists*, 91.
284   "HIS HAIR IS GRIZZLED" Burlingame, ed., *Lincoln Observed*, 13.
284   REMOVED GENERAL MCCLELLAN *LDBD, 1861–1865*, 148; CW, 5:485–86.
284   MIDTERM ELECTIONS See, for instance, Jamie L. Carson, Jeffery A. Jenkins, David W. Rohde and Mark A. Souva, "The Impact of National Tides and District-Level Effects on Electoral Outcomes: The U.S. Congressional Elections of 1862–63," *American Journal of Political Science* 45, no. 4 (October 2001): 887–98; Mark M. Krug, "Lincoln, the Republican Party, and the Emancipation Proclamation," *History Teacher* 7, no. 1 (November 1973): 48–61.
284   FOURTEEN STATES VOTED Carson et al., "Impact of National Tides," 896.
284   GOVERNORSHIPS OF NEW YORK AND NEW JERSEY Krug, "Lincoln, the Republican Party, and the Emancipation Proclamation," 58.
284   FELL FROM 59 TO 46.2 PERCENT Carson et al., "Impact of National Tides," 887.
284   THERE WERE SUNDRY REASONS See, in particular, Carson et al., "Impact of National Tides."
285   "DISASTROUS IN THE EXTREME" Burlingame, *AL*, 2:419. For a more optimistic view of the 1862–63 elections, see McPherson, *Battle Cry of Freedom*, 561–62.

285   Battle of Fredericksburg McPherson, *Battle Cry of Freedom*, 571–75.

285   exacting about thirteen thousand casualties Ibid., 572.

285   "If there is a worse" Ibid., 574. See also Weber, *Copperheads*, 73–75.

285   "the bottom would be out" *RWAL*, 322.

285   Only news of victory Weber, *Copperheads*, 76.

285   "God bless you" *CW*, 6:39.

285   Elements of the Sioux tribe Burlingame, *AL*, 2:480–81; Prucha, *Great Father*, 437–43; Michael S. Green, *Lincoln and Native Americans* (Carbondale, Ill., 2021), 69–87.

285   Encouraged by the removal Prucha, *Great Father*, 440.

285   frustrated by broken treaties Ibid.

285   "state of near starvation" Ibid., 441.

285   Native American issues See, for instance, Christopher W. Anderson, "Native Americans and the Origins of Abraham Lincoln's Views on Race," *JALA*, 37, no. 1 (Winter 2016); Burlingame, *AL*, 2:480–84; Green, *Lincoln and Native Americans*; Prucha, *Great Father*, 412–13; 417, 424, 442–43, 445, 468–70, 472.

285   1858 Senate race Prucha, *Great Father*, 413. As Prucha went on to observe: "That Lincoln's humane principles applied to Indians there can be little doubt, but he held common white views about their destiny." Ibid.

285   "simultaneously foreign and respectable" Anderson, "Native Americans and the Origins of Abraham Lincoln's Views on Race," 12.

285   Minnesota militia and the U.S. military Burlingame, *AL*, 2:481.

285   Sioux were convicted Prucha, *Great Father*, 443.

285   "We cannot hang" Ibid., 444.

286   Typically inclined to clemency Ibid., 445; Burlingame, *AL*, 2:482.

286   Told in 1864 Burlingame, *AL*, 2:483.

286   "Fellow-citizens, we cannot" *CW*, 5:537. See also Burlingame, *AL*, 2:439–43.

286   Lincoln proposed a constitutional amendment *CW*, 5:529–31.

286   "Every State, Wherein" Ibid., 530.

287   "How it makes" Burlingame, *AL*, 2:441.

287   when a Republican congressman *RWAL*, 1.

287   "Yes, I have" Ibid.

287   "Christmas is a great institution" Strong, "The Diaries, 1862," in Holzer, ed., *TLA*, 52.

287   "Public affairs unchanged" Ibid.

287   "I have made up" Burlingame, *AL*, 2:467.

287   On New Year's Day Hay and Nicolay, *AL: A History*, 6:421–29.

287   It was mid-afternoon Ibid., 429.

287   Worn out from the long Burlingame, *AL*, 2:469.

288   "could not for a moment" Ibid.

288   "I never, in my life" Emancipation Proclamation, National Archives, https://www.archives.gov/news/topics/emancipation-proclamation.

288   "Men, women, young and old" Burlingame, *AL*, 2:470.

288   "This is a great Era!" Harrold, *Lincoln and the Abolitionists*, 91.

288   "several millions" Burlingame, *AL*, 2:472.

288   "What shall we" Carolyn L. Harrell, *When the Bells Tolled for Lincoln: Southern Reaction to the Assassination* (Macon, Ga., 1997), 24.

288   "Many of my strongest" *RWAL*, 83–84.

288   British had long watched See, for instance, Amanda Foreman, *A World on Fire: Britain's Crucial Role in the American Civil War* (New York, 2011).

288   "The North may be assured" "The North and the South (1861)," from *The London*

Review, Civil War Collection: Confederate and Federal MF 824, Confederate Collection, Box 20, Folder 3, Scrapbooks—Couch, Mary E. Reel 8 Mf. Ac. No. 824, Tennessee State Archives.

288 "There is no doubt" David Colbert, *Eyewitness to America: 500 Years of American History in the Words of Those Who Saw It Happen* (New York, 1997), 214.

289 "it seems not" James M. McPherson, *The War That Forged a Nation: Why the Civil War Still Matters* (New York, 2015), 73. See also James M. McPherson, "No Peace Without Victory, 1861–1865," Presidential Address to the American Historical Association, January 3, 2004. "We may have our own opinions about slavery," William Gladstone remarked in Newcastle, "we may be for or against the South; but there is no doubt that Jefferson Davis and other leaders . . . have made an army; they are making, it appears, a navy; and they have made what is more than either; they have made a nation." Nevins, *War for the Union*, 2:268.

289 "would it not be time" McPherson, *War That Forged a Nation*, 73.

289 The Union victory Ibid., 73–75.

289 There would be no recognition Ibid., 74. In Paris, however, Napoleon III harbored hopes that he, with other European powers, could bring about a settlement that would ratify secession. "My own preference is for a proposition of an armistice of six months, with the Southern ports open to the commerce of the world," the French emperor said in October 1862. "This would put a stop to the effusion of blood, and hostilities would probably never be resumed." See, for instance, Owen F. Aldis, "Louis Napoleon and the Southern Confederacy," *North American Review* 129, no. 275 (1879): 342–60; Daniel B. Carroll, *Henri Mercier and the American Civil War* (Princeton, N.J., 1971), 239.

289 "done more for us" McPherson, *War That Forged a Nation*, 74–75.

289 "Recognition of the South" Ibid., 75.

289 "Where have you been" Elizabeth Keckley [sic], *Behind the Scenes, or, Thirty Years a Slave, and Four Years in the White House* (New York, 1868), 118–19.

289 Lincoln took up Ibid., 119.

290 "a plain working man" Harriet Beecher Stowe, "Abraham Lincoln," in Holzer, ed., *TLA*, 87.

290 the presidency of Abraham Lincoln See, for instance, Burlingame, ed., *Lincoln Observed*, 19–22.

291 "had made a great mistake" Burlingame, *AL*, 2:478.

291 "upon the brink" Ibid.

291 might lead "popular feeling" Burlingame, ed., *Lincoln Observed*, 55.

291 "In some respects" *RWAL*, 322.

291 the French episode Warren F. Spencer, "The Jewett-Greeley Affair: A Private Scheme for French Mediation in the American Civil War," *New York History* 51, no. 3 (1970): 238–68.

291 led him to "see conditions developing" Ibid., 241.

291 "the South had won" Ibid., 250.

292 shadowy figure Ibid., 246.

292 After a visit to France Ibid., 252.

292 "The French Minister" Ibid., 255–56.

292 With assistance from Seward McPherson, "No Peace Without Victory."

292 "The war must go on" Ibid.; "Prospects of the War Foreign Intervention," *NYT*, January 29, 1863.

292 "The war for the Union" Clement Vallandigham, "On the War and Its Conduct," https://teachingamericanhistory.org/document/on-the-war-and-its-conduct/.

292 "Last night to have seen Old Abe" Letter to J. G. Decker from fellow soldier,

Herman, from Evansville, Indiana, Camp Near Falmouth, April 10, 1863, ID no. mont129, Tennessee Virtual Archives.

292 RUMORS OF SECESSIONISM Weber, *Copperheads*, 79–83.

292 "THESE ARE DARK HOURS" Ibid., 81–82.

293 "STRICTLY CONFIDENTIAL" Oliver P. Morton to Abraham Lincoln [With Endorsement by Lincoln], February 9, 1863, Abraham Lincoln Papers, LOC.

293 "THE DEMOCRATIC SCHEME" Ibid.

293 OTHER "LEADING POLITICIANS" Ibid.

293 "SECRET SOCIETIES" Ibid.

293 "ARE BEING ESTABLISHED" Ibid. See also CW, 6:87–88; *LDBD, 1861–1865*, 166; "The Great Conspiracy: An Official Statement by Judge-Advocate-General Holt," *NYT*, October 16, 1864; Hay and Nicolay, *AL: A History*, 8:1–27.

293 WAS A LEADER Keehn, *Knights of the Golden Circle*, 175.

293 LONG REPORT Hay and Nicolay, *AL: A History*, 8:11.

293 "EVIDENT EXTENT AND" Ibid.

293 "AN OATH-BOUND SECRET" Ibid., 11–12.

293 "SUPREME COMMANDER" Ibid., 12.

293 "CLAIM[S] TO HAVE" Ibid. The president dispatched John Hay to St. Louis to assess the situation. Lincoln's secretary was less concerned than the president's correspondents, and Lincoln kept the threat in proportion. "The toleration with which the President regarded them, and the immunity which he allowed them in their passive treason, arose from the fact that he never could be made to believe that there was as much crime as folly in their acts and purposes," Hay and Nicolay recalled. To Lincoln's inner circle—and Hay now had firsthand experience in the matter—the Knights and their assorted heirs and allies "were sufficiently disloyal to take all manner of oaths against the Government; to declare in their secret councils they were ready to shed the last drop of their blood to abolish it. . . . But this was the limit of their criminal courage. Shedding the last drop of one's blood is a comparatively easy sacrifice—it is shedding the first drop that costs." Ibid., 10–13.

294 "VIGOROUS AND SUCCESSFUL" Morton to Lincoln, February 9, 1863, Abraham Lincoln Papers, LOC.

294 VALLANDIGHAM HAD DENOUNCED Weber, *Copperheads*, 88.

294 "IT IS BELIEVED" Hay and Nicolay, *AL: A History*, 7:13.

294 THE COURTS DISAGREED Ibid.

294 THE DRAFT WAS SEEN Ibid., 16–17.

294 CHAMPIONED BY SENATORS Ibid., 4.

294 THE CONSCRIPTION LAW McPherson, *Battle Cry of Freedom*, 600–611.

294 AS A "N——R WAR" Leslie M. Harris, "The New York City Draft Riots of 1863," https://press.uchicago.edu/Misc/Chicago/317749.html&title=The+New+York +City+Draft+Riots+of+1863&desc.

294 THE VIOLENT MOB TARGETED Hay and Nicolay, *AL: A History*, 7:20–21.

294 "DASHED WITH THE MERRIMENT" Ibid., 20.

294 LINCOLN HAD GONE Burlingame, ed., *Lincoln Observed*, 24.

294 HAY AND NICOLAY SCAMPERED Ibid.

294 JUST SHORT OF NOON Ibid., 25.

295 FURTHER ENRAGING HIS OPPONENTS Weber, *Copperheads*, 92–93.

295 "IT WAS WITH" RWAL, 501.

295 "KING LINCOLN" Hay and Nicolay, *AL: A History*, 7:331.

295 "OUR FOES HAVE GIVEN" "An Appeal to Farmers: Proclamation by the Governor of S. Carolina," *Charlotte Democrat*, March 24, 1863.

295 "Lincoln is now the President Dictator" *Mobile Advertiser and Register,* March 10, 1863.

295 Amid a blizzard *LDBD, 1861–1865,* 164.

295 "frozen crystals" Ibid.

295 General Order No. 11 Jonathan D. Sarna, *American Judaism: A History* (New Haven, Conn., 2004), 120–21.

295 "enormous outrage" "Anti-Semitism in the United States: General Grant's Infamy," https://www.jewishvirtuallibrary.org/general-grant-s-infamy.

295 "The President has no objection" *LDBD, 1861–1865,* 164.

295 To a visiting delegation of Jewish leaders "Anti-Semitism in the United States."

295 "to condemn a class" Jon Meacham, *American Gospel: God, the Founding Fathers, and the Making of a Nation* (New York, 2006), 131.

295 high-profile test See, for instance, Hay and Nicolay, *AL: A History,* 7:328–60; Burlingame, *AL,* 2:503–10.

296 "The habit of declaring" General Order No. 38, https://ohiohistorycentral .org/w/General_Order_No._38. The edict was controversial even among Burnside's staff. "Order 38 has kindled the fires of hatred and contention," James Madison Cutts wrote Lincoln. "Burnside is foolishly and unwisely excited, and if continued in command will disgrace himself, you, and the country, as he did at Fredericksburg." Hay and Nicolay, *AL: A History,* 7:329. See also Burlingame, *AL,* 2:505.

296 "wicked abolition war" Burlingame, *AL,* 2:505.

296 "I am here" Hay and Nicolay, *AL: A History,* 7:332.

296 He was convicted Burlingame, *AL,* 2:505–6.

296 The president was unhappy See, for instance, CW, 6:237, 269.

296 "Mr. Vallandigham avows" Ibid., 266.

296 Vallandigham ended up in Canada Burlingame, *AL,* 2:507.

296 "is not merely a step" Ibid., 506.

296 "attempt" CW, 6:176–77.

297 "God . . . made the world" Acts 17:24–26, KJV.

297 late-spring snows Burlingame, ed., *Lincoln Observed,* 36; *LDBD, 1861–1865,* 177. For Lincoln's note about the impending visit, see CW, 6:161.

297 a snowstorm drove *LDBD, 1861–1865,* 177.

297 "The thoughtful wife" Burlingame, ed., *Lincoln Observed,* 36.

297 A visitor among Burlingame, *AL,* 2:494–95.

297 "It was a touching scene" Burlingame, ed., *Lincoln Observed,* 41–42.

297 Falmouth, Virginia *LDBD, 1861–1865,* 178.

297 uncomfortable domestic moment Ibid.; Burlingame, *AL,* 2:495.

297 "I always felt" Burlingame, *American Marriage,* 190.

297 "You and Mary love each other" Ibid., 159–60.

297 "Think you better" CW, 6:256.

298 White House stables *LDBD, 1861–1865,* 239; Carpenter, *Inner Life of Abraham Lincoln,* 44–45.

298 "Tad explained" *LDBD, 1861–1865,* 239.

298 "When my noble little Willie" Berry, *House of Abraham,* 153.

298 "Did you ever dream" *RWAL,* 78.

298 this time from Chancellorsville McPherson, *Battle Cry of Freedom,* 640–46; *LDBD, 1861–1865,* 182–83.

298 "My plans are perfect" Burlingame, *AL,* 2:496.

298   THOUGH ONLY ABOUT HALF "Chancellorsville," Civil War Battlefield Trust, https://www.battlefields.org/learn/civil-war/battles/chancellorsville.

298   THE UNION SUSTAINED Ibid.

298   STONEWALL JACKSON WAS Ibid.

298   "HAD A THUNDERBOLT" Burlingame, ed., *Lincoln Observed*, 50. Inevitably, unhappy chatter consumed the capital. "It is so easy, you know, for a knot of critics to demolish the programme of a General, while seated around a Washington breakfast table or in an editorial sanctum," Brooks wrote, "that it is not strange that Hooker has had to 'catch it' right and left." Ibid., 51.

298   "WHAT WILL THE COUNTRY" RWAL, 44.

298   IN A STORY Ibid., 416.

299   "MY GOD, STANTON" Ibid.

299   "IF I AM NOT" Ibid.

299   "HAD FULLY MADE UP" Ibid.

299   "HAVE YOU ANY" CW, 6:293.

Chapter Twenty-two: That All Men Could Be Free

303   "I CALL THE WAR" Edward Everett, "Gettysburg Address," November 19, 1863. Voices of Democracy: The U.S. Oratory Project, University of Maryland, College Park, Maryland, https://voicesofdemocracy.umd.edu/everett-gettysburg-address-speech-text/.

303   "I HAVE GIVEN" Burlingame, AL, 2:521.

303   "THINGS" Burlingame, ed., *Oral History of Abraham Lincoln*, 57.

303   IN A CONVERSATION RWAL, 387–88.

303   "IN THE PINCH" Ibid., 388.

304   "GIGANTIC REBELLION" CW, 6:319–20.

304   "IF I HAD GONE UP" LDBD, 1861–1865, 197. By declining to pursue and destroy the Confederate forces after Gettysburg, the Union high command drove Lincoln to distraction. "I do not believe you appreciate the magnitude of the misfortune involved in Lee's escape," Lincoln wrote General Meade. "He was within your easy grasp, and to have closed upon him would, in connection with our other late successes, have ended the war. As it is, the war will be prolonged indefinitely. . . . Your golden opportunity is gone, and I am distressed immeasurably because of it." CW, 6:326–29; Burlingame, AL, 2:514. The president chose not to send the letter, but he made his basic views clear. CW, 6:328. "The fruit seemed so ripe, so ready for plucking, that it was very hard to lose it," he told Meade. Burlingame, AL, 2:514.

 In this period Lincoln received word that Alexander Stephens wanted to come to Washington. Burlingame, AL, 2:515; Donald, *Lincoln*, 456; McPherson, *Battle Cry of Freedom*, 650. The pretext for the Confederate vice president's mission to the North—he had traveled to Fortress Monroe, in Virginia—was prisoner exchange. Burlingame, AL, 2:515. Once Union and Confederate leaders were in conversation, though, there could be broader talk of a negotiated peace. McPherson, *Battle Cry of Freedom*, 650; Gienapp and Gienapp, eds., *Civil War Diary of Gideon Welles*, 237–41. The president was briefly open to seeing Stephens. "While he was opposed to having Stephens and his vessel come here," Gideon Welles told his diary, "he thought it would be well to send someone—perhaps go himself—to Fortress Monroe. Both Seward and Stanton were startled when this remark was made. Seward did not think it advisable the President should go, nor anyone else—he considered Stephens a dangerous man, who would make mischief anywhere." Gienapp and Gienapp, eds., *Civil War Diary of Gideon Welles*, 239.

Lincoln's willingness to consider speaking with Stephens is intriguing. The battlefield news was good—even glorious, for the Confederate overture came after the victories at Gettysburg and at Vicksburg. For the first time since the initial fighting at Bull Run, the Union was in a position of strength, and perhaps the president sensed it could be useful to hear from the white South firsthand. He had recently shown an openness to learning about the enemy's thinking when Colonel James F. Jaquess, a Methodist minister from Quincy, Illinois, had written to him for permission to "go into Confederate territory to seek out members of the Methodist Church and others opposed to war and to effect terms for their return to allegiance which would be acceptable to the government." "Such a mission as he proposes I think promises good, if it were free from difficulties, which I fear it cannot be," Lincoln observed. Jaquess ultimately succeeded in crossing Confederate lines and wrote Lincoln that he had "obtained *valuable* information, and proposals for *peace*," but nothing came of it. *CW*, 6:225; 236; 329.

With Stephens at Fortress Monroe, the president had a direct channel to the Confederacy at what could well have been an inflection point in the war. When he was considering Stephens's proposal over July 4 and 5, Lincoln expected that the Union's aggressive pursuit of Lee's army might end the fighting. He had known Stephens for a long time; some good might come of looking him in the eye. Welles, among others, was less sanguine. "We must not put ourselves in the wrong by refusing to communicate with these people," Welles wrote on July 5. "On the other hand, there is difficulty in meeting and treating with men who have violated their duty, disregarded their obligations, and lack sincerity." Gienapp and Gienapp, eds., *Civil War Diary of Gideon Welles*, 240. Lincoln ultimately declined to receive Stephens, informing the rebel vice president that "any *military* communication should be made through the prescribed military channels." Ibid., 241.

304 "I do not remember" *CW*, 6:326.

304 performance of Black soldiers Fredrickson, *Big Enough to Be Inconsistent*, 114–15. "The colored population is the great *available* and yet *unavailed of*, force for restoring the Union," Lincoln had written to Andrew Johnson in March. *CW*, 6:149–50. To David Hunter in April, the president had said, "I am glad to see the accounts of your colored force. . . . The enemy will make extra efforts to destroy them; and we should do the same to preserve and increase them." Ibid., 158.

304 "We needed that" Quarles, *The Negro in the Civil War*, 183.

304 a 1792 act of Congress Ibid., 184.

304 legislation in the summer of 1862 Militia Act of 1862, http://www.freedmen.umd.edu/milact.htm. Section 12 of the act read: "That the President be, and he is hereby, authorized to receive into the service of the United States, for the purpose of constructing [e]ntrenchments, or performing camp service or any other labor, or any military or naval service for which they may be found competent, persons of African descent, and such persons shall be enrolled and organized under such regulations, not inconsistent with the Constitution and laws, as the President may prescribe." Ibid.

304 Emancipation Proclamation The relevant section of the final Proclamation read: "And I further declare and make known, that such persons of suitable condition, will be received into the armed service of the United States to garrison forts, positions, stations, and other places, and to man vessels of all sorts in said service." "Transcript of the Proclamation," National Archives, https://www.archives.gov/exhibits/featured-documents/emancipation-proclamation/transcript.html. In general, see also John David Smith, *Lincoln and the U.S. Colored Troops* (Carbondale, Ill., 2013).

304 "WHEN FIRST THE REBEL CANNON" Douglass, *Autobiographies*, 778. The Massachusetts Fifty-fourth, one of two of the state's regiments of Black men, came into being at the insistence of the state's governor, John A. Andrew, who knew what he wanted from his white officers: "Young men of military experience, of firm Anti-slavery principles, ambitious, superior to the vulgar contempt of colour, and having faith in the capacity of coloured men for military service." Quarles, *The Negro in the Civil War*, 8–9. Grant was pleased. "I have given the subject of arming the negro my hearty support," the general told Lincoln in August. "This, with the emancipation of the negro, is the heaviest blow yet given the Confederacy." Burlingame, *AL*, 2:521.

Grant saw things whole. "What Vice-President Stephens acknowledges the corner stone of the Confederacy is already knocked out," Grant observed in August 1863. "Slavery is already dead and cannot be resurrected. It would take a standing army to maintain slavery in the South if we were to make peace today guaranteeing to the South all their former constitutional privileges. I was never an abolitionist, nor even what could be called Anti-Slavery, but I try to judge fairly and honestly and it became patent to my mind early in the rebellion that the North and South could never live at peace with each other except as one nation, and that without slavery. As anxious as I am to see peace reestablished I would not therefore be willing to see any settlement until this question is forever settled." Nevins, *War for the Union*, 2:524.

Frederick Douglass agreed. "Once let the black man get upon his person the brass letters *U.S.*," Douglass said, "let him get an eagle on his button, and a musket on his shoulder and bullets in his pocket, and there is no power on earth which can deny that he has earned the right to citizenship in the United States," Douglass said. Quarles, *The Negro in the Civil War*, 184. Lincoln himself was pragmatic. "We were not succeeding—at best, were progressing too slowly—without" emancipation, Lincoln had written in January 1863. "Now, that we have it, and bear all the disadvantage of it, (as we do bear some in certain quarters) we must also take some benefit from it, if practicable." *CW*, 6:56.

304 ORDERED THAT ESCAPED SLAVES Burlingame, *AL*, 2:521–22.

305 "IT IS THE DUTY" *CW*, 6:357. The order continued: "The government of the United States will give the same protection to all its soldiers, and if the enemy shall sell or enslave anyone because of his color, the offense shall be punished by retaliation upon the enemy's prisoners in our possession. It is . . . ordered that for every soldier of the United States killed in violation of the laws of war, a rebel soldier shall be executed; and for every one enslaved by the enemy or sold into slavery, a rebel soldier shall be placed at hard labor on the public works and continued at such labor until the other shall be released and receive the treatment due to a prisoner of war." Ibid. See also Burlingame, *AL*, 2:522. On General Order 252, see Gates, ed., *Lincoln on Race and Slavery*, 276.

305 MASSACRE AT FORT PILLOW McPherson, *Battle Cry of Freedom*, 748. See also Nathan W. Daniels Diary, April 11–May 3, 1864, LOC. "Great God," Nathan Daniels wrote, "that such inhuman works should be permitted by the good angel above as this horrible massacre of our brave colored troops at Fort Pillow." Ibid.

305 DELEGATION OF BLACK CLERGY *CW*, 6:401.

305 "THE OBJECT" Ibid.

305 BLACK SOLDIERS WERE PAID LESS Douglass, *Autobiographies*, 786.

305 MONDAY, AUGUST 10 See, for instance, Douglass, *Autobiographies*, 784–88; Blight, *Frederick Douglass*, 406–10; Burlingame, *AL*, 2:522–23; Foner, ed., *Life and Writings of Frederick Douglass*, 3:383–85.

305 Douglass was understandably wary Foner, ed., *Life and Writings of Frederick Douglass*, 3:383.

305 "For twenty-five years" Ibid.

306 he and Senator Samuel C. Pomeroy *LDBD, 1861–1865*, 201.

306 making their way Foner, ed., *Life and Writings of Frederick Douglass*, 3:383–84.

306 "Yes, damn it" Ibid.

306 Lincoln was seated Ibid.

306 Douglass began to explain Douglass, *Autobiographies*, 786.

306 "I know who you are" Ibid.

306 "I will tell you" Foner, ed., *Life and Writings of Frederick Douglass*, 3:383.

306 "I told [the president] that he had" Ibid., 385.

306 Black men under arms Douglass, *Autobiographies*, 786–87.

306 "had larger motives" Ibid.

306 "be willing to enter" Ibid., 787.

306 endeavor to enforce Ibid.

307 "any commission" Ibid.

307 "Though I was not" Ibid.

307 "the full belief that" Ibid., 788.

307 "We are fighting" Foner, ed., *Life and Writings of Frederick Douglass*, 3:385–86.

307 In a public letter CW, 6:406–10; *LDBD, 1861–1865*, 204. Lincoln had been invited to the event but could not make such a trip amid the war. "For a moment the President cherished the hope of going to Springfield," Hay and Nicolay recalled, "and once more in his life renewing the sensation, so dear to politicians, of personal contact with great and enthusiastic masses, and of making one more speech to shouting thousands of his fellow-citizens." Hay and Nicolay, *AL: A History*, 7:379–80. When he was asked whether he would undertake such a homecoming, he replied, "No, I shall send them a letter instead; and it will be a rather good letter." Ibid., 385.

307 "To be plain" CW, 6:407.

307 "You say you will not" Ibid., 409. James Conkling, who had read the letter to the meeting at Lincoln's request, reported the reaction. "The most unbounded enthusiasm prevailed," Conkling told the president. "The speeches of the most earnest, radical and progressive character and the people applauded most vociferously every sentiment in favor of the vigorous prosecution of the war until the rebellion was subdued—the Proclamation of Emancipation and the arming of negro soldiers and every allusion to yourself and your policy." Burlingame, *AL*, 2:562.

308 titanic September battle McPherson, *Battle Cry of Freedom*, 666–81; Keith Bohannon, "Battle of Chickamauga," *New Georgia Encyclopedia*, https://www.georgia encyclopedia.org/articles/history-archaeology/battle-of-chickamauga/.

308 Benjamin Hardin Helm Burlingame, *AL*, 2:555–56.

308 David Davis found the president "in the greatest grief" Ibid., 555.

308 She had been injured *LDBD, 1861–1865*, 194.

308 Mary took Robert and Tad Lloyd Ostendorf, "A New Mary Todd Lincoln Photograph: A Tour of the White Mountains in Summer, 1863," *Illinois Historical Journal* 83, no. 2 (1990): 109–12.

308 "All as well" CW, 6:371–72.

308 where Hay dozed off *LDBD, 1861–1865*, 203.

308 "The air is so clear" CW, 6:471–72.

309 Mary spent time with spiritualists See, for instance, Burlingame, *American Marriage*, 217–22; Nettie Colburn Maynard, *Was Abraham Lincoln a Spiritualist? Or, Curious*

Revelations from the Life of a Trance Medium (Philadelphia, 1891); Jay Monaghan, "Was Abraham Lincoln Really a Spiritualist?" *Journal of the Illinois State Historical Society (1908–1984)* 34, no. 2 (1941): 209–32. See also Elizabeth Lindsey, "Observance of the Lincoln Centennial," *Lincoln Herald* 59, 14; *LDBD, 1861–1865,* 181.

309 LINCOLN ATTENDED A FEW SÉANCES Monaghan, "Was Abraham Lincoln Really a Spiritualist?," 210.

309 "MRS CROSBY TOLD ME" Nathan W. Daniels Diary, December 27, 1863, LOC.

309 "MRS. LINCOLN WAS MORE" Monaghan, "Was Abraham Lincoln Really a Spiritualist?," 222.

309 PERFORMANCE OF *OTHELLO LDBD, 1861–1865,* 211.

309 HE HAD ENJOYED https://www.fords.org/blog/post/playbills-john-wilkes-booth -performed-at-ford-s-before-assassinating-lincoln-at-ford-s/.

309 HE SAW *FANCHON* Ibid.

309 *THE MARBLE HEART* Ibid.; *LDBD, 1861–1865,* 218.

309 "HOW DOES IT" CW, 6:513.

309 "MY MAJORITY CANNOT VARY" Ibid.

309 "HOW DOES IT" Ibid.

309 A HUNDRED-THOUSAND-VOTE LANDSLIDE "Clement Vallandigham," https://ohio historycentral.org/w/Clement_Vallandigham.

309 WERE "REBEL SYMPATHIZERS" Gienapp and Gienapp, eds., *Civil War Diary of Gideon Welles,* 309. "Gov. Curtin's reelection or defeat," Salmon Chase said, "is now the success or defeat of the administration of President Lincoln." Burlingame, AL, 2:565. Had the voters in Pennsylvania and Ohio "gone for the [Democrats]," one observer wrote in September, "then . . . a new feeling and spirit will inspire the South." Donald, *Lincoln,* 454.

310 HE HAD BEEN "NERVOUS" Gienapp and Gienapp, eds., *Civil War Diary of Gideon Welles,* 308. "I stopped in to see and congratulate the President, who is in good spirits and greatly relieved from the depression of yesterday," Gideon Welles told his diary. "He told me he had more anxiety in regard to the election results of yesterday than he had in 1860 when he was chosen." Ibid., 309.

310 "ONE HUNDRED GUNS" *NYT,* October 16, 1863.

310 "IT IS THE GREAT" Burlingame, AL, 2:565–66.

310 A SPECIAL FOUR-CAR TRAIN *LDBD, 1861–1865,* 220.

310 "WE STARTED FROM" Burlingame and Ettlinger, ed., *Inside Lincoln's White House,* 111.

310 TAD WAS ILL *LDBD, 1861–1865,* 220.

310 HE HAD DRAFTED IT Burlingame, AL, 2:569–70.

310 LINCOLN LEFT THE CAPITAL *LDBD, 1861–1865,* 220. On the Gettysburg trip, see also "Our Trip to Gettysburg," *The Pittsburgh Commercial,* November 23, 1863; Washington *Evening Star,* November 18, 1863; *Chicago Tribune,* November 25, 1863.

310 THE INVITATION HAD COME Hay and Nicolay, *AL: A History,* 8:189.

310 TO BURY THE THIRTY-FIVE-HUNDRED Gettysburg National Cemetery, Gettysburg, Pennsylvania, https://www.nps.gov/nr/travel/national_cemeteries/pennsylvania /gettysburg_national_cemetery.html.

310 SEVENTEEN STATES Hay and Nicolay, *AL: A History,* 8:189.

310 EDWARD EVERETT OF MASSACHUSETTS Ibid., 190.

310 "I DO NOT WISH" *LDBD, 1861–1865,* 220.

310 THE PRESIDENT ARRIVED Ibid., 221.

310 SPENT THE EVENING Ibid.

310 "I THANK MY GOD" Hay and Nicolay, *AL: A History,* 8:191. Slavery was one issue; respect for democracy another, related question. "When we part to-morrow night,

let us remember that we owe it to our country and to mankind that this war shall have for its conclusion the establishing of the principle of democratic government—the simple principle that whatever party, whatever portion of the community, prevails by constitutional suffrage in an election, that party is to be respected and maintained in power, until it shall give place, on another trial and another verdict, to a different portion of the people," Seward told his listeners in Gettysburg. "If you do not do this, you are drifting at once and irresistibly to the very verge of a universal, cheerless, and hopeless anarchy." Ibid.

311 "BY INQUIRY MRS. LINCOLN" *LDBD, 1861–1865*, 221.

311 AFTER BREAKFAST THE NEXT MORNING Ibid.; *The Pittsburgh Commercial*, November 23, 1863. "We had quite a pleasant chat with the President for a few moments," the newspaper reported. "He said the best course for the journals of the country to pursue, if they wished to sustain the Government, was to stand by the officers of the army, and instead of censuring them for any errors they might commit, encourage them by urging the people to render them all the aid in their power."

311 ONE VISITOR ASKED *The Pittsburgh Commercial*, November 23, 1863.

311 LINCOLN PUT THE FINISHING TOUCHES *LDBD, 1861–1865*, 221.

311 "MAGNIFICENT CHESTNUT CHARGER" Ibid.

311 "THE PROCESSION FORMED" Burlingame and Ettlinger, eds., *Inside Lincoln's White House*, 113.

311 IT WAS A FIFTEEN-MINUTE *LDBD, 1861–1865*, 221.

311 QUIET PREVAILED Ibid.

311 THE MEN IN THE AUDIENCE Ibid.

311 "A GREAT CROWD" Nathan W. Daniels Diary, November 20, 1863, LOC.

311 "MADE A PRAYER" Burlingame and Ettlinger, eds., *Inside Lincoln's White House*, 113.

311 "AS HE ALWAYS DOES, PERFECTLY" Ibid.

311 "TO LEVY WAR" Hay and Nicolay, *AL: A History*, 8:194–96.

311 "TOOK OUT" *LDBD, 1861–1865*, 222.

311 "GREAT GOD IN HEAVEN!" *The Pittsburgh Commercial*, November 23, 1863.

312 FINALLY, AT TWO P.M. *LDBD, 1861–1865*, 222.

312 "FOUR SCORE AND SEVEN YEARS" The Gettysburg Address, November 19, 1863, http://www.abrahamlincolnonline.org/lincoln/speeches/gettysburg.htm.

312 THE SPEECH WAS SO SHORT *LDBD, 1861–1865*, 222.

313 "IN A FIRM FREE WAY" Burlingame and Ettlinger, eds., *Inside Lincoln's White House*, 113.

313 THE PRESS REACTION I am indebted to Harold Holzer for this insight.

313 "WE PASS OVER THE SILLY REMARKS" "The Gettysburg Address: Contemporary Reactions," Cornell University Library, https://rmc.library.cornell.edu/gettysburg/ideas_more/reactions_p2.htm.

313 "COULD THE MOST ELABORATE" Ibid.

313 "I SHOULD BE GLAD" Dos Passos, "Lincoln and His Almost Chosen People," 713.

313 "THE DEDICATORY REMARKS" "The Gettysburg Address: Contemporary Reactions," Cornell University Library, https://rmc.library.cornell.edu/gettysburg/ideas_more/reactions_p1.htm#chicago_tribune.

313 "ABRAHAM LINCOLN IS" French, *Witness to the Young Republic*, 435.

313 "WE SUBMIT THAT" Burlingame, *AL*, 2:576–77. See also Thurow, *Abraham Lincoln and American Political Religion*, 63–87; Wills, *Lincoln at Gettysburg*, 38–39.

314 "KEPT TO HIS PULPIT" Wills, *Lincoln at Gettysburg*, 108.

314 "BY CHRISTIANITY, I MEAN" Ibid., 108–9.

314 "IN PUBLIC LIFE" George Bancroft, *The Necessity, The Reality, and the Promise of the Progress of the Human Race* (New York, 1854), 11; 35–36. See also Wills, *Lincoln at Gettysburg*, 105.

Chapter Twenty-three: Who Shall Be the Next President?

316 "I confess that" Waugh, *Reelecting Lincoln*, 17.

316 "We are fighting" *NYT*, July 29, 1864.

316 "The President," John Hay told Burlingame, ed., *Inside Lincoln's White House*, 118.

316 ten past one o'clock *LDBD, 1861–1865*, 222.

316 mild case of smallpox Ibid. See also Donald R. Hopkins, *Princes and Peasants: Smallpox in History* (Chicago, 1983), 274–83, 322–24. "The President is sick at the White House and it is rumored around the city that he has The Small Pox," Nathan Daniels wrote. "His little boy has just recovered from it and it would not be at all strange if he should be taken with the same." Nathan W. Daniels Diary, December 6, 1863, LOC.

316 "suffering from a severe" Hopkins, *Princes and Peasants*, 277. For a contemporary description of the symptoms of smallpox, see the Washington *Evening Star*, January 6, 1864.

316 "Now I have" *LDBD, 1861–1865*, 222.

316 under partial quarantine Ibid., 223.

316 by mid-December Nathan W. Daniels Diary, December 20, 1863, LOC.

316 whom Lincoln admired See, for instance, Douglas L. Wilson, "His Hour Upon the Stage," *American Scholar* 81, no. 1 (2012): 60–69; Burlingame and Ettlinger, eds., *Inside Lincoln's White House*, 76, 127–28. See also Carpenter, *Inner Life of Abraham Lincoln*, 49–52.

316 "I have rarely" Burlingame, *AL*, 2:526–27.

317 "Who shall be" Burlingame, ed., *Lincoln Observed*, 53–54.

317 "the buzzing" Waugh, *Reelecting Lincoln*, 6.

317 In a private conversation Ibid., 17–18; Burlingame, ed., *Lincoln Observed*, 216.

317 "I confess that" Burlingame, ed., *Oral History of Abraham Lincoln*, 78.

317 "I don't know but" Waugh, *Reelecting Lincoln*, 17.

318 "As to the politics" Ibid., 13.

318 When Lincoln was Carpenter, *Inner Life of Abraham Lincoln*, 38.

318 Recalling the story Ibid.

318 "If we come triumphantly out" Burlingame, *AL*, 2:646.

318 "I, like you" "Speech by Secretary Seward," *NYT*, September 7, 1864.

319 "We cannot have" *CW*, 8:100–101.

319 "The most reliable" Ibid., 149.

319 Interrupted one day at the Soldiers' Home Pinsker, *Lincoln's Sanctuary*, 52–53.

319 "the saddest face" Carpenter, *Inner Life of Abraham Lincoln*, 30–31.

319 The president would pace Ibid.

319 Carpenter . . . was reminded Ibid., 31.

319 "This war is eating" Ibid.; *LDBD, 1861–1865*, 238.

319 "A traveller on the frontier" Carpenter, *Inner Life of Abraham Lincoln*, 48–49.

320 Charles Sumner had offered W.E.B. Du Bois, *Black Reconstruction in America: An Essay Toward a History of the Part Which Black Folk Played in the Attempt to Reconstruct Democracy in America, 1860–1880* (New York, 2007), 150.

320 "Chas Sumner is" Nathan W. Daniels Diary, December 21, 1863, LOC.

320 "I pray for the advancement" Ibid., January 1, 1864.

320 Daniels had encountered Ibid., March 24, 1864.

320 "He is a drifter" Ibid.

320 Proclamation of Amnesty *CW*, 7:53–56. See also, for instance, Foner, *Reconstruction*, 35–38.

320 LARGELY SOVEREIGN Harrold, *Lincoln and the Abolitionists*, 97–98.

320 HE WOULD PARDON CW, 7:54.

320 HE WOULD RECOGNIZE Ibid., 55.

320 "ANY PROVISION" Ibid.

321 TO REVERSE Ibid., 51.

321 TO WENDELL PHILLIPS Harrold, *Lincoln and the Abolitionists*, 98.

321 "DON'T GO FORWARD" Hans L. Trefousse, *The Radical Republicans: Lincoln's Vanguard for Racial Justice* (New York, 1968), 289.

321 LIMITED BLACK SUFFRAGE Foner, *Fiery Trial*, 282–83. As Foner wrote, "The contentious issue of black suffrage first came to national attention via Louisiana." Ibid.

321 "I BARELY SUGGEST" CW, 7:243. "This was the only occasion on which Lincoln intervened in a state's Reconstruction process to promote blacks' civil or political rights rather than the abolition of slavery," Foner wrote. "Hardly a ringing endorsement of black suffrage, it nonetheless represented a major departure for him." Foner, *Fiery Trial*, 283.

321 "WHEN WAS IT EVER" Du Bois, *Black Reconstruction*, 200–201.

322 "THE REFORMER IS CARELESS" Hofstadter, *American Political Tradition*, 178–79.

322 "WHILE HE THOUGHT" Hamlin, *Life and Times of Hannibal Hamlin*, 452.

322 "WORKING LIKE A BEAVER" Burlingame, ed., *Inside Lincoln's White House*, 92. "If I were controlled by merely personal sentiments, I should prefer the reelection of Mr. Lincoln to that of any other man," Chase wrote to his son-in-law, William Sprague, "but I doubt the expediency of reelecting anybody, and I think a man of different qualities from those the President has will be needed for the next four years." Hay and Nicolay, *AL: A History*, 8:311. In the style of the time, Chase cloaked his aspirations with Cincinnatus-like pronouncements. "I am not anxious to be regarded as that man," Chase added in his letter to Sprague, "and I am quite willing to leave that question to the decision of those who agree in thinking that some such man should be chosen"—and he was quite willing to be so chosen. Ibid. In February, a pro-Chase, anti-Lincoln circular signed by Senator Samuel C. Pomeroy of Kansas was published and widely discussed. Should Lincoln be reelected, "his manifest tendency towards compromises and temporary expedients of policy will become stronger during a second term than it has been in the first, and the cause of human liberty, and the dignity and honor of the nation [would] suffer proportionally," Pomeroy argued. Ibid., 319–20.

322 "VERY BAD TASTE" Burlingame, ed., *Inside Lincoln's White House*, 93.

322 THAT PLAN FAILED Hay and Nicolay, *AL: A History*, 8:323–25; Waugh, *Reelecting Lincoln*, 120.

322 "ANY ATTEMPT TO DIVIDE" Carpenter, *Inner Life of Abraham Lincoln*, 47.

322 AT A GATHERING IN CLEVELAND Nevins, *War for the Union*, 8:72–73; "The Cleveland Convention," *NYT*, June 1, 1864; Hay and Nicolay, *AL: A History*, 9:29–51.

322 THE CLEVELAND PLATFORM Hay and Nicolay, *AL: A History*, 9:30.

323 OTHERS WONDERED WHETHER William S. McFeely, *Grant: A Biography* (New York, 1981), 163.

323 "THE QUESTION ASTONISHES ME" Waugh, *Reelecting Lincoln*, 124.

323 "NOTHING WOULD INDUCE ME" Ibid.

323 "NO MAN KNOWS" McFeely, *Grant*, 163; Rice, ed., *Reminiscences*, 390.

323 "SECESSIA" Burlingame and Ettlinger, eds., *Inside Lincoln's White House*, 128.

323 A PROBLEMATIC GUEST Berry, *House of Abraham*, 149–56; Helm, *Mary, Wife of Lincoln*, 219–33; Turner and Turner, *Mary Todd Lincoln: Her Life and Letters*, 154–56.

323 ALWAYS THE SUBJECT OF UNIONIST SUSPICION See, for instance, Mark E. Neely, Jr.,

"The Secret Treason of Abraham Lincoln's Brother-in-Law," *JALA* 17 (Winter 1996): 39–43.

323   "Mr. Lincoln and my sister" Helm, *Mary, Wife of Lincoln*, 221–22.

323   In an act of familial kindness Berry, *House of Abraham*, 150–51.

323   "I feel that my being here" Helm, *Mary, Wife of Lincoln*, 231; Berry, *House of Abraham*, 155.

323   She had cross words Berry, *House of Abraham*, 154–55.

323   The Lincolns would ultimately fall out Ibid., 173–74.

324   They kept at it Ibid.

324   During a sitting Carpenter, *Inner Life of Abraham Lincoln*, 48–51.

324   Friday, March 25 Ibid., 58–61.

324   Young Tad was dispatched Ibid., 58.

324   by William Knox "Mortality," https://www.scottishpoetrylibrary.org.uk/poem /mortality/. See also John J. Miller, "With Death on His Mind," *The Wall Street Journal*, February 11, 2012.

324   "The hand of the king" Carpenter, *Inner Life of Abraham Lincoln*, 60.

324   Here was the depressive Lincoln As noted above, see also Shenk, *Lincoln's Melancholy*.

325   He remembered, too Carpenter, *Inner Life of Abraham Lincoln*, 58–59.

325   "The mossy marbles" Ibid., 59. See also Oliver Wendell Holmes, Sr., "The Last Leaf," https://www.poetryfoundation.org/poems/44383/the-last-leaf.

325   "For pure pathos" Carpenter, *Inner Life of Abraham Lincoln*, 59.

325   In March 1864, empowered McFeely, *Grant*, 151.

325   The unassuming hero Ibid., 152–53.

325   The Grants passed Nevins, *War for the Union*, 8:7; McFeely, *Grant*, 154–55.

325   Later that evening Nevins, *War for the Union*, 8:7.

325   The diminutive Grant Ibid.

325   In the Wilderness See, for instance, Nevins, *War for the Union*, 8:18–57; McPherson, *Battle Cry of Freedom*, 718–81.

326   "Providence has decreed" Hay and Nicolay, *AL: A History*, 9:53.

326   Asked why he Edward Chase Kirkland, *The Peacemakers of 1864* (New York, 1927), 47–48.

326   "The State of Illinois" Hay and Nicolay, *AL: A History*, 9:71–72.

326   On a motion Ibid., 72.

326   The Republican platform Harold M. Hyman, "Election of 1864," in *HAPE*, 1:507; "Republican Party Platform of 1864," June 7, 1864, American Presidency Project, https://www.presidency.ucsb.edu/documents/republican-party-platform-1864.

326   the Confederacy's unconditional surrender "Republican Party Platform of 1864."

326   "the Government owes" Ibid.

326   the "speedy construction" Ibid.

326   a "liberal and just" Ibid.

326   "*Resolved*, That as slavery" Ibid.

327   On Monday, December 14, 1863 Vorenberg, *Final Freedom*, 49–50.

327   proposed the "submission" Ibid.

327   "The havoc of war" Ibid., 37.

327   An abolition amendment was approved "Thirteenth Amendment to the U.S. Constitution: Primary Documents in American History," LOC, https://guides .loc.gov/13th-amendment/digital-collections.

327   apparently been quietly supportive Vorenberg, *Final Freedom*, 91–92.

327 WANTED TIME TO GAUGE Ibid., 126–27, analyzes Lincoln's quiet seven months between Ashley's December 1863 proposal and the president's public embrace of the Republican platform in June 1864.

327 "THE UNCONDITIONAL UNION MEN" Ibid., 125; CW, 7:380.

327 WHO WAS TO BE VICE PRESIDENT? See, for instance, Burlingame, *AL*, 2:642–43; Don E. Fehrenbacher, "The Making of a Myth: Lincoln and the Vice-Presidential Nomination of 1864," *Civil War History* 41 (1995): 273–90; Annette Gordon-Reed, *Andrew Johnson* (New York, 2011), 75–78; James F. Glonek, "Lincoln, Johnson, and the Baltimore Ticket," *Abraham Lincoln Quarterly* 6 (1951): 255–71; Hay and Nicolay, *AL: A History*, 9:72–75; Matt Speiser, "The Ticket's Other Half: How and Why Andrew Johnson Received the 1864 Vice Presidential Nomination," *Tennessee Historical Quarterly* 65, no. 1 (2006): 42–69; Trefousse, *Andrew Johnson*, 176–80; Nevins, *War for the Union*, 8:75–78.

327 "GENERAL IMPRESSION" Hay and Nicolay, *AL: A History*, 9:73.

328 HAMLIN HAD HIS ADHERENTS Ibid., 72–75; Trefousse, *Andrew Johnson*, 176–80.

328 "IT WAS ... WITH MINDS" Hay and Nicolay, *AL: A History*, 9:72–73.

328 LINCOLN'S FRIEND LEONARD SWETT Ibid.

328 "WISH NOT TO INTERFERE" Ibid., 73.

328 "I HAVE LIVED" Trefousse, *Andrew Johnson*, 166. In January 1864, *The Nashville Daily Press* wrote, "No man in Tennessee ... has done more than Andrew Johnson to create, to perpetuate and embitter in the minds of the Southern people, that feeling of jealousy and hostility against the free States, which has at length culminated in rebellion and civil war. Up to 1860, he had been for 20 years among the most bigoted and intolerant of the advocates of slavery and Southernism, and the most unsparing denouncer of everything and everybody north of Mason's and Dixon's line." Ibid., 173.

328 "I AM FOR THE GOVERNMENT" Ibid., 168–69.

328 "CAN'T YOU FIND" Trefousse, *Radical Republicans*, 312.

329 A RADICAL REPUBLICAN PLAN See, for instance, Hay and Nicolay, *AL: A History*, 9:104–27.

330 REMINDING THE UNION See, for instance, ibid., 158–83; Nevins, *War for the Union*, 8:88–89; Burlingame, *AL*, 2:655–58; Thomas A. Lewis, "When Washington, D.C. Came Close to Being Conquered by the Confederacy," *Smithsonian*, July 1988, https://www.smithsonianmag.com/history/when-washington-dc-came-close-to-being-conquered-by-the-confederacy-180951994/; Charles C. Osborn, *Jubal: The Life and Times of General Jubal A. Early, CSA, Defender of the Lost Cause* (Chapel Hill, N.C., 1992), 261–93.

330 "SIGHT OF THE DOME" Lewis, "When Washington, D.C. Came Close."

330 LINCOLN WAS CONVINCED Hay and Nicolay, *AL: A History*, 9:167–69. "The lonely situation of the President's Summer residence would have afforded a tempting chance for a daring squad of rebel cavalry to run some risks for the chance of carrying off the President, whom we could ill afford to spare just now," Noah Brooks wrote. Burlingame, ed., *Lincoln Observed*, 126.

330 "OLD ABE IS IN GREAT DANGER" Nathan W. Daniels Diary, July 11, 1864, LOC.

330 A WATERBORNE ESCAPE Hay and Nicolay, *AL: A History*, 9:169.

330 THE CRUX CAME Lewis, "When Washington, D.C. Came Close."

330 LINCOLN OBSERVED THE BATTLE Ibid.; Burlingame, *AL*, 2:656.

330 "HE STOOD THERE" Donald, *Lincoln*, 518–19.

330 "GET DOWN, YOU DAMN FOOL" Lewis, "When Washington, D.C. Came Close."

330 "THE COUNTRY WAS" Frederick Douglass to Theodore Tilton, October 15, 1864,

https://civilwarnotebook.blogspot.com/2020/06/frederick-douglass-to
-theodore-tilton.html.

330 Jewett was back Hay and Nicolay, *AL: A History*, 9:185–86; Burlingame, *AL*,
2:669–74.

330 "I venture to remind" Hay and Nicolay, *AL: A History*, 9:186.

331 "If you can find" Ibid., 187–88; CW, 7:435.

331 Slated for Niagara Falls Hay and Nicolay, *AL: A History*, 9:201–21.

331 "To whom it may concern" CW, 7:451; Hay and Nicolay, *AL: A History*, 9:192.

331 "caprice of his imperial will" Hay and Nicolay, *AL: A History*, 9:194.

331 still hoped insurrection Ibid., 8:17. There was "no hope but in force," the Confederate and Knights of the Golden Circle provocateur Jacob Thompson wrote.
"The belief was entertained and freely expressed, that by a bold, vigorous, and
concerted movement, the three great Northwestern States of Illinois, Indiana,
and Ohio could be seized and held. This being done, the States of Kentucky and
Missouri could easily be lifted from their prostrate condition and placed on their
feet, and this, in sixty days, would end the war." Ibid. The operation was set to
begin on August 16, but the plot collapsed after Niagara Falls—the Confederate
representatives had no real power from Richmond—and Lincoln's letter of July 18,
which, Hay and Nicolay observed, "shocked the country to such an extent that the
leading politicians conceived the idea that Lincoln might be beaten at the ballot-
box on such an issue." Ibid., 18–19.

331 called for five hundred thousand Burlingame, ed., *Lincoln Observed*, 127.

331 Grant's campaigns in Virginia See, for instance, Stephen W. Sears, ed., *The Civil
War Papers of George B. McClellan: Selected Correspondence, 1860–1865* (New York, 1989),
524, 575–76.

331 "They must have" Ibid., 576.

332 "possible only" Ibid., 574.

332 interesting political ground Ibid., 588. When the Democrats at last met in
convention, in Chicago in late August, the party passed a peace platform for a war
nominee. In the plank that troubled McClellan the most, Clement Vallandigham
had written: "*Resolved,* That this convention does explicitly declare . . . that after
four years of failure to restore the Union by the experiment of war, . . . justice,
humanity, liberty and the public welfare demand that immediate efforts be made
for a cessation of hostilities, with a view to an ultimate convention of the States, or
other peaceable means, to the end that at the earliest practicable moment peace
may be restored on the basis of the Federal Union of the States." McClellan accepted the nomination but was more hawkish than the platform. Reconciling his
own views with those of the party whose standard he bore would be the work of a
new administration, if there were one. Ibid., 592.

332 As the seventeenth president See, for instance, Oakes, *Freedom National*, xxiv;
Burlingame, *AL*, 2:675–76, 681–84, 688–90; Bordewich, *Congress at War*, 313–16;
McPherson, *Battle Cry of Freedom*, 771–73, 775–76, 803–806; Waugh, *Reelecting Lin-
coln*, 276–361; Weber, *Copperheads*, 164–203.

332 "Constitution & laws" Sears, ed., *Civil War Papers of George B. McClellan*, 584.

332 "We are fighting for independence" *NYT*, July 29, 1864. See also, for instance,
McPherson, "The Strategy of Unconditional Surrender" in Wilentz, ed., *Best American History Essays on Lincoln*, 223. "Our doctrine is this," the Richmond-published
Southern Punch declared in September 1864: "we are fighting for independence that our great and necessary domestic institution of
slavery shall be preserved." John M. Coski, *The Confederate Battle Flag: America's Most Embattled Emblem* (Cambridge, Mass., 2005), 25.

332 "If I am elected" McPherson, *Battle Cry of Freedom*, 771.

332 "The Union is" Ibid., 776.

332 McClellan wanted Union Sears, ed., *Civil War Papers of George B. McClellan*, 584–85.

332 "The great election" Sears, *George B. McClellan*, 367.

332 "Mr. Lincoln is already" Nevins, *War for the Union*, 8:91.

333 "The fact begins" Charles Bracelen Flood, *1864: Lincoln at the Gates of History* (New York, 2009), 258.

333 "never consent" Burlingame, *AL*, 2:672.

333 "If Jefferson Davis wishes" CW, 7:501. The letter, which would not be sent, was to Charles D. Robinson of the Green Bay, Wisconsin, *Advocate*. "I am a War Democrat, and the editor of a Democratic paper," Robinson had written to Lincoln in a letter the president received on August 16. "I have sustained your Administration ... because it is the legally constituted government. I have sustained its war policy, not because I endorsed it entire, but because it presented the only available method of putting down the rebellion.... It was alleged that because I and my friends sustained the Emancipation measure, we had become abolitionized. We replied that we regarded the freeing of the negroes as sound war policy, in the depriving the South of its laborers weakened the ... Rebellion." Ibid. That, Robinson said, had been a workable and convincing argument—until Niagara. "The Niagara Falls 'Peace' movement was of no importance whatever, except that it resulted in bringing out your declaration, as we understand it, that no steps can be taken towards peace ... unless accompanied with an abandonment of slavery," Robinson wrote. "This puts the whole war question on a new basis, and takes us War Democrats clear off our feet, leaving us no ground to stand upon. If we sustain the war and war policy, does it not demand the changing of our party politics?" Ibid.

Robinson's case was a politically compelling one, and Lincoln privately struggled to maintain his antislavery policy without alienating moderate to conservative white voters. In the draft reply to Robinson the president wrote, "To me it seems plain that saying re-union and abandonment of slavery would be considered, if offered, is not saying that nothing *else* or *less* would be considered, if offered." Ibid., 499. It was far too clever a formulation. If made public, Lincoln's words would have been interpreted as a reversal of policy, a rejection of the principles he had laid out at the time of Niagara Falls.

On Friday, August 19, Lincoln received Alexander W. Randall, a former governor of Wisconsin, and the lawyer Joseph T. Mills in the White House. The president mused about how a Democratic victory would be disastrous for the Union. "The President was free & animated in conversation. I was astonished at his elasticity of spirits," Mills told his diary. Randall suggested a holiday. "Why can[']t you, Mr. P.[,] seek some place of retirement for a few weeks?"

"Aye," Lincoln replied, "3 weeks would do me no good—my thoughts my solicitude for this great country follow me where ever I go. I don't think it is personal vanity, or ambition—but I cannot but feel that the weal or woe of this great nation will be decided in the approaching canvas." He went on: "The slightest acquaintance with arithmetic will prove to any man that the rebel armies cannot be destroyed with [D]emocratic strategy. It would sacrifice all the white men of the north to do it. There are now between 1 & 200 thousand black men now in the service of the Union. These men will be disbanded, returned to slavery & we will have to fight two nations instead of one. I have tried it. You cannot conciliate the South, when the mastery & control of millions of blacks makes them sure of ultimate success." Ibid., 506–7.

333   FREDERICK DOUGLASS RETURNED Foner, ed., *Life and Writings of Frederick Douglass*, 3:422–24. "The president did not propose to take back what he had said in his Niagara letter, but wished to relieve the fears of his peace friends, by making it appear that the thing which they feared could not happen, and was wholly beyond his power," Douglass wrote in October 1864. According to Douglass, Lincoln said: "Even if I would, I could not carry on the war for the abolition of slavery. The country would not sustain such a war, and I could do nothing without the support of Congress. I could not make the abolition of slavery an absolute prior condition to the reestablishment of the Union." Douglass added: "All that the President said on this point was to make manifest his want of power to do the thing which his enemies and pretended friends professed to be afraid he would do."

It seems likely that Lincoln was making a precise—perhaps overly precise—point: That he was not proposing to abolish slavery by fiat. Ibid., 423.

334   "TREATED ME AS A MAN" Burlingame, *AL*, 2:678.

334   LINCOLN, TOO, WAS IMPRESSED Ibid.

334   "THE TIDE IS SETTING" CW, 7:517–18.

334   "WHY WOULD IT NOT BE WISE" Ibid., 517.

334   "ONE DENOUNCES MR. LINCOLN" Flood, *1864*, 261.

334   "POPULAR WITH THE PLAIN PEOPLE" Hyman, "Election of 1864," 507.

335   WROTE LETTERS SEEKING Nevins, *War for the Union*, 8:91. See also New York *Sun*, June 30, 1889.

335   "EVERYTHING IS DARKNESS" Burlingame, ed., *With Lincoln in the White House*, 152.

335   TO LINCOLN'S FRIEND Burlingame, ed., *Oral History of Abraham Lincoln*, 58.

335   "WELL" Ibid.

335   "THIS MORNING, AS FOR" CW, 7:514.

335   HE ASKED HIS CABINET Ibid.

335   "PEOPLE ARE WILD" Ibid., 515.

335   WEED REPORTED THAT Ibid.

336   "THE THING WHICH ALARMED ME" Foner, ed., *Life and Writings of Frederick Douglass*, 3:423–24.

336   "HELL IS TO PAY" Burlingame, ed., *With Lincoln in the White House*, 152.

336   "I THINK THAT TODAY" Ibid.

337   "IF THE PRESIDENT" Ibid.

337   TO SEND WORD Ibid., 153.

337   "WE MAY BE DEFEATED" RWAL, 499.

337   IF HE RETURNED CW, 7:506–8.

337   "IT HAS ALWAYS" Ibid., 542–43.

337   "I CLAIM NOT" Ibid., 282.

337   WHILE WAITING FOR A CARRIAGE Carpenter, *Inner Life of Abraham Lincoln*, 35–36.

338   "THE LORD IS WITH YOU" Ibid., 36.

338   "OLD ABE . . . MUST NOW" Nathan W. Daniels Diary, September 1, 1864, LOC.

Chapter Twenty-four: The Strife of the Election

339   "THOUSANDS OF BITS OF PAPER" Waugh, *Reelecting Lincoln*, 348; Flood, *1864*, 364.

339   "THE ONLY RUMOR" Lucy Virginia French Diary, November 20, 1864, ID no. 6059, Microfilm no. 1816, VII-M-2, Tennessee Virtual Archives.

339   "ATLANTA IS OURS" Flood, *1864*, 279; Hay and Nicolay, *AL: A History*, 9:289.

339   "GLORIOUS NEWS" Burlingame, *AL*, 2:688.

339 "Sherman has had a great battle" Nathan Daniels Diary, September 3, 1864, LOC.

339 The fall of the Georgia city CW, 7:532–33.

339 "The political skies begin" Flood, *1864*, 280. See also Hay and Nicolay, *AL: A History*, 9:352–53, and "The Political Prospect," *NYT*, September 7, 1864.

339 Lincoln agreed to remove On the Montgomery Blair episode, see, for instance, *LDBD, 1861–1865*, 282; Burlingame, *AL*, 2:689–96. "You have generously said to me more than once, that whenever your resignation could be a relief to me, it was at my disposal," Lincoln wrote Blair. "The time has come. You very well know that this proceeds from no dissatisfaction of mine with you personally or officially." Blair acceded quickly, and his brother, Francis, praised the decision, writing that, in resigning, the postmaster general "had acted his part for the good of the country and for the re-election of Mr. Lincoln in which the safety of the country is involved." *CW*, 8:18–19.

339 "had no doubt" Burlingame, *AL*, 2:692.

340 "all hesitation ought" Ibid., 683.

340 Shenandoah Valley CW, 8:73–74; *LDBD, 1861–1865*, 290–91.

340 "We have . . . a free Government" CW, 7:504–5.

340 "To the humblest" Ibid., 528–29.

340 "I wish all men" Ibid., 8:41.

340 The constitution was approved *LDBD, 1861–1865*, 292.

340 "I had rather" *RWAL*, 49.

340 the president's openness See, for instance, White, *House Built by Slaves*.

340 Sojourner Truth among them *LDBD, 1861–1865*, 292; Carleton Mabee, "Sojourner Truth and President Lincoln," *New England Quarterly* 61, no. 4 (1988): 519–29.

340 Born into slavery On Truth, see, for instance, Nell Irvin Painter, *Sojourner Truth: A Life, a Symbol* (New York, 1996).

340 referring to her as "Aunty" Mabee, "Sojourner Truth and President Lincoln," 521; Burlingame, *Black Man's President*, 179.

341 "I said, 'I appreciate you'" Sojourner Truth, *Narrative of Sojourner Truth: A Bondswoman of Olden Time* (New York, 1991), 178.

341 a seventy-two-page pamphlet See, for instance, Sidney Kaplan, "The Miscegenation Issue in the Election of 1864," *Journal of Negro History* 34, no. 3 (1949): 274–343; McPherson, *Battle Cry of Freedom*, 789–91; Burlingame, *AL*, 2:696–700.

341 "All that is needed" Kaplan, "Miscegenation Issue," 279.

341 "Abraham Africanus the First" McPherson, *Battle Cry of Freedom*, 790. The weekly was the *New-York Freeman's Journal and Catholic Register*. Ibid.

341 talk that Lincoln CW, 8:52–53; Hay and Nicolay, *AL: A History*, 9:353–54.

341 "I am struggling" CW, 8:52–53.

342 "It is said" Ibid., 75.

342 at the ballot box Burlingame, *AL*, 2:717–24; McPherson, *Battle Cry of Freedom*, 803–5; Dora L. Costa and Matthew E. Kahn, *Heroes and Cowards: The Social Face of War* (Princeton, N.J., 2009); Donald S. Inbody, *The Soldier Vote: War, Politics, and the Ballot in America* (New York, 2016); Nathan Kalmoe, *With Ballots and Bullets: Partisanship and Violence in the American Civil War* (Cambridge, UK, 2020); Jonathan W. White, *Emancipation, the Union Army, and the Reelection of Abraham Lincoln* (Baton Rouge, La., 2004).

342 many of whom voted Republican Kalmoe, *With Ballots and Bullets*, 78–81.

342 Democrats understood McPherson, *Battle Cry of Freedom*, 804.

342   THE *DETROIT ADVERTISER AND TRIBUNE* CALCULATED Kalmoe, *With Ballots and Bullets,* 79.

342   SEVERAL STATES ADOPTED ABSENTEE VOTER POLICIES Inbody, *Soldier Vote,* 27–28. "The pattern for passing soldier voting laws was clear," Inbody wrote. "In general, states with Republican governors and legislatures dominated by Republican majorities passed soldier voting laws. Those with Democrats in the majority did not. Partisan politics and concern for maintaining control of Congress and state legislatures, not to mention the presidency, trumped other concerns." Ibid., 32.

342   "THEY ARE AMERICAN CITIZENS" McPherson, *Battle Cry of Freedom,* 804.

342   INDIANA, ILLINOIS, AND NEW JERSEY Ibid.

342   WORKED TO FURLOUGH Inbody, *Soldier Vote,* 5.

342   WHEN LINCOLN WAS TOLD *LDBD, 1861–1865,* 293.

342   "LAST NIGHT CHIEF JUSTICE TANEY" Burlingame and Ettlinger, eds., *Inside Lincoln's White House,* 241. "I talked with the President one moment," Hay told his diary. "He says he does not think he will make the appointment immediately." Ibid.

343   A CHASE COURT WAS LIKELY Donald, *Lincoln,* 552. "During the next few years the most difficult cases likely to come before the Court were those involving the constitutionality of Lincoln's emancipation policies and the validity of the greenbacks with which the war was being financed," Donald wrote. "Chase's record, the President thought, put him unquestionably on the right side of these basic issues." Ibid. See also Michael A. Kahn, "Abraham Lincoln's Appointments to the Supreme Court: A Master Politician at His Craft," *Journal of Supreme Court History* 22 (July 2011): 65–78.

343   AS THE NOVEMBER ELECTION NEARED *NYT,* October 30, 1864.

343   "IT IS NOT BECAUSE" Ibid.

343   CLIPPED THE COLUMN "The Contents of Abraham Lincoln's Pockets on the Evening of His Assassination," Alfred Whital Stern Collection of Lincolniana, Rare Book and Special Collections Division, LOC.

343   RAINY, HUMID, AND LONG Burlingame, ed., *Inside Lincoln's White House,* 243–44.

343   PRIVATE WILBUR FISK Waugh, *Reelecting Lincoln,* 348; Flood, *1864,* 364.

344   "THIS IS ELECTION DAY" Nathan W. Daniels Diary, November 8, 1864, LOC.

344   "IT IS A LITTLE SINGULAR" *RWAL,* 231–32.

344   "I DON'T KNOW" Epstein, *Lincolns,* 450.

344   "I COULD HAVE GONE" Burlingame, *Inner World,* 312.

344   AT SEVEN P.M. Burlingame, ed., *Inside Lincoln's White House,* 243–44.

344   "AS THE PRESIDENT ENTERED" Ibid., 244.

344   "FORNEY IS A LITTLE" Ibid.

344   FRIED OYSTERS Ibid., 246.

344   "SHE IS MORE ANXIOUS" Ibid., 244.

345   A MUDDIED AND BEDRAGGLED Ibid., 243.

345   "FOR SUCH AN AWKWARD FELLOW" Ibid.

345   "ABRAHAM LINCOLN HAS" *LDBD, 1861–1865,* 294.

345   "WAS GRATEFUL" *RWAL,* 52.

345   THE PRESIDENT WON Hyman, "Election of 1864," 492, 515–17. See also CW, 8:98.

345   IN THE DOZEN STATES McPherson, *Battle Cry of Freedom,* 804.

345   STATIONED HIMSELF Burlingame, *Inside Lincoln's White House,* 246.

345   "HE TOOK A GLASS" Ibid.

345   "JUDGING BY THE RECENT CANVASS" CW, 8:149–50.

346   "THAT OUR NATIONAL" Hyman, "Election of 1864," 513.

346   "DEEPLY IMPRESSED" Burlingame, ed., *Inside Lincoln's White House,* 251.

346 "THE INEVITABLE DESTINY" Nathan W. Daniels Diary, November 8, 1864, LOC.

346 "GOD BE PRAISED" Ibid., November 11–12, 1864.

346 "IT HAS LONG BEEN" CW, 8:100–101.

346 "I KNOW WHAT YOU" RWAL, 52–53.

346 "THE STRIFE OF THE ELECTION" CW, 8:100–101.

347 "BEING ONLY MORTAL" RWAL, 52.

347 THE MORNING AFTER THE ELECTION Burlingame, ed., *Oral History of Abraham Lincoln*, 83.

347 IN A MEETING AFTER THE ELECTION CW, 7:514.

348 "THE PURPOSES OF" Ibid., 535.

348 "RAIN, & CLOUDS" Lucy Virginia French Diary, November 20, 1864, ID no. 36059, Microfilm Number 1816, VII-M-2, Tennessee Virtual Archives.

348 "OF COURSE I MAY ERR" CW, 8:1–2.

348 "IT WAS JUST AFTER" RWAL, 53. Superstition, William Herndon recalled of Lincoln's ethos on the frontier, was "at once their food and drink. They believed in the baneful influence of witches, pinned their faith to the curative power of wizards in dealing with sick animals, and shot the image of a witch with a silver ball to break the spell she was supposed to have over human beings. . . . The flight of a bird in at the window, the breath of a horse on a child's head, the crossing by a dog of a hunter's path, all betokened evil luck in store for someone." Lincoln was a rational being, but even he was somewhat prone, Herndon recalled, "to believe in the significance of dreams and visions." Herndon and Weik, *Herndon's Life of Lincoln*, 55–56.

349 PROPOSED ABOLITIONIST THIRTEENTH AMENDMENT CW, 8:149.

349 "IN A GREAT NATIONAL CRISIS" Ibid.

349 "I REPEAT THE DECLARATION" Ibid., 152.

Chapter Twenty-five: This Great Moral Victory

353 "LIBERTY HAS BEEN WON" Foner, *Fiery Trial*, 335.

353 "WHATEVER MAY HAVE BEEN" RWAL, 421–22.

353 "I SHOULD BE THE VERIEST" Ibid., 52.

353 "YES, AS AFFAIRS" Ibid., 89–90.

353 IN A WARTIME MEETING CW, 8:154–55.

354 "THINGS BEYOND MEN" Harrold, *Lincoln and the Abolitionists*, 105.

354 "MAN'S CAPACITY FOR" Crofts, *Lincoln and the Politics of Slavery*, 261; James Mitchell Ashley, *Duplicate Copy of the Souvenir from the Afro-American League of Tennessee to Hon. James M. Ashley, of Ohio*, ed. Benjamin W. Arnett (Philadelphia, 1894), 259.

354 "WE CAN NEVER" Foner, *Fiery Trial*, 313.

354 "I WOULD RATHER" Arnold, *Life of Abraham Lincoln*, 360.

354 "IN MY JUDGMENT" Hay and Nicolay, *AL: A History*, 10:82.

354 HIS MEN LOBBIED On the passage of the Thirteenth Amendment, see, for instance, Burlingame, *AL*, 2:745–51; Vorenberg, *Final Freedom*, is comprehensive; Foner; *Fiery Trial*, 312–14; Hay and Nicolay, *AL: A History*, 10:72–90. Arnold, *Life of Abraham Lincoln*, 342–56, details the 1864 drama, which ended in defeat, 357–60 chronicles the post-1864 election story.

354 "THE PASSAGE OF THIS AMENDMENT" Arnold, *Life of Abraham Lincoln*, 359.

354 "MONEY WILL CERTAINLY" Burlingame, *AL*, 2:749.

354 "THE GREATEST MEASURE" Donald, *Lincoln*, 554.

354 AT FOUR O'CLOCK Hay and Nicolay, *AL: A History*, 10:85–86.

354 THE HOUSE APPROVED Burlingame, *AL*, 2:750. See also Du Bois, *Black Reconstruction*, 207–8.

354 BRIEF BUT HEARTFELT REMARKS CW, 8:254–55.

355 AT THE LAST MOMENT Burlingame, *AL*, 2:749.

355 THE PROSPECT OF NEGOTIATIONS Vorenberg, *Final Freedom*, 205–6; Burlingame, *AL*, 2:749–50.

355 "SO FAR AS I KNOW" Vorenberg, *Final Freedom*, 206. See also CW, 8:248.

355 WAS SOMEWHAT RESPONSIBLE Burlingame, *AL*, 2:751–52; Hay and Nicolay, *AL: A History*, 10:93–94. After the election, Blair had proposed making peace overtures to Davis. Lincoln had demurred, saying, "Come to me after Savannah falls"—which it did, to Sherman, just before Christmas. Hay and Nicolay, *AL: A History*, 10:94.

355 BLAIR'S IDEA: END THE FIGHTING Hay and Nicolay, *AL: A History*, 10:91–112; Burlingame, *AL*, 2:751.

355 NOT FULLY INVESTED Burlingame, *AL*, 2:753. "Blair thinks something can be done, but I don't, but I have no objection to have him try his hand," Lincoln told Henry Ward Beecher on Wednesday, February 1. Ibid.

355 "READY TO RECEIVE" Burlingame, *AL*, 2:752. The president was insistent that the Union give no ground in the field. "Let nothing which is transpiring, change, hinder, or delay your Military movements, or plans," Lincoln wired Grant. CW, 8:252. And there were, Lincoln said, three "indispensable" conditions: "The restoration of the national authority throughout all the States"; "No receding, by the Executive of the United States on the Slavery question"; and "No cessation of hostilities short of an end of the war, and the disbanding of all forces hostile to the government." CW, 8:250–51; Stahr, *Seward*, 421; Burlingame, *AL*, 2:753.

355 HAD ARRIVED AT FORTRESS MONROE Stahr, *Seward*, 421–22.

355 "INDUCED BY A DISPATCH" CW, 8:256.

355 GRANT HAD WRITTEN Hay and Nicolay, *AL: A History*, 10:116–17.

355 "SAY TO THE GENTLEMEN" Ibid., 117.

355 TIRED FROM HIS JOURNEY Robert Garlick Hill Kean, "Diary, February 5, 1865," in Aaron Sheehan-Dean, ed., *The Civil War: The Final Year Told by Those Who Lived It* (New York, 2014), 573.

356 THE THREE-HOUR MEETING Ibid., 573; Burlingame, *AL*, 2:755–61. See also William C. Harris, "The Hampton Roads Peace Conference: A Final Test of Lincoln's Presidential Leadership," *JALA* 21 (Winter 2000): 30–61.

356 A BLACK MAN Stahr, *Seward*, 422.

356 "SEEMED TO BE" Burlingame, *AL*, 2:756.

356 AS HE HAD SAID Ibid.

356 STEPHENS TRIED A DIFFERENT Ibid.; Kean, "Diary, February 5, 1865," in Sheehan-Dean, ed., *Civil War: The Final Year*, 573.

356 "LINCOLN APPEARED TO" Kean, "Diary, February 5, 1865," in Sheehan-Dean, ed., *Civil War: The Final Year*, 573. See also Burlingame, *AL*, 2:756.

356 STEPHENS TRIED ONCE MORE Sheehan-Dean, ed., *Civil War: The Final Year*, 573.

356 SURRENDER WOULD BE Hay and Nicolay, *AL: A History*, 10:122–23.

356 "AS TO ALL QUESTIONS" Ibid., 123. On slavery, Lincoln is alleged to have said that he "had always himself been in favor of emancipation, but not immediate emancipation, even by the states. Many evils attending this appeared to him." RWAL, 421. He addressed Stephens directly: "Stephens, if I were in Georgia and entertained the sentiments I do—though, I suppose, I should not be permitted to stay there long with them—but if I resided in Georgia with my present sentiments, I'll tell

you what I would do if I were in your place. I would go home and get the governor of the state to call the legislature together and get them to recall all the state troops from the war, elect senators and members to Congress, and ratify [the Thirteenth] amendment *prospectively*, so as to take effect, say, in five years. Such a ratification would be valid in my opinion. I have looked into the subject and think such a prospective ratification would be valid. Whatever may have been the views of your people before the war, they must be convinced now that slavery is doomed. It cannot last long in any event, and the best course, it seems to me, for your public men to pursue would be to adopt such a policy as will avoid, as far as possible, the evils of immediate emancipation. This would be my course, if I were in your place." Ibid., 421–22. A prospective ratification of the Thirteenth Amendment seems unconstitutional and unrealistic, and scholars doubt the veracity of Stephens's recollection on this point.

356 AT ONE POINT Stahr, *Seward*, 423–25. See also Burlingame, *AL*, 2:757.

356 THE CONFEDERATES COMPLAINED Burlingame, *AL*, 2:758.

356 "TO YIELD TO" Ibid. "Seward was right," Burlingame observed. "The terms offered the South by Lincoln—reunion and emancipation—were far more limited and generous than the demands the United States would in 1945 impose on Germany and Japan, who surrendered unconditionally." Ibid.

357 "THIS ENDS THE" Kean, "Diary, February 5, 1865," in Sheehan-Dean, ed., *Civil War: The Final Year*, 575.

357 "HIS MAJESTY ABRAHAM" Hay and Nicolay, *AL: A History*, 10:130–31.

357 "INSOLENT ENEMY" Burlingame, *AL*, 2:758.

357 THE MONEY WOULD BE PAID Hay and Nicolay, *AL: A History*, 10:133–34.

357 UNANIMOUSLY OPPOSED Ibid., 133–37.

357 "IT DID NOT MEET" Ibid., 136.

357 "HOW LONG WILL" Ibid.

357 "BUT YOU ARE ALL" Ibid.

357 "THE AUDIENCE WELCOMED" Washington *Evening Star*, February 11, 1865.

358 WHICH FEATURED TWO PLAYS Lincoln Log, February 10, 1865, http://thelincolnlog .org/Results.aspx?type=CalendarMonth&year=1865&month=2.

358 "IN MANY RESPECTS" Washington *Evening Star*, February 11, 1865.

358 "A RICH LILAC" Ibid.

358 AT NOON ON SUNDAY, FEBRUARY 12, 1865 Martin B. Pasternak, *Rise Now and Fly to Arms: The Life of Henry Highland Garnet*, PhD diss., University of Massachusetts, Amherst (1981): 206; Clara Merritt DeBoer, *His Truth Is Marching On: African Americans Who Taught the Freedman for the American Missionary Association, 1861–1877* (New York, 1995), 13–15; Henry Highland Garnet, *A Memorial Discourse: Delivered in the Hall of the House of Representatives, Washington City, D.C., on Sabbath, February 12, 1865* (Philadelphia, 1865), 65.

358 THE FIRST BLACK MAN "The First African American Man to Speak in the House Chamber," https://history.house.gov/Historical-Highlights/1851-1900/The-first -African-American-to-speak-in-the-House-Chamber/.

358 WILLIAM SLADE . . . WAS AN ELDER Sweet, "A Representative 'of Our People': The Agency of William Slade," *JALA*, 27, https://quod.lib.umich.edu/j/jala/2629860 .0034.204/--representative-of-our-people-the-agency-of-william-slade?rgn =main;view=fulltext#N29.

358 DR. JOSEPH P. THOMPSON On Thompson, see "History/Biographical Note," Joseph Parrish Thompson and Leonard Bacon Correspondence, 1845–1879, Rare Book and Manuscript Library, Columbia University Library, New York. https://finding aids.library.columbia.edu/ead/nnc-rb/ldpd_9577639#history. See also Samuel C.

Pearson, "From Church to Denomination: American Congregationalism in the Nineteenth Century," *Church History* 38, no. 1 (1969): 67–87.

358 WHICH LINCOLN REPORTEDLY APPROVED Pasternak, *Rise Now and Fly*, 205; W. M. Brewer, "Henry Highland Garnet," *Journal of Negro History* 13, no. 1 (January 1928): 50.

358 "TOLD THE WHOLE STORY" DeBoer, *His Truth Is Marching On*, 15.

358 DESCRIBED AS "WORDS OF" Ibid.

359 THE YOUNGER CHANNING WAS CHOSEN Octavius Brooks Frothingham, *Memoir of William Henry Channing* (Boston, 1886), 316. Channing defeated the Right Reverend John Henry Hopkins of Vermont, who served as presiding bishop of the Episcopal Church. On Hopkins, see, for instance, Woody Register, "In Their Own Words: An Introduction to John Henry Hopkins—First Bishop of Vermont, Artist and Architect, and Defender of Slavery," *Meridiana: The Blog of the Roberson Project on Slavery, Race, and Reconciliation*, April 14, 2020. https://meridiana.sewanee.edu/2020/04/14/in-their-own-words-an-introduction-john-henry-hopkins-first-bishop-of-vermont-artist-and-architect-and-defender-of-slavery/.

359 HE "BEST REPRESENT[ED]" Frothingham, *Memoir of William Henry Channing*, 316.

359 THAT "A WOMAN'S VOICE" Ibid.

359 INVITED THE QUAKER RACHEL HOWLAND Ibid., 317.

359 "THAT A COLORED MINISTER" Ibid., 316.

359 "WHITE AND COLORED" *Memorial Discourse*, 66.

359 THE FIFTEENTH STREET PRESBYTERIAN CHOIR Ibid.

359 "GREAT GOD!" Henry Highland Garnet, "Let the Monster Perish," February 12, 1865, https://www.blackpast.org/african-american-history/1865-henry-highland-garnet-let-monster-perish/; *Memorial Discourse*, 73–74.

359 "UPON THE TOTAL" Ibid., 88.

359 "IF SLAVERY HAS BEEN" Ibid., 87.

360 THE *WEEKLY ANGLO-AFRICAN* THOUGHT "dazzling" Pasternak, *Rise Now and Fly*, 207.

360 "WE HAVE PAID SOME OF THE FEARFUL INSTALLMENTS" *Memorial Discourse*, 88.

360 "LIBERTY HAS BEEN" Foner, *Fiery Trial*, 335.

360 SPECIAL FIELD ORDER NO. 15 Ibid., 320–21.

360 SHERMAN ADDED UNION MULES Ibid., 321.

360 IN SYRACUSE, NEW YORK Blight, *Frederick Douglass*, 440–42; Foner, *Fiery Trial*, 309–10; Du Bois, *Black Reconstruction*, 233–35.

360 "WE WANT THE ELECTIVE FRANCHISE" Du Bois, *Black Reconstruction*, 234–35.

360 CENTRAL POSTWAR CONCERN Donald, *Charles Sumner and the Rights of Man*, 207. In the Senate in late February 1865, Sumner led a battle against the Louisiana constitution that denied Black men the ballot. Du Bois, *Black Reconstruction*, 153–65; Cox, *Lincoln and Black Freedom*, 46–139; Du Bois, *Black Reconstruction*, 153–65; Foner, *Reconstruction*, 45–50.

360 "NEARLY ALL THE FREE" Arnold Bertonneau, "Every Man Should Stand Equal Before the Law," April 12, 1864, https://www.blackpast.org/african-american-history/1864-arnold-bertonneau-every-man-should-stand-equal-law/.

360 ARNOLD BERTONNEAU Herbert G. Ruffin II, "E. Arnold Bertonneau (1834–1912)," https://www.blackpast.org/african-american-history/bertonneau-e-arnold-1834-1912/.

360 JEAN BAPTISTE ROUDANEZ See, for instance, "The New Orleans Tribune: America's First Black Daily Newspaper," https://neworleanshistorical.org/items/show/1546?tour=104&index=6. The paper was founded by Jean Baptiste Roudanez's younger brother, Dr. Louis Charles Roudanez. Ibid.

360 WENT TO WASHINGTON White, *House Built by Slaves*, 90–93.

360 "WE ARE MEN" Ibid., 90.

360 "THE RIGHT TO VOTE" Bertonneau, "Every Man Should Stand Equal Before the Law."

361 MOVED, LINCOLN HAD MADE White, *House Built by Slaves*, 92–93.

361 "CRIMINAL CONJUNCTION" Du Bois, *Black Reconstruction*, 162.

361 SUMNER PREVAILED Ibid., 162–63.

361 "THE FRIENDS OF FREEDOM" Ibid.

361 "I INSIST THAT" Ibid., 198–99.

362 "OF ANY PERSON" African American Refugees and Emancipation, https://www.nps .gov/cane/african-american-refugees-and-emancipation.htm.

362 "A BUREAU OF REFUGEES" Freedmen's Bureau Acts of 1865 and 1866, https://www .senate.gov/artandhistory/history/common/generic/FreedmensBureau.htm.   See also Du Bois, *Black Reconstruction*, 225–30; Foner, *Reconstruction*, 68–79; Foner, *Fiery Trial*, 321–22.

362 "AFTER MANY TRIALS" Nathan W. Daniels Diary, March 5, 1865, LOC.

362 LED BY GENERAL OLIVER O. HOWARD "Oliver O. Howard," https://www.battle fields.org/learn/biographies/oliver-o-howard.

362 "THE FREEDMEN'S BUREAU" Du Bois, *Black Reconstruction*, 219.

362 "SCARCELY ANY SUBJECT" Ibid.

362 WAS TO FEED Ibid., 225–30; Foner, *Reconstruction*, 68–79; Foner, *Fiery Trial*, 321–22.

362 "THE GREAT SHIFTER" Trefousse, *Radical Republicans*, 304.

362 "I AM SURE" Harrold, *Lincoln and the Abolitionists*, 107.

363 "THIS COUNTRY WAS" *NYT*, April 21, 1865; Du Bois, *Black Reconstruction*, 128.

Chapter Twenty-six: *The Almighty Has His Own Purposes*

364 "MEN ARE NOT FLATTERED" Hay and Nicolay, *AL: A History*, 10:146.

364 THE FRIDAY EVENING Washington *Evening Star*, March 4, 1865. See also, as noted above, Burlingame, ed., *Lincoln Observed*, 165; Brooks, *Abraham Lincoln and the Downfall of American Slavery*, 412–15; White, *Lincoln's Greatest Speech*, 29–30; Nathan W. Daniels Diary, March 5, 1865, LOC.

364 "DRIVING MISTS AND BLACK SKIES" Washington *Evening Star*, March 4, 1865.

364 FIREMEN BEARING TORCHES Ibid.

364 THE STARS AND STRIPES Ibid.

364 "ALMOST A PANDEMONIUM" Nathan W. Daniels Diary, March 5, 1865, LOC.

364 "WITHIN THE CAPITOL" Washington *Evening Star*, March 4, 1865.

365 A STATE CONVENTION Trefousse, *Andrew Johnson*, 185–87.

365 "YOU TOOK ME" Ibid., 186.

365 HE WAS NOT FEELING WELL Ibid., 188.

365 ON THE MORNING Ibid., 189.

365 TO STEADY HIMSELF Ibid.

365 "MR. HAMLIN, I AM NOT WELL" David O. Stewart, *Impeached: The Trial of President Andrew Johnson and the Fight for Lincoln's Legacy* (New York, 2009), 8.

365 HE THEN DRANK THREE Ibid.

365 NOT THE BEST OF CHOICES For accounts of the Johnson swearing-in, see, for instance, ibid., 7–12; Trefousse, *Andrew Johnson*, 189–91; Burlingame, ed., *Lincoln Observed*, 165–67; White, *Lincoln's Greatest Speech*, 38–39. Nathan Daniels, who stood outside the chamber where he could "hear but not see," had a different take. "Andy Johnson gave one of the most remarkable speeches that it was ever my privilege to

listen to," Daniels wrote. "He took up the members of the Cabinet individually, and named them, that they rec'd their power from the people, which under his administration they should not forget—and much upon the same order. . . . [I]t was surmised that he had taken too much liquor and was not himself, but this I cannot believe—I heard nothing but what was proper and all the cabinet deserved—was glad he gave it to them." Nathan W. Daniels Diary, March 5, 1865, LOC.

365 HAMLIN HAD HOPED Stewart, *Impeached*, 8.

365 "ARM IN ARM" Burlingame, ed., *Lincoln Observed*, 166.

365 "IN A STATE OF MANIFEST INTOXICATION" Ibid.

365 "JOHNSON," HAMLIN MURMURED Stewart, *Impeached*, 9.

365 "IN VAIN DID HAMLIN" Burlingame, ed., *Lincoln Observed*, 166.

365 JOHNSON FINALLY TOOK Ibid.

365 "I KISS THIS BOOK" Ibid.

365 "ALL THIS IS" Stewart, *Impeached*, 9–10.

365 "ENJOYED THE MEANEST WHISKEY" Ibid., 11.

365 "I HAVE KNOWN" Ibid.

365 "DRUNKEN BOOR" Trefousse, *Andrew Johnson*, 190.

365 "BEHAVIOR WAS THAT" Stewart, *Impeached*, 11.

366 "THE VICE PRESIDENT ELECT" Trefousse, *Andrew Johnson*, 190.

366 GIVEN THE RECENT RAIN Achorn, *Every Drop of Blood*, 203–4.

366 STANDING NEAR THE PRESIDENT Frothingham, *Memoirs of William Henry Channing*, 320–21.

366 IN HIS ADDRESS As noted above, on the Second Inaugural, see, for instance, Achorn, *Every Drop of Blood*; Black, "Ultimate Voice of Lincoln," 49–57; Thurow, *Abraham Lincoln and American Political Religion*, 88–108; Hansen, "Dimensions of Agency in Lincoln's 'Second Inaugural,'" *Philosophy and Rhetoric*, 223–54; White, *Lincoln's Greatest Speech*; Burlingame, *AL*, 2:765–72; Carwardine, *Lincoln: A Life of Purpose and Power*, 244–48; Donald, *Lincoln*, 565–68; Goodwin, *Team of Rivals*, 697–701; Hay and Nicolay, *AL: A History*, 10:132–47.

366 "TO STRENGTHEN, PERPETUATE" CW, 8:332–33.

366 "IT MAY SEEM STRANGE" Ibid., 333.

366 "JUDGE NOT, THAT YE BE" Matthew 7:1–27, KJV.

367 "'WOE UNTO THE WORLD'" Matthew 18:7, KJV.

367 "IF WE SHALL SUPPOSE" CW, 8:333.

367 "AT THE SAME TIME" Matthew 18:1–4, KJV.

367 "WHEREFORE IF THY HAND" Ibid., 18:8–9.

367 "BUT WHOSO SHALL OFFEND" Ibid., 18:6.

368 "FONDLY DO WE HOPE" CW, 8:333.

368 GURLEY HAD SPOKEN White, *Lincoln's Greatest Speech*, 139, 154–55.

368 TERM HAS BEEN THOUGHT Ibid.

368 "AND THEY SHALL MOCK HIM" Mark 10:34, KJV; see also Matthew 16:21.

368 "THEN PILATE THEREFORE" John 19:1–3, KJV.

368 "EVERY DROP OF BLOOD" CW, 8:333.

368 "'THE JUDGMENTS OF THE LORD'" Ibid.

368 "THE HEAVENS DECLARE" Psalm 19:1–14, KJV.

369 IN THE HEBREW BIBLE "What Does Judgment Mean?," http://helpmewithbiblestudy.org/1God/WorksJudgmentDef.aspx.

369 "LEARN TO DO WELL" Isaiah 1:17, KJV.

369 "MORE TO BE DESIRED" Psalm 19:10–11, KJV.

370 THE REACTION TO THE SPEECH White, *Lincoln's Greatest Speech*, 181–82; "Lincoln's

Second Inaugural: Press Reactions to the Most Eloquent Presidential Address in American History," *Journal of Blacks in Higher Education* 43 (Spring 2004): 44–46.

370 THE BLACK PEOPLE White, *Lincoln's Greatest Speech*, 181–82; *The New York Herald*, March 6, 1865.

370 "THEY SEEMED TO HANG" "Abraham Lincoln's Second Inauguration," http://www .abrahamlincolnonline.org/lincoln/education/inaugural2.htm.

370 "THE WHOLE PROCEEDING" Douglass, *Autobiographies*, 801.

370 "I EXPECT THE" *CW*, 8:356; Hay and Nicolay, *AL: A History*, 10:146.

370 *THE NATIONAL INTELLIGENCER* OFFERED From *The National Intelligencer* in the Baltimore *Sun*, March 7, 1865. "Woe to the nation that shall fall into the hands of ungodly rulers; and equal woe to the people whose rights and interests shall be involved and torn in the whirlpool created by jarring theological sects," the paper wrote. "Whatever good men may think of the providence of God in human affairs . . . nevertheless he may well beware who undertakes to say that in the sight of God he is without sin, and that his adversary should be burned as a heretic. Mr. Lincoln cannot intend to convey any such self-righteous dogma. He is merely regarding the war in its obstinacy and causelessness on the part of the rebels; he is contemplating the unlooked for magnitude of, and great social results which have unexpectedly sprung from the rebellion. . . . He certainly does not design to affirm the narrow opinion that the chastisement of Heaven which has fallen upon this nation is to be regarded by the North with the pharisaical pride which shall say, *we are without sin*." Ibid.

371 "THAT RAIL-SPLITTING LAWYER" White, *Lincoln's Greatest Speech*, 184.

371 "I AM TAKEN CAPTIVE" Burlingame, *AL*, 2:772.

371 "THE LEADING CHARACTERISTIC" *Chicago Tribune*, March 6, 1865.

371 "THE INAUGURAL WAS SHORT" Nathan W. Daniels Diary, March 5, 1865, LOC.

371 "FOUR YEARS AGO" *Janesville Daily Gazette*, March 6, 1865.

371 "HE MAKES NO BOASTS" White, *Lincoln's Greatest Speech*, 189–90.

371 "WITH A SOUL" Harrell, *When the Bells Tolled for Lincoln*, 26.

372 "DON'T FAIL TO READ" *The Spirit of Democracy* (Woodsfield, Ohio), March 15, 1865.

372 "A LITTLE SPEECH" White, *Lincoln's Greatest Speech*, 190.

372 TO CALL JEFFERSON'S WORDS *CW*, 3:375–76.

372 TOOK MRS. LINCOLN ON A DRIVE *LDBD, 1861–1865*, 318.

372 PERSEVERANCE FIRE COMPANY Lincoln Log, March 4, 1865, http://thelincoln.org /Results.aspx?type=basicSearch&terms=march+4%2c+1865&r=L1NlYXJjaC5h c3B4.

372 AS THE MARINE BAND PLAYED Ibid.

372 THOUSANDS OF WELL-WISHERS *LDBD, 1861–1865*, 318; White, *Lincoln's Greatest Speech*, 198–99.

372 FREDERICK DOUGLASS WAS AMONG Douglass, *Autobiographies*, 802–5, details the Douglass visit to the White House on the day of Lincoln's second inauguration.

372 MRS. LOUISE DORSEY Ibid., 803.

372 "I HAD FOR SOME TIME" Ibid.

372 TWO POLICEMEN Ibid.

373 "I TOLD THE OFFICERS" Ibid.

373 "OBSTRUCTING THE DOORWAY" Ibid., 803–4.

373 "WE HALTED" Ibid., 804.

373 FORTUNATELY, AT THAT POINT Ibid.

373 "HERE COMES MY FRIEND DOUGLASS" Ibid.

373 "IT CAME OUT" Ibid., 804–5.

373 "I HAVE FOUND" Ibid.

374 CHURCH SERVICES Rev. E. Barrass, "A Few Particulars in the Life of Bishop Simpson, D.D., LL.D.," *Wesley-Methodist Magazine*, Sixth Series, 107, no. 11 (November 1884): 839.

374 "PREACHED IN CAPITOL" Matthew Simpson Papers, 1865 Diary, Container 2, LOC. The biblical text came from John 12:32, KJV.

374 "PLEASANT AND CHEERFUL" Washington *Evening Star*, March 6, 1865.

374 GUESTS INCLUDED THE PRESIDENT *New-York Daily Tribune*, March 6, 1865.

374 THE CHAMBER'S FURNISHINGS "Furniture: The Walter Desk: 1857–1873," Collection of the U.S. House of Representatives, Washington, D.C.

374 FLAGS HUNG BEHIND "Old House of Representatives (about 1861). Earliest photo of interior of Capitol," Brady-Handy Photograph Collection, Library of Congress Prints and Photographs Division, Washington, D.C.

374 A SINGLE FRESCO "Arts and Artifacts: Constantino Brumidi's Fresco," Architect of the Capitol, Washington, D.C.

374 A WALKING STICK Barrass, "A Few Particulars," 839.

374 MUSIC WAS PLAYED Ibid.

374 "HE SPOKE OF" Thomas H. Pearne, *Sixty-one Years of Itinerant Christian Life in Church and State* (Cincinnati, 1898), 160–61; "Jottings from the Capital," *Hartford Daily Courant*, March 8, 1865.

375 "INSTANTLY, AS IF BY ELECTRICITY" Pearne, *Sixty-one Years*, 160–61; "Jottings," *Hartford Daily Courant*.

375 BEGAN TO RAP Pearne, *Sixty-one Years*, 160–61.

375 AND HE WEPT Ibid.

375 TWO SPIRITUALIST FRIENDS Nathan W. Daniels Diary, March 5, 1865, LOC.

375 "ENGAGED IN HIS OWN APARTMENTS" Ibid.

375 "DESCRIBED LITTLE WILLIE LINCOLN" Ibid.

375 "I HAVE BEEN UP" " 'The Honor of Your Company Is Requested': Lincoln's Second Inaugural Ball at the Patent Office," https://www.nps.gov/articles/-the-honor-of-your-company-is-requested-lincoln-s-second-inaugural-ball-at-the-patent-office.htm.

376 BLUE AND GOLD SOFAS *NYT*, March 8, 1865.

376 "UNLESS YOU SEND ME WORD" CW, 8:337.

376 LINCOLN, WHO WANTED TO USE Donald, *Charles Sumner and the Rights of Man*, 207.

376 THE PRESIDENT'S PARTY Lincoln Log, March 6, 1865, http://thelincolnlog.org/Results.aspx?type=CalendarMonth&year=1865&month=3.

376 ABOUT TEN THIRTY Ibid.

376 "MRS. LINCOLN . . . WORE" Ibid.

376 "MR. LINCOLN WAS EVIDENTLY" " 'The Honor of Your Company Is Requested': Lincoln's Second Inaugural Ball at the Patent Office." See also "The Inauguration Ball," *NYT*, March 8, 1865.

376 "SHE LOOKED EXCEEDINGLY WELL" Ibid.

376 LINCOLN WAS SHOWN Ibid.

376 OYSTERS, DUCK, BEEF Megan Gambino, "Document Deep Dive: The Menu from President Lincoln's Second Inaugural Ball," *Smithsonian*, January 15, 2013, https://www.smithsonianmag.com/history/document-deep-dive-the-menu-from-president-lincolns-second-inaugural-ball-1510874/; Andrew F. Smith, "First Suppers: A Tradition of Inaugural Meals," *Los Angeles Times*, January 14, 2009.

376 "THE FLOOR OF THE SUPPER ROOM" Gambino, "Document Deep Dive."

376 ANOTHER FOUR-HOUR AFTERNOON ENTERTAINMENT *LDBD, 1861–1865*, 320.

377   THE PRESIDENT BECAME ILL Ibid.

377   THE CABINET MET Ibid.; Gienapp and Gienapp, eds., *Civil War Diary of Gideon Welles*, 602–3.

377   A DESPERATE BID McPherson, *Battle Cry of Freedom*, 831–37. "It is better for us to use the negroes for our defense than that the Yankees should use them against us," Southern newspaper editors said. Ibid., 831.

377   "AT THE TIME" Douglass, *Autobiographies*, 800.

378   "NOT ONLY EXPEDIENT" McPherson, *Battle Cry of Freedom*, 836–37.

378   "THOSE WHO ARE" Ibid.

378   IN HIS LIFE CW, 8:360–61.

378   "CAN YOU NOT VISIT" Ibid., 367.

378   "HAD ALREADY THOUGHT" Ibid.

378   HE CHARTERED THE *River Queen* LDBD, *1861–1865*, 321.

378   "WE FEEL GREAT" CW, 8:371–72.

378   "IF HE SUFFERS" Goldwin Smith, "President Lincoln," *Macmillan's Magazine* 11 (November 1864–April 1865), 303.

379   AT ONE P.M. LDBD, *1861–1865*, 322; Lincoln Log, March 23, 1865, http://thelincoln log.org/Results.aspx?type=basicSearch&terms=march+23%2c+1865&r=L1NlYX JjaC5hc3B4. On Lincoln at the front in Virginia, see Burlingame, *AL*, 2:777–98.

379   "FURIOUS GALE" CW, 8:373.

379   APPARENTLY AFFECTED BY Ibid.; Lincoln Log, March 24, 1865, http://thelincolnlog .org/Results.aspx?type=basicSearch&terms=march+24%2c+1865&r=L1NlYXJja C5hc3B4.

379   ABOUT EIGHT HOURS Ibid.

379   EARLY THE NEXT MORNING Ibid., March 25, 1865, http://thelincolnlog.org/Results .aspx?type=basicSearch&terms=March+25%2c+1865&r=L1NlYXJjaC5hc3B4.

379   THOUGH THE PRESIDENT Ibid.

379   TOOK A MILITARY TRAIN Ibid.; Horace Porter, *Campaigning with Grant* (Bloomington, Ind., 1961), 404–5.

379   CONFEDERATE THRUST NEAR FORT STEDMAN Porter, *Campaigning with Grant*, 404–6.

379   "ROBERT JUST NOW" Ibid., 405.

379   ON HORSEBACK Lincoln Log, March 25, 1865.

379   CONSULTING A MAP Porter, *Campaigning with Grant*, 406.

379   BROUGHT SOME OF THE WOUNDED BACK LDBD, *1861–1865*, 322.

379   BACK AT GRANT'S HEADQUARTERS Porter, *Campaigning with Grant*, 406–7.

379   CHOSE NOT TO DINE Lincoln Log, March 25, 1865.

379   WOULD SPEND SIXTEEN DAYS LDBD, *1861–1865*, 322–27. He had reached City Point on Friday, March 24, and arrived back in Washington on Sunday, April 9. Ibid.

379   AWAITING THE ANTICIPATED FALL Baker, *Mary Todd Lincoln*, 240.

379   "WE ARE IN" Sears, ed., *Civil War Papers of George B. McClellan*, 629.

380   IN GRANT'S TENT AT CITY POINT Porter, *Campaigning with Grant*, 410.

380   WITH THE YOUNG WIFE Turner and Turner, *Mary Todd Lincoln: Her Life and Letters*, 206–7; Burlingame, *AL*, 2:781–85.

380   THE PRESIDENT WAS REVIEWING Turner and Turner, *Mary Todd Lincoln: Her Life and Letters*, 207.

380   ENRAGED AND SUFFERING Ibid.; Baker, *Mary Todd Lincoln*, 239.

380   "BORE IT AS CHRIST" Adam Badeau, *Grant in Peace: From Appomattox to Mount McGregor; A Personal Memoir* (Hartford, Conn., 1887), 360; Burlingame, *AL*, 2:782.

381   THE FIRST LADY RETREATED Baker, *Mary Todd Lincoln*, 240.

381   THE TENSION BETWEEN HUSBAND AND WIFE Ibid., 240–41.

381   "The battle now rages" CW, 8:381–82.

381   at Grant's request *RWAL*, 75; Burlingame, *AL*, 2:787.

Chapter Twenty-seven: Old Abe Will Come Out All Right

382   "Slavery they admit" CW, 8:387.

382   "Don't kneel to me" *RWAL*, 366; Burlingame, *AL*, 2:790.

382   "Bright and beautiful" John B. Jones, "Diary, April 2, 1865," in Sheehan-Dean, ed., *Civil War: The Final Year*, 637–38.

382   "No sound disturbed" Ibid., 641.

382   At Grace and Ninth St. Paul's Episcopal Church, Richmond, Virginia, https://www.stpaulsrva.org/ourhistory.

382   Jefferson Davis was attending Davis, *Jefferson Davis*, 603–4; Sallie Brock, "From *Richmond During the War*," in Sheehan-Dean, ed., *Civil War: The Final Year*, 641–42; Stout, *Upon the Altar of the Nation*, 435–37.

382   "mercifully to look upon" *Protestant Episcopal Church in the Confederate States of America Book of Common Prayer. Selections. Prayer Book for the Camp* (Richmond, 1863), no page number.

382   The choir sang Davis, *Jefferson Davis*, 603.

382   "Hide me, O my Savior" "Jesus, Lover of My Soul," Hymn No. 143, *The Order for Daily Morning and Evening Prayer, According to the Use of the Protestant Episcopal Church in the Confederate States of America* (Atlanta, 1863), 45.

382   "The war came" Davis, *Jefferson Davis*, 600.

382   Davis gave his wife Ibid., 601.

382   he had asked Ibid. "If I live you can come to me when the struggle is ended, but I do not expect to survive the destruction of constitutional liberty," Davis said as he arranged for his family's evacuation. Ibid., 602.

383   At about noon on this Sunday Elizabeth Wright Weddell, *St. Paul's Church: Richmond, Virginia: Its Historic Years and Memorials* (Richmond, Va., 1931), 1:241.

383   the congregation in St. Paul's were kneeling Ibid., 242.

383   "It was Sunday" Ibid., 243.

383   "a large, pompous, swaggering kind of fellow" "The Fall of Richmond," *The Richmond Dispatch*, February 2, 1902.

383   "General Lee telegraphs" Weddell, *St. Paul's Church*, 242.

383   Davis quietly slipped out Ibid., 237.

383   "There was no confusion" Ibid., 239.

383   The service ended as usual Ibid.

383   "The direful tidings" Brock, "From *Richmond During the War*," 642.

383   By late afternoon Ibid., 642–43.

383   Banks were opened Ibid., 642.

383   Prison guards left Ibid., 643.

383   By order of Ibid.

383   "In the gutters" Ibid.

383   recalled the day "The Fall of Richmond," *The Richmond Dispatch*, February 2, 1902.

383   "I remembered my" Ibid.

383   "bring up the very gates" Chesebrough, *"God Ordained This War,"* 221.

384   To John Blair Dabney Stout, *Upon the Altar of the Nation*, 432–33.

384   "The signs of the times" Ibid., 433.

384   "It is certain now" CW, 8:385.

384 "PETERSBURG AND RICHMOND!" George Templeton Strong, "Diary, April 3, 1865," in Sheehan-Dean, ed., *Civil War: The Final Year*, 650.

384 ELIZABETH KECKLY WAS Keckly, *Behind the Scenes*, 161–62.

384 TUESDAY, APRIL 4 *LDBD, 1861–1865*, 325.

384 AS LINCOLN WALKED Thomas Morris Chester, "To the *Philadelphia Press*," in Sheehan-Dean, ed., *Civil War: The Final Year*, 663–64.

384 "WHY, DOCTOR," LINCOLN TOLD Chapman, *Latest Light on Abraham Lincoln*, 500.

384 "AS SOON AS" Chester, "To the *Philadelphia Press*," 663.

385 A BLACK MAN Ibid., 656.

385 "SOME OF THE NEGROES" Ibid., 663.

385 ONE WOMAN CRIED OUT Harold Holzer, *President Lincoln Assassinated!! The Firsthand Story of the Murder, Manhunt, Trial, and Mourning* (New York, 2014), 7.

385 A FEW WERE SO MOVED Burlingame, *AL*, 2:790.

385 "DON'T KNEEL TO ME" Ibid.

385 LINCOLN INSPECTED THE HOUSE Chester, "To the *Philadelphia Press*," 663.

385 "THIS MUST HAVE BEEN" Lincoln Log, April 4, 1865, http://thelincolnlog.org/Results .aspx?type=basicSearch&terms=April+4%2c+1865&r=L1NlYXJjaC5hc3B4.

385 "THE HATED, DESPISED, RIDICULED" Charles Coleton Coffin, "Scenes in Richmond," in Holzer, *President Lincoln Assassinated!!*, 3.

385 A HUGE COMPANY Chester, "To the *Philadelphia Press*," 663.

385 "I KNOW THAT" Ibid., 665.

385 "NOTHING CAN EXCEED" Ibid., 664.

386 "THE ENTHUSIASTIC BEARING" Coffin, "Scenes in Richmond," in Holzer, *President Lincoln Assassinated!!*, 8.

386 "MEN IN HEART AND SOUL" Ibid.

386 "THOUSANDS OF MEN" Ibid.

386 MRS. LINCOLN REJOINED *LDBD, 1861–1865*, 326.

386 "EVEN OUR STATELY" Turner and Turner, *Mary Todd Lincoln: Her Life and Letters*, 220.

386 RICHMOND, SHE REMARKED Ibid., 208.

386 TOURING RICHMOND Keckly, *Behind the Scenes*, 160–61.

386 THE FLOORS WERE LITTERED Ibid., 166.

387 THE PRESIDENT MET *CW*, 8:386–87.

387 A SIX-WORD SENTENCE Ibid., 387.

387 "GEN. SHERIDAN SAYS" Ibid., 392.

387 "I ASK A SUSPENSION" Stout, *Upon the Altar of the Nation*, 440.

387 LINCOLN HAD LEFT *LDBD, 1861–1865*, 326–27.

387 HE WAS ABOARD Ibid., 327.

387 LEE WAS IN RESPLENDENT For accounts of the surrender, see, for instance, McPherson, *Battle Cry of Freedom*, 848–51; Shelby Foote, *The Civil War: A Narrative* (New York, 1958), 3:939–56. For a study of how differing views of the end of the war have shaped post–Civil War America, see Varon, *Appomattox*.

387 GRANT MENTIONED THAT Foote, *Civil War*, 3:946–47.

387 "IT IS DESIRABLE" Gideon Welles, "Diary, April 7, 1865," in Sheehan-Dean, ed., *Civil War: The Final Year*, 668–69.

387 "THERE IS NOTHING" Ibid., 671.

387 "THE SOUTH LIES" Emma LeConte, "Diary, April 21, 1865," in Holzer, *President Lincoln Assassinated!!*, 241.

387 CALLED ON A BAND Burlingame, *AL*, 2:798.

388 LINCOLN READ ALOUD Ibid., 799–800.

388 AMONG HIS SELECTIONS Ibid., 799.

388 He mused on Ibid., 799–800.

388 arrived in Washington *LDBD, 1861–1865*, 327.

388 "Peace! blessed Peace!" Sarah Morgan, "Diary, April 19, 1865," in Sheehan-Dean, ed., *Civil War: The Final Year*, 701.

388 the news of Appomattox Brooks, *Abraham Lincoln and the Downfall of American Slavery*, 450.

388 Big gun after big gun Burlingame, ed., *Lincoln Observed*, 181–82.

388 Windows in houses Ibid.

388 "The streets, horribly muddy" Ibid., 182.

388 "The very day" Burlingame, *AL*, 2:800.

388 Clerks gathered Brooks, *Abraham Lincoln and the Downfall of American Slavery*, 450.

388 A celebratory crowd CW, 8:393–94; Lincoln Log, April 10, 1865, http://the lincolnlog.org/Results.aspx?type=basicSearch&terms=April+10%2c+1865&r =L1NlYXJjaC5hc3hc3B4.

388 "The bands played" CW, 8:393.

388 A delighted Tad Burlingame, ed., *Lincoln Observed*, 182; CW, 8:393.

388 At last the president Burlingame, ed., *Lincoln Observed*, 182.

388 "radiant with happiness" Brooks, *Abraham Lincoln and the Downfall of American Slavery*, 451.

388 "of the wildest confusion" Burlingame, ed., *Lincoln Observed*, 182.

389 Far from being triumphant CW, 8:393.

389 They complied, and followed Burlingame, ed., *Lincoln Observed*, 183.

389 He wanted the new Louisiana government Donald, *Charles Sumner and the Rights of Man*, 214–15.

389 "confusion and uncertainty" Ibid., 215.

389 "A practical difficulty is this" Beverly Wilson Palmer, ed., *Selected Letters of Charles Sumner* (Boston, 1990), 2:273.

389 Typically, the president See, for instance, John C. Rodrigue, *Lincoln and Reconstruction* (Carbondale, Ill., 2013), 109–47; Burlingame, *AL*, 2:792–95; Donald, *Lincoln*, 589–92; Foner, *Fiery Trial*, 316–22. "Those who are ready to fight the President on reconstruction and thereby carry out in 1868 the radical programme for the Presidency, which failed in 1864, are only waiting for the occasion to pounce upon the President's expected clemency toward the offending rebel leaders," Brooks noted. "As yet, we have none of them to experiment upon, but the extremists are thirsting for a general hanging, and if the President fails to gratify their desires in this direction, they will be glad, for it will afford them more pretexts for the formation of a party which be shall pledged to 'a more vigorous policy.'" Burlingame, ed., *Lincoln Observed*, 184–85.

389 "Whatever aspect the question" Burlingame, ed., *Lincoln Observed*, 186.

389 the Washington darkness was rent Brooks, *Abraham Lincoln and the Downfall of American Slavery*, 450–51.

390 She had asked Keckly, *Behind the Scenes*, 174.

390 "Certainly, Lizabeth" Ibid.

390 Tad again entertained Brooks, *Abraham Lincoln and the Downfall of American Slavery*, 453.

390 Brooks held a candle Burlingame, *AL*, 2:801; Brooks, *Abraham Lincoln and the Downfall of American Slavery*, 453–54. Keckly recalled this differently, writing that Tad, not Brooks, held the light. Keckly, *Behind the Scenes*, 177.

390 "I stood a short distance" Ibid., 177–78. The next day, Mary agreed with Keckly's observation. "Yes, yes, Mr. Lincoln's life is always exposed," the First Lady said.

"Ah, no one knows what it is to live in constant dread of some fearful tragedy. The President has been warned so often, that I tremble for him on every public occasion. I have a presentiment that he will meet with a sudden and violent end. I pray God will protect my beloved husband from the hands of the assassin." Ibid., 178.

390 RECONSTRUCTION WAS LINCOLN'S CENTRAL THEME CW, 8:399–401.

390 "IT IS FRAUGHT" Ibid., 400–401.

390 A PLATFORM FOR PROGRESS Du Bois, *Black Reconstruction*, 201–2; "Seven Points," *New-York Daily Tribune*, May 30, 1865.

391 "WHEREVER I GO" Du Bois, *Black Reconstruction*, 136.

391 "IN RESPECTFUL EARNESTNESS" Ibid., 140.

391 "THE REAL CONCERN" Ibid., 201; "The President's Speech—The Question of Reconstruction," *NYT*, April 13, 1865.

391 "THE AMOUNT OF CONSTITUENCY" CW, 8:403.

391 "IT WAS JUST LIKE" Burlingame, *AL*, 2:802–3.

392 "SOME TWELVE THOUSAND" CW, 8:403–4.

393 "THERE CAN BE NO DOUBT" Du Bois, *Black Reconstruction*, 235. Foner wrote that the president's "capacity for growth" was the "essence of Lincoln's greatness." Foner, *Fiery Trial*, 336.

393 "I THINK WE HAVE REASON" Foner, *Fiery Trial*, 336.

393 LYDIA MARIA CHILD "Lydia Marie Child," National Abolition Hall of Fame and Museum, https://www.nationalabolitionhalloffameandmuseum.org/lydia-maria-child.html.

393 "WITH ALL HIS DEFICIENCIES" Foner, *Fiery Trial*, 336.

393 "MR. LINCOLN ... WAS A WISER" Greeley, *Recollections of a Busy Life*, 409.

393 JOHN WILKES BOOTH HAD BEEN ON Thomas T. Eckert, "Testimony Before the House Judiciary Committee" in Holzer, *President Lincoln Assassinated!!*, 9; Burlingame, *AL*, 2:803. See also Michael W. Kauffman, *American Brutus: John Wilkes Booth and the Lincoln Conspiracies* (New York, 2004), 210.

393 THE ACTOR HAD URGED Eckert, "Testimony Before the House Judiciary Committee" in Holzer, *President Lincoln Assassinated!!*, 9.

393 POWELL REFUSED Ibid.

393 "THAT" Ibid.

Chapter Twenty-eight: Lincoln Was Slain; America Was Meant

394 "HURRAH! OLD ABE LINCOLN" LeConte, "Diary, April 21, 1865" in Holzer, *President Lincoln Assassinated!!*, 241; Harrell, *When the Bells Tolled for Lincoln*, 59–60. See also Emma LeConte Diary, April 16–20, 1865, LeConte Papers, Southern Historical Collection, University of North Carolina, Chapel Hill.

394 "NO ONE DARE SPEAK" Pheebe Clark letter, April 22, 1865, Pheebe Clark Correspondence, LOC.

394 "OH, ASSASSINATION OF" RWAL, 73.

394 IN MARCH 1864, AGENTS OF THE CONFEDERACY Ibid., 82–83.

394 A SNIPER TRIED Pinsker, *Lincoln's Sanctuary*, 217–18.

394 "SOON AFTER I WAS NOMINATED" RWAL, 82–83.

394 "I LONG AGO" Burlingame, *AL*, 2:808.

394 "ASSASSINATION IN THE ABSTRACT" Ibid., 812.

395 AFTER LINCOLN'S REELECTION Ibid., 813.

395 "THIS DAY FOUR LONG YEARS AGO" LeConte Diary, April 13, 1865, Southern Historical Collection, University of North Carolina, Chapel Hill.

395 WITH THE ARRIVAL Lincoln Log, April 14, 1865, http://thelincolnlog.org/Results
.aspx?type=basicSearch&terms=April+14+1865&r=L1NlYXJjaC5hc3hc3B4.

396 THE PRESIDENT HAD BEEN ILL Burlingame, *AL*, 2:806; Turner and Turner, *Mary Todd
Lincoln: Her Life and Letters*, 219.

396 "MR. LINCOLN IS INDISPOSED" Ibid.

396 MARY HAD BEEN VISIBLY ANNOYED Burlingame, *AL*, 2:806–7.

396 MRS. GRANT, TOO, HAD NO INTEREST Ibid., 807.

396 "VISIT OUR CHILDREN" Ibid.

396 THE PRESIDENT HAD A BUSY MORNING *LDBD, 1861–1865*, 329; Bates, *Lincoln in the Telegraph Office*, 367.

396 EDWIN STANTON URGED Bates, *Lincoln in the Telegraph Office*, 366–67.

396 "STANTON," THE PRESIDENT ASKED Ibid., 367.

396 THE LINCOLNS WERE TO TAKE Ibid., 368; *LDBD, 1861–1865*, 330.

396 AT TEN O'CLOCK *LDBD, 1861–1865*, 329; CW, 8:411.

396 ABOUT THE SAME TIME Louis J. Weichmann, *A True History of the Assassination of Abraham Lincoln and of the Conspiracy of 1865*, ed. Floyd E. Risvold (New York, 1975), 135.

396 A HANDSOME CHILD On Booth, see, for instance, Kauffman, *American Brutus*; Weichmann, *True History*; Burlingame, *AL*, 2:810–16.

396 "LARGE LUSTROUS EYES" Weichmann, *True History*, 40.

397 BORN IN 1838 Kauffman, *American Brutus*, 82–83.

397 MARRIED IN 1851 Ibid., 88–89.

397 A GIFTED ATHLETE Weichmann, *True History*, 39.

397 ACCOMPANYING VIRGINIA MILITIAMEN John Wilkes Booth, "To Whom It May
Concern," in Holzer, *President Lincoln Assassinated!!*, 66; Kauffman, *American Brutus*,
105–6.

397 "I WAS PROUD" Booth, "To Whom It May Concern" in Holzer, *President Lincoln Assassinated!!*, 66.

397 "I THOUGHT THEN" Ibid.

397 BOOTH SET OUT Ibid., 62.

397 "I LOVE *JUSTICE*" Ibid., 66–67.

397 HE RECRUITED WITH CHARM Weichmann, *True History*, 32–35.

397 THE KIDNAPPING PLOT Ibid., 136–37; John Wilkes Booth, "Diary, April 17, 1865," in
Holzer, *President Lincoln Assassinated!!*, 62.

397 "WHAT AN EXCELLENT CHANCE" Weichmann, *True History*, 137.

397 "FOR SIX MONTHS" Booth, "Diary, April 17, 1865," 62.

398 BOOTH STOPPED OFF Weichmann, *True History*, 135.

398 "HE WAS FAULTLESSLY DRESSED" Ibid., 136.

398 ON SEEING BOOTH Ibid.

398 "HERE COMES THE HANDSOMEST MAN" Ibid.

398 "WHAT'S ON TONIGHT?" Ibid.

399 HE WALKED FROM TENTH STREET Ibid., 138.

399 STOPPING IN A RESTAURANT Ibid.

399 THE MEETING RAN FROM ELEVEN *LDBD, 1861–1865*, 329.

399 "THE GREAT QUESTION" Gienapp and Gienapp, eds., *Civil War Diary of Gideon Welles*,
622–23.

399 HE HAD HAD A DREAM Ibid., 623–24.

400 BOOTH, MEANWHILE Weichmann, *True History*, 138–39.

400 AS THEY CHATTED Ibid., 140.

400 "PALENESS, NERVOUSNESS AND AGITATION" Ibid.

400 WHICH MATTHEWS LATER DESTROYED Booth, "To Whom It May Concern," 64.

400 "Many will blame me" Ibid.

400 on a drive Lincoln Log, April 14, 1865.

400 "playfully & tenderly worded" Turner and Turner, *Mary Todd Lincoln: Her Life and Letters*, 217–18.

400 "We must be" Ibid., 218.

400 At dusk, Booth left Weichmann, *True History*, 141.

401 At eight thirty p.m. *LDBD, 1861–1865*, 330. For accounts of the assassination and Lincoln's death, see, for instance, Burlingame, *AL*, 2:809–19; Donald, *Lincoln*, 594–99; Goodwin, *Team of Rivals*, 738–45; Hay and Nicolay, *AL: A History*, 10:286–302; Martha Hodes, *Mourning Lincoln* (New Haven, Conn., 2015), 1–3; Holzer, *President Lincoln Assassinated!!*, 3–130; Kauffman, *American Brutus*, 194–230; White, *A. Lincoln*, 673–75; "Charles A. Leale, M.D., 1842–1932, First Surgeon to Reach the Assassinated President Lincoln." Memorial booklet containing Dr. Leale's official report of his service attending President Lincoln during the night of April 14–15, 1865. Certified by Secretary of War Robert Lincoln on March 2, 1885, as "a true copy" from the records of the War Department of the report given to Gen. Benjamin Butler, dated July 20, 1867. Helen Leale Harper, Dr. Leale's granddaughter, presented this document to the church on April 2, 1965, New York Avenue Presbyterian Church Archives; Charles A. Leale to Benjamin F. Butler, July 20, 1867, Box 43, Benjamin Butler Papers, LOC; James Tanner, "The James Tanner Manuscript," *Remembering Lincoln*, https://rememberinglincoln.fords.org/node/892; Horatio Nelson Taft, *Washington During the Civil War: The Diary of Horatio Nelson Taft, 1861–1865*, Horatio Nelson Taft Papers, MMC-2215, LOC. According to John O'Brien, New York Avenue Presbyterian Church Archivist, "Horatio Nelson Taft's account, as recorded in his diary, April 30, 1865, was based on newspaper accounts and reports of his son Dr. Charles Taft, who accompanied the president to Petersen House." For Charles Taft's own account, see Charles Sabine Taft, "Abraham Lincoln's Last Hours," *Century Magazine*, February 1893. On Charles Leale's sundry recollections of the night Lincoln died, see Helena Iles Papaioannou and Daniel W. Stowell, "Dr. Charles A. Leale's Report on the Assassination of Abraham Lincoln," *JALA* 34 (Winter 2013): 40–53.

401 the actors paused Donald, *Lincoln*, 595.

401 decorated with flags "Then Vs. Now: Exploring the Presidential Box," https://www.fords.org/blog/post/then-vs-now-exploring-the-presidential-box/.

401 a special rocking chair Donald, *Lincoln*, 595. The chair belonged to Harry C. Ford, brother of theater owner John Ford. Ibid.

401 Mary to his right Henry R. Rathbone, "Affidavit," in Holzer, *President Lincoln Assassinated!!*, 21.

401 In the second scene Donald, *Lincoln*, 595.

401 Booth made his way Ibid., 597; Burlingame, *AL*, 2:816–17.

401 he peered through Burlingame, *AL*, 2:817.

401 Bearing a .44-caliber "Booth's Deringer," https://www.fords.org/lincolns-assassination/booths-deringer/; Carol M. Highsmith, photographer, "Derringer Gun John Wilkes Booth Used to Assassinate Abraham Lincoln," Artifact in the Museum Collection, National Park Service, Ford's Theatre National Historic Site, Washington, D.C., https://www.loc.gov/item/2010630694/.

401 a puff of smoke Rathbone, "Affidavit," in Holzer, *President Lincoln Assassinated!!*, 21.

401 Rathbone swiveled his head Ibid.

401 Rising quickly Ibid.

401 dropped his gun "Booth's Deringer," Ford's Theatre. According to the Associated

Press's Lawrence A. Gobright, "A common single-barrelled pocket-pistol was found on the carpet" once the president was carried from the box. Lawrence A. Gobright, "Associated Press Dispatch," April 14, 1865, in ibid., 11.

401 PRODUCED A KNIFE Rathbone, "Affidavit," in ibid., 21.

401 "THE KNIFE WENT" Hodes, *Mourning Lincoln*, 48.

401 LEAPED FROM THE BOX Holzer, *President Lincoln Assassinated!!*, xix.

401 DISTANCE OF ABOUT TEN FEET "The Assassin," National Park Service, https://www.nps.gov/foth/learn/historyculture/faq-the-assassin.htm

401 HIS SPUR CAUGHT Charles A. Leale, "Report on the Death of President Lincoln," in Holzer, *President Lincoln Assassinated!!*, 29.

401 "SIC SEMPER TYRANNIS!" Ibid., 10.

401 "SITTING SIX OR EIGHT ROWS BACK" Burlingame, ed., *Oral History of Abraham Lincoln*, 90.

402 "MY HUSBAND'S BLOOD" Hodes, *Mourning Lincoln*, 2.

402 "THEREUPON THE AUDIENCE" Burlingame, ed., *Oral History of Abraham Lincoln*, 90.

402 "SOME OF THE BRAIN" Gobright, "Associated Press Dispatch," in Holzer, *President Lincoln Assassinated!!*, 11.

402 ABOUT A QUARTER PAST TEN Donald, *Lincoln*, 597; Holzer, *President Lincoln Assassinated!!*, xviii.

402 PRESENTED HIMSELF Frances "Fanny" Seward, "Diary, April 14, 1865" in Holzer, *President Lincoln Assassinated!!*, 44–53.

403 ARMED WITH A PISTOL Ibid., 46.

403 THE PLANNED ATTACK Ibid., xxiii; William E. Doster, "Argument for George Atzerodt," in Ibid., 115–18.

403 THE COUP TO DESTROY Ibid., xxii–xxiii.

403 "IN JUMPING BROKE" Booth, "Diary, April 17, 1865" in ibid., 63.

403 LINCOLN WAS CARRIED Ibid.

403 RED BRICK FEDERAL-STYLE Petersen House, https://www.fords.org/visit/historic-site/petersen-house/.

403 A TINY NINE-BY-FIFTEEN-FOOT BEDROOM Horatio Nelson Taft Diary, April 30, 1865, LOC.

403 AT FIRST LINCOLN SWALLOWED Charles Sabin Taft, "Abraham Lincoln's Last Hours," in Holzer, *President Lincoln Assassinated!!*, 36.

403 THE BULLET WOULD HAVE ENTERED "A Doctor's View of the Lincoln Assassination," http://www.abrahamlincolnonline.org/lincoln/education/medical.htm. On the medical aspects of the assassination, see also J. K. Lattimer and A. Laidlaw, "Good Samaritan Surgeon Wrongly Accused of Contributing to President Lincoln's Death: An Experimental Study of the President's Fatal Wound," *Journal of the American College of Surgeons* 182, no. 5 (May 1996): 431–48.

403 SOMETIMES TWITCHING "A Doctor's View of the Assassination."

403 ON HEARING THE NEWS Horatio Nelson Taft Diary, April 30, 1865, LOC.

403 "LAY EXTENDED DIAGONALLY" Gienapp and Gienapp, eds., *Civil War Diary of Gideon Welles*, 627.

403 "OF A SIZE WHICH ONE WOULD SCARCE HAVE EXPECTED" Ibid.

403 LINCOLN'S BREATHING LIFTED Ibid.

403 "HIS FEATURES WERE CALM" Ibid.

404 THE INCONSOLABLE MRS. LINCOLN Horatio Nelson Taft Diary, April 30, 1865, LOC.

404 THE FIRST LADY FAINTED Ibid.

404 IN THE NIGHT Gienapp and Gienapp, eds., *Civil War Diary of Gideon Welles*, 628.

404 ORDERED THE CAPITOL BUILDING CLOSED French, *Witness to the Young Republic*, 470.

404 SUMNER AND ROBERT LINCOLN Horatio Nelson Taft Diary, April 30, 1865, LOC.

404 "CRYING AUDIBLY" Ibid.

404 PHINEAS GURLEY ARRIVED Ibid. Gurley's account of the same scene was reported by many newspapers more than a year later. In "Scene at the Death-Bed of Mr. Lincoln," *The* (New York) *Evening Post,* November 8, 1866, there is this account: "At Carlisle, Pa., recently, the Presbyterian Synods of the old and new schools being in session at the same place, the two bodies met in communion with great harmony. Rev. Dr. Gurley, pastor of the church in Washington which President Lincoln usually attended, in a speech at the table, gave the following narrative, which has never before been made public:

> "When summoned on that sad night to the deathbed of President Lincoln, I entered the room fifteen or twenty minutes before his departure. All present were gathered anxiously around him, waiting to catch his last breath. The physician, with one hand upon the pulse of the dying man, and the other hand laid upon his heart, was intently watching for the moment when life should cease.
>
> "He lingered longer than we had expected. At last the physician said: 'He is gone; he is dead.'
>
> "Then I solemnly believe that for four or five minutes there was not the slightest noise or movement in that awful presence. We all stood transfixed in our positions, speechless, breathless, around the dead body of that great and good man.
>
> "At length the Secretary of War, who was standing at my left, broke the silence and said, 'Doctor, will you say anything?' I replied, 'I will speak to God.' Said he, 'Do it just now.'
>
> "And there, by the side of our fallen chief, God put it into my heart to utter this petition, that from that hour we and the whole nation might become more than ever united in our devotion to the cause of our beloved, imperiled country.
>
> "When I ceased, there arose from the lips of the entire company a fervid and spontaneous, 'Amen.'
>
> "And has not the whole heart of the loyal nation responded, 'Amen?' Was not the prayer, there offered, responded to in a most remarkable manner? When, in our history have the people of this land, been found more closely bound together in purpose and heart than when the telegraphic wires bore all over the country the sad tidings that President Lincoln was dead?" Ibid.

404 MINISTER DIVIDED HIS TIME Horatio Nelson Diary, April 30, 1865, LOC.

404 TOWARD SEVEN O'CLOCK IN THE MORNING Ibid.

404 ABOUT NINETY MINUTES AFTER SUNRISE Krick, *Civil War Weather in Virginia*, 156. Sunrise was at 5:30 A.M. on Saturday, April 15, 1865.

404 "FOR THE LAST HALF HOUR" Horatio Nelson Taft Diary, April 30, 1865, LOC.

404 IN THE END Signed Statement of Charles A. Leale, M.D., Assistant Surgeon US Volunteers, Copy in New York Avenue Presbyterian Church Archives.

404 "LET US PRAY" Charles A. Leale to Benjamin F. Butler, July 20, 1867, Box 43, Benjamin Butler Papers, LOC.

404 "ALL KNELT DOWN" Ibid.

404 AT TWENTY-TWO MINUTES AFTER SEVEN Lincoln Log, April 15, 1865, http://the

lincolnlog.org/Results.aspx?type=basicSearch&terms=April+15%2c+1865&r=L1
NlYXJjaC5hc3hc3B4; Hodes, *Mourning Lincoln*, 5.

404 "HE IS GONE" "Scene at the Death-Bed of Mr. Lincoln."

404 EDWIN STANTON BROKE THE SILENCE Ibid.

404 HIS HANDS LIFTED James Tanner Manuscript; "Tanner Also Present," *The Washington Post*, April 16, 1905.

404 "OUR FATHER AND OUR GOD" Ibid.

404 JAMES TANNER Ibid.

404 EDWIN STANTON SOBBED Ibid.

404 "SUBDUED AND TREMULOUS TONES" Ibid.

405 "THY WILL BE DONE" Ibid.

405 AT THIS, STANTON Ibid.

405 "NOW HE BELONGS" Hay and Nicolay, *AL: A History*, 10:302. Another version has Stanton's saying "He *now* belongs to the ages." Dr. Charles Sabin Taft, "Abraham Lincoln's Last Hours," *Century Magazine* 45 (February 1893): 635. On speculation that Stanton said Lincoln "belongs to the angels now," see Allen C. Guelzo, "Does Lincoln Still Belong to the Ages?" *JALA* 33, no. 1 (2012): 1–13; Adam Gopnik, "Angels and Ages," *The New Yorker*, May 28, 2007. https://www.newyorker.com/magazine/2007/05/28/angels-and-ages.

405 GURLEY WALKED TO THE PARLOR Horatio Nelson Taft Diary, April 30, 1865, LOC.

405 "THE PRESIDENT IS DEAD" Ibid.

405 "O—WHY DID YOU" Ibid.

405 GURLEY ACCOMPANIED THE FIRST LADY Ibid.

405 THEY MET HIM ON THE PORTICO Ibid.

405 CHURCH BELLS HAD BEEN TOLLING George W. Julian, "Diary, April 15–19, 1865," in Holzer, *President Lincoln Assassinated!!*, 170.

405 "WHERE IS MY PA?" Diary of Horatio Nelson Taft, April 30, 1865, LOC.

405 "TADDY" Ibid.

405 "O WHAT SHALL I DO" Ibid.

406 GURLEY HAD NOT YET WEPT Ibid.

406 "DR. GURLEY SAID THAT" Ibid.

406 THE MINISTER DID WHAT Ibid.

406 "I FELT AS THOUGH" Ibid.

406 SATURDAY WAS RAINY Gienapp and Gienapp, eds., *Civil War Diary of Gideon Welles*, 629.

406 "I WENT AFTER BREAKFAST" Ibid. Welles noticed a general grief. "Every house, almost, has some drapery—especially the homes of the poor," he observed. "Profuse exhibition is displayed on the public buildings and the houses of the wealthy, but the little black ribbon, or strip of black cloth from hovel of the poor negro, or the impoverished white, is more touching." Ibid., 631.

406 AT TEN O'CLOCK "The New President: Inauguration of Andrew Johnson," *NYT*, April 17, 1865.

406 "I SHALL ASK" Ibid.

406 "THIS BLOW WAS AIMED" Beecher, "Sermon Preached in Brooklyn," in Holzer, ed., *TLA*, 130.

406 "THE DEED OF HORROR" Burlingame, *AL*, 2:813; Kauffman, *American Brutus*, 80.

407 "THE CITY IS DRESSED" Pheebe Clark to her sister Nellie, April 17, 1865, Pheebe Clark Correspondence, LOC. There were other reports about violence retribution against those who expressed happiness at Lincoln's murder. See, for instance, Thomas P. Lowry, "Not Everybody Mourned Lincoln's Death" in Harold

Holzer, Craig L. Symonds, and Frank J. Williams, eds., *The Lincoln Assassination: Crime & Punishment, Myth & Memory* (New York, 2010); Jennifer Cain Bohrnstedt, ed., *While Father Is Away: The Civil War Letters of William H. Bradbury* (Lexington, Ky., 2003), 258; Kauffman, *American Brutus*, 236; Richtmyer Hubbell, *Potomac Diary: A Soldier's Account of the Capital in Crisis, 1864–1865*, ed. Marc Newman (Charleston, S.C., 2000), 92.

407 "IT IS YOU REPUBLICANS" Du Bois, *Black Reconstruction*, 165.

407 "THIS MORNING WHEN" Morgan, "Diary, April 19, 1865," 701–2.

407 "HURRAH! OLD ABE LINCOLN" Emma LeConte, "Diary, April 21, 1865" in Holzer, *President Lincoln Assassinated!!*, 241; Harrell, *When the Bells Tolled for Lincoln*, 59–60. See also Emma LeConte Diary, April 16–20, 1865, LeConte Papers, Southern Historical Collection, University of North Carolina, Chapel Hill.

407 A TEXAS NEWSPAPER EDITOR Harrell, *When the Bells Tolled for Lincoln*, 27. For Southern reaction to the assassination, see also Thomas Reed Turner, *Beware the People Weeping: Public Opinion and the Assassination of Abraham Lincoln* (Baton Rouge, La., 1982), 95–99.

407 "LINCOLN WAS NOT A MARTYR" Harrell, *When the Bells Tolled for Lincoln*, 68.

407 "IT IS CERTAINLY" Ibid., 84–85. Another Texas paper, *The Galveston Daily News*, wrote, "On the 14th of April Abraham Lincoln was weltering in his own life blood, and the words *sic semper tyrannis* were ringing his death knell. In the plenitude of his power and arrogance he was struck down, and his soul ushered into eternity, with innumerable crimes to answer for. . . . It does look to us . . . as if an avenging Nemesis had brought swift and inevitable retribution upon a man stained with so many bloody crimes." Ibid., 85.

407 "ANDY JOHNSON WILL" Ibid., 60; Emma LeConte Diary, 16–20 April 1865, LeConte Papers, Southern Historical Collection.

408 "REST, OH WEARY HEART" Beecher, "Sermon Preached in Brooklyn," 125.

408 "AN EASTER SUNDAY" Strong, "The Diaries, 1865," in Holzer, ed., *TLA*, 104.

408 BUILDINGS IN MANHATTAN WERE Ibid.

408 "THE WHOLE SERVICE WAS" Ibid., 105. The Reverend Francis Vinton preached extemporaneously. "He brought out clearly the thought that had occurred to me and to many others: Perhaps Lincoln had done his appointed work; his honesty, sagacity, kindliness, and singleness of purpose had united the North and secured the suppression of rebellion," Strong recalled. "Perhaps the time has come for something besides kindliness, mercy, and forbearance, even for vengeance and judgment. . . . Perhaps God's voice in this tragedy is 'Well done, good and faithful servant. Thou hast done thy work of mercy. To others is given the duty of vengeance. Thy murder will help teach them that duty. Enter thou, by a painless process of death, into the joy of the Lord.'" Ibid.

408 LINCOLN'S EMPTY PEW Isabella C. Wunderly Diary, Campbell Collection, (C-1049), Wyoming State Archives. The diarist would become first lady of Wyoming in 1872.

408 HUNDREDS OF WORSHIPPERS Letters of Albert Daggett to his mother, *Lincoln Lore*, No. 1478 (April 1961), 4, Bulletin of the Lincoln National Life Foundation, Fort Wayne, Indiana. See also Mary Henry, "Mary Henry Diary," Smithsonian Institution Archives, *Remembering Lincoln*, https://rememberinglincoln.fords.org/node/551. "The church [NYAPC] was so thronged with stranger[s] we with difficulty made our way into the building and after standing for some time were provided with seats in the [a]isle. The pulpit and gallery were dressed in black and the President's pew was closed and clothed with same sad emblem. The Dr. [Gurley] in a short

introductory address alluded to the terrible calamity which had befallen the nation and spoke in terms of true affection of the personal qualities of our beloved chief Magistrate." Ibid.

408   "THIS IS SUCH" *The National Intelligencer*, April 17, 1865.

408   "IT IS HIS PREROGATIVE" Phineas D. Gurley, "White House Funeral Sermon for Abraham Lincoln," April 19, 1865, http://www.abrahamlincolnonline.org/lincoln /speeches/gurley.htm. Quoting the Epistle to the Hebrews, Gurley said: "'Whom the Lord loveth He chasteneth.' O how these blessed words have cheered and strengthened and sustained us through all these long and weary years of civil strife. . . . True, this new sorrow and chastening has come in such an hour and in such a way as we thought not, and it bears the impress of a rod that is very heavy, and of a mystery that is very deep." Ibid.

408   "AS WE STAND HERE TODAY" Ibid.

408   "THOUGH OUR BELOVED PRESIDENT" Ibid.

408   THE PRESIDENT WAS TAKEN *NYT*, "The Obsequies," in Holzer, *President Lincoln Assassinated!!*, 234–35.

409   "IT WAS A SPLENDID SIGHT" Pheebe Clark letter, April 22, 1865, Pheebe Clark Correspondence, LOC.

409   THE MANHUNT FOR JOHN WILKES BOOTH Kauffman, *American Brutus*, 243–320; James L. Swanson, *Manhunt: The 12-Day Chase for Lincoln's Killer* (New York, 2006), is comprehensive.

409   "HERE IS A WOUNDED" Kauffman, *American Brutus*, 309.

409   TRAPPED IN A BURNING BARN Ibid., 312–20.

409   FOUR OF BOOTH'S CONSPIRATORS Ibid., 325–98.

409   "TELL MY MOTHER" Ibid., 320.

409   LINCOLN'S JOURNEY HOME Holzer, *President Lincoln Assassinated!!*, xxiv; Hodes, *Mourning Lincoln*; Burlingame, *AL*, 2:821–25; Jeremy Prichard, "'Home Is the Martyr': The Burial of Abraham Lincoln and the Fate of Illinois's Capital," *JALA* 38, no. 1 (2017): 14–42.

409   BEGINNING A WRETCHED WIDOWHOOD See, for instance, Emerson, *The Madness of Mary Lincoln*; Emerson, *Mary Lincoln's Insanity Case: A Documentary History*; Clinton, *Mrs. Lincoln*, 251–336; Catherine Clinton, "Wife Versus Widow: Clashing Perspectives on Mary Lincoln's Legacy," *JALA* 28, no. 1 (2007): 1–19.

409   MOMENTS OF GRACE White, *House Built by Slaves*, xviii.

409   AS TIME WENT ON Emerson, *The Madness of Mary Lincoln*; Emerson, *Mary Lincoln's Insanity Case: A Documentary History*; Clinton, *Mrs. Lincoln*, 251–336; Clinton, "Wife Versus Widow."

409   "I WENT UP" French, *Witness to the Young Republic*, 479.

410   WITH THOSE OF WILLIE Holzer, *President Lincoln Assassinated!!*, xxv.

410   "THOUGH A STRANGER TO YOU" Queen Victoria, "Letter to Mary Lincoln," April 29, 1865, in Holzer, *President Lincoln Assassinated!!*, 274.

410   "THE COLORED PEOPLE" Douglass, Address at Cooper Union, New York City: Manuscript, Douglass Papers, LOC.

410   "WHAT DO THE COPPERHEADS" Pheebe Clark letter, May 1, 1865, Pheebe Clark Correspondence, LOC.

410   "IT WAS A FRIGHTFUL BLOW" Laura M. Towne, "Excerpts from the Letters and Diary of Laura M. Towne," *Remembering Lincoln*, https://rememberinglincoln.fords.org/node /1194.

411   A FREED BLACK MAN Ibid.

411   "IF IT WERE TRUE" Ibid.

411   "LINCOLN DIED FOR WE" Ibid.

Epilogue: *I See Now the Wisdom of His Course*

415 "DEAD, *DEAD*, DEAD" Beecher, "Sermon Preached in Brooklyn," 133.

415 A SERMON ON THE SECOND SUNDAY Ibid., 123–34.

415 "DISENTHRALLED OF FLESH" Ibid., 133–34.

415 "IS IT NOT TRUE" Wilson and Davis, eds., *Herndon's Informants*, 3.

415 "HOW STRANGE IT IS" Sears, ed., *Civil War Papers of George B. McClellan*, 631.

415 INITIATIVES CONSIDERED OR UNDERTAKEN Hudson, "Abraham Lincoln: An African American Perspective," 533. On Reconstruction generally, see also Foner, *Reconstruction* and *Forever Free: The Story of Emancipation and Reconstruction* (New York, 2005); Douglas R. Egerton, *The Wars of Reconstruction: The Brief, Violent History of America's Most Progressive Era* (New York, 2014); George C. Rable, *But There Was No Peace: The Role of Violence in the Politics of Reconstruction* (Athens, Ga., 1984); Gregory Downs, *After Appomattox: Military Occupation and the Ends of War* (Cambridge, Mass., 2015); Richard White, *The Republic for Which It Stands: The United States During Reconstruction and the Gilded Age, 1865–1896* (New York, 2017).

416 "WHITE MEN ALONE" Foner, *Reconstruction*, 180.

416 "NO INDEPENDENT GOVERNMENT" Ibid. Foner wrote that this was "probably the most blatantly racist pronouncement ever to appear in an official state paper of an American president." Ibid.

416 "CAN A CAUSE" Chesebrough, *"God Ordained This War,"* 242.

416 WAS A MOTIVE FORCE See, for instance, Edward A. Pollard, *The Lost Cause: A New Southern History of the War of the Confederates* (New York, 1866) and *The Lost Cause Regained* (New York, 1868); Jack P. Maddex, Jr., *The Reconstruction of Edward A. Pollard: A Rebel's Conversion to Postbellum Unionism* (Chapel Hill, N.C., 1974); James Southall Wilson, "Edward Alfred Pollard," in Edwin A. Alderman, Joel C. Harris, and Charles W. Kent, eds., *Library of Southern Literature, Compiled Under the Direct Supervision of Southern Men of Letters* (Atlanta, 1907), 9:4147–50. On the Lost Cause more generally, see W. Fitzhugh Brundage, "Redeeming a Failed Revolution: Confederate Memory," in William J. Cooper, Jr., and John M. McCardell, Jr., eds., *In the Cause of Liberty: How the Civil War Redefined American Ideals* (Baton Rouge, La., 2009), 136–53; David W. Blight, *Race and Reunion: The Civil War in American Memory* (Cambridge, Mass., 2001), especially 255–99; Caroline E. Janney, *Remembering the Civil War: Reunion and the Limits of Reconciliation* (Chapel Hill, N.C., 2013), 133–96; Gary W. Gallagher and Alan T. Nolan, eds., *The Myth of the Lost Cause and Civil War History* (Bloomington, Ind., 2000); Charles Reagan Wilson, *Baptized in Blood: The Religion of the Lost Cause, 1865–1920* (Athens, Ga., 2009); Varon, *Appomattox*, especially 208–43, 252–55.

416 "ODIOUS, AND ESPECIALLY IN THE PRESENT INSTANCE" Pollard, *Lost Cause Regained*, 211.

416 "THE PRINCIPLE FOR WHICH" Ibid. 749.

416 "THE 'LOST CAUSE' NEEDS" Ibid. 214.

416 W.E.B. DU BOIS WROTE Du Bois, *Black Reconstruction*, 708.

417 IN 1876–77 Foner, *Forever Free*, 190. See also Richard White, *Republic for Which It Stands*, 325–37; Michael F. Holt, *By One Vote: The Disputed Presidential Election of 1876* (Lawrence, Kan., 2008).

417 DEDICATION OF THE FREEDMEN'S MEMORIAL See, for instance, *Inaugural Ceremonies of the Freedmen's Memorial Monument to Abraham Lincoln: Washington City, April 14, 1876*, Anacostia Community Museum Archives, Washington, D.C.; Blight, *Race and Reunion*, 196–98; Kirk Savage, *Standing Soldiers, Kneeling Slaves: Race, War, and Monuments in Nineteenth-Century America* (Princeton, N.J., 1997).

417 "IT MUST BE ADMITTED" Douglass, "Oration in Memory of Abraham Lincoln," in Holzer, ed., *TLA*, 225–27.

417   IN THESE POSTBELLUM DECADES See, for instance, Foner, *Forever Free*, 190; C. Vann Woodward, *The Strange Career of Jim Crow* (New York, 1974).

417   IN *Plessy v. Ferguson* "Plessy v. Ferguson," *Oyez*, www.oyez.org/cases/1850-1900 /163us537.

417   LYNCHINGS WENT ON UNABATED Equal Justice Initiative, "Lynching in America: Confronting the Legacy of Racial Terror," 3rd edition, 2017, https://eji.org/reports /lynching-in-america/.

417   "THE WHOLE SOUTH" Foner, *Forever Free*, 198–99.

417   "THE CRY IS" Bancroft, "Oration in Union Square," in Holzer, ed., *TLA*, 139.

417   "ABRAHAM LINCOLN WAS" W.E.B. Du Bois, "Again, Lincoln," *The Crisis* 24, no. 5 (September 1922), 200.

418   IN HIS 1963 *Letter from a Birmingham Jail* https://kinginstitute.stanford.edu/sites/mlk /files/letterfrombirmingham_wwcw_0.pdf.

418   KING STOOD ON THE STEPS Martin Luther King, Jr., "I Have a Dream . . . ," National Archives, https://www.archives.gov/files/press/exhibits/dream-speech.pdf. See also Clarence B. Jones and Stuart Connelly, *Behind the Dream: The Making of the Speech That Transformed a Nation* (New York, 2011).

418   AND ON THE STORMY MEMPHIS NIGHT Taylor Branch, *At Canaan's Edge: America in the King Years, 1965–68* (New York, 2006), 755–56.

418   KING IMAGINED Martin Luther King, Jr., "I've Been to the Mountaintop," April 3, 1968, https://www.americanrhetoric.com/speeches/mlkivebeentothemountain top.htm.

418   "EACH MAN MUST" Benjamin E. Mays, "'Martin Luther King Jr.'s Work on Earth Must Truly Be Our Own,'" *The Atlantic Monthly*, https://www.theatlantic.com /magazine/archive/2018/02/benjamin-mays-mlk-eulogy/552545/.

419   "BUT WHAT WAS A. LINCOLN" Manuscript, Frederick Douglass Papers, LOC.

419   "THERE IS NO MISTAKE" Walter M. Merrill, ed., *The Letters of William Lloyd Garrison* (Cambridge, Mass., 1979), 5:212.

419   "TO THOSE WHO HAVE" Ibid., 223.

419   "I SEE NOW" *Elizabeth Cady Stanton as Revealed in Her letters, Diary and Reminiscences*, ed. Theodore Stanton and Harriot Stanton Blatch (New York, 1922), 2:355.

420   THE SUN SET IN WASHINGTON William C. Edwards and Edward Steers, Jr., *The Lincoln Assassination: The Evidence* (Urbana, Ill., 2009), 364.

420   LINCOLN CARRIED HIS CHINA CUP Rubenstein, *Abraham Lincoln: An Extraordinary Life*, 69; D. W. Taylor to Robert T. Lincoln, November 18, 1887, Accession file 219098, National Museum of American History, Washington, D.C.

420   BORE A MOURNING RIBBON Neil Kagan and Stephen G. Hyslop, eds., *Smithsonian Civil War: Inside the National Collection* (Washington, D.C., 2013), 317.

420   IN HIS POCKET "The Contents of Abraham Lincoln's Pockets on the Evening of His Assassination," Stern Collection, LOC.

420   "ABSOLUTE TRUTH, STERN RESOLUTION" "President Lincoln's Letter to Mr. Hackett," *Liverpool Daily Post*, n.d., Stern Collection, LOC.

420   WE SEE A HUMAN FACE See, for instance, Reynolds, *Abe*, 929–32; Langston Hughes, "Lincoln Monument: Washington," in Holzer, ed., *TLA*, 515; Donald Charles Durman, *He Belongs to the Ages: The Statues of Abraham Lincoln* (Ann Arbor, Mich., 1951); Scott Sandage, "A Marble House Divided: The Lincoln Memorial, the Civil Rights Movement, and the Politics of Memory, 1939–1963," *Journal of American History* 80 (June 1993): 135–67; Barry Schwartz, *Lincoln and the Forge of National Memory* (Chicago, 2000), 284–90; Christopher A. Thomas, *The Lincoln Memorial and American Life* (Princeton, N.J., 2002).

BIBLIOGRAPHY

Manuscript Collections

Anacostia Community Museum Archives, Washington, D.C.

Buell-Brien Papers (1805–1943), Tennessee State Library and Archives, Nashville, Tennessee

Benjamin Butler Papers, Manuscript Division, Library of Congress, Washington, D.C.

Robert H. Cartmell Papers (1849–1915), Tennessee State Library and Archives, Nashville, Tennessee

Civil War Collection: Confederate and Federal, Tennessee State Library and Archives, Nashville, Tennessee

Pheebe Clark Correspondence (1865), Manuscript Division, Library of Congress, Washington, D.C.

Colored Troops Division Records, Adjutant General's Office, Record Group 94, National Archives, Washington, D.C.

Confederate Papers Collection, William R. Laurie University Archives and Special Collections, University of the South, Sewanee, Tennessee

Rachel Carter Craighead Diaries (1855–1911), Tennessee State Archives, Nashville, Tennessee

John J. Crittenden Papers, Manuscript Division, Library of Congress, Washington, D.C.

Nathan W. Daniels Diary and Scrapbook (1861–1867), Manuscript Division, Library of Congress, Washington, D.C.

Jefferson Davis Papers, Rice University, Houston, Texas

Frederick Douglass Papers, 1841–1967, Manuscript Division, Library of Congress, Washington, D.C.

Elizabeth Todd Edwards Correspondence (1860–1861), Manuscript Division, Library of Congress, Washington, D.C.

Edward Fontaine Collection, William R. Laurie University Archives and Special Collections, University of the South, Sewanee, Tennessee

Phineas Densmore Gurley correspondence and writings, annotated by John O'Brien, New York Avenue Presbyterian Church, Washington, D.C.

Phineas Densmore Gurley Papers, Presbyterian Historical Society, Philadelphia, Pennsylvania

Phineas Densmore Gurley unpublished 1858 sermon, Virginia Theological Seminary Archives, Alexandria, Virginia (now held by the Presbyterian Historical Society)

Harding-Timberlake Collection, William R. Laurie University Archives and Special Collections, University of the South, Sewanee, Tennessee

Nannie E. Haskins Diary (1863–1917), Tennessee State Library and Archives, Nashville, Tennessee

William Hawley files, Maryland Diocesan Archives, Episcopal Diocese of Maryland, Baltimore, Maryland

Andrew Johnson Papers (1846–1875), Tennessee State Library and Archives, Nashville, Tennessee

Lawrence Family Papers, 1780–1944, Tennessee State Library and Archives, Nashville, Tennessee

LeConte and Furman Family Papers, 1861–1897, The Southern Historical Collection at the Louis Round Wilson Special Collections Library, University of North Carolina, Chapel Hill

Library Broadside Collection, Tennessee State Library and Archives, Nashville, Tennessee

Abraham Lincoln Papers, Library of Congress, Washington, D.C.

Abraham Lincoln's appointment book (March 5, 1861–March 27, 1861), John F. Kennedy Presidential Library and Museum, Boston, Massachusetts

Little Pigeon Creek Baptist Church, Spencer County, Indiana, typed transcript of minute book (June 8, 1816–February 28, 1840), S.B.C. 1958, Southern Baptist Historical Library and Archives, Nashville, Tennessee

Lovell Family Collection, William R. Laurie University Archives and Special Collections, University of the South, Sewanee, Tennessee

Basil Manly Sr. Papers, Archives and Special Collections, James P. Boyce Centennial Library, Southern Baptist Theological Seminary, Louisville, Kentucky

Catherine Marshall Papers, Agnes Scott College, Decatur, Georgia

Reverend Dr. Peter Marshall and Catherine Marshall Papers, Library of Congress, Washington, D.C.

Journals of the Maryland Diocesan Conventions, 1861–1865, Maryland Diocesan Archives, Episcopal Diocese of Maryland, Baltimore, Maryland

Moton Family Papers, Series I: Robert Russa Moton Papers, 1867–1965, Manuscript Division, Library of Congress, Washington, D.C.

Records of the U.S. Naval Observatory, Record Group Number 78, National Archives, Washington, D.C.

Washington National Cathedral Archives, Washington, D.C.

Washington National Cathedral Rare Book Library, Washington, D.C.

New York Avenue Presbyterian Church Archives, Washington, D.C.

Polk Family Collection, William R. Laurie University Archives and Special Collections, University of the South, Sewanee, Tennessee

Records of the Former Commissioners of Public Buildings and Grounds, Record Group 42, National Archives, Washington, D.C.

Smith Pyne files, Maryland Diocesan Archives, Episcopal Diocese of Maryland, Baltimore, Maryland

William Jones Rhees Correspondence, 1856–1876, Manuscript Division, Library of Congress, Washington, D.C.

Vestry Minutes, Pew Register, and President's Pew *Book of Common Prayer* (1858), St. John's Episcopal Church, Washington, D.C.

Michael Shiner Diary, Michael Shiner Papers, Manuscript Division, Library of Congress, Washington, D.C.

Robert Shortelle Family Papers (1851–1866), Manuscript Division, Library of Congress, Washington, D.C.

Matthew Simpson Papers, Manuscript Division, Library of Congress, Washington, D.C.

Alfred Whital Stern Collection of Lincolniana, Rare Book and Special Collections Division, Library of Congress, Washington, D.C.

Horatio Nelson Taft Papers, Manuscript Division, Library of Congress, Washington, D.C.

Letter from D. W. Taylor to Robert T. Lincoln, National Museum of American History, Washington, D.C.

Joseph Parrish Thompson and Leonard Bacon Papers, Rare Book and Manuscript Library, Columbia University Libraries, New York

Vallandigham and Laird Family Papers, Western Reserve Historical Society, Cleveland, Ohio

Journal of the Right Reverend William R. Whittingham, Third Bishop of Maryland, Maryland Diocesan Archives, Episcopal Diocese of Maryland, Baltimore, Maryland

Isabella C. Wunderly Diary, Campbell Collection, Wyoming State Archives, Cheyenne, Wyoming

Books and Essays

Abel, E. Lawrence. *Lincoln's Jewish Spy: The Life and Times of Issachar Zacharie*. Jefferson, N.C.: McFarland, 2020.

Achorn, Edward. *Every Drop of Blood: The Momentous Second Inauguration of Abraham Lincoln*. New York: Atlantic Monthly Press, 2020.

Adams, Henry. *The Great Secession Winter of 1860–61 and Other Essays*. Edited by George Hochfield. New York: Sagamore Press, 1958.

Adams, John. *The Works of John Adams, Second President of the U.S. with a Life of the Author* [. . .]. Vol. 6. Boston: Little, Brown, 1851.

Adams, John Quincy. *Memoir: Comprising Portions of His Diary from 1795 to 1848*. Edited by Charles Francis Adams. Vol. 5. Philadelphia: J. B. Lippincott, 1874.

Ahlstrom, Sydney E. *A Religious History of the American People*. New Haven, Conn.: Yale University Press, 1972.

Alden, John Richard. *The First South*. The Walter Lynwood Fleming Lectures in Southern History. Baton Rouge: Louisiana State University Press, 1961.

Allen, Danielle. *Our Declaration: A Reading of the Declaration of Independence in Defense of Equality*. New York: Liveright, 2014.

Allen, Theodore W. *The Invention of the White Race*. 2 vols. London: Verso, 1994–1997.

Alter, Robert, trans. *The Wisdom Books: Job, Proverbs, and Ecclesiastes; A Translation with Commentary*. New York: W. W. Norton, 2010.

American Anti-Slavery Society. *Second Annual Report of the American Anti-Slavery Society: With the Speeches Delivered at the Anniversary Meeting, Held in the City of New-York on the 12th May, 1835* [. . .]. New York: William S. Dorr, 1835.

———. *Third Annual Report of the American Anti-Slavery Society: With the Speeches Delivered at the Anniversary Meeting, Held in the City of New-York, on the 10th May, 1836* [. . .]. New York: William S. Dorr, 1836.

Andrews, Eliza Frances. *The War-Time Journal of a Georgia Girl, 1864–1865*. New York: D. Appleton, 1908.

Appiah, Kwame Anthony. *The Honor Code: How Moral Revolutions Happen*. New York: W. W. Norton, 2010.

———. "Race." In *Critical Terms for Literary Study*, edited by Frank Lentricchia and Thomas McLaughlin, 274–87. Chicago: University of Chicago Press, 1990.

Armitage, David. *The Declaration of Independence: A Global History*. Cambridge, Mass.: Harvard University Press, 2007.

Armitage, Thomas. *The Past, Present, and Future of the United States: A Discourse*. New York: T. Holman, 1862.

Arnold, Isaac N. *The Life of Abraham Lincoln*. 4th ed. Lincoln: University of Nebraska Press, 1994.

Ashley, James Mitchell. *Duplicate Copy of the Souvenir from the Afro-American League of Tennessee to*

Hon. James M. Ashley, of Ohio. Edited by Benjamin W. Arnett. Philadelphia: Publishing House of the A. M. E. Church, 1894.

Astronomical and Meteorological Observations Made at the United States Naval Observatory During the Year 1865. Washington, D.C.: Government Printing Office, 1867.

Atkins, John. *A Voyage to Guinea, Brazil, and the West Indies, Etc.* 2nd ed. London: Ward and Chandler, 1737.

Ausubel, Herman. *John Bright, Victorian Reformer.* New York: Wiley, 1966.

Authentic Life of His Excellency Louis Kossuth, Governor of Hungary [. . .]. London: Bradbury and Evans, 1851.

Avlon, John. *Lincoln and the Fight for Peace.* New York: Simon and Schuster, 2022.

———. *Washington's Farewell: The Founding Father's Warning to Future Generations.* New York: Simon and Schuster, 2017.

Ayers, Edward L. *What Caused the Civil War? Reflections on the South and Southern History.* New York: W. W. Norton, 2005.

Badeau, Adam. *Grant in Peace: From Appomattox to Mount McGregor; A Personal Memoir.* Hartford, Conn.: S. S. Scranton, 1887.

Bailey, Rufus W. *The Issue, Presented in a Series of Letters on Slavery.* New York: J. S. Taylor, 1837.

Baird, Charles Washington. *Eutaxia, or, The Presbyterian Liturgies: Historical Sketches.* New York: M. W. Dodd, 1855.

Baker, Jean H. *Building America: The Life of Benjamin Henry Latrobe.* New York: Oxford University Press, 2020.

———. "Mary and Abraham: A Marriage." In *The Best American History Essays on Lincoln,* edited by Sean Wilentz, 107–28. New York: Palgrave Macmillan, 2009.

———. *Mary Todd Lincoln: A Biography.* New York: W. W. Norton, 1987.

Baldwin, James. "The Wilderness Preacher." In *The American Book of Golden Deeds,* 110–17. New York: American Book Company, 1907.

Baldwin, Samuel D. *Dominion; or, the Unity and Trinity of the Human Race [. . .].* Nashville, Tenn.: E. Stevenson and F. A. Owen, 1857.

Balserak, Jon. *Calvinism: A Very Short Introduction.* Oxford: Oxford University Press, 2016.

Bancroft, George. *The Necessity, the Reality, and the Promise of the Progress of the Human Race: Oration Delivered Before the New-York Historical Society, Nov. 20, 1854.* New York: Printed for the Society, 1854.

Baptist, Edward E. *The Half Has Never Been Told: Slavery and the Making of American Capitalism.* New York: Basic Books, 2014.

Barr, John McKee. *Loathing Lincoln: An American Tradition from the Civil War to the Present.* Conflicting Worlds: New Dimensions of the American Civil War. Baton Rouge: Louisiana State University Press, 2014.

Barrow, David. *Involuntary, Unmerited, Perpetual, Absolute, Hereditary Slavery Examined: On the Principles of Nature, Reason, Justice, Policy, and Scripture.* Lexington, Ky.: D. and C. Bradford, 1808.

Barrows, E. P., Jr. *A View of the American Slavery Question.* New York: J. S. Taylor, 1836.

Barton, William E. *The Paternity of Abraham Lincoln: Was He the Son of Thomas Lincoln? An Essay on the Chastity of Nancy Hanks.* New York: George H. Doran, 1920.

———. *The Soul of Abraham Lincoln.* New York: George H. Doran, 1920.

Bassett, John Spencer, ed. *Correspondence of Andrew Jackson.* Vol. 5. Washington, D.C.: Carnegie Institution of Washington, 1931.

Bates, David Homer. *Lincoln in the Telegraph Office: Recollections of the United States Military Telegraph Corps During the Civil War.* Lincoln: University of Nebraska Press, 1995.

Beeman, Richard R. *Our Lives, Our Fortunes, and Our Sacred Honor: The Forging of American Independence, 1774–1776.* New York: Basic Books, 2013.

Benedict, Michael Les. *The Impeachment and Trial of Andrew Johnson.* The Norton Essays in American History. New York: W. W. Norton, 1973.

Benedict, Ruth. *Race and Racism.* London: G. Routledge and Sons, 1942.

———. *Race: Science and Politics.* New York: Modern Age Books, 1940.

Bennett, Lerone, Jr. *Before the Mayflower: A History of the Negro in America, 1619–1964.* Rev. ed. A Pelican Book. Baltimore: Penguin Books, 1966.

———. *Forced into Glory: Abraham Lincoln's White Dream.* Chicago: Johnson, 2000.

Bentley, George R. *A History of the Freedmen's Bureau.* Philadelphia: University of Pennsylvania Press, 2017.

Berlin, Ira. *Many Thousands Gone: The First Two Centuries of Slavery in North America.* Cambridge, Mass.: Belknap Press of Harvard University Press, 1998.

Berry, Mary Frances. *Military Necessity and Civil Rights Policy: Black Citizenship and the Constitution, 1861–1868.* Series in American Studies. Port Washington, N.Y.: Kennikat Press, 1977.

Berry, Stephen. *House of Abraham: Lincoln and the Todds, a Family Divided by War.* Boston: Houghton Mifflin, 2007.

Berwanger, Eugene H. *The Frontier Against Slavery: Western Anti-Negro Prejudice and the Slavery Extension Controversy.* Urbana: University of Illinois Press, 1967.

Beschloss, Michael. *Presidents of War.* New York: Crown, 2018.

Bethencourt, Francisco. *Racisms: From the Crusades to the Twentieth Century.* Princeton, N.J.: Princeton University Press, 2013.

Binnington, Ian. *Confederate Visions: Nationalism, Symbolism, and the Imagined South in the Civil War.* A Nation Divided: Studies in the Civil War Era. Charlottesville: University of Virginia Press, 2013.

Binns, Henry Bryan. *The Life of Abraham Lincoln.* Everyman's Library. London: J. M. Dent and Sons; New York: E. P. Dutton, 1936.

Black Hawk. *Life of Black Hawk.* Edited by Milo Milton Quaife. New York: Dover Publications, 1994.

Blight, David W. *Frederick Douglass: Prophet of Freedom.* New York: Simon and Schuster, 2018.

———. *Frederick Douglass' Civil War: Keeping Faith in Jubilee.* Louisiana State University Press, 1991.

———. *Race and Reunion: The Civil War in American Memory.* Cambridge, Mass.: Belknap Press of Harvard University Press, 2001.

Bloom, Harold. *Shakespeare: The Invention of the Human.* New York: Riverhead Books, 1998.

Blum, Edward J., and Paul Harvey. *The Color of Christ: The Son of God and the Saga of Race in America.* Chapel Hill: University of North Carolina Press, 2014.

Blumenthal, Sidney. *All the Powers of Earth, 1856–1863.* Vol. 3 of *The Political Life of Abraham Lincoln.* New York: Simon and Schuster, 2019.

———. *A Self-Made Man, 1809–1849.* Vol. 1 of *The Political Life of Abraham Lincoln.* New York: Simon and Schuster, 2016.

———. *Wrestling with His Angel, 1849–1856.* Vol. 2 of *The Political Life of Abraham Lincoln.* New York: Simon and Schuster, 2017.

Boehm, Christopher. *Moral Origins: The Evolution of Virtue, Altruism, and Shame.* New York: Basic Books, 2012.

The Book of Brothers: Being a History of the Adventures of John W. Hutchinson and His Family In the Camps of the Army of the Potomac. Second Series. Boston: S. Chism, 1864.

The Book of Common Prayer, and Administration of the Sacraments [. . .]. New York: Stanford and Delisser, 1858.

The Book of Common Prayer, and Administration of the Sacraments [. . .]. Richmond, Va: J. W. Randolph, 1863.

Bordewich, Fergus M. *America's Great Debate: Henry Clay, Stephen A. Douglas, and the Compromise That Preserved the Union*. New York: Simon and Schuster, 2012.

———. *Congress at War: How Republican Reformers Fought the Civil War, Defied Lincoln, Ended Slavery, and Remade America*. New York: Alfred A. Knopf, 2020.

———. *The First Congress: How James Madison, George Washington, and a Group of Extraordinary Men Invented the Government*. New York: Simon and Schuster, 2016.

Boritt, Gabor S. *Lincoln and the Economics of the American Dream*. [Memphis, Tenn.]: Memphis State University Press, 1978.

———, ed. *The Lincoln Enigma: The Changing Faces of an American Icon*. New York: Oxford University Press, 2001.

———, ed. *Why The Civil War Came*. New York: Oxford University Press, 1997.

Bourke, Richard, and Quentin Skinner, eds. *Popular Sovereignty in Historical Perspective*. Cambridge: Cambridge University Press, 2016.

Bradbury, William H. *While Father Is Away: The Civil War Letters of William H. Bradbury*. Edited by Jennifer Cain Bohrnstedt and compiled by Kassandra R. Chaney. Lexington: University Press of Kentucky, 2003.

Branch, Taylor. *At Canaan's Edge: America in the King Years, 1965–68*. New York: Simon and Schuster, 2006.

Brands, H. W. *The Zealot and the Emancipator: John Brown, Abraham Lincoln, and the Struggle for American Freedom*. New York: Doubleday, 2020.

Bray, Robert. *Peter Cartwright, Legendary Frontier Preacher*. Urbana: University of Illinois Press, 2005.

———. *Reading with Lincoln*. Carbondale: Southern Illinois University Press, 2010.

Bridges, Peter. *Donn Piatt: Gadfly of the Gilded Age*. Kent, Ohio: Kent State University Press, 2012.

Bright, John. *Speeches of John Bright, M.P., on the American Question*. Boston: Little, Brown, 1865.

Broadie, Alexander, ed. *Scottish Enlightenment: An Anthology*. Canongate Classics. Edinburgh: Canongate Books, 1997.

Brockett, L. P. *The Life and Times of Abraham Lincoln, Sixteenth President of the United States* [. . .]. Philadelphia: Bradley; Rochester, N.Y.: R. H. Curran, 1865.

Brodrecht, Grant R. *Our Country: Northern Evangelicals and the Union During the Civil War Era*. The North's Civil War. New York: Fordham University Press, 2018.

Brookhiser, Richard. *Founders' Son: A Life of Abraham Lincoln*. New York: Basic Books, 2014.

Brooks, Corey M. *Liberty Power: Antislavery Third Parties and the Transformation of American Politics*. Chicago: University of Chicago Press, 2016.

Brooks, Noah. *Abraham Lincoln and the Downfall of American Slavery*. New York: G. P. Putnam's Sons, 1895.

———. *Lincoln Observed: Civil War Dispatches of Noah Brooks*. Edited by Michael Burlingame. Baltimore: Johns Hopkins University Press, 1998.

Brophy, Alfred L. *University, Court, and Slave: Proslavery Academic Thought and Southern Jurisprudence*. New York: Oxford University Press, 2016.

Brown, Charles H. *Agents of Manifest Destiny: The Lives and Times of the Filibusters*. Chapel Hill: University of North Carolina Press, 1980.

Browne, Francis Fisher. *The Every-Day Life of Abraham Lincoln*. Lincoln: University of Nebraska Press, 1995.

Bryce, James. *Race Sentiment as a Factor in History: A Lecture Delivered Before the University of London on February 22, 1915*. Creighton Lecture. [London]: Published for the University of London Press by Hodder and Stoughton, 1915.

Buchan, James. *Crowded with Genius: The Scottish Enlightenment; Edinburgh's Moment of the Mind*. New York: Perennial, 2004.

Burin, Eric. *Slavery and the Peculiar Solution: A History of the American Colonization Society*. Gainesville: University Press of Florida, 2005.

Burlingame, Michael. *Abraham Lincoln: A Life*. 2 vols. Baltimore: Johns Hopkins University Press, 2008.

———. *An American Marriage: The Untold Story of Abraham Lincoln and Mary Todd*. New York: Pegasus Books, 2021.

———. *The Black Man's President: Abraham Lincoln, African Americans, and the Pursuit of Racial Equality*. New York: Pegasus Books, 2021.

———. *The Inner World of Abraham Lincoln*. Urbana: University of Illinois Press, 1994.

———, ed. *An Oral History of Abraham Lincoln: John G. Nicolay's Interviews and Essays*. Carbondale: Southern Illinois University Press, 1996.

Burlingame, Michael, and John R. Turner Ettlinger, eds. *Inside Lincoln's White House: The Complete Civil War Diary of John Hay*. Carbondale: Southern Illinois University Press, 1997.

Burrage, Henry S. *Baptist Hymn Writers and Their Hymns*. Portland, Maine: Brown Thurston, 1888.

Burrows, Edwin G., and Mike Wallace. *Gotham: A History of New York City to 1898*. New York: Oxford University Press, 1999.

Burton, Orville Vernon, Jerald Podair, and Jennifer L. Weber, eds. *The Struggle for Equality: Essays on Sectional Conflict, the Civil War, and the Long Reconstruction*. Charlottesville: University of Virginia Press, 2011.

Busey, Samuel C. *Personal Reminiscences and Recollections of Forty-Six Years' Membership in the Medical Society of the District of Columbia and Residence in This City* [. . .]. Washington, D.C.: N.p., 1895.

Butler, Joseph. *The Analogy of Religion, Natural and Revealed, to the Constitution and Course of Nature* [. . .]. New ed. N.p.: Tegg, 1862.

———. *Fifteen Sermons Preached at the Rolls Chapel: And Other Writings on Ethics*. Edited by David McNaughton. British Moral Philosophers. Oxford: Oxford University Press, 2017.

Byrd, James P. *A Holy Baptism of Fire and Blood: The Bible and the American Civil War*. New York: Oxford University Press, 2021.

Calhoun, John C. *Remarks of Mr. Calhoun, of South Carolina, on the Reception of Abolition Petitions* [. . .]. Washington, D.C.: William W. Moore, 1837.

Candler, Allen D., comp. *The Confederate Records of the State of Georgia*. Vol. 2. Atlanta: C. P. Byrd, 1909.

Carey, Henry Charles. *The North and the South*. New York: Office of the Tribune, 1854.

Carlyle, Thomas. *The French Revolution: A History*. 2 vols. New York: Wiley and Putnam, 1846.

———. *On Heroes, Hero-Worship, and the Heroic in History: Six Lectures*. London: J. Fraser, 1841.

Carpenter, F. B. *The Inner Life of Abraham Lincoln: Six Months at the White House*. Lincoln: University of Nebraska Press, 1995.

Carpenter, Jesse T. *The South as a Conscious Minority, 1789–1861: A Study in Political Thought*. New York: New York University Press, 1930.

Carretta, Vincent. *Phillis Wheatley: Biography of a Genius in Bondage*. Athens: University of Georgia Press, 2011.

———, ed. *Unchained Voices: An Anthology of Black Authors in the English-Speaking World of the Eighteenth Century*. Expanded edition. Lexington: University Press of Kentucky, 2004.

Carroll, Daniel B. *Henri Mercier and the American Civil War*. Princeton, N.J.: Princeton University Press, 1971.

Carson, Thomas L. *Lincoln's Ethics*. New York: Cambridge University Press, 2015.

Carter, Susan B., ed. *Historical Statistics of the United States: Earliest Times to the Present*. Millennial edition. Vol. 2. New York: Cambridge University Press, 2006.

Cartwright, Peter. *Autobiography of Peter Cartwright*. Nashville, Tenn.: Abingdon Press, 1956.

Carwardine, Richard J. *Evangelicals and Politics in Antebellum America*. New Haven, Conn.: Yale University Press, 1993.

———. *Lincoln: A Life of Purpose and Power*. New York: Vintage Books, 2007.

Cash, Bill. *John Bright: Statesman, Orator, Agitator*. London: I. B. Tauris, 2012.

Catton, Bruce. *The Coming Fury*. Vol. 1 of *The Centennial History of the Civil War*. Garden City, N.Y.: Doubleday, 1961.

Catton, William, and Bruce Catton. *Two Roads to Sumter*. New York: McGraw-Hill, 1963.

Celebration by the Colored People's Educational Monument Association in Memory of Abraham Lincoln: On the Fourth of July, 1865, in the Presidential Grounds, Washington, D.C. Washington, D.C.: McGill and Witherow, 1865.

Chadwick, Bruce. *The Two American Presidents: A Dual Biography of Abraham Lincoln and Jefferson Davis*. Secaucus, N.J.: Carol Publishing Group, 1999.

Chadwick, John White. *Theodore Parker: Preacher and Reformer*. Library of American Civilization. Boston: Houghton Mifflin, 1901.

Chambers, Robert. *Vestiges of the Natural History of Creation*. Morley's Universal Library. London: Routledge, 1887.

Chapman, Ervin S. *Latest Light on Abraham Lincoln, and War-Time Memories* [. . .]. New York: Fleming H. Revell, 1917.

Chase, Salmon P. *The Salmon P. Chase Papers*. Edited by John Niven. Vol. 2, *Correspondence, 1823–1857*. Kent, Ohio: Kent State University Press, 1994.

Chesebrough, David B., ed. *"God Ordained This War": Sermons on the Sectional Crisis, 1830–1865*. Columbia: University of South Carolina Press, 1991.

———. *"No Sorrow Like Our Sorrow": Northern Protestant Ministers and the Assassination of Lincoln*. Kent, Ohio: Kent State University Press, 1994.

Cheshire, Joseph Blount. *The Church in the Confederate States: A History of the Protestant Episcopal Church in the Confederate States*. Reinicker Lectures. New York: Longmans, Green, 1912.

Chester, Thomas Morris. *Thomas Morris Chester, Black Civil War Correspondent: His Dispatches from the Virginia Front*. Edited by R.J.M. Blackett. Baton Rouge: Louisiana State University Press, 1989.

Childers, Christopher. *The Failure of Popular Sovereignty: Slavery, Manifest Destiny, and the Radicalization of Southern Politics*. American Political Thought. Lawrence: University Press of Kansas, 2012.

Chittenden, L. E. *Invisible Siege: The Journal of Lucius E. Chittenden, April 15, 1861–July 14, 1861*. San Diego: Americana Exchange Press, 1969.

———. *Recollections of President Lincoln and His Administration*. New York: Harper and Brothers, 1891.

Cimbala, Paul A., and Randall M. Miller, eds. *The Freedmen's Bureau and Reconstruction: Reconsiderations*. Reconstructing America. New York: Fordham University Press, 1999.

Clarkson, Thomas. *An Essay on the Slavery and Commerce of the Human Species, Particularly the African* [. . .]. London: J. Phillips, 1785.

Clay, Cassius Marcellus. *The Life of Cassius Marcellus Clay: Memoirs, Writings, and Speeches, Showing His Conduct in the Overthrow of American Slavery* [. . .]. New York: Negro Universities Press, 1969.

Clay, Henry. *The Life and Speeches of the Hon. Henry Clay*. Edited by Daniel Mallory. 2 vols. New York: A. S. Barnes, 1857.

Cleveland, Henry. *Alexander H. Stephens, in Public and Private: With Letters and Speeches, Before, During, and Since the War*. Philadelphia: National, 1866.

Clinton, Catherine. *Mrs. Lincoln: A Life*. New York: Harper, 2009.

Cohen, Mitchell, and Nicole Fermon, eds. *Princeton Readings in Political Thought: Essential Texts Since Plato.* Princeton, N.J.: Princeton University Press, 1996.

Colbert, David, ed. *Eyewitness to America: 500 Years of America in the Words of Those Who Saw It Happen.* New York: Pantheon Books, 1997.

Coleman, J. Winston, Jr. *A Kentucky Lincolnian: The Story of William H. Townsend's Great Collection of Lincolniana, at Lexington, Kentucky.* Harrogate, Tenn.: N.p., [1943?]. Reprinted from the *Lincoln Herald,* February 1943.

Commager, Henry Steele. *Theodore Parker.* Boston: Little, Brown, 1936.

Conroy, James B. *Lincoln's White House: The People's House in Wartime.* Lanham, Md.: Rowman and Littlefield, 2017.

Cook, Robert J., William L. Barney, and Elizabeth R. Varon. *Secession Winter: When the Union Fell Apart.* Baltimore: Johns Hopkins University Press, 2013.

Coombs, John C. "Beyond the 'Origins Debate': Rethinking the Rise of Virginia Slavery." In Douglas Bradburn and John C. Coombs, eds., *Early Modern Virginia: Reconsidering the Old Dominion,* 239–78. Charlottesville: University of Virginia Press, 2011.

Cooper, John Milton, Jr., and Thomas J. Knock, eds., *Jefferson, Lincoln, and Wilson: The America Dilemma of Race and Democracy.* Charlottesville: University of Virginia Press, 2010.

Cooper, William J., Jr. *Liberty and Slavery: Southern Politics to 1860.* New York: Alfred A. Knopf, 1983.

———. *The Lost Founding Father: John Quincy Adams and the Transformation of American Politics.* New York: Liveright, 2017.

———. *The South and the Politics of Slavery, 1828–1856.* Baton Rouge: Louisiana State University Press, 1978.

———. *We Have the War upon Us: The Onset of the Civil War, November 1860–April 1861.* New York: Alfred A. Knopf, 2012.

Cooper, William J., Jr., and John M. McCardell, Jr., eds. *In the Cause of Liberty: How the Civil War Redefined American Ideals.* Baton Rouge: Louisiana State University Press, 2009.

Coski, John M. *The Confederate Battle Flag: America's Most Embattled Emblem.* Cambridge, Mass.: Belknap Press of Harvard University Press, 2005.

Costa, Dora L., and Matthew E. Kahn. *Heroes and Cowards: The Social Face of War.* Princeton, N.J.: Princeton University Press, 2009.

Cox, LaWanda. *Lincoln and Black Freedom: A Study in Presidential Leadership.* Columbia: University of South Carolina Press, 1994.

Cox, LaWanda, and John H. Cox. *Politics, Principle, and Prejudice, 1865–1866: Dilemma of Reconstruction America.* New York: Free Press of Glencoe, 1963.

Crenshaw, Douglas. *Fort Harrison and the Battle of Chaffin's Farm: To Surprise and Capture Richmond.* Charleston, S.C.: History Press, 2013.

Crofts, Daniel W. *Lincoln and the Politics of Slavery: The Other Thirteenth Amendment and the Struggle to Save the Union.* Chapel Hill: University of North Carolina Press, 2016.

———. *A Secession Crisis Enigma: William Henry Hurlbert and "The Diary of a Public Man."* Baton Rouge: Louisiana State University Press, 2010.

Crook, William H. *Through Five Administrations; Reminiscences of Colonel William H. Crook, Body-Guard to President Lincoln.* Compiled and edited by Margarita Spalding Gerry. New York: Harper and Brothers, 1910.

Crooks, George R. *The Life of Bishop Matthew Simpson. Of the Methodist Episcopal Church.* New York: Harper and Brothers, 1891.

Crowley, John G. *Primitive Baptists of the Wiregrass South: 1815 to the Present.* Gainesville: University Press of Florida, 1998.

Cullen, Jim. *The American Dream: A Short History of an Idea That Shaped a Nation.* New York: Oxford University Press, 2003.

Cunliffe, Christopher, ed. *Joseph Butler's Moral and Religious Thought: Tercentenary Essays*. Oxford: Clarendon Press, Oxford University, 1992.

Current, Richard Nelson. *The Lincoln Nobody Knows*. New York: Hill and Wang, 1969.

Curry, Leonard P. *Blueprint for Modern America: Non-Military Legislation of the First Civil War Congress*. Nashville, Tenn.: Vanderbilt University Press, 1968.

Curtin, Philip D. *The Rise and Fall of the Plantation Complex: Essays in Atlantic History*. Studies in Comparative World History. Cambridge: Cambridge University Press, 1990.

Dalcho, Frederick. *Practical Considerations Founded on the Scriptures Relative to the Slave Population of South-Carolina*. Charleston, S.C.: A. E. Miller, 1823.

Daly, John Patrick. *When Slavery Was Called Freedom: Evangelicalism, Proslavery, and the Causes of the Civil War*. Religion in the South. Lexington: University Press of Kentucky, 2002.

Daniel, Curt. *The History and Theology of Calvinism*. Durham, UK: Evangelical Press, 2019.

Davis, David Brion. *Inhuman Bondage: The Rise and Fall of Slavery in the New World*. Oxford, UK: Oxford University Press, 2006.

——. *The Problem of Slavery in the Age of Emancipation*. New York: Alfred A. Knopf, 2014.

——. *The Problem of Slavery in the Age of Revolution, 1770–1823*. Ithaca, N.Y.: Cornell University Press, 1975.

——. *The Problem of Slavery in Western Culture*. Ithaca, N.Y.: Cornell University Press, 1966.

Davis, Jefferson. *The Rise and Fall of the Confederate Government*. 2 vols. New York: Da Capo Press, 1990.

——. *Speech of the Hon. Jefferson Davis, of Mississippi, Delivered in the United States Senate, on the 10th Day of January, 1861* [. . .]. Baltimore: J. Murphy, 1861.

Davis, Michael. *The Image of Lincoln in the South*. Knoxville: University of Tennessee Press, 1971.

Davis, Reuben. *The Duty of Parties: Speech of Hon. Reuben Davis, of Mississippi, in the House of Representatives, December 8, 1859* [. . .]. [Washington, D.C.]: [Printed at the Congressional Globe Office], 1859.

Davis, William C. *Breckinridge: Statesman, Soldier, Symbol*. Southern Biography Series. Baton Rouge: Louisiana State University Press, 1974.

——. *Jefferson Davis: The Man and His Hour*. New York: HarperCollins, 1991.

DeBoer, Clara Merritt. *His Truth Is Marching On: African Americans Who Taught the Freedmen for the American Missionary Association, 1861–1877*. Studies in African American History and Culture. New York: Garland Publishing, 1995.

DeRosa, Marshall L., ed. *The Politics of Dissolution: The Quest for a National Identity and the American Civil War*. New Brunswick, N.J.: Transaction Publishers, 1998.

Dew, Charles B. *Apostles of Disunion: Southern Secession Commissioners and the Causes of the Civil War*. A Nation Divided. Charlottesville: University Press of Virginia, 2001.

DiLorenzo, Thomas J. *The Problem with Lincoln*. Washington, D.C.: Regnery History, 2020.

Dilworth, Thomas. *Dilworth's Spelling-Book, Improved: A New Guide to the English Tongue* [. . .]. A new American ed. Philadelphia: John M'Culloch, 1796.

Dirck, Brian R. *Abraham Lincoln and White America*. Lawrence: University Press of Kansas, 2012.

——. *Lincoln and Davis: Imagining America, 1809–1865*. American Political Thought. Lawrence: University Press of Kansas, 2001.

——, ed. *Lincoln Emancipated: The President and the Politics of Race*. DeKalb: Northern Illinois University Press, 2007.

Dobak, William A. *Freedom by the Sword: The U.S. Colored Troops, 1862–1867*. Army Historical Series. Washington, D.C.: U.S. Army Center of Military History, 2011.

Domby, Adam H. *The False Cause: Fraud, Fabrication, and White Supremacy in Confederate Memory*. Charlottesville: University of Virginia Press, 2020.

Donald, David Herbert. *Charles Sumner and the Coming of the Civil War.* New York: Alfred A. Knopf, 1960.

——. *Charles Sumner and the Rights of Man.* New York: Alfred A. Knopf, 1970.

——. *Lincoln.* American Presidents and World Leaders. New York: Simon and Schuster, 1995.

——. *Lincoln's Herndon.* New York: Alfred A. Knopf, 1948.

——. *"We Are Lincoln Men": Abraham Lincoln and His Friends.* New York: Simon and Schuster, 2003.

Donaldson, Frances F. *The President's Square: The Cosmos Club's [sic] and Other Historic Homes on Lafayette Square.* New York: Vantage Press, 1968.

Douglass, Frederick. *Narrative of the Life of Frederick Douglass, an American Slave.* Edited by Benjamin Quarles. The John Harvard Library. Cambridge, Mass.: Belknap Press of Harvard University Press, 1960.

——. *Oration by Frederick Douglass, Delivered on the Occasion of the Unveiling of the Freedmen's Monument in Memory of Abraham Lincoln, in Lincoln Park, Washington, D.C., April 14th, 1876.* Washington, D.C.: Gibson Brothers, 1876.

Downs, Gregory P. *After Appomattox: Military Occupation and the Ends of War.* Cambridge, Mass.: Harvard University Press, 2015.

Draper, Nicholas. *The Price of Emancipation: Slave-Ownership, Compensation, and British Society at the End of Slavery.* Cambridge Studies in Economic History, Second Series. Cambridge: Cambridge University Press, 2010.

Duane, Anna Mae. *Educated for Freedom: The Incredible Story of Two Fugitive Schoolboys Who Grew Up to Change a Nation.* New York: New York University Press, 2020.

Du Bois, W.E.B. *Black Reconstruction in America: An Essay Toward a History of the Part Which Black Folk Played in the Attempt to Reconstruct Democracy in America, 1860–1880.* The Oxford W.E.B. Du Bois. New York: Oxford University Press, 2007.

——. *The Souls of Black Folk.* New York: Dodd, Mead, 1961.

Duff, John J. *A. Lincoln, Prairie Lawyer.* New York: Rinehart, 1960.

Durman, Donald C. *He Belongs to the Ages: The Statues of Abraham Lincoln.* Ann Arbor, Mich.: Edwards Brothers, 1951.

Earle, Jonathan H. *Jacksonian Antislavery and the Politics of Free Soil, 1824–1854.* Chapel Hill: University of North Carolina Press, 2004.

Early Kentucky Settlers: The Records of Jefferson County, Kentucky, from "The Filson Club History Quarterly." Baltimore: Genealogical, 1988.

Edgington, Frank E. *A History of the New York Avenue Presbyterian Church: One Hundred Fifty-seven Years, 1803 to 1961.* Washington, D.C.: New York Avenue Presbyterian Church, 1962.

Egerton, Douglas R. *The Wars of Reconstruction: The Brief, Violent History of America's Most Progressive Era.* New York: Bloomsbury, 2014.

——. *Year of Meteors: Stephen Douglas, Abraham Lincoln, and the Election That Brought on the Civil War.* New York: Bloomsbury Press, 2010.

Ehrlich, Walter. *They Have No Rights: Dred Scott's Struggle for Freedom.* Contributions in Legal Studies. Westport, Conn.: Greenwood Press, 1979.

Eliav-Feldon, Miriam, Benjamin Isaac, and Joseph Ziegler, eds. *The Origins of Racism in the West.* Cambridge: Cambridge University Press, 2009.

Elkins, Stanley. *Slavery: A Problem in American Institutional and Intellectual Life.* Chicago: University of Chicago Press, 1959.

Elliot, E. N. *Cotton Is King, and Pro-Slavery Arguments: Comprising the Writings of Hammond, Harper, Christy, Stringfellow, Hodge, Bledsoe, and Cartwright, on This Important Subject.* Augusta, Ga.: Pritchard, Abbott and Loomis, 1860.

Ellis, Richard E. *The Union at Risk: Jacksonian Democracy, States' Rights, and the Nullification Crisis.* New York: Oxford University Press, 1987.

Elmore, A. E. *Lincoln's Gettysburg Address: Echoes of the Bible and Book of Common Prayer.* Carbondale: Southern Illinois University Press, 2009.

Eltis, David. *The Rise of African Slavery in the Americas.* Cambridge: Cambridge University Press, 2000.

Emerson, Jason. *The Madness of Mary Lincoln.* Carbondale: Southern Illinois University Press, 2007.

———. *Mary Lincoln for the Ages.* Carbondale: Southern Illinois University Press, 2019.

———. *Mary Lincoln's Insanity Case: A Documentary History.* Urbana: University of Illinois Press, 2015.

Emerson, Ralph Waldo. *The Essential Writings of Ralph Waldo Emerson.* The Modern Library Classics. Edited by Brooks Atkinson. New York: Modern Library, 2000.

Engle, Stephen D., ed. *The War Worth Fighting: Abraham Lincoln's Presidency and Civil War America.* The Alan B. Larkin Series on the American Presidency. Gainesville: University Press of Florida, 2015.

Episcopal Church. Diocese of Virginia. Missionary Society. *Prayer Book for the Camp.* Richmond, Va: Macfarlane and Fergusson, 1863.

Epstein, Abraham. *Insecurity: A Challenge to America; A Study of Social Insurance in the United States and Abroad.* 2nd rev. ed. New York: Random House, 1938.

Epstein, Daniel Mark. *The Lincolns: Portrait of a Marriage.* New York: Ballantine Books, 2008.

Equal Justice Initiative. *Lynching in America: Confronting the Legacy of Racial Terror.* 3rd ed. Montgomery, Ala.: Equal Justice Initiative, 2017.

Escott, Paul D. *Lincoln's Dilemma: Blair, Sumner, and the Republican Struggle over Racism and Equality in the Civil War Era.* A Nation Divided: Studies in the Civil War Era. Charlottesville: University of Virginia Press, 2014.

———. *"What Shall We Do with the Negro?": Lincoln, White Racism, and Civil War America.* Charlottesville: University of Virginia Press, 2009.

———. *The Worst Passions of Human Nature: White Supremacy in the Civil War North.* A Nation Divided: Studies in the Civil War Era. Charlottesville: University of Virginia Press, 2020.

Essig, James D. *The Bonds of Wickedness: American Evangelicals Against Slavery, 1770–1808.* Philadelphia: Temple University Press, 1982.

Eubank, Damon R. *In the Shadow of the Patriarch: The John J. Crittenden Family in War and Peace.* Macon, Ga.: Mercer University Press, 2009.

Evans, William McKee. *Open Wound: The Long View of Race in America.* Urbana: University of Illinois Press, 2009.

Farrand, Max, ed. *The Records of the Federal Convention of 1787.* 3 vols. New Haven, Conn.: Yale University Press, 1911.

Fast Day Sermons: or, The Pulpit on the State of the Country. New York: Rudd and Carleton, 1861.

Faust, Drew Gilpin. *The Creation of Confederate Nationalism: Ideology and Identity in the Civil War South.* The Walter Lynwood Fleming Lectures in Southern History. Baton Rouge: Louisiana State University Press, 1988.

———, ed. *The Ideology of Slavery: Proslavery Thought in the Antebellum South, 1830–1860.* Library of Southern Civilization. Baton Rouge: Louisiana State University Press, 1981.

———. *This Republic of Suffering: Death and the American Civil War.* New York: Alfred A. Knopf, 2008.

Fehrenbacher, Don E. *The Dred Scott Case: Its Significance in American Law and Politics.* New York: Oxford University Press, 1979.

———. *The Slaveholding Republic: An Account of the United States Government's Relations to Slavery.* Completed and edited by Ward M. McAfee. New York: Oxford University Press, 2001.

Fehrenbacher, Don E., and Virginia Fehrenbacher, comps. and eds. *Recollected Words of Abraham Lincoln.* Stanford, Calif.: Stanford University Press, 1996.

Feldman, Noah. *The Broken Constitution: Lincoln, Slavery, and the Refounding of America.* New York: Farrar, Straus and Giroux, 2021.

Feller, Daniel. *The Jacksonian Promise: America, 1815–1840.* The American Moment. Baltimore: Johns Hopkins University Press, 1995.

Fields, Karen E., and Barbara J. Fields. *Racecraft: The Soul of Inequality in American Life.* London: Verso, 2014.

Findley, Paul. *A. Lincoln: The Crucible of Congress.* New York: Crown Publishers, 1979.

Finkelman, Paul. *Defending Slavery: Proslavery Thought in the Old South; A Brief History with Documents.* The Bedford Series in History and Culture. Boston: Bedford / St. Martin's, 2003.

———. *Slavery and the Founders: Race and Liberty in the Age of Jefferson.* 2nd ed. Armonk, N.Y.: M. E. Sharpe, 2001.

Fitzhugh, George. *Cannibals All! Or, Slaves Without Masters.* Edited by C. Vann Woodward. The John Harvard Library. Cambridge, Mass.: Belknap Press of Harvard University Press, 1960.

———. *Sociology for the South: or, The Failure of Free Society.* Richmond, Va.: A. Morris, 1854.

Fleischner, Jennifer. *Mrs. Lincoln and Mrs. Keckly: The Remarkable Story of the Friendship Between a First Lady and a Former Slave.* New York: Broadway Books, 2003.

Flood, Charles Bracelen. *1864: Lincoln at the Gates of History.* New York: Simon and Schuster, 2009.

———. *Grant's Final Victory: Ulysses S. Grant's Heroic Last Year.* Cambridge, Mass.: Da Capo Press, 2011.

Foner, Eric. *The Fiery Trial: Abraham Lincoln and American Slavery.* New York: W. W. Norton, 2010.

———. *Forever Free: The Story of Emancipation and Reconstruction.* New York: Alfred A. Knopf, 2005.

———. *Free Soil, Free Labor, Free Men: The Ideology of the Republican Party Before the Civil War.* Oxford: Oxford University Press, 1995.

———. *Politics and Ideology in the Age of the Civil War.* New York: Oxford University Press, 1980.

———. *Reconstruction: America's Unfinished Revolution, 1863–1877.* New American Nation Series. New York: Harper and Row, 1988.

———, ed. *Our Lincoln: New Perspectives on Lincoln and His World.* New York: W. W. Norton, 2008.

Foner, Philip S., ed. *The Life and Writings of Frederick Douglass.* 5 vols. New York: International Publishers, 1950–1975.

Foote, Shelby. *The Civil War: A Narrative.* 3 vols. New York: Random House, 1958.

Forbes, Robert Pierce. *The Missouri Compromise and Its Aftermath: Slavery and the Meaning of America.* Chapel Hill: University of North Carolina Press, 2007.

Foreman, Amanda. *A World on Fire: Britain's Crucial Role in the American Civil War.* New York: Random House, 2011.

Fornieri, Joseph R. *Abraham Lincoln, Philosopher Statesman.* Carbondale: Southern Illinois University Press, 2014.

———. *Abraham Lincoln's Political Faith.* DeKalb: Northern Illinois University Press, 2003.

Fox, Richard Wightman. *Lincoln's Body: A Cultural History.* New York: W. W. Norton, 2015.

Fox-Genovese, Elizabeth, and Eugene D. Genovese. *The Mind of the Master Class: History and Faith in the Southern Slaveholders' Worldview*. Cambridge: Cambridge University Press, 2005.

Franklin, John Hope. *The Emancipation Proclamation: The Dramatic Story of Abraham Lincoln's Greatest Document and Its Significance in American History*. Anchor Books. Garden City, N.Y.: Doubleday, 1965.

——. *The Militant South, 1800–1861*. 2nd ed. Cambridge, Mass.: Belknap Press of Harvard University Press, 1970.

Fredrickson, George M. *The Arrogance of Race: Historical Perspectives on Slavery, Racism, and Social Inequality*. Middletown, Conn.: Wesleyan University Press, 1988.

——. *Big Enough to Be Inconsistent: Abraham Lincoln Confronts Slavery and Race*. The W.E.B. Du Bois Lectures. Cambridge, Mass.: Harvard University Press, 2008.

——. *The Black Image in the White Mind: The Debate on Afro-American Character and Destiny, 1817–1914*. New York: Harper and Row, 1971.

——. *The Inner Civil War: Northern Intellectuals and the Crisis of the Union*. Harper Torchbooks. New York: Harper and Row, 1965.

——. *Racism: A Short History*. Princeton, N.J.: Princeton University Press, 2015.

Freehling, William W. *Becoming Lincoln*. Charlottesville: University of Virginia Press, 2018.

——. *Prelude to Civil War: The Nullification Controversy in South Carolina, 1816–1836*. New York: Oxford University Press, 1992.

——. *The Road to Disunion*. 2 vols. New York: Oxford University Press, 1990–2007.

——, ed. *The Nullification Era: A Documentary Record*. Harper Torchbooks. New York: Harper and Row, 1967.

Freehling, William W., and Craig M. Simpson, eds. *Secession Debated: Georgia's Showdown in 1860*. New York: Oxford University Press, 1992.

Freeman, Joanne B. *The Field of Blood: Violence in Congress and the Road to Civil War*. New York: Farrar, Straus and Giroux, 2018.

French, Benjamin Brown, Donald B. Cole, and John J. McDonough. *Witness to the Young Republic: A Yankee's Journal, 1828–1870*. Hanover, N.H.: University Press of New England, 1989.

Friedman, Benjamin M. *Religion and the Rise of Capitalism*. New York: Alfred A. Knopf, 2021.

Frothingham, Octavius Brooks. *Memoir of William Henry Channing*. Library of American Civilization. Boston: Houghton Mifflin, 1886.

——. *Theodore Parker: A Biography*. American Culture Series. Boston: J. R. Osgood, 1874.

Fuller, A. James. *Chaplain to the Confederacy: Basil Manly and Baptist Life in the Old South*. Southern Biography Series. Baton Rouge: Louisiana State University Press, 2000.

Furman, Richard. *Rev. Dr. Richard Furman's Exposition of the Views of the Baptists Relative to the Coloured Population of the United States; In a Communication to the Governor of South-Carolina*. Charleston, S.C.: A. E. Miller, 1823.

Gac, Scott. *Singing for Freedom: The Hutchinson Family Singers and the Nineteenth-Century Culture of Reform*. New Haven, Conn.: Yale University Press, 2007.

Gallagher, Gary W. *The Confederate War*. Cambridge, Mass.: Harvard University Press, 1997.

——. *The Union War*. Cambridge, Mass.: Harvard University Press, 2011.

Gallagher, Gary W., and Alan T. Nolan, eds. *The Myth of the Lost Cause and Civil War History*. Bloomington: Indiana University Press, 2000.

Galvin, Robert W. *The Genius of a People: What the Scottish Enlightenment Taught Our Founding Fathers*. [Philadelphia]: Xlibris, 2008.

Garnsey, Peter. *Ideas of Slavery from Aristotle to Augustine*. The W. B. Stanford Memorial Lectures. Cambridge: Cambridge University Press, 1996.

Garrison, William Lloyd. *The Letters of William Lloyd Garrison.* Vol. 5, *Let the Oppressed Go Free, 1861–1867.* Edited by Walter M. Merrill. Cambridge, Mass.: Harvard University Press, 1979.

Gates, Henry Louis, Jr. *The Black Church: This Is Our Story, This Is Our Song.* New York: Penguin Press, 2021.

———, ed. *Lincoln on Race and Slavery.* Princeton, N.J.: Princeton University Press, 2009.

Genovese, Eugene D. *A Consuming Fire: The Fall of the Confederacy in the Mind of the White Christian South.* Mercer University Lamar Memorial Lectures. Athens: University of Georgia Press, 1998.

———. *Roll, Jordan, Roll: The World the Slaves Made.* New York: Pantheon Books, 1974.

George, Timothy. *Theology of the Reformers.* Nashville, Tenn.: Broadman Press, 1988.

Gerbner, Katharine. *Christian Slavery: Conversion and Race in the Protestant Atlantic World.* Early American Studies. Philadelphia: University of Pennsylvania Press, 2018.

Gerhardt, Michael J. *Lincoln's Mentors: The Education of a Leader.* New York: Custom House, 2021.

Giddings, Joshua R. *History of the Rebellion: Its Authors and Causes.* New York: Follet, Foster, 1864.

Gienapp, William E., and Erica L. Gienapp, eds. *The Civil War Diary of Gideon Welles: Lincoln's Secretary of the Navy.* The Knox College Lincoln Studies Center Series. Urbana: Knox College Lincoln Studies Center and the University of Illinois Press, 2014.

Gilmore, James R. *Personal Recollections of Abraham Lincoln and the Civil War.* Boston: L. C. Page, 1898.

Glaude, Eddie S., Jr. *Democracy in Black: How Race Still Enslaves the American Soul.* New York: Crown Publishers, 2016.

———. *Exodus! Religion, Race, and Nation in Early Nineteenth-Century Black America.* Chicago: University of Chicago Press, 2000.

Gloucester, Jeremiah. *An Oration, Delivered on January 1, 1823, in Bethel Church, on the Abolition of the Slave Trade.* Philadelphia: John Young, 1823.

Goodheart, Adam. *1861: The Civil War Awakening.* New York: Alfred A. Knopf, 2011.

Goodman, Paul. *Of One Blood: Abolitionism and the Origins of Racial Equality.* Berkeley: University of California Press, 1998.

Goodrich, Thomas. *The Darkest Dawn: Lincoln, Booth, and the Great American Tragedy.* Bloomington: Indiana University Press, 2005.

Goodwin, Doris Kearns. *Team of Rivals: The Political Genius of Abraham Lincoln.* Simon and Schuster Lincoln Library. New York: Simon and Schuster, 2005.

Gordon-Reed, Annette. *Andrew Johnson.* American Presidents Series. New York: Times Books / Henry Holt, 2011.

Gossett, Thomas F. *Race: The History of an Idea in America.* Dallas: Southern Methodist University Press, 1963.

Gould, Lewis L. *Grand Old Party: A History of the Republicans.* New York: Random House, 2003.

Grant, Ulysses S. *The Papers of Ulysses S. Grant.* Edited by John Y. Simon. Vol. 1, *1837–1861.* Carbondale: Southern Illinois University Press, 1967.

Greeley, Horace. *Recollections of a Busy Life: Including Reminiscences of American Politics and Politicians* [ ] New York: J. B. Ford; Boston: H. A. Brown, 1869.

Green, Constance McLaughlin. *The Church on Lafayette Square: A History of St. John's Church, Washington, D.C., 1815–1970.* Washington, D.C.: Potomac Books, 1970.

Green, Duff. *Facts and Suggestions on the Subjects of Currency and Direct Trade: Addressed to the Chamber of Commerce of Macon, Ga.* Macon, Ga.: Printed for the Chamber of Commerce, 1861.

Green, Michael S. *Lincoln and Native Americans*. Concise Lincoln Library. Carbondale: Southern Illinois University Press, 2021.

Griessman, Gene. *The Words Lincoln Lived By: 52 Timeless Principles to Light Your Path*. New York: Simon and Schuster, 1997.

Grimshaw, William. *History of the United States, from Their First Settlement as Colonies, to the Cession of Florida* [. . .]. Rev. ed. Philadelphia, J. Grigg, 1826.

Grodzins, Dean. *American Heretic: Theodore Parker and Transcendentalism*. Chapel Hill: University of North Carolina Press, 2002.

Guelzo, Allen C. *Abraham Lincoln: Redeemer President*. Grand Rapids, Mich.: W. B. Eerdmans, 1999.

——. *Lincoln and Douglas: The Debates That Defined America*. New York: Simon and Schuster, 2008.

——. *Lincoln's Emancipation Proclamation: The End of Slavery in America*. New York: Simon and Schuster, 2004.

——. *Redeeming the Great Emancipator*. The Nathan I. Huggins Lectures. Cambridge, Mass.: Harvard University Press, 2016.

Guenther, Eileen. *In Their Own Words: Slave Life and the Power of Spirituals*. St. Louis: Morning-Star Music Publishers, 2016.

Gunderson, Robert Gray. *The Log-Cabin Campaign*. [Lexington]: University of Kentucky Press, 1957.

——. *Old Gentlemen's Convention: The Washington Peace Conference of 1861*. Madison: University of Wisconsin Press, 1961.

Gurowski, Adam. *Diary, from March 4, 1861, to November 12, 1862*. Boston: Lee and Shepard, 1862.

——. *Diary, from November 18, 1862, to October 18, 1863*. New York: Carleton, 1864.

Gutjahr, Paul G. *Charles Hodge: Guardian of American Orthodoxy*. New York: Oxford University Press, 2011.

Guyatt, Nicholas. *Providence and the Invention of the United States, 1607–1876*. New York: Cambridge University Press, 2007.

Gwynne, S. C. *Hymns of the Republic: The Story of the Final Year of the American Civil War*. New York: Scribner, 2019.

Halstead, Murat. *Three Against Lincoln: Murat Halstead Reports the Caucuses of 1860*. Edited by William B. Hesseltine. Baton Rouge: Louisiana State University Press, 1960.

Hamlin, Charles Eugene. *The Life and Times of Hannibal Hamlin*. Cambridge, Mass.: Riverside Press, 1899.

Hammond, James H. *Gov. Hammond's Letters on Southern Slavery: Addressed to Thomas Clarkson, the English Abolitionist*. Charleston, S.C.: Walker and Burke, 1845

——. *Selections from the Letters and Speeches of the Hon. James H. Hammond, of South Carolina*. New York: John F. Trow, 1866.

——. *Speech of Hon. James H. Hammond, Delivered at Barnwell Court House, October 29, 1858*. Washington, D.C.: Henry Polkinhorn, 1858.

Hammond, John Craig. *Slavery, Freedom, and Expansion in the Early American West*. Jeffersonian America. Charlottesville: University of Virginia Press, 2007.

Hanna, A. J. *Flight into Oblivion*. [Richmond, Va.]: Johnson, 1938.

Hannaford, Ivan. *Race: The History of an Idea in the West*. Washington, D.C.: Woodrow Wilson Center Press; Baltimore: Johns Hopkins University Press, 1996.

Hannah-Jones, Nikole, Caitlin Roper, Ilena Silverman, and Jake Silverstein, eds. *The 1619 Project: A New Origin Story*. New York: One World, 2021.

Harding, Vincent. *There Is a River: The Black Struggle for Freedom in America*. New York: Harcourt Brace Jovanovich, 1981.

Harper, William. *Memoir on Slavery, Read Before the Society for the Advancement of Learning, of South Carolina, at Its Annual Meeting at Columbia, 1837*. Charleston, S.C.: J. S. Burges, 1838.

Harrell, Carolyn L. *When the Bells Tolled for Lincoln: Southern Reaction to the Assassination*. Macon, Ga.: Mercer University Press, 1997.

Harris, Cicero W. *The Sectional Struggle: An Account of the Troubles Between the North and the South, from the Earliest Times to the Close of the Civil War*. Philadelphia: J. B. Lippincott, 1902.

Harris, William C. *Lincoln's Rise to the Presidency*. Lawrence: University Press of Kansas, 2007.

Harris, William L. *Address of Hon. W. L. Harris, Commissioner from the State of Mississippi: Delivered Before the General Assembly of the State of Georgia, on Monday, Dec. 17th, 1860*. Milledgeville, Ga.: Boughton, Nisbet and Barnes, 1860.

Harrison, Fairfax, ed. *Aris Sonis Focisque: Being a Memoir of an American Family, the Harrisons of Skimino and Particularly of Jesse Burton Harrison and Burton Norvell Harrison*. [New York]: [De Vinne Press], 1910.

Harrison, Lowell H., and James C. Klotter. *A New History of Kentucky*. Lexington: University Press of Kentucky, 1997.

Harrold, Stanley. *Gamaliel Bailey and Antislavery Union*. Kent, Ohio: Kent State University Press, 1986.

———. *Lincoln and the Abolitionists*. Concise Lincoln Library. Carbondale: Southern Illinois University Press, 2018.

Hastings, Thomas. *The Presbyterian Psalmodist: A Collection of Tunes Adapted to the Psalms and Hymns of the Presbyterian Church in the United States of America, Approved by the General Assembly*. Philadelphia: Presbyterian Board of Publication, 1852.

Hatch, Nathan O. *The Democratization of American Christianity*. New Haven, Conn.: Yale University Press, 1989.

Hatzenbuehler, Ronald L. *Jefferson, Lincoln, and the Unfinished Work of the Nation*. Carbondale: Southern Illinois University Press, 2016.

Hay, John. *At Lincoln's Side: John Hay's Civil War Correspondence and Selected Writings*. Edited by Michael Burlingame. Carbondale: Southern Illinois University Press, 2000.

———. *Inside Lincoln's White House: The Complete Civil War Diary of John Hay*. Edited by Michael Burlingame and John R. Turner Ettlinger. Carbondale: Southern Illinois University Press, 1999.

Haynes, Stephen R. *Noah's Curse: The Biblical Justification of American Slavery*. Religion in America Series. Oxford, UK: Oxford University Press, 2007.

Hearn, Chester G. *The Impeachment of Andrew Johnson*. Jefferson, N.C.: McFarland, 2000.

Heidler, David S. *Pulling the Temple Down: The Fire-Eaters and the Destruction of the Union*. Mechanicsburg, Pa.: Stackpole Books, 1994.

Helm, Katherine. *The True Story of Mary, Wife of Lincoln: Containing the Recollections of Mary Lincoln's Sister Emilie* [. . .]. New York: Harper, 1928.

Helper, Hinton Rowan. *The Impending Crisis of the South: How to Meet It*. New York: Burdick Brothers, 1857.

Helseth, Paul Kjoss, et al. *Four Views on Divine Providence*. Edited by Dennis W. Jowers. Counterpoints: Bible and Theology. Grand Rapids, Mich.: Zondervan, 2011.

Heng, Geraldine. *The Invention of Race in the European Middle Ages*. Cambridge: Cambridge University Press, 2018.

Herman, Arthur. *How the Scots Invented the Modern World: A True Story of How Western Europe's Poorest Nation Created Our World and Everything in It*. New York: Three Rivers Press, 2002.

Herndon, William H. *Herndon on Lincoln*. Vol. 1, *Letters*. Edited by Douglas L. Wilson and Rodney O. Davis. The Knox College Lincoln Studies Center Series. Urbana: University of Illinois Press, 2016.

———. *Herndon's Lincoln*. Edited by Douglas L. Wilson and Rodney O. Davis. The Knox College Lincoln Studies Center Series. [Galesburg, Ill.?]: Knox College Lincoln Studies Center; Urbana: University of Illinois Press, 2006.

———. *The Hidden Lincoln: From the Letters and Papers of William H. Herndon*. Edited by Emanuel Hertz. New York: Blue Ribbon Books, 1940.

Herndon, William H., and Jesse W. Weik. *Herndon's Life of Lincoln: The History and Personal Recollections of Abraham Lincoln*. New York: Da Capo Press, 1983.

Hill, Mike, ed. *Whiteness: A Critical Reader*. New York: New York University Press, 1997.

Hinks, Peter P., ed. *David Walker's Appeal to the Coloured Citizens of the World*. University Park: Pennsylvania State University Press, 2000.

Hobbes, Thomas. *Of Man, Being the First Part of Leviathan*. In Charles W. Eliot, ed., *French and English Philosophers: Descartes, Rousseau, Voltaire, Hobbes*, 323–434. Vol. 34, *The Harvard Classics*. New York: P. F. Collier and Son, 1910.

[Hobby, William J.]. *Remarks upon Slavery: Occasioned by Attempts Made to Circulate Improper Publications in the Southern States*. 2nd ed. Augusta, Ga.: Printed for the publisher, 1835.

Hodes, Martha. *Mourning Lincoln*. New Haven, Conn.: Yale University Press, 2015.

Hoffecker, W. Andrew. *Charles Hodge: The Pride of Princeton*. American Reformed Biographies. Phillipsburg, N.J.: P and R Publishing, 2011.

Hoffer, Williamjames Hull. *The Caning of Charles Sumner: Honor, Idealism, and the Origins of the Civil War*. Baltimore: Johns Hopkins University Press, 2010.

Hofstadter, Richard. *The American Political Tradition and the Men Who Made It*. New York: Vintage Books, 1989.

———. *The Paranoid Style in American Politics, and Other Essays*. Cambridge, Mass.: Harvard University Press, 1996.

Holcombe, James P. *The Election of a Black Republican President an Overt Act of Aggression on the Right of Property in Slaves: The South Urged to Adopt Concerted Action for Future Safety*. Richmond, Va.: C. H. Wynne, 1860.

Holcombe, William H. *The Alternative: A Separate Nationality, or the Africanization of the South*. New Orleans, La.: Printed at the Delta Mammoth Job Office, 1860.

Holland, Edwin C. *A Refutation of the Calumnies Circulated Against the Southern and Western States Respecting the Institution and Existence of Slavery Among Them* [. . .]. Charleston, S.C.: A. E. Miller, 1822.

Holland, J. G. *The Life of Abraham Lincoln*. Springfield, Mass.: G. Bill, 1866.

Holt, Michael F. "The Election of 1840: Voter Mobilization and the Emergence of Jacksonian Voting Behavior." In William J. Cooper, Jr., Michael F. Holt, and John M. McCardell, Jr., eds., *A Master's Due: Essays in Honor of David Herbert Donald*, 16–58. Baton Rouge: Louisiana State University Press, 1985.

———. *The Election of 1860: "A Campaign Fraught with Consequences."* American Presidential Elections. Lawrence: University Press of Kansas, 2017.

———. *The Political Crisis of the 1850s*. Critical Episodes in American Politics. New York: Wiley, 1978.

———. *The Rise and Fall of the American Whig Party: Jacksonian Politics and the Onset of the Civil War*. New York: Oxford University Press, 1999.

Holzer, Harold. *Emancipating Lincoln: The Proclamation in Text, Context, and Memory*. The Nathan I. Huggins Lectures. Cambridge, Mass.: Harvard University Press, 2012.

———. *Lincoln and the Power of the Press: The War for Public Opinion*. New York: Simon and Schuster, 2014.

———. *Lincoln at Cooper Union: The Speech That Made Abraham Lincoln President*. New York: Simon and Schuster, 2004.

———. *Lincoln President-Elect: Abraham Lincoln and the Great Secession Winter, 1860–1861*. New York: Simon and Schuster, 2008.

———, comp. *President Lincoln Assassinated!! The Firsthand Story of the Murder, Manhunt, Trial, and Mourning.* New York: Literary Classics of the United States, 2014.

———, ed., *The Lincoln Anthology: Great Writers on His Life and Legacy from 1860 to Now.* The Library of America. New York: Library of America, 2009.

———, ed., *Lincoln as I Knew Him: Gossip, Tributes, and Revelations from His Best Friends and Worst Enemies.* Chapel Hill, N.C.: Algonquin Books of Chapel Hill, 1999.

Holzer, Harold, and Sara Vaughn Gabbard, eds. *Lincoln and Freedom: Slavery, Emancipation, and the Thirteenth Amendment.* Carbondale: Southern Illinois University Press, 2007.

Holzer, Harold, and Norton Garfinkle. *A Just and Generous Nation: Abraham Lincoln and the Fight for American Opportunity.* New York: Basic Books, 2015.

Holzer, Harold, Edna Greene Medford, and Frank J. Williams. *The Emancipation Proclamation: Three Views (Social, Political, Iconographic).* Conflicting Worlds. Baton Rouge: Louisiana State University Press, 2006.

Holzer, Harold, Craig L. Symonds, and Frank J. Williams, eds. *Exploring Lincoln: Great Historians Reappraise Our Greatest President.* North's Civil War. New York: Fordham University Press, 2015.

Hopkins, Donald R. *Princes and Peasants: Smallpox in History.* Chicago: University of Chicago Press, 1983.

Horn, James. *1619: Jamestown and the Forging of American Democracy.* New York: Basic Books, 2018.

———. *A Land as God Made It: Jamestown and the Birth of America.* New York: Basic Books, 2005.

Horwitz, Tony. *Midnight Rising: John Brown and the Raid That Sparked the Civil War.* New York: Henry Holt, 2011.

Houston, David Franklin. *A Critical Study of Nullification in South Carolina.* Harvard Historical Studies. New York: Russell and Russell, 1967.

Howe, Daniel Walker. *The Political Culture of the American Whigs.* Chicago: University of Chicago Press, 1979.

———. *What Hath God Wrought: The Transformation of America, 1815–1848.* The Oxford History of the United States. New York: Oxford University Press, 2007.

Hubbell, Richtmyer. *Potomac Diary: A Soldier's Account of the Capital in Crisis, 1864–1865.* Edited by Marc Newman. Civil War History Series. Charleston, S.C.: Arcadia, 2000.

Humes, James C. *The Wit and Wisdom of Abraham Lincoln: A Treasury of More than 650 Quotations and Anecdotes.* New York: HarperCollins, 1996.

Hunt, H. Draper. *Hannibal Hamlin of Maine, Lincoln's First Vice-President.* Syracuse, N.Y.: Syracuse University Press, 1969.

Hyman, Harold M., and Leonard W. Levy, eds. *Freedom and Reform: Essays in Honor of Henry Steele Commager.* New York: Harper and Row, 1967.

Illinois Constitutional Convention (1920–1922). *Proceedings of the Constitutional Convention of the State of Illinois, Convened Jan. 6, 1920.* Vol. 1. [Springfield, Ill.]: [Illinois State Journal Co.], 1920.

Inaugural Ceremonies of the Freedmen's Memorial Monument to Abraham Lincoln: Washington City, April 14, 1876. St. Louis: Levison and Blythe, 1876.

Inbody, Donald S. *The Soldier Vote: War, Politics, and the Ballot in America.* New York: Palgrave Macmillan, 2016.

The Influence of the Slave Power: With Other Anti-Slavery Pamphlets. Westport, Conn.: Negro Universities Press, 1970.

Inskeep, Steve. *Imperfect Union: How Jessie and John Frémont Mapped the West, Invented Celebrity, and Helped Cause the Civil War.* New York: Penguin Press, 2020.

Jackson, James C. *The Duties and Dignities of American Freemen.* [Utica, N.Y.]: [Liberty Press], 1843.

Jacob, Kathryn Allamong. *Capital Elites: High Society in Washington, D.C., After the Civil War*. Washington, D.C.: Smithsonian Institution Press, 1995.

Jacobs, Harriet A. *Incidents in the Life of a Slave Girl: Written by Herself*. Edited by L. Maria Child and Jean Fagan Yellin. Cambridge, Mass.: Harvard University Press, 1987.

Janney, Caroline E. *Remembering the Civil War: Reunion and the Limits of Reconciliation*. The Littlefield History of the Civil War Era. Chapel Hill: University of North Carolina Press, 2013.

Jay, William. *A View of the Action of the Federal Government, in Behalf of Slavery*. Utica, N.Y.: J. C. Jackson, 1844.

Jefferson, Thomas. *The Writings of Thomas Jefferson: Being His Autobiography, Correspondence, Reports, Messages, Addresses, and Other Writings, Official and Private*. Edited by H. A. Washington. 9 vols. Cambridge: Cambridge University Press, 2011.

Jenkins, William Sumner. *Pro-Slavery Thought in the Old South*. The University of North Carolina. Social Study Series. Chapel Hill: University of North Carolina Press, 1935.

Johannsen, Robert W. *Stephen A. Douglas*. Illini Books Edition. Urbana: University of Illinois Press, 1997.

Johnson, J. F. *Proceedings of the General Anti-Slavery Convention: Called by the Committee of the British and Foreign Anti-Slavery Society and Held in London from Tuesday, June 13th to Tuesday, June 20th, 1843*. London: J. Snow, 1843.

Johnson, Reinhard O. *The Liberty Party, 1840–1848: Antislavery Third-Party Politics in the United States*. Antislavery, Abolition, and the Atlantic World. Baton Rouge: Louisiana State University Press, 2009.

Johnson, Samuel. *Taxation No Tyranny: An Answer to the Resolutions and Address of the American Congress*. London: Printed for T. Cadell, 1775.

Jones, Clarence B., and Stuart Connelly. *Behind the Dream: The Making of the Speech That Transformed a Nation*. New York: Palgrave Macmillan, 2011.

Jones, Edgar De Witt. *The Influence of Henry Clay upon Abraham Lincoln*. Lexington, Ky.: Henry Clay Memorial Foundation, 1952.

———. *Lincoln and the Preachers*. New York: Harper, 1948.

Jones, J. B. *A Rebel War Clerk's Diary at the Confederate States Capital*. 2 vols. Philadelphia: J. B. Lippincott, 1866.

Jordan, Ryan P. *Church, State, and Race: The Discourse of American Religious Liberty, 1750–1900*. Lanham, Md.: University Press of America, 2012.

Jordan, Serepta. *The Diary of Serepta Jordan: A Southern Woman's Struggle with War and Family, 1857–1864*. Edited by Minoa D. Uffelman, Ellen Kanervo, Phyllis Smith, and Eleanor Williams. Voices of the Civil War. Knoxville: University of Tennessee Press, 2020.

Jordan, Winthrop D. *White over Black: American Attitudes Toward the Negro, 1550–1812*. Chapel Hill: Published for the Institute of Early American History and Culture at Williamsburg, Virginia, by the University of North Carolina Press, 1968.

Julian, George W. *The Life of Joshua R. Giddings*. Chicago: A. C. McClurg, 1892.

Jung, Patrick J. *The Black Hawk War of 1832*. Campaigns and Commanders. Norman: University of Oklahoma Press, 2007.

Kagan, Neil, and Stephen G. Hyslop, eds. *Smithsonian Civil War: Inside the National Collection*. Washington, D.C.: Smithsonian Books, 2013.

Kagan, Robert. *Dangerous Nation*. New York: Alfred A. Knopf, 2006.

Kalmoe, Nathan P. *With Ballots and Bullets: Partisanship and Violence in the American Civil War*. Cambridge: Cambridge University Press, 2020.

Kantor, MacKinlay. *If the South Had Won the Civil War*. New York: Bantam Books, 1961.

Kateb, George. *Lincoln's Political Thought*. Cambridge, Mass.: Harvard University Press, 2015.

Katz, Jacob. *From Prejudice to Destruction: Anti-Semitism, 1700–1933*. Cambridge, Mass.: Harvard University Press, 1980.

Kauffman, Michael W. *American Brutus: John Wilkes Booth and the Lincoln Conspiracies*. New York: Random House, 2004.

Kaye, Harvey J. *Thomas Paine and the Promise of America*. New York: Hill and Wang, 2005.

Kean, Robert Garlick Hill. *Inside the Confederate Government: The Diary of Robert Garlick Hill Kean, Head of the Bureau of War*. Edited by Edward Younger. New York: Oxford University Press, 1957.

Keckley [as published], Elizabeth. *Behind the Scenes: or, Thirty Years a Slave, and Four Years in the White House*. New York: G. W. Carleton, 1868.

Keehn, David C. *Knights of the Golden Circle: Secret Empire, Southern Secession, Civil War*. Conflicting Worlds. Baton Rouge: Louisiana State University Press, 2013.

Keith, LeeAnna. *When It Was Grand: The Radical Republican History of the Civil War*. New York: Hill and Wang, 2020.

Kendi, Ibram X. *Stamped from the Beginning: The Definitive History of Racist Ideas in America*. New York: Nation Books, 2016.

Kentucky, State of. *Text of Kentucky Constitutions of 1792, 1799, and 1850*. Frankfort, Ky.: Legislative Research Commission, 1965.

Ketcham, Ralph. *James Madison: A Biography*. Charlottesville: University of Virginia Press, 1990.

Kirk, Elise K. *Music at the White House: From the 18th to the 21st Centuries*. 2nd ed. Washington, D.C.: White House Historical Association, 2017.

Kirkham, Samuel. *English Grammar in Familiar Lectures: Accompanied by a Compendium [. . .]*. New York: Robert B. Collins, 1829.

Kirkland, Edward Chase. *The Peacemakers of 1864*. New York: Macmillan, 1927.

Kirwan, Albert Dennis. *John J. Crittenden: The Struggle for the Union*. Westport, Conn.: Greenwood Press, 1974.

Klein, Herbert S. *The Atlantic Slave Trade*. 2nd ed. Cambridge: Cambridge University Press, 2010.

Klement, Frank L. *Lincoln's Critics: The Copperheads of the North*. Edited by Steven K. Rogstad. Shippensburg, Pa.: White Mane, 1999.

Kline, Michael J. *The Baltimore Plot: The First Conspiracy to Assassinate Abraham Lincoln*. Yardley, Pa.: Westholme, 2008.

Klinkner, Philip A., with Rogers M. Smith. *The Unsteady March: The Rise and Decline of Racial Equality in America*. Chicago: University of Chicago Press, 1999.

Klotter, James C. *Henry Clay: The Man Who Would Be President*. New York: Oxford University Press, 2018.

Knoles, George H. *The Crisis of the Union, 1860–1861*. [Baton Rouge]: Louisiana State University Press, 1965.

Koch, Adrienne, and William Peden, eds. *The Life and Selected Writings of Thomas Jefferson*. New York: Modern Library, 1998.

Kohn, Hans. *American Nationalism: An Interpretive Essay*. New York: Collier Books, 1961.

Kovacevich, Michael. *Hannibal Hamlin: The Story of the Anti-Slavery and Civil War Vice President Who Might Have Changed History*. Parker, Colo.: Outskirts Press, 2010.

Krick, Robert K. *Civil War Weather in Virginia*. Tuscaloosa: University of Alabama Press 2007.

Kytle, Ethan J. *Romantic Reformers and the Antislavery Struggle in the Civil War Era*. New York: Cambridge University Press, 2014.

Lamon, Ward Hill. *Recollections of Abraham Lincoln, 1847–1865*. Edited by Dorothy Lamon Teillard. Bison Books edition. Lincoln: University of Nebraska Press, 1994.

Lankford, Nelson. *Richmond Burning: The Last Days of the Confederate Capital*. New York: Viking, 2002.

Lee, Elizabeth Blair. *Wartime Washington: The Civil War Letters of Elizabeth Blair Lee*. Edited by Virginia Jeans Laas. Urbana: University of Illinois Press, 1991.

Leech, Margaret. *Reveille in Washington, 1860–1865*. New York: Harper and Brothers, 1941.

Lehrman, Lewis E. *Lincoln at Peoria: The Turning Point; Getting Right with the Declaration of Independence*. Mechanicsburg, Pa.: Stackpole Books, 2008.

Leland, Henry Martyn. *Abraham Lincoln: The Important Collection of the Late Henry M. Leland; Unrestricted Public Auction, Thursday Evening, June 2, 1932 [. . .]*. Chicago: Chicago Book and Art Auctions, 1932.

Levine, Bruce. *Confederate Emancipation: Southern Plans to Free and Arm Slaves During the Civil War*. Oxford: Oxford University Press, 2005.

———. *Thaddeus Stevens: Civil War Revolutionary, Righter for Racial Justice*. New York: Simon and Schuster, 2021.

Lincoln, Abraham. *The Collected Works of Abraham Lincoln*. Edited by Roy P. Basler. 9 vols. New Brunswick, N.J.: Rutgers University Press, 1953–1955.

———. *In Lincoln's Hand: His Original Manuscripts*. Edited by Harold Holzer and Joshua Wolf Shenk. New York: Bantam Dell, 2009.

———. *Lincoln on Democracy*. Edited by Mario M. Cuomo and Harold Holzer. New York: HarperCollins, 1990.

———. *The Living Lincoln: The Man, His Mind, His Times, and the War He Fought, Reconstructed from His Own Writings*. Edited by Paul M. Angle and Earl Schenck Miers. New York: Barnes and Noble, 1992.

———. *Selected Writings*. New York: Barnes and Noble, 2013.

———. *Speeches and Writings, 1832–1858: Speeches, Letters, and Miscellaneous Writings, the Lincoln-Douglas Debates*. Compiled by Don E. Fehrenbacher. The Library of America. New York: Literary Classics of the United States, 1989.

———. *Speeches and Writings, 1859–1865: Speeches, Letters, and Miscellaneous Writings, Presidential Messages and Proclamations*. Compiled by Don E. Fehrenbacher. The Library of America. New York: Literary Classics of the United States, 1989.

Lincoln, Abraham, and Stephen A. Douglas. *The Lincoln-Douglas Debates*. Edited by Rodney O. Davis and Douglas L. Wilson. The Knox College Lincoln Studies Center Series. Urbana: Knox College Lincoln Studies Center, University of Illinois Press, 2008.

Lincoln, C. Eric, and Lawrence H. Mamiya. *The Black Church in the African-American Experience*. Durham, N.C.: Duke University Press, 1990.

Lincoln, Waldo. *History of the Lincoln Family: An Account of the Descendants of Samuel Lincoln, of Hingham, Massachusetts, 1637–1920*. Worcester, Mass.: Commonwealth Press, 1923.

Litwack, Leon F. *Been in the Storm So Long: The Aftermath of Slavery*. New York: Alfred A. Knopf, 1979.

———. *North of Slavery: The Negro in the Free States, 1790–1860*. [Chicago]: University of Chicago Press, 1961.

Locke, John. *Two Treatises of Government: And a Letter Concerning Toleration*. Edited by Ian Shapiro. Rethinking the Western Tradition. New Haven, Conn.: Yale University Press, 2003.

Lorant, Stefan. *Lincoln: A Picture Story of His Life*. Revised and enlarged edition. New York: W. W. Norton, 1969.

Lott, Tommy Lee. *The Invention of Race: Black Culture and the Politics of Representation*. Malden, Mass.: Blackwell, 1999.

Lowance, Mason I., ed. *Against Slavery: An Abolitionist Reader*. Penguin Classics. New York: Penguin Books, 2000.

Lowenstein, Roger. *Ways and Means: Lincoln and His Cabinet and the Financing of the Civil War.* New York: Penguin Press, 2022.

Lowry, Richard S. *The Photographer and the President: Abraham Lincoln, Alexander Gardner, and the Images That Made a Presidency.* New York: Rizzoli Ex Libris, 2015.

Lowry, Thomas P. "Not Everybody Mourned Lincoln's Death." In *The Lincoln Assassination: Crime and Punishment, Myth and Memory,* edited by Harold Holzer, Craig L. Symonds, and Frank J. Williams, 95–114. New York: Fordham University Press, 2010.

Lucas, Marion B. *A History of Blacks in Kentucky: From Slavery to Segregation, 1760–1891.* Lexington: Kentucky Historical Society, 2003.

Lynch, Christopher, and Jonathan Marks, eds. *Principle and Prudence in Western Political Thought.* SUNY Series in the Thought and Legacy of Leo Strauss. Albany: State University of New York Press, 2016.

Mackay, Alexander. *The Western World: or, Travels in the United States in 1846–47, Exhibiting Them in Their Latest Development [. . .].* 2nd ed. Vol. 1. Philadelphia: Lea and Blanchard, 1849.

Mackay, Charles. *Extraordinary Popular Delusions and the Madness of Crowds.* Philadelphia: Templeton Foundation Press, 1999.

MacPherson, Ryan C. *Debating Evolution Before Darwinism: An Exploration of Science and Religion in America, 1844–1859.* Mankato, Minn.: Into Your Hands, 2015.

Maddex, Jack P., Jr. *The Reconstruction of Edward A. Pollard: A Rebel's Conversion to Postbellum Unionism.* The James Sprunt Studies in History and Political Science. Chapel Hill: University of North Carolina Press, 1974.

Magness, Phillip W., and Sebastian N. Page. *Colonization After Emancipation: Lincoln and the Movement for Black Resettlement.* Columbia: University of Missouri Press, 2011.

Maier, Pauline. *American Scripture: How America Declared Its Independence from Britain.* London: Pimlico, 1997.

Mansfield, Stephen. *Lincoln's Battle with God: A President's Struggle with Faith and What It Meant for America.* Nashville, Tenn.: Thomas Nelson, 2012.

Marrs, Elijah P. *Life and History of the Rev. Elijah P. Marrs.* Louisville, Ky.: Bradley and Gilbert, 1885.

Marshall, Catherine. *A Man Called Peter: The Story of Peter Marshall.* New York: McGraw Hill, 1951.

———. *To Live Again.* New York: McGraw Hill, 1957.

Marshall, Peter, and David Manuel. *Sounding Forth the Trumpet.* Grand Rapids, Mich.: Fleming H. Revell, 1999.

Mason, George. *The Papers of George Mason, 1725–1792.* Edited by Robert A. Rutland. Vol. 1, *1749–1778.* Chapel Hill: University of North Carolina Press, 1970.

Masur, Kate. *An Example for All the Land: Emancipation and the Struggle over Equality in Washington, D.C.* Chapel Hill: University of North Carolina Press, 2010.

———. *Until Justice Be Done: America's First Civil Rights Movement, from the Revolution to Reconstruction.* New York: W. W. Norton, 2021.

Masur, Louis P. *Lincoln's Hundred Days: The Emancipation Proclamation and the War for the Union.* Cambridge, Mass.: Belknap Press of Harvard University Press, 2012.

———. *Lincoln's Last Speech: Wartime Reconstruction and the Crisis of Reunion.* New York: Oxford University Press, 2015.

Mathis, Ray, ed. *In the Land of the Living: Wartime Letters by Confederates from the Chattahoochee Valley of Alabama and Georgia.* Troy, N.Y.: Troy State University Press, 1981.

May, Robert E. *John A. Quitman: Old South Crusader.* Southern Biography Series. Baton Rouge: Louisiana State University Press, 1985.

———. *Manifest Destiny's Underworld: Filibustering in Antebellum America.* Chapel Hill: University of North Carolina Press, 2002.

——. *The Southern Dream of a Caribbean Empire, 1854–1861.* 2nd paperback edition. Gainesville: University Press of Florida, 2002.

Mayer, Henry. *All on Fire: William Lloyd Garrison and the Abolition of Slavery.* New York: St. Martin's Press, 1998.

Maynard, Nettie Colburn. *Séances in Washington: Abraham Lincoln and Spiritualism During the Civil War.* Edited by Irene McGarvie. Rev. ed. Toronto: Ancient Wisdom Publishing, 2009.

——. *Was Abraham Lincoln a Spiritualist? Or, Curious Revelations from the Life of a Trance Medium.* Philadelphia: Rufus C. Hartranft, 1891.

McCardell, John. *The Idea of a Southern Nation: Southern Nationalists and Southern Nationalism, 1830–1860.* New York: W. W. Norton, 1979.

McClure, Alexander Kelly, ed. *The Annals of the Civil War.* New York: Da Capo Press, 1994.

McCurry, Stephanie. *Confederate Reckoning: Power and Politics in the Civil War South.* Cambridge, Mass.: Harvard University Press, 2010.

McFeely, William S. *Grant: A Biography.* New York: W. W. Norton, 1981.

McGovern, George. *Abraham Lincoln.* The American Presidents Series. Times Books / Henry Holt, 2009.

McKitrick, Eric L. *Andrew Johnson and Reconstruction.* [Chicago]: University of Chicago Press, 1960.

McKivigan, John R. *The War Against Proslavery Religion: Abolitionism and the Northern Churches, 1830–1865.* Ithaca, N.Y.: Cornell University Press, 1984.

McKivigan, John R., and Mitchell Snay, eds. *Religion and the Antebellum Debate over Slavery.* Athens: University of Georgia Press, 1998.

McPherson, James M. *Abraham Lincoln.* Oxford: Oxford University Press, 2009.

——. *Abraham Lincoln and the Second American Revolution.* New York: Oxford University Press, 1990.

——. *Battle Cry of Freedom: The Civil War Era.* The Oxford History of the United States. New York: Oxford University Press, 1988.

——. *Embattled Rebel: Jefferson Davis as Commander in Chief.* New York: Penguin Press, 2014.

——. *The Negro's Civil War: How American Negroes Felt and Acted During the War for the Union.* New York: Pantheon Books, 1965.

——. *Ordeal by Fire: The Civil War and Reconstruction.* New York: Alfred A. Knopf; New York: Random House, 1982.

——. *The War That Forged a Nation: Why the Civil War Still Matters.* New York: Oxford University Press, 2015.

——, ed. *"We Cannot Escape History": Lincoln and the Last Best Hope of Earth.* Urbana: University of Illinois Press, 1995.

McWhirter, Christian. *Battle Hymns: The Power and Popularity of Music in the Civil War.* Chapel Hill: University of North Carolina Press, 2012.

Meacham, Jon. *American Gospel: God, the Founding Fathers, and the Making of a Nation.* New York: Random House, 2006.

——. *American Lion: Andrew Jackson in the White House.* New York: Random House, 2008.

——. *The Soul of America: The Battle for Our Better Angels.* New York: Random House, 2018.

——. *Thomas Jefferson: The Art of Power.* New York: Random House, 2012.

Mead, Margaret, Theodosius Dobzhansky, Ethel Tobach, and Robert E. Light, eds. *Science and the Concept of Race.* New York: Columbia University Press, 1968.

Meltzer, Milton. *Slavery: A World History.* 2 vols. New York: Da Capo Press, 1993.

Merry, Robert W. *A Country of Vast Designs: James K. Polk, the Mexican War, and the Conquest of the American Continent.* New York: Simon and Schuster, 2009.

Miers, Earl Schenck, ed. *Lincoln Day by Day: A Chronology, 1809–1865.* 3 vols. Washington, D.C.: U.S. Lincoln Sesquicentennial Commission, 1960.

Miles, James Warley. *The Relation Between the Races at the South.* Charleston, S.C.: Presses of Evans and Cogswell, 1861.

Mill, John Stuart. *On Liberty.* Luton, UK: Andrews UK, 2011.

Miller, John C. *The Federalist Era, 1789–1801.* New American Nation Series. New York: Harper and Row, 1960.

Miller, Perry, ed. *The Transcendentalists: An Anthology.* Cambridge, Mass.: Harvard University Press, 1950.

Miller, William Lee. *Arguing About Slavery: John Quincy Adams and the Great Battle in the United States Congress.* New York: Vintage Books, 1998.

———. *Lincoln's Virtues: An Ethical Biography.* New York: Alfred A. Knopf, 2002.

———. *President Lincoln: The Duty of a Statesman.* New York: Alfred A. Knopf, 2008.

Milton, John. *Complete Poems and Major Prose.* Edited by Merritt Y. Hughes. New York: Macmillan, 1957.

Monaghan, Jay. *Abraham Lincoln Deals with Foreign Affairs: A Diplomat in Carpet Slippers.* Lincoln: University of Nebraska Press, 1997.

Montagu, Ashley. *Man's Most Dangerous Myth: The Fallacy of Race.* 2nd ed. New York: Columbia University Press, 1945.

Moore, A. Y. *The Life of Schuyler Colfax.* Philadelphia: T. B. Peterson and Brothers, 1868.

Moore, Frank, ed. *The Rebellion Record: A Diary of American Events, with Documents, Narratives, Illustrative Incidents, Poetry, Etc.* American Culture Series. Vol. 10. New York: D. Van Nostrand, 1867.

Moorhead, James H. *Princeton Seminary in American Religion and Culture.* Grand Rapids, Mich.: W. B. Eerdmans, 2012.

Morel, Lucas E. *Lincoln and the American Founding.* Concise Lincoln Library. Carbondale: Southern Illinois University Press, 2020.

———. *Lincoln's Sacred Effort: Defining Religion's Role in American Self-Government.* Lanham, Md.: Lexington Books, 2000.

———, ed. *Lincoln and Liberty: Wisdom for the Ages.* Lexington: University Press of Kentucky, 2015.

Moreno, Paul D., and Johnathan O'Neill, eds. *Constitutionalism in the Approach and Aftermath of the Civil War.* The North's Civil War. New York: Fordham University Press, 2013.

Morgan, Edmund S. *American Slavery, American Freedom: The Ordeal of Colonial Virginia.* New York: W. W. Norton, 1975.

Morgan, Kenneth. *Slavery and Servitude in Colonial North America: A Short History.* New York: New York University Press, 2001.

Morgenthau, Hans J., and David Hein. *Essays on Lincoln's Faith and Politics.* Edited by Kenneth W. Thompson. American Values Projected Abroad. Lanham, Md.: University Press of America, 1983.

Mörner, Magnus. *Race Mixture in the History of Latin America.* Boston: Little, Brown, 1967.

Morris, Roy, Jr. *The Long Pursuit: Abraham Lincoln's Thirty-Year Struggle with Stephen Douglas for the Heart and Soul of America.* [Washington, D.C.]: Smithsonian Books; New York: Collins, 2008.

Morrison, Chaplain W. *Democratic Politics and Sectionalism: The Wilmot Proviso Controversy.* Chapel Hill: University of North Carolina Press, 1967.

Morrison, Michael A. *Slavery and the American West: The Eclipse of Manifest Destiny and the Coming of the Civil War.* Chapel Hill: University of North Carolina Press, 1997.

Mott, Frank Luther. *Golden Multitudes: The Story of Best Sellers in the United States.* New York: Macmillan, 1947.

Murray, Lindley. *The English Reader: or, Pieces in Prose and Poetry, Selected from the Best Writers Designed to Assist Young Persons to Read with Propriety and Effect [. . .].* Philadelphia: Bennett and Walton, 1826.

Mushkat, Jerome. *Fernando Wood: A Political Biography*. Kent, Ohio: Kent State University Press, 1990.

Myers, Robert Manson, ed. *The Children of Pride: A True Story of Georgia and the Civil War*. New Haven, Conn.: Yale University Press, 1972.

Nagel, Paul C. *One Nation Indivisible: The Union in American Thought, 1776–1861*. New York: Oxford University Press, 1964.

Nash, Gary B. *The Forgotten Fifth: African Americans in the Age of Revolution*. Nathan I. Huggins Lectures. Cambridge, Mass.: Harvard University Press, 2006.

———. *Race and Revolution*. The Merrill Jensen Lectures in Constitutional Studies. Madison, Wis.: Madison House, 1990.

———. *Red, White, and Black: The Peoples of Early America*. Prentice-Hall History of the American People Series. Englewood Cliffs, N.J.: Prentice-Hall, 1974.

Needleman, Jacob. *The American Soul: Rediscovering the Wisdom of the Founders*. New York: J. P. Tarcher / Putnam, 2002.

Neely, Mark E., Jr. *The Last Best Hope of Earth: Abraham Lincoln and the Promise of America*. Cambridge, Mass.: Harvard University Press; San Marino, Calif.: Huntington Library; Springfield: Illinois State Historical Society, 1993.

Neely, Mark E., Jr., and R. Gerald McMurtry. *The Insanity File: The Case of Mary Todd Lincoln*. Carbondale: Southern Illinois University Press, 1986.

Nevins, Allan. *The Emergence of Lincoln*. 2 vols. New York: Scribner, 1950.

———. *Ordeal of the Union*. 2 vols. New York: Scribner, 1947.

———. *The War for the Union*. 4 vols. New York: Scribner, 1959–1971.

New York Avenue Presbyterian Church (Washington, D.C.). *The Centennial of the New York Avenue Presbyterian Church, Washington, D.C.* [Washington, D.C.?]: [The Church?], 1904.

Nicholas, Roy Franklin. *The Disruption of American Democracy*. New York: Macmillan, 1948.

Niebuhr, Gustav. *Lincoln's Bishop: A President, a Priest, and the Fate of 300 Dakota Sioux Warriors*. New York: HarperOne, 2014.

Niebuhr, H. Richard. *Christ and Culture*. Harper Torchbooks. New York: Harper, 1951.

———. *The Kingdom of God in America*. Chicago: Willett, Clark, 1937.

Niebuhr, Reinhold. *Faith and History: A Comparison of Christian and Modern Views of History*. New York: Charles Scribner's Sons, 1949.

———. *The Irony of American History*. New York: Charles Scribner's Sons, 1952.

Nisbet, Robert. *History of the Idea of Progress*. Harper Colophon Books. New York: Basic Books, 1980.

Noll, Mark A. *America's God: From Jonathan Edwards to Abraham Lincoln*. New York: Oxford University Press, 2005.

———. *The Civil War as a Theological Crisis*. The Steven and Janice Brose Lectures in the Civil War Era. Chapel Hill: University of North Carolina Press, 2006.

———. *One Nation Under God? Christian Faith and Political Action in America*. San Francisco: Harper and Row, 1988.

Nord, David Paul. "The Evangelical Origins of Mass Media in America, 1815–1835." *Journalism Monographs* 88 (May 1984). 39 pp. ERIC number: ED245260.

Nott, Josiah C. *Two Lectures on the Natural History of the Caucasian and Negro Races*. Mobile, Ala.: Dade and Thompson, 1844.

Nott, Josiah C., and George R. Gliddon. *Types of Mankind; or, Ethnological Researches; Based upon the Ancient Monuments, Paintings, Sculptures, and Crania of Races* [. . .]. Philadelphia: Lippincott, Grambo, 1854.

Nowlin, William Dudley. *Kentucky Baptist History, 1770–1922*. [Louisville, Ky.]: Baptist Book Concern, 1922.

Nye, Russel B. *Fettered Freedom: Civil Liberties and the Slavery Controversy, 1830–1860.* [East Lansing]: Michigan State University Press, 1963.

Oakes, James. *The Crooked Path to Abolition: Abraham Lincoln and the Antislavery Constitution.* New York: W. W. Norton, 2021.

———. *Freedom National: The Destruction of Slavery in the United States, 1861–1865.* New York: W. W. Norton, 2013.

———. *The Radical and the Republican: Frederick Douglass, Abraham Lincoln, and the Triumph of Antislavery Politics.* New York: W. W. Norton, 2007.

———. *The Scorpion's Sting: Antislavery and the Coming of the Civil War.* New York: W. W. Norton, 2014.

Oates, Stephen B. *With Malice Toward None: A Biography of Abraham Lincoln.* New York: Harper Perennial, 2011.

Official Proceedings of the Democratic National Convention, Held in 1860, at Charleston and Baltimore [. . .]. Cleveland, Ohio: Nevins' Print, 1860.

Oliver, Frederick Scott. *The Alternatives to Civil War.* London: Murray, 1913.

Onstot, T. G. *Pioneers of Menard and Mason Counties: Made Up of Personal Reminiscences of an Early Life in Menard County* [. . .]. Forest City, Ill.: T. G. Onstot, 1902.

The Order for Daily Morning and Evening Prayer, According to the Use of the Protestant Episcopal Church in the Confederate States of America [. . .]. Atlanta, Ga.: R. J. Maynard, 1863.

Osborn, Charles C. *Jubal: The Life and Times of General Jubal A. Early, CSA, Defender of the Lost Cause.* Chapel Hill, N.C.: Algonquin Books of Chapel Hill, 1992.

Otis, James. *A Vindication of the Conduct of the House of Representatives of the Province of the Massachusetts-Bay* [. . .]. Boston: Edes and Gill, 1762.

Pachter, Marc, ed. *Abroad in America: Visitors to the New Nation, 1776–1914.* Reading, Mass.: Published in association with the National Portrait Gallery, Smithsonian Institution by Addison-Wesley, 1976.

Pagden, Anthony. *The Fall of Natural Man: The American Indian and the Origins of Comparative Ethnology.* Cambridge Iberian and Latin American Studies. Cambridge: Cambridge University Press, 1982.

Page, Elwin L. *Abraham Lincoln in New Hampshire.* Boston: Houghton Mifflin, 1929.

Paine, Thomas. *Collected Writings.* Edited by Eric Foner. The Library of America. New York: Literary Classics of the United States, 1995.

Painter, Nell Irvin. *The History of White People.* New York: W. W. Norton, 2010.

———. *Sojourner Truth: A Life, a Symbol.* New York: W. W. Norton, 1996.

Palmer, Colin A. *Slaves of the White God: Blacks in Mexico, 1570–1650.* Cambridge, Mass.: Harvard University Press, 1976.

Paludan, Phillip S. *The Presidency of Abraham Lincoln.* Lawrence: University Press of Kansas, 1994.

Parent, Anthony S., Jr. *Foul Means: The Formation of a Slave Society in Virginia, 1660–1740.* Chapel Hill: Published for the Omohundro Institute of Early American History and Culture, Williamsburg, Virginia, by the University of North Carolina Press, 2003.

Parker, Theodore. *The Collected Works of Theodore Parker* [. . .]. Edited by Francis Power Cobbe. Vol. 2, *Sermons. Prayers.* London: Trubner, 1863.

———. *The Works of Theodore Parker.* Centenary edition. Vol. 4, *Sermons of Religion.* Edited by Samuel A. Eliot. Boston: American Unitarian Association, 1908.

Paskoff, Paul F., and Daniel J. Wilson, eds. *The Cause of the South: Selections from "De Bow's Review," 1846–1867.* Library of Southern Civilization. Baton Rouge: Louisiana State University Press, 1982.

Pearne, Thomas H. *Sixty-one Years of Itinerant Christian Life in Church and State.* Cincinnati: Curts and Jennings, 1898.

Pearson, Elizabeth Ware, ed. *Letters from Port Royal Written at the Time of the Civil War*. Boston: W. B. Clark, 1906.

Peraino, Kevin. *Lincoln in the World: The Making of a Statesman and the Dawn of American Power*. New York: Crown Publishers, 2013.

Peters, William G., ed. *Sermons of the Confederacy*. Vol. 2, *1863–1865*. Morrisville, N.C.: Lulu Press, 2014.

Peterson, Merrill D. *Lincoln in American Memory*. New York: Oxford University Press, 1994.

———. *Olive Branch and Sword: The Compromise of 1833*. Walter Lynwood Fleming Lectures in Southern History. Baton Rouge: Louisiana State University Press, 1982.

Phillips, Wendell. *Can Abolitionists Vote or Take Office Under the United States Constitution?* New York: American Anti-Slavery Society, 1845.

Piatt, Donn. *Memories of the Men Who Saved the Union*. New York: Belford, Clarke, 1887.

Pinckney, Henry L. *An Oration, Delivered in the Independent, or Congregational Church, Charleston: Before the State Rights and Free Trade Party, the State Society of Cincinnati* [. . .]. Charleston, S.C.: A. E. Miller, 1833.

Pinel, Stephen L. *The Work-List of Henry Erben, Organ Builder in Nineteenth-Century New York*. OHS Monographs in American Organ History. Villanova, Pa.: OHS Press, Organ Historical Society, 2021.

Pinsker, Matthew. *Lincoln's Sanctuary: Abraham Lincoln and the Soldiers' Home*. New York: Oxford University Press, 2003.

Pitch, Anthony S. *"They Have Killed Papa Dead!": The Road to Ford's Theatre, Abraham Lincoln's Murder, and the Rage for Vengeance*. Hanover, N.H.: Steerforth Press, 2008.

Pollard, Edward A. *The Lost Cause: A New Southern History of the War of the Confederates* [. . .]. New York: E. B. Treat, 1866.

———. *The Lost Cause Regained*. New York: G. W. Carleton, 1868.

Porter, Horace. *Campaigning with Grant*. Edited by Wayne C. Temple. Civil War Centennial Series. Bloomington: Indiana University Press, 1961.

Potter, David M. *The Impending Crisis, 1848–1861*. Completed and edited by Don E. Fehrenbacher. Harper Colophon Books. New York: Harper and Row, 1976.

———. *Lincoln and His Party in the Secession Crisis*. New Haven, Conn.: Yale University Press, 1962.

Pratt, Richard H. "The Advantages of Mingling Indians with Whites." In Francis P. Prucha, ed., *Americanizing the American Indians: Writings by the "Friends of the Indian," 1880–1900*, 260–71. Cambridge, Mass.: Harvard University Press, 2013.

Presbyterian Church in the U.S.A. General Assembly. *Extracts from the Minutes of the General Assembly, of the Presbyterian Church, in the United States of America* [. . .]. Philadelphia: Thomas and William Bradford, 1820.

Presbyterian Church in the U.S.A. Synod of South Carolina and Georgia. *Report of the Committee to Whom Was Referred the Subject of the Religious Instruction of the Colored Population of the Synod of South-Carolina and Georgia* [. . .]. Charleston, S.C.: Observer Office Press, 1834.

Price, James S. *The Battle of New Market Heights: Freedom Will Be Theirs by the Sword*. The History Press Civil War Sesquicentennial Series. Charleston, S.C.: History Press, 2011.

Prucha, Francis Paul. *The Great Father: The United States Government and the American Indians*. 2 vols. Lincoln: University of Nebraska Press, 1984.

Quarles, Benjamin. *Lincoln and the Negro*. New York: Oxford University Press, 1962.

———. *The Negro in the Civil War*. New York: Da Capo Press, 1989.

———. "The Revolutionary War as a Black Declaration of Independence." In Ira Berlin and Ronald Hoffman, eds., *Slavery and Freedom in the Age of the American Revolution*, 283–301. Charlottesville: Published for the United States Capitol Historical Society by the University Press of Virginia, 1983.

Rable, George C. *But There Was No Peace: The Role of Violence in the Politics of Reconstruction.* Athens: University of Georgia Press, 1984.

———. *The Confederate Republic: A Revolution Against Politics.* Civil War America. Chapel Hill: University of North Carolina Press, 1994.

———. *Damn Yankees! Demonization and Defiance in the Confederate South.* Walter Lynwood Fleming Lectures in Southern History. Baton Rouge: Louisiana State University Press, 2015.

———. *God's Almost Chosen Peoples: A Religious History of the American Civil War.* The Littlefield History of the Civil War Era. Chapel Hill: University of North Carolina Press, 2010.

Raboteau, Albert J. *Canaan Land: A Religious History of African Americans.* New York: Oxford University Press, 2001.

———. *Slave Religion: The "Invisible Institution" in the Antebellum South.* New York: Oxford University Press, 2004.

Randall, James G. *Lincoln, the President.* 4 vols. New York: Dodd, Mead, 1945–1955.

Randall, Ruth Painter. *Mary Lincoln: Biography of a Marriage.* Boston: Little, Brown, 1953.

Ransom, Roger L. *The Confederate States of America: What Might Have Been.* New York: W. W. Norton, 2005.

Redpath, James. *Echoes of Harpers Ferry.* Boston: Thayer and Eldridge, 1860.

Reese, George H., ed. *Proceedings of the Virginia State Convention of 1861, February 13–May 1.* 4 vols. Richmond, Virginia State Library, 1965.

Remini, Robert V. *Henry Clay: Statesman for the Union.* New York: W. W. Norton, 1991.

———. *John Quincy Adams.* The American Presidents Series. New York: Times Books; New York: Henry Holt, 2002.

Rex, John, and David Mason, eds., *Theories of Race and Ethnic Relations.* Comparative Ethnic and Race Relations. Cambridge: Cambridge University Press, 1986.

Reynolds, David S. *Abe: Abraham Lincoln in His Times.* New York: Penguin Press, 2020.

———. *John Brown, Abolitionist: The Man Who Killed Slavery, Sparked the Civil War, and Seeded Civil Rights.* New York: Alfred A. Knopf, 2005.

Rice, Allen Thorndike, ed. *Reminiscences of Abraham Lincoln by Distinguished Men of His Time.* New York: North American Review, 1888.

Richards, Leonard L. *The Life and Times of Congressman John Quincy Adams.* New York: Oxford University Press, 1986.

Richardson, H. Edward. *Cassius Marcellus Clay: Firebrand of Freedom.* The Kentucky Bicentennial Bookshelf. Lexington: University Press of Kentucky, 1976.

Richardson, Heather Cox. *How the South Won the Civil War: Oligarchy, Democracy, and the Continuing Fight for the Soul of America.* New York: Oxford University Press, 2020.

———. *To Make Men Free: A History of the Republican Party.* New York: Basic Books, 2014.

———. *West from Appomattox: The Reconstruction of America After the Civil War.* New Haven, Conn.: Yale University Press, 2007.

Richardson, James D., ed. *A Compilation of the Messages and Papers of the Confederacy: Including the Diplomatic Correspondence, 1861–1865.* 2 vols. Nashville, Tenn.: United States Pub. Co., 1906.

Riddle, Donald W. *Congressman Abraham Lincoln.* Urbana: University of Illinois Press, 1957.

———. *Lincoln Runs for Congress.* New Brunswick, N.J.: Rutgers University Press, 1948.

Riley, James. *An Authentic Narrative of the Loss of the American Brig Commerce, Wrecked on the Western Coast of Africa, in the Month of August, 1815.* Edited by Anthony Bleecker. New York: T. and W. Mercein, 1817.

Ripley, C. Peter, ed. *The Black Abolitionist Papers.* 5 vols. Chapel Hill: University of North Carolina Press, 1985–1992.

Ripley, Eliza. *Social Life in Old New Orleans: Being Recollections of My Girlhood.* New York: D. Appleton, 1912.

Robbins, Hollis, and Henry Louis Gates, Jr., eds. *The Portable Nineteenth-Century African American Women Writers*. Penguin Classics. New York: Penguin Books, 2017.

Roberts, Justin. *Slavery and the Enlightenment in the British Atlantic, 1750–1807*. New York: Cambridge University Press, 2013.

Rodrigue, John C. *Lincoln and Reconstruction*. Concise Lincoln Library. Carbondale: Southern Illinois University Press, 2013.

Rogers, James A. *Richard Furman: Life and Legacy*. [Macon, Ga.]: Mercer University Press, 1985.

Rossiter, Clinton. *The American Quest, 1790–1860: An Emerging Nation in Search of Identity, Unity, and Modernity*. The Founding of the American Republic. New York: Harcourt Brace Jovanovich, 1971.

Rubenstein, Harry R. *Abraham Lincoln: An Extraordinary Life*. [Washington, D.C.]: Smithsonian Books, 2008.

Ruffin, Edmund. *The Diary of Edmund Ruffin*. Edited by William Kauffman Scarborough. 3 vols. Baton Rouge: Louisiana State University Press, 1972–1989.

Russell, William Howard. *My Diary North and South*. 2 vols. London: Bradbury and Evans, 1863.

Safire, William. *The First Dissident: The Book of Job in Today's Politics*. New York: Random House, 1992.

Salter, Darius. *"God Cannot Do Without America": Matthew Simpson and the Apotheosis of Protestant Nationalism*. Wilmore, Ky.: First Fruits Press, 2017.

Salter, William. *The Life of James W. Grimes: Governor of Iowa, 1854–1858; A Senator of the United States, 1859–1869*. New York: D. Appleton, 1876.

Sandburg, Carl. *Abraham Lincoln: The Prairie Years*. 2 vols. New York: Harcourt, Brace, 1926.

———. *Abraham Lincoln: The War Years*. 4 vols. New York: Harcourt, Brace, 1939.

Sandel, Michael J. *Democracy's Discontent: America in Search of a Public Philosophy*. Cambridge, Mass.: Belknap Press of Harvard University Press, 1996.

———. *Justice: What's the Right Thing to Do?* New York: Farrar, Straus and Giroux, 2009.

———. *Public Philosophy: Essays on Morality in Politics*. Cambridge, Mass.: Harvard University Press, 2005.

———, ed. *Justice: A Reader*. New York: Oxford University Press, 2007.

Sarna, Jonathan D. *American Judaism: A History*. New Haven, Conn.: Yale University Press, 2004.

Savage, Kirk. *Standing Soldiers, Kneeling Slaves: Race, War, and Monument in Nineteenth-Century America*. Princeton, N.J.: Princeton University Press, 1997.

Schlesinger, Arthur M., Jr. *The Age of Jackson*. Boston: Little, Brown, 1945.

———. *War and the American Presidency*. New York: W. W. Norton, 2004.

Schoonover, Thomas David. *Dollars over Dominion: The Triumph of Liberalism in Mexican–United States Relations, 1861–1867*. Baton Rouge: Louisiana State University Press, 1978.

Schwartz, Barry. *Abraham Lincoln and the Forge of National Memory*. Chicago: University of Chicago Press, 2000.

Scott, Morgan. *History of the Separate Baptist Church: With a Narrative of Other Denominations*. Indianapolis: Hollenbeck Press, 1901.

Scripps, John Locke. *The First Published Life of Abraham Lincoln*. [Detroit]: [Cranbrook Press], 1900.

Seabrook, Whitemarsh B. *A Concise View of the Critical Situation and Future Prospects of the Slave-Holding States in Relation to Their Coloured Population*. Charleston, S.C.: A. E. Miller, 1825.

Seale, William. *The President's House: A History*. Washington, D.C.: White House Historical Association with the cooperation of the National Geographic Society, 1986.

Sears, Stephen W. *George B. McClellan: The Young Napoleon*. New York: Ticknor and Fields, 1988.

———, ed. *The Civil War Papers of George B. McClellan: Selected Correspondence, 1860–1865*. New York: Ticknor and Fields, 1989.

Secord, James A. *Victorian Sensation: The Extraordinary Publication, Reception, and Secret Authorship of "Vestiges of the Natural History of Creation."* Chicago: University of Chicago Press, 2000.

Sellers, Charles G. *The Market Revolution: Jacksonian America, 1815–1846*. New York: Oxford University Press, 1991.

Seward, William H. *The Works of William H. Seward*. Edited by George E. Baker. New ed. 5 vols. Boston: Houghton, Mifflin, 1884.

Shenk, Joshua Wolf. *Lincoln's Melancholy: How Depression Challenged a President and Fueled His Greatness*. Boston: Houghton Mifflin, 2005.

Shepherd, Massey Hamilton, Jr. *History of St. James' Church, Chicago, A.D. 1834–1934*. [Chicago]: Lakeside Press, R. R. Donnelley and Sons, 1934.

Sidney, Algernon. *Discourses Concerning Government*. Edited by Thomas G. West. Rev. ed. Indianapolis: Liberty Fund, 1996.

Simms, W. Gilmore. "The Morals of Slavery." In *The Pro-Slavery Argument: As Maintained by the Most Distinguished Writers of the Southern States* [. . .], 175–285. Charleston, S.C.: Walker, Richards, 1852.

Simon, James F. *Lincoln and Chief Justice Taney: Slavery, Secession, and the President's War Powers*. Simon and Schuster Lincoln Library. New York: Simon and Schuster, 2006.

Simon, Paul. *Lincoln's Preparation for Greatness: The Illinois Legislative Years*. Urbana: University of Illinois Press, 1971.

Simpson, Brooks D., Stephen W. Sears, and Aaron Sheehan-Dean, eds. *The Civil War*. 4 vols. New York: Library of America, 2011–2014.

Sinha, Manisha. *The Counterrevolution of Slavery: Politics and Ideology in Antebellum South Carolina*. Chapel Hill: University of North Carolina Press, 2000.

———. *The Slave's Cause: A History of Abolition*. New Haven, Conn.: Yale University Press, 2016.

Six Women's Slave Narratives. With an introduction by William L. Andrews. The Schomburg Library of Nineteenth-Century Black Women Writers. New York: Oxford University Press, 1988.

Smiley, David L. *Lion of White Hall: The Life of Cassius M. Clay*. Madison: University of Wisconsin Press, 1962.

Smith, Elbert B. *Francis Preston Blair*. New York: Free Press, 1980.

Smith, John David. *Lincoln and the U.S. Colored Troops*. Concise Lincoln Library. Carbondale: Southern Illinois University Press, 2013.

Smith, Margaret Bayard. *The First Forty Years of Washington Society, Portrayed by the Family Letters of Mrs. Samuel Harrison Smith (Margaret Bayard)* [. . .]. Edited by Gaillard Hunt. New York: Charles Scribner's Sons, 1906.

Smith, William Ernest. *The Francis Preston Blair Family in Politics*. 2 vols. New York: Macmillan, 1933.

Solomos, John, and Les Back. *Race, Politics, and Social Change*. London: Routledge, 1995.

South Carolina Convention. *The Address of the People of South Carolina, Assembled in Convention, to the People of the Slaveholding States of the United States*. Charleston, S.C.: Evans and Cogswell, 1860.

———. *Speeches Delivered in the Convention of the State of South-Carolina, Held in Columbia, in March, 1833* [. . .]. Charleston, S.C.: E. J. Van Brunt, 1833.

A South-Carolinian. *Remarks on the Ordinance of Nullification, the President's Proclamation, the President's Last Message, and the Enforcing Bill, Reported by the Judiciary Committee of the Senate* [. . .]. Charleston, S.C.: A. E. Miller, 1833.

Southern Baptist Theological Seminary. *Report on Slavery and Racism in the History of the Southern Baptist Theological Seminary*. Kentucky: Southern Baptist Theological Seminary, 2018.

Spencer, J. H. *A History of Kentucky Baptists: From 1769 to 1885.* 2 vols. Cincinnati: J. H. Spencer, 1886.

Stahr, Walter. *Seward: Lincoln's Indispensable Man.* New York: Simon and Schuster, 2012.

Stampp, Kenneth M. *And the War Came: The North and the Secession Crisis, 1860–1861.* [Baton Rouge]: Louisiana State University Press, 1970.

———. *The Imperiled Union: Essays on the Background of the Civil War.* New York: Oxford University Press, 1980.

Stanton, Elizabeth Cady. *Elizabeth Cady Stanton as Revealed in Her Letters, Diary and Reminiscences.* Edited by Theodore Stanton and Harriot Stanton Blatch. 2 vols. New York: Harper and Brothers, 1922.

Stanton, William. *The Leopard's Spots: Scientific Attitudes Toward Race in America, 1815–59.* Chicago: University of Chicago Press, 1960.

Staples, Laurence C. *Washington Unitarianism: A Rich Heritage.* Northampton, Mass.: Metcalf, 1970.

Stashower, Daniel. *The Hour of Peril: The Secret Plot to Murder Lincoln Before the Civil War.* New York: Minotaur Books, 2013.

Staudenraus, P. J. *The African Colonization Movement, 1816–1865.* New York: Columbia University Press, 1961.

Stauffer, John. *The Black Hearts of Men: Radical Abolitionists and the Transformation of Race.* Cambridge, Mass.: Harvard University Press, 2002.

———. *Giants: The Parallel Lives of Frederick Douglass and Abraham Lincoln.* New York: Twelve, 2008.

Steiner, Bernard C. *Life of Roger Brooke Taney: Chief Justice of the United States Supreme Court.* Baltimore: Williams and Wilkins, 1922.

Steiner, Mark E. *An Honest Calling: The Law Practice of Abraham Lincoln.* DeKalb: Northern Illinois University Press, 2009.

———. *Lincoln and Citizenship.* Concise Lincoln Library. Carbondale: Southern Illinois University Press, 2021.

Stephen, Leslie, and Sidney Lee, eds. *Dictionary of National Biography.* 66 vols. London: Smith, Elder, 1885–1901.

Sterling, Dorothy. *The Making of an Afro-American: Martin Robison Delany, 1812–1885.* New York: Da Capo Press, 1996.

Stern, Philip Van Doren. *An End to Valor: The Last Days of the Civil War.* Boston: Houghton Mifflin, 1958.

Stevens, Frank E. *The Black Hawk War, Including a Review of Black Hawk's Life.* Chicago: F. E. Stevens, Press of Blakely Printing Co., 1903.

Stevenson, Louise L. *Lincoln in the Atlantic World.* New York: Cambridge University Press, 2015.

Stewart, David O. *Impeached: The Trial of President Andrew Johnson and the Fight for Lincoln's Legacy.* New York: Simon and Schuster, 2009.

Stewart, John W., and James H. Moorhead, eds. *Charles Hodge Revisited: A Critical Appraisal of His Life and Work.* Grand Rapids, Mich.: W. B. Eerdmans, 2002.

Stoddard, William O. *Inside the White House in War Times.* New York: Charles L. Webster, 1890.

Stout, Harry S. *Upon the Altar of the Nation: A Moral History of the American Civil War.* New York: Viking, 2006.

Stowe, Harriet Beecher. *A Key to Uncle Tom's Cabin.* The American Negro, His History and Literature. New York: Arno Press, 1968.

———. *Uncle Tom's Cabin.* With an introduction by James M. McPherson. Library of America Paperback Classics. New York: Library of America, 2010.

Striner, Richard. *Father Abraham: Lincoln's Relentless Struggle to End Slavery.* Oxford: Oxford University Press, 2007.

———. *Lincoln and Race.* Concise Lincoln Library. Carbondale: Southern Illinois University Press, 2012.

Stuart, Moses. *Conscience and the Constitution: With Remarks on the Recent Speech of the Hon. Daniel Webster in the Senate of the United States on the Subject of Slavery.* Boston: Crocker and Brewster, 1850.

Stucker, Augustin. *Lincoln and Davis: A Dual Biography of America's Civil War Presidents.* N.p.: Authorhouse, 2011.

Sumner, Charles. *The Selected Letters of Charles Sumner.* Edited by Beverly Wilson Palmer. 2 vols. Boston: Northeastern University Press, 1990.

Swanson, James L. *Bloody Crimes: The Chase for Jefferson Davis and the Death Pageant for Lincoln's Corpse.* New York: William Morrow/HarperCollins, 2010.

———. *Manhunt: The Twelve-Day Chase for Lincoln's Killer.* New York: Harper Perennial, 2007.

Takaki, Ronald. *A Different Mirror: A History of Multicultural America.* Boston: Little, Brown, 1993.

Tarbell, Ida M. *In the Footsteps of the Lincolns.* New York: Harper and Brothers, 1924.

Tate, N[ahum], and N[icholas] Brady. *A New Version of the Psalms of David, Fitted to the Tunes Used in Churches.* London: Printed by M. Clark for the Company of Stationers, 1696.

Taylor, Gary. *Buying Whiteness: Race, Culture, and Identity from Columbus to Hip-hop.* New York: Palgrave Macmillan, 2005.

Taylor, John M. *William Henry Seward: Lincoln's Right Hand.* New York: HarperCollins, 1991.

Teed, Paul E. *A Revolutionary Conscience: Theodore Parker and Antebellum America.* Lanham, Md.: University Press of America, 2012.

Temple, Wayne C. *Abraham Lincoln: From Skeptic to Prophet.* Mahomet, Ill.: Mayhaven Publishing, 1995.

———. *Lincoln's Confidant: The Life of Noah Brooks.* Edited by Douglas L. Wilson and Rodney O. Davis. The Knox College Lincoln Studies Center Series. Urbana, Ill.: Published by the Knox College Lincoln Studies Center and the University of Illinois Press, 2019.

Thomas, Benjamin P. *Abraham Lincoln: A Biography.* New York: Alfred A. Knopf, 1952.

Thomas, Christopher A. *The Lincoln Memorial and American Life.* Princeton, N.J.: Princeton University Press, 2002.

Thomas, Louisa. *Louisa: The Extraordinary Life of Mrs. Adams.* New York: Penguin Press, 2016.

Thornwell, J. H. *Hear the South! The State of the Country, An Article Republished from the "Southern Presbyterian Review."* New York: D. Appleton, 1861.

———. *Our Danger and Our Duty.* Confederate Imprints, 1861–1865. Columbia, S.C.: Southern Guardian Steam-Power Press, 1862.

Thurow, Glen E. *Abraham Lincoln and American Political Religion.* Albany: State University of New York Press, 1976.

Tise, Larry E. *Proslavery: A History of the Defense of Slavery in America, 1701–1840.* Athens: University of Georgia Press, 1987.

Tocqueville, Alexis de. *Democracy in America.* Translated and edited by Harvey C. Mansfield and Delba Winthrop. Chicago: University of Chicago Press, 2000.

———. *A Fortnight in the Wilderness.* Delray Beach, Fla.: Levenger Press, 2003.

Tomasello, Michael. *A Natural History of Human Morality.* Cambridge, Mass.: Harvard University Press, 2016.

Tomek, Beverly C., and Matthew J. Hetrick, eds. *New Directions in the Study of African American Recolonization.* Southern Dissent. Gainesville: University Press of Florida, 2017.

Tooley, Mark. *The Peace That Almost Was: The Forgotten Story of the 1861 Washington Peace Conference and the Final Attempt to Avert the Civil War.* Nashville, Tenn.: Nelson Books, 2015.

Townsend, William H. *Lincoln and His Wife's Home Town*. Indianapolis: Bobbs-Merrill, 1929.

Tragle, Henry Irving, comp. *The Southampton Slave Revolt of 1831: A Compilation of Source Material*. Amherst: University of Massachusetts Press, 1971.

Trask, Kerry A. *Black Hawk: The Battle for the Heart of America*. New York: Owl Books, 2007.

Trefousse, Hans L. *Andrew Johnson: A Biography*. New York: W. W. Norton, 1989.

———. *Impeachment of a President: Andrew Johnson, the Blacks, and Reconstruction*. Knoxville: University of Tennessee Press, 1975.

———. *The Radical Republicans: Lincoln's Vanguard for Racial Justice*. New York: Alfred A. Knopf, 1968.

Trevelyan, George Macaulay. *The Life of John Bright*. The Making of the Modern Law. Boston: Houghton Mifflin, 1913.

Troy, Gil, Arthur M. Schlesinger, Jr., and Fred L. Israel, eds. *History of American Presidential Elections, 1789–2008*. 4th ed. Vol. 1, *1789–1868*. Facts on File Library of American History. New York: Facts on File, 2012.

Trueblood, Elton. *Abraham Lincoln: The Spiritual Growth of a Public Man: Excerpts from "Abraham Lincoln: Theologian of American Anguish."* Trinity Forum Reading. Burke, Va.: Trinity Forum, 1993.

———. *Abraham Lincoln: Theologian of American Anguish*. New York: Harper and Row, 1973.

Trumbull, Lyman. *Great Speech of Hon. Lyman Trumbull, on the Issues of the Day: Delivered in Chicago, Saturday, August 7, 1858*. [Chicago]: [Press and Tribune], 1858.

Truth, Sojourner. *Narrative of Sojourner Truth: A Bondswoman of Olden Time*. Edited by Olive Gilbert. The Schomburg Library of Nineteenth-Century Black Women Writers. New York: Oxford University Press, 1991.

Tucker, Beverley. *The Partisan Leader: A Tale of the Future*. Southern Literary Classics Series. Chapel Hill: University of North Carolina Press, 1971.

Turnbull, Robert J. *The Crisis, or, Essays on the Usurpations of the Federal Government*. Charleston, S.C.: A. E. Miller, 1827.

Turner, Justin G., and Linda Levitt Turner. *Mary Todd Lincoln: Her Life and Letters*. New York: Alfred A. Knopf, 1972.

Turner, Thomas Reed. *Beware the People Weeping: Public Opinion and the Assassination of Abraham Lincoln*. Baton Rouge: Louisiana State University Press, 1982.

Tyler, Samuel. *Memoir of Roger Brooke Taney, LL.D.: Chief Justice of the Supreme Court of the United States*. Baltimore: J. Murphy, 1872.

United States War Department. *The War of the Rebellion: A Compilation of the Official Records of the Union and Confederate Armies*. 128 vols. Washington, D.C.: Government Printing Office, 1880–1901.

Vallandigham, Clement L. *Speeches, Arguments, Addresses, and Letters of Clement L. Vallandigham*. New York: J. Walter, 1864.

Van Deusen, Glyndon G. *Horace Greeley: Nineteenth-Century Crusader*. Philadelphia: University of Pennsylvania Press, 1953.

———. *William Henry Seward*. New York: Oxford University Press, 1967.

Van Evrie, J. H. *White Supremacy and Negro Subordination; or, Negroes a Subordinate Race, and (So-Called) Slavery Its Normal Condition [. . .]*. 2nd ed. New York: Van Evrie, Horton, 1868.

Van Natter, Francis Marion. *Lincoln's Boyhood: A Chronicle of His Indiana Years*. Washington, D.C.: Public Affairs Press, 1963.

Varon, Elizabeth R. *Appomattox: Victory, Defeat, and Freedom at the End of the Civil War*. Oxford: Oxford University Press, 2014.

———. *Armies of Deliverance: A New History of the Civil War*. New York: Oxford University Press, 2019.

Vaughan, Alden T. *The Roots of American Racism: Essays on the Colonial Experience*. New York: Oxford University Press, 1995.

Vile, John R. *The Bible in American Law and Politics: A Reference Guide*. Lanham, Md.: Rowman and Littlefield, 2020.

Volney, C. F. *The Ruins, or, Meditation on the Revolutions of Empires; and the Law of Nature*. New York: Peter Eckler, 1890.

Von Drehle, David. *Rise to Greatness: Abraham Lincoln and America's Most Perilous Year*. New York: Henry Holt, 2012.

Vorenberg, Michael. *Final Freedom: The Civil War, the Abolition of Slavery, and the Thirteenth Amendment*. Cambridge Historical Studies in American Law and Society. Cambridge: Cambridge University Press, 2001.

Wakelyn, Jon L. *Confederates Against the Confederacy: Essays on Leadership and Loyalty*. Westport, Conn.: Praeger, 2002.

———, ed. *Southern Pamphlets on Secession, November 1860–April 1861*. Civil War America. Chapel Hill: University of North Carolina Press, 1996.

Walker, William. *The War in Nicaragua*. Mobile, Ala.: S. H. Goetzel, 1860.

Wallace, Anthony F. C. *Prelude to Disaster: The Course of Indian-White Relations Which Led to the Black Hawk War of 1832*. Springfield: Illinois State Historical Library, 1970.

Wallace, Dewey D., Jr., Wilson Golden, and Edith Holmes Snyder, eds. *Capital Witness: A History of the New York Avenue Presbyterian Church in Washington D.C.* Franklin, Tenn.: Plumbline Media, 2011.

Wallenstein, Peter. *From Slave South to New South: Public Policy in Nineteenth-Century Georgia*. The Fred W. Morrison Series in Southern Studies. Chapel Hill: University of North Carolina Press, 1987.

Waller, Douglas. *Lincoln's Spies: Their Secret War to Save a Nation*. New York: Simon and Schuster, 2019.

Walsh, John Evangelist. *The Shadows Rise: Abraham Lincoln and the Ann Rutledge Legend*. Urbana: University of Illinois Press, 1993.

Walther, Eric H. *The Fire-Eaters*. Baton Rouge: Louisiana State University Press, 1992.

———. *The Shattering of the Union: America in the 1850s*. The American Crisis Series. Wilmington, Del.: Scholarly Resources, 2004.

———. *William Lowndes Yancey and the Coming of the Civil War*. Civil War America. Chapel Hill: University of North Carolina Press, 2006.

Warren, Louis Austin. *Abraham Lincoln's Gettysburg Address: An Evaluation*. Columbus, Ohio: C. E. Merrill Co., 1946.

———. *Lincoln's Parentage and Childhood: A History of the Kentucky Lincolns Supported by Documentary Evidence*. New York: Century Co., 1926.

———. *Lincoln's Youth: Indiana Years, Seven to Twenty-one, 1816–1830*. Indianapolis: Indiana Historical Society, 1959.

———. *The Romance of Thomas Lincoln and Nancy Hanks*. [Indianapolis]: N.p., [1934?]

———. *The Slavery Atmosphere of Lincoln's Youth*. Fort Wayne, Ind.: Lincolniana Publishers, 1933.

———. *Three Generations of Kentucky Lincolns*. [Louisville, Ky.]: N.p., 1938.

Washington, John E. *They Knew Lincoln*. New York: Oxford University Press, 2018.

Washington, Joseph R., Jr. *Anti-Blackness in English Religion, 1500–1800*. Texts and Studies in Religion. New York: E. Mellen Press, 1984.

Watkins, Sam R. *"Co. Aytch": Maury Grays, First Tennessee Regiment, or, a Side Show of the Big Show*. 2nd ed. Chattanooga, Tenn.: Times, 1900.

Watts, Isaac. *The Psalms of David Imitated in the Language of the New Testament* [. . .]. London: Printed for J. Clark, 1719.

Waugh, John C. *Reelecting Lincoln: The Battle for the 1864 Presidency*. New York: Crown, 1997.

Weber, Jennifer L. *Copperheads: The Rise and Fall of Lincoln's Opponents in the North*. New York: Oxford University Press, 2006.

Webster, Daniel, and Robert Young Hayne. *The Webster-Hayne Debate on the Nature of the Union: Selected Documents.* Edited by Herman Belz. Indianapolis: Liberty Fund, 2000.

Weed, Thurlow. *Life of Thurlow Weed Including His Autobiography and a Memoir.* 2 vols. Vol. 1, *Autobiography of Thurlow Weed,* edited by his daughter, Harriet A. Weed. Vol. 2: *Memoir of Thurlow Weed,* edited by his grandson, Thurlow Weed Barnes. [Boston]: Houghton Mifflin, 1883–1884.

Weems, M. L. *The Life of George Washington: With Curious Anecdotes, Equally Honourable to Himself and Exemplary to His Young Countrymen.* 7th ed. Philadelphia: Printed for the author, 1808.

Weicek, William M. *The Sources of Antislavery Constitutionalism in America, 1760–1848.* Ithaca: Cornell University Press, 1977.

Weichmann, Louis J. *A True History of the Assassination of Abraham Lincoln and of the Conspiracy of 1865.* Edited by Floyd E. Risvold. New York: Alfred A. Knopf, 1975.

Weik, Jesse W. *The Real Lincoln: A Portrait.* Boston: Houghton Mifflin, 1922.

Weld, Theodore Dwight, comp. *American Slavery as It Is: Testimony of a Thousand Witnesses.* New York: American Anti-Slavery Society, 1839.

West, Cornel, and Eddie S. Glaude, Jr., eds. *African American Religious Thought: An Anthology.* Louisville, Ky.: Westminster John Knox Press, 2003.

White, Jonathan W. *Emancipation, the Union Army, and the Reelection of Abraham Lincoln.* Conflicting Worlds: New Dimensions of the American Civil War. Baton Rouge: Louisiana State University Press, 2014.

———. *A House Built by Slaves: African American Visitors to the Lincoln White House.* Lanham, Md.: Rowman and Littlefield, 2022.

White, Ronald C., Jr. *A. Lincoln: A Biography.* New York: Random House, 2009.

———. *Lincoln in Private: What His Most Personal Reflections Tell Us About Our Greatest President.* New York: Random House, 2021.

———. *Lincoln's Greatest Speech: The Second Inaugural.* New York: Simon and Schuster, 2002.

White, Walter. "The Paradox of Color." In Alain Locke, ed., *The New Negro: An Interpretation,* 361–68. New York: Albert and Charles Boni, 1925.

Whitney, Ellen M., comp. and ed. *The Black Hawk War, 1831–1832.* 4 vols. Springfield: Illinois State Historical Library, 1970–1978.

Widmer, Ted. *Lincoln on the Verge: Thirteen Days to Washington.* New York: Simon and Schuster, 2020.

Wilentz, Sean. *No Property in Man: Slavery and Antislavery at the Nation's Founding.* Cambridge, Mass.: Harvard University Press, 2018.

———. *The Politicians and the Egalitarians: The Hidden History of American Politics.* New York: W. W. Norton, 2016.

———. *The Rise of American Democracy: Jefferson to Lincoln.* New York: W. W. Norton, 2005.

———, ed. *The Best American History Essays on Lincoln.* New York: Palgrave Macmillan, 2009.

Williams, David. *Bitterly Divided: The South's Inner Civil War.* New York: New Press, 2008.

———. *Rich Man's War: Class, Caste, and Confederate Defeat in the Lower Chattahoochee Valley.* Athens: University of Georgia Press, 1998.

Williams, Frank J., and Michael Burkhimer, eds. *The Mary Lincoln Enigma: Historians on America's Most Controversial First Lady.* Carbondale: Southern Illinois University Press, 2012.

Williams, Glenn F. *Dunmore's War: The Last Conflict of America's Colonial Era.* Yardley, Pa.: Westholme Publishing, 2017.

Williams, Robert C. *Horace Greeley: Champion of American Freedom.* New York: New York University Press, 2006.

Wills, Garry. *Lincoln at Gettysburg: The Words That Remade America.* New York: Simon and Schuster, 1992.

Wilson, Charles Reagan. *Baptized in Blood: The Religion of the Lost Cause, 1865–1920*. Athens: University of Georgia Press, 2009.

Wilson, Douglas L. *Honor's Voice: The Transformation of Abraham Lincoln*. New York: Vintage Books, 1999.

Wilson, Douglas L., and Rodney O. Davis, eds. *Herndon's Informants: Letters, Interviews, and Statements About Abraham Lincoln*. Urbana: University of Illinois Press, 1998.

Wiltse, Charles M. *John C. Calhoun, Sectionalist, 1840–1850*. Indianapolis: Bobbs-Merrill, 1951.

Wineapple, Brenda. *The Impeachers: The Trial of Andrew Johnson and the Dream of a Just Nation*. New York: Random House, 2019.

Winger, Stewart. *Lincoln, Religion, and Romantic Cultural Politics*. DeKalb: Northern Illinois University Press, 2003.

Winkle, Kenneth J. *The Young Eagle: The Rise of Abraham Lincoln*. Dallas, Tex.: Taylor Trade Publishing, 2001.

Wolf, William J. *The Almost Chosen People: A Study of the Religion of Abraham Lincoln*. Garden City, N.Y.: Doubleday, 1959.

Wood, Forrest G. *Black Scare: The Racist Response to Emancipation and Reconstruction*. Berkeley: University of California Press, 1968.

Wood, Gordon S. *Empire of Liberty: A History of the Early Republic, 1789–1815*. The Oxford History of the United States. Oxford: Oxford University Press, 2009.

Wood, Leonora W. *Abraham Lincoln: Fatalist, Skeptic, Atheist, or Christian, as Revealed Through Records of Church and State*. Piedmont, W.V.: Herald Printing House, 1942.

Woodard, Colin. *Union: The Struggle to Forge the Story of United States Nationhood*. [New York]: Viking, 2020.

Woodson, Carter G. *The Negro in Our History*. 7th ed. Washington, D.C.: Associated Publishers, 1941.

Woodward, C. Vann. *The Burden of Southern History*. Rev. ed. Baton Rouge: Louisiana State University Press, 1968.

———. *The Strange Career of Jim Crow*. 3rd rev. ed. New York: Oxford University Press, 1974.

Woodward, Colin Edward. *Marching Masters: Slavery, Race, and the Confederate Army During the Civil War*. A Nation Divided: Studies in the Civil War Era. Charlottesville: University of Virginia Press, 2014.

Yacovone, Donald. *Teaching White Supremacy: America's Democratic Ordeal and the Forging of Our National Identity*. New York: Pantheon, 2022.

———, ed. *Freedom's Journey: African American Voices of the Civil War*. Chicago: Lawrence Hill Books, 2004.

Yanoff, Stephen G. *Turbulent Times: The Remarkable Life of William H. Seward*. Bloomington, Ind.: AuthorHouse, 2017.

Young, Andrew. *An Easy Burden: The Civil Rights Movement and the Transformation of America*. New York: HarperCollins, 1996.

Young, John Russell. *Around the World with General Grant: A Narrative of the Visit of General U.S. Grant, Ex-President of the United States, to Various Countries in Europe, Asia, and Africa, in 1877, 1878, 1879*. 2 vols. New York: American News Co., 1879.

Zornow, William Frank. *Lincoln and the Party Divided*. Norman: University of Oklahoma Press, 1954.

Periodical Articles

Abbott, Martin. "Southern Reaction to Lincoln's Assassination." *Abraham Lincoln Quarterly* 7, no. 3 (September 1952): 111–27.

Aldis, Owen F. "Louis Napoleon and the Southern Confederacy." *North American Review* 129, no. 275 (October 1879): 342–60.

Anderson, Christopher W. "Native Americans and the Origin of Abraham Lincoln's Views on Race." *Journal of the Abraham Lincoln Association* 37, no. 1 (Winter 2016): 11–29.

Arendt, Hannah. "Race Thinking Before Racism." *Review of Politics* 6, no. 1 (January 1944): 36–73.

Arnold, Dean A. "The Ultimatum of Virginia Unionists: 'Security for Slavery or Disunion.'" *Journal of Negro History* 48, no. 2 (April 1963): 115–29.

Aurer, J. Jeffrey. "Lincoln's Minister to Mexico." *Ohio State Archaeological and Historical Quarterly* 59 (April 1950): 115–28.

Bancroft, Frederic. "The Final Efforts at Compromise, 1860–61." *Political Science Quarterly* 6, no. 3 (September 1891): 401–23.

Barbee, David R. "The Musical Mr. Lincoln." *Abraham Lincoln Quarterly* 5, no. 8 (December 1949): 435–54.

———. "President Lincoln and Doctor Gurley." *Abraham Lincoln Quarterly* 5, no. 1 (March 1948): 3–24.

Barrass, E. "A Few Particulars in the Life of Bishop Simpson, D.D., LL.D." *Wesleyan-Methodist Magazine*, November 1884, 834–40.

Beard, Rick. "Lincoln's Panama Plan." *The New York Times*, August 16, 2012.

Belz, Herman. "Lincoln's Construction of the Executive Power in the Secession Crisis." *Journal of the Abraham Lincoln Association* 27, no. 1 (Winter 2006): 13–38.

Berry, Mary Frances. "Lincoln and Civil Rights for Blacks." *Papers of the Abraham Lincoln Association* 2 (1980): 46–57.

Black, C. Clifton "American Scriptures." *Theological Today* 67, no. 2 (July 2010): 127–68.

Black, Edwin. "The Ultimate Voice of Lincoln." *Rhetoric and Public Affairs* 3, no. 1 (Spring 2000): 49–57.

Blankenhorn, David. "'Better Angels' in Our Past." *American Interest*, July 4, 2019. https://www.the-american-interest.com/2019/07/04/better-angels-in-our-past/.

Bray, Robert. "What Abraham Lincoln Read: An Evaluative and Annotated List." *Journal of the Abraham Lincoln Association* 28, no. 2 (Summer 2007): 28–81.

Brewer, W. M. "Henry Highland Garnet." *Journal of Negro History* 13, no. 1 (January 1928): 36–52.

Bridges, C. A. "The Knights of the Golden Circle: A Filibustering Fantasy." *Southwestern Historical Quarterly* 44, no. 3 (January 1941): 287–302.

Brown, Christopher L. "Empire Without Slaves: British Concepts of Emancipation in the Age of the American Revolution." *William and Mary Quarterly* 56, no. 2 (April 1999): 273–306.

Brussel, James A. "Mary Todd Lincoln: A Psychiatric Study." *Psychiatric Quarterly* 15, supp. 1 (January 1941): 7–26.

Bryant, A. Christopher. "Stopping Time: The Pro-Slavery and 'Irrevocable' Thirteenth Amendment." *Harvard Journal of Law and Public Policy* 26, no. 2 (Spring 2003): 501–49.

Cady, John F. "The Religious Environment of Lincoln's Youth." *Indiana Magazine of History* 37, no. 1 (March 1941): 16–30.

Calhoun, Samuel W., and Lucas E. Morel. "Abraham Lincoln's Religion: The Case for His Ultimate Belief in a Personal, Sovereign God." *Journal of the Abraham Lincoln Association* 33, no. 1 (Winter 2012): 38–74.

Carden, Allen. "Religious Schism as a Prelude to the American Civil War: Methodists, Baptists, and Slavery." *Andrews University Seminary Studies* 24, no. 1 (Spring 1986): 13–29.

Carrington, Paul D. "Teaching Law and Virtue at Transylvania University: The George Wythe Tradition in the Antebellum Years." The Carl Vinson Lecture delivered on

October 18, 1989 at Mercer University Law School in Macon, Georgia. *Mercer Law Review* 41 (1990): 673–99.

Carson, Jamie L., Jeffery A. Jenkins, David W. Rohde, and Mark A. Souva. "The Impact of National Tides and District-Level Effects on Electoral Outcomes: The U.S. Congressional Elections of 1862–63." *American Journal of Political Science* 45, no. 4 (October 2001): 887–98.

Carwardine, Richard J. "Lincoln, Evangelical Religion, and American Political Culture in the Era of the Civil War." *Journal of the Abraham Lincoln Association* 18, no. 1 (Winter 1997): 27–55.

——. "'Simply a Theist': Herndon on Lincoln's Religion." *Journal of the Abraham Lincoln Association* 35, no. 2 (Summer 2014): 18–36.

Cashdollar, Charles D. "The Social Implications of the Doctrine of Divine Providence: A Nineteenth-Century Debate in American Theology." *Harvard Theological Review* 71, no. 3/4 (July–October 1978): 265–84.

Chapman, G. Clarke, Jr. "Lincoln, Bonhoeffer, and Providence: A Quest for Meaning in Wartime." *Union Seminary Quarterly Review* 55, no. 3/4 (2001): 129–49.

Chesebrough, David B. "The Civil War and the Use of Sermons as Historical Documents." *OAH Magazine of History* 8, no. 1 (Fall 1993): 26–29.

Chesebrough, David B., and Lawrence W. McBride. "Sermons as Historical Documents: Henry Ward Beecher and the Civil War." *History Teacher* 23, no. 3 (May 1990): 275–91.

Clark, Allen C. "Abraham Lincoln in the National Capital." *Records of the Columbia Historical Society, Washington, D.C.* 27 (1925): 1–174.

Clark, Robert D. "Bishop Matthew Simpson and the Emancipation Proclamation." *Mississippi Valley Historical Review* 35, no. 2 (September 1948): 263–71.

Clinton, Catherine. "Wife Versus Widow: Clashing Perspectives on Mary Lincoln's Legacy." *Journal of the Abraham Lincoln Association* 28, no. 1 (Winter 2007): 1–19.

"Congress Versus the Constitution." *Southern Review* 4, no. 7 (July 1868): 72.

Crenshaw, Ollinger. "The Knights of the Golden Circle: The Career of George Bickley." *American Historical Review* 47, no. 1 (October 1941): 23–50.

Crocker, Lionel. "Lincoln and Beecher." *Southern Speech Journal* 26, no. 2 (1960): 149–59.

Crofts, Daniel W. "Secession Winter: William Henry Seward and the Decision for War." *New York History* 65, no. 3 (July 1984): 229–56.

Curtis, Michael K. "The 1859 Crisis over Hinton Helper's Book, the Impending Crisis: Free Speech, Slavery, and Some Light on the Meaning of the First Section of the Fourteenth Amendment." Symposium on the Law of Slavery: Constitutional Law and Slavery. *Chicago-Kent Law Review* 68, no. 3 (June 1993): 1113–77.

Daly, Walter J. "The 'Slows': The Torment of Milk Sickness on the Midwest Frontier." *Indiana Magazine of History* 102, no. 1 (March 2006): 29–40.

Daniel, W. Harrison. "Virginia Baptists and the Negro in the Early Republic." *Virginia Magazine of History and Biography* 80, no. 1 (January 1972): 60–69.

Danoff, Brian. "Lincoln and the 'Necessity' of Tolerating Slavery Before the Civil War." *Review of Politics* 77, no. 1 (Winter 2015): 47–71.

Davis, Damani. "Slavery and Emancipation in the Nation's Capital: Using Federal Records to Explore the Lives of African American Ancestors." *Prologue Magazine* 42, no.1 (Spring 2010), National Archives https://www.archives.gov/publications/prologue /2010/spring/dcslavery.html.

Dawes, Henry L. "Two Vice-Presidents: John C. Breckinridge and Hannibal Hamlin." *Century Magazine*, July 1895, 463–67.

——. "Washington the Winter Before the War." *The Atlantic Monthly*, August 1893, 160–67.

Dillon, Merton Lynn. "The Antislavery Movement in Illinois, 1824–1835." *Journal of the Illinois State Historical Society* 47, no. 2 (Summer 1954): 149–66.

Dirck, Brian. "Lincoln's Kentucky Childhood and Race." *Register of the Kentucky Historical Society* 106, no. 3/4 (Summer/Autumn 2008): 307–32.

Donald, David. "The Proslavery Argument Reconsidered." *Journal of Southern History* 37, no. 1 (February 1971): 3–18.

Dueholm, James A. "Lincoln's Suspension of the Writ of Habeas Corpus: An Historical and Constitutional Analysis." *Journal of the Abraham Lincoln Association* 29, no. 2 (Summer 2008): 47–66.

Ecelbarger, Gary. "Before Cooper Union: Abraham Lincoln's 1859 Cincinnati Speech and Its Impact on His Nomination." *Journal of the Abraham Lincoln Association* 30, no. 1 (Winter 2009): 1–17.

"Editorial." *De Bow's Review*, July 1868, 665–69.

Edwards, Owen. "The Death of Colonel Ellsworth." *Smithsonian Magazine*, April 2011. https://www.smithsonianmag.com/history/the-death-of-colonel-ellsworth-878695/.

Egerton, Douglas R. "'Its Origin Is Not a Little Curious': A New Look at the American Colonization Society." *Journal of the Early Republic* 5, no. 4 (Winter 1985): 463–80.

Ehrlich, Walter. "Was the Dred Scott Case Valid?" *Journal of American History* 55, no. 2 (September 1968): 256–65.

Eighmy, John Lee. "The Baptists and Slavery: An Examination of the Origins and Benefits of Segregation." *Social Science Quarterly* 49, no. 3 (December 1968): 666–73.

Ellis, James W. "Spirituals and Gospel Songs: Messages of Unity, Hope, and Deliverance." *International Journal of Arts and Social Science* 4, no. 2 (March–April 2021): 42–57.

Eltis, David. "Europeans and the Rise and Fall of African Slavery in the Americas: An Interpretation." *American Historical Review* 98, no. 5 (December 1993): 1399–1423.

Etcheson, Nicole. "'A Living, Creeping Lie': Abraham Lincoln on Popular Sovereignty." *Journal of the Abraham Lincoln Association* 29, no. 2 (Summer 2008): 1–25.

Featherman, A. "Our Position and That of Our Enemies." *De Bow's Review*, July 1861, 17–35.

Fehrenbacher, Don E. "Lincoln's Wartime Leadership: The First Hundred Days." *Journal of the Abraham Lincoln Association* 9, no. 1 (1987): 1–18.

———. "The Making of a Myth: Lincoln and the Vice-Presidential Nomination of 1864." *Civil War History* 41, no. 4 (December 1995): 273–90.

———. "The Origins and Purpose of Lincoln's 'House-Divided' Speech." *Mississippi Valley Historical Review* 46, no. 4 (March 1960): 615–43.

Field, Peter S. "Our Shrinking Lincoln: The Sixteenth President and the 'Meaning of America.'" *Australasian Journal of American Studies* 40, no. 1 (July 2021): 33–48.

Finkelman, Paul. "Garrison's Constitution: The Covenant with Death and How It Was Made." *Prologue Magazine*, Winter 2000. National Archives. https://www.archives.gov/publications/prologue/2000/winter/garrisons-constitution-1.html.

———. "The Revolutionary Summer of 1862: How Congress Abolished Slavery and Created a Modern America." *Prologue Magazine* 49, no. 4 (Winter 2017–18). National Archives. https://www.archives.gov/publications/prologue/2017/winter/summer-of-1862.

Fisher, Miles Mark. "Friends of Humanity: A Quaker Anti-Slavery Influence." *Church History* 4, no. 3 (September 1935): 187–202.

Fisher, Walter R. "The Failure of Compromise in 1860–1861: A Rhetorical View." *Speech Monographs* 33, no. 3 (August 1966): 364–71.

Fitzhugh, George. "Origin of Civilization—What Is Property?—Which Is the Best Slave Race?" *De Bow's Review*, December 1858, 653–64.

————. "The Times and the War." *De Bow's Review*, July 1861, 1–13.

Flagg, Edmund. "Disappointment at Vandalia." *Journal of the Illinois State Historical Society* 41, no. 3 (September 1948): 312–14.

Foner, Eric. "The Education of Abraham Lincoln." *The New York Times*, February 10, 2002.

————. "Was Abraham Lincoln a Racist?" *Los Angeles Times*, April 9, 2000.

————. "The Wilmot Proviso Revisited." *Journal of American History* 56, no. 2 (September 1969): 262–79.

Franklin, John Hope. "The Use and Misuse of the Lincoln Legacy." *Papers of the Abraham Lincoln Association* 7 (1985): 30–42.

Fredrickson, George M. "A Man but Not a Brother: Abraham Lincoln and Racial Equality." *Journal of Southern History* 41, no. 1 (February 1975): 39–58.

"From Washington: Charles Sumner on the Barbarism of Slavery." *The New York Times*, June 5, 1860.

"The Future of Our Confederation." *De Bow's Review*, July 1861, 35–40.

Gambino, Megan. "Document Deep Dive: The Menu from President Lincoln's Second Inaugural Ball." *Smithsonian Magazine*, January 15, 2013. https://www.smithsonianmag.com/history/document-deep-dive-the-menu-from-president-lincolns-second-inaugural-ball-1510874/.

Glass, Maeve Herbert. "Bringing Back the States: A Congressional Perspective on the Fall of Slavery in America." *Law and Social Inquiry* 39, no. 4 (Fall 2014): 1028–56.

————. "Slavery's Constitution: Rethinking the Federal Consensus." *Fordham Law Review* 89, no. 5 (April 2021): 1815–40.

Glonek, James F. "Lincoln, Johnson, and the Baltimore Ticket." *Abraham Lincoln Quarterly* 6, no. 5 (March 1951): 255–71.

Gopnik, Adam. "Angels and Ages." *The New Yorker*, May 28, 2007. https://www.newyorker.com/magazine/2007/05/28/angels-and-ages.

"The Great Conspiracy: An Official Statement by Judge-Advocate-General Holt." *The New-York Times*, October 16, 1864.

Grimsley, Elizabeth Todd. "Six Months in the White House." *Journal of the Illinois State Historical Society* 19, no. 3/4 (October 1926–January 1927): 43–73.

Guelzo, Allen C. "Abraham Lincoln and the Doctrine of Necessity." *Journal of the Abraham Lincoln Association* 18, no. 1 (Winter 1997): 57–81.

————. "Does Lincoln Still Belong to the Ages?" *Journal of the Abraham Lincoln Association* 33, no. 1 (Winter 2012): 1–13.

————. "How Abe Lincoln Lost the Black Vote: Lincoln and Emancipation in the African American Mind." *Journal of the Abraham Lincoln Association* 25, no. 1 (Winter 2004): 1–22.

————. "Lincoln, Cobden, and Bright: The Braid of Liberalism in the Nineteenth Century's Transatlantic World." *American Political Thought* 4, no. 3 (Summer 2015): 391–411.

————. "The Prudence of Abraham Lincoln," *First Things: A Monthly Journal of Religion and Public Life* no. 159 (January 2006): 11–13.

Guyatt, Nicholas. " 'An Impossible Idea?': The Curious Career of Internal Colonization." *Journal of the Civil War Era* 4, no. 2 (June 2014): 234–63.

Hacker, J. David. "A Census-Based Count of the Civil War Dead." *Civil War History* 57, no. 4 (December 2011): 307–48

Hansen, Andrew C. "Dimensions of Agency in Lincoln's 'Second Inaugural.' " *Philosophy and Rhetoric* 37, no. 3 (2004): 223–54.

Harper, Keith. " 'And All the Baptists in Kentucky Took the Name United Baptists': The Union of the Separate and Regular Baptists of Kentucky." *Register of the Kentucky Historical Society* 110, no. 1 (Winter 2012): 3–31.

———. "'A Strange Kind of Christian': David Barrow and Involuntary, Unmerited, Perpetual, Absolute, Hereditary Slavery, Examined; On the Principles of Nature, Reason, Justice, Policy, and Scripture." *Ohio Valley History* 15, no. 3 (Fall 2015): 68–77.

Harris, William C. "The Hampton Roads Peace Conference: A Final Test of Lincoln's Presidential Leadership." *Journal of the Abraham Lincoln Association* 21, no. 1 (Winter 2000): 30–61.

Hart, Charles Desmond. "Why Lincoln Said 'No': Congressional Attitudes on Slavery Expansion, 1860–1861." *Social Science Quarterly* 49, no. 3 (December 1968): 732–41.

Hickey, James T., and Sam Haycraft. "Robert Todd Lincoln and the 'Purely Private' Letters of the Lincoln Family." *Journal of the Illinois State Historical Society* 74, no. 1 (Spring 1981): 58–79.

Hodge, Charles. "The State of the Country." *Biblical Repertory and Princeton Review* 33, no. 1 (January 1861): 1–36.

Holliday, Carl Boyd. "Lincoln's God." *South Atlantic Quarterly* 18, no. 1 (January 1919): 15–23.

Howe, Daniel Walker. "Why Abraham Lincoln Was a Whig." *Journal of the Abraham Lincoln Association* 16, no. 1 (Winter 1995): 27–38.

Hudson, Gossie Harold. "Black Americans vs. Citizenship: The Dred Scott Decision." *Negro History Bulletin* 46, no. 1 (January–February–March 1983): 26–28.

Hudson, J. Blaine. "Abraham Lincoln: An African American Perspective." *Register of the Kentucky Historical Society* 106, no. 3/4 (Summer/Autumn 2008): 513–35.

———. "References to Slavery in the Public Records of Early Louisville and Jefferson County, 1780–1812." *Filson Club History Quarterly* 73, no. 4 (October 1999): 325–54.

Hunt, Eugenia Jones. "My Personal Recollections of Abraham and Mary Todd Lincoln." *Abraham Lincoln Quarterly* 3, no. 5 (March 1945): 235–52.

Jeansonne, Glen. "Southern Baptist Attitudes Toward Slavery, 1845–1861." *Georgia Historical Quarterly* 55, no. 4 (Winter 1971): 510–22.

Johnson, Albert E. H. "Reminiscences of the Hon. Edwin M. Stanton, Secretary of War." *Records of the Columbia Historical Society, Washington, D.C.* 13 (1910): 69–97.

Jordan, Philip D. "The Death of Nancy Hanks Lincoln." *Indiana Magazine of History* 40, no. 2 (June 1944): 103–10.

Kahn, Michael A. "Abraham Lincoln's Appointments to the Supreme Court: A Master Politician at His Craft." *Journal of Supreme Court History* 22, no. 2 (December 1997): 65–78.

Kaplan, Sidney. "The Miscegenation Issue in the Election of 1864." *Journal of Negro History* 34, no. 3 (July 1949): 274–343.

"Kentucky's Drive for Statehood." *Journal of Applied Research in Economic Development.* Council for Community and Economic Research. http://journal.c2er.org/history/vol-1-part-1-chapter-4-statehood-creating-a-state-policy-system-h-kentuckys-drive-to-statehood/.

Knox, Clinton Everett. "The Possibilities of Compromise in the Senate Committee of Thirteen and the Responsibility for Failure." *Journal of Negro History* 17, no. 4 (October 1932): 437–65.

"Kossuth Before Ohio Legislature." *Ohio History Journal* 12, no. 2 (April 1903): 114–19.

Krug, Mark M. "Lincoln, the Republican Party, and the Emancipation Proclamation." *History Teacher* 7, no. 1 (November 1973): 48–61.

Kubal-Komoto, James. "Abraham Lincoln: The Balance Between Moral Certainty and Moral Humility." *Seattle Times*, February 19, 2012.

Kull, Irving Stoddard. "Presbyterian Attitudes Toward Slavery." *Church History* 7, no. 2 (June 1938): 101–14.

Ladu, Arthur I. "The Political Ideas of Theodore Parker." *Studies in Philology* 38, no. 1 (January 1941): 106–23.

Lattimer, John K., and Angus Laidlaw. "Good Samaritan Surgeon Wrongly Accused of Contributing to President Lincoln's Death: An Experimental Study of the President's Fatal Wound." *Journal of the American College of Surgeons* 182, no. 5 (May 1996): 431–48.

Lee, Robert, and Tristan Ahtone. "Land-Grab Universities." *High Country News*, March 30, 2020. https://www.hcn.org/issues/52.4/indigenous-affairs-education-land-grab-universities.

Levine, Bruce. "Conservatism, Nativism, and Slavery: Thomas R. Whitney and the Origins of the Know-Nothing Party." *Journal of American History* 88, no. 2 (September 2001): 455–88.

Lewis, Thomas A. "When Washington, D.C. Came Close to Being Conquered by the Confederacy." *Smithsonian Magazine*, July 1988. https://www.smithsonianmag.com/history/when-washington-dc-came-close-to-being-conquered-by-the-confederacy-180951994/.

"Lincoln's Second Inaugural: Press Reactions to the Most Eloquent Presidential Address in American History." *Journal of Blacks in Higher Education* 43 (Spring 2004): 44–46.

Lindsey, Elizabeth. "Observance of the Lincoln Centennial." *Lincoln Herald*, Fall 1957.

Ludwig, Charles. "Lincoln and His Pastor." *Christianity Today*, January 21, 1966, 34–37.

Mabee, Carleton. "Sojourner Truth and President Lincoln." *New England Quarterly* 61, no. 4 (December 1988): 519–29.

MacLean, William Jerry. "Othello Scorned: The Racial Thought of John Quincy Adams." *Journal of the Early Republic* 4, no. 2 (Summer 1984): 143–60.

Magness, Phillip W. "Benjamin Butler's Colonization Testimony Reevaluated." *Journal of the Abraham Lincoln Association* 29, no. 1 (Winter 2008): 1–28.

Mallory, Stephen P. "Last Days of the Confederate Government." *McClure's Magazine*, December 1900, 99–107; January 1901, 239–48.

Manning, Chandra. "The Shifting Terrain of Attitudes Toward Abraham Lincoln and Emancipation." *Journal of the Abraham Lincoln Association* 34, no. 1 (Winter 2013): 18–39.

Masur, Kate. "The African American Delegation to Abraham Lincoln: A Reappraisal." *Civil War History* 56, no. 2 (June 2010): 117–44.

———. "Color Was a Bar to the Entrance: African American Activism and the Question of Social Equality in Lincoln's White House." *American Quarterly* 69, no. 1 (March 2017): 1–22.

Mays, Benjamin E. "'Martin Luther King Jr.'s Unfinished Work on Earth Must Truly Be Our Own.'" *The Atlantic*, Special King Issue, n.d. https://www.theatlantic.com/magazine/archive/2018/02/benjamin-mays-mlk-eulogy/552545/.

McMurtry, R. Gerald. "The Lincoln Migration from Kentucky to Indiana." *Indiana Magazine of History* 33, no. 4 (December 1937): 385–421.

McPherson, James M. "Lincoln the Devil." *The New York Times*, August 27, 2000.

———. "No Peace Without Victory, 1861–1865." *American Historical Review* 109, no. 1 (February 2004): 1–18.

Melton, Julius. "A View from the Pew: Nineteenth-Century Elders and Presbyterian Worship." *American Presbyterians* 71, no. 3 (Fall 1993): 161–74.

Miller, John J. "With Death on His Mind." *The Wall Street Journal*, February 11, 2012.

Monaghan, Charles. "The Murrays of Murray Hill: A New York Quaker Family Before, During, and After the Revolution." *Quaker History* 87, no. 1 (Spring 1998): 35–56.

Monaghan, Jay. "Was Abraham Lincoln Really a Spiritualist?" *Journal of the Illinois State Historical Society* 34, no. 2 (June 1941): 209–32.

Monroe, Haskell. "South Carolinians and the Formation of the Presbyterian Church in the Confederate States of America." *Journal of Presbyterian History* 42, no. 4 (December 1964): 219–43.

Morris, J. Brent. "'We Are Verily Guilty Concerning Our Brother': The Abolitionist Transformation of Planter William Henry Brisbane." *South Carolina Historical Magazine*, July–October 2010, 118–50.

Morrison, Larry R. "The Religious Defense of American Slavery Before 1830." *Journal of Religious Thought* 37, no. 2 (Fall 1980/Winter 1981): 16–29.

Morrow, Ralph E. "The Proslavery Argument Revisited." *Mississippi Valley Historical Review* 48, no. 1 (June 1961): 79–94.

Murphy, Joseph T. "The British Example: West Indian Emancipation, the Freedom Principle, and the Rise of Antislavery Politics in the United States, 1833–1843." *Journal of the Civil War Era* 8, no. 4 (December 2018): 621–46.

Murr, J. Edward. "Lincoln in Indiana." *Indiana Magazine of History* 14, no. 1 (March 1918): 13–75.

Najar, Monica. "'Meddling with Emancipation': Baptists, Authority, and the Rift over Slavery in the Upper South." *Journal of the Early Republic* 25, no. 2 (Summer 2005): 157–86.

Neely, Mark E., Jr. "The Secret Treason of Abraham Lincoln's Brother-in-Law." *Journal of the Abraham Lincoln Association* 46 (Winter 1996): 39–43.

"The New Heresy." *Southern Punch*, September 19, 1864, 2.

Nichols, Robert Hastings. "Lincoln's Leadership in War." *Christianity and Crisis*, February 9, 1942, 2–5.

Nicklason, Fred. "The Secession Winter and the Committee of Five." *Pennsylvania History: A Journal of Mid-Atlantic Studies* 38, no. 4 (October 1971), 372–88.

Nye, Russel B. "The Slave Power Conspiracy: 1830–1860." *Science and Society* 10, no. 3 (Summer 1946): 262–74.

Oakes, James. "The Ages of Jackson and the Rise of American Democracies." *Journal of the Historical Society* 6, no. 4 (December 2006): 491–500.

Oakleaf, J. B. "Azel W. Dorsey: Lincoln's School Teacher in Indiana Buried in Illinois." *Journal of the Illinois State Historical Society* 22, no. 3 (October 1929): 447–50.

O'Brien, John A. "Seeking God's Will: President Lincoln and Rev. Dr. Gurley." *Journal of the Abraham Lincoln Association* 39, no. 2 (Summer 2018): 29–54.

Ostendorf, Lloyd. "A New Mary Todd Lincoln Photograph: A Tour of the White Mountains in Summer, 1863." *Illinois Historical Journal* 83, no. 2 (Summer 1990): 109–12.

Paludan, Phillip Shaw. "Lincoln and Colonization: Policy or Propaganda?" *Journal of the Abraham Lincoln Association* 25, no. 1 (Winter 2004): 23–37.

Papaioannou, Helena Iles, and Daniel W. Stowell. "Dr. Charles A. Leale's Report on the Assassination of Abraham Lincoln." *Journal of the Abraham Lincoln Association* 34, no. 1 (Winter 2013): 40–53.

Pearson, Samuel C., Jr. "From Church to Denomination: American Congregationalism in the Nineteenth Century." *Church History* 38, no. 1 (March 1969): 67–87.

Peck, Graham Alexander. "Abraham Lincoln and the Triumph of an Antislavery Nationalism." *Journal of the Abraham Lincoln Association* 28, no. 2 (Summer 2007): 1–27.

Pfau, Michael William. "The House That Abe Built: The 'House Divided' Speech and Republican Party Politics." *Rhetoric and Public Affairs* 2, no. 4 (Winter 1999): 625–51.

Phipps, William E. "Lincoln's Presbyterian Connections." *Journal of Presbyterian History* 80, no. 1 (Spring 2002): 17–28.

Pinsker, Matthew. "Senator Abraham Lincoln." *Journal of the Abraham Lincoln Association* 14, no. 2 (Summer 1993): 1–21.

Pollack, Sheldon D. "The First National Income Tax, 1861–1872." *Tax Lawyer* 67, no. 2 (Winter 2014): 311–30.

Posey, Walter B. "The Baptists and Slavery in the Lower Mississippi Valley." *Journal of Negro History* 41, no. 2 (April 1956): 117–30.

Potter, Lee Ann, and Wynell Schamel. "The Homestead Act of 1862." *Social Education* 61, no. 6 (October 1997): 359–64.

Prichard, Jeremy. "'Home Is the Martyr': The Burial of Abraham Lincoln and the Fate of Illinois's Capital." *Journal of the Abraham Lincoln Association* 38, no. 1 (Winter 2017): 14–42.

Putnam, Elizabeth Duncan. "Governor Joseph Duncan of Illinois." *Tennessee Historical Magazine* 7, no. 4 (January 1922): 243–51.

Ramsdell, Charles W. "Lincoln and Fort Sumter." *Journal of Southern History* 3, no. 3 (August 1937): 259–88.

Rietveld, Ronald D. "The Lincoln White House Community." *Journal of the Abraham Lincoln Association* 20, no. 2 (Summer 1999): 17–48.

Sandage, Scott A. "A Marble House Divided: The Lincoln Memorial, the Civil Rights Movement, and the Politics of Memory, 1939–1963." *Journal of American History* 80, no. 1 (June 1993): 135–67.

Saum, Lewis O. "Providence in the Popular Mind of Pre–Civil War America." *Indiana Magazine of History* 72, no. 4 (December 1976): 315–46.

Schafer, Ronald G. "He Became the Nation's Ninth Vice President. She Was His Enslaved Wife." *The Washington Post*, February 7, 2021. https://www.washingtonpost.com/history/2021/02/07/julia-chinn-slave-wife-vice-president/.

Scheips, Paul J. "Gabriel Lafond and Ambrose W. Thompson: Neglected Isthmian Promoters." *Hispanic American Historical Review* 36, no. 2 (May 1956): 211–28.

Schouler, James. "Abraham Lincoln at Tremont Temple in 1848." *Proceedings of the Massachusetts Historical Society* 42 (January 1909): 70–83.

Scott, Kenneth. "Lincoln's Home in 1860." *Journal of the Illinois State Historical Society* 46, no. 1 (Spring 1953): 7–12.

Sinha, Manisha. "Did He Die an Abolitionist? The Evolution of Abraham Lincoln's Antislavery." *American Political Thought* 4, no. 3 (Summer 2015): 439–54.

Sloat, James M. "The Subtle Significance of Sincere Belief: Tocqueville's Account of Religious Belief and Democratic Stability." *Journal of Church and State* 42, no. 4 (Autumn 2000): 759–79.

Smith, Andrew F. "First Suppers: A Tradition of Inaugural Meals." *Los Angeles Times*, January 14, 2009.

Smith, Goldwin. "President Lincoln." *Macmillan's Magazine*, February 1865, 300–305.

Smith, John David. "'Gentlemen, I Too, Am a Kentuckian': Abraham Lincoln, the Lincoln Bicentennial, and Lincoln's Kentucky in Recent Scholarship." *Register of the Kentucky Historical Society* 106, no. 3/4 (Summer/Autumn 2008): 433–70.

Smith, L. Scott. "Religion, Politics, and the Establishment Clause: Does God Belong in American Public Life?" *Chapman Law Review* 10, no. 2 (2007): 299–358.

Soloveichik, Meir Y. "The Theologian of the American Idea." *Commentary*, December 2017, 13–14.

Sotos, John G. "'What an Affliction': Mary Todd Lincoln's Fatal Pernicious Anemia." *Perspectives in Biology and Medicine* 58, no. 4 (Autumn 2015): 419–43.

Speiser, Matt. "The Ticket's Other Half: How and Why Andrew Johnson Received the 1864 Vice Presidential Nomination." *Tennessee Historical Quarterly* 65, no. 1 (Spring 2006): 42–69.

Spencer, Warren F. "The Jewett-Greeley Affair: A Private Scheme for French Mediation in the American Civil War." *New York History* 51, no. 3 (April 1970): 238–68.

Stampp, Kenneth M. "Lincoln and the Strategy of Defense in the Crisis of 1861." *Journal of Southern History* 11, no. 3 (August 1945): 297–323.

Steell, Willis. "Mrs. Abraham Lincoln and Her Friends." *Munsey's Magazine*, February 1909, 617–23.

Stein, Stephen J. "George Whitefield on Slavery: Some New Evidence." *Church History* 42, no. 2 (June 1973): 243–56.

Sterner, Eric. "The Siege of Fort Laurens, 1778–1779." *Journal of the American Revolution*, December 17, 2019. https://allthingsliberty.com/2019/12/the-siege-of-fort-laurens-1778-1779/#google_vignette.

Stoler, Ann L. "Racial Histories and Their Regimes of Truth." *Political Power and Social Theory* 11 (1997): 183–206.

Stowe, Harriet Beecher. "Abraham Lincoln." *Christian Watchman and Reflector*, January 7, 1864. Reprinted in *Littell's Living Age*, February 6, 1864, 282–84.

Sweet, Natalie. "A Representative 'of Our People': The Agency of William Slade, Leader in the African American Community and Usher to Abraham Lincoln." *Journal of the Abraham Lincoln Association* 34 (Summer 2013): 21–41.

Sydnor, James Rawlings. "Sing a New Song to the Lord: An Historical Survey of American Presbyterian Hymnals." *American Presbyterians* 68, no. 1 (Spring 1990): 1–13.

Taft, Charles Sabine. "Abraham Lincoln's Last Hours." *Century Magazine*, February 1893, 634–36.

Tarrants, Charles. "Carter Tarrant (1765–1816): Baptist and Emancipationist." *Register of the Kentucky Historical Society* 88, no. 2 (Spring 1990): 121–47.

A Texan. "The South and Progress." *De Bow's Review*, February 1859, 214–16.

Tillery, Tyrone. "The Inevitability of the Douglass-Garrison Conflict." *Phylon* 37, no. 2 (2nd Quarter, 1976): 137–49.

Towers, Frank. "Another Look at Inevitability: The Upper South and the Limits of Compromise in the Secession Crisis." *Tennessee Historical Quarterly* 70, no. 2 (Summer 2011): 108–25.

Trainor, Kathleen. "'But the Choir Did Not Sing': How the Civil War Split First Unitarian Church." *Washington History* 7, no. 2 (Fall/Winter, 1995/1996): 54–71.

Turner, Edward Raymond. "The First Abolition Society in the United States." *Pennsylvania Magazine of History and Biography* 36, no. 1 (1912), 92–109.

Turner, Justin G., and H. E. Barker. "Lincolniana: The Grimsley Trunk." *Journal of the Illinois State Historical Society* 66, no. 4 (Winter 1973): 455–59.

Upshur, Abel P. "Domestic Slavery." *Southern Literary Messenger* 5 (October 1839): 677–87.

Vishneski, John S., III. "What the Court Decided in Dred Scott v. Sandford." *American Journal of Legal History* 32, no. 4 (October 1988): 373–90.

Vorenberg, Michael. "Abraham Lincoln and the Politics of Black Colonization." *Journal of the Abraham Lincoln Association* 14, no. 2 (Summer 1993): 22–45.

Wade, Richard C. "The Vesey Plot: A Reconsideration." *Journal of Southern History* 30, no. 2 (May 1964): 143–61.

Walker, Samuel R. "Cuba and the South." *De Bow's Review*, November 1854, 519–25.

Warren, Louis A. "Abraham Lincoln, Senior, Grandfather of the President." *Filson Club History Quarterly* 5, no. 3 (July 1931): 136–52.

———. "The Grave of David Elkin." *Indiana Magazine of History* 22, no. 2 (June 1926): 203–204.

Weatherman, Donald V. "James Buchanan on Slavery and Secession." *Presidential Studies Quarterly* 15, no. 4 (Fall 1985): 796–805.

Wheeler, Samuel P. "Solving a Lincoln Literary Mystery: 'Little Eddie.'" *Journal of the Abraham Lincoln Association* 33, no. 2 (Summer 2012): 34–46.

Widmer, Ted. "The Capitol Takeover That Wasn't." *The New York Times*, January 8, 2021.

Wilentz, Sean. "Who Lincoln Was." *The New Republic*, July 15, 2009, 24–47.

Williams, Mary Wilhelmine. "Letter from Colonel John T. Pickett, of the Southern Confederacy, to Senor Don Manuel De Zamacona, Minister of Foreign Affairs, Mexico." *Hispanic American Historical Review* 2, no. 4 (November 1919): 611–17.

Wilson, Douglas L. "His Hour upon the Stage." *American Scholar* 81, no. 1 (Winter 2012): 60–69.

———. "What Jefferson and Lincoln Read: An Essay on Literacy and Achievement." *The Atlantic,* January 1991, 51–57, 60–62.

Winchcole, Dorothy Clark. "The First Baptist Church in Washington, D.C." *Records of the Columbia Historical Society, Washington, D.C.* 57/59 (1957/1959): 44–57.

Woods, Michael E. "Popularizing Proslavery: John Van Evrie and the Mass Marketing of Proslavery Ideology." *Journal of the Civil War Era,* May 26, 2020. https://www.journalofthecivilwarera.org/2020/05/popularizing-proslavery-john-van-evrie-and-the-mass-marketing-of-proslavery-ideology/.

Zaeske, Susan. "Hearing the Silences in Lincoln's Temperance Address: Whig Masculinity as an Ethic of Rhetorical Civility." *Rhetoric and Public Affairs* 13, no. 3 (Fall 2010): 389–419.

Zarefsky, David. "Lincoln and the House Divided: Launching a National Political Career." *Rhetoric and Public Affairs* 13, no. 3 (Fall 2010): 421–53.

———. "'Public Sentiment Is Everything': Lincoln's View of Political Persuasion." *Journal of the Abraham Lincoln Association* 15, no. 2 (Summer 1994): 23–40.

Zietlow, Rebecca E. "James Ashley's Thirteenth Amendment." *Columbia Law Review* 112, no. 7 (November 2012): 1697–1731.

Zilversmit, Arthur. "Lincoln and the Problem of Race: A Decade of Interpretations." *Papers of the Abraham Lincoln Association* 2 (1980): 22–45.

Zimmer, Ben. "'Supremacist': A Proxy for Racism Since Its Early Days." *The Wall Street Journal,* October 1, 2020.

Sermons

Chane, John Bryson. "Lincoln and Divine Providence." Sermon delivered at Washington National Cathedral, Washington, D.C., n.d.

Channing, William Henry. "The Birth of a New Nation." Sermon delivered at the First Unitarian Church, Washington, D.C., January 15, 1865.

Elliott, Stephen. *"New Wine Not to Be Put into Old Bottles": A Sermon Preached in Christ Church, Savannah, on Friday, February 28th, 1862* [. . .]. Savannah: Press of J. M. Cooper, 1862.

———. *Our Cause in Harmony with the Purposes of God in Christ Jesus: A Sermon Preached in Christ Church, Savannah, on Thursday, September 18th, 1862* [. . .]. Savannah, Ga.: Power Press of John M. Cooper, 1862.

Freeman, George W. *The Rights and Duties of Slave-Holders: Two Discourses, Delivered on Sunday, November 27, 1836; In Christ Church, Raleigh, North-Carolina.* Charleston, S.C.: A. E. Miller, 1837.

Garnet, Henry Highland. *"Let the Monster Perish": The Historic Address to Congress of Henry Highland Garnet.* Address delivered on February 12, 1865. Louisville, Ky.: Westminster John Knox Press, 2020.

———. *A Memorial Discourse: Delivered in the Hall of the House of Representatives, Washington City, D.C., on Sabbath, February 12, 1865.* Philadelphia: Joseph M. Wilson 1865

Garrison, William Lloyd. *No Compromise with Slavery: An Address Delivered to the Broadway Tabernacle, New York, February 14, 1854.* New York: American Anti-Slavery Society, 1854.

Gurley, P. D. "Address of Rev. P. D. Gurley, D.D." Address of Phineas Densmore Gurley to the American Colonization Society. Published in *African Repository* 40, no. 2 (February 1864): 57–60.

———. *The Voice of the Rod: A Sermon Preached on Thursday, June 1, 1865, in the New York Avenue Presbyterian Church, Washington, D.C.* Washington, D.C.: W. Ballantyne, 1865.

Marshall, Catherine. "The Lincoln Tradition." Sermon delivered at the New York Avenue Presbyterian Church, Washington, D.C., circa February 1950. Copy in the Catherine Marshall Papers, Agnes Scott College Archives, Decatur, Georgia.

Marshall, Peter. "The Dome Above the Ruins." Sermon delivered at the New York Avenue Presbyterian Church, Washington, D.C., November 1, 1942.

———. "From Laurie to Lincoln." Sermon delivered on February 19, 1939. Washington, D.C.: New York Avenue Presbyterian Church, 1939.

———. "A Man of the Ages." Sermon delivered on February 11, 1940. [Washington, D.C.]: [New York Avenue Presbyterian Church], 1940.

———. "A Text by Lincoln." Sermon delivered at the New York Avenue Presbyterian Church on February 14, 1943. Published in *The Wartime Sermons of Dr. Peter Marshall.* Edited by Peter J. Marshall. Dallas, Tex.: Clarion Call Marketing, 2005.

Palmer, B. M. *The South: Her Peril, and Her Duty: A Discourse, Delivered in the First Presbyterian Church, New Orleans, on Thursday, November 29, 1860.* New Orleans, La.: True Witness and Sentinel, 1860.

Parker, Theodore. *A Discourse on the Transient and Permanent in Christianity: Preached at the Ordination of Mr. Charles C. Shackford in the Hawes Place Church in Boston, May 19, 1841.* Boston: Freeman and Bolles, 1841.

Prentiss, William O. *A Sermon Preached at St. Peter's Church, Charleston, by the Rev. William O. Prentiss, on Wednesday, November 21, 1860* [. . .]. Charleston, S.C.: Evans and Cogswell, 1860.

Ruffner, William Henry. *The Oath: A Sermon on the Nature and Obligation of the Oath, with Special Reference to the Oath of Allegiance.* Lexington, [Va.]: Printed at the Gazette Office, 1864.

Schenck, William E. *In Memoriam: A Discourse Commemorative of the Life, Labours and Character of the Late Rev. Phineas D. Gurley, D.D., Pastor of New York Avenue Presbyterian Church of Washington, D.C., Delivered in Said Church . . . Dec. 13, A.D. 1868* [. . .]. Washington, D.C.: W. Ballantyne, 1869.

Thornwell, J. H. *The Rights and the Duties of Masters: A Sermon Preached at the Dedication of a Church Erected in Charleston, S.C., for the Benefit and Instruction of the Coloured Population.* Charleston, S.C.: Walker and James, 1850.

Walker, John Thomas. "Abraham Lincoln: A Suffering Servant." Sermon delivered at the dedication of Abraham Lincoln Bay at Washington National Cathedral, February 12, 1984. Published in *Cathedral Age,* Summer 1984, 18–19.

Wishart, Alfred Wesley. "Lincoln as a Man of God." Sermon delivered at Powers' Theatre, Grand Rapids, Michigan, February 13, 1921. [Grand Rapids, Mich.]: [Dean-Hicks], 1921.

Scholarly Papers

Herrick, Michael J. "Kentucky and Slavery: The Constitutional Convention of 1792." Master's thesis, Dalhousie University, 2010.

Kelley, Jim. "The Paradox of Theodore Parker: Transcendentalist, Abolitionist, and White Supremacist." Master's thesis, Georgia State University, 2015.

McWhirter, Christian. "'Liberty's Great Auxiliary': Music and the American Civil War." PhD diss., University of Alabama, Tuscaloosa, 2009.

Pasternak, Martin B. "Rise Now and Fly to Arms: The Life of Henry Highland Garnet." PhD diss., University of Massachusetts, Amherst, 1981.

Sinha, Manisha. "The Counter-Revolution of Slavery: Class, Politics, and Ideology in Antebellum South Carolina." PhD diss., Columbia University, 1994.

Stockwell, Clinton Earl. "A Better Class of People: Protestants in the Shaping of Chicago, 1833–1873." PhD diss., University of Illinois, Chicago, 1992.

Online Resources

"Abraham Lincoln's Second Inauguration." Abraham Lincoln Online. http://www .abrahamlincolnonline.org/lincoln/education/inaugural2.htm.

Africanus, S. M. "The Fugitive Slave Law," 1850. African American Odyssey, Library of Congress. https://memory.loc.gov/ammem/aaohtml/exhibit/aopart3b.html.

Alexander, Kerri Lee. "Elizabeth Freeman." National Women's History Museum. https:// www.womenshistory.org/education-resources/biographies/elizabeth-freeman.

"An Act for the Gradual Abolition of Slavery (1780)." The President's House in Phila-delphia. https://www.ushistory.org/presidentshouse/history/gradual.php.

"An Act of April 16, 1862 (For the Release of Certain Persons Held to Service or Labor in the District of Columbia)." National Archives, https://catalog.archives.gov/id /299814.

"African American Refugees and Emancipation." National Park Service. https://www.nps .gov/cane/african-american-refugees-and-emancipation.htm.

Allen, Erin. "Here Comes the Sun: Seeing Omens in the Weather at Abraham Lincoln's Second Inauguration." Library of Congress Blog, March 4, 2015. https://blogs.loc.gov /loc/2015/03/here-comes-the-sun-seeing-omens-in-the-weather-at-abraham -lincolns-second-inauguration/.

Allen, William C. "History of Slave Laborers in the Construction of the United States Capitol." Report of the Architect of the Capitol, June 1, 2005. DC Emancipa-tion Day. https://emancipation.dc.gov/sites/default/files/dc/sites/emancipation /publication/attachments/History_of_Slave_Laborers_in_the_Construction_of _the_US_Capitol.pdf.

"Ann Sprigg." Bytes of History. http://bytesofhistory.com/Collections/UGRR/Sprigg_ Ann/Sprigg_Ann-Biography.html.

"Anti-Semitism in the United States: General Grant's Infamy." Jewish Virtual Library: A Project of AICE [American-Israeli Cooperative Enterprise]. https://www.jewish virtuallibrary.org/general-grant-s-infamy.

Arnold, Matthew. "Dover Beach." Poetry Foundation. https://www.poetryfoundation .org/poems/43588/dover-beach.

Bertonneau, Arnold. "Every Man Should Stand Equal Before the Law," 1864. BlackPast, January 28, 2007. https://www.blackpast.org/african-american-history/1864-arnold -bertonneau-every-man-should-stand-equal-law/.

Blake, John. "Did Black Lives Matter to Abraham Lincoln? It's Complicated." CNN, March 14, 2021. https://www.cnn.com/2021/03/14/us/abraham-lincoln-racism-blake /index.html.

"Booth's Deringer." Ford's Theatre. https://www.fords.org/lincolns-assassination/booths -deringer/.

Bouie, Jamelle. "The Enlightenment's Dark Side: How the Enlightenment Created Modern Race Thinking, and Why We Should Confront It." *Slate,* June 5, 2018. https://slate.com/news-and-politics/2018/06/taking-the-enlightenment-seriously -requires-talking-about-race.html.

"Brown's Indian Queen Hotel, Washington City [. . .]." Library of Congress. https:// www.loc.gov/item/93506552.

Bryant, William Cullen. "Thanatopsis." Poetry Foundation. https://www.poetryfoundation .org/poems/50465/thanatopsis.

Buchanan, James. "Inaugural Address." The American Presidency Project, University of

California, Santa Barbara. https://www.presidency.ucsb.edu/documents/inaugural
-address-33.

Burke, Edmund. "Edmund Burke, Speech to the Electors of Bristol." University of Chicago Press. https://press-pubs.uchicago.edu/founders/documents/v1ch13s7.html.

Burns, Michael. "The Second Battle of Bull Run." Essential Civil War Curriculum.
https://www.essentialcivilwarcurriculum.com/the-second-battle-of-bull-run.html.

Burton, Brian K. "The Seven Days Battles." Essential Civil War Curriculum. https://
www.essentialcivilwarcurriculum.com/the-seven-days-battles.html.

Campbell, Randolph B. "Mike." "Knights of the Golden Circle." Texas State Historical
Association Handbook of Texas. https://archive.ph/L5xpk#selection-379.25-391.27.

"Chancellorsville." American Battlefield Trust. https://www.battlefields.org/learn/civil
-war/battles/chancellorsville.

Clay, Henry. "Market Speech." Ashland: The Henry Clay Estate. http://henryclay.org/wp
-content/uploads/2016/02/Market-Speech.pdf.

"Clement Vallandigham." Ohio History Central, Ohio History Connection. https://
ohiohistorycentral.org/w/Clement_Vallandigham.

"Clocks and Bells: The Bell Tower of St. Michael's Church." St. Michael's Church,
Charleston, South Carolina. https://stmichaelschurch.net/clock-bells/.

"Constitution of the American Anti-Slavery Society." Library of Congress. https://www
.loc.gov/resource/llst.052/?st=gallery.

"Constructing a National Symbol." United States Senate. https://www.senate.gov/artand
history/history/minute/ConstructingaNationalSymbol.htm.

Coon, Diane Perrine. "Emancipationists in Northern Kentucky." Historybyperrine.
November 4, 2014. http://www.historybyperrine.com/emancipationists-northern
-kentucky/.

Davis, Jefferson. "Jefferson Davis' Resolutions on the Relations of States." The Papers of
Jefferson Davis, Rice University. https://jeffersondavis.rice.edu/archives/documents
/jefferson-davis-resolutions-relations-states.

"Davis, Jefferson, 1808–1889." History, Art and Archives, United States House of Representatives. https://history.house.gov/People/Detail/11970.

"The Death of Willie Lincoln." Abraham Lincoln Online. http://www.abrahamlincoln
online.org/lincoln/education/williedeath.htm.

"A Doctor's View of the Lincoln Assassination." Abraham Lincoln Online. http://www
.abrahamlincolnonline.org/lincoln/education/medical.htm.

Douglass, Frederick. "The Dred Scott Decision." University of Rochester Frederick
Douglass Project. https://rbscp.lib.rochester.edu/4399.

———. "Frederick Douglass to Theodore Tilton, October 15, 1864." Civil War Notebook.
https://civilwarnotebook.blogspot.com/2020/06/frederick-douglass-to-theodore
-tilton.html.

———. "'If There Is No Struggle, There Is No Progress,'" 1857. BlackPast, January 25,
2007. https://www.blackpast.org/african-american-history/1857-frederick-douglass
-if-there-no-struggle-there-no-progress/.

"Dred Scott, Plaintiff in Error, v. John F. A. Sandford." Legal Information Institute, Cornell Law School. https://www.law.cornell.edu/supremecourt/text/60/393.

Drexler, Ken. "Compromise of 1850." Primary Documents in American History, Library
of Congress Research Guides. Last modified April 11, 2019. https://guides.loc.gov
/compromise-1850.

"Edwards, Ninian, 1775–1833." Biographical Directory of the United States Congress.
https://bioguide.congress.gov/search/bio/E000078.

Emerson, Ralph Waldo. "Divinity School Address." EmersonCentral.com. https://

emersoncentral.com/texts/nature-addresses-lectures/addresses/divinity-school
-address.

———. "Power." EmersonCentral.com. https://emersoncentral.com/texts/the-conduct
-of-life/power.

Everett, Edward. "Gettysburg Address." Voices of Democracy, The U.S. Oratory Project,
University of Maryland, College Park. https://voicesofdemocracy.umd.edu/everett
-gettysburg-address-speech-text/.

"Expulsion Case of John C. Breckinridge of Kentucky (1861)." United States Senate.
https://www.senate.gov/about/powers-procedures/expulsion/038Breckinridge
_expulsion.htm.

Finefield, Kristi. "The Washington Monument: A Long Journey to the Top." Picture This:
Library of Congress Prints and Photos Blog, September 19, 2019. https://blogs.loc.gov
/picturethis/2019/09/the-washington-monument-a-long-journey-to-the-top/.

"The First Confiscation Act." Freedmen and Southern Society Project, University of
Maryland History Department. Last modified February 4, 2022. http://www.freedmen
.umd.edu/conact1.htm.

"Free Soil Party Platform of 1848." The American Presidency Project, University of California, Santa Barbara. https://www.presidency.ucsb.edu/documents/free-soil-party
-platform-1848.

"Freedmen's Bureau Acts of 1865 and 1866." Senate Historical Office, United States
Senate. https://www.senate.gov/artandhistory/history/common/generic/Freedmens
Bureau.htm.

"From Thomas Jefferson to Roger Chew Weightman, 24 June 1826." Founders Online, National Archives. https://founders.archives.gov/documents/Jefferson/98-01
-02-6179.

"The Gardiner Spring Resolutions." Historic Documents in American Presbyterian
History, PCA Historical Center. https://www.pcahistory.org/documents/gardiner
spring.html.

Garner, Bryan A. "Remembering Lindley Murray, an Inspirational Lawyer-Grammarian."
ABA Journal, October 1, 2013. https://www.abajournal.com/magazine/article
/remembering_lindley_murray_an_inspirational_lawyer-grammarian.

Garnet, Henry Highland. "Let the Monster Perish," 1865. BlackPast, January 28, 2007.
https://www.blackpast.org/african-american-history/1865-henry-highland-garnet
-let-monster-perish/.

Garrison, William Lloyd. "No Compromise with the Evil of Slavery," 1854. BlackPast,
November 7, 2011. https://www.blackpast.org/african-american-history/1854-william
-lloyd-garrison-no-compromise-evil-slavery/.

"General Order No. 38." Ohio History Central, Ohio History Connection. https://ohio
historycentral.org/w/General_Order_No._38.

"The Generals and Admirals: David Hunter (1802–1886)." Mr. Lincoln's White House.
http://www.mrlincolnswhitehouse.org/residents-visitors/the-generals-and
-admirals/generals-admirals-david-hunter-1802-1886/.

"Germantown Quaker Petition Against Slavery." National Park Service. Last modified
April 5, 2016. https://www.nps.gov/articles/quakerpetition.htm.

"The Gettysburg Address: Contemporary Reactions." Cornell University Library
https://rmc.library.cornell.edu/gettysburg/ideas_more/reactions_p1.htm#chicago
_tribune.

"Gettysburg National Cemetery, Gettysburg, Pennsylvania." National Park Service.
https://www.nps.gov/nr/travel/national_cemeteries/pennsylvania/gettysburg
_national_cemetery.html.

"Hardin County (KY) Slaves, Free Blacks, and Free Mulattoes, 1850–1870." Notable Kentucky African Americans Database. https://nkaa.uky.edu/nkaa/items/show/2360.

Harris, Leslie M. "The New York City Draft Riots of 1863." University of Chicago Press. https://press.uchicago.edu/Misc/Chicago/317749.html&title=The+New+York+City+Draft+Riots+of+1863&desc=.

Henry, Mary. "Mary Henry Diary." Remembering Lincoln, Ford's Theatre. https://rememberinglincoln.fords.org/node/551.

Henry, Natasha L. "Slavery Abolition Act: United Kingdom (1833)." *Encyclopaedia Britannica*. Last modified July 25, 2021. https://www.britannica.com/topic/Slavery-Abolition-Act.

Highsmith, Carol M., photographer. "Derringer Gun John Wilkes Booth Used to Assassinate Abraham Lincoln. [. . .]." Library of Congress, May 28, 2007. https://www.loc.gov/item/2010630694.

"Historical Highlights: The First African American to Speak in the House Chamber." History, Art, and Archives, United States House of Representatives. https://history.house.gov/Historical-Highlights/1851-1900/The-first-African-American-to-speak-in-the-House-Chamber/.

"Historical Highlights: Joint Session to Count 1860 Electoral College Votes." History, Art, and Archives, United States House of Representatives. https://history.house.gov/Historical-Highlights/1851-1900/1861_02_13_Joint_Session_Electoral_Votes/.

Holm, April. "As the Churches Go, So Goes the Nation? Evangelical Schism and American Fears on the Eve of the Civil War." *Muster: How the Past Informs the Present* (blog). *Journal of the Civil War Era*, May 14, 2019. https://www.journalofthecivilwarera.org/2019/05/as-the-churches-go-so-goes-the-nation-evangelical-schism-and-american-fears-on-the-eve-of-the-civil-war/.

Holmes, Oliver Wendell, Sr. "The Last Leaf." Poetry Foundation. https://www.poetryfoundation.org/poems/44383/the-last-leaf.

"'The Honor of Your Company Is Requested': Lincoln's Second Inaugural Ball at the Patent Office." National Park Service. Last modified June 25, 2021. https://www.nps.gov/articles/-the-honor-of-your-company-is-requested-lincoln-s-second-inaugural-ball-at-the-patent-office.htm.

"Horace Greeley, 'A Prayer for Twenty Millions,' *New-York Daily Tribune*, August 20, 1862." Northern Visions of Race, Region, and Reform, American Antiquarian Society. https://www.americanantiquarian.org/Freedmen/Manuscripts/greeley.html.

Jefferson, Thomas. "First Inaugural Address." The Avalon Project, Lillian Goldman Law Library, Yale Law School. https://avalon.law.yale.edu/19th_century/jefinau1.asp.

——. "From Thomas Jefferson to John Breckinridge, 12 August 1803." Founders Online, National Archives. https://founders.archives.gov/documents/Jefferson/01-41-02-0139.

"John J. Crittenden." Tulane University. https://www.tulane.edu/~sumter/Crittenden.html.

"John Van Evrie and Scientific Racism." Center for the History of Medicine at Countway Library, Harvard University. https://collections.countway.harvard.edu/onview/exhibits/show/this-abominable-traffic/john-van-evrie.

"Joshua Speed." National Park Service. https://www.nps.gov/abli/learn/education/upload/JoshuaSpeed2.pdf.

"Josiah Clark Nott." Penn and Slavery Project, University of Pennsylvania. http://pennandslaveryproject.org/exhibits/show/medschool/southerndoctors/josiahnott.

King, Martin Luther, Jr. "Letter from a Birmingham Jail." Martin Luther King, Jr. Papers Project, The Martin Luther King Jr. Research and Education Institute, Stan-

ford University, 2004. https://kinginstitute.stanford.edu/sites/mlk/files/letterfrom
birmingham_wwcw_0.pdf.

———."I've Been to the Mountaintop." Speech Delivered 3 April 1968, Mason Temple
(Church of God in Christ Headquarters), Memphis, Tennessee. https://www.american
rhetoric.com/speeches/mlkivebeentothemountaintop.htm.

Knox, William. "Mortality." Scottish Poetry Library. https://www.scottishpoetrylibrary
.org.uk/poem/mortality/.

Lankford, Nelson. "Virginia Convention of 1861." *Encyclopedia Virginia*. Virginia Humanities. Last modified February 1, 2021. https://encyclopediavirginia.org/entries/virginia
-convention-of-1861/.

Lester, Connie L. "Peter Cartwright." *Tennessee Encyclopedia*. Tennessee Historical Society.
Last modified, March 1, 2018. https://tennesseeencyclopedia.net/entries/peter
-cartwright/.

"The Library and Abraham Lincoln." Illinois State Library Heritage Project, Office of
the Illinois Secretary of State. https://www.ilsos.gov/departments/library/heritage
_project/home/chapters/the-early-years-1840-to-1850/the-library-and-abraham
-lincoln/.

Lincoln, Abraham. "Emancipation Proclamation." National Archives. Last modified December 28, 2021. https://www.archives.gov/news/topics/emancipation-proclamation.

"Lincoln and Churchill: Peace and Unconditional Surrender." The Lehrman Institute.
https://lincolnandchurchill.org/peace-unconditional-surrender/.

The Lincoln Log: A Daily Chronology of the Life of Abraham Lincoln. http://www.the
lincolnlog.org/.

"Louis Agassiz." Department of Earth and Planetary Sciences, Harvard University.
https://eps.harvard.edu/louis-agassiz.

Luebke, Peter. "Seven Pines, Battle of." *Encyclopedia Virginia*. Virginia Humanities. Last
modified February 12, 2021. https://encyclopediavirginia.org/entries/seven-pines
-battle-of/.

"Lydia Maria Child." National Abolition Hall of Fame and Museum. https://www.nation
alabolitionhalloffameandmuseum.org/lydia-maria-child.html.

"Martin Luther King, Jr." National Archives at New York City. Last modified February 2,
2022. https://www.archives.gov/nyc/exhibit/mlk.

"Massachusetts Constitution." The General Court of the Commonwealth of Massachusetts. https://malegislature.gov/laws/constitution.

"The Militia Act of 1862." Freedmen and Southern Society Project, University of Maryland History Department. Last modified February 4, 2022. http://www.freedmen
.umd.edu/milact.htm.

Mintz, Steven. "Historical Context: Facts About the Slave Trade and Slavery." The
Gilder Lehrman Institute of American History. https://www.gilderlehrman.org
/history-resources/teaching-resource/historical-context-facts-about-slave-trade
-and-slavery.

"Missouri State Archives: Dred Scott; 150th Anniversary Commemoration." Missouri
Digital Heritage. Missouri Office of the Secretary of State, Missouri State Library.
https://www.sos.mo.gov/archives/resources/dredscott.asp.

"Missouri State Archives: Missouri's Dred Scott Case, 1846–1857." Missouri Digital
Heritage. Missouri Office of the Secretary of State, Missouri State Library. https://
www.sos.mo.gov/archives/resources/africanamerican/scott/scott.asp.

"A Monument More Durable Than Brass: The Donald and Mary Hyde Collection of Dr.
Samuel Johnson." Houghton Library, Harvard University. https://library.harvard.edu
/sites/default/files/static/onlineexhibits/johnson/index.html.

Morden, Peter J. "British Baptists and Slavery." Baptist Heritage and Identity Commission, Baptist World Alliance. https://bwa-baptist-heritage.org/wp-content/uploads/2016/07/British-Baptists-and-Slavery.pdf.

Morgan, James A. "The Battle of Ball's Bluff." Essential Civil War Curriculum. https://www.essentialcivilwarcurriculum.com/the-battle-of-balls-bluff.html.

"Native Americans and the Homestead Act." National Park Service. Last modified November 29, 2021. https://www.nps.gov/home/learn/historyculture/native-americans-and-the-homestead-act.htm.

"Nebraska Trailblazer," no. 6. Nebraska State Historical Society. https://history.nebraska.gov/sites/history.nebraska.gov/files/doc/ntb6.pdf.

"Northwest Ordinance." Primary Documents in American History, Library of Congress Web Guides. Last modified February 18, 2020. https://www.loc.gov/rr/program//bib/ourdocs/northwest.html.

"Notable Visitors: John J. Crittenden (1787–1863)." Mr. Lincoln's White House. http://www.mrlincolnswhitehouse.org/residents-visitors/notable-visitors/notable-visitors-john-j-crittenden-1787-1863/.

"Notable Visitors: Thomas T. Eckert (1825–1910)." Mr. Lincoln's White House. http://www.mrlincolnswhitehouse.org/residents-visitors/notable-visitors/notable-visitors-thomas-t-eckert-1825-1910/.

"Notable Visitors: Thurlow Weed (1797–1882)." Mr. Lincoln's White House. http://www.mrlincolnswhitehouse.org/residents-visitors/notable-visitors/notable-visitors-thurlow-weed-1797-1882/.

Noyalas, Jonathan A. "'Like a Wind from the Mountains': Stonewall Jackson's 1862 Valley Campaign." Essential Civil War Curriculum. https://www.essentialcivilwarcurriculum.com/like-a-wind-from-the-mountains-stonewall-jacksons-1862-valley-campaign.html.

"Object of the Month: 'A Covenant with Death and an Agreement with Hell.'" Massachusetts Historical Society, July 2005. https://www.masshist.org/object-of-the-month/objects/a-covenant-with-death-and-an-agreement-with-hell-2005-07-01.

"Oliver O. Howard." American Battlefield Trust. https://www.battlefields.org/learn/biographies/oliver-o-howard.

"Petersen House." Ford's Theatre. https://www.fords.org/visit/historic-site/petersen-house/.

"Plessy v. Ferguson." Oyez. www.oyez.org/cases/1850-1900/163us537.

"The Politicians: John J. Hardin (1810–1847)." Mr. Lincoln and Friends. http://www.mrlincolnandfriends.org/the-politicians/john-hardin/.

Pope, Alexander. "An Essay on Man: Epistle I." Poetry Foundation. https://www.poetryfoundation.org/poems/44899/an-essay-on-man-epistle-i.

"The Pratt Street Riot." National Park Service. Last modified, February 26, 2015. https://www.nps.gov/fomc/learn/historyculture/the-pratt-street-riot.htm.

"The Preachers: Peter Cartwright (1785–1872)." Mr. Lincoln and Friends. http://www.mrlincolnandfriends.org/the-preachers/peter-cartwright/.

"President Jackson's Proclamation Regarding Nullification, December 10, 1832." The Avalon Project, Lillian Goldman Law Library, Yale Law School. https://avalon.law.yale.edu/19th_century/jack01.asp#1.

Register, Woody. "In Their Own Words: An Introduction [to] John Henry Hopkins—First Bishop of Vermont, Artist and Architect, and Defender of Slavery." Meridiana: The Blog of the Roberson Project on Slavery, Race, and Reconciliation, April 14, 2020. https://meridiana.sewanee.edu/2020/04/14/in-their-own-words-an-introduction-john-henry-hopkins-first-bishop-of-vermont-artist-and-architect-and-defender-of-slavery/.

Reifsnyder, Richard. "Charles Hodge: A Conservative Theologian Finds His Way to Emancipation." Presbyterian Historical Society, April 17, 2018. https://www.history.pcusa.org/blog/2018/04/charles-hodge-conservative-theologian-finds-his-way-emancipation#_edn12.

"Republican Party Platform of 1864." The American Presidency Project, University of California, Santa Barbara. https://www.presidency.ucsb.edu/documents/republican-party-platform-1864.

Ruffin, Herbert G., II. "E. Arnold Bertonneau (1834–1912)." BlackPast, January 17, 2007. https://www.blackpast.org/african-american-history/bertonneau-e-arnold-1834-1912/.

"The Sack of Lawrence, Kansas, 1856." EyeWitness to History. http://www.eyewitnesstohistory.com/lawrencesack.htm.

"Samuel George Morton." Penn and Slavery Project, University of Pennsylvania. http://pennandslaveryproject.org/exhibits/show/medschool/southerndoctors/samuelmorton.

"The Second Confiscation Act." Freedmen and Southern Society Project, University of Maryland History Department. Last modified February 4, 2022. http://www.freedmen.umd.edu/conact2.htm.

"Seventh Congressional District Election Returns (1846)." 100 Most Valuable Documents at the Illinois State Archives: The Online Exhibit, Office of the Illinois Secretary of State. https://www.ilsos.gov/departments/archives/online_exhibits/100_documents/1846-seventh-congress-election-more.html.

Seward, William Henry. "Speech to the United States Senate." National Humanities Center. http://nationalhumanitiescenter.org/pds/triumphnationalism/america1850/text3/seward.pdf.

"Significant Scots: Hugh Blair." Electric Scotland. https://www.electricscotland.com/history/other/blair_hugh.htm.

"Sixteen Months to Sumter: Newspaper Editorials on the Path to Secession; Chronology of Major Events Leading to Secession Crisis." American Historical Association. https://www.historians.org/teaching-and-learning/teaching-resources-for-historians/sixteen-months-to-sumter/chronology.

Smith, Timothy B. "The Battle of Shiloh." Essential Civil War Curriculum. https://www.essentialcivilwarcurriculum.com/the-battle-of-shiloh.html.

Stanford, Eleanor. "Martin R. Delany (1812–1885)." *Encyclopedia Virginia*. Virginia Humanities. Last modified December 22, 2021. https://encyclopediavirginia.org/entries/delany-martin-r-1812-1885/.

Stephens, Alexander H. "Cornerstone Speech." American Battlefield Trust. https://www.battlefields.org/learn/primary-sources/cornerstone-speech.

Tanner, James. "Tanner Manuscript." Remembering Lincoln, Ford's Theatre. https://rememberinglincoln.fords.org/node/892.

"Then vs. Now: Exploring the Presidential Box." Ford's Theatre. https://www.fords.org/blog/post/then-vs-now-exploring-the-presidential-box/.

"13th Amendment to the U.S. Constitution: Primary Documents in American History." Library of Congress Research Guides. https://guides.loc.gov/13th-amendment/digital-collections.

"Thomas Lincoln." National Park Service. Last modified April 18, 2020. https://www.nps.gov/abli/learn/historyculture/thomas-lincoln.htm.

"Union to Disunion: New Testament." Michigan State University. http://projects.leadr.msu.edu/uniontodisunion/exhibits/show/scripture-passages/new-testament.

Vallandigham, Clement. "On the War and Its Conduct." Teaching American History, Ashbrook Center at Ashland University. https://teachingamericanhistory.org/document/on-the-war-and-its-conduct.

Wakelyn, Jon L. "Secession." *South Carolina Encyclopedia*. University of South Carolina, Institute for Southern Studies. https://www.scencyclopedia.org/sce/entries/secession/.

Washington, George. Letter to Phillis Wheatley. (February 28, 1776). https://founders.archives.gov/documents/Washington/03-03-02-0281.

———. "Transcript of President George Washington's Farewell Address (1796)." Our Documents. https://www.ourdocuments.gov/doc.php?flash=false&doc=15&page=transcript.

"Webb, Edwin B." Papers of Abraham Lincoln Digital Library, Abraham Lincoln Presidential Library. https://papersofabrahamlincoln.org/persons/WE04514.

Webster, Daniel, and Robert Y. Hayne. "The Webster-Hayne Debates." Edited and introduced by Jason W. Stevens. Teaching American History, Ashbrook Center at Ashland University. https://teachingamericanhistory.org/document/the-webster-hayne-debates.

Wesley, John. *Thoughts upon Slavery*, 1778. Electronic edition. Documenting the American South, University of North Carolina at Chapel Hill. https://docsouth.unc.edu/church/wesley/wesley.html.

Wiley, John M. "The Baptists' Parallel Revolution." John M. Wiley: A Blog for Theology and History, November 14, 2015. https://johnmichaelwiley.wordpress.com/2015/11/14/the-baptists-parallel-revolution/.

Withington, Charles F. "Building Stones of Our Nation's Capital." United States Department of the Interior Geological Survey. USGS: INF-74-35. https://pubs.usgs.gov/gip/70039206/report.pdf.

Wyatt-Brown, Bertram. "American Abolitionism and Religion." Divining America: Religion in American History, TeacherServe. National Humanities Center. http://nationalhumanitiescenter.org/tserve/nineteen/nkeyinfo/amabrel.htm.

Periodicals

The Alabama Beacon (Greensboro, Alabama)
Albany (New York) *Evening Journal*
Alton (Illinois) *Observer*
American Heritage
The Atlantic Monthly
Boston Daily Advertiser
Boston Daily Journal
Buffalo (New York) *Commercial Advertiser*
Century Magazine
Charleston (South Carolina) *Mercury*
Charlotte (North Carolina) *Democrat*
Chicago Daily Journal
Chicago Tribune
The Daily Constitutionalist and Republic (Augusta, Georgia)
The Daily Express (Petersburg, Virginia)
Daily Missouri Republican (St. Louis)
Daily Morning News (Savannah, Georgia)
Daily National Republican (Washington, D.C.)
Daily Patriot and Union (Harrisburg, Pennsylvania)
The Daily Picayune (New Orleans, Louisiana)
Daily Richmond (Virginia) *Examiner*
De Bow's Review
Detroit Advertiser and Tribune

The Evening Post (New York)
The Evening Star (Washington, D.C.)
The Examiner (Louisville, Kentucky)
Frank Leslie's Illustrated Newspaper
Freedom's Journal
The Galveston (Texas) *Daily News*
Harper's Weekly
Hartford (Connecticut) *Daily Courant*
Illinois Journal
Illinois Register (Springfield)
Illinois State Gazette (Shawneetown)
Janesville (Wisconsin) *Daily Gazette*
Jeffersonian Democrat (Chardon, Ohio)
The Liberator (Boston, Massachusetts)
Lincoln Herald
Lincoln Lore
Liverpool Daily Post
The London Review
Los Angeles Times
Louisville (Kentucky) *Daily Courier*
Macmillan's Magazine
Mobile (Alabama) *Advertiser and Register*
The Morning Star (London)
Nashville (Tennessee) *Centennial Whig*
The Nashville (Tennessee) *Daily Press*
The National Era (Washington, D.C.)
The National Intelligencer (Washington, D.C.)
The National Republican (Washington, D.C.)
The New Orleans Bee
The New York Herald
The New York Times
The North Star (Rochester, New York)
The Pantagraph (Bloomington, Illinois)
The Philadelphia Inquirer
The Philadelphia Press
The Pittsburgh Commercial
The Press and Tribune (Chicago)
Providence (Rhode Island) *Daily Journal*
Putnam's Monthly
Raleigh (North Carolina) *Register*
The Richmond (Virginia) *Dispatch*
Richmond (Virginia) *Enquirer*
The Richmond (Virginia) *Whig*
The Texas Republican (Marshall, Texas)
The True American (Lexington, Kentucky / Cincinnati, Ohio)
St. Johnsbury (Vermont) *Caledonian*
Sangamo Journal (Springfield, Illinois)
Seattle Times
Slate
Smithsonian

Southern Literary Messenger (Richmond, Virginia)
Southern Standard (McMinnville, Tennessee)
The Spirit of Democracy (Woodsfield, Ohio)
The Sun (Baltimore)
The Times (London)
Vermont Telegraph (Brandon, Vermont)
The Wall Street Journal
The Washington Post
Washington (Kansas) *Republican*
Weekly Anglo-African (New York)
The Weekly Globe (Lexington, Kentucky)
Wesley Methodist Magazine
Wisconsin Daily State Journal (Madison)
The World (New York)

AUTHOR'S NOTE AND ACKNOWLEDGMENTS

"No man knows—no one in the future can ever know Abraham Lincoln," Bram Stoker once remarked to Walt Whitman. "He was much greater—so much vaster even than his surroundings—What is not known of him is so much more than what is, that the true man can never be known on earth." Yet we try, and in trying we find ourselves grappling with enduring questions about the American struggle to live up to the nation's noblest ideals in a world that is all too often ignoble.

My primary debt is to the Lincoln scholars and historians who generously replied to my queries and gave of themselves and of their time to read all or part of the manuscript. Michael Burlingame, author of what he fondly calls the "Green Monster," his million-word masterpiece *Abraham Lincoln: A Life*, was welcoming, gracious, and insightful. The author of several fine books about the White House in different eras, James Conroy advised on the details of the Lincolns' domestic world in Washington. Eddie Glaude, Jr., is my friend, a brilliant scholar, and a valuable interlocutor. Doris Kearns Goodwin is always engaging and illuminating; our conversations about history have been unfolding for decades, and I value them beyond measure. Allen C. Guelzo was a kind consultant on several aspects of Lincoln and religion. Harold Holzer gave me a lovely afternoon in the Roosevelt House on Sixty-fifth Street in New York and offered incisive comments about the manuscript. Sean Wilentz is a long-standing friend whose careful reading of my draft rescued me from several debacles of my own making; I am in his debt both for his works on the American experience and for his invaluable counsel. James Oakes was also generous with his time and insights. Ronald C. White, Jr., a fine biographer of Lincoln and a scholar of religion and politics, helped me with several theological nuances. David W. Blight was helpful on matters related to Frederick Douglass, the subject of his Pulitzer Prize—winning book *Prophet of Freedom*.

For kindnesses large and small, my thanks to Gordon Belt, Director of Public Services for the Tennessee State Library and Archives; Sidney Blumenthal, author of a still-unfolding landmark series on Lincoln; James F. Byrd, professor of American religious history and Cal Turner Chancellor's Chair in Wesleyan Studies at Vanderbilt University; Heath W. Carter, associate professor of American Christianity, Princeton Theological Seminary; Matthew Costello, Vice President of the David M. Rubenstein National Center for White House History and Senior Historian for the White House Historical Association; Anthea M. Hartig, Elizabeth MacMillan Director of the Smithsonian Institution's Museum of American History; Walter Isaacson; John McCardell, Vice Chancellor emeritus and professor of history at the University of the South; Stewart McLaurin, president of the White House Historical Association; James M. McPherson, the George Henry Davis '86 Professor of United States History Emeritus at Princeton University; the Honorable Nancy Pelosi, who arranged for a historical tour of Lincoln's Capitol; Woody Register, the Francis S. Houghteling Professor of American History at the University of the South; Harry Rubenstein, longtime chair of the Smithsonian Institution's National Museum of American History's Division of Politics and Reform; Joe Scarborough; Paul E. Teed, biographer of Theodore Parker and professor of history at Saginaw Valley State University; Minoa D. Uffelman, professor of history at Austin Peay State University; Matthew Wasniewski, Historian of the United States House of Representatives; and Jonathan W. White, associate professor of American Studies at Christopher Newport University.

For archival assistance and advice on various points, I am grateful to John A. O'Brien, Church Historian of the New York Avenue Presbyterian Church and president of the Lincoln Group of the District of Columbia (not least for generously sharing a trove of his research on Phineas Gurley); Dr. Richard F. Grimmett, Church Historian of St. John's Episcopal Church, Lafayette Square; Stephen Buzard, Director of Music at St. James Cathedral in Chicago; Diane Ney, Head Archivist of Washington National Cathedral; Casey S. Westerman, College Archivist and Librarian at Agnes Scott College; Bill Sumners, Director Emeritus of the Southern Baptist Historical Theological Library and Archives in Nashville; B. J. Gooch, University Archivist and Special Collections Librarian Emerita at Transylvania University; Dr. Mitzi Jarrett Budde, Head Librarian and the Arthur Carl Lichtenberger Chair for Theological Research, and Christopher Pote, Seminary Archivist, at Virginia Theological Seminary; Mary Klein, Archivist of the Episcopal Diocese of Maryland; Julia Edmundson Randle, Registrar and Historiographer of the Episcopal Diocese of Virginia; Harry E. Salyards, M.D., and Phyllis Shannon Salyards, M.D., of the Episcopal Diocese of Nebraska; the Reverend Linda LeSourd Lader; Mandi Johnson, Director of University Archives and Special Collections at the University of the South, and Matthew Reynolds, Associate Director; Dr. David R. Bains, professor of religion, Samford University; Dr. Edward M. Nassor, Cathedral Carillonneur, Washington National Cathedral; and the Reverend Dr. Shawn Strout, Associate Dean of Chapel and Assistant Professor of Worship at Virginia Theological Seminary.

At the Library of Congress, my thanks to Jeffrey Flannery, Head of Reference and Reader Services, Manuscript Division; Andrea Tietjen Merrill, editor, Federal Research Division; and Michelle Krowl, Civil War and Reconstruction specialist, who pointed the way to several valuable collections, including those of Nathan W. Daniels, Pheebe Clark, Elizabeth Todd Edwards, William Jones Rhees, and Robert Shortelle.

At Vanderbilt University, where I am fortunate to teach, my thanks to John Geer, Daniel Diermeier, Nick Zeppos, Michael Eric Dyson, Samar Ali, Alan Wiseman, Joshua Clinton, and Gray Sasser.

For research, particularly in sundry archives, thanks to Mike Hill, Margaret Shannon, Victoria Hinshaw, Angelo Ryu, Hannah Hicks, Michael E. Shepherd, and Sarah Jean Caver. Jack Bales expertly conjured his usual bibliographic magic. Merrill Fabry was the fact-checking catcher in the rye. Any mistakes that survive are of course my own responsibility.

I am also grateful to Samuel Adkisson, Rachel Adler, Emily Berret, Andy Brennan, Will Byrd, Elizabeth Dias, Barbara DiVittorio, Sabrina Huffman, Beth Laski, Lisa and Richard Plepler, Teresa Smith, May Smythe, Mary Catherine Sullivan, Oscie Thomas, and Amanda Urban. As ever, Carol Poticny did splendid work on photographs and other visual elements.

At Random House, deepest thanks to Kate Medina, Andy Ward, Noa Shapiro, Avideh Bashirrad, Benjamin Dreyer, Dennis Ambrose, Rebecca Berlant, Simon Sullivan, Richard Elman, Maria Braeckel, Susan Corcoran, Barbara Fillon, Michelle Jasmine, Michael Hoak, Robbin Schiff, Lucas Heinrich, and Louisa McCullough.

This book is dedicated to Gina Centrello, the president and publisher of Random House. Loyal, wise, incisive, and candid—*always* candid—Gina is a gift to the republic of letters, an architect of the literature of history, and the most stalwart of friends.

Michael Beschloss and Evan Thomas are steadfast counselors and friends; their readings were vital. And my family—Keith, Mary, Maggie, and Sam—are perennially indulgent as I move between present and past. Their patience and their love are ever-sustaining.

ILLUSTRATION LIST AND CREDITS

Photograph insert 1

Page 1

Page 2

Page 3

Page 4

· Early portrait of Abraham Lincoln, attributed to Nicholas H. Shepherd, 1846/47. © CORBIS/GETTY IMAGES
· *Autobiography of Peter Cartwright, the Backwoods Preacher,* 1857. LIBRARY OF CONGRESS, LOC CONTROL NUMBER 12003514
· American Colonization Society, James Madison membership certificate, 1816. LIBRARY OF CONGRESS, MANUSCRIPT DIVISION, JAMES MADISON PAPERS, ITEM MJM018373
· Theodore Parker, Unitarian clergyman and social reformer. HULTON ARCHIVE/ GETTY IMAGES

Page 5

· Anti-slavery poster by Reverend Theodore Parker, 1851. PETER NEWARK AMERICAN PICTURES/BRIDGEMAN IMAGES
· Ralph Waldo Emerson photogravure by A. W. Elson and Company. APIC/ GETTY IMAGES
· Robert Chambers, Scottish publisher and naturalist, engraving circa 1861. WORLD HISTORY ARCHIVE/ALAMY STOCK PHOTO
· *Vestiges of the Natural History of Creation* and *Explanations: A Sequel to Vestiges of the Natural History of Creation* by Robert Chambers, 1844/1845. HERITAGE AUCTIONS, HA.COM

Page 6

· Basil Manly, Sr. ARCHIVES AND SPECIAL COLLECTIONS, JAMES P. BOYCE CENTENNIAL LIBRARY, THE SOUTHERN BAPTIST THEOLOGICAL SEMINARY, LOUISVILLE, KY
· James Henley Thornwell, frontispiece of *The Life and Letters of James Henley Thornwell* by B. M. Palmer, 1875. INTERNET ARCHIVE/PRINCETON THEOLOGICAL SEMINARY LIBRARY
· Stephen A. Douglas, Brady-Handy Photograph Collection, circa 1855–1865. LIBRARY OF CONGRESS, PRINTS AND PHOTOGRAPHS DIVISION, LOC CONTROL NUMBER 2017895894

Page 7

· Roger B. Taney, Brady-Handy Photograph Collection, circa 1855–1865. LIBRARY OF CONGRESS, PRINTS AND PHOTOGRAPHS DIVISION, LOC CONTROL NUMBER 2017896009
· James Buchanan, fifteenth president of the United States. BETTMANN/GETTY IMAGES
· John C. Breckinridge, vice president, senator from Kentucky, Confederate States Secretary of War. NIDAY PICTURE LIBRARY/ALAMY STOCK PHOTO

Page 8

· William Henry Seward. LIBRARY OF CONGRESS, PRINTS AND PHOTOGRAPHS DIVISION, LOC CONTROL NUMBER 2004672783
· Jefferson Davis, president of the Confederate States of America. HULTON ARCHIVE/GETTY IMAGES
· Confederate Pro-Slavery Patriotic Cover, Unite or Die envelope depicting an image of a snake in segments representing the Confederate states, circa 1863.

Jefferson Davis quote reads "SLAVE STATES, once more let me repeat, that the only way of preserving our slave property, or what we prize more than life, our LIBERTY, is by a UNION WITH EACH OTHER." HERITAGE AUCTIONS, HA.COM
· Alexander Hamilton Stephens, by McClees & Vannerson, 1858. NATIONAL PORTRAIT GALLERY, SMITHSONIAN INSTITUTION; TRANSFER FROM THE SMITHSONIAN INSTITUTION LIBRARIES; GIFT OF ROGER F. SHULTIS, 1986

Page 9

· William Lowndes Yancey, by unidentified artist, circa 1858. NATIONAL PORTRAIT GALLERY, SMITHSONIAN INSTITUTION
· William Walker, president of Nicaragua, training his soldiers at Virgin Bay, circa 1856. BETTMANN/GETTY IMAGES
· William Walker, by Mathew Brady. MIXPIX/ALAMY STOCK PHOTO
· South Carolina representative Preston S. Brooks beating abolitionist Massachusetts senator Charles Sumner in the U.S. Senate Chamber, 1856, lithograph by J. L. Magee. NEW YORK HISTORICAL SOCIETY/GETTY IMAGES

Page 10

· President Lincoln with his private secretaries, John Nicolay and John Hay, 1863. EVERETT COLLECTION/BRIDGEMAN IMAGES
· President Lincoln with his son Thomas (Tad), by Alexander Gardner, 1865. BRIDGEMAN IMAGES
· Reverend Phineas D. Gurley, pastor of the New York Avenue Presbyterian Church, Washington, DC. PRESBYTERIAN HISTORICAL SOCIETY, PHILADELPHIA, PA

Page 11

· President Lincoln and General George McClellan in the general's tent following the Battle of Antietam on September 17, 1862, by Alexander Gardner. EVERETT COLLECTION
· Major General George McClellan and Mrs. McClellan. © CORBIS/GETTY IMAGES
· General Ulysses Simpson Grant at his headquarters, City Point, during the Civil War, by Mathew Brady. GETTY IMAGES

Page 12

· President Jefferson Davis, the Cabinet of the Confederate States of America, and Confederate general Robert E. Lee. SCIENCE HISTORY IMAGES/ALAMY STOCK PHOTO
· Sergeant Alex Rogers with the battle flag, Army of the Potomac, circa 1863. HERITAGE IMAGES/GETTY IMAGES

Page 13

· Sojourner Truth. HI-STORY/ALAMY STOCK PHOTO
· Emilie Todd Helm. HELM AND TODD FAMILY PHOTOGRAPHS AND PAPERS COLLECTION/UNIVERSITY OF KENTUCKY LIBRARIES SPECIAL COLLECTIONS RESEARCH CENTER
· John Bright, by Henry Joseph Whitlock, 1862. © NATIONAL PORTRAIT GALLERY, LONDON/ART RESOURCE, NY

- Horace Greeley, by Mathew Brady, circa 1860–1865. NATIONAL ARCHIVES AND RECORDS ADMINISTRATION, COLLEGE PARK, MD, NATIONAL ARCHIVES IDENTIFIER 526061

Page 14

- Lydia Maria Child, abolitionist, author, and women's rights advocate, by John Adams Whipple, circa 1865. LIBRARY OF CONGRESS, PRINTS AND PHOTOGRAPHS DIVISION, LOC CONTROL NUMBER 2018645032
- Copperhead ticket for President George McClellan and Vice President George Pendleton, 1864. LINCOLN BROADSIDES, BROWN DIGITAL REPOSITORY, BROWN UNIVERSITY LIBRARY. HTTPS://REPOSITORY.LIBRARY.BROWN.EDU/STUDIO/ITEM/BDR:76983/
- Andrew Johnson, second-term vice president under Abraham Lincoln, by Mathew Brady, between 1860–1875. LIBRARY OF CONGRESS, PRINTS AND PHOTOGRAPHS DIVISION, LOC CONTROL NUMBER 96524285
- Hannibal Hamlin, first-term vice president under Abraham Lincoln, Mathew Brady Studio, 1860s. GLASSHOUSE IMAGES/ALAMY STOCK PHOTO

Page 15

- President Lincoln delivering his second inaugural address at the U.S. Capitol, by Alexander Gardner, March 4, 1865. LIBRARY OF CONGRESS, PRINTS AND PHOTOGRAPHS DIVISION, LOC CONTROL NUMBER 00650938
- John Wilkes Booth, by Alexander Gardner, circa 1865. LIBRARY OF CONGRESS, PRINTS AND PHOTOGRAPHS DIVISION, LOC CONTROL NUMBER 2008680389
- Theory. Practice. Effect. George Bickley, head of the Knights of the Golden Circle, John Wilkes Booth, the assassin, Abraham Lincoln, the Martyr President, 1865. LIBRARY OF CONGRESS, RARE BOOK AND SPECIAL COLLECTIONS DIVISION, ALFRED WHITAL STERN COLLECTION OF LINCOLNIANA, LOC CONTROL NUMBER 2020771056

Page 16

- The "death coach," on which the coffin of President Lincoln was carried, April 1865. POPPERFOTO/GETTY IMAGES
- President Lincoln's house in Springfield, Illinois, April 1865, draped in black after his assassination. MPI/GETTY IMAGES

Photograph insert 2

Page 1

- The Penny Image of Abraham Lincoln, by William Willard, 1864. NATIONAL PORTRAIT GALLERY, SMITHSONIAN INSTITUTION, GIFT OF MR. AND MRS. DAVID A. MORSE

Page 2

- Artist's idea of the appearance of Abraham Lincoln's mother, Nancy Hanks Lincoln, by Lloyd Ostendorf, 1963. LINCOLN FINANCIAL FOUNDATION COLLECTION, COURTESY OF THE INDIANA STATE MUSEUM
- Mary Todd Lincoln in inaugural ball gown, color tinted photograph, 1861. BETTMANN/GETTY IMAGES

Page 3

· The Lincoln family: President Lincoln, Mary Todd Lincoln and their sons, Tad, Robert, and Willie, by Thomas Kelly. WHITE HOUSE COLLECTION, WHITE HOUSE HISTORICAL ASSOCIATION

Page 4

· Joseph Butler, bishop of Durham, by John Vanderbank. COURTESY OF THE AUCKLAND PROJECT AND THE CHURCH COMMISSIONERS
· Absalom Jones, by Raphaelle Peale, circa 1810. BALFORE ARCHIVE IMAGES/ALAMY STOCK PHOTO
· Frederick Douglass, color-tinted daguerreotype by Samuel J. Miller, mid-nineteenth century. GRANGER COLLECTION

Page 5

· William Lloyd Garrison, by Edwin Tryon Billings. © NEW-YORK HISTORICAL SOCIETY/PURCHASE, THE LOUIS DURR FUND/BRIDGEMAN IMAGES
· "The Liberator Commenced . . ." William Lloyd Garrison abolitionist banner, 1831. © MASSACHUSETTS HISTORICAL SOCIETY/BRIDGEMAN IMAGES

Page 6

· "Distinguished Colored Men," by A. Muller & Company, circa 1883. WORLD HISTORY ARCHIVE/ALAMY STOCK PHOTO

Page 7

· Henry Clay, by Theodore Sydney Moise, 1843. HERITAGE IMAGES/GETTY IMAGES
· John C. Calhoun, by Henry F. Darby, circa 1858. THE HISTORY COLLECTION/ALAMY STOCK PHOTO
· Senator Charles Sumner by George Peter Alexander Healy. HERITAGE AUCTIONS, HA.COM

Page 8

· Poster for *Uncle Tom's Cabin* by Harriet Beecher Stowe, 1859. BETTMANN/GETTY IMAGES
· Nathaniel Beverley Tucker portrait. SPECIAL COLLECTIONS RESEARCH CENTER, WILLIAM & MARY LIBRARIES
· *The Partisan Leader: A Novel, and an Apocalypse of the Origin and Struggles of the Southern Confederacy* by Beverley Tucker, originally published in 1836, republished and edited by Thomas A. Ware, 1862. COURTESY OF HATHITRUST/UNIVERSITY OF NORTH CAROLINA AT CHAPEL HILL

Page 9

· John Brown, by Ole Peter Hansen Balling, 1872. NATIONAL PORTRAIT GALLERY, SMITHSONIAN INSTITUTION
· John J. Crittenden, by George Peter Alexander Healy, 1857. NIDAY PICTURE LIBRARY/ALAMY STOCK PHOTO

Page 10

· Inauguration of Jefferson Davis at Montgomery, Alabama, February 18, 1861, Strobridge Lithography Company after a painting by James Massalon, based on

a photograph by Archibald Crossland McIntyre, 1878. NATIONAL PORTRAIT
GALLERY, SMITHSONIAN INSTITUTION
· Jefferson Davis Patriotic Cover, envelope depicting a seven-star First National
flag inscribed "A Secession Envelope." HERITAGE AUCTIONS, HA.COM

Page 11

· The First Reading of the Emancipation Proclamation before the Cabinet, by
Alexander Hay Ritchie, after a painting by Francis Bicknell Carpenter, 1866.
NATIONAL PORTRAIT GALLERY, SMITHSONIAN INSTITUTION
· Emancipation Proclamation, published 1888. STROBRIDGE/ALAMY STOCK PHOTO

Page 12

· *The Hour of Emancipation,* by William Tolman Carlton, 1863. PHOTO
© CHRISTIE'S IMAGES/BRIDGEMAN IMAGES

Page 13

· Frederick Douglass appealing to President Lincoln and his cabinet to enlist
African Americans in the Union Army, mural by William Edouard Scott.
PHOTO BY CAROL M. HIGHSMITH/BUYENLARGE/GETTY IMAGES
· Martin Robison Delany, by unidentified artist, after Abraham Bogardus, circa
1865. NATIONAL PORTRAIT GALLERY, SMITHSONIAN INSTITUTION

Page 14

· Broadside for the 1864 presidential campaign of George McClellan. HERITAGE
AUCTIONS, HA.COM
· *The Peacemakers* by George Peter Alexander Healy, 1868. From left to right:
Major General William Tecumseh Sherman, Lt. General Ulysses S. Grant,
President Abraham Lincoln, and Rear Admiral David D. Porter meet aboard
the *River Queen,* March 1865, City Point, Virginia. WHITE HOUSE COLLECTION,
WHITE HOUSE HISTORICAL ASSOCIATION

Page 15

· Emma LeConte Furman, LeConte Furman Carter Family Papers, Collection
Number ms3027, Box 13, Folder 4. COURTESY OF HARGRETT RARE BOOK AND
MANUSCRIPT LIBRARY, UNIVERSITY OF GEORGIA LIBRARIES
· The capture and shooting of John Wilkes Booth in the barn of Garrett's farm,
Kimmell & Forster. LIBRARY OF CONGRESS, PRINTS AND PHOTOGRAPHS DIVISION,
LOC CONTROL NUMBER 2003666961

Page 16

· Apotheosis of Abraham Lincoln, "In Memory of Abraham Lincoln. The
Reward of the Just," published by William Smith of Philadelphia, 1865.
HERITAGE AUCTIONS, HA.COM

INDEX

ABOUT THE AUTHOR

JON MEACHAM is a Pulitzer Prize–winning biographer. The Carolyn T. and Robert M. Rogers Chair in the American Presidency at Vanderbilt University, he is the author of the *New York Times* bestsellers *His Truth Is Marching On: John Lewis and the Power of Hope; The Soul of America: The Battle for Our Better Angels; Destiny and Power: The American Odyssey of George Herbert Walker Bush; Thomas Jefferson: The Art of Power; American Lion: Andrew Jackson in the White House; American Gospel: God, the Founding Fathers, and the Making of a Nation;* and *Franklin and Winston: An Intimate Portrait of an Epic Friendship.* A fellow of the Society of American Historians, Meacham lives in Nashville.

About the Type

This book was set in Requiem, a typeface designed by the Hoefler Type Foundry. It is a modern typeface inspired by inscriptional capitals in Ludovico Vicentino degli Arrighi's 1523 writing manual, *Il modo de temperare le penne*. An original lowercase, a set of figures, and an italic in the chancery style that Arrighi (fl. 1522) helped popularize were created to make this adaptation of a classical design into a complete font family.